CHILD PSYCHOLOGY

Second Edition

CHILD

PSY

Wallace A. Kennedy, FLORIDA STATE UNIVERSITY

CHOLOGY

PRENTICE-HALL, INC., *Englewood Cliffs, New Jersey*

Library of Congress Cataloging in Publication Data

Kennedy, Wallace A.
   Child psychology.

   Bibliography: p.
   Includes index.
    1. Child study—Addresses, essays, lectures.
I. Title. [DNLM: 1. Child psychology. WS105 K353c]
BF721.K415 1975   155.4   74-23198
ISBN 0-13-131169-7

Cover photographs and photograph facing page 170 by John Okladek

CHILD PSYCHOLOGY, second edition
Wallace A. Kennedy

Printed in the United States of America

10 9 8 7 6 5 4 3 2 1

Prentice-Hall International, Inc., *London*
Prentice-Hall of Australia Pty. Ltd., *Sydney*
Prentice-Hall of Canada, Ltd., *Toronto*
Prentice-Hall of India Private Limited, *New Delhi*
Prentice-Hall of Japan, Inc., *Tokyo*

DEDICATED TO MY STUDENTS

Contents

10 THE CLINICIAN'S NOTEBOOK ON CHILD-REARING   445

Illustrations

Tables

Preface

During the past four years, hundreds of students and professors have taken time to write me about the first edition of CHILD PSYCHOLOGY. Most of these responded favorably to the informal, folksy, commonsense style of the first edition, which has encouraged me to extend this style into the second.

Two areas lightly covered in the first edition reflect an emerging interest of students of child psychology: the development of early cognitive style and the application of behavior techniques to the everyday problems of children. At birth and during the neonatal period, the child is bombarded with sensations emanating from his environment. This Tower of Babel surrounding the child is confusing, evidently somewhat unsettling, and demands some sort of classification and interpretation on the part of the child. As each of his sensory organs begins to function, the child discovers and makes sense out of his world. Chapter 4, a new look at cognitive development, describes the transitional period between this early sensory bombardment and the later intellectual manipulation. This chapter addresses the mystery of how the child moves from primitive sensory response to language.

Chapter 10, The Clinician's Notebook, is derived from an accumulation of my clinical experience as a practicing child psychologist over the last twenty years. It emphasizes common, vexing behavior problems that children almost routinely perform for their parents, teachers, and counselors. These are not the rare, strange, bizarre textbook cases, but predictable, manageable problems frequently encountered by all of us in daily contact with children.

Chapter 5, on intelligence, has been revised to take into account an increasing awareness of the pernicious effect of poverty. For a time, the controversy stirred up by Shockley, Jensen, and Herrnstein appeared to be one of semantic arguments and hysteria; public policy appeared to be unaffected by this jurisdictional dispute over the nature of intelligence. But additional studies, which related more to achievement than to intelligence, gave a staggering blow to remedial and compensatory programs. This controversy could not be pushed aside without sharing with the student the importance of public policy decisions affecting the concept of intelligence, its measurement, application, and utility over the next decade.

The nature-nurture controversy surrounding intelligence, which has continued to grow, has called attention to the considerable advances made in the area of behavioral genetics during the past decade. Chapters 1, 2, and 3 cover heredity, environment, and maturation to present the powerful influence of genetic and familial factors on the child during the first decade of his life. Clearly, genetic, prenatal, and early maturational changes set the pace for all later development: the past four years have seen enormous advances in our understanding of these changes.

In addition, the remaining chapters have been updated to take advantage of the growth in the field of child psychology since 1971, particularly in the field of learning and achievement.

During preparation of the Second Edition I received helpful comments from Professor Louis A. Marton, Miami-Dade Community College, South, Professor Gordon N. Cantor, University of Iowa, and Professor Bernardine English, Broward Community College, for which I express my appreciation.

WALLACE A. KENNEDY

January, 1975

Acknowledgments

Appreciation is expressed to the following authors, institutions, and publishers who granted permission for the use of their material in this book:

Albert Bandura
Nancy Bayley
Cedric O. Carter
L. Erlenmeyer-Kimling
Irwin Feifer
Melvin M. Grumbach
Harry F. Harlow
Louis M. Heil
Lissy F. Jarvik
Arthur T. Jersild
Berwind P. Kaufman

Gerald S. Lesser
D. MacCarthy
Maud A. Merrill
O. Hobart Mowrer
Willard C. Olson
Marion B. Powell
Landrum B. Shettles
Stephen J. Suomi
Vernon Van De Riet
James C. White, Jr.

American Association for the Advancement of Science
American Psychological Association
British Medical Association
The Carnegie Foundation for the Advancement of Teaching
Clark University
Cleveland Health Museum
John Philip Company
The National Foundation—The March of Dimes
The Society for Research in Child Development, Inc.

Appleton-Century-Crofts, Inc.
General Learning Corporation
Harcourt Brace Jovanovich, Inc.
Houghton-Mifflin Company
The Journal Press
McGraw-Hill Book Company

Macmillan Publishing Company, Inc.
The Ronald Press Company
Rupert Hart-Davis Ltd.
Shocken Books, Inc.
Teachers College Press

A brief history of child psychology

Child psychology is said to have a long past and a short history. Its past begins with the great philosophers, Plato, Aristotle, Locke, and Rousseau, and its history begins with the laboratory of G. Stanley Hall and his students. Yet past and history each begin at the same place: with the child; with a concern about the nature of his childhood and the process by which his maturity comes about.

CHILD PSYCHOLOGY'S PAST

Adults have always been curious about the child, concerned with his growth and development into adulthood. The emphasis in child psychology's past was for

the teacher to arrange circumstances so that the child was brought with understanding and efficiency to the threshold of the adult's world.... The theme of the philosophers was the reduction of childish variety to the requirements of responsible adult life [Kessen, 1965, p. 57].

Plato (427–347 B.C.)

Concerned with the good of the republic, the Greek philosopher Plato turned his attention to the problem of selecting and shaping children to fill the needs of the state. He addressed himself to devising some sort of large-scale aptitude testing of children from which the principle of best fit could be applied to shape children into vocations most needed by the state. Plato considered that often these fits would be close; but if not, then the task of pounding square pegs into round holes took place.

This pounding process of Plato is not unlike our contemporary selection, recruitment, and placement of garbage men. That any child, in his early formative years, would wake up one morning and run to his father, crying, "At last, Papa, I have selected my life's vocation, I want to be a garbage collector," is highly doubtful. But even if he should, his father would unlikely leap with joy at the prospect of a son's having made such a vocational choice.

But the state needs garbage men. So society, following the advice of Plato, sets in motion some social pressures that ultimately drive the square peg of a man, who might well want to be a truck driver and who might well have all the talents and abilities to become one, into the round hole of garbage collector—through the device of economic pressure (not enough jobs for all aspiring truck drivers), and bribes (the garbage man often makes a surprising salary), and brute force (an unemployed truck driver may find that only by working on a garbage truck can he protect his family, since he cannot draw unemployment compensation without standing on the street corner dressed and waiting for a job, and the first job that comes along is alley man on the garbage truck). Plato's concept of the supremacy of the state, or authority, has many takers today; it is not a dead issue.

Aristotle (384–322 B.C.)

Aristotle, a Greek philosopher, pupil of Plato, and tutor of Alexander the Great, had essentially the same focus, the supremacy of society's needs, but he proposed a model different from that of Plato. Aristotle was aware that Plato's dream of a universal aptitude test was just that, a dream. He proposed the apprenticeship system, also alive and well today, which had the great advantage of producing stably and efficiently the mainstay journeymen necessary to any society.

The apprenticeship model was a highly visible journeyman-craftsman, such as a stone cutter. Youths were apprenticed to him for a try at also becoming skilled craftsmen. They would start at the most rudimentary tasks; as they developed skills, they progressed through more and more complex aspects of the role. Through a process of natural selection, those who did not reveal talent or drive or interest were sent home and others took their place.

Parents arranged for their children to have the most prestigious apprenticeships they could provide, both in terms of the prestige of the master and of the job. Then, what happened next was up to the child: if he did not make the first apprenticeship, he floated downward to his highest level of competence. This selection by apprenticeship had many advantages over the aptitude selection device proposed by Plato and figures prominently in today's discussions on the use of aptitude testing in industry, which bitter complaints often describe as a tyranny that tests not aptitude, but social class.

John Locke (1632–1704)

At the end of the seventeenth century, an English philosopher espoused a basic philosophy directly related to one of today's burning controversies. John Locke (1693), partly on theological grounds and partly as a result of his own observations, proposed that children by nature are perverted by their wild, native instincts, which are not adaptive to social living. He proposed that rigid controls be applied to children to alter their baseness. He felt that society had the duty to modify the behavior of the child from its natural, perverted state into a socially compliant, controlled, and productive state. Society could not afford the luxury of allowing children to run wild.

Modern-day behaviorism tends to follow his philosophy. The principle of behavior modification is predicated upon the assumption that children's behavior requires modification. The assumption remains that the normal behavioral repertoire of young children is inherently maladaptive and demands curbing.

Jean Jacques Rousseau (1712–1778)

About fifty years later, a Swiss-born French philosopher, Jean Jacques Rousseau, took exactly the opposite tack. Rousseau held that children are basically adaptive, naturally good, that the very act of socialization by society leads to their badness. "God makes all things good; man meddles with them and they become evil" (1762 [1911, p. 5]).

Rousseau proposed that children should grow up in a free, unstructured environment that allows open expression, exploration, and experimentation and that makes no demands regarding the control of behavior other than minimum conformity—the principle of protecting the freedom of others by limiting one's own. Rousseau could have written the script for *Summerhill,* in which Alexander Neill (1960) describes his forty years' experience administering a free school that boasted little structure, curriculum, or behavior modification but instead encouraged and observed children developing on their own in a way that would have made Rousseau proud.

Summary

Obviously, those psychologists with a bias stemming from the tradition of Plato, Aristotle, and Locke would look at the basic needs of society, in terms both of community structure and individual function, and would build a science of behaviorism aimed at rendering the process of behavior shaping most effective. Out of this tradition have come the testing movement, behavior modification, remedial education, vocational training, and mass, consolidated education. On the other hand, those psychologists who follow in the tradition of Rousseau would ally themselves with the child development movement, free schools, and a naturalistic approach to childhood. These latter investigators would study the nature of children through unobtrusive measurement, performed in a natural, unstructured environment; the former would study the modification of behavior according to the needs and demands of contemporary society. The major emphasis that makes for the difference is the concept of freedom and the degree to which children and society need structure for survival.

CHILD PSYCHOLOGY'S HISTORY

Over the years two profound changes occurred in man's thinking about the child. First, individual differences became interesting and important, which obviously led to a seeking of the sources of variety. And second, a proposition evolved that "childhood is a time of construction";

that the child is "what he is made" (Kessen, 1965, p. 58). Certainly interest in the child became increasingly important and to discover the child became the goal of child psychology.

THE BIOGRAPHY

Once the goals of child psychology were established, the question remained of the method by which these goals were to be obtained. An obvious first step that faced the early child psychologists was to define the nature of children. At the very beginning, some method was needed to objectify the study of children.

From antiquity, descriptions of the childhoods of great leaders, prophets, and healers have been available, but these are suspect, retrospective accounts based on memory, often replete with signs evidencing the greatness of the individual even as a child. Some court physicians kept daily ledgers of their charge, the prince, later to be king of all the land, but the authenticity of these documents is also doubtful: a court physician who valued his freedom would be unlikely to provide much illumination regarding slowness to toilet train, bed-wetting, temper tantrums, night terrors, weaning problems, and the like, of an heir apparent to the throne. No, a relatively unbiased, skilled observer was needed, one who would describe the child in his usual environment without holding back unfavorable comments and without overemphasizing signs of his impending greatness. The first method, then, of child psychology was the biographical method, and the first of the great biographers was Dietrich Tiedemann.

Dietrich Tiedemann (1748–1803)

At the time of the American Revolution, Tiedemann ([1787], trans. Murchison and Langer, 1927), a German philosopher-educator, kept a daily ledger describing the first two and a half years of a child's life, with special emphasis upon his mental development. That Tiedemann made some erroneous conclusions about the mental growth of the child was due both to his naiveté about the interpretation of behavior and to his generally favorable attitude toward this special child, his son. But the document stands on its own merit as a starting place for modern child psychology.

The clarity of Tiedemann's observations was striking. For example, he noted on the eighteenth day of the child's life:

> If, when he was crying, the boy was laid upon his side in the position of nursing, or if he felt a soft hand upon his face, he subsided and sought the breasts. Here the association of ideas is visible: the feeling of the particular posture or of the soft hand awakened the image of nursing and of the breasts; so he had formed thereof a definite image, that is to say, he had retained a few traces of previous impressions, which were revived upon receiving a proper sensory stimulus, and through the inner mental powers were transformed into images again [Murchison and Langer, 1927, p. 209].

Obviously a primitive but accurate description of classical conditioning, the implications of this observation did not appear for over a hundred years.

Charles Darwin (1809–1882)

A second great child biographer was the English naturalist Charles Darwin, who, in 1877, published a detailed daily ledger he had begun keeping on his son in 1840.

> M. Taine's very interesting account of the mental development of an infant, translated in the last number of *Mind* (p. 252), has led me to look over a diary which I kept thirty-seven years ago with respect to one of my own infants [Darwin, 1877, p. 286].

This ledger brought to bear Darwin's great observational power upon his own son, with whom he had almost daily contact. As was his bias, Darwin concentrated more upon emotional development, studying his son's expressions of anger, fear, pleasure, and affection. In describing fear and its development, he wrote:

> Before the present one was four and a half months old I had been accustomed to make close to him many strange and loud noises, which were all taken as excellent jokes, but at this period I one day made a loud snoring noise which I had never done before; he instantly looked grave and then burst out crying [p. 288].

Wilhelm Preyer (1841–1897)

Darwin's skill in unobtrusive observation ranks him near the top of any list of biographers of children, but the top of the list is reserved for Wilhelm Preyer, a German philosopher and physiologist. Like Darwin and Tiedemann, he kept a daily ledger on his own son. Preyer (1881) organized his three-year diary into the three psychological classifications, Senses, Will, and Intellect. The focus of Preyer's book was a detailed study of the origin of adult functions; that is, what are the precursors of adult behavior and when do they appear? This bias was good for developmental psychology, but subject to the anthropomorphic error of too soon attributing to children's often simplistic behavior sophisticated adultlike interpretations. Nevertheless, Preyer's generally accurate calibration of the sequence of such behavior as smiling gave clear insight into the maturational process of important social phenomena.

Summary

The biography, then, had several distinct advantages, among them, the intensity and extensity of the observation of a young child for many hours each day, in his own home with his own parents, by an observer totally familiar with the child. The disadvantages were equally obvious, including the lack of representativeness of the sons of these great scientists and the obvious parental biases, as well as the fact that the vast amounts of data, difficult to place into any objective format, made biography a cumbersome method unsuitable for gathering adequate normative data.

THE QUESTIONNAIRE

Although the baby biographies provided an excellent beginning for the solution of the question "What is the nature of children?" the method was too cumbersome to apply to the general population or to speak to the point of the average child. Probably no one found the question of normality more vexing than did the baby doctor who, thousands of times, must answer the question "How is my child doing?"

Pediatricians, through instruction and experience, had developed an implied normal growth rate; parents were informed if their child was a little slow or a little fast: but this was based more upon a tradition fraught with subjectivity than upon reliable scientific study. The more obvious factors, such as day of sitting, walking, talking, were so highly variable and so unrewarding as predictors of future success, that it became all too apparent that something else was needed.

Stanford Chaille (1830–1911)

A Louisiana pediatrician in the mid-1800s, Stanford E. Chaille, set about doing something about the problem of normalcy. He developed the second major method of child psychology almost simultaneously with G. Stanley Hall, although with a slightly different focus. On the basis of the raw score obtained from a series of questions he asked the child and his parents, Chaille (1887) determined whether or not the child was slow. The questions, arranged by age level, were of fact, of ability, and of performance. Children were asked to perform little tasks, or their parents were asked if they could perform specific tasks; they were questioned on their general fund of information and checked off on abilities.

From this new method, suitable for mass usage, broad norms were developed in the teaching hospitals. Since mental retardation was the primary focus of the questionnaire, mental tasks and the fine visual-motor coordination of the child were emphasized over the usual measurements of physical abilities. Chaille's instrument, similar to the *Vineland Social Maturity Scale* in general use today, was a landmark signaling a significant change in the direction of data gathering about children.

G. Stanley Hall (1844–1924)

While Chaille was focusing upon social, emotional, and mental development in the preschool years, G. Stanley Hall, the father of child psychology, and his associates were focusing upon reading readiness, or intellectual maturity related to school performance. The kinds of general abilities children brought forward to the beginning days of school were not known; the development of normative data upon which to base a judgment of mental maturity, or school readiness, was greatly needed. Hall, publishing "The Contents of Children's Minds" in 1883 and "The Contents of Children's Minds on Entering School" in 1891, developed the questionnaire method for schoolchildren.

Henry Goddard (1886–1957) and Edgar Doll (1889–1968)

After Chaille and Hall had established the questionnaire as a useful method, Henry H. Goddard, a student of Hall's, and Edgar A. Doll, working at the Vineland Training School, the first modern training school for the retarded, became interested in correctly classifying residents on the basis of their disability. Together they devised a questionnaire, now refined into the *Vineland Social Maturity Scale,* that, largely because of the prodigious effort of Doll (1953), has become a standard for the measurement of social competence.

Generally administered to the parents of a disabled child, or at least to someone who has had daily contact with him, the questionnaire establishes both the degree and the type of disability suffered. The genius of the method is in its avoidance of the direct evaluation process that causes many children to give a poorer than average performance. The questionnaire focuses upon habitual performance on a day-to-day basis: The question is "Does he usually put on his own socks?" not "Will he, on the day he comes to see the psychologist in a strange building with a great deal of strange activity going on around him, put on his socks?"

This method survives today not only in the *Vineland,* but in the form of personality inventories and sociograms, initiated through the work of Jacob Moreno (1953), a social psychologist interested in group structure and the social position of children.

Summary

The clear advantage of the questionnaire is its high validity. Independent of any hidden meanings or higher order inferences, a great deal of factual information, which needs to be known about children, can best be gathered by a straightforward, articulate, commonsense questionnaire. Its disadvantage is the possibility of deliberate or accidental biases being implanted in the questionnaire, depending upon the biases, prejudices, and attitudes of both the examiner and the respondent: there can be a vast discrepancy between the way parents say they rear their children and the way they actually rear them. But as an efficient, effective, and relatively inexpensive technique for gathering data, the questionnaire has few equals. It survives in scientific literature today essentially in the same form as it was developed by Chaille, Hall, and Doll.

THE CASE HISTORY

Closely resembling the biographical technique, but generally written after the fact, the case history method usually is concerned with strange, unusual, ill, or bizarre people. Medical case histories have dated from antiquity as a primary teaching method.

Jean-Marc Itard (1774–1838)

One of the best case histories related to children was the work of a French physician and amateur anthropologist, Jean Itard (1801, 1807), a student of Phillippe Pinel, the great medical reformer who was head of the Saltpetriere and Bicetre mental hospitals in Paris. Pinel (1745–1826) advocated more humane treatment for the mentally ill, urged study of mental disease, stressed the role of passions in mental illness, and established the custom of maintaining accurate psychiatric case histories for research.

Itard was a young, twenty-three-year-old, bootstrap-trained physician, desperately trying to stay out of Napoleon's army and eager to please the Minister of the Interior, who asked him to take charge of a boy, about twelve years old, who had been captured in the Aveyron woods outside Paris, where he allegedly had been running wild for about six years.

The term *allegedly* refers to the perennial problem of feral children. Somehow, an emotional need of man is filled by the idea of children being raised by animals. But such reports turn out to be exaggerated, somewhat romanticized notions that do not fit all the known facts. Never has a case been well documented of a child of six living successfully with animals, although primitive, dull, abandoned children have lived off of garbage and the land, surviving by theft and stealth until captured.

The Wild Boy of Aveyron was probably such a case; in fact, scars on his body suggested that he had been a beggar's ploy, used to attract pity, whose throat had been cut when he became no longer useful. Nevertheless, he was brought to Itard, who devoted the next five years to an attempt both to study and to domesticate him.

In performing his heroic and only partially successful act of socialization, Itard kept a precise record of the Wild Boy's every move and carefully documented his successes and failures in the boy's treatment. To review all the avenues of cause and modification, Itard developed what was at that time a sophisticated case history, such that 170 years later, each step in the remediation effort can be followed precisely. The degree to which Itard's methods predicted the successful efforts of today's special education is amazing. The problem, however, was that Itard's set of looking at the Wild Boy as one raised by animals rather than as retarded colored his observations to the point where the basic accomplishments and failures of his method were obscured.

Sigmund Freud (1856–1939)

Sigmund Freud (1909), who never actually worked with a child, nevertheless wrote a superior case history of Little Hans, a preschool child afraid of going outside, afraid of being bitten by a horse, and afraid of his father. The history, written on the basis of reports from the father, was consistent with the psychoanalytic interpretation of the cause of neurosis: Freud found all the things he expected to find and neatly confirmed his theory. In spite of its great thoroughness, the case history of Little Hans is strongly prejudiced by Freud's preconceived interpretation of the boy.

Bruno Bettelheim (b. 1903)

This after-the-fact bias is most particularly noticeable in the work of Bruno Bettelheim (1967), a psychoanalyst at the Orthogenic School in Chicago. Bettelheim probably has worked with more schizophrenic children than any person other than Lauretta Bender (1947, 1955, 1956). He long has ascribed the cause of childhood schizophrenia to the schizophrenogenic mother, a theory holding that a certain type of mother, noted for her ambivalence, aloofness, and general lack of warmth in her relationship with her child, is largely responsible for the production of this terrible childhood illness. Bettelheim (1959), then, in his case history of the Mechanical Boy, produces just such a mother; and in fact, the general tenor of all his case histories makes such assertions about the history of his patients.

Thus, in spite of significant evidence to suggest that childhood schizophrenia follows a pattern similar to that of recessive genetic diseases (Kallmann and Roth, 1956), that the schizophrenic child shows biochemical disturbances (Goldfarb, 1970), that from birth the schizophrenic child shows restrictions in perceptual, perceptuomotor, and cognitive responses, which evidence dysfunction of the central nervous system (Fish, 1959, 1961; Fish and Alpert, 1962; Goldfarb, 1961), that the schizophrenic child frequently has normal older and younger siblings (Kallmann and Roth, 1956), that his behavior pattern is so bizarre as to demand an explanation far more complex than the ambivalent, cold-mother theory, particularly since many ambivalent, cold mothers do not produce schizophrenia in their children, the case history goes on, and Bettelheim, one of the grand medical investigators of the disease in this century, continues to find evidence of the schizophrenogenic mother.

Summary

The case history method does not seem sensitive to the difference between cause and effect. It does not recognize the possibility of an alternative explanation for the fact that a mother, who finds herself trying to deal with a fretful, nonverbal, hyperactive, rhythmically moving, aggressive, hostile, and often bizarre child who seems never to sleep when the family sleeps, after two years gradually turns away from this child and becomes detached and perhaps cold, and, after reading the constant damnation of herself as a mother in the women's press, does indeed confirm the doctor's theory.

THE PSYCHOMETRIC

Next upon the scene, psychometry endeavored to measure mental traits, abilities, and processes.

Francis Galton (1822–1911)

The psychometric method was founded and greatly influenced by Francis Galton (1870, 1874, 1888), who began with a strong conviction that human intelligence is a biologically determined, organic ability best measured in terms of sensory reaction time. Galton felt that the unifying principle of human intelligence was the reaction time of the nervous system reflected through the five senses; he placed a high premium upon the concept that speed equals intelligence. This quickness bias led him to devise a large number of measurements of timed judgments based upon sight, hearing, feeling, tasting, and smelling.

These sensory tasks of Galton, which also emphasized memory and vocabulary, began a tradition referred to as the psychometric method.

Although Galton's instruments generated a great deal of interest, considerable conversation, and theory building, they had little practical utility, since the major problem relating to intelligence in children was the prediction of academic success. His sensory-motor tasks failed to discriminate between the successful and the unsuccessful, but Galton became convinced of a biological, physically based intelligence that had great significance for survival.

Alfred Binet (1857–1911) and Theophile Simon (1873–1961)

Chaille and Hall addressed themselves to the rate of mental development, and Hall was interested in school readiness, but Alfred Binet and Theophile Simon (1905, 1905–1908, 1916) were the first to take on the task of relating intelligence tests to the actual prediction of intelligence and, thereby, school performance. They were hired by the school district of Paris to help classify academically retarded youngsters into two groups: bright children who were poorly motivated and retarded youngsters who needed special classes. Evidently the Paris school teachers felt they had an answer for low motivation that was more direct than special education. The problem, then, was to conserve space in remedial special education programs for those who really needed it.

Binet's work began with the simple notion of developmental tasks: that is, what is the functional nature of school success? What does a child have to do to succeed in the first grade? By skillful observation and careful analysis, Binet identified several prerequisite skills for academic success on the basis of the requirements laid down by teachers for adequate performance. He found that children in the first grade must have a certain level of small muscle/visual motor coordination; they must have both short-range and long-range memory; they must have certain number concepts; and they must have a certain attention span.

Binet devised a test to measure these skills, which he ordered according to the age at which they should be ready for use. The Binet instrument from the very beginning was designed to overlap items demanded for school performance. It was a broad test of achievement that measured prerequisite skills for scholastic performance, rather than scholastic performance itself.

The Binet instrument was an immediate success. This built-in overlap with school performance, the face validity of the instrument, guaranteed a high level of success in predicting academic achievement. It was, of course, biased in the direction of the middle-class school and in terms of academic talent, but as a first of its kind, it was a classic.

Henry Goddard (1886–1957)

The psychometric method was brought to America by Henry Goddard (1910), at the Vineland Training School, who simply made a translation of Binet's test without taking into account the cultural difference between the Parisian school children and retarded children and adults in New Jersey. He soon found that Binet's test poorly predicted the life adjustment of his retardates. It did, of course, confirm the diagnosis of mental retardation, but within that grouping, it did little to classify the nature or the severity of the disability.

Lewis Terman (1877–1956)

Although Goddard's attempted utilization of an English translation of Binet's test left him less than enamored with the usefulness of the instrument, his effort attracted the attention of a bright young doctoral student of G. Stanley Hall at Clark University. Lewis Terman, whose dissertation was concerned with the study of genius, needed an instrument that would track mental growth over a span of years.

Terman recognized the need for a general standardization of Binet's test on Americans. Thus, beginning in 1916 and continuing for the rest of his life, he conveyed the Binet test from an obscure, hand-tooled, modest instrument designed for the special education placement of Parisian schoolchildren to the benchmark of intelligence testing, the *Stanford-Binet Intelligence Scale* (Terman, 1916; Terman and Merrill, 1937, 1960). Terman is due considerable credit for his prodigious effort; but his success contributed to an overselling of the concept of IQ as a measure of biological potential.

Arnold Gesell (1880–1961)

A fellow student of Terman's at Clark University, also working on his doctorate under Hall, Arnold Gesell advanced the psychometric movement by turning back to the approach Galton had pursued. Gesell attempted to develop an instrument at Yale Medical School to measure biological intelligence. Like Galton, Gesell believed that intelligence was inherent in the genes and functional in survival, but he felt that the key to the mystery of biological intelligence was the developmental rate of the nervous system. He devised a number of scales to measure the expanding functions of the developing motor-sensory system and, on the basis of these instruments, he projected the long-term development of the child (Gesell and Amatruda, 1962).

The instrument he perfected was effective in early childhood, but like Galton's sensory-motor tasks, it provided little useful information about the schoolreadiness of the child. It seemed to be most effective at the extremes of the continuum, with severely slow children or with very advanced children. Gesell, however, provided the model and the encouragement for other infant tests of intelligence, such as those developed by Psyche Cattell (1960) and Nancy Bayley (1969).

Summary

One of the most effective methods developed by psychology, psychometry represents many of the good points and the bad points of the fledgling science. Because of the lack of general knowledge about children and the need for accurate information, early child psychologists tended to seize upon any method that worked as the cornerstone of the science. In the early days, the psychometric evaluation of children became the major preoccupation of psychology. The IQ concept became the rallying point of the new breed of applied psychologists who began to offer services to mankind, first through the IQ test and finally through a proliferation of instruments for the measurement of intelligence, achievement, personality, vocational aptitude, diagnosis, and treatment requirements. By the end of World War II, testing was almost synonymous with child psychology in the United States.

THE OBSERVATION

The observational method was next developed in child psychology. Although the biographic method involved observing children, it lacked a systematic control of the observation, thus could not provide data applicable to the scientific method. A method was needed to reduce the typical periodic activity periods of children to manageable potentials.

Karl Pratt (b. 1899)

Since motor development was one of the earliest interests of psychologists, and since the vast individual differences in children's activity rates were assumed to have some significance, the first observational method was developed to measure activity rates of children. In the 1930s, Karl C. Pratt and his associates (Pratt, A. Nelson, and Sun, 1930) developed the stabilimeter to measure infant activity rates. An enclosed crib balanced upon a pivot, the stabilimeter recorded every movement of the infant. Thus, the twenty-four-hour activity pattern of infants could be studied without the necessity of constant vigilance on the part of the investigator.

B. F. Skinner (b. 1904)

Although the stabilimeter was a crude instrument, sensitive only to activity rate, it was the predecessor of the baby box developed by B. F. Skinner (1959) as a controlled environment for young children. The Skinner Box was designed such that not only could constant recordings be made of the activity rate, but the sensory stimulation of the child could be controlled in terms of lights, shapes, sounds, and so on. The child could be maintained for long periods in a controlled environment of maximum mental stimulation.

Arnold Gesell (1880–1961)

At the time Pratt was developing his stabilimeter, Arnold Gesell (1934), who wanted to make controlled observations in a natural setting, was developing a photographic dome, a room within a room. Screen wire, painted white to reflect light, covered a dome-shaped form inside a room that could be darkened. Developed before the utilization of one-way glass, the dome served the same purpose: the high intensity lighting inside the screened dome, contrasted with the darkened room, enabled one individual or a whole class to observe a child undisturbed at play, or with his parents in some specific activity under study. Gesell also developed photography techniques with movie cameras that enabled him to study in slow motion the development of motor sequences.

This photo-dome technique has been greatly sophisticated with the utilization of one-way glass, TV, and videotape observations of children. But ever present is the problem of coding the data into a useful form. Continuous camera and tape recording produces so much data that some kind of selectivity is required, if it is to be put to any significant use.

Willard Olson (b. 1899)

Willard Olson, proposed time-sampling, a technique derived from statistics, as a solution to too much data pouring out of the new techniques of observation. To have all of the data is not necessary, he reasoned, if one can be sure that the data one does have are representative.

Olson and Cunningham (1934) proposed the time-sampling technique as a method to utilize small, but representative time blocks, such as one-minute intervals ten minutes apart. If the one-minute time sample can be considered a representative sample of the behavior, then intensive examination of this period can generate invaluable hypotheses about the whole time frame.

For example, not so long ago parents, who knew of cases of stuttering in the family tree, were highly sensitive to the beginnings of stuttering in their children and frequently were horrified to find that at about age four, their child began to stutter. However, time-sampling of the speech patterns of a large group of normal children growing up demonstrated that all children go through a stage, at about four, where, because of developmental sequences, they are able to think ahead of their ability to speak; they repeat one word in five as a natural result. Thus all children could be said to show signs of stuttering at age four. Parents who are worried about stuttering thus are spared this confirmation of their fears. By not focusing on this developmental sequence, they spare their child being identified as a stutterer, which, by the way, may be the primary cause of stuttering.

Olson conducted the same kind of study on tics, aggression, masturbation, withdrawal, crying, and many other social and emotional behaviors of children. The relative efficiency and accuracy of the method used by trained observers makes possible large-scale studies of whole populations in a natural setting.

Summary

Although all observational techniques suffer from a common affliction, high cost, there is something remarkably informative about an eyeball-to-eyeball contact between the child psychologist and his prey. The great cost of the observational techniques is due to the need for breaking down an enormous amount of data into objective form. This data crunching, or changing auditory and visual scanning into a reasonable numerical form, is a severe challenge to most investigators. Literally hundreds of laboratories around the country contain file drawers jammed with reams of observational notes, plots, tapes, films, and photographs. And in many of these laboratories, this vast array has not been reduced to a single published study.

THE EXPERIMENT

The most contemporary method of child study, the experimental method, combines the methodology of modern experimental psychology with the problems of child psychology.

John Watson (1878–1958)

Probably the earliest investigator in experimental child psychology, John B. Watson studied the development of emotional responses in children through conditioning. He and Rosalie Rayner (1920) demonstrated that a child, initially unafraid of a white rat, could be conditioned to fear the rat simply by pairing the presentation of the rat with a loud clang made by striking a steel bar with a hammer.

This demonstration and a subsequent one by Mary Cover Jones (1924b), that a fear response could be deconditioned by associating the fear stimulus with a positive experience, made the study of emotions the proper purview of the experimentalist. Although Watson probably oversimplified the development of emotions, he did provide a methodology for making significant advances in the field.

Jean Piaget (b. 1896)

While Watson and his followers were performing laboratory studies of emotions, learning, and behavior in general, Jean Piaget, a Swiss investigator, became interested in the development of logical thinking. Piaget, using a kindergarten as his laboratory and a relatively small number of children, began a systematic study of the origin of certain logical principles, such as the conservation of mass, weight, and space. Much of Piaget's work involved skillful, insightful observation of children, from which he developed a theory about the developmental sequences of thinking that resembled the motor-development theory of Gesell, and the sexual-stages-development theory of Freud (Piaget, 1952b).

These stages of logical thinking were presumed to develop as a result of some kind of inborn unfolding process, which is modified only slightly by experience and opportunity. This latter statement is not without challengers, but as we shall see in Chapter 4, Piaget is a formidable advocate.

Beth Wellman (1895–1952)

No history of experimental child psychology would be complete without mentioning Beth Wellman (1945), who was responsible for the founding of the Iowa Child Welfare Station and the application of systematic learning theory to developmental psychology. She and her students, Harold Skeels and Marie Skodak, made monumental strides in the translation of experimental findings obtained upon laboratory animals to the problems of children. This methodology, coupled later with the findings of Skinner, made a vast difference in the practical application of psychological principles to child growth and development.

Albert Bandura (b. 1925)

Although there are hundreds, perhaps thousands of experimental child psychologists today, one further individual will serve as an introduction to a contemporary thrust of experimental child psychology. One of the dimensions lacking both in the operant strategy proposed by B. F. Skinner and the classic strategy proposed by John Watson and Ivan Pavlov was the principle of modeling and imprinting. Clearly, many of the complex tasks children must learn would never be mastered if reinforcement of the correct response were the only learning device; the correct response, if highly complex, might never appear in the natural repertoire of the child. Albert Bandura called attention to the combination of a good model and conditioning as an efficient and parsimonious method of teaching most of the behavior needed in children (Bandura and Walters, 1963).

Summary

Clearly, the advantage of the experimental method is the control of variables. At any given moment in a child's life, so many events affect his growth and development that to bring these variables under control in a natural or clinical setting is extremely difficult. But the experimenter frequently can do so, thereby studying the cause-and-effect relationship between the powerful influences in a child's life.

The limitations of the experimental method are as obvious. The experimental scientist, in restricting the variables, produces an unnatural situation, which brings into question the applicability of the laboratory findings to real life. Nevertheless, the complexity of children's behavior demands this kind of sorting out: without the experimental child psychologists, the field will move but little.

THE PSYCHOBIOLOGIC

The final methodology in child psychology, the psychobiological method, emphasizes the ontogenetic sweep through the immediate-preconception/prenatal/immediate-postnatal period: this perinatal period is the most important time span of one's life. A clear understanding of this methodology and its findings is the most appropriate beginning for a study of child psychology; therefore, the first three chapters concentrate on heredity and environment and the biological-medical methodology of child psychology.

Child Psychology's Past

From two views of children and society come two views of child psychology, education, and child-rearing. One views society, the group, as paramount; only in the context of a successful group structure can the individual best be fulfilled. Children are viewed as the responsibility of adults, who, to the best of their ability and love, should guide them through their maturation to adulthood with the goal of producing productive, responsible citizens working for the good of society in general.

The second emphasizes the individual above society; proposes unstructured, free schools, allowing children to grow, learn, mature as they will. Self-fulfillment, self-"honesty," self-understanding are seen as more important than the needs of society in general.

The basic difference between the two viewpoints is the structure deemed necessary for society and for children. The first holds that children grow and mature to more healthy intellectual, emotional, and social adulthood under structured guidance; the second, that complete freedom and lack of interference in childhood produces the free adult. The first holds that society needs structure for survival; the second, that the less structure in society, the better. The first holds that the individual is responsible to and for the group; the second, that the individual is responsible to and for himself.

Child Psychology's History

The Biography A few child biographers, outstanding for their sensitivity and observational abilities, brought scientific skill and curiosity to bear on the development of their infants, thereby adding greatly to the literature on individual maturation. But the biography is a cumbersome method not at all suitable for gathering data on numbers of children.

The Questionnaire More suitable for gathering data on many children, even though subject to biases of the examiner and the examinee, the questionnaire is an efficient, effective, and relatively inexpensive technique.

The Case History Used mostly for the unusual, bizarre, or ill, the case history long has been a method of study, although hampered by an inability to distinguish cause and effect.

The Psychometric Designed to measure mental traits, abilities, and processes, the psychometric represents the good and the bad of psychology's methodology: testing, by the end of World War II, was synonymous with psychology.

The Observation The observational technique, although extremely expensive, provides valuable information about the child. Its greatest drawback is the difficulty presented by so much data. Evidently few researchers have the ability to digest these data into a format productive of theories or conclusions: collecting the data is much easier than formulating results.

The Experiment Experimental methodology in child psychology usually involves a laboratory situation. Rather than simply observing what happens naturally as the child matures, the experimenter says, "what if," and proceeds to set up a situation under controlled conditions to see what happens *if*.

The Psychobiologic The psychobiological method in child psychology recognizes that the child is whole, made up of many parts. His experiences affect his emotions; so do his central nervous and his endocrine systems, and his nutrition, for that matter. To understand the child, one must understand him biologically, emotionally, intellectually, socially.

NAMES TO KNOW

Child Psychology's Past

PLATO (427–347 B.C.) Plato, concerned with the good of the state, viewed the goal of education, of child-rearing, to be the production of adults with efficiencies and skills that enhanced the state. Not a champion of individual freedom at the expense of the group, Plato thought children should be molded, taught responsibility and values, their individual skills and differences shaped to the needs of the many, the state.

ARISTOTLE (384–322 B.C.) A pupil of Plato and the tutor of Alexander the Great, Aristotle proposed that children be apprenticed to skilled adults as models for their learning—models who could show the correct, the easiest way to accomplish goals; models who could tie the present task of the child to his performance as an adult; models who were examples of a task accomplished. Plato and Aristotle both realized the need for responsible, productive adults working toward filling the needs of the state. Plato proposed an aptitude matching; Aristotle, an apprenticeship learning; both proposed the careful molding of children to responsible adulthood.

JOHN LOCKE

as being born perverse, wild, even base. He saw education as a duty to change the very nature of children to make them acceptable adults. Plato and Aristotle recognized the responsibility of adults to guide children as they matured. Locke proposed more than guidance: complete change of their nature as he saw it was his recommended goal.

JEAN JACQUES ROUSSEAU (1712–1778) Rousseau said "Nonsense!" to Locke's philosophy. Children are born good; man makes them evil. Unlike Locke, Rousseau would not change children; unlike Plato or Aristotle, he would not guide children. Rousseau would leave them to mature as they would, unfettered, unguided, uncontrolled, under the necessity of minimum conformity: Rousseau recognized that one's own freedom can result only from the protection of the freedom of others.

Child Psychology's History

the biography

DIETRICH TIEDEMANN (1748–1803) Tiedemann's biography of his infant son emphasized mental development. He may have been the first to describe classical conditioning, although its implications did not become apparent for a hundred years.

CHARLES DARWIN (1809–1882) Darwin's bias in the biography of his infant son concentrated upon emotional development, where he added understanding of the effect of maturation upon the behavior of young children.

WILHELM PREYER (1841–1897) Perhaps the most thorough child biographer, Preyer organized his observations into the development of the senses, the will, and the intellect.

the questionnaire

STANFORD CHAILLE (1830–1911) A pediatrician, Chaille developed a questionnaire to determine a child's maturational level, the diagnosis of mental retardation being the main focus. His instrument, suitable for mass use with norms developed in large teaching hospitals, signaled a significant change in the methodology of data gathering about children.

G. STANLEY HALL (1844–1924) Hall, interested in intellectual development, designed a questionnaire to test what sorts of abilities and information children brought to the first grade. His instrument provided an objective measurement of mental maturity.

HENRY GODDARD (1886–1957) and **EDGAR DOLL** (1889–1968) Goddard and Doll developed the *Vineland Social Maturity Scale,* a questionnaire focused upon habitual performance and a standard today for the measurement of social competence.

the case history

JEAN-MARC ITARD (1774–1838) Charged with the rehabilitation of the Wild Boy of Aveyron, Itard provided remarkably precise records of his efforts to socialize and educate the boy, a methodology that provided a basis for the success of today's special education efforts.

SIGMUND FREUD (1856–1939) The case history of Little Hans, although famous, illustrates the basic weakness of the method in Freud's preconceived interpretation of the boy.

BRUNO BETTELHEIM (b. 1903) Bettelheim's case histories illustrate his prejudice toward behavioral causes of schizophrenia.

the psychometric

FRANCIS GALTON (1822–1911) A giant in psychometry, Francis Galton was convinced that differences in the speed of sense reactions would delineate the true differences among individuals; he was convinced that human intelligence was biologically determined, therefore biologically measureable.

ALFRED BINET (1857–1911) and **THEOPHILE SIMON** (1873–1961) Assuming intelligence to be that something in an individual that allows him to benefit from experience, Binet and Simon, by carefully discovering the prerequisites of school performance, designed a test of intelligence that would predict academic achievement.

HENRY GODDARD (1886–1957) The psychometric method was brought to the United States by Henry Goddard, who translated Binet's test.

LEWIS TERMAN (1877–1956) Terman took the test of Binet and Simon, standardized it on an American population, and made it the benchmark of intellectual measurement, *The Stanford-Binet Intelligence Scale.*

ARNOLD GESELL (1880–1961) Following the thinking of Galton, Gesell calibrated the physical maturation of the infant and young child, providing the model for today's tests of infant intelligence and maturation.

KARL PRATT (b. 1899) Motor development held primary interest, so the first observational instrument, developed by Karl Pratt, was the stabilimeter to measure the activity rates of infants.

B. F. SKINNER (b. 1904) B. F. Skinner's baby box was a more sophisticated apparatus still focused on the behavior of infants under various stimulation.

ARNOLD GESELL (1880–1961) Gesell developed a photo dome for observing infants and young children undisturbed in their natural activity.

WILLARD OLSON (b. 1899) Time-sampling, a concept introduced by Willard Olson, assumed that representative time periods could be observed carefully and general behavior extrapolated from these.

the experiment

JOHN WATSON (1878–1958) Watson asked, "Can you make a child afraid?" And answered, "Indeed you can." So, Mary Cover Jones asked, "Can you make him unafraid?" And answered, "Some methods do not help a frightened child, but others are most effective in diminishing his fears." And in asking these laboratory questions, these two researchers demonstrated how many of man's emotions are learned and how they are learned.

JEAN PIAGET (b. 1896) Piaget is interested in the cognitive development of children: how do they think? He is a strong advocate for his developmental sequences of logical thinking, a theory developed from long hours of observing children at problem solving.

BETH WELLMAN (1895–1952) Wellman asked, "Can children's measured intelligence, their IQ, be changed by schooling? Does environment affect IQ?" Her answer was a resounding "Yes."

ALBERT BANDURA (b. 1925) Bandura is concerned with how children learn. "Are operant conditioning and classical conditioning sufficient to explain the child maturing to adulthood?" Bandura felt not, and his research has centered around the importance of modeling for the maturing child.

Heredity

Once the mystery of impregnation was solved before the dawn of recorded history, the attention of man turned with considerable excitement and concern to the essential elements of procreation. The relationship between hereditary predispositions and influences of the environment, even to the prenatal influences on the fetus, became of paramount concern in the study of children. Of course, the relative influence attributed to heredity or to environment has waxed and waned through the centuries, with interesting correlates in social customs, law, and family structure. The drama of impregnation, child carrying, and child rearing has had an almost mystical quality from time immemorial.

After a brief historical sweep through the nature-nurture discussion in child psychology, Chapters 1 and 2 will present the genetic, prenatal, environmental, and early postnatal conditions that are a part of the psychobiochemical interaction between parents and child, in addition to reviewing the hereditary and environmental factors related to general health, intelligence, personality, and constitution. Chapter 3 will look at the genetically regulated maturational process, particularly with regard to the sequence of development in the nervous, endocrine, and skeletal systems. Chapter 3, ending with the critical period hypothesis, will draw implications from the data presented for the practical management of conception, pregnancy, and early child care as they are affected by the developmental timetable.

Clearly, just in terms of the many Nobel Prizes awarded to researchers in genetics in the last fifteen years, startling changes have taken place in our understanding of the genetic process and its relation to body chemistry. These changes have altered our understanding of behavior genetics and the biochemical processes of conception, pregnancy, and maturation. To grasp the intricate unfolding of child growth and development, and to understand the contributions of behavior genetics to child psychology, a review of the history of genetics as it relates to our contemporary understanding is important.

Undoubtedly, more progress has been made in understanding the complex relationship between heredity and environment in the last twenty years than in all past history. A whole new concept of the environment to include biochemical environment affecting life before birth is now prominent. Once we thought environment began at birth; and then at conception; and now, environmental influences of drugs, radiation, and malnutrition are known to have their effects long before the parents themselves are born.

To understand child psychology fully demands, then, some understanding of the sweep of genetics, the impact of nutritional and biochemical environment, as well as the implication of perinatal events surrounding the miracle of procreation, pregnancy, and birth. The early philosophers and theorists were quite as interested in heredity as men are today.

Aristotle (384–322 B.C.)

The prevailing view of genetics in Aristotle's time, and certainly the view adopted by Aristotle as an early scientific philosopher, was one that grossly depreciated the value of women in the procreation process. In Aristotle's concept of the prenatal period, the woman's role was essentially that of a nurturing incubator to provide the heat and substance needed by the offspring: "What the male contributed to generation is the form and the efficient cause, while the female contributes the material" (*De generatione animalium* 1.20.729a10–11).

That some children resembled their mother much more than their father, or that sharp differences were evidenced between some siblings, seemed not to matter to Aristotle. All of these evidences inconsistent with his theory were dismissed as accidents of nature.

> Presumably nature seeks to reproduce the parent exactly in the offspring, but fails in different degrees. The ideal would be for male to produce male only; the first fall from this is the production of females, and thence we can proceed by gentle gradations to freaks [translator's note to 4.3.767b1–6].

Jan Swammerdam (1637–1680)

So strong was the influence of Aristotle, and so weak contradictory information, that Aristotle's theory survived essentially intact well into the seventeenth century, when Jan Swammerdam, using the recently developed compound microscope, noticed life in semen. From his belief that he observed microscopically small babies in the semen, he developed a preformation theory that the live sperm cells were the preformed young, with the egg merely providing nourishment. This theory, entirely consistent with Aristotle's belief, tended to retain the assumption that the apparent transmittal of features of the mother to the child was merely an accident of nature, or some type of vague influence or markings, which the mother could make upon the preformed youngsters.

Regner de Graaf (1641–1673)

Regner de Graaf, searching diligently for some form of germ cell in the female comparable to the male sperm cell, located a protuberance in the ovaries, which he thought to be eggs and which today bear his name, Graafian follicles. The first to appreciate the role of the female, de Graaf correctly surmised that the egg breaks away from the ovaries, links up with a sperm cell, and is thus fertilized. He further surmised that the fertilized egg then migrates to the uterus for development.

Kaspar Wolff (1733–1794)

Not until the late eighteenth century was the first adequate histological study made of the fertilization process. Kaspar Wolff determined, from his observations of chick embryos, that the germ cells contained substances that became differentiated after fertilization; thus, after fertilization, some undifferentiated substances developed potential for body organs, legs, and wings. He demonstrated, by scooping out nearly microscopic portions of the fluid mass, from specific parts of the mass and at critical periods in the development just before and just after fertilization, that he could make drastic but specific deformities occur at will. He could remove a wing or leg, or cause deformed wings or legs, simply by interfering with the small fluid mass that developed into the wing or leg. His theory, known as epigenesis and similar to our present-day general conception of heredity, was a monumental step in the understanding of the role of both sexes in the reproductive process. He essentially put to rest the theory of preformation.

Jean Lamarck (1744–1829)

At about the same time that Wolff was working on his theory of epigenesis, Jean Lamarck presented one of the most tenacious theories in genetics. Lamarck's theory of the inheritance of acquired characteristics is important because, although it apparently was disproved in the early part of the twentieth century, recent work on protein molecules has opened the possibility that environmental influences on heredity may yet need to be taken into account. Lamarck believed in the power of experience to make modification in the body that could be transmitted to the next generation.

Companion to Lamarck's theory of the inheritance of acquired characteristics is his disuse theory—organs not used eventually become less and less pronounced with each generation, until they no longer appear. Proof is taken from the cavefish, which in sunlight have functional eyes but which, when introduced into a dark cave, develop into a nearly pure breed of eyeless fish in very few generations. Lamarck explains this as atrophy caused by disuse. He postulated that evolution occurred in this way: through the gradual acquisition of a characteristic developed during one's ancestors' lifetimes, and through the gradual eroding away of organs and functions disused from generation to generation. Modern research has demonstrated that only characteristics resulting from biochemical experience are acquired from one generation to the next. The environment definitely can influence heredity. But it does so only through the avenue of the body chemistry that affects the DNA-RNA organization in the chromosomes. No evidence whatsoever indicates that behavioral experiences that do not affect body chemistry have any influence on heredity.

Charles Darwin (1809–1882)

Charles Darwin represents the first massive infusion of genetic theory into the thinking of man. Until his time, the theories of genetic scientists had little impact on science as a whole and certainly no effect on the thinking of Western man, who for the most part rested content in his feeling that the Book of Genesis contained all that was necessary for understanding the vast proliferation of God's creatures on earth.

A trip around the world led Darwin, an English clergyman by training and a naturalist by hobby, to the observation that remarkable changes did indeed occur in the species of the world: and though he vigorously rejected Lamarck's conceptions—"Heaven forfend me from Lamarck's nonsense of a tendency to progression" (quoted by Winchester, 1951, p. 25)—he was forced to conclude that some principle governed the development of variations. Stimulated by Thomas Robert Malthus's book on overpopulation, which indicated that only a small fraction of the reproductive potential of any species survived to maturity, Darwin hit upon the essentials of his idea of natural selection: given an overproduction of offspring and a hostile environment in which all but a small fraction die before reproducing themselves, those offspring that have the best adaptive characteristics survive and reproduce.

Not fathoming the concept of genotypic mutations (actual random changes in the hereditary units themselves) that accompany the phenotypic changes (changes in obvious outward appearance), Darwin attempted to understand the inheritance of the adaptive mechanism. Thus he developed the concept of pangenesis: the existence of hereditary units, located in all parts of the body, which circulate to and from the reproductive organs. The arms of a blacksmith, Darwin thought, are represented in his germ cells by a substance that he called pangenes and that, he believed, could be altered by the development of the organ in which they are produced and in which they circulate. Hence, by constantly circulating from the arms to the testes, the arm pangenes of the blacksmith become overdeveloped and the blacksmith's child is born with arms that are potentially large. This is similar to Lamarck's "nonsense," but the similarity never seemed apparent to Darwin. Darwin also maintained that not all the pangenes are used by every generation; thus he explained how some family characteristics could skip a generation.

August Weismann (1834–1914)

Two additional giant steps forward bring us to the beginning of modern genetics and the work of Gregor Mendel. The first of these was the germ-plasm theory of August Weismann, who distinguished somatoplasm, the type of cell that makes up all of the body except the reproductive cells, from germ plasm, which is isolated even after the first divisions in the embryonic period and is solely responsible for reproduction. He believed in a continuity of cell division from one generation to another, a continuity unaffected by any life experience.

Although Weismann believed in natural selection, he demolished Darwin's theory of pangenesis by cutting the tails of mice for many generations, so that there could be no migration of pangenes, yet finding no change in the tail length in subsequent generations. Thus his major contribution was in greatly diminishing the influence of the concepts of pangenesis and the inheritance of acquired characteristics. He obviously overemphasized the isolation of the germ plasm, but his concept of its continuity was a foundation for modern genetics.

Hugo De Vries (1848–1935)

The second great step leading toward Mendel was taken by Hugo De Vries, who, from his observation of the primrose, provided, through his mutation theory, the essential explanation of varieties of species. He determined that any living organism infrequently but consistently produces new types of offspring through sudden changes, or mutations in the hereditary mechanism. Thus, evolution was neither a gradual eroding away of some unused organ nor the gradual development of some desirable characteristic, but a series of discrete jumps. This, together with the knowledge that most mutations are fatal, could account for the changes resulting from a small portion of desirable mutations.

It matters little that the changes in primroses observed by De Vries in 1909 were not in fact mutations, or new species, but rather recessive characteristics; the fact remains that his basic idea was a sound one and became a firm foundation for modern genetics. As important as this work was, however, perhaps De Vries's most significant contribution to genetics was his rediscovery and popularization of Mendel's concept, which ushered in the modern study of genetics.

FOUNDATIONS OF MODERN GENETICS

Concepts of heredity have changed through the years as man has learned more and more about himself and his world. As research methods became more sophisticated, and as more and more men became researchers, our knowledge and understanding of the process of heredity grew, based on the firm foundation provided by Gregor Mendel, Thomas Hunt Morgan, George W. Beadle, and Edward L. Tatum.

Gregor Mendel (1822–1884)

Noting the ready availability of a number of pure varieties of garden peas, so shaped that the reproductive organs, protected by the petals, were self-pollinating, Gregor Mendel began his study of heredity. With a background in mathematics and natural history, the Moravian monk was uniquely qualified for his work. The care with which he kept his records, his knowledge of mathematics, and his shrewd guesses put Mendel far ahead of his time. Using twenty-two varieties of peas that produced fertile hybrids, during eight years of careful work Mendel formulated the five major points of modern genetics.

1. Factors, christened genes by Hugo De Vries, are the transmitting agents.
2. A mature plant has two of each type of factor.
3. When these are different (hybrid), one will be dominant and the other latent, or recessive.
4. In the germ cells, the factors divide such that each gamete or daughter cell carries only one of the pair.
5. A random union of these gamete cells results in the variations seen [Winchester, 1951, p. 61].

Mendel's discoveries, first published in 1866 in the proceedings of a provincial natural-history society, had a major impact on the thinking of the world's geneticists. The concept of the independence of "characters," or hereditary traits, such that they combine as do chips of marble instead of blending like paint pigments, made modern genetics possible. The idea that each parent has a pair of each "character," and that chance alone determines which of the pair is transmitted to a given offspring, made the developing mathematics of probability a tool of genetics. The concept that hybrids, which show no surface or phenotypic evidence of a given trait, are still carriers of that characteristic in a recessive position clarified the old mystery of the sudden reappearance of characteristics that have skipped several generations—of why, for example, a family may have no color-blind members for five generations, and suddenly produce four color-blind sons.

Thomas Hunt Morgan (1866–1945)

Thomas Hunt Morgan, working with the vinegar fly, made the discovery that the "characters" mentioned by Mendel are in fact actual structures carried in the chromosomes of the cell nucleus. Morgan also determined that the independence of factors was somewhat limited, in that the genes within chromosomes tend to be transported in groups, like beads on a string rather than like chips of marble. That is, genes are transported in a linked fashion, and where they go is not determined by pure chance (see Figure 1). This finding was in turn complicated somewhat by the observation, made with the electron microscope, that some of the genes cross over from one chromosome to another during cell division. However, these genes that cross over are few, considering that man normally has twenty-three pairs of chromosomes and that each of these probably contains thousands of genes:

> By grouping genes in chromosomes and yet allowing them some freedom to change their lodgings, nature reconciles two conflicting requirements of inheritance and evolution. On the one hand, total disorganization of the genes in a cell would make the reproduction of cells exceedingly difficult. The tiny vinegar fly has something of the order of 10,000 genes. If they were loose in the cell nucleus, like buckshot, the problem of passing them on in exactly equal number to every daughter cell would be formidable. The problem is reduced to manageable proportions by the fact that the genes are grouped in four pairs of chromosomes: thus the cell has only eight objects to cope with, instead of 10,000. On the other hand, if the genes were

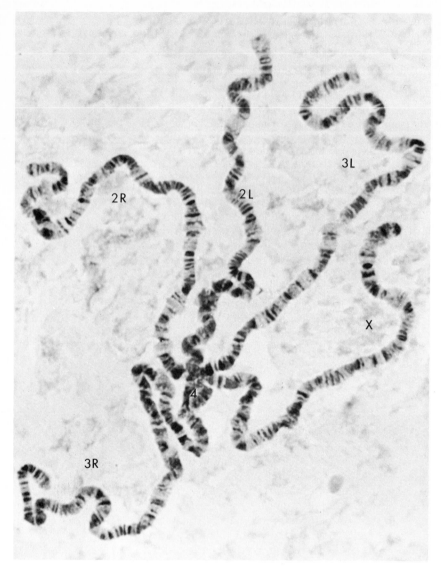

Figure 1
Photomicrograph of salivary-gland chromosomes of *Drosophila melanogaster*. Courtesy of Berwind P. Kaufmann, Professor Emeritus, Department of Zoology, University of Michigan, Ann Arbor.

forever bound in the same chromosomes, the organism would lack the flexibility for recombination of genes which is essential for evolutionary development [N. Horowitz, 1956, p. 82].

George Beadle (b. 1903) and Edward Tatum (b. 1909)

George Beadle and Edward Tatum, winners of the Nobel Prize for Medicine in 1958 for their work with DNA (deoxyribonucleic acid) and RNA (ribonucleic acid) protein molecules, discovered that genes act by regulating definite chemical events: i.e., the genes control metabolic reactions. Their hypothesis of one-gene/one-enzyme found experimental support. They established that each gene has a "specific action, in some cases limited to control over only a portion of the synthesis of some chemical" (Goodnight, Goodnight, and P. Gray, 1964, p. 465). Obviously, any changes in the genes would affect the chemical balance in the body.

BIOLOGICAL CONCEPTS

To review a few basic principles of biology as they relate to behavior is appropriate to our fully realizing the critical importance of the contribution of modern genetics to our understanding of child psychology. These biological concepts, related to the reproductive and hereditary processes, are introduced according to their function in the developmental process of the growing child. Genetic constitution is expressed in development. Human biology is intricately associated with human behavior. To understand the latter, we need a rudimentary understanding of the former.

Alleles

Mendel discovered genes and developed the concept of dominant versus recessive genes. Biologists today have discovered alleles, the twin, altered states of the same gene, which make the building blocks for the gene combinations that explain hereditary variations.

Each gene consists of a pair of alleles that separate in the germ cells during the reduction division of the chromosomes: each germ cell donates one allele to each daughter cell, making possible several gene combinations in the fertilized germ cell. If for any given hereditary characteristic (such as eye color, for instance), identical pairs come from the parents (two blue-eyed alleles), the daughter cell is homozygous; if an unlike pair combines (one blue-eyed allele and one brown-eyed), the daughter cell is heterozygous and the dominant allele will produce the phenotype (brown eyes).

Dominance

The recognition of this allele concept, plus the concept of dominance, made possible an understanding of the concept of an hereditary trait carrier. A dominant characteristic will be expressed physically even when represented by a heterozygous cell. A recessive characteristic is expressed only through a homozygous cell.

Eye color demonstrates this phenomenon: two alleles for eye color are brown (B), which is dominant, and blue (b), which is recessive. Two brown-eyed parents, then, can represent any combination of Bb, except bb; they can be BB or Bb. Assuming for the moment that they are both heterozygous for brown eyes, Bb, then they will produce an equal number of B alleles and b alleles, with the result that they should have an equal number of children who are BB and bb, and twice as many who are Bb. This combination, then, would produce three times as many brown-eyed children as blue-eyed children, since both BB and Bb are brown-eyed.

This same logic forms the basis for blood type; type A is dominant; O, recessive. Thus a child who received a type A allele from the father and a type O from his mother will have type A blood, but will be a carrier of type O. We are making, then, a distinction between the phenotype, which is the physical expression of the characteristic, and the genotype, which is the genetic combination that produced the phenotype.

Incomplete Dominance

Concomitant with a concept of dominance in heredity is the concept of incomplete dominance, which occurs most frequently when the characteristic or phenotype is carried by several genes located on different chromosomes, such as skin pigment, and height, and hair color, and freckles, all of which usually seem to produce some intermediate condition rather than an exact reproduction of the parent: in the case of one very dark-skinned and one very light-skinned parent, the skin of the offspring is usually between the two extremes.

Accompanying this principle of incomplete dominance is one developed by Galton referred to as the law of filial regression, which operates both from a statistical distribution model and from the incomplete dominance in many inherited factors in humans. The law of filial regression holds that parents at the extreme of any distribution produce offspring that tend back toward the mean. For example, two extremely tall parents tend to have children shorter than either of them; two very bright parents tend to have children duller than either of them; extremely dark parents tend to have children lighter than either of them.

The converse of this is also true, such that dull parents have brighter children than they, etc. This is one of the reasons why population control would not be a productive answer for extreme cases, such as mental retardation. Most mentally retarded children do not have parents who are retarded, and most mentally retarded parents have children who are not mentally retarded. There are exceptions of course, but they are not the usual rule.

Sex-linked Traits

The sex-linked concept refers to characteristics carried on the sex pair of chromosomes. Sex-linked conditions can be dominant or recessive, and usually are carried on the X chromosome. Man has two sex chromosomes, paired in the female (XX) and unpaired in the male (XY); all other chromosomes are autosomes. Man has twenty-two pairs of autosomes and two sex chromosomes.

Color Blindness

The best example of a sex-linked characteristic is color blindness, carried on the X chromosome but recessive to dominant color perception. If a female carrier (only one of her X chromosomes carries the affliction) mates with a man who is not color-blind, the probability is that half her sons will have the affliction and half her daughters will be carriers. An afflicted male who mates with a noncarrier female will have no color-blind sons, but all his daughters will be carriers (see Figure 2).

Male color-blind	X Y +				
Female color-blind ..		X X			
	X	+	X	=	Color-blind daughter
	X	+	X	=	Color-blind daughter
	Y	+	X	=	Color-blind son
	Y	+	X	=	Color-blind son
Male color-blind	X Y +				
Female carrier		X X			
	X	+	X	=	Color-blind daughter
	X	+	X	=	Carrier daughter
	Y	+	X	=	Color-blind son
	Y	+	X	=	Normal son
Male color-blind	X Y +				
Female normal		X X			
	X	+	X	=	Carrier daughter
	X	+	X	=	Carrier daughter
	Y	+	X	=	Normal son
	Y	+	X	=	Normal son
Male Normal	X Y +				
Female color-blind ..		X X			
	X	+	X	=	Carrier daughter
	X	+	X	=	Carrier daughter
	Y	+	X	=	Color-blind son
	Y	+	X	=	Color-blind son
Male Normal	X Y +				
Female carrier		X X			
	X	+	X	=	Carrier daughter
	X	+	X	=	Normal daughter
	Y	+	X	=	Color-blind son
	Y	+	X	=	Normal son
Male Normal	X Y +				
Female normal		X X			
	X	+	X	=	Normal daughter
	X	+	X	=	Normal daughter
	Y	+	X	=	Normal son
	Y	+	X	=	Normal son

Figure 2
Schematic diagram of the inheritance of color blindness.

What is important, and critically so, is that color blindness be recognized early to prevent a child from being penalized on reading readiness tests and other color-coded learning tools, and to spare him the frustration of trying to comprehend the discriminations his teacher can make but which are completely unintelligible to him. Many of the better tests of reading readiness are no longer color-coded for this very reason.

Hemophilia

Only about one boy in ten thousand is born with hemophilia, a disease involving a defect in blood coagulation because of a deficiency of antihemophilic globulin. It is a classic example of a disorder transmitted by the X chromosome. Several European royal families have suffered from the disease.

Man has twenty-three pairs of chromosomes. In the cell division of the germ cells, each daughter cell, each gamete, receives only one of each pair of chromosomes. This cell division is meiosis.

Mitosis, on the other hand, is the cell division process for all body cells other than germ cells. Mitosis ensures a full complement of chromosomes for each gamete somatic cell; each daughter cell is a carbon copy with 46 chromosomes. The variation in humankind results from meiosis rather than mitosis, from the elaborate interaction of the haploid cells (containing half the chromosomes) from both parents combining.

Occasionally the reduction division, the meiosis, of chromosomes in the germ cells does not, for some reason, result in a neat division. Such a chromosomal aberration is Down's syndrome, where the error is related to the twenty-first chromosome. Sex chromosome anomalies are related to the twenty-third pair. Single-gene defects that are recessive, dominant, or X-linked also cause disturbances or changes in the naturally expected order of heredity.

> By 1971, the total number of disorders proven to be caused by abnormal recessive genes had reached 366, according to Dr. Victor A. McKusick, of Johns Hopkins University School of Medicine [with another 421 probables]. . . . Dr. McKusick's 1971 count showed 418 disorders resulting from abnormalities in dominant genes, with 528 additional probables. . . . [He] listed 86 disorders proven to be caused by X-linked genes, with 65 more probables [Apgar and Beck, 1972, pp. 75, 78, 79].

A chromosome error involves more genetic material than a single gene. In Down's syndrome, for instance, every cell in the body carries the chromosomal aberration of forty-seven instead of forty-six. Chromosomal errors usually produce multiple and severe abnormalities, and, like single-gene defects, are preprogrammed into the genetic material of the unborn child. All the possible causes for these defects, mutations, and chromosome errors are not known; but some are.

Down's Syndrome

Down's syndrome seems to relate to extra, probably fragmented pieces of chromosome becoming attached to the twenty-first pair of chromosomes, giving the appearance of a triplet chromosome (see Figure 3). At least one researcher feels that the cause of this abnormality may lie in the early environment of the fetus.

> Our research over the last 25 years has established beyond doubt that mongolism is a prenatal growth deficiency in which central growth regulation is at fault. The child with mongolism suffers from a deceleration of growth during the prenatal period which results in a highly complex, multidimensional disorder in which every organ is involved. . . . While a hereditary-genetic disorder and a spontaneous gene mutation can be excluded as causes of mongolism, we and other investigators have accumulated a wealth of material which indicates that the condition of the mother—either at the time of conception or shortly thereafter—is responsible for the occurrence [Benda, 1960, pp. 188, 194].

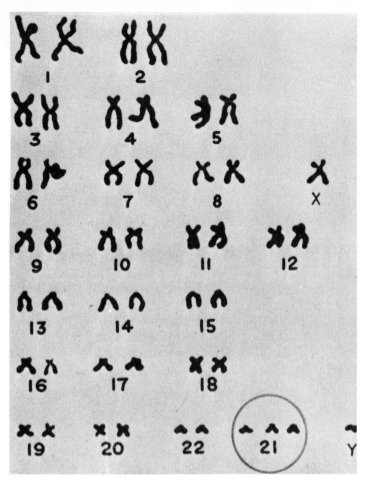

Figure 3

Down's syndrome. Reprinted, by permission of Melvin
M. Grumbach and The National Foundation, from *Chemis-
try, Chromosomes, and Congenital Anomalies* (New York:
The National Foundation-March of Dimes, n.d.), p. 5.

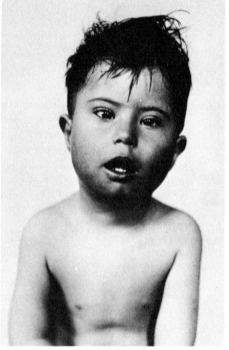

There are instances of mongolism where the number of chromosomes is correct, but one of the forty-six is longer than it should be. It is possible that the extra chromosome is attached there. Interestingly enough, this long D chromosome has been noted frequently in the parents of mongoloids, but balanced by the absence of a G chromosome. The parents show no mongoloid symptoms, but must be carriers. The probability that children of such parents will be mongoloid is one in three.

The incidence of Down's syndrome is estimated variously, from about one in seven-hundred births to about one in five-hundred. Table 1 shows its relationship to maternal age.

Table 1

Risk of Down's Syndrome by Maternal Age

	Risk of Down's Syndrome in Child	
Age of Mother	At Any Pregnancy	After the Birth of a Mongoloid
–29	1 in 3,000	1 in 1,000
30–34	1 in 600	1 in 200
35–39	1 in 280	1 in 100
40–44	1 in 70	1 in 25
45–49	1 in 40	1 in 15
All mothers	1 in 665	1 in 200

Reprinted, by permission of the authors and the publisher, from Cedric O. Carter and D. MacCarthy, Incidence of mongolism and its diagnosis in the newborn, *British Journal of Social Medicine*, 1951, 5, 83–90.

Children suffering from Down's syndrome are identified at birth by their characteristic appearance—almond-shaped eyes and rather roundish heads. They are mentally retarded and usually die young, although their life expectancy has increased fourfold in the last generation with the availability of antibiotics to treat the respiratory infections to which they are especially susceptible. They also have a higher susceptibility to congenital heart disease and leukemia. "They are usually delightful children, easy to manage, and, for some inexplicable reason, love music" (Emery, 1968, p. 52). The picture of children with Down's syndrome is one of overall developmental retardation. The child shown in Figure 3 has the typical upward-slanted eyes and short neck; his karyotype shows forty-seven chromosomes.

Research on Down's syndrome has left the impression that "the defect resulting in the Down's syndrome resides in the fertilized egg and therefore, presumably, in some defect in ova or sperm, but the defect is apparently not a mutation of a Mendelian gene" (Knudson, 1965, p. 63). In studying pairs of twins at least one of whom shows Down's syndrome, A. Smith (1960) found (with only two exceptions) that both monozygotic twins are invariably affected (concordant), while the other of the dizygotic twins is always unaffected (discordant). "Down's syndrome is the only common malformation where, with one exception, the monozygotic co-twins of affected individuals have always also been affected, indicating complete genetic determination" (C. Carter, 1964, pp. 306–307). The consistency of the older average age of mothers of children with Down's syndrome focuses attention on the egg rather than the sperm as the site of the defect.

Klinefelter's Syndrome

The typical Klinefelter's syndrome male child (XXY) has both masculine and feminine secondary sexual characteristics. He is tall and usually somewhat frail, lacks masculine hair and hair pigmentation, and has small, undeveloped testicles. Usually he is infertile in adulthood, often accompanied by larger than normal breast development and a higher pitched voice than that of the usual male. The condition occurs about once in every four-hundred male births and accounts for 1 to 2 percent of the institutionalized mentally retarded males.

Not all Klinefelter's syndrome children are retarded, and not all are infertile, but both conditions prevail in the usual case. Although many Klinefelter's syndrome children have normal intelligence and can develop useful, productive lives, through help in appearance and behavior by male hormone treatment during adolescence, no specific treatment of the condition is known. Sensitivity on the part of the parents and physician to the child's discomfort in situations such as the locker room at P.E. will aid in the child's acceptance and adjustment.

Turner's Syndrome

In the female child, a parallel condition to Klinefelter's syndrome is Turner's syndrome (XO), which is far less common because a human fetus rarely survives with a missing chromosome. Most Turner's syndrome children are aborted spontaneously; less than 3 percent survive until birth. One in every two- to three-thousand live-born female babies carries the XO condition. This is five to seven times less frequent than Klinefelter's syndrome.

The usual symptom pattern is swelling in the extremities, which disappears with age, leaving flabby folds of skin and webbing, particularly in the neck area (see Figure 4). This swelling leaves distorted ridges in the fingerprints, a useful stigmata of the condition. In early adolescence, more obvious sexual differences appear in the form of small, immature breast development, abnormal ovary development, and a lack of secondary sexual changes in hair and contour. Turner's syndrome children are generally of normal intelligence, small in stature, and subject to abnormal heart and metabolism development.

The appearance of the two-year-old girl in Figure 4 is typical of Turner's syndrome. There is considerable edema of her extremities, a frequent sign. Her neck is short, with loose folds of skin over the nape. She also has a high-arched palate, a triangular-shaped mouth, and low-set, deformed

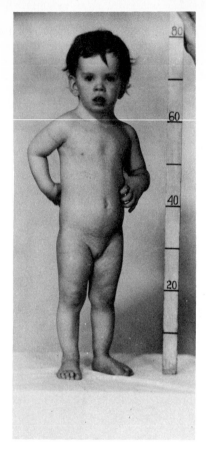

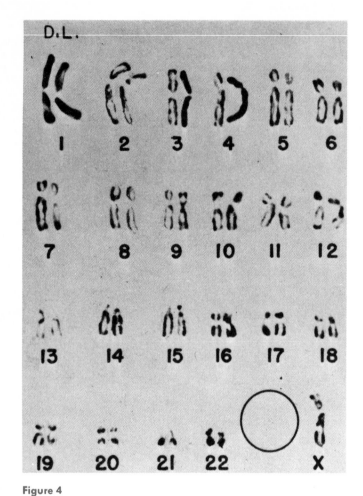

Figure 4

Turner's syndrome. Reprinted, by permission of Melvin M. Grumbach and The National Foundation, from *Chemistry,* *Chromosomes, and Congenital Anomalies* (New York: The National Foundation–March of Dimes, n.d.), p. 6.

ears. Her karyotype bears out the clinical findings; she has forty-five chromosomes: twenty-two pairs and only a single X chromosome (XO).

XYY Syndrome

The XYY syndrome, or the super male, was for some time believed to be associated with abnormal aggressiveness and criminal proneness in the male, but scientific observations made upon individual cases in prisons have not confirmed this. Persons afflicted with the XYY condition are tall, given to excessive acne as adults, and have a much higher than normal tendency to develop abnormal electrical patterns in the brain, with concomitant seizures.

Overproduction of Germ Cells

A sixth biological concept is that of an oversupply of germ cells. In the female fetus, by six weeks after conception, the primary oocytes, or special germ cells out of which the ova are formed, already are developed, some 600,000 in number. These germ cells, located in the ovary area, begin a process of reduction division, meiosis, at about the third fetal month. During this process, the cells line up as they were at fertilization, with the father-donated chromosomes exactly parallel to the mother-donated. During this period, the process of crossing-over occurs, such that the new daughter cells, or oocytes, have new combinations, but each contains the full number of chromosomes. At about the fifth month of prenatal life, the meiosis process is arrested and remains arrested until puberty.

At birth, there are about two million oocytes in existence, but only about 350 to 400 will mature into fully developed ova. Of these 350, on an average in the United States, only 2 are fertilized to develop into a fetus. Only a fraction of the potential ova participate in the reproductive process.

One theory of the cause of Down's syndrome, or mongolism, is the so-called tired-ovum theory. Younger mothers, less than thirty years old, have been noted to have a risk factor of only 1 in 3,000 of producing a Down's syndrome child; whereas older mothers, thirty to thirty-four, have a risk factor of 1 in 600, and mothers between thirty-five and thirty-nine, a risk factor of 1 in 280. The theory is that ova in older women have a greater possibility of some kind of change that produces the abnormality.

During puberty, a second stage of meiosis begins. This time the daughter cells do not follow the usual process of duplication before division; instead, the chromosomes divide before duplication. This is, of course, after the so-called cross-over that occurred in the prenatal period, and, in the female, results in the formation of two kinds of daughter cells, both with only twenty-three of the chromosomes, one from each of the pair. One daughter cell, much smaller and with less of the cytoplasm, called a polar body, quickly is reabsorbed by the body. The other, the ovum located in a follicle in the ovary, continues to expand in terms of cytoplasm, and finally, in the process called ovulation, is released into the fluid of the abdominal cavity by the ovary, where it becomes a target of the sperm cells, which also, by the process of reduction division, meiosis, have only half the chromosome number, one from each pair.

The ova contain only X chromosomes of course, while the sperm contain either an X or a Y chromosome. The male reduction division does not result in the production of polar bodies; many more sperm cells are produced than ova. In fact, a normal, healthy male is estimated to deposit three to five-hundred million sperm into the vagina at a single ejaculation.

Fertilization

Fertilization of the single haploid ovum, by one of the millions of haploid sperm, occurs in the fallopian tube to produce the diploid zygote, which rapidly develops into the blastocyst implanted in the nurturing wall (the endometrium) of the uterus. From this single fertilized cell, already growing phenomenally as it becomes firmly attached to its life-supply source, comes the child. Half of his inherited potential comes from his mother, half from his father. His growth and development in utero will depend not only upon his inherited genotype, but also upon the health of his mother, her nutrition, and the absence of toxic agents in her blood stream.

Twinning

Multiple births essentially occur in two ways. First, through the process of single ovum division occurring shortly after fertilization, the identical twinning process; each of these twins, called monozygotes, has identical genetic components. They most frequently are born in a single placenta and share the same outer chorion, but have separate amniotic sacs. The only sure determination of identical twinning is with rather complex blood grouping and skin patch tests, since it is not only difficult after a twin birth to determine if there was a single placenta, but some identical twins do have different placentas. There can, of course, be identical triplets, quadruplets, and perhaps even quintuplets, but this is not the more common form of multiple birth.

More common is the simultaneous ovulation and fertilization of two or more ova, fraternal twinning or heterozygotic twinning. In this case, from a genetic point of view, these twins have no greater similarity than do ordinary brothers and sisters.

Obviously, even though their development in the uterus is simultaneous, twins do not have precisely the same environment. They have different nutrition, oxygen, and waste systems, and at times, more or less input into the placenta. They are subject to different potential in infection, injury, and birth sequence. There are subtle differences even in identical twins, such as fingerprints, and mirror image placement of some physical features, or birth marks. Twins represent a mild but significantly greater risk than nontwins in the prenatal life and birth process simply because they place an added stress on the life-support system.

HEREDITARY METABOLIC DISEASES

Research in hereditary metabolic diseases was pioneered by an eminent physician, Archibald Garrod (1909), whose concept of inborn errors of metabolism pushed genetics another step forward. A genetically determined biochemical disorder, an inborn error hinders metabolism through a specific enzyme defect that produces a toxic effect.

Phenylketonuria (PKU)

One out of seventy American parents is estimated to carry the recessive gene for phenylketonuria; but since it is recessive, PKU occurs in only one birth out of every twenty thousand. It is associated predominantly with the Caucasian population groups (Reisman and Matheny, 1969). In spite of its rarity, the effect of phenylketonuria is so hazardous, if neglected, that all babies are routinely checked for this disease by a simple blood test at birth, the Guthrie test.

PKU is caused by an inability to manufacture a specific enzyme, the result of which is the production of a waste byproduct of milk and milk products, phenylalanine, which is damaging to the growing brain. The damage begins in the first few days after the infant ingests protein in formula or from breast feeding. Unchecked, the brain damage is so severe that 90 percent of the afflicted children have to be institutionalized. In addition to causing brain damage, the blocked metabolism prevents the production of skin pigment, resulting in an albinolike quality to the skin, hair, and eyes.

If the Guthrie test is positive for PKU, the major treatment is the restriction of phenylalanine in the diet, which is most difficult because of the great need of the developing child for protein. Special PKU diets are being produced to maintain the child through the critical first four years of life, after which many children are returned to a normal diet, since the accumulation of phenylalanine seems to have its main effect during the period of rapid growth of the brain.

Occasionally the Guthrie test gives false positives on children with a temporary buildup of phenylalanine due to reasons other than PKU. The diet also produces problems. Phenylalanine is in so many essential foods that a constant manipulation of the diet is necessary to insure no deficiencies in proteins. Because of the complexity of the treatment, special PKU clinics manage the cases of most PKU children, rather than the family doctor.

Galactosemia and Lactosemia

Two related conditions were more recently discovered. Galactosemia is the inability to convert galactose into glucose and energy, and lactosemia is the inability to convert lactose into glucose and energy. In both cases, the buildup of excess unmetabolized milk sugar causes damage to the liver, spleen, eyes, and brain. Perhaps as many as 12 percent of all infants in the United States, and a much higher percentage in some Eastern countries, are unable to metabolize milk, which is touted as a universal food. Some of the frequent digestive problems and general health problems of infants probably stem from this inability to properly digest milk foods. The lack of the enzymes galactase and lactase may account for problems in infant health to a greater degree than was once believed.

Recent investigators, who have identified the defect as a recessive trait carried on one chromosome, suggest that a woman who is a carrier and pregnant with a baby who might have inherited two abnormal genes should probably limit the intake of milk in her own diet to reduce the prenatal effect of the disease. Certainly the child's intake of milk and milk products should be reduced.

Recent cross-cultural studies of the absence of lactase indicate vast genetic differences in the ability to produce this enzyme.

> Lactose is milk sugar; the enzyme lactase breaks it down. For want of lactase most adults cannot digest milk. In populations that drink milk the adults have more lactase, perhaps through natural selection [Kretchmer, 1972, p. 71].

The capacity to digest lactose probably occurred as a mutation in the group of individuals who became animal herders, less than ten thousand years ago. Lactose tolerance obviously is transmitted genetically and is dominant, but interestingly enough, intolerance is also transmitted genetically and is probably a recessive trait.

It would appear that in racial groups with a long tradition of herdsmanship, such as Swedish, Swiss, Finnish, and U.S. white, the population has a high tolerance to lactose; populations without the herding tradition as a main food staple, Yoruba and Chinese, for instance, have almost a total intolerance to lactose.

> By 1970 enough data had been accumulated to indicate that many more groups all over the world are intolerant to lactose than are tolerant. As a matter of fact, real adult tolerance to lactose has so far been observed only in northern Europeans, approximately 90 per cent of whom tolerate lactose, and in the members of two nomadic pastoral tribes in Africa, of whom about 80 per cent are tolerant [Kretchmer, 1972, pp. 73–74].

Long-range implications of these findings for world health situations and food supply will have to await further research, but presently it would appear that milk is far from the univeral good food for infants that it was once presumed to be.

Sickle-cell Anemia

In addition to the general tendency for PKU and other metabolism problems to have discernible geographic and racial distributions, other syndromes follow definite racial origins and probably relate to an early mutation in that cultural group. One of the most significant of these is sickle-cell anemia, carried by 10 percent of the blacks in the United States. This recessive disorder is caused by defective DNA, which carry incorrect instructions for the production of hemoglobin, a protein foundation of red blood cells. This slight error in the DNA causes an abnormally shaped red blood cell: the cell is sickle-shaped rather than rounded.

Sickling of the blood cells seems to occur most frequently in blood vessels with low oxygen content. Thus the progressive nature of the disease, since the abnormal shape of the cells causes them to carry little oxygen, to group together in a clog, which further reduces the amount of oxygen in the blood stream, which produces a higher rate of sickling.

The condition causes two main problems: first, the anemia caused by the rapid destruction of the red blood cells; and second, the coagulation caused by the clumping together of the sickled cells. The symptoms of the disease begin in the young child with swelling in the extremities, thickening of the bones in the fingers and toes, and compression of the bone marrow. The effects, noticeable at age two, are accompanied by severe pain during the crisis period, followed by enlargement of the heart and progressive anemia and blood stagnation. Complications of advanced stages are unhealing sores, neurological breakdown, and general symptoms of severe anemia.

Before the disease was identified, fully half of the children afflicted with sickle-cell anemia died by the age of twenty, few lived longer than age forty. Now with early detection, good treatment, and consistent medical care, the probability of a normal life span has been increased greatly. The disease is not restricted exclusively to black children, but because of the high incidence of carriers in black America, routine screening of all young black children is indicated.

Diabetes

Although the most common hereditary metabolic disease, diabetes is not as predictable as other genetic disturbances. In fact, because of the difficulty in developing an adequate model of its operation, diabetes frequently is referred to as the "geneticist's nightmare." Presently, the major functional utility of knowing that diabetes is a hereditary disease is simply to insure a great deal of additional checking when diabetes is present in the family.

Fully 10 percent of all diabetics are children, and children's diabetes is far more serious and more closely related to hereditary factors than is diabetes contracted late in life. The precise cause of diabetes is unknown; but evidently, in persons suffering from diabetes, the quality of insulin manufactured in the body is such that it does not effectively metabolize sugars and starches. Evidence also supports the contention that childhood diabetes is more likely to be an insufficient production of insulin rather than an improper release, as is the case with adults.

Insulin was extracted from the pancreas in 1921 (Sawin, 1969). Manufactured in the islets of Langerhans in the pancreas, insulin increases cell permeability to glucose. Anoxia and exercise mimic insulin in that they also increase glucose permeability, but insulin is necessary for this to happen.

The overall effect of insulin on the body is to diminish the use of fatty acids as an energy source and to increase their storage in adipose tissue. At the same time, the burning of amino acids for energy is inhibited and their corporation into protein enhanced—the protein-sparing effect of carbohydrate. The main determinant of insulin secretion is the level of blood glucose. Diabetes mellitus is caused by a lack of enough insulin to get glucose speedily out of the blood and into the tissue, yet it is more complex than that.

One out of four persons in the United States is estimated to be a carrier of diabetes, which is peculiarly recessive: even if two carriers marry, the chances of their child having the disease is only one in four. Unfortunately, no scientific basis has been discovered to indicate who is a carrier; the only cue comes from the family history.

When two diabetics marry, all of their children eventually will develop diabetes, although not necessarily in childhood. If a diabetic marries a carrier, half of their children will develop the condition, if they live long enough: only half of the potential diabetics live long enough for the condition to develop.

No reliable report has identified babies with diabetes at birth. The peak years for the development of diabetes in childhood are between the ages of eight and twelve. One child in every twenty-five hundred is diabetic.

Obviously, diabetic tests are desirable for all children during this age period; treatment should be started immediately upon discovery. The major problem is in establishing a good balance of insulin. Complications from diabetes include problems with circulation, healing of sores, infections, hardening of the arteries, and blindness.

The fetal months of the baby carried by a diabetic mother are extremely hazardous. The risk is progressive to the point where most physicians prefer to induce early labor rather than run the risk of toxemia in the last month. Diabetic parents should be alert to the risk of their children developing the condition, and should exercise extremely careful management of pregnancy.

SUMMARY

Genetic research has taught us much about man. We know that inheritance is chemical. Therefore, we know that good nutrition and an absence of toxic agents are prerequisites for healthy children. Granted this base, man reproduces himself faithfully with relatively little influence exerted by his behavior, so long as his behavior does not affect the chemical balance of his body. But once his body chemistry is affected, faithful reproduction is no longer possible; the viability of the fetus is in inverse proportion to the magnitude of the change.

The complex process of the reproduction of replacement cells both in the body and in the reproductive organs is guided and regulated by the chemical structure, or chemical memory, of DNA. These protein molecules are arranged into long strings of substructures with discrete sections, each of which contains chemical instructions regarding cell growth through the manufacture of new and varied enzymes and proteins of increasing complexity and specificity. DNA and RNA within genes within chromosomes control metabolic reactions. Each gene has a specific chemical action; but each gene represents a specific location, or order, in the long strings of nucleic acid, rather than a specific compound.

Understanding that inheritance is chemical, even without understanding all the complex interactions, is enough to point out that the health of the parents is an all important factor in the health of the child. Understanding the implications of biology, even without understanding all the facts of biology, gives a basis for a beginning for understanding the child.

In spite of the great similarity among all babies, each is unique, and each will use and react differently to his environment. Born with uniqueness not only in genetic makeup, but in intrauterine environment, each child will grow, develop, and mature according to his own genetic constitution, proclivity, propensity, stimulation, nurture, and models.

Man is not just a product of his heredity and his environment. Man is the result of how he uses and incorporates his heredity and environment. And the child is not just a little man. He is a child, given certain heredi-

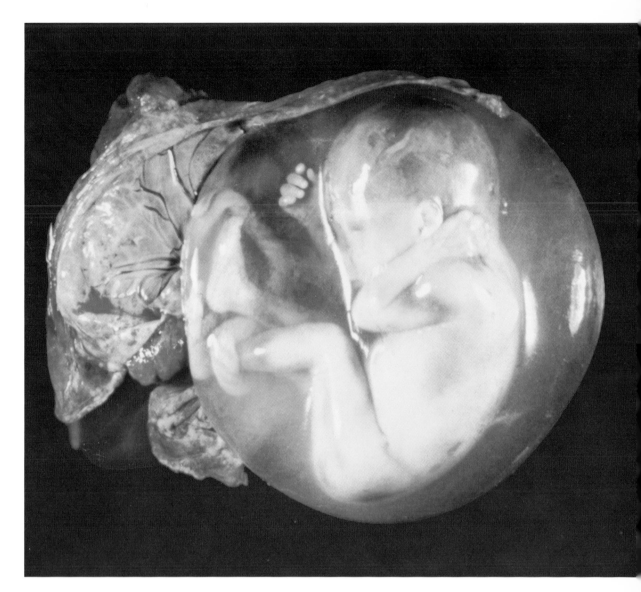

FIGURE 5
Fetus in utero. Photograph courtesy of
Dr. Landrum B. Shettles, The Presbyterian Hospital,
Columbia-Presbyterian Medical Center, New York.

tary propensities, set in a specific environment surrounded by specific influences, learning how to cope, to use, to assimilate, and to incorporate all that is available to him as he matures, grows, and changes according to his genetic potential for maturation and his experiences.

REPRODUCTION

The miracle of reproduction, in spite of all our knowledge, is just that—a miracle. Man is ever in awe of the newborn infant. So, accepting the miraculous, let us discover its order.

THE ENDOCRINOLOGY OF REPRODUCTION

Before we approach reproduction itself, to review the background that makes it possible is appropriate. The endocrinology of reproduction includes the female ovaries, the male testes, the pituitary, the placenta (in pregnancy), the hypothalamus, and the central nervous system. The endocrinology of reproduction begins in utero. The production of maternal hormones determines whether the pregnancy will be maintained. The combination of maternal and fetal hormone production sets the stage in utero for the spectacular changes of puberty. Although endocrination is discussed more fully in Chapter 3, the endocrinology of reproduction cannot be ignored here.

> Successful reproduction depends not only on normal gonads [ovary or testis] but also on the proper growth and development of the central nervous system and external genitalia.... Sexual behavior and gonadotropin secretion at puberty are dependent upon the central nervous system and are "built into" the brain during fetal life. Whether or not the fetus is exposed to testosterone makes a great deal of difference later on.... In adulthood, human sexual behavior depends on the gonadal hormones secreted and their effect on the central nervous system. Once the behavior pattern is established, its maintenance apparently depends on the central nervous system; libido beyond puberty is in large part psychologically determined. Still, normal adult sexual behavior probably requires proper conditioning of the central nervous system, preferably in utero [Sawin, 1969, pp. 149, 150].

Most growth of genitalia takes place at puberty, but development and initial growth in utero must be normal for pubertal changes to occur. The fetal testes, for example, produce testosterone, the androgen responsible for proper development of the male external genitalia. The gonadotropin that stimulates the testosterone secretion probably comes from the placenta. After birth, there is little gonadal activity until puberty.

Puberty

The magical age of change, puberty is a trying time for the child. Change is rapid, and rather phenomenal. And all of these changes come about because of the endocrine system and the central nervous system.

The exact trigger for the release of gonadotropin at puberty is not known. It is known that the stimulus for puberty comes from within the central nervous system; a girl who is blind has an earlier puberty than other girls. And it is known that gonadotropin secretion precedes ovarian or testicular development and secretion. And it is known that hypothalamic stimulation is necessary for the secretion of pituitary hormones, the follicle-stimulating hormone and the luteinizing hormone. The central nervous system and the hypothalamus together trigger the phenomenon known as puberty.

At puberty, growth of pubic hair is stimulated by an adrenal androgen. In girls, there is an increased secretion of estrogen, which soon becomes cyclic and which stimulates development of breasts and genitalia. Perhaps for nutritional reasons, the age of menarche (the onset of menstruation) is decreasing. In the United States in the last fifty years, menarche has dropped from 14.2 to 12.9 years (Sawin, 1969, p. 151).

Boys at puberty, through increased secretion of testosterone, show development of facial hair, growth of genitalia, and seminal emission with production of spermatozoa. In puberty, growth rate increases for both boys and girls.

The Female

Reproduction in the female centers around the ovary, the secretions of which are cyclic. In the earlier follicle stage, the secretions are predominantly estrogens, with progestins predominant in the later luteal stage: the follicle secretes in the first stage; the corpus luteum in the second.

Estrogens act on the ovary, stimulate motility of the fallopian tube, act on the uterus, induce secondary characteristics—such as the proper growth and development of the reproductive tract, breast development, menstruation, feminine fat distribution, and feminine hair distribution—and estrogens affect the central nervous system: feminine behavior is built in early life.

Progestins aid in maintaining pregnancy. Progesterone, the principal progestin, acts on the female reproductive tract by decreasing the motility of the oviduct (the fallopian tube); acts on the uterus by decreasing uterine contractility, enhancing estrogen stimulation of overall uterine growth, causing differentiation of the endometrium of the uterus so that it is ready for the implantation of the blastocyst (the fertilized ovum); acts on the central nervous system by inhibiting ovulation, by stimulating maternal behavior, and by, in combination with estrogen, causing estrus behavior. The secretion of progesterone is essential for maintaining pregnancy.

Thus, the cyclic ovary first produces estrogens to prepare for pregnancy and then progestins to maintain pregnancy.

The cycling of ovarian hormone secretion, along with the luteinizing hormone of the anterior pituitary, results in the periodic release of an ovum, the growth and development of which is unaffected by gonadotropins; only the follicle itself is stimulated by gonadotropins. Estrus occurs about the time of ovulation. The menstrual flow begins about fourteen days after ovulation. Normally, humans release only one egg (ovum) per month.

FSH, the follicle-stimulating hormone of the anterior pituitary, stimulates the growth of the follicle. LH, the luteinizing hormone of the anterior pituitary, augments the growth effect of FSH and also increases RNA and protein synthesis, gradually increases estrogen secretion, which stimulates endometrial protein synthesis and growth in the placenta. Estrogen and progesterone from the ovary combine to increase LH production, which causes the follicle to open and release the ovum. Thus, the hormones of the ovary and anterior pituitary act on each other in producing ovulation.

After ovulation, the empty follicle is transformed into the corpus luteum, which secretes estrogen and progesterone. LH is required for this to happen, thus its name, luteinizing hormone.

The corpus luteum lasts two weeks. The estrogen it secretes seems to be essential as a priming agent for the secretory stage of the endometrium of the uterus and, therefore, for the implantation of the blastocyst. If implantation does not occur, the corpus luteum decreases in function. The secondary endometrium can no longer be maintained, because of the drop in secretion of progesterone and estrogen; it is sloughed and menstruation occurs.

If implantation does occur, the placenta forms, the corpus luteum continues to function and to secrete progesterone, which is essential for the maintenance of pregnancy at this point. The placenta probably stimulates the continuing functioning of the corpus luteum through its production of human chorionic gonadotropin (HCG) and human placental lactogen (HPL).

After two months, the corpus luteum is no longer needed, but it persists for about six months. The placenta, at about two months, takes over the function of the corpus luteum.

Lactation requires breast development, milk secretion, and milk release from the breast. The initial breast development is due to estrogens. In pregnancy, breast development is due to estrogen and progesterone, placental hormones, and to prolactin from the pituitary. The anterior pituitary is essential for both the initiation and maintenance of lactation, as are good nutrition and a proper mental state. The hypothalamus hormone, oxytocin, stimulates the release of milk. Suckling enhances the secretion of both prolactin and oxytocin.

Thus, in the female the ovarian hormones are stimulated, enhanced, and aided by the anterior pituitary (the follicle-stimulating and luteinizing hormones and prolactin), the placenta (in pregnancy), and the hypothalamus (oxytocin).

The Male

Male reproduction centers around the testis, which makes spermatozoa and secretes hormones. A descended testis is necessary because sperm production requires a temperature lower than the central body temperature. Descent normally occurs before birth and requires testosterone. FSH, the follicle-stimulating hormone of the anterior pituitary, is required for spermatogenesis.

LH, the luteinizing hormone of the anterior pituitary, also is required in males to stimulate testosterone secretion. LH is identical in males and females, thus the name is retained in males, although it was named for its function in females. LH and FSH are both needed for spermatogenesis and effective seminal emission.

The Leydig, or interstitial, cells of the testis secrete testosterone, which is both androgenic—causes secondary male sex characteristics—and anabolic—increases the net protein synthesis by the body. Anabolic functions stimulate bone growth and, with the growth hormone from the anterior pituitary, the pubertal growth spurt; stimulate closure of bone epiphyses (ending further growth—a function of estrogen in girls); and stimulate red blood cell production. Androgenic functions stimulate the growth and function of genitalia; stimulate increased hair growth in the male pattern; have direct effects on the central nervous system through the stimulation of more aggressive behavior, increased sexual desire and sexual activity; stimulate increased muscle mass and strength and increased skeletal growth; stimulate overall growth, changes in fat distribution, and deepening of the voice.

The androgenic effect of testosterone on the central nervous system requires testosterone exposure in utero for optimal development. The functioning of the hypothalamus is critical.

Summary

In males and in females, although the gonads, the testes and ovaries, play the principal role in reproduction and in sexuality, without being aided and abetted by the central nervous system, the hypothalamus, and the anterior pituitary, they would be ineffectual indeed. Maleness and femaleness, seeded in utero, flowers in puberty. Although exposure to appropriate sexual models aids childhood identification, hormonal activity determines how the child views the models. The central nervous system is primed in utero, by placental and fetal hormones, for maleness and femaleness.

Mating behavior is determined hormonally as a result of the effect of gonadal hormones on the central nervous system. Without the central nervous system effects of the estrogens, progestins, and androgens, no reproduction would occur.

One might add here that even so powerful an effect as that of the hormones and central nervous system seems to be affected by a critical period in development. Babies who are loved, fondled, carried about, stroked, and caressed are much more likely to grow to an emotional maturity that allows them to enjoy their maleness or femaleness in mutual sensitivity, understanding, and need with their partner.

FERTILIZATION

The perinatal period of man's life, perhaps the most important period in his life, usually is considered to begin with fertilization. It includes not only the intrauterine stages of development, but also the period of the neonate, the newborn. Granted the healthy growth and maturation of the germ cells in the parents' bodies, a new, unique life begins with the union of the female egg and the male sperm.

The sperm cells released in the vagina at the neck of the cervix are microscopically small; one hundred thousand sperm weigh as much as a single ovum. They penetrate the mucus plug of the cervix, move upward through the uterus and the fallopian tubes and often outward into the abdominal cavity. The ovum, released by the process of ovulation into the abdominal cavity, is gently siphoned into the fallopian tube, where it encounters a swarm of sperm cells. When one of these sperm cells penetrates the outer shell and enters the cytoplasm of the ovum, fertilization takes place. Almost instantly, by a process not yet understood, a chemical reaction prevents other sperm cells from penetrating the ovum.

Once penetration is effected, the center of the sperm cell, containing the cytoplasm and the chromosomes, detaches itself from the tail and moves toward the center of the ovum; the second stage of the meiotic division, union, is completed. Within twelve hours the new cell nucleus has been formed in the center of the ovum, microscopic parts of which contain the complete program for the development of a new human being. Obviously, with the ability of genes to cross over, plus all the combinations possible from twenty-three pairs of chromosomes, each carrying hundreds of genes, production of a unique individual is assured.

During the twelve hours that the new cell is readying itself for its first division, it is moved down into the uterus. Within two weeks, the ovum, now a fertilized blastocyst, attaches itself to the uterus wall where it has become soft, highly vasculated, and engorged with blood. Shortly it is encapsulated into a bonded layer of tissue, consisting of the amniotic sac, the chorion layer, and the lumen, which becomes its primary link to the mother, the placenta.

THE INTRAUTERINE PERIODS

The growth and development that take place in utero are phenomenal. From the union of two haploid cells into the fertilized ovum, which contains all that is necessary for the production of hair and eyes, fingernails and toes, endocrine glands and lungs, brain and brawn, comes the child. Before he is the child, he is the ovum, the embryo, the fetus, the neonate, the infant. At every stage, his growth and development, as outlined by his genetic makeup, must be encouraged and enhanced by an appropriate, nurturing environment.

The Ovum

From the time of fertilization, usually in the fallopian tube but possibly in the abdominal cavity, until about the seventh day, the ovum is pretty much on its own, as far as nutrition and oxygen are concerned. It floats gradually down the fallopian tube, undergoing primitive increases in size through simple cell divisions. Identical twinning would occur during this first week; thus, the cell divisions are evidently into equipotential cells. Timing, however, is critical, since after the seventh day the ovum cannot feed off its cell and must have an adequate input of oxygen and nutrients.

At the end of this period, the ovum comes to rest on the surface of the uterus, usually in the upper quadrant, most frequently in the back. The surface of the uterus has cycled for optimal nesting, becoming thick and spongy, engorged with blood. The implantation act is somewhat difficult to account for, because in a very real sense, this small body of cells represents foreign protein, and normally the body is programmed to reject such as an infection. In fact, 50 percent of fertilized ova fail to make this life-supporting contact.

The Embryo

This nesting or implantation signals the beginning of the period of the embryo. Two important processes begin immediately. First is the construction of the placental barrier, the interface between mother and embryo. This process involves a penetration of the wall of the uterus by villi from the ovum. These rootlike structures, vascular processes to absorb nutrients, make broad contact with the maternal blood supply, rooting aside some maternal cells, destroying others, which are ingested by the villi, and in general making an effective tap on the maternal blood supply, while forming on the wall of the uterus a thin, blisterlike sac, the rudimental placenta.

At this point, the embryo, still microscopic in size, about the size of the head of a pin, has begun its biochemical dance with the mother. This small cell cluster, dwarfed as it is by the maternal biochemical system, nevertheless secretes a chorionic gonadotropin hormone that prevents the completion of the menstrual cycle by the mother and in essence gains control of much of the maternal hormonal system, which will spend the next nine months pretty much at the beck and call of this demanding fetus.

The major event of the next eight weeks, the period of the embryo, is the development of the placenta. The outside layer, on the maternal side, the chorion, is a balloonlike sac whose outside surface is covered with thin, hairlike villi that penetrate the surface of the uterus to become the major source of input and output on the maternal side. The middle tissue, or lumen, is the filter layer of the placenta. On the inner side, the amnion becomes attached to the fetus through the umbilical cord. This permeable placenta supplies the life support for the fetus.

Only chemicals can cross the placental barrier; between mother and fetus are no direct neural connections. Through the placenta pass nutrients and oxygen from the mother and wastes from the fetus. Dual in development as well as in operation, the placenta is made up of tissues coming both from the mother and the embryo. It contributes to the well-being of both.

> For the unborn infant, the placenta does the work of lungs, kidneys, intestines, liver and hormone-producing glands. To the mother, the placenta contributes hormones essential to the maintenance of the pregnancy and for the production of milk after childbirth [Apgar and Beck, 1972, p. 62].

During these eight weeks, the growth of the embryo is rapid, with 95 percent of the body's parts becoming differentiated, a 2,000,000 percent increase in size. During this period, the embryo first becomes differentiated into three specialized tissue layers: an outer layer, the ectoderm, of baby skin and surface tissue, such as sweat glands, hair, and nervous system; a middle section, the mesoderm, that is the rudiment of the skeletal, muscular, and circulatory systems; and an inner layer, the endoderm, that, for the most part, becomes the viscera.

During this period of rapid growth, the majority of major birth defects are formed. As a general rule, the greater the defect, the earlier it is formed. This is a time of great shifts in specialization, high speed of meiosis and mitosis, and rampant changes in biochemistry. This is also the period when the mother should take the greatest care with regard to her chemical and nutritional intake; unfortunately, as often as not, the whole process occurs without the mother knowing she is pregnant.

During the first month, the nervous system develops from a flat neural plate into a long tube, which becomes the spinal cord and nerves. The upper end begins to thicken into a more solid mass, which becomes the brain. At the same time, the heart is establishing a regular 65-beat-per-minute rhythm and actually begins to circulate the blood. Limb buds appear and the rudiments of hands and feet begin. This first month repre-

Figure 6

Diagram of a fetus in utero.

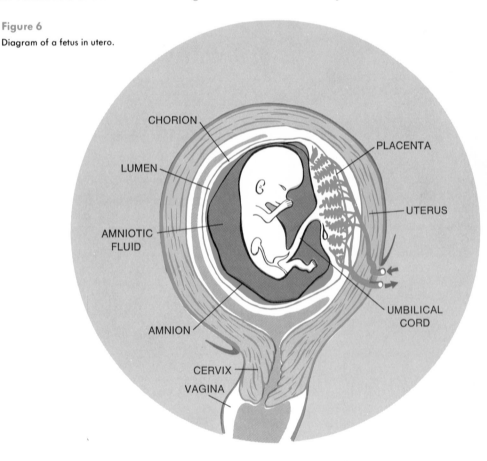

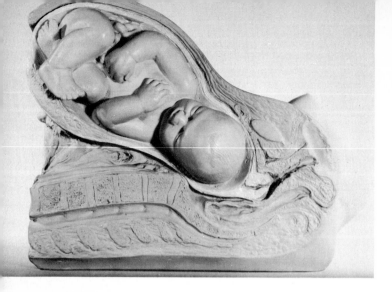

Figure 7

Six stages in the process of childbirth. Courtesy of the Cleveland Health Museum, 8911 Euclid Avenue, Cleveland, Ohio.

A. The uterus at term: cervix not dilated.

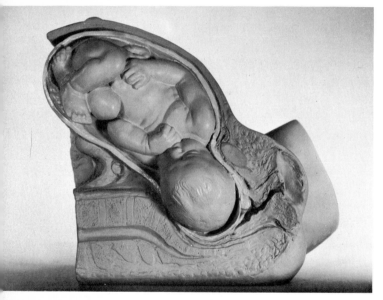

B. Cervix dilating as the uterus contracts.

C. Progress of the head to pelvic floor.

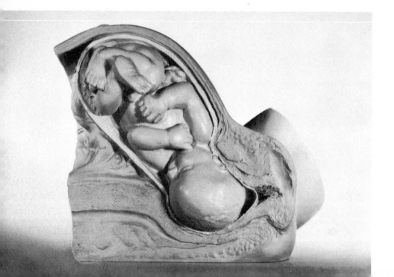

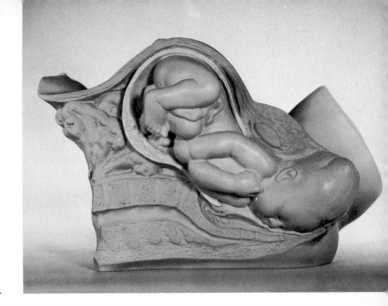

D. Emergence of the head as it rotates.

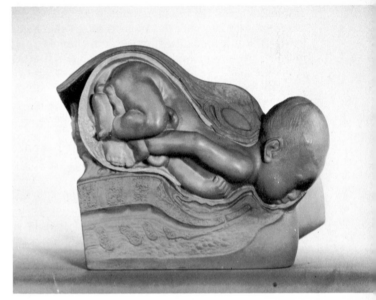

E. The further extension of the head.

F. The shoulder begins its emergence.

sents phenomenal growth. Still less than half an inch long, the embryo is already ten thousand times bigger.

During the second month, liver, digestive tract, kidneys, and a beating heart all have operational potential. The yoke sac, though relatively small, is producing a rapidly increasing blood supply through the child's body and also through the network of villi in the placenta. The waste disposal system is now functioning and the mother's blood is bringing in a rich supply of oxygen and nutrients through the placenta. The brain is developing rapidly. A cephalocaudal growth pattern, with the most rapid growth at the head, is established, and a proximodistal pattern, with more rapid growth at the midline. Eyes, eyelids, ears, and other discrete features, such as lips, are now clearly distinguishable. The brain is in its period of most rapid growth.

The Fetus

During the third month, the now one-ounce human infant is beginning to drink the amniotic fluid, which surrounds him, acts as a shock absorber, and prevents fluid loss through the highly porous skin of the fetus. His intestinal tract and kidneys are beginning to function. His muscles are developing, with spontaneous movements of arms and legs. His sex is easily distinguishable.

By the end of the fourth month, virtually all of the major changes in the fetus have taken place. The fully functioning fetus begins to place a heavier and heavier demand upon the placenta, the major source of nutrition and oxygen. The biochemical interchange between mother and fetus now becomes critical, with both bodies rushing toward separation.

BIRTH

Three out of four pregnancies end within 11 days of 266 days after conception. Birth normally occurs at the optimal time for the infant's development: he is ready to live independently.

But to enable him to do so, dramatic changes take place at birth. His lungs must begin to breathe air. His circulatory system must be rechanneled to pick up oxygen from his lungs. His body must maintain a stable temperature. And he must adjust to the effects of gravity.

> Safely born, his heartbeat and breathing well established, the newborn infant is a remarkably capable individual. He can cry, yawn, cough, sneeze. He can open and shut his eyes, distinguish light and dark.... He is able to suck—his thumb or his mother's breast. His fingers will grasp anything that touches the palm of his hand with a grip strong enough to support his own weight.
>
> Even on the first day of life, the newborn baby is capable of learning, remembering and altering his behavior on the basis of his new knowledge. His personality and temperament show clearly that he is different from all other infants in the newborn nursery of the hospital. He is distinctly, uniquely himself, just as the fertilized egg cell from which he has grown—increasing in size from one cell to hundreds of millions—contained unique and distinctly individual genetic instructions [Apgar and Beck, 1972, pp. 70–71].

Establishing the age of the human fetus at birth is difficult because the day of conception rarely is known accurately. The usual formula for establishing the age of the fetus is the so-called conception age—fifteen days added to the date of the first day of the last menstrual period. Conception is assumed to have occurred about the time the next ovulation should have occurred. However, there is a great degree of irregularity in the menstrual cycle itself, and many reasons why a cycle might be skipped altogether—including, for example, psychological stress. Thus, the maturity of an infant is judged on the basis of his birth weight. Generally, any baby who weighs less than five-and-a-half pounds is considered premature.

Even with advances in care and feeding, the premature infant has a bad time of it. Although adequate comparisons are difficult to make, we know that premature infants have two to three times as many physical defects, 50 percent more illnesses, and a significantly higher number of neurological impairments. In the most premature group, those weighing three pounds or less, fully one-quarter have a major neurological defect. Nearly one-third of the children with cerebral palsy were premature infants. Children sent to reading clinics because of difficulty in elementary school show a high incidence of prematurity. In a study on a black population, Braine, Heimer, Wortis, and A. Freedman (1966) found a significant relationship between the degree of impairment and the degree of prematurity. They also found significant sexual differences in the amount of impairment, which appear to indicate that males are more vulnerable.

The mother's diet, whether and how much she smokes, and her economic status are closely related to the maturity or prematurity of her infant. Wortis, Heimer, Braine, Redlo, and Rue (1963), in a study in Brooklyn, found that all 445 premature infants were from lower socioeconomic families with concomitant poor housing, poor medical care, poor nutrition, poor health habits. Simpson (1957) and Frazier, G. Davis, Goldstein, and Goldberg (1961) found twice as high an incidence of prematurity in infants of cigarette-smoking mothers. The latter study found that the rate of prematurity grew increasingly higher as the rate of smoking increased.

> One of our prime problems ... is prematurity. In 1900 the prematurity rate was 16 to 20 per cent. In 1963 the prematurity rate in the State of California was 12 to 14 per cent in county hospitals and 6 to 7 per cent in private hospitals. Associated with prematurity is a 4- to 10-fold higher incidence of major anomalies than observed in term babies. These abnormalities derive in part from antenatal difficulties and in part from inability of the infant to adapt to the postnatal environment.... Since the mother will house the fetus for approximately 40 weeks, the health of these individuals is of utmost importance.... All the data indicate that good prenatal care decreases the rate of prematurity by a factor of one-half [Kretchmer, 1964, pp. 19, 29].

In studying perceptual acuity in infants, Lipsitt (1970) raises an interesting question concerning premature infants. Noting that the premature infant has handicaps that seem to persist, Lipsitt wonders if perhaps the understimulation necessitated by the baby's biologic prematurity might not affect his ultimate maturation. Ordinarily the premature in-

fant receives less handling than the normal infant, who soon is out of the
hospital, home in the midst of his family, enjoying the usual fond attention
of the newborn. For the premature infant, this attention may be delayed
by weeks, or even months.

SUMMARY

We appear to have gone the full circle in our conception of conception, from a belief that the child is highly susceptible to every evil event that
occurs in the world, from a fear that the mother's being frightened by ugly
scenes would leave a mark on the child, to a belief that the fetus is like an
egg and the mother merely a cantankerous, somewhat whimsical incubator, and now back again to the view that all nutritional and physical
events during pregnancy can indeed mark a child, and that even emotional
events can be translated chemically through the placenta and, prior to
birth, produce gross emotional lability in the baby.

There is no doubt, then, that the relationship between environmental
and genetic influences is a complex one that begins even before the moment
of conception. There is every reason to believe that nutritional, radiologi-
cal, infectious, and other biochemical influences can definitely alter, in a
permanent way, the genetically determined characteristics of the developing
embryo and fetus. Never before have we been so acutely aware of the importance of the first few moments and hours of conception.

Although child psychology in the main is concerned with behavioral
events that occur after birth, in the effort to understand, predict, and control the behavior of children, child psychologists have become increasingly
aware of the need to investigate, in great detail, the relationship between
the prenatal environment and the newborn child. More sophisticated
electronic and chemical techniques of analysis make study of the fetus in
utero increasingly possible. As these investigations proceed, we will understand more clearly the role of the prenatal environment and its long-range
influence upon human behavior.

REVIEW

Early Genetic Theories

Disuse Theory A corollary of Jean Lamarck's
theory of the inheritance of acquired characteristics: organs not used ultimately become less and
less pronounced with each generation until they
finally disappear.

Epigenesis Theory Kaspar Wolff's theory that
undifferentiated substances in the germ cell after
fertilization develop potential for becoming different parts of the body; in contradistinction to
the theory of preformation.

Germ-plasm Theory August Weismann distinguished between germ plasm, which is isolated
even after the first divisions in the embryonic state
and is solely responsible for reproduction, and

somatoplasm, the type of cell that makes up all of
the body except the sexual reproductive cells.

Inheritance of Acquired Characteristics Theory
Jean Lamarck's theory that experience has the
power to make modifications in the body that can
be transmitted to the next generation.

Mutation Theory Hugo De Vries's theory that
any living organism infrequently but consistently
produces new types of offspring through sudden
changes, or mutations, in the hereditary mechanism.

Natural Selection Theory Charles Darwin's
theory that, given an overproduction of offspring
and a hostile environment that causes all but a
small fraction to die before they reproduce themselves, those offspring with the best adaptive
characteristics will survive and reproduce.

Pangenesis Theory Darwin's theory that hereditary units, located in all parts of the body, circulate to and from the reproductive organs.

Preformation Theory Jan Swammerdam's theory that live sperm cells were the preformed young, the egg merely providing nourishment.

Foundations of Modern Genetics

DNA Deoxyribonucleic acid, the nucleic acid of chromosomes in which genetic information is coded. Chromosomes are composed of DNA on a framework of sugar phosphate. The DNA molecule contains four bases: adenine, thymine, guanine, and cytosine. The DNA molecular structure is something like a spiral staircase—the phosphates and sugars are the frame, the bases the steps. DNA contains the genetic code that regulates RNA.

Five Major Bases of Modern Genetics (1) Genes are the transmitters of heredity; (2) adult organisms have two of each; (3) when these two are hybrid, one is dominant; (4) germ cells divide such that each gamete has only one of each pair of genes; (5) random union of gametes accounts for phenotypic variation.

Gene Units of heredity composed of segments of DNA molecules arranged in linear fashion along the chromosomes, each gene having a precise position or locus; genes tend to be transported in groups, like beads on a string. Genes act by regulating and controlling metabolic reactions.

RNA Ribonucleic acid, a specific catalyst for the production of the infinite variety of protein substances in the body. RNA is regulated by DNA.

Biological Concepts

Alleles The two factors of Mendel are defined as alleles in modern biology: each gene in the mature adult has two alleles that separate in the germ cells during cell division; one of the alleles is dominant, the other recessive. For a recessive trait to be expressed, two recessive alleles are required, one from each parent. A gamete with identical alleles for a trait is homozygous; a gamete with an unlike pair of alleles is heterozygous.

Dominance A dominant characteristic will be expressed even when represented by a heterozygous cell. A recessive trait is expressed only through a homozygous cell.

Down's Syndrome (also known as trisomy 21 and mongolism) A genetic deficiency such that chromosome pair 21 is defective, appearing as a triple chromosome; the clinical picture is one of overall retardation of development. The mother's age is a critical factor.

Fertilization Fertilization of an ovum occurs when a sperm enters the cell; the two haploid cells, the ovum and sperm, become a single diploid cell, the zygote, which rapidly develops into the blastocyst implanted in the nurturing wall of the uterus. From this single fertilized cell comes the child, half of his inherited potential from his mother and half from his father.

Incomplete Dominance Incomplete dominance of inherited traits occurs most frequently when the characteristic is carried by several genes located on different chromosomes, e.g., pigment or height.

Klinefelter's Syndrome An anomaly of the sex chromosomes such that the child has two normal X chromosomes and a Y chromosome (XXY); he has mostly male primary characteristics but many female secondary characteristics.

Meiosis/Mitosis Meiosis, the cell division of the germ cells in which each gamete receives only one of each pair of chromosomes; mitosis, the cell division of all body cells, except germ cells, in which each gamete receives both of a pair of chromosomes. The continuity of cell division is a basis of heredity; discontinuity results in severe aberrations, such as Down's syndrome, Turner's syndrome, and Klinefelter's syndrome.

Overproduction of Germ Cells An oversupply of germ cells, both male and female, is a biological fact: the female produces about 350 to 400 mature ova, only 2 of which, on the average, are fertilized; the male releases about 300 to 500 million sperm at a single ejaculation.

Sex-linked Traits The sex-linked concept refers to characteristics carried on the sex pair of chromosomes, such as color blindness and hemophilia, both carried on the X chromosome.

Turner's Syndrome An anomaly of the sex chromosomes such that the child has only one X chromosome, the other being inactivated (X0); the Barr body is missing. These girls are greatly reduced in sex differentiation.

Twinning Multiple births result from the division of a single fertilized ovum (monozygotes) or from the simultaneous fertilization of two ova (heterozygotes). Twins do not have the same environment though developing simultaneously.

XYY Syndrome An anomaly of the sex chromosomes such that the child has an X chromosome and two Y chromosomes; greater height, excessive acne, and a tendency toward seizures characterize this syndrome.

Hereditary Metabolic Diseases

Diabetes A common but unpredictable hereditary metabolic disease, diabetes affects the body's manufacture of insulin such that sugars and starches are ineffectively metabolized.

Galactosemia and Lactosemia Hereditary metabolic diseases involving the metabolism of milk, galactosemia and lactosemia have discernible geographic and racial distributions that seem to be related to a tradition of herdsmanship.

Inborn Error of Metabolism A genetically determined biochemical disorder in which a specific enzyme defect produces a metabolic block that may have pathological consequences.

Phenylketonuria (PKU) A hereditary metabolic disease transmitted through genetic action. The inability to manufacture an enzyme results in a waste product that damages the brain cells, damage that can be controlled by early detection and strict diet.

Sickle-cell Anemia A recessive disorder caused by defective DNA, sickle-cell anemia is carried by 10 percent of the blacks in the United States. Sickling of the red blood cells prevents an adequate supply of oxygen in blood vessels.

Reproduction

the endocrinology of reproduction

Anabolic The anabolic function of the endocrine glands increases protein synthesis; stimulates bone growth; stimulates, along with the growth hormone of the anterior pituitary, the pubertal growth spurt; stimulates closure of bone epiphyses; and stimulates red blood-cell production.

Androgenic The androgenic function of the endocrine glands causes secondary male sex characteristics; stimulates growth and function of the genitalia; stimulates hair growth in male pattern; stimulates central nervous system, conditioned in utero by testosterone exposure, for increased male behavior; stimulates increased muscle mass and strength and skeletal growth; stimulates overall growth; changes fat distribution; and deepens the voice.

Anterior Pituitary Secretes LH, luteinizing hormone; FSH, follicle-stimulating hormone; prolactin, lactation stimulation and maintenance hormone; and growth hormone as part of the endocrinology of reproduction.

Breast Development Initially stimulated by estrogens, breast development during pregnancy is stimulated by estrogen, progesterone, the placental hormones, and prolactin. Milk release

during lactation is stimulated by oxytocin from the hypothalamus.

Corpus Luteum After ovulation, the follicle of the ovary is transformed into the corpus luteum, which secretes progestins in second stage of ovarian cycle, and secretes estrogen necessary for implantation of the blastocyst in uterine wall. If implantation does not occur, the corpus luteum decreases in function and menstruation occurs; if implantation does occur, the corpus luteum continues to function and to secrete progesterone, which is essential for maintenance of pregnancy. The continued function of the corpus luteum is stimulated by HCG and HPL, human chorionic gonadotropin and human placental lactogen.

Endocrine System of Reproduction The endocrinology of reproduction, which includes the female ovaries and male testes, the pituitary, the placenta (in pregnancy), the hypothalamus, and the central nervous system, begins in utero. The combination of maternal and fetal hormone production sets the stage for the spectacular changes of puberty: sexual behavior and gonadotropin secretion at puberty are dependent upon the central nervous system and are built into the brain during fetal life.

Estrogen Estrogen functions in the endocrinology of reproduction by acting on the ovary and uterus to prepare for pregnancy, as well as stimulating the motility of the fallopian tube; induces secondary sexual characteristics, such as feminine fat distribution, growth and development of the reproductive tract, breast development, menstruation, and feminine hair distribution; affects the central nervous system for feminine behavior; and stimulates closure of bone epiphyses.

Female Reproduction Reproduction in the female centers around the cyclic ovaries. In the earlier, follicle stage, ovarian secretions are predominantly estrogens; in the later luteal stage, predominantly progestins. Reproduction in the female includes the central nervous system, the hypothalamus, anterior pituitary, ovaries, and placenta (in pregnancy): estrogens, progestins (both gonadotropins), FSH, LH, prolactin, oxytocin, HCG, and HPL.

Follicle The follicle of the female ovary is stimulated by gonadotropins; its growth is enhanced by FSH, the follicle-stimulating hormone of anterior pituitary, augmented by LH, the luteinizing hormone of the anterior pituitary. Ovulation is stimulated by estrogen, progesterone, and LH. After ovulation, the follicle becomes the corpus luteum.

FSH The follicle-stimulating hormone of the anterior pituitary, FSH is required for spermatogenesis and seminal emission in the male.

Gonadotropic A hormonal function that supports and stimulates the function and growth of the gonads, the ovaries, and testes.

Hypothalamus In the endocrinology of reproduction, the hypothalamus stimulates secretions of the anterior pituitary at puberty and secretes oxytocin, the lactation milk-release hormone.

LH The luteinizing hormone of the anterior pituitary; production of LH is stimulated by estrogen and progestin from the ovary, which causes the follicle to open and release the ovum. LH augments the growth effect of FSH, increases RNA and protein synthesis, and aids in transformation of the follicle to the corpus luteum after ovulation. LH stimulates testosterone secretion in testes and aids in seminal emission.

Male Reproduction Reproduction in the male centers around the testes, which produce the sperm. Reproduction in the male includes the central nervous system, hypothalamus, anterior pituitary, and testes: testosterone, FSH, and LH.

Mating Behavior Mating behavior is determined hormonally through the effect of gonadal hormones on the central nervous system.

Menarche The first menstrual period; establishment of menstruation.

Ovary Cyclic in function, the ovary first produces estrogens to prepare for pregnancy (follicular stage), then produces progestins to maintain pregnancy (luteal stage). The ovaries are stimulated, aided, and enhanced by the anterior pituitary, placenta (in pregnancy), and hypothalamus.

Ovum The periodic release of an ovum is controlled by cyclic ovarian secretions (gonadotropins) and LH, the luteinizing hormone of the anterior pituitary. The growth and development of an ovum is unaffected by gonadotropins; only the follicle, which houses the ovum, is stimulated by gonadotropins.

Placenta The placenta acts as a filter for nourishment from the mother and wastes from the fetus. It secretes HCG, human chorionic gonadotropin, and HPL, human placental lactogen.

Progestin In the endocrinology of reproduction, progestin maintains pregnancy by decreasing the motility of the fallopian tube, enhancing uterine growth, aiding in the implantation of the blastocyst, inhibiting ovulation, and stimulating maternal behavior.

Prolactin Secreted by the anterior pituitary, prolactin stimulates breast development during pregnancy and maintains lactation; its secretion is enhanced by suckling.

Puberty The age at which an individual is first capable of sexual reproduction, puberty is a magical period of change. The exact trigger for puberty is not known, but the stimulus comes from the central nervous system, conditioned in utero, and from the hypothalamus.

Sexuality Maleness and femaleness, seeded in utero, flowers in puberty. Although exposure to appropriate sexual models aids childhood identification, hormonal activity determines how the child views the models. The central nervous system is primed in utero, by placental and fetal hormones, for maleness or femaleness. But even so powerful an effect as that of the hormones and central nervous system seems to be affected by a critical period in development. Babies who are loved, fondled, carried about, stroked, and caressed are much more likely to grow to an emotional maturity that allows them to enjoy their maleness or femaleness in mutual sensitivity, understanding, and need with their partner.

Testes The testes, which produce sperm, are descended because sperm production requires lower than body temperature. For descent, testosterone is required in utero. The testes secrete the gonadotropin hormone, testosterone, that has anabolic and androgenic functions.

Testosterone Secreted by the Leydig (interstitial) cells of the testes, testosterone is androgenic (causes secondary male sex characteristics) and anabolic (increases protein synthesis in the body).

fertilization

Blastocyst Within two weeks, the fertilized ovum is a blastocyst attached to the uterus wall, where it is encapsulated in a bonded layer of tissue, consisting of the amniotic sac, the chorion layer, and the lumen, which becomes the placenta, the primary link to the mother.

Fertilization When a sperm cell penetrates the outer shell and enters the cytoplasm of the ovum, fertilization takes place. Once penetration is effected, the center of the sperm cell, containing the cytoplasm and the chromosomes, detaches itself from the tail and moves toward the center of the ovum; the second stage of the meiotic division, union, is completed.

Ovum The ovum, released by the process of ovulation into the abdominal cavity, is gently siphoned into the fallopian tube, where it encounters a swarm of sperm cells.

Perinatal Period   Perhaps the most important period of man's life, the perinatal period usually is considered to begin with fertilization—the beginning of unique life with the joining of the female ovum and male sperm.   The perinatal period includes not only the intrauterine stages of development, but also the period of the neonate, the newborn.

Sperm   The sperm cells released in the vagina at the neck of the cervix are microscopically small; 100,000 sperm weigh as much as a single ovum. They penetrate the mucus plug of the cervix, move upward through the uterus and the fallopian tubes and often outward into the abdominal cavity.

the intrauterine periods

Amnion   The placental layer that makes up the umbilical cord.

Cephalocaudal   A pattern of growth and maturation with most rapid development at the head.

Chorion   The outside placental layer on the maternal side, the chorion taps maternal blood supply and is source of maternal input.

Diploid   Having two complementary sets of chromosomes.

Ectoderm   The outer layer of specialized tissues developed during the period of the embryo, the ectoderm consists of baby skin and surface tissue, such as sweat glands, hair, and nervous system.

Embryo   On implantation on the surface of the uterus, the ovum becomes the embryo.   The major event of the next eight weeks, the period of the embryo, is the development of the placenta. Growth of the embryo is rapid: 95 percent of the body's parts become differentiated.   During this period, the embryo develops three specialized tissue layers: the ectoderm, mesoderm, and endoderm.   The embryo is particularly susceptible to teratogenesis during this period of phenomenal growth.   The nervous system and brain begin developing during this first month, and the heart develops a regular rhythmic beat.   The growth pattern is cephalocaudal and proximodistal.

Endoderm   The inner layer of specialized tissues developed during the period of the embryo, the endoderm becomes, for the most part, the viscera.

Fetus   During the third month, the embryo has developed into a fetus with an easily distinguishable sex.   By the end of the fourth month virtually all major changes in the fetus have taken place. Teeth, fingernails, hair become differentiated; fetal movement is initiated; fetal heart circulates blood drawn from placenta.   About twenty-eight weeks after fertilization, the fetus is capable of living out-side the uterus, although the fetus has not yet reached optimal intrauterine maturation.

Haploid   Having a single set of chromosomes.

Intrauterine Periods   (1) Period of the ovum lasts about the first seven days, while the ovum is self-sufficient; (2) period of the embryo lasts about two months, during which the placenta is formed and growth and development is phenomenal: the period of the embryo is a time of great susceptibility to teratogenesis; (3) period of the fetus covers the remainder of the intrauterine time as the fetus develops strength and maturation great enough to be self-sustaining.

Lumen   The middle filter layer of the placenta.

Mesoderm   The middle layer of specialized tissues developed during the period of the embryo, the mesoderm is the rudiment of the skeletal, muscular, and circulatory systems.

Ovum   The ovum, consisting of the two haploid cells from mother and father joined into one diploid cell, begins to increase in size even as it moves toward the uterus.   For about the first seven days, the ovum is capable of sustaining itself nutritionally, but by the end of that period it needs support.

Placenta   Upon implantation of the embryo on the uterus wall, the important process of constructing the placenta begins.   Made up of tissues from both mother and embryo, the placenta is composed of three layers: (1) the chorion, outside layer on maternal side, which taps maternal blood supply and is source of maternal input; (2) the lumen, which is the filter layer; and (3) the amnion, which is the umbilical cord.   The placenta allows only chemicals to cross between mother and fetus; there are no direct neural pathways. Nutrients and oxygen from the mother and wastes from the fetus are passed through the placenta.

Proximodistal   A pattern of growth and maturation where the most rapid development is at the midline, with the central nervous system and internal organs functioning more rapidly and precisely than the extremities.

Teratogenesis   The production of defects and malformations.

Uterus   By the end of seven days, the fertilized ovum comes to rest on the surface of the uterus, which has cycled for optimal nesting, becoming thick and spongy, engorged with blood.

Birth

Birth   Three out of four pregnancies end within 11 days of 266 days after conception.   Birth normally occurs at the optimal time for the infant's development: he is now ready to live independently.

Prematurity

Prematurity   Generally, a baby who weighs less than five-and-a-half pounds at birth is considered premature. Premature infants are at greater risk than mature infants: they have more physical defects, more illnesses, and more neurological impairments. Concomitant with the physical problems of the premature infant are those caused by his missing the fondling, handling, rocking, caressing that greets the usual newborn, a deprivation that seems to leave permanent scars.   An infant's maturity at birth is affected by his mother's smoking habits as well as her health and her nutrition.

NAMES TO KNOW

Early Genetic Theories

ARISTOTLE (384–322 B.C.) A Greek philosopher who believed in the overwhelming importance of the male as the provider of the essential aspects of heredity, the female serving merely as the incubator.

JAN SWAMMERDAM (1637–1680) A Dutch anatomist and entomologist who developed the theory of preformation, i.e., that the live sperm cells are the preformed young, the egg merely providing nourishment.

REGNER DE GRAAF (1641–1673) A Dutch anatomist who discovered the Graafian follicles in the female ovaries and surmised the fertilization of the female egg by the male sperm.

KASPAR WOLFF (1733–1794) In the eighteenth century, Kaspar Wolff discovered that specific parts of the egg mass, after fertilization, develop into specific body parts. His epigenesis theory put to rest the hardy but incorrect theory of preformation.

JEAN LAMARCK (1744–1829) A French naturalist who believed in the inheritance of acquired characteristics, i.e., the theory that experience has the power to make modifications in the body that can be transmitted to the next generation; and in the theory of disuse, i.e., that organs not used ultimately become less and less pronounced with each generation until they finally disappear.

CHARLES DARWIN (1809–1882) "To Charles Darwin belongs the credit for the far-reaching and plausible theory of the evolutionary origin of species. . . . Like many great ideas, it is extremely simple when reviewed in retrospect; its greatness lies in its adequacy, its novelty, and in the degree to which it ran counter to the accepted belief of the time" (Boring, 1950, p. 470). An English naturalist, Darwin presented the ideas of natural selection, i.e., given an overproduction of offspring and a hostile environment that causes all but a small fraction to die before reproducing themselves, those offspring with the best adaptive characteristics will survive and reproduce; and pangenesis, the theory that hereditary units, located in all parts of the body, circulate to and from the reproductive organs.

AUGUST WEISSMANN (1834–1914) A German biologist who developed the germ-plasm theory, i.e., that germ plasm and somatoplasm are different. He believed in a continuity of cell division from one generation to another unaffected by any life experience, and demolished Darwin's theory of pangenesis.

HUGO DE VRIES (1848–1935) A Dutch botanist who was responsible for the mutation theory, that is, any living organism infrequently but consistently produces new types of offspring through sudden changes or mutations in the hereditary mechanism, and for the rediscovery of Gregor Mendel.

Foundations of Modern Genetics

GREGOR MENDEL (1822–1884) A Moravian monk, Austrian biologist, and founder of modern genetics, Mendel formulated the five major bases of modern genetics: (1) genes (named by De Vries) are the transmitting agents of heredity; (2) adult organisms have two of each; (3) when these two are hybrid (different), one will be dominant, the other recessive; (4) in germ cells, the genes divide such that each gamete (daughter cell) has only one of the pair; (5) the random union of these gamete cells upon fertilization accounts for phenotypic variation.

THOMAS HUNT MORGAN   866–1945) A zoologist who won the Nobel Prize for Medicine in 1933 for his discovery that chromosomes are the "characters" mentioned by Mendel, Morgan demonstrated that genes are carried on chromosomes in groups, like beads on a string, rather than individually; that heredity is not totally haphazard, even though each of man's forty-six chromosomes contains thousands of genes (freckles, for instance and simplistically, tend to go with red hair).

GEORGE BEADLE (b. 1903) and EDWARD TATUM (b. 1909) Beadle, a biologist, and Tatum, a biochemist, won the Nobel Prize for Medicine in 1958 for their work with DNA and RNA protein molecules and their discovery that genes act by regulating definite chemical events, i.e., that genes control metabolic reactions.

Hereditary Metabolic Diseases

ARCHIBALD GARROD A physician who pioneered research in hereditary metabolic diseases, Garrod proposed the concept of inborn errors of metabolism.

Environment

Thus far we have explored the biological aspects of human heredity and reproduction: the mechanics of undisturbed physical and chemical processes. We have discussed what makes up the individual's genetically determined potentialities. Now we move to the environmental effects that can alter this potential. Heredity determines our potential. Environment determines whether or not the given potential will be fulfilled. The nourishment, protection, and development of the fertilized egg, embryo, and fetus are environmental effects upon genetic potential.

PERINATAL TERATOGENES

The relationship between mother and fetus is indeed critical. In addition to the special vulnerability of the child to such infections of the mother as rubella, or German measles, during the first few months of pregnancy, her diet and general health can affect him: "That many children are born handicapped by prenatal deprivations reveals the profound influence of socio-economic, biological, and psychological factors on the individual even before he is born" (Haimowitz and Haimowitz, 1966, p. 126). Various congenital abnormalities can occur in infants born to diabetic mothers and to mothers who have taken certain drugs during pregnancy. Microcephaly, accompanied by severe mental retardation, is due to a rare recessive gene, but may also result from the fetus being exposed to radiation during pregnancy. Clearly, a child inherits not only a genotype and phenotype, but an environment. Heredity is the dynamic interaction of the two.

A part of the embryo undergoing rapid developmental changes can suffer defect whether the damage is caused by an external agent or by gene action. Fraser (1959) has summed up the causes of congenital malformations in human beings:

1. A minority of congenital malformations have a major genetic cause.
2. A minority of congenital malformations have a major environmental cause.

3. Most malformations probably result from complicated interactions between genetic predispositions and subtle factors of the intrauterine environment.

"Any agent which produces a malformation, or raises the incidence of a malformation in a population, is said to be teratogenic (i.e., malformation-producing)" (J. Thompson and M. Thompson, 1966, p. 189). Wilson (1961) lists five general principles of teratology:

1. The embryologic stage at the time an agent acts determines which tissues are susceptible to teratogenesis.
2. Teratogenic agents interfere with particular phases of metabolism, thus often produce characteristic patterns of malformations.
3. Teratogenic agents often, if not always, act in a complementary fashion with the genotype of the embryo to produce malformations.
4. Intrauterine mortality tends to vary directly with the rate of malformations.
5. An agent which is very damaging to the embryo may be relatively harmless to the mother.

The best known teratogenes in man are viruses, radiation, and drugs. To be effective a teratogenic agent must affect some specific metabolic process in the developing embryo and usually causes malformations only if exposure occurs at a time when the embryo is sensitive to its effects: "The drugs used by the pregnant mother, her nutrition, her endocrine status, emotional life, and activity level may very likely contribute to the shaping of the physical status, the behavior patterns, and the postnatal progress of the child" (Montagu, 1954, p. 19).

Rubella

Rubella, when infecting the mother during the first three months of pregnancy, seems to have a serious effect on those fetal parts undergoing a critical phase of development. The eyes, ears, and other sense organs, as well as the heart, may be severely affected. Rhodes (1961) has found that the incidence of major defects in infants following the mother's infection with rubella during pregnancy falls from 50 percent, if the infection occurs in the first four weeks of pregnancy, to 17 percent if it occurs in the third month, to near zero thereafter.

> Surveys have shown that if a pregnant woman contracts the disease during the early weeks of pregnancy there is a 60 percent chance that her child will be abnormal in some way. The main abnormalities are deafness (in about 50 percent), congenital heart disease (in just less than 50 percent), and eye defects (in about 30 percent) [Emery, 1968, p. 206].

Gammaglobulin injections have made immunization of the mother possible when she knows she has been exposed to the usually harmless childhood disease.

Drugs

Another far-reaching danger to the growing fetus has been recognized in the many powerful drugs being used. One of the most tragic instances was the massive deformity associated with the sleeping compound, thalidomide. The affected child, if not stillborn, is born with very small, deformed, useless arms and hands. Yet thalidomide causes these and other deformities only when taken during early pregnancy.

Other drugs can also affect the unborn child. Congenital deafness has been traced to the mother's use of quinine. Morphinism is reported in infants whose mothers are morphine addicts. Heavy sedation of the mother can cause asphyxiation of the fetus. And preliminary studies are showing chromosomal damage in animals when the mother is given LSD (lysergic acid diethylamide):

> There are available today over a dozen drugs which definitely or presumably cause fetal injury, and the list will extend as additional drugs are introduced and our studies grow more perceptive. . . . Epidemiologically, much of the problem rests with the fact that many people do not recognize that they are taking drugs. A woman who has put a dropper of nose drops in each nostril nightly for two years will deny that she is "taking any pills." Yet the effect of the vasospastic drugs on the vessels of the placenta and placental bed is well known. The meticulous housewife who sprays her kitchen regularly with an insecticide is likewise not "taking any drugs" as she sees it. The woman who omits her contraceptive pill or jelly for one night and thereby becomes pregnant, only to return to the regular use of these chemicals, not knowing of conception, presents a maximal fetal hazard. The effect of the progestins orally is well known and a jelly strong enough to be spermaticidal may well have an effect on the conceptus. One such is known to be actively absorbed through the vaginal epithelium and is teratogenic in laboratory animals. It is being over-innocent to believe that prenatal care alone can obviate all such chemical contacts and the hope would seem to lie in childhood training of the public and medical school training of the physician, which produce an abstemious attitude toward drug consumption [Barnes, 1964, pp. 380–381].

Radiation

Muller and Stadler's work on the effect of radiation on the genetic mechanism has demonstrated that even the smallest exposure may produce a mutation. There is no safe dose of radiation, only necessary and unavoidable dosages. Any increase in the level of radiation affecting the ovaries and testes that is not mandatory for the health and well-being of the parent is too much. And the risk pyramids rather than summates.

Maternal Effects

Drugs and radiation can cause malformations in the father's germ cells, as well as in the mother's or in the undeveloped embryo. Rubella obviously affects the unborn child through the mother, as do other aspects of the mother's health and habits as she carries the child. Other diseases are potentially dangerous, as are her drug and alcoholic intake, her smoking habits, her diet, even her emotional health.

Blood Oxygen Level

Although the placenta serves as a rather effective filter, its very nature as an exchange point requires that it allow a large variety of chemical transfers to take place. All of the waste products of the child's system must be discharged through the placenta, and all of the nutrition and oxygen must be admitted from the mother's side of the barrier. In addition, certain hormones must be allowed to pass through, because much of the sensitive timing regarding the shifts in functions that occur before and during birth depend upon the signaling between mother and child.

The fetus is dependent upon the richness of oxygen in the mother's blood in order to maintain the oxygen balance vital to its own system. It responds to a signal from the brain centers with a sudden squirming action that would in most instances free the umbilical cord if it were being pinched by the fetus's position against the bone structure of the mother. This sensitivity is to a drop in the percentage of oxygen in the blood, and not to the amount of oxygen being transmitted. For example, if the mother is exercising rapidly, say riding a bicycle, she will gradually build up the oxygen level in her blood because her own breathing becomes more efficient. When the mother stops exercising and her oxygen level is returning to normal, the fetus's brain evidently is registering not the fact that there is a return to normal, but that there is a relative drop, with the result that the fetus begins to squirm strongly in response to the threat of asphyxiation. A prolonged deficit in the oxygen level, of course, can cause severe mental retardation in the child.

Emotional State

This sensitivity to a subtle change in the oxygen level is similar to the reaction of the fetus to the mother's smoking, or drinking alcohol, or simply being in an upset condition much of the time. Since the upset mother would be pumping adrenalin into her own system, it follows that the fetus is experiencing a physiological state similar to his mother's upset state. It is, of course, impossible to determine whether the fetus is capable of emotional response or whether the response is purely physiological. Mothers who are upset, anxious, and emotional during the final stages of pregnancy have a high incidence of hyperactive, irritable infants who sleep and eat poorly in the first few weeks. Although the effects of the hormones in the child's system would quickly disappear after birth, a child who has an upset mother and who himself is upset at birth can easily suffer from his poor eating, sleeping, and nursing habits, as well as his general irritability. Studies of the mother's emotional state during pregnancy and the child's adjustment after birth have uncovered a significant relationship between the two. About the child, Montagu writes:

> He is to all intents and purposes a neurotic infant when he is born—the result of an unsatisfactory fetal environment. In this instance he has not had to wait until childhood for a bad home situation or other cause to make him neurotic. It has been done for him before he has even seen the light of day [1954, p. 19].

Prolonged nervous and emotional disturbance of the mother during the later months of pregnancy seems to be related directly to early feeding difficulties and to an irritable and hyperactive autonomic nervous system in the infant. The autonomic nervous system of the fetus seems to become sensitized through the hyperactivity of the mother's nervous and endocrine systems acting through the fluid medium of her blood. Jost and Sontag (1944) found a greater similarity in the functioning of the autonomic nervous systems of twins than of siblings, and of siblings than an unrelated group, which suggests that the autonomic constitution may be at least partially inherited.

Even the process of ovulation, which is regulated by the woman's endocrine glands, is actually influenced by her emotional condition as well. Her attitudes, feelings, and relationship with her husband, parents, and children, all tend to influence the secretion of the hormones that in turn influence ovulation.

Alcoholic Intake

Moderation seems to be a good byword for all sorts of human activities. Certainly in pregnancy, moderation in alcoholic consumption is essential, and abstinence would not be a bad idea. K. Jones, D. Smith, Ulleland, and Streissguth (1973, p. 1267) found a "similar pattern of craniofacial, limb, and cardiovascular defects associated with prenatal-onset growth deficiency and developmental delay" in children born to chronic alcoholics in three different ethnic groups. All the children were retarded. The fact that these were serious defects caused by chronic alcoholism is pertinent, even though most mothers are not alcoholics. No one knows how much alcohol is too much. And one would assume that no mother would wish to test the possibility that she has crossed the line between no effect to little effect to gross effect. When the health of the child is at stake, a little effect is too much.

Smoking

Excessive smoking by the mother seems to be related to more than just irritability of the fetus. There is the possibility that smoking affects the heart as well as the whole cardiovascular system of the fetus, since the mother's smoking increases the heart rate of the fetus. "But the choice between a dessicated weed and a well cultivated seed seems often to be a quite difficult one" (H. Bernard, 1962, p. 43).

Simpson (1957) reported, in a retrospective study of 7,449 patients, that heavy smokers are twice as likely to have premature babies as nonsmokers. This does not prove that the smoking causes the prematurity; it might be that the woman who smokes heavily during pregnancy smokes for reasons that in turn cause prematurity. Nevertheless, the finding is significant.

Following up the Simpson study, Frazier, G. Davis, Goldstein, and Goldberg (1961) studied 2,736 pregnant black women and found a significant relationship between prematurity and smoking: the rate of premature deliveries was 11.2 percent for nonsmokers, 13.6 percent for those who became smokers during pregnancy, and 18.6 percent for smokers. Moreover, the incidence of prematurity increased with the amount smoked. Frazier et al. also found that the infants of smokers weigh less than the infants of nonsmokers regardless of the duration of the pregnancy, which suggests a fetal developmental mechanism rather than an early onset of labor. The difference between infants of smokers and nonsmokers was independent of the mother's age, blood-group type, initial hemoglobin level, work history, education, and score on a psychosomatic-complaint scale, as well as the sex of the child.

Diet

Another highly relevant environmental influence during the prenatal period is the mother's diet. Many studies have shown the high correlation between the nutritional state of the mother and the health of the fetus. Most investigators have found a definite relationship between dietary deficiencies during pregnancy, especially of protein and vitamins, and the incidence of spontaneous abortions, premature births, stillbirths, and neonatal deaths. A Baltimore study showed that stillbirths and major deformities, as well as the length and weight of the newborn, were all highly related to the mother's prenatal diet (Knobloch and Pasamanick, 1966; Pasamanick and Knobloch, 1966).

In all studies of conditions relating to conception and birth, the general findings have been that the earlier the effect of the environmental deficiency upon the fetus, the more serious the damage that results. Diet may be an exception, since in the earliest stages of the pregnancy it appears that the fetus can, so to speak, rob the mother of vital minerals and nutrients. But later in the pregnancy, the needs of both can become so acute that, even though the child may get the lion's share of some of the vital minerals and vitamins, there still are not enough and the child may be born with rickets, for example. Still Warkany (1947) suggests that maternal malnutrition in the early stages of fetal growth is a decisive factor in the production of certain physical abnormalities. Ebbs, Brown, Tisdall, Moyle, and Bell (1942), working in Canada, found that the fetus of a mother on a poor diet suffered more than the mother and that, in every way, the mothers on a good diet, and their offspring, did better than the mothers on a poor diet, and their offspring.

A shortage of vitamin B would seem to affect mental ability. Studies, which supplemented the diet of mothers in a depressed socioeconomic group, resulted in their having brighter children than mothers in the same socioeconomic group who did not receive the supplement. An extensive study of children in well-baby clinics across the nation (Bayley, 1965) has replicated these well-established findings that there is a relationship between the mother's nutrition and the infant's general intellectual and physical development. And a study conducted by the World Health Organization Expert Committee on Maternal and Child Health has shown that a high rate of premature births is associated with poor prenatal care, poor nutrition, and the stressful conditions of life associated with poverty (Wortis, 1963).

Age

The age of the mother is also important to the health of the baby. Congenital hydrocephalus is significantly correlated with advanced maternal age. Two-egg twinning increases with the age of the mother. Birth weight and the incidence of a number of miscellaneous congenital deformities vary with the age and the parity of the mother. So does the incidence of dizygotic twins, which might be considered an indirect effect of maternal age on, for instance, birth weight.

The best-known instance in man is the incidence of Down's syndrome. The dependence of Down's syndrome on maternal age itself, independent of parity, is very clear: every increase of five years after the age of twenty-five more than doubles the probability that a child suffering from Down's syndrome will be born.

Disease

One of the benefits of medical care of pregnant women stems from the recognition of maternal disease. The discovery that syphilis, disorders of the thyroid, subclinical or prediabetes, cyanotic heart disease, or other disease is present—even taking the history of previous reproductive events —all enable the physician to contribute to the health of the child as well as the mother.

Rhodes (1961) has reported a substantial increase in malformations of children born after their mothers contracted influenza—3.6 percent of the children had malformations, as against 1.5 percent of those whose mothers had not had influenza. Rhodes cites the Dublin study of Coffey and Jessop (1959), who found that the risk of malformation in the child following the mother's contracting influenza varied with the trimester of pregnancy: in the first trimester the risk of malformation was 7.4 percent; in the second, 4.3 percent; in the third, 2.0 percent.

Rhodes also cites a Finnish study of mumps made by Ylinen and Jarvinen (1953), who found that 22.6 percent of the babies born to mothers who contracted mumps in the first three months of pregnancy had malformations, as against 10 percent when the disease occurred in the second and third trimesters. "Influenza and mumps occurring early in pregnancy seem to increase the incidence of 'run of the mill' malformations. They seldom cause the cataracts and deafness so characteristic of the rubella syndrome. It would appear that rubella is a specific teratogenic agent" (Rhodes, 1961, pp. 111–112).

Diabetes is a special problem: "The children of insulin-treated diabetic mothers evince a relatively high proportion of malformations, for which we must blame either the mother's high blood sugar or the action of insulin on the early embryo, or both" (Corner, 1961, pp. 14–15).

NUTRITION

By now overwhelming evidence indicates that the nutritional level of the population—both male and female prior to procreation, and female during gestation and lactation—is the most critical single variable affecting the production of genetically and physically sound children. The evidence is clear that malnutrition, and the accompanying absence of essential vitamins and minerals, is the greatest single determinant of defects in children.

The need for adequate nutrition not only for survival but for full growth and normal physiological function has been demonstrated experimentally in many studies. Recently a series of animal studies has centered around the effects of maternal undernutrition during gestation and lactation. Physiological and behavioral abnormalities have been evidenced in the progeny: stunted growth, retarded neuromotor development, poor metabolism, impaired ability to learn, lowered exploratory drive, heightened irritability and emotional lability, and marked antisocial behavior (Chow, Simonson, Hanson, and Roeder, 1971).

Timing of the Undernutrition

Studies of animals have indicated that the timing of undernutrition is a critical factor. Undernourishment after weaning and throughout life results in a decreased growth rate as well as less maximum growth, delays in maturational development and earlier death (M. Ross, 1959; Berg and Simms, 1960). But temporary undernutrition in animals does not seem to affect their ability to recover: weight losses and impaired metabolic activities caused by dietary restrictions in adulthood were restored to normal with adequate nutrition (Barrows and Roeder, 1961). Even extreme deficits in body weight and size and alterations in biochemical and behavioral characteristics caused by undernourishment in young animals after weaning were corrected upon being refed (Barrows and Roeder, 1963; S. Yeh and B. Weiss, 1963; Dickerson and Walmsley, 1967).

Early undernutrition, on the other hand, during lactation, can result in permanent nutritional influences, even when an adequate diet is available after weaning (Roeder and Chow, 1972). Maternal nutritional deprivation during gestation alone causes similar though less drastic effects as deprivation during gestation and lactation (Blackwell, Blackwell, T. Yeh, Weng, and Chow, 1969).

Chow and Stephan concluded that "in rats an imprint is made *in utero* on the growth potential of the progeny that is determined by the maternal diet during gestation" (1971, p. 254). Hanson and Simonson found "an increased liability to disruption of behavior due to prenatal undernourishment" (1971, p. 307).

The earlier a nutritional stress is imposed, the poorer the recovery, probably due to interferences with cell replication, thought Winick and Noble (1966). Stephan, however, felt that probably "the previously observed learning and behavioral deficits" are not due to impaired cellular development, but rather "that these psychological changes might be related to the disturbed hormonal pattern" (1971, p. 257).

Simonson et al. concluded that "fetal deprivation can cause lasting behavioral damage to the offspring not correctable by subsequent feeding" (Simonson, Stephan, Hanson, and Chow, 1971, p. 335). Hsueh, R. Blackwell, and Chow (1970) suggest that dietary restriction during gestation and lactation causes a metabolic derangement in the offspring that affects their ability to utilize subsequent diets, even though adequate, thus suggesting a critical period in the development of metabolizing capacity, which, if passed, is never regained. The research team did not find a similar metabolic derangement when malnourishment was during the lactation period alone.

This study had been prompted by a preliminary study of eleven-year-old children in Formosa where the research team observed that

> a dietary intake sufficient to permit normal weight gain in children from adequately fed families caused weight loss in children from poorly fed families.... The study has demonstrated a hitherto unrecognized phenomenon of food wastage in a certain group of children, a group characterized by economic and, hence, dietary deprivation of both their mothers and themselves [Chow, Blackwell, Blackwell, Hou, Anilane, and Sherwin, 1968, pp. 677, 675].

Diet Content

R. Davis, Hargen, and Chow (1972) found that progeny of animals fed a diet of 35 percent sucrose during gestation and lactation were significantly heavier than controls even though both groups had adequate diets after weaning and the control dams had an adequate diet during gestation and lactation. The researchers concluded that the sucrose in the maternal diet had a geneticlike effect in controlling the metabolism of glucose throughout the life of the progeny.

Chow, Simonson, Hanson, and Roeder (1971) found specific vitamin deficiencies to produce marked behavioral impairments in rats. And maternal protein deficiency during gestation and lactation was found to affect the subsequent metabolism of the progeny, regardless of quality of diet after weaning (Chow, Blackwell, Blackwell, Hou, Anilane, and Sherwin, 1968).

Studying metabolism of protein, Lee and Chow found that the progeny of underfed mothers could utilize "good-quality protein as efficiently as the unrestricted progeny," but that they "did not utilize a poorer quality protein" (1968, p. 20). An earlier study concluded that

> protein is the critical dietary component ... which, when deficient, results in the previously reported growth-stunting of the progeny.... Restoration of vitamins and minerals failed to influence the effect of restriction. Restoration of the caloric intake by the addition of sucrose resulted in less marked but still significant growth-stunting [Hsueh, Agustin, and Chow, 1967, p. 195].

Results of Undernutrition

Chow and Rider (1973) summarize research on dietary influences in rats as indicating that maternal malnutrition during pregnancy and lactation affects not only the viability of the progeny, but sets the pattern for subsequent growth and rate of development and affects behavioral and intellectual performance, no matter how well fed the progeny after weaning. Malnutrition suffered shortly after birth causes permanent and obvious effects on subsequent growth and development, but effects of malnutrition later in life can be reversed by an adequate diet. The earlier the malnutrition is suffered, the more permanent and more serious its effects.

Research on malnutrition in humans is not so easy to come by as that with animals. And often the data we do have are confounded with other variables concomitant to the condition that produced the malnutrition. But the evidence of the importance of good nutrition is overwhelming. Suspicions that malnutrition in early childhood retarded normal development have been realized in studies throughout the world.

Winick and Rosso, responding to the suspicion of retarded brain growth in malnourished children, studied the cellular structure of the brains of Chilean children accidentally killed compared with those who died of malnutrition. They found a decided difference. The brains of the undernourished children were "reduced in weight and in nucleic acid and protein content. These data indicate that severe early malnutrition retards cell division in the human brain" (1969*a*, p. 184).

In relating these findings to ways in which pediatricians check the growth and development of infants, Winick and Rosso found that

> in marasmic infants who died as a result of their severe malnutrition, brain weight and protein were reduced proportionally to head circumference. DNA content was reduced as much as [or] more than head circumference. These data strongly support the validity of using changes in head circumference as a measure of postnatal brain growth in normal and malnourished infants [1969*b*, p. 774].

Along the same line, the Perinatal Research Committee found head circumference to correlate significantly with measured intelligence at age four: at birth, head circumference correlated .15 with four-year IQ; at four months, head circumference correlated .15 with four-year IQ; at eight months, .13; at one year, .13; and at four years, head circumference correlated .14 with four-year IQ. Maternal education (.38), socioeconomic status (.38), prenatal care (.21), all were found to have high correlations with four-year IQ, and all would be concomitant to the condition that would cause undernourishment.*

K. Nelson and Deutschberger, corroborating Winick's suggestion of the appropriateness of measurements of head circumference as indicators of normal maturation and growth, found that no boy with a head circumference less than 43 cm at one year, or girl with less than 42 cm, achieved a four-year IQ of 120 or more (1970, p. 493).

Winick (1969) asked three questions: (1) does malnutrition produce significant brain changes? (2) if so, are they functionally important? and (3) is the brain more susceptible to change from malnutrition at specific times? The answer to all three is yes (Cravioto and Robles, 1965; Champakam, Srikantia, and Gopalan, 1968; Chase and Martin, 1969; Ricciuti, 1970; Brockman and Ricciuti, 1971), although to isolate effects of malnutrition from other consequences of poverty is difficult. More and more

---

*Unpublished data from the collaborative study, "Cerebral Palsy, Mental Retardation, and Other Neurological and Sensory Disorders of Infancy and Early Childhood," carried out by the National Institute of Neurological Diseases and Stroke.

data indicate that malnutrition in infancy permanently affects the minds of children.

The problem is the self-perpetuating nature of poverty. Begun in infancy, condemned to marginal functioning, there seems to be no extrication from an environment that will produce the same "disease" in the next generation. We know that the earlier the malnutrition, the more severe and permanent the damage. Perhaps as much emphasis should be given to improving the nutrition of pregnant women and infants as to providing adequate school lunches. By school age, the harm has been done.

It is indeed ironic that the central cause of a major problem to children, a problem that affects both their physical and mental health and, in turn, their ability to produce healthy children, should be so easily identified, should be well within the capacity of the world's resources to eliminate, and yet should continue to be the central cause of birth defects. While we are preoccupied with research into the causes and elimination of the rare diseases that kill children (a preoccupation justified by the resources at our disposal), we seem to forget the importance of three balanced meals a day as a major deterrent to gross defects.

INTELLIGENCE

Much effort has been expended to isolate the action of environment upon genetic predisposition in two areas of the child's behavior—intelligence and personality. Intelligence refers to his ability to profit from past experience in solving present problems. Personality refers to the characteristic way of behaving that defines his uniqueness in a social setting. Let us review some of these research efforts.

Early Theories

Charles Darwin early considered the relationship between intelligence and genetics. He believed intelligence to be one of those characteristics of survival that permitted certain family groups and races to become prominent and powerful. His theories laid the groundwork for the study and speculation of his cousin, Sir Francis Galton, who systematically investigated the nature of intelligence and its relationship to heredity. Galton (1870) examined in some detail the family history of the leaders of the British Commonwealth, men of great reputation in science, education, government, and law. He found that these men came from a few closely related families that had held positions of leadership in England for generations. Galton, who himself came from one of these families, seemed to have no hesitation in attributing their remarkable success to superior heredity. He chose to ignore the superior education, cultural background, and special opportunity for advancement that was their birthright as members of the British aristocracy.

Galton's law of filial regression, the tendency to return to the mean, was a convenient way of dealing with the children of these families of great stature who did not measure up. These black sheep Galton considered to be merely examples of his law, a return to the mean, to the mediocre, to the common. He believed that the offspring of parents who are far above average will have a tendency to be more like the mean than either of their parents.

A second advocate of the effect of heredity on intelligence was H. H. Goddard, who founded the Vineland Training School in New Jersey and authored a famous study of familial retardation. In his study of the Kallikak family (1912), Goddard revealed generation after generation of pathology, which he assumed to be a result of poor heredity. The tracing of family trees to study the influence of heredity on intelligence was relatively short-lived in psychology, however, because of the tremendous difficulty in obtaining accurate material.

Twin Studies

A research design using four basic groups of children, now replicated many times, provides most of our stable information about heredity and intelligence: identical twins reared together, identical twins reared apart, fraternal twins reared together, and siblings reared together. Statistical correlations are used to describe the degree of relatedness between the scores of the children in different groups. These correlations can be positive (as one score increases, the other increases), negative (as one score increases, the other decreases), and zero (no covariation). A perfect relationship is indicated by a correlation of 1. Typical correlations obtained from psychological research on intelligence vary from .97, the correlation between the IQs obtained on two similar intelligence tests administered to an individual on the same day (Wechsler, 1955, p. 13), to .21, the correlation between an intelligence test administered to a two-year-old child and then readministered when he is fourteen (Honzik, MacFarlane, and Allen, 1948, p. 323, Table 3). Ireton, Thwing, and Gravem (1970) report significant correlations between four-year IQ and eight-month mental score: .28 for males; .23 for females.

Presumably, to return to twins and siblings, if heredity plays a large part in intelligence, the correlation between the IQs of identical twins should be higher than that between fraternal twins, and that between fraternal twins should be no higher than that between other brothers and sisters. Since identical twins result from the early cleavage of a single fertilized egg, there is every reason to believe that their heredity is identical. Since four independent hereditary units are involved in the case of fraternal twins, their heredity is no more alike than that of nontwin brothers and sisters.

A great many studies have compared the similarities of IQ in twins living under different environmental conditions: identical twins living together, identical twins living apart, and fraternal twins reared together. Six of these typify the results: Newman, Freeman, and Holzinger (1937), Burt (1958), Shields (1962), D. Freedman and Keller (1963), Nichols (1965), and a review by Erlenmeyer-Kimling and Jarvik (1963). In these six studies, representing a total of fifty-seven studies of identical twins reared apart and identical and fraternal twins reared together, the same trends are reported: whether identical twins were reared together or apart,

Table 2

Reported Correlations of the IQs of Twins

Group	Newman, Freeman, and Holzinger (1937)	Burt (1958)	Shields (1962)
Identical twins reared together	.91	.93	.76
Identical twins reared apart	.67	.88	.77
Fraternal twins reared together	.64	.55	.51

Data from col. 1, table 96, p. 347; col. 2, table 1, p. 6; and col. 3, table 37, p. 139.

their IQs were more similar. The correlations reported in three of these studies are listed in Table 2.

The correlations between the IQs of fraternal twins reared together and siblings reared together are nearly identical: fraternal twins reared together, .55; siblings reared together, .54; siblings reared apart, .52 (Burt, 1958, Table 1, p. 6). The great similarity between fraternal twins reared together and siblings reared together is that much more remarkable when one considers the more identical environment of twins. This more similar environment for twins is due to two factors. The first is timing. Many events can occur and substantially alter the environment in the two years or so that separate the average siblings. Second, twins are generally dressed alike and treated alike in the formative years of life in most families.

Since identical twins reared apart do not have as similar an environment as fraternal twins reared together, the effect of heredity is clearly indicated by the comparison of these two groups. Shields, whose study is more recent than the other two reported in Table 2, and who used the largest number of subjects, found virtually no difference between the IQ correlations of identical twins reared apart and identical twins reared together. He did find substantial differences between identical twins reared apart and fraternal twins reared together.

D. Freedman and Keller (1963) used an infant population, made up of twenty pairs of same-sex twins reared together, eleven fraternal and nine identical. Using the *Bayley Mental and Motor Scales*, they found that the differences between the monozygotic twins were significantly less. They concluded that

> heredity plays a role in the development of positive social orientation and in the fear of strangers. Our evidence for this is that identical twins show greater concordance than fraternal twins ... over the first year of life. There seems to be no reasonable alternate explanation of these results [D. Freedman, 1965, p. 159].

Nichols (1965) studied 1,507 pairs of same-sex twins located and identified through the National Merit Scholarship Qualifying Test. The correlation of the test scores of the monozygotic twins was .87, and of the dizygotic twins, .63. Nichols also reviewed nine studies of twins, including his own. One reported substantially lower correlations: .75 between the scores of identical twins and .39 between the scores of fraternal twins. The remaining eight studies reported correlations of .87 to .92 between intelligence test scores of identical twins and of .52 to .70 between those of fraternal twins.

Erlenmeyer-Kimling and Jarvik (1963) have made a comprehensive review of 52 heterogeneous studies from eight countries, four continents, and covering a time span of more than two generations, and whose sample populations differed in size, age, socioeconomic, and ethnic groupings. Figure 8 is their summary of the results of these studies. The figure is arranged with the utmost clarity, starting at the top with unrelated people reared apart and ending at the bottom with identical twins reared together. Theoretically, the correlations should start at 0 and gradually increase toward 1, which they do. The range of the studies is indicated from left to right, the median for each group being indicated by a vertical line.

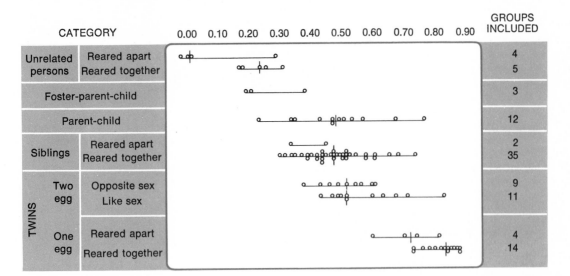

Figure 8
Summary of Erlenmeyer-Kimling and Jarvik review of studies on intelligence in twins. Reprinted, by permission of the authors and publisher, from L. Erlenmeyer-Kimling and Lissy F. Jarvik, Genetics and intelligence: a review, *Science*, 1963, 142, Figure 1, p. 1478. Copyright © 1963 by the American Association for the Advancement of Science.

Erlenmeyer-Kimling and Jarvik comment that "considering only ranges of the observed measures, a marked trend is seen toward an increasing degree of intellectual resemblance in direct proportion to an increasing degree of genetic relationship, regardless of environmental communality" (1963, p. 1477). The medians of these studies, as listed in Table 3, clearly support this statement.

These studies support the contention that there is a hereditary component of intelligence. But it must be remembered that we are talking now, not about cause but about probability. The environmentalists were able to demonstrate beyond any question that intelligence is modifiable by environmental manipulation. Once this was established, they went on to suggest that the overwhelming majority of the differences in intelligence may be environmentally determined.

Table 3

Median Group Correlations of Erlenmeyer-Kimling and Jarvik Review of Studies on Intelligence in Twins

Correlation	Group
.01	Unrelated persons reared apart
.20	Foster-parent and child
.23	Unrelated persons reared together
.49	Siblings reared together
.50	Parent and child
.53	Dizygotic twins, of opposite and like sex
.75	Monozygotic twins reared apart
.87	Monozygotic twins reared together

Environmental Studies

The work of two eminent researchers in the field, Marie Skodak and Harold Skeels (1949), presents a sterling example of the evidence for the environmentalist's view. Marie Skodak vividly describes her first encounter with two infants in an Iowa orphanage: "They were scrawny little girls. They couldn't sit up, or make a sound except to whine or cry.... They were miserable pieces of humanity." Although they were thirteen and sixteen months old, their mental performance was that of children of six and seven months: they obtained IQs of 46 and 35. Their hereditary background was wretched. Both children had mentally deficient mothers (one was also psychotic) and unknown fathers.

Because the orphanage was overcrowded and these two babies were considered unplaceable, they were transferred to an institution for the mentally retarded when they were fifteen and eighteen months old. In the institution, the children were placed in the care of retarded women on an adult women's ward. These women lavished affection, attention, and care upon the girls. Within six months, when the babies were retested by Skodak, their general emotional health had greatly improved and their IQs had risen to 77 and 87. A year later the children were retested. The child who had at first had an IQ of 35, then 87, now had an IQ of 88; and the child whose IQ had first been 46, then 77, now had an IQ of 100, precisely normal—the result, Skodak believed, of nothing more specific than the tender loving care of a retarded woman who had "adopted" the child during this critical period of her life.

Intrigued by the amazing results, Skodak and Skeels replicated the study by sending thirteen more orphanage children to live with adult retardates, and using twelve children as a control or contrast group in the orphanage. The results, discussed by Skeels (1966), were similar, if not as dramatic. The contrast group in the orphanage had on the first test a mean IQ of 86.7; on the last, a mean IQ of 60.5—an obvious deterioration in three years. The transferred children had on the first test a mean IQ of 64.3; on the last a mean IQ of 91.8—an obvious improvement.

The most interesting aspect of the study was a follow-up evaluation of the two groups after twenty-one years. All of the children were located and tested, with the exception of one in the control group who had died at fifteen in an institution. The early findings were vindicated: the children who had been boarded with retarded foster mothers were still functioning in the normal range, and the institutionalized children were still functioning in the defective range.

While it is obvious that the children studied by Skeels and Skodak cannot be considered either typical or random samples of institutionalized, mentally retarded children, the conclusion is inescapable that it was only the intervention of the two psychologists that enabled these children to make a normal adjustment. Those who were not removed from the orphanage remained, or became mental defectives. The study serves to expose as a self-fulfilling prophesy the practice of using "bad" heredity as an excuse for raising the children of retarded parents in institutions where they live out their lives as retarded adults: "It has become increasingly evident that the prediction of later intelligence cannot be based on the child's first observed developmental status. Account must be taken of his experiences between test and retest" (Skeels, 1966, p. 56).

To examine the influence of genetic and environmental variables on the IQ, Moss and Kagan (1959) analyzed and compared data from both the Fels Institute middle-class sample from rural Ohio and the Berkeley middle-class sample from California. They concluded that the mother's education is superior to the father's in predicting the child's IQ (significantly so at age three with the Fels data and at ages six and ten with the Berkeley data). Also, the mother's education is a better predictor of a daughter's IQ than a son's (significantly better at ages six and ten with the Berkeley data and ages three and ten with the Fels data).

Studying the effect of environment on intelligence, Bayler and Schaefer (1960) examined maternal behavior and its effect upon the child's IQ. They rated maternal behavior in such areas as equalitarianism, irritability, expression of affection, punishment, control through fear, strictness, fostering of independence, and intrusiveness, and then correlated these with the child's IQ. Their study revealed differences according to the age and sex of the child, but they concluded that girls' intelligence was probably genetically determined and that boys' intelligence was more environmentally determined. The authors discuss the notion that the genetic structure of girls is much less modifiable than that of boys.

Where we might say of the boys that earlier mothering pays off in the long run, for girls we would have to say that so far as intelligence is concerned these early "good" mother-daughter interactions are of little avail, and that genetic inheritance appears to be the important determiner for later intellectual growth [Bayley and Schaefer, 1964, p. 68].

However, Honzik (1963) pointed out that girls mature intellectually earlier than boys and that girls' intelligence test scores resemble their parents' at a much earlier age than boys'. The fact that girls mature earlier may well affect their modifiability; that is, there is a longer period in which boys can be modified.

More recently, Butterfield and Zigler (1970) studied IQ changes among institutionalized retarded youngsters according to the level of their preinstitutional social deprivation. They found that greater losses in IQ occurred after institutionalization among those children with the least social deprivation before institutionalization. They attributed this finding to the hypothesis that IQ changes reflect changes in motivational factors rather than in cognitive functioning per se.

Race Studies

Investigators who support the primacy of the genetic component of intelligence are likely to use the results of the twin studies reviewed earlier and to indicate that intelligence is due mostly to genetic predisposition. Nowhere has the controversy about the effect of heredity on intelligence been so bitter and so long in resolution than in the relationship between race and intelligence. In the United States the argument has revolved around the intelligence of the American black—and whether or not there are, on the basis of race, genetic differences that account for the obtained differences in IQs calculated from standardized intelligence tests. We must remember, at the outset, what ethnologists have pointed out—that there is no such thing as a pure race and that American blacks are a polymorphic ethnic group.

However, after seventy-five years of intensive investigation, thousands of empirical studies, several major theories, and a controversy that ripped asunder the tranquility of the whole testing movement, the question remains today essentially unanswered: Are there real differences in intelligence to be found among races? If not, why is it to be assumed that this variable is immune, when so many others seem free to range? No one today would seriously question that within races and between races there are many genotypic idiosyncrasies that lead to phenotypic differences in height, weight, skin pigment, facial characteristics, texture and color of hair, and even susceptibility to disease. It follows naturally that there could be some genetic variations that might lead to variations in potential intelligence.

One view is that there are genetic predispositions of intelligence, as shown in the research on identical and fraternal twins. Evidence for the other view, the environmentalist's view, begins with the early and controversial Iowa studies (Wellman, 1932–1933) that demonstrated that for certain, young, deprived children, intelligence was modifiable by so simple a thing as nursery-school attendance (Wellman, 1945). This approach, that intelligence is dependent upon cultural rather than genetic factors,

was the basis for the Head Start Program and has received considerable
support from most psychologists and educators.

The differences in performance on intelligence tests between black and white children in experimental studies has been pointed up in reviews of the literature by Shuey (1958, 1966), Dreger and K. Miller (1960, 1968), Kennedy, V. Van De Riet, and White (1963), and Kennedy (1969). To review the findings briefly, a 20-point deficit has been demonstrated in the intelligence of black children when compared to the national norm on standardized intelligence tests (Kennedy, Van De Riet, and White, 1963, Figure 2, p. 68). This pattern is well-established at the first-grade level and does not change appreciably in the school years. Moreover, after the first grade there is a 20 percent deficit in achievement, as measured by standard achievement tests. The percentage remains constant throughout the grades, although the deficit represents more months of achievement as the child moves upward through the grades in school (Kennedy, Van De Riet, and White, 1963, p. 109).

Two other observations are pertinent. The first is that at birth and during the first two years of life, tests of mental ability do not demonstrate a deficit in the intelligence of blacks. Several studies, Bayley's (1965) being the most notable, have demonstrated a slight superiority of black infants at birth—and this despite the important findings of Pasamanick and Knobloch (1958) that one of the major effects of cultural deprivation and its concomitant poor prenatal nutritional and medical care is the production of sickly, underweight, and often premature infants who begin life at an inferior level of intelligence.

The correlation between infant intelligence tests and school-age intelligence tests is very low, so low that it is obvious these tests measure different variables: the tests of infant intelligence sample mostly motor and perceptual skills, while the school-age tests sample mostly verbal and numerical skills. Nevertheless, shortly after two years of age, a slight but significant decline begins in the measured IQ of black children. This decline becomes extremely sharp between four and five years of age, so that the 20-point deficit in the mean IQ is well-established by the age of five. It seems, then, that differences between measured white and black intelligence either appear after two years of age or are based on differences that are not measurable earlier than four.

The second observation is that any kind of massive cultural infusion or environmental stimulation on a steady basis can be expected to hold the IQs of black children at a higher level during the critical years of two to four, or to restore lost IQ points in the late preschool period. Whereas the average black child's IQ is dropping from 100 to 80 during the three's, four's, and five's, children in programs of cultural enrichment seem to lose only half as much.

S. Gray and Klaus (1965) report an average rise in IQ from 87.6 at 40.7 months to 97.1 at 59.3 months of age, when children are in a culturally enriched program. In 1968, they reported an IQ of 98.1 at 83.3 months. But in 1970, the final measured IQ at 106.0 months was 86.7. In their control group, on the other hand, the mean IQ was 86.9 at 40.3 months and 80.8 at 59.6 months (Klaus and S. Gray, 1968, Table 3,

p. 28); at 82.9 months, the control IQ was 84.6 and at 96.2 months, the control IQ was 77.7 (S. Gray and Klaus, 1970, Table 2, p. 913). The Gray and Klaus intervention program consisted of only ten-week summer sessions and weekly visits to the home the remainder of the year. They concluded:

> In 1968 we wrote: "The most effective intervention programs for preschool children that could possibly be conceived cannot be considered a form of inoculation whereby the child forever after is immune to the effects of a low-income home and of a school inappropriate to his needs. Certainly, the evidence on human performance is overwhelming in indicating that such performance results from the continual interaction of the organism with its environment. Intervention programs, well conceived and executed, may be expected to make some relatively lasting changes. Such programs, however, cannot be expected to carry the whole burden of providing adequate schooling for children from deprived circumstances; they can provide only a basis for future progress in schools and homes that can build upon the early intervention."
>
> In 1969 we saw no reason to alter this statement. Our seventh-year results only serve to underscore its truth [S. Gray and Klaus, 1970, pp. 923–924].

Thus far we have been reviewing data about which there can be no serious question, unless one is willing to attack the whole concept of measured intelligence. The intercorrelations of all measures of intelligence, the predictive power of intelligence tests, the relationship between test performance and academic performance, as well as the confounding, now, of predictive variables and criteria in intelligence testing, would indicate that dealing with the problem of a deficit in the IQ of the black by attacking intelligence tests per se is simply an exercise in futility. There can be no doubt that a problem of measurement exists. No one suggests that there is a measure of intelligence that is culture-free. But as predictors of academic achievement and job placement, these tests stand on their own merit. The current fad of damning intelligence tests will last only so long as the damners are not asked to provide an acceptable alternative.

At issue is the moral question of what is right rather than what is correct. The intelligence test points up inequalities, deficiencies, and unfairness in our society. It does so on excellent theoretical and empirical grounds. It comes to the core of the issue. But the issue of social equality, of equal opportunity, of justice, will not be dealt with effectively in the midst of a donnybrook over the assessment of intelligence. No decision-making process today stands on better theoretical and empirical grounds than does the classification of children by levels of intelligence.

PERSONALITY

Let us now move from our study of the role of genetics in predisposing intelligence and shift to a brief look at the role of genetics in predisposing personality. To begin again with Sir Francis Galton is entirely appropriate, this time with his book, *English Men of Science* (1874). Galton made a detailed examination of letters written by scientific Englishmen and their families. After discussing their personality in general, including such variables as their energy level, perseverance, truthfulness, independence, and orderliness, Galton, relying only on anecdotal material, much of which was second-hand, arrived at conclusions that have been substantiated by subsequent research. Fuller and W. Thompson (1960, p. 231), in summarizing Galton's work, cite a key reference: "a love of science might be largely extended by fostering and not thwarting innate tendencies" (Galton, 1874, p. 225). Obviously, Galton felt that some men who were born scientists occasionally were prevented from becoming scientists by the ineptness of those managing their environment. Galton's work was followed by many descriptive, anecdotal studies of family trees of eminent scholars, scientists, and giants of industry in England.

Twin Studies

A personality test with a respectable degree of objectivity was not available until the early 1930s. This test, the *Bernreuter Personality Inventory*, consisted of a series of scales designed to measure neuroticism, introversion, dominance, and self-sufficiency, all then considered definable characteristics that had external meaning. That is, some people were thought to be obviously introverted, tending to be shy and retiring, keeping to themselves, while others could be classified as extroverted, gregarious in seeking the companionship of other people, outgoing, and boisterous. In addition to having such external references, these characteristics were also considered definable in terms of test items that seemed to be correlated.

Not all the data in the 1930s were consistent, but there was a tendency, at least, for the scores of daughters to be more highly correlated with their parents' scores, particularly the mother's, than the scores of sons; for mothers and daughters to resemble each other quite sharply; for sisters to resemble each other rather well; for fathers and daughters to resemble each other only slightly less well; and for sons to tend to be rather independent of either their mother's or father's personality. Because the correlations were relatively low however, and because environmental influences are difficult if not impossible to control, the family resemblances with regard to personality detected by the *Bernreuter* in the 1930s were not impressive. Better demonstrations of the effect of heredity on personality were required.

However, one researcher using the *Bernreuter* and the twin-control method to study the inheritance of personality should be mentioned. Harold Carter (1933, 1935) studied 133 pairs of twins, 55 of whom were identical. Without exception, the monozygotic pairs showed greater personality similarity. As would be expected of the fraternal twins, those of like sex were more similar in personality than those of different sexes. His work is convincing evidence that the personality characteristics studied by the *Bernreuter* are influenced by heredity.

A later study of the personality of twins, one emphasizing sociological and environmental factors, reached a similar conclusion. Richard Smith (1965) studied 164 pairs of adolescent white twins of like sex: 90 monozygotic, and 74 dizygotic. With respect to habits, activities, personal preferences, parental treatment, and self-images, he found monozygotic twins to be more similar to each other than dizygotic twins.

Somatotype Studies

Another mechanism for the transmission of personality characteristics through hereditary action is based on the well-known fact that physique is one of the most stable and reliable of family characteristics. It is obvious even to the casual observer that members of a family resemble each other in their physical proportions even more than they do in facial appearance. In the early 1940s, William H. Sheldon and his colleagues became convinced that definite personality characteristics were associated with body types or physiques (Sheldon and Stevens, 1942). The argument for such a relationship has been clearly summarized by Lindzey (1965).

Possibly the same family factors that influence body proportion, or morphology, also affect the developing personality. The fact that a mother is constantly obsessed with feeding her child, stuffing him with sweets, bread, cake, always making sure that plenty of "goodies" are in the house, certainly affects the bodily proportion of the child—he will be fat as a pig. In addition, this kind of nurture would be expected to affect his personality, affect his attitude toward eating, restrict his exercise, make him more content to sit around and nibble. By the same token, a child brought up under the care of a physical-culture faddist, who was routed out of bed every morning for a brisk run at daylight, constantly exercising, running, keeping in physical trim, eating only natural foods, getting only essential vitamins, would probably have a lithe body and also be different in personality from his counterpart, who was raised to sit around looking at TV and eating.

Some physical conditions directly or indirectly restrict or facilitate an individual's behavior. The ninety-seven-pound sophomore with brittle bones is unlikely to become a four-letter varsity football player, and a five-foot freshman is not apt to go out for basketball. On the other hand, boys with superior physiques would be hounded out of junior high school by the scorn of their classmates if they did not go out for athletics.

The indirect effect of a particular set of physical characteristics, such as early maturation, has been demonstrated many times, as in the Berkeley Growth Study (H. Jones and Bayley, 1941). Girls who reach puberty at eleven are propelled into a faster social life and earlier dating experiences. Early maturation tends to run their social clocks ahead by several years. Just so, girls with exceptional figures tend to have more social opportunities than girls who lack this attribute.

Society has built up certain expectations about behavior based on appearance. The redhead, known for his fiery temper, is expected to have one. The fat man is supposed to be jolly, the lean man aggressive. Because he is treated differently and allowed different privileges depending on his physical type, most individuals tend to fall readily into the expected role.

A last and most important mechanism, if one considers the effect of heredity to be significant, is the theory, propounded by Sheldon, of joint genetic determination of body behavior and physique; that is, both behavior and physical stature are governed by heredity. Sheldon makes a clear and vigorous argument for the crucial importance of the physical structure of the body as a primary determinant of behavior.

Sheldon has defended his thesis by making comparisons between body types and personality characteristics. He has isolated three body types, or somatotypes: (1) the endomorph, or soft, flabby person with underdeveloped bones and muscles and a tendency toward fat; (2) the mesomorph, with highly developed bone and muscle structure, a hard, firm physique, and a tendency toward an athletic build; and (3) the ectomorph, who is linear and fragile, characterized by flatness of chest and delicacy of bone structure, thin and slightly muscled, with a great deal of energy, a high metabolic rate, but little strength. Sheldon, who has compared the personalities of individuals with these body types, has encountered considerable criticism, mainly because of two inherent problems.

First, highly reliable, independent estimates of body proportions are most difficult to obtain. Few people represent pure physical types; one usually is dealing with a mixture of characteristics that perhaps tend to resemble one type. The problem of judgment enters. Sheldon's group has been most successful with those with so-called pure physiques, least successful with the mixed types.

Second, judging personality characteristics is also complex. Disagreements over personality ratings occur easily and often. Objective tests of personality also have limitations because of the necessity for demonstrating the meaning of the scores. When dealing with two complex variables there is obviously room for error and argument, and there would appear to have been considerable of both in the history of this movement. However, let's examine a few studies that make Sheldon's point as clearly as it can be made.

Child (1950) subjected 414 Yale sophomores to a self-rating of personality traits on multiple-choice items and to a physical rating by Sheldon and another rater. Of some ninety-six predictions made on the basis of Sheldon's theory, 77 percent were confirmed, suggesting that somatotype is a determinant of personality. However, the sample was limited in scope: Yale sophomores are hardly a representative sample; even so, the sophomores in the sample were selected on the basis of the ease in classifying them.

The subjects of a second study were 125 children attending the Gesell Institute Nursery School. They represented the total population of the nursery school excepting "children having physical handicaps, children falling clearly outside the intelligence distribution of the rest of the group, children of nonwhite racial background, children whose stay in school was too short to permit teachers' ratings, and children who refused to be photographed" (Walker, 1962, p. 75). The children were rated on a personality scale by their teachers, and comparisons were then made between these ratings and their physiques. The conclusions were similar to Child's, but the findings were not as striking and there were more errors, indicating that in children the tendency for body build and temperament to be related is not as strong.

The final study, performed by Glueck and Glueck (1950), was an inquiry into the relationship between physique and delinquency. The subjects were 500 persistent delinquents and 500 proven nondelinquents, matched in age, intelligence, ethnic background, and place of residence. The Gluecks found that delinquents tended to have a mesomorphic rather than an ectomorphic physique, and that they tended to have a slow growth rate until they were fourteen and then a rapid increase in growth rate until they were considerably larger than average. Interestingly, bodily disproportion was less frequent among the delinquents than the nondelinquents.

Any discussion of constitutional differences in personality should include a pair of studies by Shirley (1933) and Neilon (1948). For two years, Shirley studied the early development of the motor abilities of twenty-five children. On the basis of her familiarity with the children over a two-year span, she wrote personality sketches for nineteen of these youngsters. These sketches, somewhat anecdotal in nature, were descriptions of how the children responded, the uniqueness of their personality, how they behaved in most situations. They were a minor part of Shirley's study of the development of motor skills, but they aroused the curiosity of another investigator some fifteen years later.

Neilon administered two personality tests to the now seventeen-year-old subjects, as well as a self-rating personality scale. She interviewed the adolescents and their mothers, who also rated the subjects on a personality scale. And then Neilon wrote personality sketches for the adolescent subjects. She was able to gather partial data for all nineteen subjects and full data on fifteen: five sketches of adolescent girls were to be matched with six infant sketches; ten sketches of adolescent boys, with thirteen infant sketches. Ten judges matched the girls; five, the boys. Of the ten judges, three correctly matched personality sketches for four of the girls; six matched three correctly; and one matched two correctly. For the boys, one judge correctly matched five sketches; one correctly matched three; two correctly matched two; and one matched only one sketch correctly. Looking at the data from the point of view of the subjects, Neilon found that one girl was correctly matched by all ten judges, and one was never correctly matched. For the five girls, one was matched correctly ten times; one, nine times; one, seven times; one, six times; and one, zero times.

Neilon concluded that individual personality remains fairly stable over time and that some individuals are relatively more stable in personality than others: the personalities of some individuals are readily identifiable by age two. An individual's personality, then, can be concluded to persist over a period of time even though the methods of measurement are rather crude. That stable characteristics in children's personalities appear to be well established at a young age argues for the existence of some constitutional basis for differences in personality.

Proband Studies

Another equally important type of study is the so-called proband method, which begins with some readily diagnosed pathology or behavior pattern such as, for instance, manic-depressive psychosis—a psychosis that involves enormous swings in mood, from giddiness, great excitement, and exuberance to the depths of depression. A person who has this condition, then, would be called a proband. The researcher simply studies the family tree of a proband to determine in what percentage of his family the same illness has been diagnosed; he then compares that percentage with the frequency within the population of the country as a whole. The emotional conditions most frequently studied by this method are: (1) schizophrenia, a gross mental disorder which involves a disturbance in thinking, (2) manic-depressive psychosis, (3) involutional psychosis, a severe depression in men and women of late middle age, (4) homosexuality, and (5) psychosomatic disorders—that is, physical disorders that seem to be psychological in origin.

Kallmann's work on schizophrenia (1946) is a reasonable example of such research. Kallmann used the familiar design of the twin study to determine the relationship between heredity and mental disease. He was successful in locating a large number of identical twins, living apart, at least one of whom had developed schizophrenia. He found not only a high probability that the other twin likewise would be affected, but a tendency for schizophrenia to occur in families (see Table 4).

Table 4

Summary of Kallmann's Findings on the Probability of Schizophrenia

Group	Probability of Occurrence (%)
Children with normal parents	0.9
Children with one schizophrenic parent	16.4
Children with two schizophrenic parents	68.1
Siblings	14.3
Fraternal twins of like sex	17.6
Identical twins	85.8
Identical twins, living together	91.5
Identical twins, living apart	77.6

The living conditions of a child with two schizophrenic parents could hardly be considered normal. The wonder is that all of the children in the family do not develop the disease, whether or not one subscribes to the environmental or hereditary point of view. When one considers that the child has two models from which to choose in developing his own personality, and that both are schizophrenic, one would expect less chance than Kallmann found for the child to develop normally. Nevertheless, the striking differences between fraternal and identical twins certainly indicate a heredity component in schizophrenia.

The facts and theories in contemporary child psychology related to the effects of heredity and environment upon the behavior of children suggest that each has its part in influencing the whole. Perhaps Boyd McCandless best summarizes the present generally accepted position.

> When each of two conditions or states is required for the existence of a phenomenon, neither can be more important than the other. Heredity and environment begin to exert their influence at the time a child is conceived. They can not meaningfully be separated from each other [1967, p. 339].

In this vein let us review what is known in both areas.

Genetic Facts

Although we still are a long way from a complete understanding of the mechanisms of inheritance, certain facts now seem well established. For instance, we can list some means by which changes can take place from one generation to the other.

1. During the separation of the chromosomes, when the reproductive cell contains only half the required number (the other half coming from the other parent), certain errors in cell division can occur and fragments of the chromosomes may become lost. A wide variety of mostly negative results can occur.
2. The absence of certain vitamins and minerals at critical periods, due either to the failure of the diet to furnish them or of the system to break them down, causes certain malformations of the cells.
3. Radiation of the cell structure during critical periods in the life of the reproductive cell, either prior to or immediately following conception, can result in drastic and nearly always fatal mutations.
4. Certain chemicals ingested by either mother or father prior to conception, but most particularly by the mother during the early days of pregnancy, can alter the chemical balance within the DNA, again with drastic and usually fatal results.
5. The joining of certain cells permits the expression of recessive characteristics seldom seen in the population; the characteristic may not appear in the family tree from generation to generation until a chance mating with another carrier of the characteristic results in its overt expression.
6. Certain diseases, when contracted during a critical phase of pregnancy, lead to chemical changes within the DNA substance that result in defects in the fetus.

Environmental Facts

From the facts at hand, we can recognize the challenge that every child has the right to be well born. The following steps obviously are vital, both to the individual child and to the group to which the child belongs. Any nation, concerned with the welfare of its children and its future generations, would be wise to heed.

1. NUTRITION. Strong evidence suggests that the nutritional level of the population during the childbearing years, as well as nutritional support

of the infant and mother during gestation, lactation, and early childhood, is the most critical single variable affecting the production of genetically, intellectually, physically, and emotionally sound children. Strong evidence from animal studies, and more complex, but equally convincing evidence from human studies during famine years, indicates that malnutrition and the accompanying absence of essential vitamins, minerals, and most particularly protein, is the greatest single determinant of defects in the population.

That protein is the scarcest and most costly food, and is the first of the foods to be sacrificed during periods of economic deprivation, is perhaps obvious. Often a shortage of essential foods is accompanied by environmental and infectious pressures that preclude adequate metabolism of the few nutrients available.

2. MEDICAL CARE. Adequate medical care during the child-bearing years, particularly for women, would seem to be the second most essential answer to the problem of giving birth to unhealthy children. Adequate prenatal care is often a luxury to be enjoyed by those who can pay, but common sense and rudimentary economics show that good preventive medical care of the pregnant woman is justified even if one eliminates humanistic concerns. Its small cost is dwarfed by the expense of the prolonged care and custody required for mentally deficient and physically deformed children who often become wards of the state when they have exhausted the meager financial resources of their parents.

Although most defects in children result from prenatal deficiencies in oxygen or food supply, some of these are correctable or manageable if diagnosed promptly. And some occur during the birth process itself. Adequate medical care for the infant during birth, and intensive care during the first few hours after birth, are essential to avoid late-appearing defects or congenital diseases that could have been prevented or corrected by alert attention during and after birth. Home deliveries and deliveries in poorly equipped hospitals greatly increase the risk of defects in children.

3. EMOTIONALITY. Efforts to reduce the psychological distress of mothers during the childbearing years would seem warranted by the evidence of the relationship between the mother's and the child's emotional health, even at birth. At no time is the mother's health more important than during pregnancy and the first few months of motherhood, and this is often a time when there is so much focus on the pregnancy itself that emotional problems are given little consideration. The fact that the placenta readily transmits hormones makes the fetus liable to the emotional state of the mother.

4. DRUGS. In this age of rapid discovery of exotic new drugs that, because of great demand and economic competition, are rushed onto the market, federal drug-regulating agencies need to insist upon long-range, supervised testing of their side-effects before allowing them to be placed in general use. It is a responsibility not only of the government but of the pharmaceutical industry, if catastrophes such as that caused by thalidomide are to be avoided in the future. Although the most critical risk stems from the mother who takes drugs during pregnancy, the effect on the germ plasm of both sexes needs to be considered. All kinds of drugs—

including alcohol and even cigarettes—are known, at the very least, to be not beneficial during pregnancy, and the preponderance of evidence at this point suggests that they are harmful.

5. Genetic Counseling. Sufficient information already is available to make genetic counseling useful in avoiding certain undesirable inheritable characteristics and genetic diseases. Clearly some couples, because they are carriers of highly destructive, latent genes, should not have children, since there is almost no possibility that they may have normal children. An example would be carriers of Duchenne muscular dystrophy, a sex-linked recessive disease, which becomes manifest after an apparently normal birth and early childhood, and which always leads to the death, at about age five, of all the male children in the family.

More frequently, genetic counseling can identify conditions, such as phenylketonuria, before the disease has ravaged the child. The Coombs test commonly is used for the identification of probable difficulties in pregnancies involving an Rh-negative mother and an Rh-positive father. The test, which measures the degree to which the mother is sensitized, allows for early transfusion of the baby's blood and greatly reduces the likelihood of brain damage. Recently, immunization of the mother has become a preventive technique in Rh mismatches. Rh-immune globulin administered to the Rh-negative mother after every delivery of an Rh-positive baby, and after every abortion or miscarriage, will prevent the formation of Rh antibodies in the mother. Used properly, the vaccine is nearly 99 percent effective.

Sickle-cell anemia and diabetes are also serious genetic diseases that can be substantially helped by early identification and planning. Genetic counseling is society's responsibility; genetic planning is not society's right.

6. Radiation. The restriction of the spread of radioactive materials in the atmosphere and greater precautions in the use of X-rays certainly are required, since a high correlation has been demonstrated between the amount of radiation absorbed and the probability of mutations. Most mutations are harmful rather than helpful; indeed, most are lethal. Recent public health surveys have shown that many of the X-ray units in use expose the subject to far more radiation than necessary.

Implications

Studies of the child have demonstrated that his genetic potential, his physical makeup, his constitution, his emotionality, his intelligence, all affect how he interacts with his environment. Given that he is well born and that his is an environment that provides all the prerequisites to normal, healthy growth and maturation—good nutrition, nurture and love, stimulation and models—he himself will react to, assimilate, incorporate, and use his environment in his own unique understanding of himself.

Perinatal Teratogenes

Drugs Drugs ingested by the mother can have disastrous effects upon the fetus: thalidomide effects are well known; quinine, morphine, and other drugs are known to affect the fetus.

Maternal Age The age of the mother is important to the health of the baby. Increased maternal age is significantly correlated with congenital hydrocephalus, two-egg twinning, Down's syndrome, and others.

Maternal Alcoholic Intake Chronic alcoholism in the mother produces mental retardation and physical defects in the child.

Maternal Blood Oxygen Level A prolonged deficit in the oxygen level can cause severe mental retardation in the child.

Maternal Diet Many studies have demonstrated the high correlation between the nutritional state of the mother and the health of the fetus.

Maternal Disease Specific diseases contracted by the mother during pregnancy are known to produce defects in the baby. Of these, rubella is the most serious by far. Influenza, mumps, and diabetes are all risk-producing.

Maternal Effects Mother's diet, drug and alcoholic intake, smoking habits, emotional and physical health, all can affect the unborn child.

Maternal Emotional State Through placental transfer of hormones, the fetus experiences a physiological state similar to that of its mother. Mothers who are upset, anxious, and emotional during the final stages of pregnancy have a high incidence of hyperactive, irritable infants who sleep and eat poorly in the first few weeks.

Maternal Smoking Prematurity, birth weight, and infant irritability all seem related to maternal smoking.

Radiation Radiation can produce drastic mutations, usually lethal.

Rubella Also known as German measles, rubella exposure during the first trimester of pregnancy produces serious defects—deafness, congenital heart disease, and eye defects.

Teratogene An agent that produces malformation, a teratogene affects a specific metabolic process to cause malformation if exposure occurs at a time when the embryo is sensitive to its effect.

Teratological Principles

(1) The embryonic stage at the time a teratogene acts determines which tissues are susceptible. (2) Teratogenes interfere with particular phases of metabolism, and thus produce characteristic malformations. (3) Teratogenes act with the genotype to produce malformations. (4) Intrauterine mortality varies directly with the rate of malformation. (5) A teratogene very damaging to the embryo may be relatively harmless to the mother.

Nutrition

Nutrition The most critical single variable affecting the health of our children is nutrition: the nutritional level of the population as a whole, and of the mother during gestation and lactation. Malnutrition is the greatest single determinant of defects in children.

animal studies

Animal Studies Animal studies have demonstrated emphatically the importance of maternal nutrition: both physiological and behavioral abnormalities develop in the progeny of mothers undernourished during gestation and lactation.

diet content

Sucrose Sucrose in the maternal diet has a geneticlike effect in controlling the metabolism of glucose throughout the life of the progeny: the progeny of animals fed a diet of 35 percent sucrose during gestation and lactation were significantly heavier than controls even though both groups had adequate diets after weaning and the control dams had adequate diets during gestation and lactation.

Vitamins Specific vitamin deficiencies produced marked behavioral impairments in rats.

Protein Maternal protein deficiency during gestation and lactation was found to affect the subsequent metabolism of the progeny, regardless of quality of diet after weaning.

Results of Undernutrition Maternal malnutrition during pregnancy and lactation affects not only the viability of the progeny, but sets the pattern for subsequent growth and rate of development and affects behavioral and intellectual performance, no matter how well fed the progeny after weaning. Malnutrition suffered shortly after birth causes permanent and obvious effects on subsequent growth and development, but effects of malnutrition later in life can be reversed by an adequate diet. The earlier the malnutrition is suffered, the more permanent and more serious its effects.

timing of the undernutrition

After Weaning Undernourishment after weaning and throughout life results in a decreased growth rate as well as less maximum growth, delays in maturational development, and an earlier death. But temporary undernutrition in animals does not seem to affect their ability to recover. Even extreme deficits in body weight and size and alterations in biochemical and behavioral characteristics caused by undernourishment in young animals after weaning were corrected upon being refed.

During Lactation Early undernutrition during lactation can result in permanent nutritional influences, even when an adequate diet is available after weaning.

During Gestation and Lactation Maternal nutritional deprivation during gestation alone causes similar though less drastic effects as deprivation during gestation and lactation. Dietary restriction during gestation and lactation causes a metabolic derangement in the offspring that affects their ability to utilize subsequent diets, even though adequate, thus suggesting a critical period in the development of metabolizing capacity, which, if passed, is never regained.

During Gestation In rats an imprint is made in utero on the growth potential of the progeny that is determined by the maternal diet during gestation. Prenatal undernourishment produces an increased liability to disruption of behavior.

human studies

Human Studies Human studies of malnutrition usually produce data confounded with concomitant variables—poor medical care, inadequate housing, etc.—yet the evidence of the importance of good nutrition is overwhelming. Malnutrition during gestation, lactation, and early infancy produces permanent scars, physically, intellectually, and emotionally.

Malnutrition Severe early malnutrition retards cell division in the human brain, affects head circumference, and affects intelligence.

Intelligence

Early Theories Early theorists viewed intelligence mainly as an inherited trait.

Environmental Studies Environmental studies demonstrated that measured intelligence could change with a significant environmental change. These studies also demonstrated that predictions of later intelligence made on a child's early developmental status must take into account his experiences between the two measurements. More recent studies have suggested that preschool educational experiences change not so much the child's intelligence as his motivation to achieve.

Race Studies Race studies in the United States clearly demonstrate the effect of poverty upon intelligence; they do not demonstrate the effect of heredity upon intelligence. Because of the confounding of race, poverty, lack of opportunity, and deprivation, race studies consistently have found an IQ deficit of about 20 points in black children, with an obvious concomitant deficit in achievement. This IQ deficit, which appears before age four, has been attributed to a lack of cognitive development due to environmental influences, or more precisely, the lack of environmental influences. That these deficits in intelligence and achievement are real handicaps to be dealt with seriously seems obvious; damning intelligence tests will not change the handicap.

Twin Studies Twin studies of intelligence illustrated that the closer the genetic relationship, the closer the measured intelligence: the IQs of identical twins are more similar than those of fraternal twins.

Personality

Ectomorph A somatotype described by Sheldon as the thin, poorly muscled, highly energetic person.

Endomorph A somatotype described by Sheldon as the soft, flabby person with a tendency toward fat and underdeveloped muscles and bones.

Mesomorph A somatotype described by Sheldon as the athlete.

Proband A person who has a readily diagnosed pathology or behavior pattern.

Proband Studies Proband studies, particularly

Franz Kallmann's study on schizophrenia, indicate the tendency for some traits to run in families.

Somatotype Body type, designated by Sheldon as endomorphic, mesomorphic, and ectomorphic.

Somatotype Studies Somatotype studies also have shown the inheritability of personality traits. Gardner Lindzey (1965) gives five supportive arguments for Sheldon's theory of the relationship between somatotype and personality:

(1) possibly the family factors that influence body size also influence personality; (2) some physical conditions restrict or facilitate an individual's behavior and, therefore, his personality; (3) maturational changes in body proportions have been demonstrated to affect personality; (4) expectations for certain behaviors go along with certain appearances—society tends to type-cast; (5) possibly behavior and physique are jointly determined genetically.

Twin Studies Twin studies of personality have demonstrated, as in studies of intelligence, that monozygotic twins are more similar than dizygotic twins.

Summary

environmental facts

Emotionality Efforts to reduce the psychological distress of mothers during the childbearing years would seem warranted by the evidence of the relationship between the mother's and the child's emotional health, even at birth.

Drugs In this age of rapid discovery of exotic new drugs that are rushed onto the market because of great demand and economic competition, federal drug-regulating agencies need to insist upon long-range, supervised testing of their side-effects before allowing them to be placed in general use. Although the most critical risk stems from the mother who takes drugs during pregnancy, the effect on the germ plasm of both sexes needs to be considered.

Genetic Counseling Sufficient information already is available to make genetic counseling useful in avoiding certain undesirable inheritable characteristics and genetic diseases.

Medical Care Adequate medical care during the childbearing years, particularly for women, would seem to be the second most essential answer to the problem of giving birth to unhealthy children.

Nutrition Strong evidence suggests that the nutritional level of the population during the childbearing years, as well as nutritional support of the infant and mother during gestation, lactation, and early childhood, is the most critical single variable affecting the production of genetically, intellectually, physically, and emotionally sound children.

Radiation The restriction of the spread of radioactive materials in the atmosphere and greater precautions in the use of X-rays certainly are required, since a high correlation has been demonstrated between the amount of radiation absorbed and the probability of mutations.

Genetic Facts Genetically, we know that errors in chromosomal cell division can result in aberrations: whether these errors in cell division are spontaneous or result from teratogenesis we do not know—yet. Someday research may have the answer; in the meantime, we make every effort to provide good nutrition, good medical care, and an absence of toxic agents for the developing fetus.

Chemical Interference Chemical interference in reproduction can be caused by toxic agents in the mother's blood stream; even alcohol consumption and cigarette smoking have an effect.

Hereditary Diseases Certain hereditary diseases are carried on recessive genes; genetic counseling can help to prevent the mating of two such recessive genes.

Maternal Illness Maternal illnesses during pregnancy, illnesses relatively harmless to the mother, can produce drastic weaknesses or malformations in the child.

Nutrition Poor nutrition, both of mother and fetus, can cause permanent damage to the developing cells of the fetus.

Radiation Radiation of germ cells can cause mutations, nearly always fatal.

Heredity/Environment Influences Although the simultaneous influences of heredity and environment make up the child, these influences can be separated to the child's advantage: hereditary diseases can be identified and prevented or controlled; environmental influences can be managed to the best advantage of the child. The more research in each area, the better able we will be to provide children with the necessary prerequisites for healthy adulthood.

Implications Studies of the child have demonstrated that his genetic potential, his physical makeup, his constitution, his emotionality, his intelligence, all affect how he interacts with his environment. Given that he is well born and that his is an environment that provides all the prerequisites to normal, healthy growth and maturation—good nutrition, nurture and love, stimulation and models—he himself will react to, assimilate, incorporate, and use his environment in his own unique understanding of himself.

Names To Know

Intelligence

early theories

CHARLES DARWIN Charles Darwin viewed intelligence as a characteristic of survival that made certain families, groups, and races prominent and powerful.

FRANCIS GALTON Darwin's cousin, Francis Galton believed heredity to be the key to greatness. He saw intelligence as an inherited trait that could be measured by the quickness of the senses. The tendency to return to the mean, Galton described as the law of filial regression.

H. H. GODDARD Through his study of the Kallikak family, Goddard considered intelligence to be an inherited trait.

twin studies

ERLENMEYER-KIMLING and JARVIK L. Erlenmeyer-Kimling and Lissy Jarvik reviewed studies of IQ similarities in twins and found a marked trend toward an increasing degree of intellectual resemblance in direct proportion to increasing degree of genetic relationship, regardless of environmental communality.

environmental studies

SKODAK AND SKEELS Harold Skeels and Marie Skodak, early researchers at the Iowa Child Welfare Station at the State University of Iowa, studied the effect of early deprivation on children's IQs. They discovered that removing young children from orphanages and placing them under the care of institutionalized, retarded mothers increased the children's IQs phenomenally. Retesting of the children as adults confirmed the original conclusion: those children raised by foster mothers were normal; those remaining in the institution were retarded.

race studies

BETH WELLMAN Beth Wellman was a researcher and team captain of the group at the Child Welfare Research Station at Iowa, which defended the role of environment in intelligence and proved an anchor point for the environmentalists in the nature-nurture controversy.

AUDREY SHUEY Audrey Shuey, controversial scholar from Randolph-Macon Women's College, through her publication of extensive reviews of the literature on differences in the measured intelligence of blacks and whites, has done much to focus the attention of researchers upon the problems of intelligence of deprived groups.

KENNEDY, VAN DE RIET, and WHITE In a large-scale study of the intelligence and achievement of American blacks, Kennedy, Van De Riet, and White found a mean deficit of 20 points among black children on nationally standardized intelligence tests and a 20-percent deficit on nationally standardized achievement tests. Kennedy's five-year follow-up study of one-fifth of the sample confirmed the conclusions.

KLAUS and GRAY Susan Gray and Rupert Klaus carried out an intervention program for preschoolers from which they concluded, "The most effective intervention programs for preschool children that could possibly be conceived cannot be considered a form of inoculation whereby the child forever after is immune to the effects of a low-income home and of a school inappropriate to his needs."

Personality

FRANCIS GALTON Francis Galton, in his early study of the personalities of English men of science, although relying on anecdotal material only, arrived at conclusions substantiated by subsequent research. Galton felt that an inherited tendency, toward scientific interests, for example, could be thwarted by an unnurturing, unencouraging environment.

twin studies

HAROLD CARTER Harold Carter, using the *Bernreuter Personality Inventory* and studying 133 pairs of twins, without exception found greater similarity in personality between the monozygotic twins than between the dizygotic twins.

92

WILLIAM SHELDON William Sheldon demonstrated the similarity, or the tie-in, between physique and personality. And studies of maturation emphasized the effect of physical characteristics upon personality. Sheldon separated three body types, or somatotypes: the endomorph, mesomorph, and ectomorph. An obvious problem with Sheldon's thesis is that so few individuals fall neatly into his somatotypes; most of us are a happy mixture.

SHIRLEY and NEILON Mary Shirley and Patricia Neilon provided an interesting insight into the consistency of personality traits when Neilon found traits easily discernible in infancy and early childhood still prevalent fifteen years later; such stableness of personality traits argues for some constitutional basis for differences in personality.

proband studies

FRANZ KALLMANN Franz Kallmann used identical twins in his long-term medical research on the relationship between schizophrenia and heredity. He found a high probability that if one identical twin had developed schizophrenia, the other twin would develop it also. He concluded that a tendency for schizophrenia to occur in families is evident.

Maturation

T hus far, we have been dealing with perinatal events as they affect the physical, intellectual, and psychological growth of the child. We have discussed the human embryo and fetus in terms of pre-conceptional and prenatal changes that result from the interaction of genetic and environmental factors. However, not all of the effects of the genetic, prenatal, and immediate postnatal events are demonstrated during the period of the neonate. Some of the genetically programmed developmental sequences are dormant at birth and only begin to express themselves during the childhood growth patterns. The postnatal, physical, developmental sequence of change, which follows the instructions built into the genetic code, is referred to as maturation—changes that occur within the cells, and between the cells, changes that affect the development of the child, particularly in terms of the complex interaction between the psychological and physical growth sequences.

The process of maturation is discussed on the basis of four simultaneous growth processes: cerebration, myelination, endocrination, and skeletonation. These four events, under the control of the genetic code, have a great deal to do with the development of social, emotional, intellectual, and sexual identity. Early versus late maturity, large versus small stature, high versus low energy level, dominant versus submissive personality, all seem to be strongly influenced by the maturational process, which has a complex relationship to psychological development during childhood.

Obviously the maturational process also affects the growth and development of the child during the fetal period, but since the major thrust of child psychology, as opposed to that of obstetrics, concerns itself with the child after birth, the discussion of the maturational process essentially begins with the moment of birth and goes through puberty changes that set the stage for adolescence, the upper limit of childhood. Naturally, adolescence, identified as the beginning of the menstrual cycle in the female child and the beginning of pubic hair pigmentation in the male, covers the most spectacular natural changes in the whole lifetime, but many maturational changes that occur during childhood have significant and lasting effects upon psychological development.

In the child, maturation and growth are not distinct. The child does not simply increase in size. There also is a change in proportion, function, complexity, and relationship, all of which relate to the prescheduled unfolding of the human body as a function of cellular and tissue changes. The human clock, influenced as it is by the environment, particularly the nutritional environment, is nevertheless largely a function of genetically determined changes in capacity to cope with the demands of the environment.

There are critical periods in maturation when, if changes do not occur, viability is threatened: for example, the fetal heart must begin to beat to circulate fetal blood carrying essential nutrients and oxygen; the newborn lungs must begin to breathe to provide the life-giving oxygen. This delicate timing must be observed although the thinking part of the fetal and newborn brain appears to be totally inactive. There is no evidence that the baby is able to make any decisions in terms of comfort or discomfort at this moment: his primitive nervous system must respond effectively to the environment in the absence of the ability to reason.

There are other critical periods in the first few years of life. Certain changes in the pattern of adjustment must be made, or the growing child will be unable to cope with the problems submitted by life. These critical changes, known as maturation, dependent upon a stable supply of basic physical necessities, and, perhaps, a supply of basic emotional necessities, serve as the building materials employed by the maturational process.

Carmichael's (1926) classic experiment with salamanders relates to the maturational process of young children. Leonard Carmichael, concerned with demonstrating that maturation alone provides lower organisms with all that is necessary for the development of their behavior repertoire, used the amblystoma, a form of salamander or spring lizard. He placed a large number of salamander eggs in groups in tanks of sterile water. In all but one of these sterile tanks he mixed a small amount of an anesthetic called chlorotone, which has the property of paralyzing the motor apparatus of the animal while leaving his breathing intact. Carmichael then waited until the control group of amblystoma, those in the tank of pure water, had learned to swim by the laborious process of wiggling and squirming inefficiently and ineffectively for five days, a long time in an amblystoma's life.

At this point one of the experimental groups was freed from the chlorotone solution, washed in clear water, and dropped into the same tank. Initially they remained inert as the effect of the anesthetic wore off, but in a short period of time—in fact, often in only a minute or two—they began to swim well. Within the hour, they could not be distinguished from the control group, which had been moving freely for five days.

Later Carmichael added many environmental controls, placing the experimental animals in various settings during their drugged period—noisy or quiet laboratory settings, light or dark ones, and so on. From Carmichael's work with primitive organisms the conclusion is inescapable that with the phylogenetic responses, those characteristic of a species, the period of practice serves only as exercise. Learning takes place only after maturation has provided the nervous system with the ability necessary for the behavior.

The human child is a much more complex organism than a spring lizard. Most of his adaptive responses are predicated upon an extremely sophisticated, complex nervous system that provides the ability to develop finely coordinated movements and speech. His maturational unfolding, involving the simultaneous development of the cortical, endocrine, neural, and skeletal systems, provides a necessary and often sufficient stimulus, in and of itself, for his rapid development in behavior. The process of adaptation is dependent upon this evolutionary, instinctive unfolding. A study of the maturational process affords not only an understanding of the nature of growth, but it also provides a convenient instrument by which to measure rate of growth in the human child.

CEREBRATION

Considerable evidence indicates that during the intrauterine period, the major control of the behavior of the fetus is in the subcortical nuclei, as they respond to the stimulation of the biochemical system of the mother. The basic sensory processes of tasting, hearing, and light sensitivity, as well as sensitivity to oxygen level and hormonal stimulation, are all present prior to birth; but the primitive motor response of the fetus does not require significant functioning of the cortex. Even at birth, this highly significant part of the human brain is still dormant; many of the basic rhythms of the cortex are absent shortly after birth.

However, the brain is programmed for maturational changes just as any other aspect of the body. The process of cerebration provides one of the most interesting unfoldings of the infant, as well as critical signposts of his developmental process. The timely appearance of certain reflexes and their gradual suppression by more complex reflexes are not as important in and of themselves as they are important as indicators that maturation is progressing orderly, sequentially, appropriately. We have little evidence that these primitive reflexes are adaptive now, but it is possible to comment upon their previous adaptive significance.

Moro Reflex

An infant responds to loud noises or a sudden loss of support with the Moro reflex, a fanning of the arms in a more or less clutching fashion while arching the back. With a little imagination we can see the usefulness of the Moro reflex to the newborn infant: it would enable an infant carried on either hip of the mother to be caught easily. Thus one could make a strong case for the survival value of the Moro reflex in prehistoric times, when infants were carried, perhaps, from tree to tree. During maturation the Moro reflex becomes the startle reflex of the adult.

The Moro reflex can be modified somewhat by experience and suppressed by training. It does, however, reappear under the proper stimulus, even in the adult. Its significance in child psychology is minimal, except that it serves as a marker reflex to test the neurological development of very young children. The failure of the Moro reflex to mature into the startle reflex would be an early indication of a serious lag in the child's development.

The infant's grasp reflex allows him to grip firmly, even without the strength of his opposable thumb, any object laid in his hand. Newborn infants have been known to sustain their own weight, being literally picked up out of bed by an adult who places his index finger in the palm of the child's hand. Later, the reflex is modified so that the thumb comes into play, which of course adds considerable strength. Doting grandmothers who have had a sweet little child reach up and grasp a handful of hair and hang on for dear life can well understand that the grasp reflex would have enabled a Neanderthal child to hang onto his mother while he was nursing, and so free her hands for other activities.

Like the Moro reflex, the grasp or palmar reflex is an extremely potent automatic response. It follows upon any stimulation to the palm of the child's hand. The grasp reflex gradually subsides with maturity, becomes voluntary in nature, and by twelve months has disappeared except as a voluntary action. Thus it also serves as a marker reflex by which to measure maturity and determine when neurological growth is accelerated or retarded.

Swimming Reflex

A third subcortical reflex, and one perplexing to observe, is the swimming reflex. It occurs in children under six months of age and provides the infant with the ability to swim without training. The child swims head down, and does not breathe except to exhale slowly through the mouth. His mobility, lasting for a rather extensive period of time, and his ability to keep water out of his lungs, make for easy rescue of children younger than one year.

Having been raised myself to swim from infancy and having also raised my children to swim, I had read with considerable puzzlement the frequent newspaper accounts of children of about two-and-a-half drowning in small, shallow, backyard swimming pools. These drownings were incomprehensible to our outdoor family, when most of the babies had fallen off our river dock or been jostled off accidentally only to swim for shore in outraged indignation. How, in a four-foot wide, two-foot deep wading pool, could a child possibly drown?

Some years ago, friends from the city visited our summer cottage on the river. Their three-year-old daughter went out on the dock and, mystified by the crystal-clear water, leaned too far over. As had happened so often before to other children, she fell in headfirst. But there the resemblance ended abruptly. This little girl, too old to possess the swimming reflex and never taught to swim, sank and lay flat on the bottom of the river in crystal-clear water only two feet deep. She had blown out her air in panic as she hit the water and so had no natural buoyancy to lift her up. My wife hesitated, waiting for her to surface with the usual outraged cry, but there was no such response. In sheer terror the child lay quietly on the bottom and made no effort to move or surface; she didn't so much as wiggle a finger. It was necessary to jump in and pick her up, or she surely would have sucked water into her lungs and drowned, drowned without a single effort at movement—just as children do in their small wading pools.

One of the better traditional studies illustrating swimming movements as a function of age was conducted by Myrtle McGraw (1943), who trained raters to identify reflex swimming movements, disorganized or struggling activity, and deliberate or voluntary swimming movements. They observed forty-two infants from eleven days to two-and-one-half-years of age. They made a total of 445 observations. McGraw found that reflexive swimming was at its peak at birth and then fell off rather steeply until, at 250 days, it was almost unobserved; that disorganized, struggling activity began to appear reliably at 100 days, reached a peak at 175 days, and slowly declined through the two-and-one-half age limit of her subjects; and that deliberate or voluntary movements began to appear at about 200 days, reached a peak at 300 days, and remained constant for the remaining portion of the study.

Thus, it would appear that if parents want to make use of the swimming reflex, it must be done before the child is a year old, and the sooner the better. The evidence seems to indicate that if the child has had experience swimming reflexively, he can make a smooth transition to voluntary swimming.

The swimming reflex is similar in appearance to the reflex seen in grand mal epilepsy. The victim of a grand mal seizure is usually on his back. The noise made by his gradual, forced exhaling is somewhat distressing, but imagine him face down in the water: slight, thrashing movements would tend to keep him afloat, and the gradual exhalation would keep water out of his lungs. This is, then, the swimming reflex, but a more primitive version, one that would be stimulated by a sudden shock, such as falling into cold water. These seizures are seldom induced in modern man by the events of life, unless one is hypersensitive to them as is the epileptic. However, flashing strobe lights, high temperature, or electric stimulation of the brain can induce this reflex in anyone.

Babinski Reflex

A fourth subcortical response is the Babinski reflex—a fanning of the toes in response to any stimulation to the sole of the foot. Since it begins to disappear at four to six months as neural control shifts from the subcortical nuclei to the cortex, it provides a convenient way to note the progress of the process of cerebration. The persistence of this reflex indicates a neurological problem that is usually the result of a malfunction in myelination.

Sphincter Reflex

A fifth subcortical response is the sphincter reflex that makes bowel and bladder control possible. Initially, this control center is located in the brain stem and the infant has no voluntary control over either defecation or urination. The signal of a full bladder or a full colon, in and of itself, is sufficient to set off the reflex, which releases the sphincter muscles and allows evacuation to take place.

Bladder control in identical twins has been used by McGraw (1940) to illustrate the timing of the shift from subcortical to cortical control.

She started one twin on an early training program, almost from birth, and waited with the other until the first showed evidence of 90 percent success in bladder control. At this point, the second twin was trained: from the beginning of his training, there was almost no difference between them.

In McGraw's data one sees clearly that sufficient maturation must take place before toilet training can be successful. Her data support the recommendation that toilet training be started when the child is about two, if the greatest advantage is to be taken of his neurological development. Her results are almost identical to those of Carmichael. Both the voluntary swimming of the salamander and the voluntary bladder control of the child must await the shift of control within the nervous system from subcortical to cortical centers, and must also await myelination.

MYELINATION

Concurrently with cerebration of the central nervous system, a second neurological event takes place. This maturational change, myelination, is in the structure of the nerve cells themselves.

Immature Nerve Cells

At birth the overwhelming majority of the motor nerve cells are rather small, with long, thin axons, or conducting parts. These nerve fibers are slow to produce action, because the transmission of the nervous impulse involves a cumbersome electrochemical change in the composition of the cell wall that causes a wave of energy to pass down the cell. These long, thin-walled cells carry impulses at a slow rate, much like a long chain of slow-burning powder. And it takes an equally long time for the cell to chemically regenerate so that it can carry a second pulse. This slow, cumbersome process accounts for the newborn infant's responses being so primitive in nature, so slow in recovery, and so generalized rather than specific.

Servomechanism

The concept of the servomechanism, which contains a feedback loop, can help us to understand the developing nervous system. In the human body, feedback involves a receptor, any nerve in the body capable of detecting changes in physical energy in the vicinity, and an effector, any type of cellular activity that produces a change in physical energy in its vicinity.

Let us take, as a simple illustration, a cold boy and a warm fire. Outdoors, the boy detected the stinging cold, and for some time he has been anxiously seeking out warmth. Now he is in a room with a blazing fire. His receptors, which noted the cold and impelled him indoors, now note the warmth. The boy goes close to the fire. But as he stands there, his receptors no longer notice the cold and begin, instead, to notice the heat. He backs off to a corner of the room. The fire begins to die down, and he is again cold. He moves back to the fire. Back and forth, back and forth he vacillates, in a continuing process of trying to maintain a balance between heat and cold—his two systems, the receptors and effectors, inter-acting with each other to maintain this balance.

Now, the external events we have described with our model of the cold boy and the fireplace are slow and cumbersome. There are servomecha-nisms in the body—heart, lungs, chemical interactions—that require incredible balance between the two systems, a balance that can only take place when the receptors and the effectors are in communication with each other through the brain at a high rate of speed. The simple act of touching one's finger to the tip of one's nose requires a feedback loop that involves a three-dimensional tension in the skeletal system plus a com-plex sensor system located in the skin; it also requires a complex memory of the relationship between the end of the finger and certain kinesthetic feelings. Thus the simple act of closing one's eyes and pointing to one's nose with one's index finger involves a feedback loop that requires a major development of the primitive nervous system with which we are born.

Schwann's Sheaths

As the nervous system develops, certain of the axons—the long, thin, transmitting parts of the nerve cells—are surrounded by other cells, myelin, called Schwann's sheaths (Figure 9). A Schwann's sheath begins to slowly wrap itself, bandage-like, around the axon. As it grows, the liquid-filled part of the cell is compressed into a smaller and smaller area,

Figure 9

Nerve cell showing Schwann's sheath and nodes of Ranvier.
Reprinted, by permission of the publisher, from Diana C.
Kimber, Carolyn E. Gray, Caroline E. Stackpole, and Lutie C.
Leavell, *Textbook of Anatomy and Physiology,* 12th ed. (New
York: Macmillan, 1950), Figure 134, p. 193. Copyright
© 1950 by the Macmillan Company.

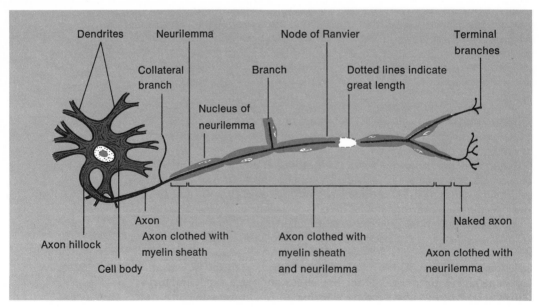

leaving a long sheath that wraps around and around the cell. Schwann's sheaths are about a millimeter wide and do not overlap, so that the axon is not continuously wrapped in myelin but has small gaps at the points where one sheath ends and another begins. These gaps are nodes, the nodes of Ranvier (see Figure 9).

Mature Nerve Cells

Now we can see the usefulness of the myelin and how it changes the function of the cell. Initially, an impulse in the cell axon moved slowly, by a process of chemically changing the wall of the cell to allow an electrical pulse to move its length. Now, with Schwann's sheaths acting as insulators over perhaps 99 percent of the cell, with the nodes of Ranvier, or openings on the outside of the cell, now occurring only at one-millimeter junctures, the pulse no longer moves slowly down the outside of the cell, polarizing as it goes. It jumps from node to node, increasing its speed a hundredfold. A very small myelinated nerve fiber can carry messages and signals at incredible speeds; also, for reasons peculiar to the nodes of Ranvier, it can regenerate with lightning speed to carry the next impulse. Very complex messages now become possible.

Myelination is a necessary condition for complex behavior, particularly for motor skills that form the essence of early intelligence. The nervous system's degree of myelination serves as a measure of its maturity and its ability to transmit messages. Certain diseases attack the nervous system by breaking down Schwann's cells, that is, by destroying the myelin: when this occurs, the nervous system loses its high-speed facility and regresses to the primitive state of the newborn.

One measure of the progress of myelination in the nervous system, as mentioned earlier, is the Babinski reflex—a reflex that occurs in the absence of myelin in the pyramidal tracts of the brain. The Babinski reflex is a primitive, slow-moving, toe-fanning response to tactile stimulation to the bottom of the foot. It appears at birth and disappears when the pyramidal tracts have been myelinated.

ENDOCRINATION*

The endocrine system of ductless glands, consisting of the hypothalamus, the pituitary, the adrenals, the pancreas, the thyroid, the parathyroid, the thymus, and the ovaries or testes (see Figure 10), as well as the central nervous system, is a neurochemical system that plays a key role in growth, contour, general sexual delineation, even personality, as well as being the wellspring of energy that enables a person to make massive physical responses to emergencies.

Hypothalamus

The hypothalamus and pituitary function as an integrated unit. The hypothalamus controls appetite, temperature, thirst, the posterior pitu-

*I am indebted to Harry J. Lipner, Ph.D., and Clark T. Sawin, M.D., for assistance in the following discussion.

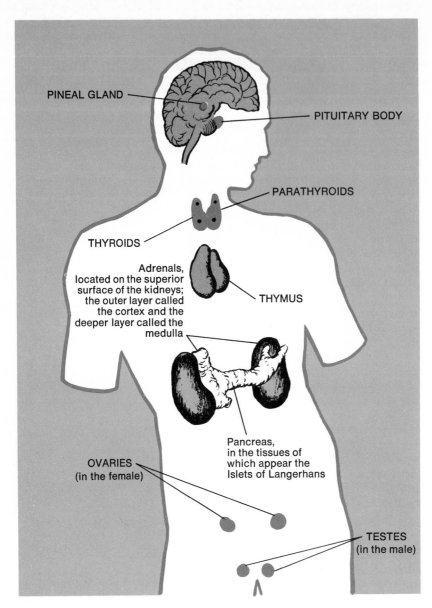

PINEAL GLAND

PITUITARY BODY

PARATHYROIDS

THYROIDS

Adrenals,
located on the superior
surface of the kidneys;
the outer layer called
the cortex and the
deeper layer called the
medulla

THYMUS

Pancreas,
in the tissues of
which appear the
Islets of Langerhans

OVARIES
(in the female)

TESTES
(in the male)

Figure 10
The endocrine system.
Adapted from Floyd L.
Ruch, *Psychology and
Life*, 6th ed. (Glenville,
Ill.: Scott, Foresman,
1963), p. 48.

itary, and the anterior pituitary (because all of the blood supply of the anterior pituitary comes through portal vessels from the hypothalamus). The hypothalamus contains releasing or inhibiting factors for all the hormones of the anterior pituitary.

The hypothalamus and central nervous system are important in bringing about puberty. FSH and LH, pituitary hormones, are completely dependent upon hypothalamic stimulation for their secretion.

104

By far the most important of the endocrine glands, the pituitary is a dual gland whose anterior and posterior lobes serve quite separate functions.

Anterior

The anterior lobe of the pituitary is influenced by the central nervous system. Functioning as an integrated unit with the hypothalamus, the anterior pituitary secretes six major hormonal substances. Four of these control the activities of the whole endocrine system; the other two operate chiefly to alter metabolism and growth, yet have minor significance in stimulating the other glands in the system. These six hormones are of critical importance in the maturation of the child.

Two of these hormones are gonadotropic: the follicle-stimulating hormone (FSH) and the luteinizing hormone (LH). FSH is mainly concerned with stimulating development of the ovarian follicle (not the ovum) in the female; in the male, FSH stimulates development of testicles and the maintenance and differentiation of spermatozoa. LH in the female causes formation of the corpus luteum, stimulates estrogen secretion, and causes ovulation. LH induces luteinization, the physical process by which the ovum is released, and the secretion of the female gonadal hormone, progesterone, vital in the cycle of pregnancy. In the male, LH (sometimes called ICSH—interstitial-cell stimulating hormone) stimulates the development of tissues of the testes and the androgen secretion, testosterone, the male gonadal hormone. Estrogen and testosterone are related to the secondary sexual characteristics of the child. Also in the male, LH, or ICSH, causes androgen secretions that produce spermatocytes, which in turn release the sperm production cycle.

The two regulating hormones, thyrotropin (TSH—thyroid-stimulating hormone) and adrenocorticotropin (ACTH), are essential for the normal growth and secretory functions of the thyroid and the adrenal glands, respectively.

The lactogenic hormone, prolactin, is responsible for the beginning and continuation of the lactation process in the breasts of the female, after they have been conditioned by the secretions of the ovarian hormones. Prolactin maintains the corpus luteum, allowing it to secrete progesterone. Estrogen plays the primary role in female differentiation during development; progesterone contributes to the later development of mammary glands, uterine development and secretions, and controls uterine muscle activity.

The growth hormone (GH) is responsible for the acceleration and deceleration of the growth of bones and tissues. This particular hormone, if secreted meagerly or superabundantly, causes abnormality in growth, such as that of midgets and giants. Good nutrition stimulates growth; poor nutrition stunts growth, produces small brain size and poor cerebral functioning. Chronic illness stunts growth. Worldwide, poor nutrition may well be the most common cause of poor growth. But genetic constitution is as important in determining human growth as the state of nutrition and the endocrine glands: all three factors interact for the sum total of man's height. Normal growth requires the proper amount, neither too much nor too little, of thyroxine (from the thyroid), hydrocortisone (adrenal cortex), and insulin (pancreas), in addition to growth hormone from the anterior pituitary. At puberty, the gonadal hormone is necessary. And the hypothalamus is the mediator of growth hormone secretion.

Numerous other regulatory functions, having to do with the metabolism of various vitamins and minerals, are also under the control of the anterior lobe of the pituitary gland, whose major functions are the regulation of growth and metabolism and the development of sexual characteristics. It controls these functions both by the production of its own secretions and by stimulating the secretions of other glands in the endocrine system.

Posterior

The anterior lobe of the pituitary, generally functioning through chemical reactions and chemical interchanges, involves few neural pathways. The posterior lobe on the other hand, is richly innervated, with nerve pathways leading directly from the hypothalamus, the primitive life-regulating center of the brain.

ADH, an antidiuretic hormone secreted by the posterior lobe of the pituitary, plays a key role in the maintenance of the water balance within the body. Damage to the posterior lobe can lead to disastrous changes in the fluid balance and produce transient diabetes insipidus, which frequently is terminal in the child. If the hypothalamus is damaged also, the diabetes insipidus is permanent. ADH, or vasopressin, which stimulates water retention by the kidney, probably originates in the hypothalamus and is stored in the posterior pituitary.

The second hormone secreted by the posterior lobe, oxytocin, stimulates lactation-release of milk in the female.

Adrenal

Just as the pituitary gland has two separate and distinct parts, both structurally and functionally, so does the adrenal gland. The largest substructure of the gland, the adrenal cortex, is predominantly chemical in nature and surrounds almost completely the adrenal medulla, which, highly innervated, is intimately connected with the sympathetic nervous system.

Adrenal Cortex

The adrenal cortex serves the major function of producing secretions essential for the metabolism of body protein and carbohydrates. Failure of the adrenal gland to function usually leads to death in five to fifteen days, unless substitutes are introduced into the body.

The adrenal cortex is the source of two essential steroids: glucocorticoid, associated with metabolism of carbohydrates, and mineralcorticoid, associated with regulating sodium retention and the loss of potassium. Death is swift following damage to the adrenal cortex due to the loss of the latter, causing an inability to metabolize salt. The adrenal cortex also secretes hydrocortisone, active in carbohydrate and protein metabolism.

There is a close relationship between the adrenals and the ovaries or testes. Loss of the adrenals causes sodium loss in the urine and decreased blood volume, a tendency to hypoglycemia, poor resistance to infection or shock, poor stamina, poor water secretion and sodium handling by the kidneys, poor fat mobilization and utilization, psychic changes such as depression, mild psychosis, lack of alertness, and decreased memory. These effects are reversed by giving hydrocortisone and aldosterone: both must be given. Addison's disease is caused by adrenal insufficiency.

Adrenal Medulla

The adrenal medulla, connected with the sympathetic nervous system, secretes epinephrine and norepinephrine. Epinephrine raises the blood pressure, stimulates the heart muscle, accelerates heart rate, and increases cardiac output. Norepinephrine is contained in all of the sympathetic nervous system in nerve endings. The two are catecholamine hormones responsible for emergency reactions. The catecholamines are responsible for the sudden, fantastic burst of free energy that occurs in situations of panic. The rise in blood pressure releases massive amounts of energy for action during crises. It is the epinephrine poured into the blood stream by the adrenal medulla that permits heroic bursts of speed and feats of great strength in emergencies. Almost everyone has read of some act, such as that of the New Jersey driver who, finding a car afire, its driver pinned in the front seat, bent the steering column upward with his bare hands and back muscles, permitting the driver to escape moments before the car exploded. The best estimate of the physical strength required was two thousand pounds, which exceeds by tenfold man's normal exertion power.

Epinephrine, connected with the sympathetic nervous system, has enormous survival value in physical emergencies, even though it is not particularly useful in many of the alarming situations confronting modern man—situations requiring a cold, rational approach rather than a powerful, physical response. Epinephrine helps the young child to maneuver out of some difficult situations, however. For example, it enables him to extricate himself from tangled bedclothing and to sustain a considerable amount of activity to draw attention to an emergency.

Crib deaths frequently are reported in the newspapers as though the child became entangled in the bedclothes and smothered, but rare indeed is the case where becoming entangled in the bedclothes actually induced death. Such deaths are usually the result of fast-moving viral infections, which, through vomiting and diarrhea, induce dehydration, rising temperatures, and sudden death. The child is put to bed at night, after having lost considerable fluid during the day. His temperature is high but not extraordinary; around 104°. During the night, while the parents are sleeping the child's temperature spikes and maintains this spike for some time, becoming 105°, 106°, 107°. The diarrhea continues, the stomach is empty of fluids, and the child goes into a terminal convulsion caused by brain damage from the dehydration. In the last spasm of this convulsion, he wraps himself in the sheet, and the parents assume that the child probably smothered in the night. If a pillow accidentally rolled on top of a child's face he would gasp, fight, struggle, roll, toss, cry out, and exert an extraordinary amount of physical energy—far too much for the average half-pound of feathers in a muslin sack to resist.

Recent observation in a hospital nursery suggests that the sudden infant death syndrome (SIDS) may be a disturbance in the central nervous system identifiable by EEG evaluation. Serendipitous observation in the hospital nursery of infants who suffered this syndrome indicated that, if observed at the onset, these infants could be revived. Steinschneider's (1972) preliminary report suggests two phases: deep sleep and sudden loss of the breathing reflex. Preventive medication may save these children in the future.

Pancreas

The pancreas secretes only one hormone, insulin, first extracted in 1921. Diabetes mellitus is caused by the failure of the pancreas to produce insulin, a protein produced by the islets of Langerhans, which comprise only about 2 percent of the total bulk of the pancreas.

Insulin plays a key role in the metabolism of carbohydrates and fats. Normally it functions in relation to the concentration of glucose in the blood: the higher the concentration of glucose, the higher the discharge of insulin. Diabetes, evidenced in terms of excessive desire for water, a marked loss of weight, and large amount of sugar in the urine, has come more and more under the control of medication. In many cases capsules administered orally are able to maintain the diabetic without the necessity of subcutaneous injections of insulin. Although this disease was formerly fatal, only a small percentage of diabetics cannot now live a nearly normal life.

Early detection of failure of the pancreas is important. Blood sugar or urine tests should be a regular part of the pediatric examination. There is every reason to believe that diabetes is hereditary, although the specific mechanisms are not known. In families where parents or grandparents had diabetes early in their lives, extra care should be given to studying the child at least yearly.

Thyroid

The thyroid gland, located in the neck close to the larynx, with two small lobes on either side of the trachea, or windpipe, contains an extraordinarily high concentration of iodine, necessary for growth. In the adult, the thyroid serves the function of regulating the metabolic rate; in the child it controls the metabolic rate and normal growth and development. The failure of a child's thyroid to function adequately has severe consequences, leading to cretinism, a condition characterized by a dwarfed appearance, small size, and severe mental deficiency. Cretinism is now a rare disease that can be avoided by a substitute therapy for thyroxine, the main hormone of the thyroid.

Iodine is the crucial element and the key to thyroid hormones. The thyroid selectively and actively takes up iodine. Removal of the thyroid results in low oxygen consumption, decreased metabolic rate, poor growth, poor maturation and development in many body systems, and poor central nervous system development and function. The thyroid hormone, given before too much damage has been done, reverses these effects.

Hypothyroidism, a shortage of thyroxine, produces a general slowing of the metabolic rate, a reduction in heart efficiency and blood circulation, and a general and diffuse sluggishness in responding to external stimuli. Much more common is an excessive secretion of the thyroid gland, called hyperthyroidism, which results in an elevated metabolic rate, a high rate of activity, restlessness, anxiety, hypersensitivity to external stimuli, and irritability. Malfunction of the thyroid can be controlled medically by prescribing synthetic thyroxine for hypothyroidism and by surgically removing parts of the gland for hyperthyroidism.

The thyroid hormone, thyroxine, stimulates an increase in carbohydrate turnover, fat turnover, cholesterol turnover, milk production during lactation, calcium mobilization from bone, magnesium turnover, heart rate and contractility, total-peripheral resistance, red cell production, hydrocortisone secretion, and growth hormone secretion. The thyroid stimulates the pituitary to secrete growth hormone; and the pituitary, through its thyrotropin hormone (TSH), stimulates the thyroid.

In addition to thyroxine, the thyroid produces thyrocalcitonin (TCT), which reduces serum calcium when it rises too high, thereby working with the parathyroid to maintain calcium balance in the body.

Parathyroid

The parathyroid gland is located near or within the thyroid, yet is independent in origin and function. The hormone secreted by the gland has recently been identified and named parathyroid hormone (PTH). An insufficiency results in an inability to metabolize calcium and phosphates. This condition produces extreme hyperirritability of the nervous system, leading to convulsions and death. Removal of the parathyroid causes tetany, a spastic twitching of the muscles, which calcium injections will reverse. Vitamin D, known as the skin hormone, is necessary, as well as PTH, to have normal serum calcium. Vitamin D is made in the skin whenever sunlight or ultraviolet light strikes it. Absence of vitamin D causes rickets.

Thymus

One gland, the thymus, completes its usefulness at about age eleven, and is virtually unidentifiable in the adult. This gland serves the function of developing the complex cellular immunities that enable the body to deal with the vast amounts of foreign agents that must be processed through the body. Evidently, as the cellular immunity is fully developed, the feedback diminishes, and the gland atrophies, a classic example of the difference between growth and maturation.

Ovaries/Testes

In the female, the ovarian secretions are cyclic: during the earlier stages of the cycle, estrogen predominates; later, progesterone. During the first stage, the follicles produce estrogen; later, the corpus luteum, progesterone.

Estrogen acts on the fallopian tube and uterus, in preparation for pregnancy, and induces secondary sex characteristics. Progesterone maintains pregnancy. FSH and LH, secreted by the pituitary, aid in the preparation for and the maintenance of pregnancy. The hypothalamus, through oxytocin secretion, also plays an important role in the female by stimulating release of milk in lactation.

In the male, the testes produce testosterone and androsterone, both important in producing male secondary sex characteristics and spermatogenesis. FSH and LH are also necessary in the male for complete spermatogenesis.

SKELETONATION

The final factor related to the process of maturation is skeletonation, or calcification of the skeletal system. We have mentioned earlier the presumed relationship between body contour and personality. The present discussion is concerned with the rate of growth and rate of calcification as it affects other variables in the life of the child. The child's relative size and rate of growth are important in the development of his self-image and his friendships. With the exception of the modification that occurs in severe dietary deficiency, his growth rate and calcification rate are strictly under the influence of hereditary characteristics.

Growth Trends

Growth trends are studied in a number of ways, principally by systematic annual or semiannual measurement of height and weight, X-ray studies of the calcification process, and studies of endocrine gland secretion. Longitudinal study, following the same children year after year, is particularly important in the study of growth. A cross-sectional study can provide for the simultaneous study of children of all age groups, different children representing each age or stage, but only the longitudinal approach provides a true picture of the nature of physical growth and skeletonation. Children tend to have spurts of growth at different ages. A cross-sectional approach masks any subtle trend by grouping the data. Thus, if you use data from a cross-sectional study to plot growth in inches of height during the first eighteen years, you get a curve that looks like the hypothetical one in Figure 11—a steady increase in almost a straight line, with no indication of any slowing down during the preadolescent period.

Actually, during these years children do not grow at a steadily progressive rate. As illustrated in the hypothetical curve in Figure 12, a longitudinal study shows that children grow rapidly in childhood, slow down during preadolescence, and spurt suddenly during adolescence. The

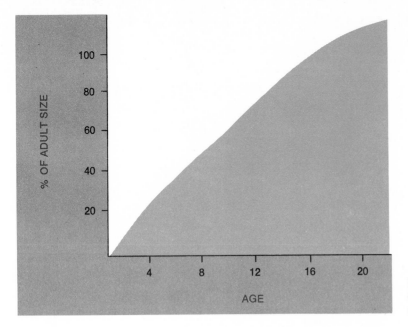

Figure 11
Growth trend, from a cross-sectional study of height.

Figure 12
Growth trend, from a longi-tudinal study of height.

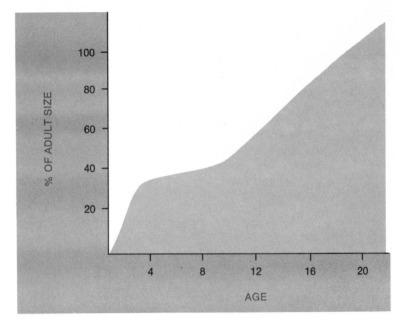

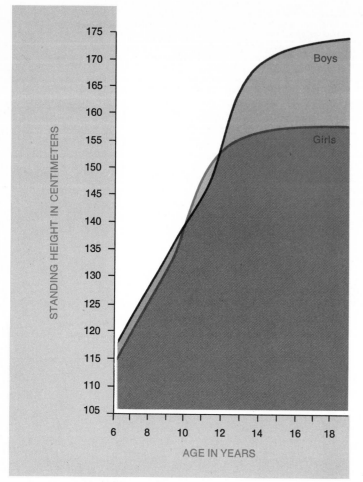

Figure 13

Average height of boys and girls at different ages. Adapted, by permission of the publisher, from Frank K. Shuttleworth, The physical and mental growth of girls and boys, age six to nineteen, in relation to age at maximum growth, *Monographs of the Society for Research in Child Development*, 1939, 4 (3), No. 22, Figure 8, p. 16. Copyright © 1939 by the Society for Research in Child Development, Inc.

plateau that occurs from about five to nine is completely lost when the data is studied in the cross-sectional manner.

Even more striking is the difference between the growth patterns of boys and girls when viewed as a function of the onset of puberty. Figure 13 illustrates this clearly. Girls enter puberty early, at about eleven; boys do not begin their growth spurt until about the thirteenth year. Often girls have completed their growth and attained their full adult height before the boys' growth spurt begins.

Figure 13 shows the growth of boys and girls in terms of an annual increase in inches, but a far more illuminating method of presenting the difference is in terms of gains per year for boys and for girls. Figure 14 illustrates a remarkable difference.

Notice that the growth rate has been uniformly dropping, for both boys and girls, from year six to ten-and-a-half. Then there is a steep increase in the growth of girls, while the boys' growth rate continues to drop until about fourteen, when they enter their adolescent growth cycle. Still, all these charts do not present as clear a picture as a school party at the end of the seventh grade. There you see the tremendous differences—in height, sexual maturity, and social maturity—between the boys and the girls. One can readily believe in the two-year lag between the sexes.

Some of the variation in height and contour is a function of environmental influences. Greatly improved pediatric care, vitamin-enriched diets, child labor laws, and informed parents have done much to avoid environmental factors that could stunt the growth of children. Thus, children have become more and more apt today to realize their full potential for growth. The greatest variance in physical growth, however, is accounted for by the genetic predispositions carried by the mother and father. The law of filial regression has the regulatory effect of bringing extreme cases back toward the mean, but in the main one's height and body contour are inherited.

Growth and Social Adjustment

We have discussed the relationship between physique and personality. The relationship between growth patterns and personality is no less important. And at no point is this relationship in clearer focus than in investigations of the personality and social problems of boys and girls who mature earlier or later than average (Tanner, 1970). Early maturation and late maturation affect adolescent boys and girls differently.

Figure 14

Average height gains per year for boys and girls. Adapted, by permission of the publisher, from Frank K. Shuttleworth, The physical and mental growth of girls and boys, age six to nineteen, in relation to age at maximum growth, *Monographs of the Society for Research in Child Development*, 1939, 4 (3), No. 22, Figure 24, p. 39. Copyright © 1939 by the Society for Research in Child Development, Inc.

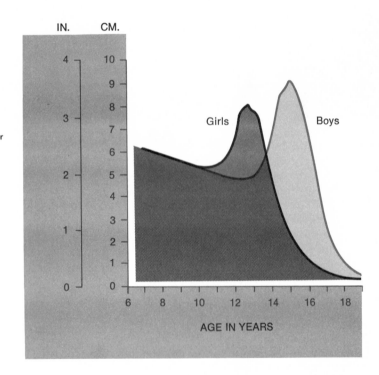

Early-maturing girls, who have spectacular social success in junior high school, experience a social problem in senior high for which neither they nor their parents are prepared. These girls attract the attention of older boys shortly after they reach puberty, when their early maturity is made obvious by their breast, hip, and waist development. Their early sexual development gives them status among their peers, but, more importantly, it gives them the social mobility to move upward into a relationship with teenagers who are considerably older.

Since the average boy reaches puberty some two years later than the average girl, the girls who mature early are often attractive to and attracted by boys who are three or four years older than they. To find girls in the seventh and eighth grades socially engaged with senior-high school boys is not unusual. They thus are propelled into activities for which they are not yet emotionally prepared. These girls feel considerable contempt for their age-group peers, who retaliate by considering them to be "fast" and perhaps "loose." As a result of this hardening of relationships, the early-maturing girl is thoroughly and completely cut off from her own age group.

During junior high school this makes little difference to her: she is satisfied with the friendship of older adolescents. The problem she encounters in senior high school is twofold. First, she has already had social experiences that other girls her age will not be having for two more years. She has moved through the logical sequence of group parties, double dates, single dates, necking, petting, and quite possibly more involved sexual interplay. By the tenth grade, when other girls and boys her age have begun to move into this same pattern, it is all "old hat" to this girl. Furthermore, the boys with whom she was socially engaged are now going off to college, taking jobs, getting married—and our early developer is still stuck in the tenth grade studying world history, algebra, English, and biology. It is little wonder that such girls lose interest in school, are socially isolated in their senior years, are somewhat rebellious and recalcitrant about obeying rules and regulations, and have the highest probability of marriage, pregnancy, and dropping out of school.

Although this phenomenon is as old as time itself, it creeps up on each generation unawares. I have spent many an evening talking with parent-teacher groups at junior high schools, explaining the hazard of early social stimulation of early-maturing girls, a hazard greatly aggravated by the formal dances that occur at the end of the sixth or seventh grade and the boy-girl parties with minimum chaperones and adult-type entertainment. All to no avail. Parents of junior-high school early-maturing girls find them responsible and mature, and they take great pride in the fact that their daughters are so advanced compared to other children. Since the ill-effects of social acceleration do not occur for three more years, the cause-and-effect relationship is difficult to perceive and hard to communicate.

Longitudinal growth studies make the problem abundantly clear. So long as there are fixed hurdles of twelve years of grade school and four years of college, now almost a necessity, together with the poor success history of teenage marriages, precocious development of early adolescent girls must be considered a significant hazard worthy of sensible parental precautions. Guidelines and rules, particularly those adopted by the school as a whole, can effectively slow down social stimulation and allow the early-maturing girl a quiescent adolescence in which to develop emotional maturity to match her physical maturity, and thereby allow her to assume the responsibility and leadership that her early maturation has thrust upon her.

C. P. Stone and Barker (1939), studying attitudes and interests of pre- and post-menarcheal girls, found that the sexually mature girls showed greater heterosexual interest, greater interest in self-adornment and in daydreaming, and less interest in physical exertion. Excluding those differences due to endocrine activity, the two groups of girls were markedly similar in interests and attitudes. The authors suggested that the total impact of sexual maturation is to be noted not so much in its immediate effects as in long-term effects observable over a period of years.

Late-maturing Boys

The late-maturing boy represents nearly a diametrically opposite problem. At twelve he is small. And since status is usually directly related to physical size, the late-maturing boy tends to have little status within his group. Consequently, he suffers from feelings of inferiority. Sometimes late-maturing boys compensate for their relatively small size and, by heroic effort, excel in some form of recreation or sport. But more often, they are insecure and inept isolates with few friends. Their tendency to associate with children two or three years younger than they keeps them socially isolated from their own age group. This in turn forces them to give up any leadership potential that they might have had in their group and encourages instead antisocial behavior.

The Glueck and Glueck (1950) study shows that many delinquents were late maturers, although in adolescence they had superior physiques. Evidently their late maturation and the antisocial feelings generated by being on-the-outside-looking-in make some contribution to the development of delinquent behavior. The more likely case, however, is that late-maturing boys are encouraged to engage in immature behavior. Probably, as M. Jones and Bayley (1950) suggest, because people tend to treat them as immature, they tend to behave more immaturely in their efforts to attract attention, and thus often become that much more socially undesirable because of their bratty behavior. Mussen and M. Jones (1957), studying the self-conceptions of early- and late-maturing boys, suggest that the social and psychological environment to which the late-maturing boy is exposed can indeed have adverse effects upon his personality.

Early-maturing Boys

The early-maturing boy, on the other hand, is propelled into a position of social responsibility. He is treated more like an adult by adults. He is allowed more privileges and more responsibility. It is simply assumed that he is going to behave in a responsible fashion and, as is often

the case, "the role makes the man." These early-maturing boys have a far
easier time coming into manhood than their late-maturing counterparts.

116
MATURATION

> The early-maturing were much more likely to get and maintain the kind of prestige
> accorded to athletes and officeholders.... Those who are physically accelerated
> are usually accepted and treated by adults and other children as more mature.
> They appear to have relatively little need to strive for status. From their ranks come
> the outstanding student body leaders in senior high school. In contrast, the physi-
> cally retarded boys exhibit many forms of relatively immature behavior: this may
> be in part because others tend to treat them as the little boys they appear to be
> [M. Jones and Bayley, 1950, p. 146].

Late-maturing Girls

Late-maturing girls, who are somewhat shy and retiring, go relatively
unnoticed. But their burst into adolescence, which comes two to four years
late, is often spectacular, giving them some of the advantages of a new girl
in the neighborhood. They are the typical spindly-legged ugly ducklings
who suddenly attract considerable attention because of the phenomenal
change. Often they are propelled from ugly ducklinghood into full social
life with considerable interest and attention from the male species. Often
they have enjoyed their childhood, had excellent peer relationships, and
have seemed to experience none of the social upheaval that accompanies
the development of the early-maturing girl.

Summary

We have seen a definite relationship between the rate of physical
growth, as determined by maturation, and both the personality and social
development of the child. Obviously there are glaring exceptions to the
general rule. There are many early-maturing girls who maintain their
friendships with others of their own age while they socialize with older
children. These girls maintain their stability throughout adolescence and
enter adulthood as mature, responsible young women. There are also
late-maturing boys who manage to enjoy childhood a little longer than
most and who move into the adult world with great speed and stability at
puberty, showing little evidence of their early immaturity. What Nancy
Bayley and the other researchers in the California Growth Studies have
shown is the general trend. Parents should be concerned sufficiently about
children who are in the high-risk group to make appropriate adjustments
to prevent unnecessary trauma during adolescence.

A follow-up study of early- and late-maturing boys after they reached
adulthood shows that these trends remain fairly constant. Although the
difference in the physical size of the two groups is less noticeable in adulthood, it is still there. The effects on personality are also still apparent.
The late maturers are more insecure, feel less able to make a good impression on others, and are not as responsive, responsible, cooperative, enter-
prising, social, or warm. One of the most important findings is the observation that good-impression scores, i.e., scores that represent positive
attributes of social development, correlated .50 with the level of skeletal
maturity measured eighteen years earlier. The tendency of boys who ma-

ture early to manifest greater sociability, greater self-control, leadership, and responsibility continues through adulthood. Mary Cover Jones concludes that "the adolescent handicaps and advantages associated with late or early maturing appear to carry over into adulthood to some extent, and perhaps to a greater extent in the psychological than in physical characteristics" (1957, p. 128).

The studies upon which the data for our discussion of growth and maturation are based were conducted some time ago, yet the picture they present is accurate for the 1970s. Growth rates are similar, with perhaps a difference in overall height. Girls still mature earlier than boys, and rate of maturation still affects the entire child.

> All the skills, aptitudes and emotions of the growing child are rooted in or conditioned by his bodily structure. Behind each stage of learning lies the development of essential cell assemblies in the brain; behind each social interaction lies a body-image conditioned by the facts of size and early or late sexual maturation [Tanner, 1970, p. 77].

SUBCORTICAL TO CORTICAL CONTROL

According to the theory presented by Myrtle McGraw, the human brain has two major divisions: the cerebral cortex and the subcortical nuclei. The first center, because it is both dominant at birth and more primitive, is composed of the subcortical nuclei. These nuclei are primitive nerve centers located in the brain stem and spinal trunk as well as in the diencephalon area of the brain itself. They are part of a vast, complex, autonomic, and reflexive network that functions in the absence of any voluntary control. All of the important functions of the body and most of the reflexes of the body are controlled at birth by these subcortical centers.

Some responses are controlled throughout life by these subcortical centers. Most of the basic reflexes—eye blink, withdrawal reflex, heart beat, breathing, in fact the full range of involuntary reflexes that are part of our biological heritage—seldom and only with a great deal of effort come under the full control of the cortex.

Some of the responses of the newborn appear to be valueless to the organism and are perhaps the residue of prehistoric adaptive mechanisms. These reflexes are often replaced, as the child grows, by an equivalent adaptive response under the control of the cortex. The primitive Babinski reflex, which does nothing to aid the child's adaptation, is, for example, replaced by a complex weight-shifting reflex, which enables an adult, when unexpectedly stepping on a sharp rock, to shift balance in a split second, place some weight on the other foot, and so prevent the affected foot from absorbing his full weight. Another example is the shift in the grasp reflex, which at first does not make use of the opposable thumb, to a more advanced grasp response, which does.

The cephalocaudal trend in development refers to the more rapid development of certain areas of the brain, particularly the motor area. Development associated with the head, such as facial expression, eye movement, tongue thrusting, lip smacking, occurs earlier and with more specificity. Essentially, there is a period of time in childhood in which the subcortical centers are dominant, a period in which the cortical centers inhibit the subcortical centers and the behavior patterns are rather disorganized, and a final stage in which the cortical centers are dominant.

This slow, unsteady shifting of control from the subcortical centers to the cortical centers, or from involuntary reflexes to voluntary and purposeful control, suggests several conclusions regarding child rearing practices.

The Role of Maturation in Training Children

Training a child, for whatever activity, is nonproductive until the cortical development required for the task has been completed. The fine coordination necessary for walking, for example, is quite impossible before the motor cortex and cerebellum have developed sufficiently. With a minimum of training and a slight amount of practice, children learn easily a task for which they have sufficient cortical facility.

An excellent example of the operation of this first principle is afforded by a Hopi Indian child-rearing practice. The Hopi child spends much of his first two years on a cradle board, and has almost no practice in standing, creeping, or crawling. Yet he walks at a normal age (Dennis and Dennis, 1940). The Hopi child follows the lesson of Carmichael's salamanders in that early training or practice is of negligible importance in learning how to walk. When a child is ready to walk, he walks. Parents who spend hours trying to teach their child to walk when he seems a bit slow and then find their efforts crowned with success have simply occupied themselves with a pleasant task while awaiting the cortical development required for the voluntary control of walking.

Much of the behavior repertoire of the child during the first year of life results from the physiological maturational changes within his nervous and muscular systems. Only later do environmental influences, such as stimulation and training, have major effect. Dennis and Dennis, after a detailed environmental control study of fraternal twins, concluded that "practically all of the common responses of the first year of life may be developed autogenously. That is, infants will develop these responses without encouragement or instruction, without reward or example" (1951, p. 130).

Periods of Regression in Training Children

Periods of disorganization and regression can be expected as the level of control shifts from subcortical to cortical. This apparent regression is what Gesell (1954) refers to as the spiral effect in growth. Growth does not proceed at a uniform rate. The enormous concentration required for shifting from one stage to another would seem to account for much of the regression that occurs at such a time.

Research has indicated that speech development slows down while the child's control over locomotion is shifting from subcortical to the cortical, voluntary control required for walking. Speech is again slowed down, and at times regresses, as the shift is made from the predominantly large-muscle performance required in walking to the predominantly small-muscle control demanded as the child begins school. The regression in speech noticed when a left-handed child is trained to righthandedness is probably the source of the rather persistent folk tale that changing handedness causes stuttering.

Ample opportunity should be provided for exercising a newly developing function. Such practice can accelerate specific achievement beyond what would normally be expected, although too early training cannot. Parents should be encouraged, for example, to talk with their child as he begins to learn how to express himself verbally, and discouraged from the use of baby talk.

INFANT MORPHOLOGY

Arnold Gesell was concerned with the general neurological development of children. His concept of morphology, the science of form, led Gesell into a description of the overt behavior of infants, which he felt closely paralleled their neurological development and from which he contended he could draw various principles with psychomorphological implications: the principles of (1) developmental direction, (2) reciprocal interweaving, (3) functional asymmetry, (4) individuating maturation, and (5) self-regulatory fluctuation.

Developmental Direction

Gesell's principle of developmental direction refers to the observable trend in children of cephalocaudal and proximodistal orderly motor development. Cephalocaudal development refers to the fact that head movement comes under the infant's control long before he can stand squarely upon his feet. Proximodistal motor development infers that parts of the body are brought under coordinated control from the center outward. These trends in infant development seem to be under the regulation of neurological unfolding.

Reciprocal Interweaving

The principle of reciprocal interweaving describes the relapses that occur as a child progresses to more and more complex behavior. For instance, as the child begins to become preoccupied with speech, a sharp regression in his motor development occurs. Gesell observed that as the infant progresses from immature to more mature states, a new development in his motor ability is frequently accompanied by a regression in some other area of his behavior.

Functional Asymmetry

Functional asymmetry refers to the bilateral nature of the newborn infant that, with increasing maturation, gives way to unilateral preferences and skills. For example, when, at an early age, the child tries to reach with one hand, the other is actively reaching also. Later he easily uses only one hand at a time.

Individuating Maturation

Individuating maturation is all-important to Gesell, who places responsibility for differences in the growth patterns of children squarely on their inherited maturational clock. For childhood behaviors, Gesell believes maturation is solely responsible. He gives little or no credit to learning.

> Growth is a unifying concept which resolves the dualism of heredity and environment. Environmental factors support, inflect, and modify; but they do not generate the progressions of development.... The maturational matrix is the primary determinant of child behavior [Gesell, 1954, p. 358].

Self-regulatory Fluctuation

The principle of self-regulatory fluctuation refers to the activity and rest states readily observable in infants. This fluctuation is:

> a normal expression of the self-regulatory mechanisms of development.... Such progressive fluctuations, culminating in a more stable response, are characteristic of all behavior development. The fluctuations, instead of being regarded as undesirable or fortuitous irregularities, should be interpreted as effortful attempts on the part of the organism to accomplish increasingly mature adjustments [Gesell, 1954, pp. 359, 364].

Maturation

For Gesell, maturation is a progressive organization of behavior forms. In a sense, maturation is the name for the regulating mechanism of the growth process, which is so intricate and sensitive that intrinsic factors must preserve the total pattern and stabilize the direction of growth. Gesell was so impressed, in fact, by the predictability of the child's development that he gave little credence to learning as an important factor in behavioral change.

HANDEDNESS

The maturational change in handedness has, in and of itself, an interesting pattern. At first cerebral dominance was thought to be responsible for handedness, but this theory was disposed of quickly. In an early critique, Dennis (1935) concluded that anatomical research had revealed a slight asymmetry of structure in all parts of the body, not merely in the cortex. This fact suggested that a single-cause explanation of handedness was unreasonable.

Later Hildreth (1949) concurred. She found that children show only a slight preference for either hand at first. Then the preference increases rather sharply until the child reaches about two-and-a-half, when almost 90 percent of all children show a preference for the right hand that continues for the rest of their lives.

Studies of children and adults alike have revealed that handedness is not an all-or-none proposition. Children should be given adequate training in the use of both hands. Considerable evidence exists that children have mixed dominance—one eye may play the major role in determining the focus, the opposite leg may well be the stronger, and the hand preferred may differ with the task.

In a study of handedness in children from sixteen weeks to ten years old, Gesell and Ames (1947) found that even in those children who eventually established a clearcut right-handedness, marked shifts in handedness occurred, particularly in the first year of life. Around one-and-a-half, children tend to be markedly bilateral; at two, a dominant preference appears; from two-and-a-half to three-and-a-half, bilaterality is again exhibited; and by four, the dominant hand is usually determined, although at seven a transient period of bilaterality may appear.

Well-established patterns of use are sometimes difficult to change—for instance, a great deal of unlearning is required for a person proficient in the two-finger, hunt-and-peck system to learn touch typewriting—but there is no reason to doubt that changes can be made. If there is a desire to change the child's writing hand from left to right, no severe problem should be encountered. Hildreth (1948) believes that right handedness is a learned behavior, initiated largely through the use of eating implements.

SUMMARY OF MATURATION

One issue in the concept of maturation, although somewhat technical, is nevertheless important to the understanding of many of the developmental theories in general use today. Is development, both physiological and psychological, a continuous process or is it a series of discrete stages? The answer is of some consequence.

Sigmund Freud (1910*b*), Sullivan (1953), and Piaget (1952*b*, 1954, 1960, 1961) all describe a process of development that consists of distinct shifts from stage to stage with a minimum of overlap, of shading—a pulse-like progression. Piaget established to his satisfaction a predictable pattern of development:

1. All development proceeds in a unitary direction.
2. Developmental progressions are in order and can readily be described by criteria marking five distinct developmental phases.
3. There are distinct organizational differences between childhood and adult behavior in all areas of human functioning.
4. All mature aspects of behavior have their beginnings in infant behavior and evolve through all subsequent patterns of development.
5. All developmental trends are interrelated and interdependent; developmental maturity means the final and total integration of all the developmental trends [Maier, 1969, p. 154].

In Freudian terminology, the oral stage is both a psychological phenomenon and a neurophysiological one. At one stage in the child's life, the mouth is the center of his universe and the feeding process the major preoccupation. Sigmund Freud assumed that during this stage, the mouth was the nerve center of the body, and he found good physiological support for his contention. With the advent of sphincter control and the beginning

of toilet training, the process of elimination moved to center stage, and
evacuation became the major preoccupation of the child and, for that matter, of his parents. What went in was no longer so important, but how and
when it was eliminated. This is the anal stage. A major neurological shift,
both at the site and in the controlling brain, accompanied this psychological shift.

Jean Piaget viewed the shift in the complexity of a child's logical
thinking as being just as abrupt. One morning the child is incapable of a
certain kind of thinking. The next, as his mind has developed and undergone maturational changes, he discovers a cognitive process that had
eluded him on the previous day. The shift is not a gradual one. Underlying these assumptions of discrete stages is the assumption that there is a
process of change in the behavior of the child as well as an accompanying
change in the neurological network of the brain—an assumption similar to
McGraw's theory of a shift from subcortical to cortical control.

Even though Harry Stack Sullivan believed that social interaction is
the key to personality development, and so placed little emphasis on
physiological processes, he affirmed that maturation of the nervous system
made the developmental shifts possible. Until the language center in the
brain becomes functional, the child cannot talk; until he can talk, he cannot shift from the prelanguage stage to the language stage. And the language stage, according to Sullivan, represents an important and dramatic
shift in personality organization.

In contradistinction to this idea of discrete shifts from one psychological stage to another, shifts that depend upon underlying pulsations in the
functioning of the maturing brain, is the idea that although development is
irregular, it is not discrete. Even though the child develops at various rates
from time to time, and at times does seem to grow into a more advanced
stage overnight, the growth is always typical rather than unique. This is
the concept of reciprocal interweaving advanced by Olson (1959) and
Gesell (Gesell, Halverson, H. Thompson, Ilg, Castner, Ames, and Amatruda, 1940) who see growth as a continuous development that involves
only a shift in emphasis.

In a sense the argument is similar to a discussion of the process of
walking. No one really questions that in walking directly from here to the
corner, one is engaged in some continuous behavior, but the psychologist
who believes in growth by discrete stages is arguing that you cannot pick
up your right foot until you put your left foot on the ground; and further,
that you must first shift your entire weight to that foot. The psychologist
who views growth as a continuous process argues that growth is more like
riding a bicycle to the corner. Although it is true that at some point one is
pushing more with his left foot than with his right, it is most difficult to say,
at any moment, whether one is propelling the bicycle with his left or with
his right foot. The more important questions, he adds, are how fast is the
bicycle moving, in what direction, and with what skill?

The argument is not a trivial one. The concepts of fixation, regression, and progression do, in a very real sense, depend upon discrete stages
or pulses of development, and they are the antitheses of the concepts of
overlapping, interlocking, reciprocal interweaving of skills, and neurological development.

The basic assumption underlying the concept of maturation is that a biochemical trend in the development of the brain, nervous system, endocrine system, and skeleton provides both stimulation to and regulation of human growth in intellectual, emotional, and social dimensions. The ever-increasing activation of the cerebral cortex gradually reduces the significance and activity rate of the subcortical brain centers and the child becomes, for the rest of his life, a cerebral being. Thinking, reasoning, language, all of which are dependent upon the complex associations possible on the surface of the cerebral cortex, are the major vehicles through which cultural accumulation is transmitted.

Along with the development of the cortex comes a basic structural change in the nervous system itself. Myelination increases the speed of communication a hundredfold and enables complex cerebral mechanisms to interrelate literally thousands of discrete events stored as chemical bonds throughout the nervous system.

The unfolding drama of human form is delicately regulated and balanced by the interconnections of the extraordinarily complex hormonal system that provides for the incredible range in temperament, physique, drive level, and activity that defines humanness, maleness, and femaleness under the pressures of social shaping. At the same time, the gross physical dimensions of the body, regulated in the main by the genetic code, are both servant to and master of the human personality. For, although man controls his body and the cortex is supreme, the size, shape, and proportion of the human body exert great influence on the nature of human experience.

At this moment in time we are for the most part spectators to the drama of maturation. Though it is true that some gross abnormalities can be curbed or eliminated through chemical or dietary intervention, the great pacemaker that regulates the development of man, from the first cell division through all the stages of man until death, does so relatively immune to any intervention by man. Human maturation may well be the last frontier and the key to enormous changes in the whole nature of human experience.

The focus, then, of child psychology at this point in history has little to do with intervention in the maturational process. Rather, the task of the psychologist is to know, understand, and take advantage of the process of maturation, to be alert to periods of great opportunity and periods of high risk, and to capitalize upon and reinforce this great maturational stability so that optimal psychological development can be achieved. For it is true, as Brutus has said, "there is a tide in the affairs of men/which, taken at the flood, leads on to fortune;/omitted, all the voyage of their life/ is bound in shallows and in miseries" (Shakespeare, *Julius Caesar*, Act 4, sc. 3).

CRITICAL-PERIOD HYPOTHESIS

Any adequate discussion of maturation must of necessity take into account the critical-period hypothesis and how it might relate to the early development of children. By critical period, we mean a stage in development, a specific time, when certain events are supposed to occur in normal maturation. If these events do not occur, maturation to appropriate adultness is, in many instances, permanently inhibited. The critical period is a maturational stage of "limited duration during which a particular influence, from another area of the developing organism, or from the environment, evokes a particular response" (Tanner, 1970, p. 131). Examples of critical periods are: the fetal heart taking over blood circulatory responsibilities, the newborn lungs breathing air, the stimulus from the central nervous system and the hypothalamus for the onset of puberty. These are mostly physical responses, but there are also critical periods in the development of healthy emotionality, language facility, and even conceptualization.

Research into the critical periods of maturation is important. The initial and perhaps most definitive work to date has been performed with animals, mostly birds.

IMPRINTING

Birds seem to have the best-established instincts—that is, they seem to have some of the most highly developed and complex unlearned, or imprinted, responses, from migration to nest building. And birds also provide experimental controls that are undesirable for human infants, particularly since the long-range effects of such experiments are largely unknown.

Konrad Lorenz

The first research in imprinting was performed by Konrad Lorenz (1937), the distinguished European naturalist who coined the term, and who shared the 1973 Nobel Prize for Physiology and Medicine, for discoveries in the individual and social behavior patterns of birds and bees in relation to natural selection and survival of the species, with two other eminent researchers (Karl von Frisch and Nikolaas Tinbergen). Lorenz demonstrated that there is a relatively short period of time early in the life of a goose when it is searching for some class of stimuli, some object, some shape or form not well defined. When this stimulus or a reasonable version of it is encountered, the goose responds to it in a preprogrammed, unlearned, instinctive manner.

Lorenz found that young birds do not instinctively recognize and choose other members of their own species as their companions. They learn to do this during a particular, critical period in their early life. If during this critical period they happen to see a man walking by instead of their mother, they will follow him. Lorenz demonstrated that the first social contact of greylag geese was the company they consistently preferred. Male geese whose first social contact was with their human caretaker made no sexual overtures toward female members of their own species, but courted instead their human caretaker.

Eckhard Hess

Lorenz's line of research has been advanced in America by Eckhard Hess (1959), who demonstrated that if a baby duckling is exposed to a

decoy 13 hours after leaving the shell, he will lock onto this decoy and follow it around for the rest of his life, paying little attention to a real mother
duck. Imprinting seems to be different from other learning in that "it
occurs very rapidly, it occurs only in a very limited part of the animal's
life, and it is irreversible, or, at least, it is difficult to extinguish" (Ramsay
and E. Hess, 1954, p. 197).

EARLY MOTHERING EXPERIENCE

There is a specific maturational time in a child's life that is the optimal time for the development of certain critical functions. If the appropriate model and stimulation for this development are absent from the
child's environment, the resulting deficit in development is permanent, or
at least very difficult to restore. This is true for the emotional, intellectual,
and social aspects of the child's developing personality.

Harry Harlow

The concept of critical early experience can be followed also in the
work of Harry Harlow with young monkeys and their experience with
mothering. Harlow chose the monkey, instead of the human infant, to
study the nature of the affectionate response or, as he called it, love, because:

> Unfortunately the human neonate is a limited experimental subject for such re-
> searches because of his inadequate motor capabilities. By the time the human
> infant's motor response can be precisely measured, the antecedent determining
> condition cannot be defined, having been lost in a jumble and jungle of confound-
> ing variables [1958, p. 674].

Harlow's preliminary work led him to the belief that contact comfort, or
the response of baby monkeys to cloth or fur against their skin, was one
of the key elements in their early security.

Harlow raised infant monkeys under three mothering conditions: the
natural mother, a wire surrogate, and a cloth surrogate. The wire and
cloth surrogate mothers were essentially the same barrel-shaped objects—
with a head, a midline nipple that provided milk, and a broad base that
provided a place for the baby monkey to sleep. Because of the superior
diet, vitamins, iron extract, penicillin, chloromycetin, 5 percent glucose,
and constant tender, loving care, both of the artificial mothers had a higher
success rate in raising their babies than the natural mothers, but of the
two, the babies fostered by the terrycloth mother had a significantly lower
rate of mortality.

In a follow-up study of the mature monkeys, Harlow and Harlow
(1962) found that the artificial mothering had some unexpected long-range
effects. The experimental adult monkeys were socially and sexually aberrant. The nourishment and contact comfort provided by the nursing cloth-
covered mother in infancy did not provide the necessary ingredients for the
production of a normal adolescent or adult. The orphaned monkeys' early
social deprivation permanently impaired their ability to relate to other
monkeys.

Harlow has pointed out the importance of certain experiences in the first few weeks of life in shaping the future behavior of young monkeys. And he has demonstrated that even the elusive abstraction of mothering can be reduced in complexity by the diligent and imaginative scientist.

Ashley Montagu

Following Harlow's line of thinking about the nature of love, Ashley Montagu (1971) reminds us that most people are not aware that the need for touching is basic, utterly necessary for survival. In fact, a baby's need for it is so compelling that if skin stimulation were denied entirely, he would die. Montagu emphasizes the need for motherly love—caressed, cuddled, and comforted infants—to insure healthy emotionality in the adult. We learn to love not by instruction, but by being loved: a mother who does not fondle and cuddle her baby fails to communicate to him that he is loved.

The feeling of being loved, of being secure as an infant and young child, is important in the child's sexual development. He cannot love others if he feels unloved himself. Being tenderly loved as a child lays the groundwork for the adult to love tenderly.

Montagu lists the physiological advantages of nursing infants, but he emphasizes that the good that comes to the infant from nursing is more than an adequate diet "perfectly timed and adjusted to the physiological development of the infant's digestive system.... [Nursing] provides him with an emotional environment of security and love in which his whole being can thrive" (1971, pp. 71, 74). The mother's relationship with her infant establishes the foundation for all his future social human relationships.

Margaret Ribble

In 1943, Ribble described vividly but in rather unscientific language the special importance of breast feeding. Her thesis, which she called "the rights of infants," emphasized that breast feeding was of far more importance emotionally than nutritionally. Although Ribble viewed nursing as important to the child's psychological development, the implications in her work of the importance of mothering were mild indeed when compared with those drawn by Spitz.

René Spitz

Interest in institutionalized infants was probably first aroused by the dismal reports of René Spitz, a psychoanalyst-physician, about the adverse effects of depriving infants of their mothers. Spitz (1949) studied two groups of children born to women prisoners. The conditions of the groups differed, he said, "in one single factor—the amount of emotional interchange offered." In one institution the children were raised by their own mothers. In the second, they were raised from the third month by overworked nursing personnel: one nurse had to care for from eight to twelve children.

Spitz found that the group raised by their own mothers did much better by all standards of development. They were healthier, had a lower mortality rate, grew faster, were better adjusted, and were happier than the babies in the foundling home. The most striking finding was the mortality rate. In the group that stayed with their mothers, there were no deaths during the two-year period of the study, whereas in the foundling home 37 percent of the infants died. Spitz, who coined the term marasmus to describe this, reports that "the high mortality is but the most extreme consequence of the general decline, both physical and psychological, which is shown by children completely starved of emotional interchange" (1949, p. 149).

Spitz's research led him to conclude that the most important psychosocial factor in the infant's life is his emotional interchange with his mother. The most susceptible age, he believed, was the second half of the first year. Burlingham and Anna Freud (1942), in reporting on London infants separated from their parents during World War II, also concluded that separation in the second half of the first year produced the most trauma.

Spitz found the institutional conditions, intermittent mothering by a fluctuating group of nursery attendants, disastrous for the psychological growth and general mental and physical health of the infants. The institutionalized infants displayed a marked deceleration in perceptual-motor development, became socially withdrawn and depressed, and failed to make normal progress in physical growth. Despite good nutrition and excellent sanitation and physical care, the mortality rate was alarmingly high. Anaclitic, or dependency-related, depression was Spitz's diagnosis of the infants' response to separation from their mothers (Spitz and Wolf, 1946).

Spitz's reports stirred considerable controversy. Critics pointed out that the cause of assignment of the mothers to one institution or the other could have biased the groups, and that an unexplained virus could have affected one of the groups and not the other. George Thompson, summarizing studies in the 1950s, observed that "the Spitz and Ribble hypotheses had a bad time of it in this year's literature" (1959, p. 32). Pinneau (1955) concluded, on the basis of statistical, methodological, and theoretical considerations, that Spitz's studies did not present scientific evidence supporting his hypothesis that institutionalized infants develop psychological disorders as a result of separation from their mothers.

> Pinneau raises questions and points out defects in design, methodology, and statistics that would seem to leave Spitz's conclusions, at best, only suggestive.... Spitz (1955), in this reviewer's opinion, fails adequately to meet the questions that have been raised. While most of us will continue to believe in the importance of mothering during infancy, we must recognize that this belief has more the characterstics of a faith and less the basis of demonstrated fact [Eriksen, 1957, pp. 194–195].

But most important was some explanation of the mechanism. How could the absence of mothering have such a drastic effect? Interpreting Spitz's conclusions presented somewhat of a problem. The possibility that they might be correct precluded an experimental study duplicating the situation. But obviously they needed to be followed up in some manner. Neilon's study, following up Shirley's motor studies, made a good case for the permanence of early personality characteristics. Spitz's findings could not be ignored, whatever the disposition of the critics.

Anna Freud

Anna Freud also published striking findings about the effect of early separation of children from their mothers (Burlingham and A. Freud, 1942). Her study was conducted in England during the London bombings of World War II. Some of the children could be evacuated from London to the countryside of Scotland, while others had to remain in the city and endure the night after night of sleeping in bomb shelters under the constant harassment of air attacks. The children in London remained with their mothers, and the children who were evacuated were kept by farm families or in large foster-home settings not unlike the foundling home that Spitz studied. Anna Freud found that the children who remained with their mothers were better able to develop and, like Spitz's group, had less illness, a lower mortality rate, and no incidence of the anaclitic depression found in the evacuated group.

This oft-quoted study, which supports Spitz's controversial work, is seldom criticized. Nevertheless, one of its weaknesses is a failure to account for the great environmental differences between London and Scotland. The children evacuated from London often came from steamy tenement houses. In northern Scotland, they lived in little stone cottages inside the Arctic Circle, where the cold was really oppressive. Changes in the living conditions of the children might well have had something to do with their health and the incidence of colds, pneumonia, and the like. When any area of research has such a dramatic beginning as the study of the effect of mothering upon infants, it takes years for the careful scientist to sort enthusiasm from fact.

William Goldfarb

Along with the work of Spitz and Freud came supporting studies by Goldfarb (1945) and Bowlby (1951, 1960), which tended to confirm the devastating effect of the absence of early mothering. In the middle 1940s, Goldfarb published a series of papers concerned mainly with the effect of this absence on intellectual and emotional development. He concluded that it results in a basic defect in total personality expressed in both intellect and feeling, and that the neglected child is fixated at a level of extreme immaturity and insecurity for his whole life. He found the children apathetic, intellectually impoverished, and weak in the will or drive to understand and reorganize external experiences. Obviously Goldfarb feels that the absence of mothering not only affects the adjustment of children, but permanently scars their intellectual and emotional growth—a neglected child can never become a well-adjusted adult.

John Bowlby

Appointed by the World Health Organization to study homeless children, Bowlby (1951, 1960) surveyed the literature and made a personal investigation in many countries on the effect of lack of mothering. He concluded that Spitz, Freud, and Goldfarb had, if anything, understated the case. His own finding was that this early deprivation leads to permanently impaired intellectual and emotional development.

Lawrence Casler

A number of reviewers have been critical of these studies of children deprived of mothering, and contradictory evidence has been reported. One of the most detailed and careful reviews was carried out by Casler.

> A large number of authors ... agree that, if a young child is separated from its mother and placed in an institution, it will suffer severe physical, emotional, and intellectual disturbance, no matter how "hygienic" its environment may be.... It is my contention that these studies are, virtually without exception, neither conclusive nor particularly instructive, because of their failure to take into account certain critical variables. The first of these concerns the age at which the separation occurred. Since ill effects may result not from the maternal deprivation itself, but from the rupture of an already existing emotional bond with the mother, only those separations beginning before the establishment of this bond can furnish data regarding the effects of deprivation per se [1961, p. 3].

Casler also felt that the institution involved should be named and adequately described and that much more detailed consideration should be given to how the sample was chosen, why the babies were in the institution, when they were first enrolled, their previous health, their parents' health, and so forth. He felt that ample evidence was available to demonstrate that prior to six months of age, infants had not sufficiently matured emotionally to establish deep emotional ties with their mothers. After that age emotional ties were a serious factor to be considered.

Casler reports that "despite its serious inadequacies in coverage and interpretation, one of the chief sources of information about institutional studies has been the summary compiled by Bowlby (1951)" (1961, p. 4). Of the forty-five studies listed by Bowlby, nineteen either did not list the age of separation, or gave it as after six months of age; fourteen did not name or describe the institution; even more gave no information about the children.

Even Goldfarb's studies, which present the most data about the subjects and the best control data, involved a small number of children. In fact, as Casler has pointed out, at least five of Goldfarb's nine studies involved the same group of fifteen institutionalized children and fifteen controls, and the criteria for the selection of the two groups were not made clear. Moreover, considerable doubt is cast on Goldfarb's personality studies because he used a personality test difficult to validate. The Rorschach test makes predictions about personality organization rather than behavior, how a person is rather than how he will behave in a particular situation. For example, the Rorschach might indicate that the person shows "shallow affective reserve," meaning he does not seem to have a rich emotional repertoire. But since there is no prediction of behavior against which to check the interpretation, its correctness is not open to validation.

Casler also criticizes Spitz's study because of a considerable drop in the number of children in the foundling home. Were the children who were left so undesirable, because of physical, emotional, or intellectual deficits, that they were not placeable? Other critics have pointed out that much of the most serious decline in the children in the foundling home occurred before their separation from their mothers. It is also important to note that the objective tests used by Spitz were not standardized.

Casler concludes his review with this summary:

> Emotional, physical, and intellectual malfunctioning is known to occur with frequency among children in many institutions. Some authors have alleged that this malfunctioning is attributable to the deprivation of maternal love. It is more likely, however, that deprivation of maternal love can have ill effects only after specific affective responsiveness has been achieved by the child (usually at about the age of six months). Ill effects found in children maternally deprived before this age probably have some other cause. Evidence is accumulating, both on the human and the animal level, that this "other cause" is perceptual deprivation—the absolute or relative absence of tactile, vestibular, and other forms of stimulation. These forms of social stimulation necessary for proper language development, etc., can be provided within an institutional setting [1961, p. 49].

ENVIRONMENTAL EXPERIENCE

Using the greylag goose, Konrad Lorenz demonstrated that social modeling of his own species is not innate, but at a critical period in his life, a young gosling is imprinted with an instinct to attach himself emotionally to the living thing he finds close to him in his environment. In the ordinary way of things, this would be his mother, but should it be a human caretaker instead, the goose always is unable to make social contact with his own species.

Working with monkeys, Harry Harlow gave a convincing demonstration of the necessity of mother love in enabling youngsters to grow to healthy emotional adulthood. Harlow theorized that basic to emotional security is the sense of touch, the satisfaction and security derived from the mother's cuddling of the infant. Ashley Montagu declares the need for touching basic to the human infant.

René Spitz concluded that the lack of mothering caused the high mortality rate of infants completely starved of emotional interchange. He concluded that the emotional interchange between an infant and his mother is the most important psychosocial factor in his life. In spite of questions concerning the complete scientific basis for Spitz's conclusions, he raised an issue that could not be ignored.

William Goldfarb and John Bowlby concluded that early emotional deprivation has permanent detrimental effects upon intellectual as well as emotional development—a neglected child can never be a well-adjusted adult. These reports prompted other researchers to look into the effect of environment on the young child.

Some studies do not support the contention that undesirable effects result from an absence of mothering per se. An early study by Dennis and Dennis (1951) deals with the effect of limited mothering. The Dennises took over the care of two-month-old female twins and kept them through the fourteenth month. The children were raised, during this thirteen-month period, under restricted conditions and with a minimum of social stimulation. The two writers exercised complete control over the infants, who saw no other children and few other adults. They did not make any social responses in the subjects' presence, and did not reward, punish, or instruct them. They provided little opportunity for imitation or learning. The basic needs of the children for food, clothing, exercise, and fresh air were met, but the mothering, which Spitz and Goldfarb believed essential to normal development, was not provided. The children evidenced no adverse effects from the experience, either emotionally or intellectually.

The Dennises concluded that most of the responses of infants in the first two years of life are a function of maturation, and not of learning or imitation. Admittedly, some behavior was slow to develop in the children, such as sitting and speech development, but such behavior requires practice for mastery. The autogenous responses that develop during the first year, the Dennises concluded, are prerequisite and crucial to the later development of socialized responses. But the Dennises provide no report of these girls in adulthood. The lasting effects of their study are not known.

Results of a later study of children in three Iranian orphanages (Dennis, 1960) seemed to contradict Dennis's earlier studies. In his studies of the twins and of Hopi Indian children, Dennis had found that environmental deprivation had little effect. In his Iranian study, he reported that major consequences can ensue from them. Dennis felt that the difference was accounted for by the kind and severity of the deprivations involved.

> The results of the present study challenge the widely held view that motor development consists in the emergence of a behavior sequence based primarily upon maturation. Shirley's chart of the motor sequence is a textbook favorite. It shows sitting alone at 7 months, creeping at 10 months, and walking alone at 15 months. The present study shows that these norms are met only under favorable environmental conditions.... These facts seem to indicate clearly that experience affects not only the ages at which motor items appear but also their very form. No doubt the maturation of certain structures, which as yet cannot be identified, is necessary before certain responses can be learned, but learning also is necessary. Maturation alone is insufficient to bring about most postnatal developments in behavior [Dennis, 1960, p. 57].

Dennis, in collaboration with Najarian (1957), performed yet another study on the effect of early environmental deprivation, this time in Lebanon. Again using children in a foundling home with a staff-to-child ratio of 1-to-10, about the same as that reported by Spitz, Dennis and Najarian found differences that seemed to relate to the early deprivation. The children in the crowded nursery setting were given a minimum of mothering. The practice of skills was slight because of lack of staff. The children spent much of their early months on their backs even when being fed. They were constantly swaddled.

The study of institutionalized infants in Lebanon revealed the infants to be normal in development at two months but progressively more retarded through the remainder of their first year. By the time they had reached four to six years of age, their development lag was no longer noticeable. The early retardation seemed to be most pronounced in activities affected by practice, experience, and stimulation.

The children exhibited no evidence of a loss of emotional attachment and no evidence of emotional shock or anaclitic depression. The effects of the retardation were not longstanding, being made up by the end of the third year, even if they remained in a relatively deprived environment. The authors concluded that the early retardation of motor performance is a function of the kind of skill required by the task, and not a generalized retardation. That is, if the task requires skills best developed in situations where imitation, practice, and instruction are helpful, a pronounced retardation is evidenced; if the skill is an autogenous part of the reflexive, genetic repertoire of the child, the effect is unnoticeable. The authors then concluded that infant intelligence tests tend to sample behavior directly related to practice and experience and to ignore many of the more fundamental processes.

SUMMARY

What, then, are we to conclude about the critical nature of the first year of life in terms of the interaction of cortical development and experience? Evidently, cortical development related to intellectual and emotional growth is affected by the quality and amount of early experiences. The most pronounced effect of early deprivation seems to be on the affective responses and language development. There also appears to be a critical period in the development of certain intellectual skills and concepts: one of the most glaring effects of early deprivation is a retardation in intellectual growth. And perhaps even more important, early deprivation of human social contacts leaves the child always unable to develop interpersonal relationships with other humans.

Part of the confusion in the literature regarding social deprivation is due to the confounding of variables. Social deprivation is accompanied by both nutritional and physical deprivation in most of its natural occurrences. To take a simple example, a child, propped up in bed and fed a bottle from a retaining rack, is not cuddled. Is he nourished? He experiences social deprivation, but he also experiences something else. He experiences gas bubbles that result in his terminating his sucking. He belches and emits a milk culture into his inner ear. He fails to experience the usual jostling about that develops muscle tone.

Thus, if the child becomes socially maladjusted later, is it because of the psychological effect of his lack of social experience, as suggested by the work of Harlow, Bowlby, or Spitz? Or could it be that the child is socially inadequate because he can't hear well in consequence of an ear infection resulting from the sour milk chronically in his ear? Or is he socially inadequate because his muscle tone is poor, since he repeatedly failed to receive any stimulation?

Man is a social being. A child's basic needs are met in a social environment. Even the most highly structured early child environment, the Skinner box, allows for constant social monitoring and social interaction. Thus far, man has not developed any way of providing all of the physical needs of a child safely and reliably in other than a social environment. When human contact is withdrawn, some form of physical neglect invariably occurs. There is no doubt that children who are socially neglected are emotionally stunted, as well as stunted in social and intellectual development.

But the question remains as to why. The fascinating animal research of Lorenz, Beach (Beach and Jaynes, 1954), and Eckhard Hess remains just that—fascinating animal research. It generates interesting speculation about the imprinting of social responses in humans, but the definitive study has not been done. It is questionable whether the cues to the critical period of human imprinting can be identified, even if they exist. However, there is sufficient evidence to warrant careful attention to the early social and emotional stimulation of children, whether it be causative or correlative in relation to healthy emotional maturation. The exact nature and extent of the critical period in the development of the cortex is yet to be determined, but it is certain that cortical development in itself plays an important role in early intellectual and emotional development. The lack of proper stimulation during this period seems to result in a permanent deficit, or at least one difficult to restore.

The major difficulty in conducting definitive research is that a responsible investigator using human subjects cannot perform research of the quality conducted by Harlow with monkeys. And this is the kind of precision required to answer the question in definitive terms. On the other hand, on those few occasions when the necessity or the misconduct of particular parents leads to the kind of neglect that might answer the question, a conglomeration of conflicting and contaminating variables clouds the picture. The effect of heredity, disease, vitamin deficiencies, or physical neglect would all tend to prevent any definitive analysis of the cause of any intellectual or emotional aberrations noted in the child.

A number of studies have been performed on so-called feral, or wild, children, children who presumably were raised by animals, or who experienced grotesque neglect the first few months or years of their lives. These cases have been covered by several excellent reviews and, without exception, a careful scrutiny of the child's history indicates that he was not normal at birth, had a genetic history that was highly questionable, and suffered from some type of major illness or neurological defect. These so-called feral children were merely severely retarded children who were abandoned by their parents and later found by other humans, generally only a few hours or a few days after they had been abandoned. Any inferences drawn from the behavior and ability of these children must take into account all the contaminating factors.

Dennis (1941, 1951) has seriously questioned the reports of wild children. Zingg, who authored or co-authored several reports on feral children (Zingg, 1940, 1941; Singh and Zingg, 1942), disagreed emphatically with Dennis. But Lorenz, in a discussion reported by Inhelder (1953), vehemently attacked Zingg on the reports of the two wolf girls of India (Squires, 1927; Kellogg, 1934; Stratton, 1934; Zingg, 1940; Gesell, 1941; and Singh and Zingg, 1942):

> I am sorry but I must lodge a passionate resistance against Amala and Kamala. I'll take my oath, and I want to drop dead this minute, if these children have really been raised by animals, and if you try to get hold of Gesell—as I did—he doesn't want to talk about it. Mr. Singh and Mr. Zingg, I am sorry to say, are people to whom the German saying applies "*Wer einmal lugt, dem Glaubt man nicht, und wenn er auch die Wahrheit spricht*" [Once a liar, always a liar]. If somebody assures me that a child raised by wolves has green luminous eyes, then I don't believe a word he says any more [quoted by Inhelder, 1953, p. 95].

SUMMARY

Genetic research has given us a rich heritage of information regarding the relationship between human heredity and the growth, development, and behavior of children. Clearly, man is ultimately a product of his heredity and his environment: each is essential to his well-being.

A healthy infant is born with potential to love, to learn, to communicate, to develop, and to grow. Without an environment that stimulates, protects, and nurtures his innate potential, it fails to thrive: without maternal love and cuddling as a model in infancy, man never is able to love; without stimulation and opportunity for concept training, man never is able to learn; without models, stimulation, and opportunity early in life, man never is able to verbalize; without exercise and nutrition, man never is able to grow.

But an infant must also have the opportunity to be well born before he can utilize the best of all environments, and this pushes the effect of environment on his heredity back generation upon generation. Inheritance is chemical: good nutrition and an absence of toxic agents are absolute prerequisites for healthy children. Granted this base, man reproduces himself faithfully with relatively little influence exerted by his behavior, so long as it does not affect the chemical balance of his body.

REVIEW

Maturation · Maturation is the postnatal, physical, developmental sequence of change that follows the instructions built into the genetic code; change within the cells and between cells; change that affects the development of the child psychologically, emotionally, intellectually, and physically. Maturation is four growth processes—cerebration, myelination, endocrination, and skeletonation—all under control of the genetic code and all in control of the child's social, emotional, intellectual, and sexual identity. Maturation is a change in proportion, in function, in complexity, in relationship, as well as in size, all related to the genetically prescheduled unfolding capacity to cope with the demands of the environment.

Cerebration

Babinski Reflex   A fanning of the infant's toes in response to stimulation to sole of the foot, the Babinski reflex begins to disappear at four to six months. Its persistence beyond this age indicates a neurological problem.

Cerebration   Initially, the subcortical nuclei maintain the major control of the brain. Cerebration is the slow but constant shift from subcortical nuclei to the cortex, from automatic, reflexive responses to deliberate, controlled responses. This cerebration process provides critical signposts of the child's development as reflexes appear and disappear in the orderly, sequential, appropriate progression of maturation.

Grasp Reflex   A grasping with the fingers, minus the opposable thumb, of any object laid in the infant's hand. Gradually, the opposable thumb comes into play. The response becomes entirely voluntary by twelve months.

Moro Reflex   A fanning of the infant's arms in a more or less clutching fashion in response to loud noises or sudden loss of support. The Moro reflex develops into the startle reflex of the adult and is used as an indicator of the neurological development of the young child.

Sphincter Reflex   The voluntary control over this reflex, which makes bowel and bladder control possible, follows the necessary neurological development.

Swimming Reflex   An early reflex that enables an infant to stay afloat in water with dry lungs for a period of time; gradually subsides by about eight months and is followed by disorganized, struggling activity in water, and then voluntary movements.

Myelination

Axon   The appendage of the neuron (nerve cell) that transmits impulses away from the cell.

Feedback Loop   A term borrowed from computer programming, feedback loop implies continuous, automatic furnishing of data concerning the output of the mechanism to an automatic device that controls and actuates the mechanism.

Myelination   Myelination is the maturation of the nerve cells from long, thin, exposed axons, which carry nerve impulses at a slow rate, to axons covered by Schwann's sheaths (myelin) with nodes of Ranvier, so that impulses jump from node to node with incredible speed. From infantile, primitive, generalized responses, the child matures to complex reactions to subtle stimuli. The Babinski reflex is used to measure the extent of myelination in individual children.   This reflex occurs when there is no myelination and disappears when myelination is complete.   The myelination process provides a necessary condition for complex behavior to occur, particularly the motor skills that form the essence of early intelligence.

Nodes of Ranvier   Gaps between the Schwann's sheaths wrapped around mature nerve cells. Nodes of Ranvier enable nerve cells to regenerate at incredible speed.

Schwann's Sheaths   The myelin wrapped around mature nerve cells, Schwann's sheaths enable nerve impulses to travel at incredible speed.

Servomechanism   A control system in which the mechanism is actuated and controlled by a specific signal. A servomechanism refers to a connected sensor and effector such that the sensor controls the effector and the effector controls the sensor.   In its simplest terms it is the relationship between a floor furnace and a thermostat.

Endocrination

ACTH   Adrenocorticotropin, secreted by the anterior pituitary, regulates the normal growth and secretory function of the adrenals.

ADH   The antidiuretic hormone secreted by the posterior lobe of the pituitary, ADH is essential for maintenance of the water balance in the body.

Adrenals   A dual gland, the adrenals' growth and secretory function is regulated by the anterior pituitary and thyroid.

   Adrenal Cortex   The adrenal cortex is predominantly chemical; surrounds the adrenal medulla; and is essential for metabolism of body proteins and carbohydrates.   The adrenal cortex secretes glucocorticoid, mineral corticoid, and hydrocortisone.

   Adrenal Medulla   The adrenal medulla is highly innervated; is closely connected with the sympathetic nervous system; secretes catecholamine hormones responsible for emergency reactions: epinephrine and norepinephrine.

Adrenocorticotropin ACTH

Androsterone Secreted by the testes, androsterone produces secondary male sex characteristics.

Antidiuretic Hormone ADH

Autonomic Nervous System The autonomic nervous system, closely related to the endocrine system, consists of the **parasympathetic nervous system,** responsible for bodily repair and maintenance during normal resting states, and the **sympathetic nervous system,** which takes precedence in moments of stress, shutting off peripheral, nonessential activities, such as digestion, to prepare for flight or fight.

Endocrination The endocrine system of ductless glands consists of the hypothalamus, the pituitary, the adrenals, the pancreas, the thyroid, the parathyroid, the thymus, the ovaries or testes, and the central nervous system. Maturation and development related to size, contour, and general sexual delineation is controlled and regulated by the endocrine glands.

Endocrine System
    Adrenals
        Adrenal cortex—Glucocorticoid; Hydrocortisone; Mineral corticoid.
        Adrenal medulla—Epinephrine; Norepinephrine
    Central nervous system
    Hypothalamus
    Ovaries—Estrogen; Progesterone
    Pancreas—Insulin
    Parathyroid—PTH (parathyroid hormone)
    Pituitary
        Anterior—ACTH (adrenocorticotropin); FSH (follicle-stimulating hormone); GH (growth hormone); LH (luteinizing hormone); Prolactin; TSH (thyrotropin).
        Posterior—ADH (antidiuretic hormone); Oxytocin
    Testes—Androsterone; Testosterone
    Thymus
    Thyroid—Thyrocalcitonin; Thyroxine

Epinephrine Secreted by the adrenal medulla, epinephrine raises blood pressure, stimulates the heart muscle, accelerates the heart rate, and increases cardiac output in cases of emergency reaction.

Estrogen Produced by the ovarian follicles in the early stages of ovarian cycle, estrogen is responsible for female secondary sex characteristics and acts on the fallopian tube and uterus in preparation for pregnancy.

Follicle-stimulating Hormone FSH

FSH The follicle-stimulating hormone secreted by the anterior pituitary, FSH is gonadotropic, stimulating development of the ovarian follicle in the female and development of the testicles and spermatozoa in the male.

GH The growth hormone secreted by the anterior pituitary, GH is responsible for acceleration and deceleration of the growth of bones and tissues.

Glucocorticoid Secreted by the adrenal cortex, glucocorticoid is responsible for metabolism of carbohydrates.

Growth Normal growth requires good nutrition and good health, growth hormone from the anterior pituitary, thyroxine from the thyroid, hydrocortisone from the adrenal cortex, and insulin from the pancreas, the gonadal hormone at puberty (estrogen or testosterone), and hypothalamic functioning mediating the anterior pituitary: all of these interact with the genotype to produce the phenotype.

Growth Hormone GH

Hydrocortisone Secreted by the adrenal cortex, hydrocortisone is responsible for carbohydrate and protein metabolism.

Hypothalamus The hypothalamus functions as an integrated unit with the pituitary; controls appetite, temperature, and thirst; stimulates secretion of FSH and LH by the anterior pituitary; combines with the central nervous system, conditioned in utero, to bring about puberty; and is the primitive, life-regulating center of the brain.

Insulin Secreted by the pancreas, insulin is essential for metabolism of carbohydrates and fats. It functions in relation to the concentration of glucose in the blood. Insufficiency results in diabetes.

Lactation Lactation requires progesterone from the ovary, oxytocin from the posterior pituitary, prolactin from the anterior pituitary, and thyroxine from the thyroid.

LH The luteinizing hormone secreted by the anterior pituitary, LH is gonadotropic, causing formation of the corpus luteum and ovulation in the female, stimulating estrogen and progesterone secretion in the female, stimulating development of the testes in the male, and stimulating testosterone secretion and spermatogenesis in the male.

Luteinizing Hormone LH

Mineral Corticoid Secreted by the adrenal cortex, mineral corticoid regulates sodium retention and loss of potassium.

Norepinephrine Secreted by the adrenal medulla, norepinephrine is contained in all the sympathetic nervous system in nerve endings.

Ovaries The female ovaries are cyclic in function, producing estrogen and progesterone.

Oxytocin Secreted by the posterior lobe of the pituitary, oxytocin stimulates lactation release of milk.

Pancreas The pancreas secretes insulin in the islets of Langerhans. Failure of the pancreas to function adequately causes diabetes mellitus.

Parathyroid The parathyroid is necessary for metabolism of calcium and phosphates. It secretes parathyroid hormone (PTH).

Parathyroid Hormone PTH

Pituitary The most important endocrine gland, the pituitary is a dual gland whose anterior and posterior lobes serve distinctly separate functions.

    Anterior Influenced by the central nervous system, the hypothalamus, and the thyroid, the anterior pituitary controls endocrine system functioning, sexual differentiation, metabolism, and growth. It functions through chemical reactions and secretes six major hormones: two gonadotropic—FSH and LH; two regulating—TSH and ACTH; one lactogenic—prolactin; and one growth—GH.

    Posterior Richly innervated with nerve pathways leading directly from the hypothalamus, the posterior pituitary controls water balance in the body and secretes two hormones: one antidiuretic—ADH; and one lactogenic—oxytocin.

Pregnancy Maintenance Maintenance of pregnancy requires progesterone from the corpus luteum of the ovary and FSH and LH from the anterior pituitary.

Progesterone Produced by the corpus luteum in the late stage of the ovarian cycle, progesterone maintains pregnancy, is responsible for later development of mammary glands, stimulates uterine development, and controls uterine muscle activity.

Prolactin Secreted by the anterior pituitary, prolactin is the lactogenic hormone responsible for the beginning and continuation of lactation and the maintenance of the corpus luteum.

PTH The parathyroid hormone, PTH is necessary for metabolism of calcium and phosphates.

Sexual Differentiation General and secondary sexual delineation requires central nervous system conditioning in utero, hypothalamus and central nervous system functioning at puberty, FSH and LH from the anterior pituitary, and estrogen and testosterone from the ovaries and testes.

Spermatogenesis Spermatogenesis requires androsterone and testosterone from the testes and FSH and LH from the anterior pituitary, as well as descended testicles.

Testes The male testes produce testosterone and androsterone, responsible for male secondary sex characteristics and spermatogenesis.

Testosterone Secreted by the testes, testosterone has both androgenic and anabolic functions.

Thymus The thymus is active only until about age eleven as it develops bodily immunities.

Thyrocalcitonin Secreted by the thyroid, thyrocalcitonin works with the parathyroid to maintain calcium balance.

Thyroid Regulated by the anterior pituitary, the thyroid concentrates iodine, necessary for growth; regulates metabolic rate in the adult and controls metabolic rate and normal growth and development in the child; secretes thyroxine and thyrocalcitonin.

Thyrotropin TSH

Thyroxine Secreted by the thyroid, thyroxine stimulates carbohydrate turnover, fat turnover, cholesterol turnover, milk production during lactation, calcium mobilization from bone, magnesium turnover, heart rate and contractility, red cell production, hydrocortisone secretion, and growth hormone secretion.

TSH Secreted by the anterior pituitary, thyrotropin regulates the normal growth and secretory function of the thyroid.

Skeletonation

Early-maturing Boys Propelled into situations of responsibility, early-maturing boys become responsible; they come into manhood much more easily than late-maturing boys.

Early-maturing Girls Spectacular social successes in junior high, early-maturing girls experience difficulty in senior high for which neither they nor their parents are prepared; accelerated social experiences leave them socially isolated in high school, bored, rebellious, and recalcitrant.

Growth Trends Children do not grow at a steady rate: growth is rapid in early childhood, slows down during preadolescence, and spurts at adolescence; girls reach the adolescent growth spurt before boys. Early or late maturation can have permanent effects upon children, with early-maturing girls and late-maturing boys at greater risk.

Late-maturing Boys Exactly opposite to the situation of early-maturing girls, late-maturing boys have little social status; they are treated as if they are immature and consequently tend to act immature.

Late-maturing Girls Late-maturing girls seem to suffer none of the social handicaps of late-maturing boys or early-maturing girls; like early-maturing boys, they move into adulthood with relative ease.

Skeletonation The calcification of the skeletal system, skeletonation, with the exception of gross dietary deficiency, is under the influence of hereditary characteristics. Bodily growth, controlled and regulated for the most part by the genetic code, directly affects, as does endocrination, a child's personality, social adjustment, and interaction with his environment.

Infant Morphology

Developmental Direction The observable developmental trend in children of cephalocaudal and proximodistal orderly motor development, developmental direction seems to be under the regulation of neurological unfolding.

Functional Asymmetry The bilateral nature of the newborn, which, with increasing maturation, gives way to a unilateral preference and skill, functional asymmetry is predictable in all children.

Individuating Maturation The all-important morphological principle for Gesell, who placed responsibility for differences in the growth patterns of children squarely on their inherited maturational clock, individuating maturation implies that although all children follow a predictable pattern of growth, they do so at their own individual rate.

Reciprocal Interweaving The lapses that occur as a child progresses to more and more complex behavior, reciprocal interweaving corresponds to McGraw's periods of regression.

Self-regulatory Fluctuation The activity and rest states, observable in all children, which fluctuate and change as the child matures, self-regulatory fluctuation is evidence of the child's changing attempts to adjust to his environment as he matures.

Handedness

Handedness Studies of handedness in children recognize a slight asymmetry in all parts of the body that probably indicates handedness to be more than a learned phenomenon. Hand preference varies as children mature, becoming dominant by about four years of age.

Summary of Maturation

Concept of Maturation The basic assumption underlying the concept of maturation is that a biochemical trend in the development of the brain, nervous system, endocrine system, and skeleton provides both stimulation to and regulation of human growth in intellectual, emotional, and social dimensions.

The ever-increasing activation of the cerebral cortex gradually reduces the significance and activity rate of the subcortical brain centers and the child becomes, for the rest of his life, a cerebral being. Thinking, reasoning, language, all of which are dependent upon the complex associations possible on the surface of the cerebral cortex, are the major vehicles through which cultural accumulation is transmitted.

The unfolding drama of human form is delicately regulated and balanced by the interconnections of the extraordinarily complex hormonal system that provides for the incredible range in temperament, physique, drive level, and activity that defines humanness, maleness, and femaleness under the pressures of social shaping.

The gross physical dimensions of the body, regulated in the main by the genetic code, are both servant to and master of the human personality. Although man controls his body and the cortex is supreme, the size, shape, and proportion of the body exert great influence on the nature of human experience.

Continuous Maturation Arnold Gesell and Willard Olson argue that maturation is a continuing phenomenon that involves overlapping, interlocking, and reciprocal interweaving of skills dependent upon neurological, physical, social, and emotional growth. For them, maturation is comparable to riding a bicycle to the corner: at no specific point is one foot more important than the other.

Discrete-stages Maturation Sígmund Freud, Harry Stack Sullivan, and Jean Piaget argue that maturation develops in discrete stages, with steps of fixation, regression, and progression from one stage to another. For them, maturation is comparable to walking to the corner using one foot at a time.

Critical-period Hypothesis

Critical Period A critical period is a stage in development, a specific time, when certain events should occur in normal maturation, when a specific influence should evoke a specific response; if these events do not occur, growth to appropriate adultness is, in many instances, permanently inhibited. There is a specific maturational time in a child's life that is the optimal time for the development of certain critical functions. If the appropriate model and stimulation for this development are absent from the child's environment, the resulting deficit in development is permanent, or at least very difficult to restore. This is true for the emotional, intellectual, and social aspects of the child's developing personality, as well as for his developing physical health, i.e., the permanent effects of malnutrition during gestation and lactation.

Imprinting Imprinting is learning quite resistant to extinction that occurs very early in life.

Summary Early emotional deprivation permanently impairs social development and early deprivation in perceptual and intellectual stimulation permanently impairs conceptual development. Infants need not only adequate nutritional and physical care, but adequate emotional attachments and adequate intellectual stimulation to grow and mature into healthy adulthood.

NAMES TO KNOW

LEONARD CARMICHAEL In his classic experiment with amblystoma, Leonard Carmichael demonstrated that maturation alone provides lower organisms with all that is necessary for the development of their behavior repertoire. With phylogenetic responses, those characteristic of a species, the period of practice serves only as exercise; learning takes place only after maturation has provided the nervous system with the ability necessary for the behavior.

Cerebration

MYRTLE McGRAW Using identical twins, Myrtle McGraw conducted an experiment somewhat similar to Carmichael's. Almost from birth she began training one twin in bladder control. The other twin received no training until the first had achieved 90 percent successful bladder control. The second twin achieved equal success in bladder control almost immediately. Like Carmichael, McGraw demonstrated the necessity for maturation before specific learning could effectively change behavior patterns. Once the child was capable of bladder control, learning could occur; prior to that, training was ineffective.

Subcortical to Cortical Control

MYRTLE McGRAW Myrtle McGraw theorizes that maturation is based upon the development of the nervous system, and that the shift from subcortical to cortical control is the enabling agent. Effective training of children must await this cortical shift. Too-early training creates only frustration for both the parent and child. And because the shift to cortical control is a gradual process, periods of regression can be perfectly normal and understandable as children master more and more mature behavior.

Infant Morphology

ARNOLD GESELL   Arnold Gesell's theory of maturation involves five principles with psychomorphological implications: developmental direction, reciprocal interweaving, functional asymmetry, individuating maturation, and self-regulatory fluctuation. For him, maturation is a progressive organization of behavior forms. He was so impressed by the predictability of childhood development that he gave little credence to learning as an important factor in behavior change.

Critical-period Hypothesis

imprinting

KONRAD LORENZ   Using the greylag goose, Konrad Lorenz demonstrated that social modeling of his own species is not innate, but at a critical period in his life, a young gosling is imprinted with an instinct to attach himself emotionally to the living thing he finds close to him in his environment. In the ordinary way of things, this would be his mother, but should it be a human caretaker instead, the goose always is unable to make social contact with his own species.

ECKHARD HESS   Eckhard Hess found imprinting to occur rapidly, during a short time span, and to be nearly irreversible.

early mothering experience

HARRY HARLOW   Harry Harlow's exciting and long-term research on the effects of mothering in monkeys has demonstrated clearly that infant monkeys who miss normal mothering, the most important aspect of which is touch, mature to be socially and sexually aberrant adults. Early social deprivation permanently impaired their ability to relate to other monkeys.

ASHLEY MONTAGU   The importance of touch to human infants in relationship to their later emotional and social adjustment is stressed by Ashley Montagu, who underscores Harlow's work. Montagu says we learn to love by being loved; and early love for the infant is physical: being held, rocked, caressed, fed, kept warm, clean, and dry. Both Harlow and Montagu emphasize that the mother's relationship with her infant establishes the foundation for all his future social human relationships.

MARGARET RIBBLE   Margaret Ribble and Montagu both stressed the importance of nursing for reasons above and beyond nutrition by providing an environment of security and love for the infant through his being held close and cuddled. Although her study probably was lacking in technique, her thesis—that the emotional interaction between mother and child is as important as the nutritional interaction—has proved to be one worth noticing. Children who do not learn early to interact emotionally with others never seem to develop this very necessary human quality.

RENE SPITZ   René Spitz, preceding Montagu, arrived at the same conclusion: emotional contact and stimulation are necessary for an infant's survival. Spitz was the controversial researcher who emphatically pointed out the tragic consequences of raising infants in overcrowded and understaffed institutions. Although not yet defined adequately by rigorous research, a specific time of great sensitivity in human maturation nevertheless seems to exist, when adequate social and intellectual stimulation as well as physical nurture are required, or the opportunity for maximum emotional and intellectual development is forever lost.

SAMUEL PINNEAU   Samuel Pinneau specifically criticized Spitz's studies on rather solid scientific grounds. And Spitz could not adequately answer the charges.

ANNA FREUD   Reporting on British children during the bombing of London in World War II, Anna Freud found evidence that, in spite of the nightly bombings, the children who remained with their mothers in London fared better than those who were sent for safekeeping to foster homes in northern Scotland. Being deprived of their mothers was considered to be the basic factor in the decline of the removed children. Since then, researchers have suggested that environment too may well have played a large role.

WILLIAM GOLDFARB   William Goldfarb's studies of maternal deprivation are often quoted in the literature as evidence of the devastating consequences—permanent impairment of intellectual and emotional growth—incurred when children are deprived of their mothers. Unfortunately, his studies, although considerably better designed than earlier ones, still lacked the rigor required for the conclusion that maternal deprivation was the sole cause of the traumatic effect he reported.

JOHN BOWLBY   John Bowlby conducted a worldwide study of homeless children. He concluded, from personal investigation and a review of the literature, that early deprivation leads to permanent impairment of intellectual and emotional development.

LAWRENCE CASLER   Lawrence Casler reported, in a

comprehensive review of maternal deprivation studies, that the conclusions were not scientifically supported. A critical reader could not sort out the evidence and reach an intelligent conclusion. He did not state that their thesis was necessarily false, only that it was necessarily unproven.

early environmental experience

WAYNE DENNIS   Wayne Dennis has conducted several studies of the effects of early environment upon human development. He investigated the effect of the Hopi Indians' cradling practice upon their youngsters' learning to walk, and concluded that being bound on a cradle board for long hours each day did not noticeably affect the advent of walking among Hopi children.

He raised a pair of infant twins under environmentally restricted conditions: they were given adequate physical care but no social or play interaction with adults. He concluded that most changes in infant behavior occurring in the first year are genetically determined and are little affected by environment. He also concluded, however, that practice and stimulation facilitate even genetically determined behavior changes.

In studies of institutionalized infants in Iran and Lebanon, Dennis found evidence to support his theory that most early maturational changes are prescheduled, genetically controlled behavior, some of which is obviously enhanced through practice, stimulation, and experience, and that, therefore, a lack of practice, stimulation, and experience can be debilitating.

Early perceptual and cognitive development

At birth, the child functions at a subcortical response level, on a reflexive or instinctive basis: no perceptual or cognitive processing of stimuli from the external or internal environment is evident. Nevertheless, the newborn infant, coming from a sensory-deprived situation, insulated by the thick, deadening walls of the uterus, is sensitive to a wide band of sensations, which are, in effect, unconditioned stimuli that produce an undifferentiated, but massive response on his part.

These stimuli provoking a response from the infant are usually of a high magnitude or intensity and are usually nonspecific, such as a loud noise, a bright flash of light, an electrical pulse, a sharp taste, a heavy vibration, or other assorted, intense tactile stimulations. To these, the child generally offers an unspecific response, the startle pattern or Moro reflex, which involves a massive, general response, including diaphragm, arms, legs, neck, trunk, and head; a response that demonstrates little differentiation, an all-or-none phenomenon.

Unless the stimuli are intense, they are not responded to at all; but if sufficiently intense, or at the threshold of the child, they are responded to with a full-blown reaction. The human infant at birth exhibits an absence of coordinated responses, except those related to eating: sucking and swallowing, coughing and retching.

At the interface between the child's senses, particularly touch, and the world are some highly discrete responses under subcortical control. These responses, obviously unconditioned, but nevertheless highly refined, are the basis for the beginning of the proprium; they provide a sense of bodily self, the first of seven aspects of selfhood that Gordon Allport (1961) describes as the proprium, or selfness, of an individual (C. Hall and Lindzey, 1970, pp. 268–269).

In addition to the coordinated responses related to eating, searching, in response to hunger or stimulation of the midline of the upper lip, and eyeblinking represent rather sophisticated unconditioned responses. These few reflexes or unconditioned responses, mediated in the subcortical centers of the nervous system, do not meet the criteria for being perceptions or cognitive responses. At birth, the child literally makes no cognitive analysis of sensory events that surround him.

Between birth and the functional use of language, at about two-and-a-half to three years, a rapid prerequisite development of his perceptual and cognitive faculties enables the child to cope effectively with his increasingly complex world. This process of cognition and the related perceptual organization play a vital role in the difference in intellectual growth noted in children from deprived and enriched environments. The primary focus of the present chapter is on this process of sensory organization, perception, and cognition.

The early development of the thinking process of the child has two important dimensions. First is the sensory process by which the child becomes aware of his surroundings and begins to attend to discriminated stimuli in a world that is subjecting him to massive stimulus bombardment, after the prenatal period of sensory deprivation and isolation. Second is the process by which these now distinct sensory impressions are combined into meaning. This latter perceptual and cognitive development Piaget refers to as transformations; the process of knowing the stimuli in one's environment takes place by combining, taking apart, reassembling, and displacing both the raw sensation and often the material object that produces the sensation. These cognitive manipulations of the raw, incoming sensory data form the building blocks upon which later intelligence is built. Not only the stimulus richness but also the sensory manipulation are the bases that develop intelligence.

Sensory deprivation, whether from a deprived, bleak environment or from massive, sensory-motor deficits that block reception or manipulation, is probably one of the major determinants of abnormal or primitive thinking in the child, and may well be one significant cause of mental subnormality. One has only to watch a young child at work, examining, manipulating, modifying, losing, finding a simple sensory object such as a rattle, to understand this process of transformation. In a matter of moments, the rattle becomes a fan, a club, a sucker, a light, a brush, a speck, a pry bar, a flag, a baton, a hammer, and so on endlessly as it is handled, manipulated, and experienced in the transforming of this external object into an internal one, or in what the Gestalt psychologist refers to as psychophysical parallelism.

The present chapter will examine the onset of cognitive and perceptual development, its relation to environmental stimulation as well as to genetic predispositions, and thus lead up to the age of three, at which time most authorities believe begins the operation of a language structure inherent to adult intelligence. This area of child psychology, still somewhat speculative, owes considerable debt to a few brilliant investigators who have spent an extensive amount of time in face-to-face interaction with the developing infant as he apprehends his environment. The best data come from those investigators who have concentrated on observing the child in his natural environment with minimum intrusion into his perceptual world. Long, tedious hours of observation of young children at work on the task of deciphering and experiencing their world make up the laboratory of the cognitive psychologist.

The focus of the chapter will be on the nature of the response mechanism of the developing infant as he apprehends the various degrees and kinds of early environmental stimulation, and on the cognitive style that enables the child to translate the raw sensory data into the conceptual framework of intelligence. Not truly language development, cognition is the acquisition of the operations or processes by which the prelinguistic conceptual building blocks are laid.

SENSORY ACUITY OF THE INFANT

"Experience and practice teach us to use our senses and perceive correctly" (Dietrich Tiedemann, 1787, trans. Murchison and Langer, 1927, p. 205). And the newborn infant immediately begins the process of learning what his senses have to teach him. Our discussion of the child's perceptual and cognitive development begins with the sensory processes of the neonate.

VISION

Although various levels of maturity at birth make for individual differences in infants, convincing evidence suggests that the newborn visually is sensitive and responsive mainly to level of illumination: generally, the child's behavior is inhibited by light and enhanced by darkness. The pupillary reflex, present at birth, is not yet refined: "during the infant's first day or two, only a light or a dark room will make the infant's pupils contract or dilate, and even then the reflex may operate slowly" (Sutton-Smith, 1973, p. 121). Within a few weeks of birth, moderate changes in illumination stimulate the pupillary reflex (Pratt, 1934, 1954).

Any clarity of retinal image in the neonate is unlikely: the fovia and ocular motor muscles are not yet fully developed and the eyeball itself has not yet achieved mature proportions. The adult eye is approximately double in size and weight.

In spite of some tracking movement of the eyes, such attending by the neonate is rather passive, uncontrolled, and slow, giving the impression of being under the control of the optic nerve reflexes rather than under voluntary control. The same is true of the pupillary reflex and blinking, which gives the glass-eye stare so typical of the newborn child.

Eye control obviously improves with maturation: in the newborn, sustained or accurate fixation is rare; the newborn has little capacity for smooth pursuit movements or binocular fixation. "But infants of only two or three days will follow a flashlight's beam" (Sutton-Smith, 1973, p. 121).

Convergence, focusing of both eyes to produce one image, functions at about two months. During the first four weeks the infant focuses on objects only about eight inches away. At eight weeks, he begins accommodating for greater distances. At sixteen weeks, he can accommodate as well as an adult.

During the first eight to twelve weeks, the infant is attracted visually to objects with movement, contour lines, and sharp contrasts. After six months, sometimes as early as four months, he can recognize things and people. As early as ten weeks he can recognize depth, and at six months he is sure enough to trust his judgment about depth (Gibson and Walk, 1960): further research has indicated that infants may learn depth perception (Walk, 1966).

Various estimates have been made of the visual acuity of young children, but technical problems and measurement difficulties make these estimates somewhat crude. However, most investigators estimate the Snellen notation of the newborn to be approximately 20/150 (Spears and Hohle, 1967, p. 68); the infant sees at 20 feet about what the average adult sees at 150 feet. The visual acuity of the human infant is slow to develop, unstable, and not as significant to the sensory proprium of the infant as are several other of his senses (Champneys, 1881; G. S. Hall, 1891b; Pratt, Nelson, and Sun, 1930; Ling, 1942; Pratt, 1954; Dayton and M. H. Jones, 1964; Hershenson, 1964; I. Mann, 1964; Doris and Cooper, 1966; Spears and Hohle, 1967; Kessen, Haith, and Salapatek, 1970).

Color Discrimination

Even so, long after a child demonstrates a rather well-developed visual acuity, stable color discrimination is lacking, probably resulting to some extent from the difficulty in controlling for brightness, although Albrecht Peiper, Professor Emeritus of Leipzig University, felt that he had demonstrated the Purkinje effect in infants; Peiper felt that the brightness value of colors was similar for infants and adults. The best evidence suggests that color discrimination per se probably does not appear until three months, and is not stable until four-and-a-half to five months.

This slowness in color discrimination may account for the lack of agreement regarding color preference, which has plagued the literature. Although many studies suggest a preference for one color over another, agreement is so slight that these results must be explained upon the basis of methodological problems and random errors, or perhaps upon individual differences or a lack of consistency even in a particular child; researchers do agree, however, that infants prefer color to noncolor (Trincker and Trincker, 1955; Spears and Hohle, 1967).

Shape Discrimination

Perhaps this lack of stability in color discrimination and preference results from the child's decided use of form or shape as the dominant dimension in matching or making choices. Not until he is almost four does color play a major role in the child's matching procedure, and then only for about a two-year period, during which color utilization becomes heavy, only to revert to an inferior position to form by the time the child is school age. This choice of form over color is perhaps social in origin, since little of our world is color coded; most information comes to the child from changes in the figure-ground patterns and not from color contrasts (Brian and Goodenough, 1929).

Summary

A curious set of conditions interacts to affect the utilization of the young child's sense of sight, which refers not only to visual acuity, but also to color and brightness discrimination. The first, probably neurological in origin, relates directly to the development of the neurosensory system according to the preprogrammed genetic unfolding we call maturation. During the first few weeks of childhood, the sense of sight, from a strictly neurological and mechanical point of view, is unstable, nonacute, poorly differentiated, and not at all well calibrated. The second, affecting the young child's utilization of his sense of sight, centers around the functional utility of this sense in his life space. In early childhood, the sense of sight is of little adaptive significance to the child.

The lack of neurological stability and maturity, together with a lack of functional utility, tends to retard the development of the sense of sight, as such conditions would retard any psychophysical process. The use-it-or-lose-it phenomenon is never more sharply in focus than in relation to sensory acuity.

In those situations where, to affect his well-being the child does need to make meaningful discrimination of objects in his environment, his other senses provide more helpful information. In fact, for the first three months, the sense of sight provides the least helpful information in making these important judgments.

Take the problem of discriminating mother, a vital person, who feeds, bathes, rocks, soothes, and in short, meets the critical needs of the child during his early childhood. But she never looks the same. She changes her clothes, consequently her color, at least once a day, and often, thanks to the behavior of the child, she may change all or part of her clothes two or three times a day, each change bringing a different set of colors, none of which is color-coded for information. The shading of her clothes and skin also changes during the day, depending upon the surrounding light. Her shape changes greatly, in relation to position, profile, dress, and hair style. In short, mother never is mother because of the way she looks. Only much later in the child's life does he learn that how she looks, meaning the facial expression she maintains, does indeed affect his well-being.

Reading Readiness

With the beginning of early childhood, the sense of sight—visual acuity and color perception—has great significance for the development of the capacity we refer to as reading readiness, the prereading skill that involves a high degree of visual acuity and color discrimination. The child deficient in his visual sense is indeed handicapped; if not given remediation or compensation, he will fall seriously behind other children in normal intellectual and academic development.

Valid estimates of the child's visual acuity and color discrimination during early childhood are important to his well-being. During the preschool years, visual acuity moves into great significance in our society. Learning to read demands a high degree of visual-motor perceptual development. Parents, teachers, and other workers with children should pay close attention to the development of visual acuity in the young child, particularly when indications suggest genetic or perinatal factors, or an environment devoid of sensory stimulation that may cause a tendency toward a visual defect.

Many visual problems are indeed hereditary, and several diseases of prenatal life and early childhood tend to affect sight. Although rubella, German measles, contacted by the mother during the early months of pregnancy is one of the most prominent causes of childhood visual problems, blood incompatibility, such as an Rh mismatch, and venereal diseases of a less common type can contribute to the risk of visual defects. Certainly parents, who themselves had early-appearing visual problems, or find such conditions in close relatives, should pay close attention to the early development of their children, watching for signs of extreme nearsightedness, lack of recognition of familiar persons and objects, and difficulty in hand-eye coordination when picking up objects.

The importance of this early detection is underlined by studies of both animals and humans regarding the critical-period hypothesis of neurological development, which suggests that certain visual abilities result from experiences that alter the perceptual fields of the brain. Absence of these experiences in early childhood may well alter the long-range capability of the child. The newborn is able to attend visually and to respond differentially to different visual stimulation. Lipsitt (1970) points to visual stimulation of the young child as being perhaps as important to his later reading ability as tactile stimulation is to his later sociability.

AUDITION

At birth, the hearing mechanism of the human infant is not very efficient. The outer-ear chamber is filled with residual amniotic fluids from the long aqueous period of the child's life, and the middle-ear cavity is filled both with fluid and residual connective tissue that has not yet been absorbed. Because the middle ear is fluid-filled and interspersed with residual tissue, the ossicles, the mechanical part of the middle ear, are unable to function properly. Because of these physical conditions, the newborn child long had been assumed to be functionally deaf. Certainly the child responds to loud and sharp sounds, but the assumption had been that the child was responding not to sound waves per se, but to the resulting tactile vibrations of the skin and bones; that the "hearing" was a direct bone-conductance activation of the auditory nerve, rather than true hearing.

While this observation still appears to be technically correct, the child does have functional hearing long before he is born. Good evidence indicates that both the fetus and the newborn child respond to the full range of frequencies, although the threshold is rather high until the outer ear drains, or is cleared manually, and the middle ear absorbs the fluid and connective tissues that block the operation of the ossicles.

Within the first few days of birth, good behavioral evidence of hearing is present in terms of sound localization and specific threshold to tones. The very young child can be observed turning his head to track the changing location of a sound source (Pratt, Nelson, and Sun, 1930; Stubbs, 1934;

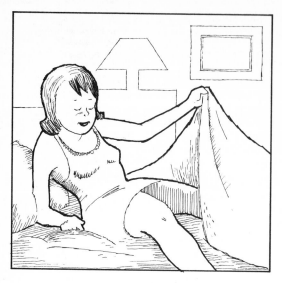 

L. Weiss, 1934). Not only continuous light stimulation but also continuous sound stimulation reduces the level of activity and arousal in infants (Stubbs, 1934; L. Weiss, 1934; Bartoshuk, 1962; Birns, Blank, Bridger, and Escalona, 1965; Brackbill, Adams, Crowell, and M. Gray, 1966; Spears and Hohle, 1967).

Where hearing acuity is questioned, either because of hereditary hearing defects or prenatal exposure to illness, the measurement of gross hearing loss in children is relatively simple. The most common methods involve sound-source location through the use of a bell or clacker, or the use of classical conditioning (described in more detail in Chapter 7), which consists of repeatedly pairing a tone with a mild shock to the foot of the child. Once the child has been conditioned to twitch his foot in anticipation of the shock following the tone, an accurate audiogram on the newborn child can be plotted relatively simply by varying both the volume and the pitch of the sound.

This technique is limited, however, in that several types of receptive aphasias (sensory-input confusion) do not involve pure-tone reception, but rather, complex sounds; thus, a child may be able to hear pure tones, but not be able to discriminate complex ones. At present, considerable research attempting to solve this measurement problem is underway; presently, the only way to be sure the child is hearing normally is through accurate behavioral observations of the child as his hearing becomes more functional.

Considerable evidence indicates that very early the child makes functional use of hearing. Quite early he learns to detect the sounds of mother or father on the way. Just the rustling sounds of mother or father stirring out of bed, the swish of bedroom slippers on the floor, or the rattle of bottles and warmers in the kitchen, are enough to start a relief response on the part of a hungry child. On the other hand, strange sounds that indicate something different in the child's world often are reacted to with consider-

able distress. The child, then, quickly learns that his sense of hearing provides useful information about his comfort, and thus he attends well to the sounds and vibrations around him. Some of his earliest concepts are formed in relationship to sounds.

Language Readiness

Although probably obvious, its importance makes it worth repeating, the major problem with poor hearing in infancy is what this defect does to the development of speech. Children who are deaf, or hard of hearing, or who have the condition of confused, garbled hearing, which we call receptive aphasia, are at a severe disadvantage and are frequently misdiagnosed as retarded or emotionally disturbed. The importance of adequate hearing in the infant cannot be overemphasized; its importance justifies repeated examination when there is any reason to question the child's sense of hearing.

Granted, most of the time, when a mother takes her young son to the pediatrician because "Doctor, he doesn't seem to hear me when I call him," it usually turns out to be what our pediatrician termed a serious case of selective hearing—hardheaded little boys who are resisting being tamed. But the embarassment on the part of the parent in facing the bemused comment of the long-suffering pediatrician that "He hears you all right" pales into insignificance when one finds something seriously wrong with the child's reception or processing of that vital stimulus, sound.

Summary

The sense of hearing is essential to the normal development of language in children. Just as healthy emotional maturation has a critical period in development, when, through his senses, an infant must learn to trust and love another, so speech and language have a critical period, when, through his sense of hearing a child must learn that oral, verbal communication is productive in affecting his environment for the better: a child learns speech first through his sense of hearing, and the effectiveness of careful, precise, considered language through verbalized interaction with those around him. A hearing deficiency is a heavy handicap indeed.

GUSTATION

Gustation, or the sense of taste, is probably the best-developed sense of the newborn. Very early in the fetal period, the fetus shows evidence of monitoring the taste of his environment; he draws the amniotic fluid in and out of his mouth, instantly responsive to changes in its taste. When, on occasion, the production of amniotic fluid is too great, to the point where the uterus is distended, the pressure can be regulated by the simple device of injecting saccharin into the fluid, which results in the fetus swallowing quantities of the solution. The concentration of saccharin seems to determine the amount that is swallowed. The swallowed fluid is then concentrated by the fetus and discharged through the umbilical cord, thereby reducing the pressure upon the mother and fetus, a phenomenon demonstrated as early as the fourth month of fetal life.

In addition, premature infants demonstrate distinctly different responses to salt-sour, bitter, and sweet tastes. The salt-sour taste provokes a tongue-thrusting, spitting kind of response; the bitter provokes a puckering, frowning response; and the sweet provokes a licking, smacking response. That these responses are subcortical in nature, under the control of the primitive centers of the brain, has long been known. However, recent studies of the behavior of children born without any brain, except the brain stem, indicate well-developed responses to these three tastes. These infants, both premature and brainless, gave a well-developed discrimination demonstration on a behavioral basis.

The four basic tastes, salt, sour, bitter, and sweet, appear to be detectable to young children. Both operant and classical conditioning can be used to demonstrate thresholds for each of these tastes. The combination of behavioral differences in responses and conditioning demonstrations makes the functioning of this basic sense of taste clearly evident long before any of the other senses are operating.

Note, however, that in the newborn human infant, to separate the sense of smell from that of taste is difficult, but undoubtedly, as the newborn infant surveys the world around him for the first time, his sense of taste is his most dependable receptor. No one who has observed a young child popping everything he can manage into his mouth can doubt the confidence with which children taste things; no one who has given a child a taste of bitter medicine can doubt that this outrage was fully recorded by the sensory process of the child.

Children obviously are dependent upon tasting to help them begin the necessary process of discriminating eatable objects. But this process is made much more complex by modern mechanical and synthetic food processing. That the old studies, which demonstrated the so-called wisdom of the body in the self-selection of a balanced diet by children, could be replicated today is doubtful. Synthetic odors, seasoning, coloring, and sweetening certainly have gone beyond the capacity of the infant's sense of taste.

OLFACTION

Evidently the sense of smell is well developed at birth, but the problem of measurement has prevented any sharp picture of the range and sensitivity of the child's perception of odors by this sense alone, in the absence of the sense of taste. Research in both embryology and physiology tends to suggest that the sense of smell, mediated as it is by the oldest, most primitive part of the brain, would be expected, along with the sense of taste, to be highly developed at birth. The recent studies of totally subcortical reception of smell and taste suggest that these senses are indeed very primitive phylogenetically.

These two senses are difficult to separate in psychological evaluations. For the sense of smell, the major difficulty is the absence of a clearly defined, unconditioned response to any smell that is not stringent and not subject to the contamination of taste. In addition to that problem, which is formidable enough, the human sense of smell suffers from a deterioration we refer to as accommodation—the process of adapting to an odor, such as chlorine or sulfur in the water, to the point where it is undetectable. This process is not simple nonattention, but an actual change in the receptor that makes for a lack of sensitivity.

Most studies of children's sense of smell, following the suggestion of Lipsitt, use the child's activity rate as an indication of threshold. That is, when stimulated by a faint odor, the child seems to begin an overall response of generally increased activity. His respiration rate increases, arms and legs thrash around, heart rate increases, pupils slightly dilate, and he begins to sniff, all of which suggest that he is sensitive to the given level of odor. The newborn has a wide range of discrimination power related to distinct odors; part of the food-seeking behavior of the child relates to his sense of smell.

An interesting side observation is that one of the most striking features of a psychotic child is his heightened sense or preoccupation with smell. Autistic children, those showing the earliest form of psychotic behavior, typically spend hours sniffing people and things in their environment. They are strongly attracted to stringent, dank odors and attempt to sniff body crevices and orifices as well as fecal material, all of which suggest a much more active functioning of the brain at a primitive level. This acute disturbance in a basic physiological process is one of the mainstays in the argument that childhood schizophrenia is probably an organically caused, genetic disease, and not just a learned emotional problem.

TOUCH

Good evidence seems to indicate that of all the human senses, the sense of touch is the most important from the point of view of the general psychological adjustment of the infant. The magic of touch comes both from the information touch provides the child about the nature of his world as he comes into contact with it, and from the all-important role touch plays in the social and emotional bond between the child and the significant others in his environment. Of course, the former is important. The child, after all, is protected by a thin and fragile outer shell; that he be able to sense rapidly those changes in his external world that forbode hazard or succor is imperative: the newborn child makes good use of his skin in sensing his world.

However, the latter, the social-emotional aspect, is probably the most critical to the development of human personality. Observations made of children born without a sense of touch indicate that they have serious emotional problems, particularly in forming close emotional ties with people around them. Of course, scientific caution would suggest that since such a sensory deprivation is so aberrant, other causes than the loss of touch may be responsible for the problem. Even so, lack of maternal body contact does indeed have serious consequences for the child as he matures.

The fetal period of life is, of course, a skin-to-skin period. In the normal course of human development, throughout the critical period of formation of human personality, the first two years of life, the child receives a great deal of his emotional contact through the skin. Breast feeding, bathing, fondling, kissing, stroking, rocking, brushing, swaddling, holding, bouncing, all of which are the normal experiences of most infants, convey to the child security, warmth, affection, and love. Montagu (1971), one of the most significant investigators of mother-child relationships, recently has written a scientifically valid, but poetic book, *Touching: The Human Significance of the Skin*, which elaborates the evidence of the critical importance of the sense of touch. The Harlows have spent a lifetime in careful research on the mother-child interaction through their investigation of the pattern of mothering in monkeys.

Significantly, touching the skin elicits the first response of the human fetus. By eight weeks of fetal age, a light stroke of a bristle on the midline of the upper lip produces a broad spectrum of motor response, as well as a rather specific puckering response, which is the precursor of the first adaptive behavior, sucking. At the time of birth, a wide range of responses can be elicited from the infant by stroking, blowing air, or brushing. Carmichael, one of the world's leading experts on the development of the behavior of the human infant, has concluded that,

> given a stimulus just above the lower threshold and a quiescent fetus in a standard posture, there is typically *one behavior act* or *reflex* set off by the stimulation of each cutaneous area. These cutaneous "push buttons" are remarkably specific in their behavioral relations when the complexity of the central nervous system is considered [1954, p. 142].

Shortly after birth, this network of neurological push buttons loses much of its specificity, replaced by many, highly variable, voluntary movements. During the fetal period and during the immediate postbirth phase of human life, the skin serves as the most important communication network between the child and his protectors. Whether the communication of emotions occurs during the final stages of pregnancy, as Montagu supposes, or not, certainly this vast and effective network has critical importance. Once the child is born, he depends upon his sense of touch for the development of his emotional ties. Simply watching a child in contact with his world through his skin, observing his obvious pleasure on physical contact, the importance of texture and temperature, all give convincing evidence of the importance of his sense of touch.

Since the early 1950s, Harlow and his associates have applied rigorous experimental techniques to the most fundamental problem in child psychology: the dimension of mother love. Harlow's study of monkeys and their babies provided the procedural control necessary to study empirically a poetic quality. They studied a single complex dimension of the mothering process, the skin contact between the two, from the point of view of the kinesthetic and warmth interaction. Their results indicate that in the process of mothering, at least as it is displayed in its primitive form between monkeys and their infants, the single dimension of tactile stimulation clearly seemed to be the most critical.

Even when all of the physical needs of the baby monkeys were met, adequate food, warmth, isolation from infection, and the like, they failed to thrive: the maternal warmth and the tactile stimulation provided by a fur-like surface proved to be indispensable for normal growth. These observations led Harlow to assume that skin-to-skin contact provided the essential building block upon which the mother-child relationship is founded. Those monkeys raised on a terry-cloth surrogate mother did well except in certain social situations, where the absence of imitation learning made these monkeys socially and sexually aberrant. The males in particular were inept and disinterested in mating, when they had not had social contact during infancy; and the females failed as mothers when they had not had social contact during infancy.

Although Harlow reports that body contact between infant and mother is of overpowering importance, in the intervening years since his first publication on the nature of love, he has observed additional elements in monkey mothering—elements which, although not as crucial as the tactile stimulation element, are nevertheless important. Harlow has shown that emotional security provided for the infant by the mother allows the infant to explore strange situations and participate in play, which "is the variable of primary importance in the development of normal social, sexual, and maternal functions." Harlow's data "imply that an infant visually responds to the earliest version of mother he encounters, that the mother he grows accustomed to is the mother he relies upon."

He has found rocking motion to be "a variable of more than statistical significance, particularly early in the infant's life, in binding the infant to the mother figure." And warmth was a significant variable for the very young infant. Being raised with a warm surrogate mother, as contrasted with a cold one, affected the monkey's later behavior. More comfort is provided for infant monkeys by warm and mobile mothers than by cold and stationary ones.

Note in Harlow's recent article, in addition to the factual information and the implications of his research, the style of scientific writing. Harlow has mastered this incredible style of writing precisely, correctly, and scientifically, while at the same time writing so as to provide a high level of interest, entertainment, and scientific seductiveness.

The intriguing concept of imprinting continues to be important in Harlow's work: most, if not all, of our primary emotional responses are learned in a classical-conditioning paradigm. The basic physiological stimulation provided an infant may have much to do with his ultimate unfolding as a human being.

Because of the seminal importance of his work and his brilliant writing style, Harlow's permission was obtained to reprint this summary of his lifetime effort.

NATURE OF LOVE—SIMPLIFIED[1]

Harry F. Harlow and Stephen J. Suomi
University of Wisconsin

The cloth surrogate and its wire surrogate sibling (see Figure 1) entered into scientific history as of 1958 (Harlow, 1958). The cloth surrogate was originally designed to test the relative importance of body contact in contrast to activities associated with the breast, and the results were clear beyond all expectation. Body contact was of overpowering importance by any measure taken, even contact time, as shown in Figure 2.

However, the cloth surrogate, beyond its power to measure the relative importance of a host of variables determining infant affection for the mother, exhibited another surprising trait, one of great independent usefulness. Even though the cloth mother was inanimate, it was able to impart to its infant such emotional security that the infant would, in the surrogate's presence, explore a strange situation and manipulate available physical objects (see Figure 3), or animate objects (see Figure 4). Manipulation of animate objects leads to play if these animate objects are age-mates, and play is the variable of primary importance in the development of normal social, sexual, and maternal functions, as described by Harlow and Harlow (1965). It is obvious that surrogate mothers, which are more docile and manipulative than real monkey mothers, have a wide range of experimental uses.

SIMPLIFIED SURROGATE

Although the original surrogates turned out to be incredibly efficient dummy mothers, they presented certain practical problems. The worst of the problems was that of cleanliness. Infant monkeys seldom soil their real mothers' bodies, though we do not know how this is achieved. However, infant monkeys soiled the bodies of the original cloth surrogates with such efficiency and enthusiasm as to present a health problem and, even worse, a financial problem resulting from laundering. Furthermore, we believed that the original cloth surrogate was too steeply angled and thereby relatively inaccessible for cuddly clinging by the neonatal monkey.

In the hope of alleviating practical problems inherent in the original cloth surrogate, we constructed a family of simplified surrogates. The simplified surrogate is mounted on a rod attached to a lead base 4 inches in diameter, angled upward at 25°, and projected through the surrogate's body for 4 inches, so that heads may be attached if desired. The body of the simplified surrogate is only

Reprinted, by permission of the authors and the publisher, from Harry F. Harlow and Stephen J. Suomi, Nature of love—simplified, *American Psychologist*, 1970, 25, 161–168.

[1] This research was supported by United States Public Health Service Grants MH-11894 and FR-0167 from the National Institutes of Health to the University of Wisconsin Primate Laboratory and Regional Primate Research Center, respectively.

Requests for reprints should be sent to Harry F. Harlow, Regional Primate Research Center, University of Wisconsin, Madison, Wisconsin 53706.

Cloth and wire surro-
gate mothers

Figure 2
Contact time to cloth and wire surrogate

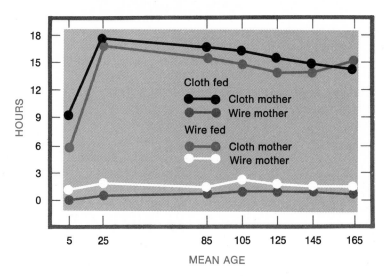

6 inches long, 2½ inches in diameter, and stands approximately 3 inches off the ground. Figure 5 shows an original cloth surrogate and simplified surrogate placed side by side.

As can be seen in Figure 6, infants readily cling to these simplified surrogates of smaller body and decreased angle of inclination. Infant monkeys do soil the simplified surrogate, but the art and act of soiling is very greatly reduced. Terry cloth slipcovers can be made easily and relatively cheaply, alleviating, if not eliminating, laundry problems. Thus, the simplified surrogate is a far more practical dummy mother than the original cloth surrogate.

lactation

Although the original surrogate papers (Harlow, 1958; Harlow and Zim-mermann, 1959) were written as if activities associated with the breast, partic-

SURROGATE
VARIABLES

Figure 3
Infant monkey se-
curity in presence of
cloth surrogate

Figure 4
Infant play in presence of surrogate

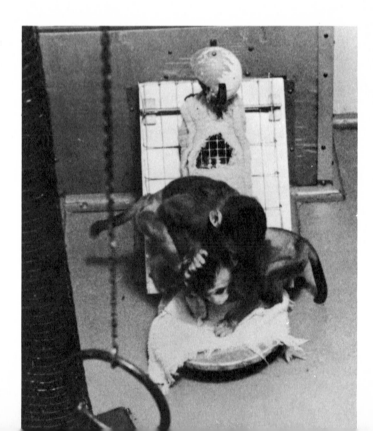

ularly nursing, were of no importance, this is doubtlessly incorrect. There were no statistically significant differences in time spent by the babies on the lactating versus nonlactating cloth surrogates and on the lactating versus nonlactating wire surrogates, but the fact is that there were consistent preferences for both the cloth and the wire lactating surrogates and that these tendencies held for both the situations of time on surrogate and frequency of surrogate preference when the infant was exposed to a fear stimulus. Thus, if one can accept a statistically insignificant level of confidence, consistently obtained from four situations, one will properly conclude that nursing is a minor variable but one of more than measurable importance operating to bind the infant to the mother.

To demonstrate experimentally that activities associated with the breasts were variables of significant importance, we built two sets of differently colored surrogates, tan and light blue; and using a 2 × 2 Latin square design, we arranged a situation such that the surrogate of one color lactated and the other did not. As can be seen in Figure 7, the infants showed a consistent preference for the lactating surrogate when contact comfort was held constant. The importance of the lactational variable probably decreases with time. But at least we had established the hard fact that hope springs eternal in the human breast and even longer in the breast, undressed.

facial variables

In the original surrogates we created an ornamental face for the cloth surrogate and a simple dog face for the wire surrogate. I was working with few available infants and against time to prepare a presidential address for the 1958 American Psychological Association Convention. On the basis of sheer intuition, I was convinced that the ornamental cloth-surrogate face would become a stronger fear stimulus than the dog face when fear of the unfamiliar matured in the monkeys from about 70 to 110 days (Harlow and Zimmermann, 1959;

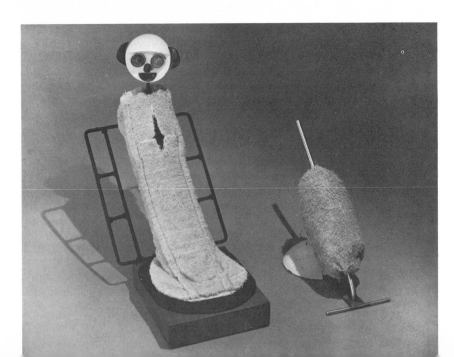

Figure 5
Original surrogate and
simplified surrogate

Figure 6
Infant clinging to simplified surrogate

Figure 7
Infant preference for lactating cloth surrogate

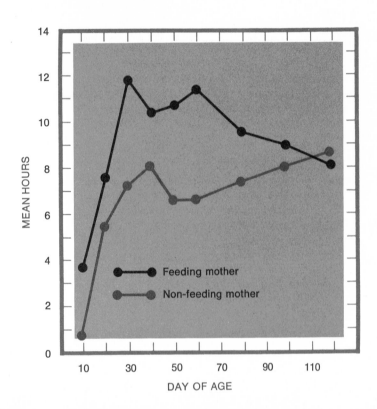

Sackett, 1966). But since we wanted each surrogate to have an identifiable face and had few infants, we made no effort to balance faces by resorting to a feebleminded 2 × 2 Latin square design.

Subsequently, we have run two brief unpublished experiments. We tested four rhesus infants unfamiliar with surrogate faces at approximately 100 days of age and found that the ornamental face was a much stronger fear stimulus than the dog face. Clearly, the early enormous preference for the cloth surrogate over the wire surrogate was not a function of the differential faces. Later, we raised two infants on cloth and two on wire surrogates, counterbalancing the ornamental and dog faces. Here, the kind of face was a nonexistent variable. To a baby all maternal faces are beautiful. A mother's face that will stop a clock will not stop an infant.

The first surrogate mother we constructed came a little late, or phrasing it another way, her baby came a little early. Possibly her baby was illegitimate. Certainly it was her first baby. In desperation we gave the mother a face that was nothing but a round wooden ball, which displayed no trace of shame. To the baby monkey this featureless face became beautiful, and she frequently caressed it with hands and legs, beginning around 30–40 days of age. By the time the baby had reached 90 days of age we had constructed an appropriate ornamental cloth-mother face, and we proudly mounted it on the surrogate's body. The baby took one look and screamed. She fled to the back of the cage and cringed in autistic-type posturing. After some days of terror the infant solved the Medusa-mother problem in a most ingenious manner. She revolved the face 180° so that she always faced a bare round ball! Furthermore, we could rotate the maternal face dozens of times and within an hour or so the infant would turn it around 180°. Within a week the baby resolved her unfaceable problem once and for all. She lifted the maternal head from the body, rolled it into the corner and abandoned it. No one can blame the baby. She had lived with and loved a faceless mother, but she could not love a two-faced mother.

These data imply that an infant visually responds to the earliest version of mother he encounters, that the mother he grows accustomed to is the mother he relies upon. Subsequent changes, especially changes introduced after maturation of the fear response, elicit this response with no holds barred. Comparisons of effects of baby-sitters on human infants might be made.

body-surface variables

We have received many questions and complaints concerning the surrogate surfaces, wire and terry cloth, used in the original studies. This mountain of mail breaks down into two general categories: that wire is aversive, and that other substances would be equally effective if not better than terry cloth in eliciting a clinging response.

The answer to the first matter in question is provided by observation: Wire is not an aversive stimulus to neonatal monkeys, for they spend much time climbing on the sides of their hardware-cloth cages and exploring this substance orally and tactually. A few infants have required medical treatment from protractedly pressing their faces too hard and too long against the cage sides. Obviously, however, wire does not provide contact comfort.

In an attempt to quantify preference of various materials, an exploratory study[2] was performed in which each of four infants was presented with a choice between surrogates covered with terry cloth versus rayon, vinyl, or rough-grade sandpaper. As shown in Figure 8, the infants demonstrated a clear preference for the cloth surrogates, and no significant preference difference between the other body surfaces. An extension of this study is in progress in which an attempt is being made to further quantify and rank order the preference for these materials by giving infants equal exposure time to all four materials.

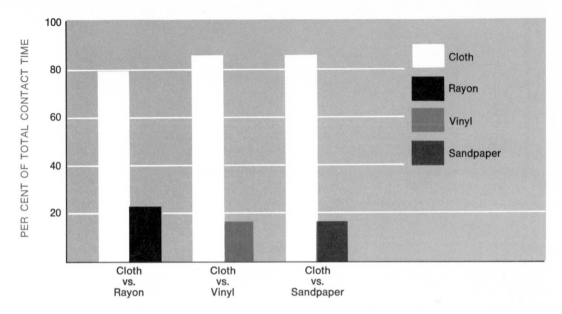

Figure 8
Effect of surface on surrogate contact

motion variables

In the original two papers, we pointed out that rocking motion, that is, proprioceptive stimulation, was a variable of more than statistical significance, particularly early in the infant's life, in binding the infant to the mother figure. We measured this by comparing the time the infants spent on two identical planes, one rocking and one stationary (see Figure 9), and two identical cloth surrogates, one rocking and one stationary (see Figure 10).

[2] We wish to thank Carol Furchner, who conducted this experiment and the described experiment in progress.

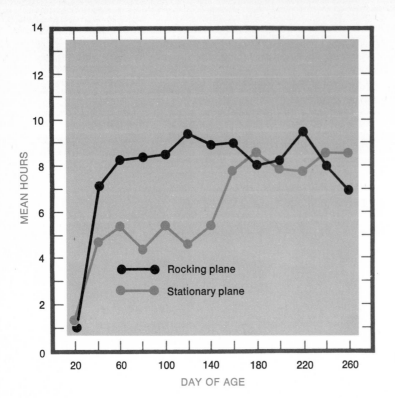

Figure 9
Infant contact to stationary and rock-ing planes

Figure 10
Infant contact to stationary and rock-ing surrogates

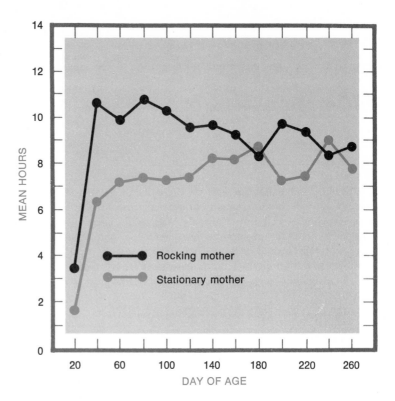

To study another variable, temperature, we created some "hot mamma" surrogates. We did this by inserting heating coils in the maternal bodies that raised the external surrogate body surface about 10°F. In one experiment, we heated the surface of a wire surrogate and let four infant macaques choose between this heated mother and a room-temperature cloth mother. The data are presented in Figure 11. The neonatal monkeys clearly preferred the former. With increasing age this difference decreased, and at approximately 15 days the preference reversed. In a second experiment, we used two differentially colored cloth surrogates and heated one and not the other. The infants preferred the hot surrogate, but frequently contacted the room-temperature surrogate for considerable periods of time.

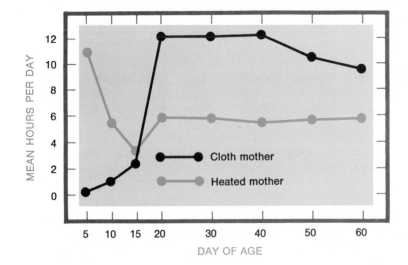

Figure 11
Infant contact to heated-wire and
room-temperature cloth surrogates

More recently, a series of ingenious studies on the temperature variable has been conducted by Suomi, who created hot- and cold-running surrogates by adaptation of the simplified surrogate. These results are important not only for the information obtained concerning the temperature variable but also as an illustration of the successful experimental use of the simplified surrogate itself.

The surrogates used in these exploratory studies were modifications of the basic simplified surrogate, designed to get maximum personality out of the minimal mother. One of these surrogates was a "hot mamma," exuding warmth from a conventional heating pad wrapped around the surrogate frame and completely covered by a terry cloth sheath. The other surrogate was a cold female; beneath the terry cloth sheath was a hollow shell within which her life fluid—cold water—was continuously circulated. The two surrogates are illustrated in Figure 12, and to the untrained observer they look remarkably similar. But looks can be deceiving, especially with females, and we felt that in these

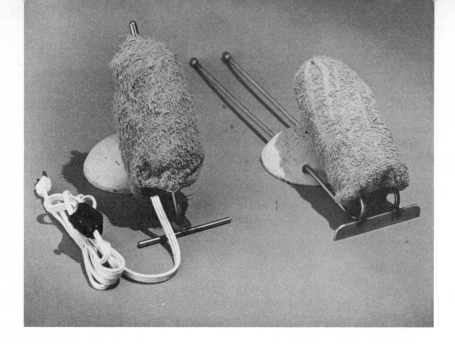

EARLY PERCEPTUAL
AND COGNITIVE
DEVELOPMENT

Figure 12
Warm (left) and cold
simplified surrogates

similar-looking surrogates we had really simulated the two extremes of woman-hood—one with a hot body and no head, and one with a cold shoulder and no heart. Actually, this is an exaggeration, for the surface temperature of the hot surrogate was only 7°F. above room temperature, while the surface tempera-ture of the cold surrogate was only 5°F. below room temperature.

In a preliminary study, we raised one female infant from Day 15 on the warm surrogate for a period of four weeks. Like all good babies she quickly and completely became attached to her source of warmth, and during this time she exhibited not only a steadily increasing amount of surrogate contact but also began to use the surrogate as a base for exploration (see Figure 13). At the end of this four-week period we decided that our subject had become spoiled enough and so we replaced the warm surrogate with the cold version for one week. The infant noticed the switch within two minutes, responding by huddling in a corner and vocalizing piteously. Throughout the week of bitter maternal cold, the amount of surrogate contact fell drastically; in general, the infant avoided the surrogate in her feeding, exploratory, and sleeping behaviors. Feeling some-what guilty, we switched surrogates once more for a week and were rewarded for our efforts by an almost immediate return to previously high levels of sur-rogate contact. Apparently, with heart-warming heat, our infant was capable of forgiveness, even at this tender age. At this point, we switched the two sur-rogates daily for a total two weeks, but by this time the infant had accepted the inherent fickle nature of her mothers. On the days that her surrogate was warm, she clung tightly to its body, but on the days when the body was cold, she gen-erally ignored it, thus providing an excellent example of naïve behaviorism.

With a second infant we maintained this procedure but switched the sur-rogates, so that he spent four weeks with the cold surrogate, followed by one week with the warm, an additional week with the cold, and finally a two-week period in which the surrogates were switched daily. This infant became anything

Figure 13
Infant clinging to and
exploring from warm
simplified surrogate

Figure 14
Typical infant reactions
to cold simplified sur-
rogate

but attached to the cold surrogate during the initial four-week period, spending most of his time huddling in the corner of his cage and generally avoiding the surrogate in his exploratory behavior (see Figure 14). In succeeding weeks, even with the warm surrogate, he failed to approach the levels of contact exhibited by the other infant to the cold surrogate. Apparently, being raised with a cold mother had chilled him to mothers in general, even those beaming warmth and comfort.

Two months later both infants were exposed to a severe fear stimulus in the presence of a room-temperature simplified surrogate. The warm-mother infant responded to this stimulus by running to the surrogate and clinging for dear life. The cold-mother infant responded by running the other way and seeking security in a corner of the cage. We seriously doubt that this behavioral difference can be attributed to the sex difference of our subjects. Rather, this demonstration warmed our hopes and chilled our doubts that temperature may be a variable of importance. More specifically, it suggested that a simple linear model may not be adequate to describe the effects of temperature differences of surrogates on infant attachment. It is clear that warmth is a variable of major importance, particularly in the neonate, and we hazard the guess that elevated temperature is a variable of importance in the operation of all the affectional systems: maternal, mother-infant, possibly age-mate, heterosexual, and even paternal.

Recently we have simplified the surrogate mother further for studies in which its only function is that of providing early social support and security to infants. This supersimplified surrogate is merely a board 1½ inches in diameter and 10 inches long with a scooped-out, concave trough having a maximal depth of ¾ inch. As shown in Figure 15, the supersimplified surrogate has an angular deviation from the base of less than 15°, though this angle can be increased by the experimenter at will. The standard cover for this supremely simple surrogate mother is a size 11, cotton athletic sock, though covers of various qualities, rayon, vinyl (which we call the "linoleum lover"), and sandpaper, have been used for experimental purposes.

> Linoleum lover, with you I am through
> The course of smooth love never runs true.

This supersimplified mother is designed to attract and elicit clinging responses from the infant during the first 15 days of the infant's life.

We have designed, but not yet tested, a swinging mother that will dangle from a frame about 2 inches off the floor and have a convex, terry cloth or cotton body surface. Observations of real macaque neonates and mothers indicate that the infant, not the mother, is the primary attachment object even when the mother locomotes, and that this swinging mother may also elicit infantile clasp and impart infant security very early in life. There is nothing original in this day and age about a swinger becoming a mother, and the only new angle, if any, is a mother becoming a swinger.

Additional findings, such as the discovery that six-month social isolates will learn to cling to a heated simplified surrogate, and that the presence of a surrogate reduces clinging among infant-infant pairs, have substantiated use of the surrogate beyond experiments for its own sake. At present, the heated

PROSPECTIVES

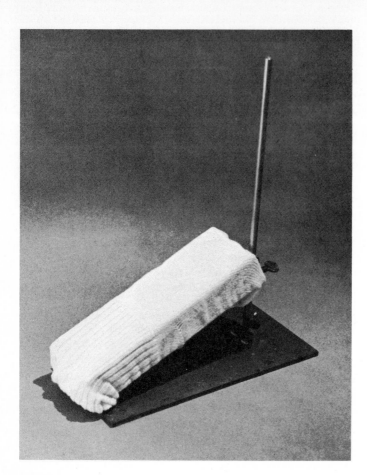

Figure 15
The supersimplified surrogate

simplified surrogate is being utilized as a standard apparatus in studies as varied as reaction to fear, rehabilitation of social isolates, and development of play. To date, additional research utilizing the cold version of the simplified surrogate has been far more limited, possibly because unused water faucets are harder to obtain than empty electrical outlets. But this represents a methodological, not a theoretical problem, and doubtlessly solutions will soon be forthcoming.

It is obvious that the surrogate mother at this point is not merely a historical showpiece. Unlike the proverbial old soldier, it is far from fading away. Instead, as in the past, it continues to foster not only new infants but new ideas.

HARLOW, H. F. 1958. The nature of love, *American Psychologist*, 13:673–85.
HARLOW, H. F., AND M. K. HARLOW. 1965. The affectional systems, in A. M. Schrier, **REFERENCES**

H. F. Harlow, and F. Stollnitz, eds., *Behavior of nonhuman primates*, Vol. 2. New York: Academic Press.

HARLOW, H. F., AND R. R. ZIMMERMANN. 1959. Affectional responses in the infant monkey, *Science*, 130: 421–32.

SACKETT, G. P. 1966. Monkeys reared in visual isolation with pictures as visual input: Evidence for an innate releasing mechanism, *Science*, 154: 1468–72.

KINESTHESIA

The kinesthetic sense, the sense of body movement, plays an important part in the early psychological adjustment of the human infant. His response to motion not only appears to provide important orienting information, but provides pleasure, comfort, and security at a stage when other forms of interpersonal communication are weak and somewhat ineffectual. Children early have a sense of motion and rhythm, and not only respond to but produce body movements that seem to have important meaning to themselves, as well as enabling them to communicate to significant others in their world.

The comforting of infants by rocking is, of course, an obviously important dimension of early parent-child interaction, but the rather startling tendency for some children, particularly premature infants, to be rockers or headbangers gives rise to some interesting speculation regarding the relationship between the security of the child and the amount and kind of body motion encountered in the last few weeks of fetal life. In the last two months of the period in the uterus, the weight of the fetus, combined with the general loosening of the structure of the pelvic girdle and a sagging of the muscles that hold up the uterus, results in a rapid increase in the amount and kind of movement the child experiences. This swaying, rocking sensation seems to play an important part in the development of the emotional dimension of a child's total personality.

Many children, particularly premature children, are given to rocking back and forth when placed in a prone position with their knees drawn up under them; these same children often will move forward in the bed until their head is at the headboard and then rock and bang against the headboard until they cause every screw and joint of the bed to loosen and collapse. Children, who develop normally as far as we can determine, will bang their heads against the headboard for hours at a time. Some hospitals have placed premature infants in special rocking incubators so that they can experience several weeks of rather vigorous rocking, and thereby prevent the child from becoming a head-banger, and at the same time produce a more comfortable and evidently happier child.

Obviously, then, the human infant is programmed to expect, to seek, to create, and to enjoy kinesthetic stimulation, which provides a necessary input into the healthy infant during the first few months of life. How this sense operates is not generally understood, except that it obviously is related to the deep-muscle movement in accommodation to postural changes and sway. How it functions is not so important as the fact that it does function and is a significant dimension of child-rearing and personality development.

Obviously, the newborn child is fully in touch with his environment at the moment of birth. He has at his disposal, coming in through his sensory organs, with little or no voluntary control at first, a vast range of information about his environment. This sensory input is massive, multiple-dimensioned, and evidently somewhat traumatic to a child who has been living in a rather quiet, static environment.

Sensory flooding through multiple sense organs would seem to be a fact of life. At first the child lacks the ability to suppress, enhance, or divert attention from one modality to another. Whatever stimulation is the largest, sharpest, or the greatest deviation from the background seems to predominate in the child's world; the art of attending takes him some little while to develop.

JEAN PIAGET

The child's development of the ability to process his world has attracted the attention of many investigators, who have addressed themselves to studying how the child makes sense out of his senses: how he learns to deal effectively with the important events in his life.

Obviously the sensory world of a child requires special study. For many years we knew little about the beginnings of the process by which sensory input becomes cognitive material upon which the operations of reasoning, thinking, and creativity are performed. For a time, the early cognitive world of the child defied scientific inquiry. How was the scientist to penetrate the child's world when the child lacked the elaborate language capacity with which to explain how he goes through the process of interpreting his rich sensory world?

In 1927, a Swiss zoologist, taxonomist, and epistemologist, concerned about the process of classifying behavior into a logical system, became interested in the behavior of young children. Jean Piaget, like the famous zoologist Charles Darwin before him, began his scientific inquiry into the cognition of childhood through the vehicle of his own children.

Piaget became insatiably curious about the manner in which the child learns to process his environment, and spent many hours, in the best tradition of the naturalist, in unobtrusive observation of young children, singly and in small groups, as they developed styles of operations by which they made meaning out of the crowded sensory pathways. Only after years of careful observation of the natural behavior of children at play did he begin his tradition of research, which is itself a form of child's play by which Piaget injects himself into the logic system of very young children.

Never really interested in the large, normative studies of intellectual growth that dominated American research in the early 1930s and 1940s, Piaget's most useful function has been as a catalyst, stimulating the thinking of other investigators. Nor is Piaget without his detractors; from the beginning, he was engaged in a controversy regarding his basic tenet.

For thinking to develop in discrete stages is fundamental to Piaget's genetic approach to cognitive development in children. Even though most other physiological and perceptual aspects of human development seem to to continuous in nature, and in fact seem to be given to a great deal of fluctuation, with advancement and regression being the rule, such is not the case with logical thinking, so says Piaget. The development of logical thinking represents, according to Piaget, the application of a set of operations that either are used or not used; but once they are placed in use, the whole cognitive style of the child is altered permanently.

To use a crude analogy from motor performance, once the child has learned to pick up small objects between his thumb and forefinger, he will never again pick them up between his elbows. The principle of manual opposition between these powerful and versatile tools in operation is so vivid, so effective, and so obviously necessary, that the child is forever changed by his discovery. Just so, according to Piaget, the genetically determined but serendipitously applied mental operation that represents a state in cognitive development is so dominant an experience that reversibility is inconceivable.

Whether these stages are indeed discrete, and particularly, whether they are irreversible, is certainly open to question, both from a theoretical point of view and from a commonsense point of view; the argument is not a frivolous one: but the theoretical implications are far more important than the practical ones. The focus of this book is, of course, upon the practical implications.

To take but a moment, however, to understand the nature of these theoretical arguments, in the early 1940s, Huang (1943) and Oakes (1945) attacked the discrete-stage idea through the simple demonstration that even the most intelligent adult uses all stages of logic, depending upon his knowledge in a particular area and also upon his emotionality level. All of us are aware of the degree of primitive thinking that can accompany high frustration: many sophisticated adults, even child psychology professors, have been known to speak in "unknown tongues" to a stalled car in the morning rush-hour; at such times the logical operations are indeed primitive—Neanderthal in fact. These early detractors, and others since, simply have been unwilling to accept the discreteness, purity, and irreversibility of cognitive operations. Just as the Freudian stages of sexual development have failed to demonstrate either theoretical cause or practical proof of discreteness and irreversibility, so the Piaget tradition has failed to demonstrate this discreteness as fact.

While on the subject of detractors, also fundamental to Piaget's argument is a biological-clock tradition that assumes great significance for maturation at each stage: until the hereditary sequence of readiness is passed, specific development is not possible; and conversely, if the hereditary stage arrives and is not utilized, the opportunity is lost almost irretrievably. A number of investigators have demonstrated that training can alter the natural developmental rate of logical thinking; but note that most of these arguments come from research with children in the late preschool years, rather than with children under two.

PIAGET'S LANGUAGE

Before we discuss Piaget's concept of prelanguage cognitive development, we need to look at Piaget's language. For Piaget, some words have meaning unique to his theory (Beard, 1969; Furth, 1969; Phillips, 1969).

Schema

The structural units in Piaget's cognitive development system, schemas are well-defined sequences of physical or mental actions that form the basic building blocks of intelligence. In its simplest form, a schema is a reflex; in its more complex form, a general, connected pattern of internal or external responses.

For Piaget, a schema begins with the mental connection between two previously independent cognitive or sensory-motor events. When a schema has been constructed, a functional relationship has been found in the cognitive or sensory-motor world of the child. No distinction is made in levels of consciousness, awareness, or deliberateness. A schema can be active or passive, have a high or low probability of influence, be verbal or nonverbal. A schema is a personal discovery that once made is never truly lost.

Schemas generally are labeled by the behavioral sequence to which they refer, i.e., the schema of sucking. However, the label that refers to the overt behavior does not restrict the concept of schema, which refers to the whole cognitive, symbolic, sensory-motor act and, finally, the underlying plan of action or stragegy, the scheme.

Function

When Piaget refers to the biologically inherited manner of interacting with the environment, he uses the term *function*, which refers to those general intellectual capacities that cut across all ages: motor-memory process, sensory-memory process, and perceptual-memory process. Piaget holds that function remains invariant, but as the child develops, structure changes systematically.

> To use a simple and somewhat imprecise capsule definition, *function* is concerned with the manner in which any organism makes cognitive progress; *content* refers to the external behavior which tells us that functioning has occurred; and *structure* refers to the inferred organizational properties which explain why this content rather than some other content has emerged [Flavell, 1963, p. 18].

Content

For Piaget, content refers to the observable input and output of the child, what the behaviorists call the stimulus-response sequence. The content, the overt events in the child's world—what is happening—allows for research on the cognition of the child because content provides the basic data from which the inferences regarding structure and function are made.

Structure

Structures are the mediators between the invariant basic biological functions of the child and his rapidly changing behavioral and sensory content. Structures, the organizational pattern of intellect, are the basic stuff of cognition; although not directly observable, they can be understood through observing the behavior of children. In describing the nature of structure, Piaget has made his greatest contribution.

Piaget uses organization and the two components of adaptation, assimilation and accommodation, to isolate the abstract properties of intelligence-in-action, to define function.

Organization

"Every act of intelligence presumes some kind of intellectual structure, some sort of organization, within which it proceeds" (Flavell, 1963, p. 46). The specific characteristics of this organization vary from stage to stage in development.

Organization of experience is an expansion of adaptation by means of a wide variety of mental activities such as memory, perception, and experimentation. In the process of organization, many schemas are combined into larger and larger schematic systems to deal with an increasingly complex environment. As the child grows older, he becomes increasingly aware of organization and begins consciously to engage in the process.

Organization consists of a constant interplay of discrimination (noticing differences) and generalization (noticing similarities) of environmental elements that can be manipulated by schemas. The pervasive controlling schema, the temper tantrum, which sometimes works and sometimes doesn't, gradually is understood by Waldo as a mechanism; he learns to read the signs correctly: he learns that a temper tantrum just as mother and daddy are leaving for an important engagement with daddy's boss provides him with chances about 8 to 5, and probably 9 to 1, that he can stay up and look at two more TV shows and maybe extend that to include an ice cream, without the slightest risk to himself.

Piaget believed that external actions as well as thought processes have logical organization, that "logic stems from a sort of spontaneous organization of acts" (Flavell, 1963, p. 2).

Organization is inseparable from adaptation: They are two complementary processes of a single mechanism.... These two aspects of thought are indissociable:

It is by adapting to things that thought organizes itself and it is by organizing it-self that it structures things [Piaget, 1952b, pp. 7–8, as quoted by Flavell, 1963, pp. 47–48].

Adaptation

Organization of experience cannot be effective without the reception and registration of experience—adaptation, the adjustment to the environment through assimilation (incorporation of new objects and experiences) and accommodation (modification according to experience). Adaptation occurs when, as a result of experience, the child is better able to cope with similar future experiences. Adaptation represents a perceptual reorganization of the child's mentality, which is fundamental to learning. Adaptation refers to the process by which the child adjusts his perceptual skills to the peculiarity of an object in his world.

Assimilation

When a child utilizes and incorporates something from his environment, he is assimilating, which changes the stimulation and the child. We perceive an object as we know it is, even though distance, light, or angle of view changes the way it actually looks. We invest objects with meaning, such as familiarity, beauty, utility, and thus perceive them, even though others may see them quite differently. We assimilate these objects.

A conceptual component of adaptation, assimilation is the process of restructuring events in the environment to make them more readily usable by the child. No event in the world is used by the child as it "really" is, but must be transformed to fit the perceptual network of the child.

> Associationism [or conditioning] conceives the relationship between stimulus and response in a unilateral manner: $S \rightarrow R$; whereas the point of view of assimilation presupposes a reciprocity: $S \rightleftarrows R$; this is to say, the input, the stimulus, is filtered through a structure that consists of action-schemes (or, at a higher level, the operations of thought), which in turn are modified and enriched when the subject's behavioral repertoire is accommodated to the demands of reality. The filtering or modification of the input is called *assimilation;* the modification of internal schemes to fit reality is called *accommodation* [Piaget and Inhelder, 1969, pp. 5–6].

Accommodation

Through a process of modifying the schemas and the signal system related to the schemas, the child becomes adapted to his environment. This coping process, essential to the healthy development of the child, is never-ending: he is never perfectly adapted since his environment changes, his ability to cope with his environment changes, and his own need system changes.

A child making changes in his behavior according to his past experience is accommodating, is learning through experience. Accommodation changes the schemas themselves as a result of new experiences, a gradual learning process involving trial and error, exploration, questioning, probing, and, in the broadest sense, experimentation. By combining motor and

sensory responses into complex schemas, the child succeeds in solving some problem that had been insoluble. Waldo learns to unwrap Christmas candy because he finds it tastes better with the cellophane removed. The process of clutching candy, unwrapping candy, and putting candy in his mouth becomes locked in forever. "Intelligent activity is always an active, organized process of assimilating the new to the old and of accommodating the old to the new" (Flavell, 1963, p. 17).

Equilibrium

Piaget conceives organisms as constantly seeking a state of equilibrium, which other authors might call health or maturity. Equilibration is the process by which organisms change from one state to another, the underlying regulatory process that continuously is changing, balancing, and unifying development and experience. A child grows, develops, matures, learns, because of a genetically compelling push for equilibrium with the environment.

Transformation

Piaget's concept of cognition makes him a perceptualist: he does not feel a valid distinction exists between subject and object. Transformation represents an interaction between the object and the child's ability to transform it. In a simple example, concepts such as hot and cold emerge from a sensory acuity, a temperature tolerance, and a biochemical dimension of the human body, not solely from the physical property of the object—temperature: the perception by the body and the property of temperature are transformed into a concept of hot or cold.

Internalization

A young child first internalizes the outside world through eidetic imagery: visual images stored in the mind for instant replay. Because eidetic memories can become fused, transposed, and changed, early internalization is subject to distortions that with maturation gradually disappear.

Construction

The child early develops the capacity for constructions, for the creation of new dimensions and concepts of his world. Constructions depend upon a coordinated, repeated act and some dimension of the object in the environment to produce new understanding, i.e., the manner in which the concept of permanence is discovered by the child.

During the process of losing and finding a ball, the child begins to see a factor of permanence in the ball; he begins to understand that it may be that the ball is not lost, but he himself. Young Waldo, "lost" in the supermarket, wants to know if anyone has seen a mother who is lost. He is not lost, he is here; she is lost.

Operation

With the passage of time, and with increased experience, certain sensory-motor cognitive sequences become more and more stable and more highly structured. The connection between the outside stimulus-response events and the internal cognitive events becomes highly stylized, almost reflexive and unthinking, such as the process of avoiding obstacles when walking across a room. When these cognitive structures reach this highly organized, stable, and useful state, they are called operations by Piaget. Operations, then, become a stable part of the behavioral repertoire of the child, thereby freeing up psychic energy for newer, less predictable events in his world.

PIAGET'S STAGES OF COGNITIVE DEVELOPMENT

Piaget and his theory of cognitive development are important in the study of prelinguistic stages of development. We are concerned primarily with Piaget's Stage I, the Sensory-Motor Period, which covers approximately the first eighteen months of a child's life. Piaget's second stage extends from eighteen months through about eleven or twelve years, the Period of Concrete Operations of Classes, Relations, and Numbers. The third period, Formal Operations, achieves full development at about fifteen.

Each of Piaget's three stages of development has two essential phases or periods, formation and attainment. The formation period represents the maturational process by which the genetically determined neurological development prerequisite to the mental operation takes place. The attainment period, on the other hand, represents the mental operations being put together and becoming functional.

A stage then represents three separate sequences occurring simultaneously: the attainment of one stage, the neurological development for the next stage, and the disintegration of the operations of the previous stage. Stages are considered to be discrete and to follow one another in orderly sequence. Even though the exact age of attainment of a stage may be slightly different from one child to another, depending upon genetic predisposition, motivation, cultural stimulation, and opportunity, the sequence of development never varies, and the genetic factors predominate. During the shift from one stage to another, most of the previous operations are lost; but the process of loss proceeds through integration into more sophisticated operations, rather than through what might be called amnesia.

Remember the discussion in Chapter 3 of the differences between cross-sectional and longitudinal studies? Piaget's method demands longitudinal investigation: the orderly sequence of development from one stage to another frequently is obscured by the fact that children enter phases at slightly different ages. Averaging out these differences across groups would cause the sharpness of the transition to be lost completely.

Piaget's theory does indeed imply a continuity of growth: operations at one stage are prerequisite for operations at another stage. His argument for discreteness of stages comes from his concept of insight, of discovery of the new operations; but, the new operations represent an independent or discrete type of transformation of the sensory world.

Before beginning a detailed presentation of the first stage of the development of logical thinking, the Sensory-Motor Period, a brief overview of the full range of stages outlined by Piaget is appropriate. Piaget organizes cognitive development into three major stages in which there are rather sharp qualitative differences in thought strategies. These stages are subdivided into substages, as outlined in Table 5.

Table 5

Piaget's Stages of Cognitive Development

Developmental Stage	Age
I. Sensory-motor	0 mo.–18 mo.
A. Reflex exercises	0 mo.– 1 mo.
B. Primary circular schemas	1 mo.– 4 mo.
C. Secondary circular schemas	4 mo.– 8 mo.
D. Coordination of secondary schemas	8 mo.–12 mo.
E. Tertiary circular schemas	12 mo.–18 mo.
F. Invention of new schemas	18 mo.–24 mo.
II. Concrete operations of classes, relations, numbers	18 mo.–12 yr.
A. Preoperational	18 mo.– 7 yr.
1. Preconceptual	18 mo.– 4 yr.
2. Intuitive	4 yr. – 7 yr.
B. Concrete operations	7 yr. –12 yr.
III. Formal operations	12 yr. –15 yr.

 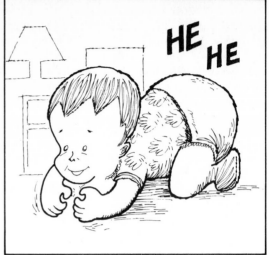

I. Sensory-Motor

The Sensory-Motor Stage, essentially a prelanguage developmental stage, is concerned with the organization of sensory input and the co-ordination of sensory-motor responses. It is a period of great interest in and preoccupation with sensory-motor mastery. The child spends an in-ordinate amount of time experiencing his environment, mastering simple motor responses, and repeating them ad infinitum; such as, for instance, picking up bits of fluff with his fingers, falling backward on a pillow, and blowing. Such simple motor mastery, together with sensory manipula-tions, bring cackles of delight. The logical operations at this stage are simple, relating directly to sensory-motor processing, controlling, master-ing, repeating. Piaget often refers to this stage as the period of reversible action or repetition, and he notes that it is a period of highly unstable operations.

II. Concrete Operations

The second stage, Concrete Operations of Classes, Relations, and Numbers, includes preschool and elementary school ages, in which occur the most rapid changes in the development of a child's thinking processes. He is gradually solving problems of logical error. As he resolves one level of error, he moves to another, more subtle and with more and more correct elements; that is, he is only partially in error: clouds do bring rain, but not because it's a picnic day and they are being mean.

A. *Preoperational*

The preoperational period bridges the interim between the sensory-motor stage and the first operations. Halfway between the two, it is a preparatory stage that demonstrates a great many concrete operations that are productive but do not yet produce generalizations in the child's thinking.

The preoperational period is characterized by egocentric thinking. Waldo learns that the black kitten scratches and the white one doesn't; therefore the white one can be dragged around the house by his tail. This saves Waldo's hide from considerable mistreatment, but doesn't offer him much help in judging how to treat the Andersons' old white alley cat with the raggedy ears. Waldo may develop delusions of grandeur regarding his power over white animals (egocentric thinking), which old Tom wouldn't hesitate to straighten out for him; nobody hauls an old white alley cat with chewed-up ears by the tail more than once.

1. PRECONCEPTUAL. In the preconceptual stage of logical development, the child learns the basic use of language for simple communication and the rudiments of symbolism, although he remains tied to action rather than symbols in his everyday life. During this period he is not able to form what Piaget refers to as true concepts. Concepts come into use loosely;

they do not represent the fine interplay of discrimination and generalization observed in later stages. During this period several systematic errors in basic logic are easily identified in the child's thinking.

The error of transduction involves reasoning from particular to particular without generalization. Thus Waldo reasons that Spot will jump up on you, because he has; and Brownie will jump up on you because he is frisky like Spot; but Red will not jump up on you because he is too big. No concept that dogs tend to jump up on you is derived. As a matter of fact, Red is the most jumping-up-on-you dog in the whole neighborhood.

The error of syncretism involves the linking together of unrelated ideas: Waldo believes that getting a haircut is just like Jenny's coming over because they both occur on Monday. Thus two unrelated events are connected and Waldo wants another haircut so Jenny will come over.

The error of realism refers to the conviction of children that every-

thing they see is seen in the same way by other people. Waldo is sure his parents understand the special quality of his bedtime silk scarf that makes it unacceptable when it has been machine-washed, just as the average adult is sure that any fool can see that an apple is red. The that's-the-way-it-is argument is compelling to children during this stage.

The error of artification is related to the belief that the world is created and maintained by the performance of people. Young children believe that it gets dark because the lights have been turned off.

2. INTUITIVE. The intuitive stage is still without true concepts. Thinking and reasoning are evident, but operational thinking is absent. The ability to make mental comparisons in other than a serial fashion is lacking. A consistent error in the use of concepts is present; the context in which the concept occurs alters it significantly.

The child is unable to maintain in his thinking more than one relationship at a time, which results in a number of limitations: (1) inconsistency in explanation; (2) lack of sequence in argument; (3) egocentric explanation (arbitrary, illogical certainty); (4) lack of comprehension of constants (for instance, a boy must learn that if he has a brother, his brother has a brother).

B. Concrete Operations

During the period of concrete operations of logical development, the last substage of Piaget's second stage of cognitive development, both given the same name by Piaget, the child learns to deal with six relationship groupings that greatly increase his power to think logically. These six classes form the foundation for the final stage in logical thinking, which develops during adolescence, Formal Operations.

1. Hierarchy of classes. The child learns to distinguish animals and birds; further, he learns that animals can be broken down into cats and dogs, and dogs can be classified into bulldogs, setters, terriers, bird dogs, and other breeds.
2. Order of succession. Objects, the child learns, may be ordered by size, alphabetical order, how far they live away from school, and so on.
3. Substitution. Children learn that various combinations of numbers make the same total, and various combinations of coins add up to the same amount.
4. Symmetrical relations. The child learns the reciprocity of relationships: two brothers are brothers to each other.
5. Multiplication of classes. The child learns that an object can belong simultaneously to many classes; it can be a red fruit, beginning with the letter *a*, that comes from a grocery store.
6. Multiplication of series. Children understand that an object can belong to two series at once. The game Battleship, in which a square is designated by a number down and a letter across, is an example of this process.

From these six relationship groupings with which children classify phenomena during the Concrete Operations Period, Piaget has drawn five laws that form the basis for relationships.

1. The law of closure or composition. When two elements combine, they form a new element of the same kind: dogs and cats are both animals.

2. The law of associativity. All combinations that are additive are the same: dogs and cats as well as horses are animals is the same as dogs and horses as well as cats are animals.
3. The law of inversion. Just as two elements can combine, they can be reduced: given the information in Law 1, what is another animal besides dogs? Cats.
4. The law of identity. An operation combined with its converse is annulled: if you add two dogs to the family and take two dogs away, how many dogs do you have? The number you started with.
5. The law of tautology. Adding identities yields identities: dogs plus dogs equals dogs.

III. Formal Operations

Formal operations, phenomena of adolescence, normally do not occur in childhood and therefore will not be discussed in this text.

Summary

According to Maier, six generalizations summarize Piaget's concept of cognitive development:

1. There is an absolute continuity of all developmental processes.
2. Development proceeds through a continuous process of generalization and differentiation.
3. This continuity is achieved by a continuous unfolding. Each level of development finds its roots in a previous phase and continues into the following one.
4. Each phase entails a repetition of processes of the previous level in a different form or organization (schema). Previous behavior patterns are sensed as inferior and become part of the new superior level.
5. The differences in organizational pattern create a hierarchy of experiences and actions.
6. Individuals achieve different levels within the hierarchy, although "... there is in the brain of each individual the possibility for all these developments but they are not all realized" (Piaget, 1950, p. 156) [Maier, 1965, p. 102].

SENSORY-MOTOR STAGE

According to Piaget, the first stage in the development of cognitive ability is the Sensory-Motor Stage, the prelanguage stage; estimates of its duration range from the first eighteen to twenty-four months of early childhood.

Stage One of Piaget's cognitive development sequence involves three maturational processes: (1) voluntary control of reflexive actions, (2) selective attention and memory, and (3) perceptual-motor actions that transform the environment. The third group of activities represents physical and mental manipulations, such as connecting, combining, displacing, assembling, and disassembling, as the child copes with his environment. Stage One begins with the capacity for a few reflexes and ends with the first appearance of symbolic ways of representing the world.

Prior to the development of functional language, intelligence is properly referred to as sensory-motor. This stage of intellectual development, occurring during the first two years of life, serves as the foundation upon which adult intelligence is based. Extremely important, sensory-motor intelligence sets the stage for the quality of thinking the child will continue to use throughout his lifetime; this prelanguage period in a child's life may well set attitudes, patterns, and styles of thinking that are irreversible. The critical-period hypothesis suggests that during this early period, a child is open to certain styles of learning on an imprinting basis; if these sensory experiences are absent or impoverished, the child's intellectual growth may be stunted permanently.

We need, then, to examine the sensory-motor development of the child from a neurobehavioral basis. Some children, by reason of late neurological maturation or mild brain impairment due to nutritional or oxygen deficiency during the prenatal and lactation periods, do not have the sensory-motor acuity to process adequately the stimuli in their environment; they repeatedly miss cues that would suggest possible organization of their world.

Take the simple operation of figure-ground distinction. Most of us have had the experience of solving an embedded-figure problem, such as, for instance, a picture of a fawn and her mother hiding in the woods. Once you spot the figure, it seems to jump out at you, so obvious, you wonder why it was so difficult to detect. The trick is to develop a scanning technique to break the figure out of the background, and then to be able to make some sense out of the figure, when it is broken out.

The experience cue, which aids in developing a set or organization, also is required for early sensory-motor development. If a child has the double handicap of a slight developmental lag in perceptual-motor acuity and a lack of cueing by significant experiences and people in his environment, he begins to lose confidence in the environment's meaningfulness. In order for the child to develop his maximum potential, his environment during his first two years should provide him with maximum experience in successful processing of its meaning. All his senses should be stimulated so that he can learn to organize what they teach him. Just as a child learns to put pieces of a puzzle together to form a whole, so he must learn to integrate his experiences in early childhood.

In describing the Sensory-Motor Stage, Piaget makes liberal use of some language concepts unique to him and his associates. To understand these in his terms is necessary because they have a different connotation for Piaget than in normal usage.

Piaget describes six substages of the Sensory-Motor Period. These are identified by the developmental complexity of the sensory-motor processes of each substage, beginning with the simple variations of the sucking reflex, by which the child "learns" to suck some things because they are "pleasant" and not to suck other things because they are "unpleasant." The sixth substage represents abstract problem-solving; the child makes mental manipulations or vicarious motor responses rather than the actual motor responses. At this substage, some subvocal muttering is evident, suggesting some attempt to "think in words."

A. Reflex Exercises

During the first few months after birth, the ability to release and to bind a reflex voluntarily is observed in the human infant: the reflex of sucking at stimulation of the mouth is restrained when the child places an unpleasant object into his mouth. Shortly after birth, the child closes his eyes, not merely as a blink reflex, but because the light is painful. He opens his eyes and looks, or closes his eyes and does not look, and thus by a motor manipulation, the child has learned to alter the sensory input from his environment; the first schema goes into operation.

To wax eloquent about what the child is thinking when the light goes on would be an anthropomorphic error in logic. We do not know whether the child makes a few mental comments about people flipping on the lights in the middle of the night, but we do know that the child possesses the power to leave his eyes open or to close them, and that he chooses to close them to reduce the glare and pain of too rapid accommodation to light.

The child, then, carries out of Substage A the ability to control voluntarily some motor responses to some sensory inputs; and this can be a rather complex sensory-motor processing. At the end of Substage A of the Sensory-Motor Period, the rudiments of voluntary control are in operation; more importantly, the beginnings of conceptual thinking appear. The child can learn, for example, that certain movements on his part operate on his environment, and the primitive form of cause is acquired.

B. Primary Circular Schemas

In Substage B, these voluntary, coordinated movements become reliable; the child, at about one month of age, can perform the operations of Substage B with great precision and total reliability. Instead of serendipitous movements, the patterns of sensory-motor responses become habitual. Piaget refers to these as "the first acquired adaptations."

At the same time, the child begins to develop some broad scanning strategies by which he effectively locates objects in his environment. He learns to look in specific quadrants of the visual field as a result of certain sounds. He thus has tandem use of a combination of sensory systems: his looking becomes more effective because he knows where to look on the basis of sound, and on the basis of the effectiveness of previous scanning cycles. These sweeps of the environment Piaget refers to as primary circular reactions, which clearly demonstrate the beginning of an effective memory, an effective sensory-motor cycle, and the rudiments of causality.

Language still is noneffective, but these complex sensory-motor sequences serve the same purpose as a concept: the sensory-motor process of nursing equals concept of relief from hunger. Later these sensory-motor sequences will be subsumed under the complex association to the word *mother*, but in Substage B, the sensory-motor building stage, the texture of mother, the motor sequences of mother, the smell of mother, the sound of mother, the taste of mother, and the sight of mother are all being manipulated in exploratory sequences that are far from integrated. Note that some sense of time is important in Substage B because sequence is necessary.

During Substage B, imitation is evidenced; the child moves from the crying-for-help stage to social interaction. At this age, he begins to seek out and enjoy repetition of motor responses that are social in nature; the crying becomes deliberate, social, and modulated: the sensory-motor process of emotional behavior comes under some voluntary control even at this early age.

C. Secondary Circular Schemas

Substage C of the Sensory-Motor Period represents a stabilizing of the circular reactions into reliable, repeated operations that produce an effect on the environment. During this substage, imitations become not only deliberate and systematic, but more functional. The child also seems to use cause-and-effect reasoning: he calls, and often cackles when he hears his mother answer. Thus he is not only effective in manipulating his environment, but he enjoys the new-found power of control and anticipation.

This gives rise to endless games of repetition, such as sweeping toys off the high-chair tray, knowing that the parent will replace them, only to be knocked off again. A great deal of laughing, gurgling, and bilateral movement accompany this behavior. Thus, although there is inefficiency, there is reliable manipulation.

During this substage and fundamental to it are a sense of time delay, a sense of permanence in an object's occupation of space, and some sense of physical causality. The child, after sweeping objects from the table top, looks on the floor to see where they landed. He looks under objects, such as napkins, knowing that an object can be covered.

This is a period, then, of the building up of a vast repertoire of perceptual-motor concepts that involve objects, relations, cause and effect. It is a time of development of basic strategies, and the true origin of intelligent behavior. This play period of Substage C is probably one of the most important building periods of basic intellectual strategy.

D. Coordination of Secondary Schemas

Substage D of the Sensory-Motor Period of the development of logical thinking involves a progressively complex coordination of secondary schemas. It is characterized by a logical operation that involves the concept of detour. That is, during this period, the child learns to reach a goal not immediately obtainable via an indirect or intermediate means. Taking a piece of foil-wrapped candy out of his mouth, opening it with his hands, and then returning it to his mouth is an example of the child's coordination of schemas. The direct action of taking the candy and placing it in his mouth did not work; the child learned to interrupt the candy-in-the-mouth schema with the candy-unwrapping schema; they become blended into a single coordinated schema: unwrapping-candy-then-putting-it-in-the-mouth-to-eat.

As is often the case in the development of new schemas, the principle of combination, detour, and intermediate steps is broadened into an across-the-board strategy to the point where the child now rearranges many of his schemas into these sequences; many rituals appear in the child's daily activities, rituals he is extremely fond of.

Since the child suddenly shifts into this fourth stage with the discovery of the importance of sequence, this discovery becomes a compelling dimension in his life. Going to bed becomes a compulsive ritual; put the doll on the chair, then tuck the covers up, then sing a good-night song, then kiss the child, then kiss the doll, then turn the light out, then say good night. And, at that stage in a child's life, woe be unto the parent who, in a hurry to go to a dinner party, skips the doll-kissing and finds that nothing will suffice but to do the whole thing over again.

E. Tertiary Circular Schemas

Substage E of the Sensory-Motor Period involves the testing of schemas, the tertiary circular reaction stage. Variation and experimentation with the sequences developed in Substage D occur during this substage. The child develops long chains of rituals with slight variations, and seems delighted with the effects of these variations. A concept of physical causality is evident; the child knows, for example, that in the domino-chain game, great care must be taken to prevent the dominoes from falling until the right moment. The child, in placing large numbers of toys on a balance beam prior to knocking them off, knows that unless they are placed carefully, they will fall "not at the right time."

This is a stage of great concentration in child's play, and a period in which the adult may find playing with the child difficult, because the adult seems always to be obviously doing something wrong that breaks the sequence, much to the annoyance of the child. Ritualistic, solitary, and/or parallel play is the essential characteristic of this period. The child neither needs nor appreciates anything except an audience or a puppet; he does not want any "help." Mother,-I-would-rather-do-it-myself is the characteristic look of anger given by children who are helped during this period, which is again a period of significant development in non-verbal concepts that will serve as a foundation for the later verbal conceptualizations.

F. Invention of New Schemas

Substage F of the Sensory-Motor Period, the final substage, represents a transition into Piaget's Stage II of cognitive development, Concrete Operations. Substage F, taking us through the beginning of year two, consists of a mental tracing of sensory-motor actions that greatly increases the efficiency of the process.

The child at this stage begins to make significant representations of the outside world in terms of eidetic or picture memories and symbols, with which he can operate without the necessity of making the related motor movements. This is the beginning of abstract reasoning and is a major step on the way to a functional language. The child spends less time in sensory-motor tasks and more time in reviewing, integrating, and reliving these sensory-motor memories. It is a period of great expansion of intellectual capacity and, as the Kelloggs (1933) found when raising their son and a chimp as nursery mates in their home, it is a time of rapid change in both style and quantity of intellectual development. Prior to this stage, many animal infants are superior to human infants, but at this point, a rapid, almost explosive increase in the abstract ability of the human infant leaves the animal far behind.

IMPLICATIONS

At birth, the human infant has at his disposal a wide range of sensory receptors and a reasonably effective motor-response system that enables him to interact with his environment in the critical dimension of the feeding process: his first significant sensory-motor sequences are related to the nursing response. Initially, the searching, nuzzling, sucking response, tied into sight, taste, smell, sound, tactile, and kinesthetic qualities of the mother and her breast, together with probing, drooling, nuzzling, sucking, spitting, swallowing, squirming, snuggling, become the first of a series of sensory-motor processes that develop during the first two years of life to set the stage for an adaptive behavior referred to as intelligence.

SENSE DEPRIVATION

Obviously, that all of these sensory processes are operational is important. If they are not, some form of compensation initiated by the parents or the child is essential, if the child is to develop normally.

Hearing

Hearing is critical for imitation of the preverbal sequences of sounds with which the child develops confidence in the power of language. Defective hearing is significant; and prompt attention through sound amplification or substitution of tactile stimulation is highly important in the early months of the child's life. If the child is to develop functional speech, in all cases where deafness is suspected, prompt referral to a speech and hearing clinic is essential. Pediatricians are competent to make initial rough screening, but have neither the skills nor the equipment for fine diagnosis of hearing deficits. At times, simply speaking directly to the child, or speaking loudly, can greatly aid the child in hearing the critical dimensions of the human voice. When the child is hard of hearing, medical intervention may improve the condition, or hearing devices may alter the state, but occasionally expert auditory help is needed.

The parent should recognize that hearing is a pump-priming phenomenon that needs to occur during the first few months, if the child is to make full use of his potential. If the child is not receiving meaningful communication through sound, he turns off this sense; he no longer attends to sound, which precludes the development of normal speech, greatly hampers the early development of cognitive ability, and produces what is often referred to as a pseudoretarded child—a child who acts and often is treated as though he were retarded, when such is not the case.

Research on the expectancy effect, to be discussed in more detail in Chapter 6, suggests the possibility of a child misidentified as retarded actually becoming retarded through the treatment from those around him, just by their expectancy of his performance. Each year in the developmental clinics around the country, many cases are seen of children, normal in cognitive potential, who have suffered from being thought retarded when actually they were simply hard of hearing. Correct diagnostic evaluation by the combined efforts of the pediatrician, audiologist, and psychologist often can lead to remediation. But many such children, not correctly diagnosed in time, actually become retarded because they have missed so much in their environment.

Psycholinguists have long postulated a critical period during the second year of life, a period in which the language activation center of the brain is stimulated by hearing speech. Now, some argue as to how specific the language activation center is regarding built-in grammatical sequences, but all agree that the center goes dormant without stimulation. Regardless, then, of whether one believes, as does Noam Chomsky, that formal grammatical structure is an instinctive maturational process within the brain, it is apparent that failure to identify hearing deficiencies in this critical period does lead to muteness, with concomitant and considerable problems in language, syntax, and logical thinking.

Sight

Although the effects do not appear as soon as those caused by a hearing deficiency, poor visual acuity does indeed hamper the early intellectual and social development of a child. Some visual defects are hereditary and some result from prenatal infection. When any of these is suspected, early evaluation of the child's vision is necessary. In most cases, the child should have a visual examination before beginning kindergarten. Forewarned about uncorrectable problems, such as mirror vision, and treated for correctable visual defects, the child has a much better chance of beginning school in a normal fashion. A child can be misidentified as slow, when in fact he has a visual defect. Great progress has been made during the past few years in testing very young children for visual problems.

Smell/Taste

Disturbances in the senses of smell and taste are extremely rare and usually closely related to serious brain impairment. Little information is available toward remediation of these defects. The parent and teacher should work closely with a child neurologist in such cases, to insure the child the most effective remedial program.

Touch

A lack of remedial alternatives is also true for the sense of touch and the kinesthetic sense, where the deficiency results from a major defect in the brain, usually involving the cranial nerves at the base of the brain.

Summary

What, then, can the average parent do to encourage the optimal use of the major sensory channels of the child in the development of his intellectual capacity. Obviously, the first step is a reasonable vigilance regarding sensory deficiencies. But beyond that is the need to provide a broad range of stimulation, as well as discrimination training in the use of the senses. Walks in the woods, with encouragement to listen, to feel, to taste, to smell, as well as to see, serve as the model; discrimination training in the use of the senses is the process: the more guided experience, the better the learning. This discrimination training can best be effected when extraneous stimulation is low, when the environment is otherwise relatively quiet: the child needs help in learning to concentrate on what you are trying to teach him. He cannot be expected to discriminate two different birdcalls when an angry bull is bellowing in the next field, even though he can clearly hear the birds.

STIMULUS DEPRIVATION

A frequently used term in the literature, *cultural deprivation*, or *stimulus deprivation*, probably generates more heat than light in scientific discourse; yet some aspects of the problem are clear. Cultural deprivation in the usual sense refers to those children who by reason of poverty live in an extremely restricted sensory environment. The restriction is not only in the amount and kind of sensory stimulation but also in the cueing quality of the stimulation that is received. That is, an impoverished child, living in a two-room apartment without functional plumbing, without a bed of his own, without curtains, and with three generations of the family, for a total of sixteen within the walls, is not understimulated. There is much to see, much to hear, much to taste, much to smell, and much to feel; but there is little in the way of differentiation or discrimination. It is as though five different channels of a TV were showing on the screen at one time. The problem of signal-to-ground contrast is so extensive that the child is flooded by stimulation but unable to make sharp discriminations.

When a child is not given early sensory discrimination training, he falls into the protective mechanism of accommodation; he becomes generally unresponsive, generally unwilling to take in the environment, retreating to a safer, quieter level of noise. Children from such an environment need to be reintroduced as early as possible in the school setting to the fine-tuned discrimination learning that so many middle-class children experience on a daily basis.

The evidence is overwhelming that children need not only multimedia, multisensual stimulation in as broad a range as possible, but simultaneously need discrimination training in order to organize this complex signal system. In a confusing, disorganized environment, the child experiences the same deprivation he would experience in an environment with no stimulation at all. The critical dimension is discrimination experience; thus any significant training needs to make somewhat gaudy contrasts during this period.

Solitary and group games that involve the constant interplay of sensory discrimination and generalization provide a honing of the senses in preparation for the essential cognitive set for breaking the code of the environment. During the critical period from eighteen months to three years, these sensory discriminations play a most important role in preparing the child for language utilization. During this period, the child identifies sensations and perceptions that he will gradually learn to name with words.

Learning the feel of rough versus soft texture provides the essential underpinning for the words *soft* and *rough*, and with experiences of *softness* come *fluffy, filmy, puffy, silky, cottony, billowy, satiny*, and so on, with each word having a slightly different connotation and meaning, and each accompanied by a sensory experience. Multiple sensory experiences encourage the development of multiple concepts, which in turn provide the tools for complex thought. Particularly in multiple and related sensory experiences are the higher-level concepts first experienced and cast into the behavioral repertoire of the child. The more complex and related the child's experiences, the more complex his concepts; and the more complex his concepts, the more complex his thought patterns; and the more complex his thought patterns, the more he is able to benefit from experience, the more intelligent he is.

SUMMARY

Piaget and his detractors do not agree upon whether shifts in substages can be hurried. From reading Piaget, one has the distinct impression that he, like Freud, feels that a maturational clock controls intellectual and emotional development, that logical thinking follows a critical-period schedule just as do the motor activities upon which it is based. Just as a child cannot be taught to walk until the neurological development necessary for walking is complete, so a child cannot learn to perform mental combinations until a similar development in the brain is complete.

On the other hand, evidence from studies of environmental deprivation suggests that age and the accompanying neurological development in the brain provide a necessary but not a sufficient condition for the development of logical thinking: clearly, children who receive focused experience in the development of schemas are more likely to acquire the schemas, and also are more likely to use them, if given guided experience. The more the schemas are used, the more fluent the access to them becomes, to the point where thinking itself is faster and more versatile. Thus, the significant work of Lewis Lipsitt suggests that a rich, sensory environment, with stimulating and mildly frustrating experiences in early infancy and childhood, encourages the development of a larger, more fluent set of schemas; thus a child in a rich, stimulating, challenging environment can be expected to enter into the verbal period of his life with a large number of schemas that await only labeling to become language.

Parents who play sensory-motor games with their children, who afford them a wide variety of multiple sensory experiences with a world always exceeding the grasp of the child, are being more than doting parents with nothing better to do. Instead, significant evidence indicates that they are expanding a capacity of the child's behavioral repertoire that will later provide significant underpinnings for late-childhood intelligence, underpinnings that do not appear without the experience.

In 1800, when Jean-Marc Itard took over the education of the Wild Boy of Aveyron, the secretary of the newly founded Society of Observers of Man wrote:

> It is indeed very important for the advance of mankind's knowledge that a devoted and impartial observer take the boy in charge and . . . examine the totality of his acquired ideas, study his manner of expressing them, and determine if the state of man in isolation is incompatible with the development of the intelligence [G. Hervé, quoted by Lane, 1973].

Itard labored long to educate the Wild Boy, with some but not overwhelming success. Following Etienne Condillac's philosophy that a child becomes a man by acquiring knowledge through the senses, Itard felt that the Wild Boy had to be taught to see, to hear, to touch, to attend, to remember, to judge.

Pinel labeled the Wild Boy as an incurable idiot. Itard referred to him as a so-called idiot. Lane quotes current descriptions of the Wild Boy that would indicate some intelligence at least, and he quotes Itard describing how the Wild Boy achieved a correct order for the alphabet, not by at first noting the individual letters, but by noting the order in which the practice letters were removed from the frames. The Wild Boy stacked the letters in such a way that he could always replace them in the frames in the correct order.

Yet most of the reports indicate "so many examples of sensory and intellectual skills that the boy lacks, . . . it boggles the mind of even the most confirmed empiricist" (Lane, 1973). He could not discriminate between painted objects, three-dimensional objects, and mirrored objects; he did not respond to loud noises; he could discriminate edible foods only by smell, not by sight; he had no vocal behavior. Itard set out "to bring to bear all the resources of . . . present knowledge in order to develop the boy physically and morally" according to Condillac's hypothesis that all our ideas come from our senses.

And Itard was extremely skilled and ingenious at his self-appointed task. Yet he was unsatisfied with his results. Lane suggests that Itard's error was the error of many pedagogues—that education provides all and the child nothing. Lane suggests that the child is no more a pristine receptacle for society's wisdom than he is simply a biological unfolding of behavior. Yet there are those today who would agree wholeheartedly with James Mill (circa 1829), "if education cannot do everything, there is hardly anything it cannot do" (quoted by Burt, 1958, p. 2).

It is probably true that intellectual ability, particularly in the middle range of intelligence, can be significantly manipulated by the heightening of experience in childhood. It is also true that early intervention programs, such as early childhood education for the children of poverty, should make full use of the information provided by Piaget, spending considerable concentration upon the encouragement, stimulation, and acquisition of schemas. The children of the poor frequently are understimulated in terms of sensory-motor acquisition. That they lack multimedia stimulation, multiconceptual development, multisensual discrimination, and general opportunity and encouragement to explore their perceptual environment is obvious. Whether or not one can hurry the process, one obviously can render more effective the utilization of the senses. And one can do this with the critical-period hypothesis in mind, for missed opportunities just may never be regained.

REVIEW

Early Development of Cognition The stimuli richness of the environment and the sensory manipulations of the child are the basis for developing intelligence. Lack of these, sensory deprivation, whether from a bleak environment or from sensory-motor deficits, is a fundamental cause of subnormal intelligence. Intelligence begins with the use of our senses; experience and practice teach us to perceive correctly.

Early Experiences The experiences of the young child are important in his continuing growth: this process of cognition and perceptual organization differentiates the intellectual abilities of children from deprived and enriched environments. In the cognition process, the child first learns to discriminate his surroundings through his senses. Then he learns to organize these sensations into meaningful relationships.

Status at Birth At birth, the child's behavior is automatic, with no deliberate reasoning involved. Yet he is sensitive to a wide range of external and internal stimuli that produce an undifferentiated but massive response.

Sensory Acuity of the Infant

vision

Color Discrimination Color discrimination, developing more slowly than visual acuity, becomes stable at about five months.

Convergence At about two months, an infant is able to focus both eyes to produce one image.

Depth As early as ten weeks an infant can recognize depth. At six months he trusts his judgment of depth, which has been suggested to be a learned phenomenon.

Focus During first four weeks, an infant focuses on objects only about eight inches away. At eight weeks, he begins accommodating for greater distances. At sixteen weeks, he can accommodate as well as an adult.

Pupillary Reflex Present at birth, only a dark or a light room will trigger the pupillary reflex; within a few weeks, moderate changes in illumination stimulate the pupillary reflex.

Reading Readiness Visual acuity is important to the young child as he matures in his reading readiness. Visual ability should be checked and defects corrected: poor vision offers a severe handicap to the developing intellect. Lewis Lipsitt believes that visual stimulation of the young child is as important to his later intellectual development as is tactile stimulation to his later sociability.

Shape Discrimination Shape discrimination is preferred by the young child; form or shape is the dominant dimension in his matching or choice discriminations.

Status at Birth At birth, the child's vision is not his most acute sense, being sensitive mainly to levels of illumination: his behavior is inhibited by light and enhanced by darkness.

Tracking Movement Although the movement is jerky and uncontrolled, an infant nevertheless is able to track the beam of a flashlight held within his visual range.

audition

Attending The child learns early that his sense of hearing provides useful information about his environment; he attends well to the sounds and vibrations around him, reacting strongly to strange or unexpected sounds. Some of his earliest concepts are formed in relationship to sound.

Language Readiness The child's sense of sound is all important in his development of language ability. His hearing ability should be monitored as he grows, with any defects being corrected early, since language has a critical period of development just as does emotional development.

Status at Birth At birth, the infant's sense of hearing is not acute due to the physical state of the ear as it adjusts from being in an aqueous state to life outside the womb. But hearing acuity develops rapidly and is important in the child's adaptation to his environment.

gustation

Status at Birth The sense of taste is probably the best developed sense of the newborn. Important to the newborn and the young child in getting to know his environment, taste is a subcortical response that seems to be developed in the fetus before any other sense.

olfaction

Status at Birth The newborn's sense of smell, like his sense of taste, seems well developed, although separating the sense of smell from the sense of taste is difficult.

touch

Status at Birth The sense of touch is highly important to the newborn; touch stimulation of the infant is necessary for his survival, says Ashley Montagu; and Harry Harlow found it to be the very basis of mothering in monkeys. The sense of touch is the necessary foundation for the development of emotional ties.

kinesthesia

Prematurity An infant needs rocking as well as fondling. One of the lasting problems of prematurity is that the infant's precarious physical strength usually precludes the normal handling, rocking, and fondling that is enjoyed by the full-term, healthy infant. This deprivation seems to leave permanent scars.

Status at Birth The kinesthetic sense, the sense of body movement, plays an important part in the early psychological adjustment of the human infant. His response to motion not only appears to provide important orienting information, but provides pleasure, comfort, and security at a stage when other forms of interpersonal communication are weak and somewhat ineffectual.

Sensory Processing of the Child

Status at Birth The newborn child is fully in touch with his environment. He has at his disposal a vast range of information about his environment coming in through his sensory organs, with little or no voluntary control at first. At first he lacks the ability to suppress, enhance, or divert attention from one modality to another. Whatever stimulation is the largest, sharpest, or the greatest deviation from the background seems to predominate in the child's world; the art of attending takes him some little while to develop.

Piaget's language

Accommodation A child making changes in his behavior according to his past experience is accommodating, is learning through experience. Accommodation changes the schemas themselves as a result of new experiences; "the modification of internal schemes to fit reality is called accommodation." "Intelligent activity is always an active, organized process of assimilating the new to the old and of accommodating the old to the new."

Adaptation Organization of experience cannot be effective without the reception and registration of experience—adaptation, the adjustment to the environment through assimilation (incorporation of new objects and experiences) and accommodation (modification according to experience).

Assimilation When a child utilizes and incorporates something from his environment, he is assimilating, which changes the stimulation and the child. A conceptual component of adaptation, assimilation is the process of restructuring events in the environment to make them more readily usable by the child. "The filtering or modification of the input is called assimilation."

Construction The child early develops the capacity for constructions, for the creation of new dimensions and concepts of his world. Constructions depend upon a coordinated, repeated act and some dimension of the object in the environment to produce new understanding.

Content "Content refers to the external behavior which tells us that functioning has occurred"; content refers to the observable input and output of the child, what the behaviorists call the stimulus-response sequence.

Equilibrium Equilibration is the process by which organisms change from one state to another, the underlying regulatory process that continuously is changing, balancing, and unifying development and experience. A child grows, develops, matures, learns, because of a genetically compelling push for equilibrium with the environment.

Function "Function is concerned with the manner in which any organism makes cognitive progress"; function refers to the biologically inherited manner of interacting with the environment.

Internalization A young child first internalizes the outside world through eidetic imagery: visual images stored in the mind for instant replay. Because eidetic memories can become fused, transposed, and changed, early internalization is subject to distortions that gradually disappear with maturation.

Invariant Functions Piaget uses organization and the two components of adaptation, assimilation and accommodation, to isolate the abstract properties of intelligence-in-action, to define function.

Operation When cognitive structures reach a highly organized, stable, and useful state, they are called operations by Piaget. Operations, then, become a stable part of the behavioral repertoire of the child, thereby freeing up psychic energy for newer, less predictable events in his world.

Organization "Every act of intelligence presumes some kind of intellectual structure, some sort of organization, within which it proceeds." The specific characteristics of this organization vary from stage to stage in development.

Schema The structural units in Piaget's cognitive development system, schemas are well-defined sequences of physical or mental actions that form the basic building blocks of intelligence. In its simplest form, a schema is a reflex; in its more complex form, a general, connected pattern of internal or external responses.

Structure "Structure refers to the inferred organizational properties which explain why this content rather than some other content has emerged"; structure refers to the organizational pattern of intellect.

Transformation Transformation represents an interaction between the object and the child's ability to transform it to his use.

Piaget's stages of cognitive development

Piaget's stages of cognitive development are discrete and orderly; the sequence never varies; genetic factors predominate: Sensory-Motor, Concrete Operations, Formal Operations.

Concrete Operations Period The last substage of Piaget's second stage of cognitive development, in the concrete operations period the child learns to deal with six relationship groupings that greatly increase his power to think logically. These six classes form the foundation for the final stage in logical thinking, Formal Operations, which develops during adolescence: hierarchy of classes, order of succession, substitution, symmetrical relations, multiplication of classes, and multiplication of series.

Concrete Operations Stage (18 mo.–12 yr.) The second of Piaget's three stages of cognitive development, Concrete Operations covers the preconceptual and intuitive stages of the child's development.

Error of Artification An error in logic that occurs during the preconceptual period, the error of artification is believing that the world is created and maintained by the performance of people.

Error of Realism An error in logical thinking that occurs during the preconceptual period, the error of realism is conceiving that everything is seen the same way by everybody.

Error of Syncretism   An error in logical thinking that occurs during the preconceptual period, the error of syncretism is linking together unrelated ideas.

Error of Transduction   An error occurring in the preconceptual period, the error of transduction is reasoning from particular to particular without generalization.

Formal Operations Stage   (12–15 yr.) The third of Piaget's three stages of cognitive development, Formal Operations covers the development of mature, logical thinking.

Hierarchy of Classes   During the final period of the Concrete Operations Stage in cognitive development, the child learns to distinguish animals and birds; further, he learns that animals can be broken down into cats and dogs, and dogs can be classified into bulldogs, setters, terriers, bird dogs, and other breeds.

Intuitive   The second phase of the preoperational period of the Concrete Operations Stage of cognitive development, the intuitive stage is still without true concepts.   Thinking and reasoning are evident, but operational thinking is absent.   The ability to make mental comparisons in other than a serial fashion is lacking.   A consistent error in the use of concepts is present; the context in which the concept occurs alters it significantly.   The child is unable to maintain in his thinking more than one relationship at a time, which results in a number of limitations: inconsistency in explanation; lack of sequence in argument; egocentric explanation (arbitrary, illogical certainty); and a lack of comprehension of constants.

Law of Associativity   One of Piaget's five laws that form the basis for relationships, the law of associativity says that all combinations that are additive are the same: dogs and cats as well as horses are animals is the same as dogs and horses as well as cats are animals.

Law of Closure or Composition   One of Piaget's five laws that form the basis for relationships, the law of closure or composition says that when two elements combine, they form a new element of the same kind: dogs and cats are both animals.

Law of Identity   One of Piaget's five laws that form the basis for relationships, the law of identity says that an operation combined with its converse is annulled: if you add two dogs to the family and take two dogs away, how many dogs do you have? The number you started with.

Law of Inversion   One of Piaget's five laws that form the basis for relationships, the law of inversion says that just as two elements can combine, they can be reduced: given the information that dogs and cats are both animals, what is another animal besides dogs? Cats.

Law of Tautology   One of Piaget's five laws that form the basis for relationships, the law of tautology says that adding identities yields identities: dogs plus dogs equals dogs.

Multiplication of Classes   During the final period of the Concrete Operations Stage in cognitive development, the child learns that an object can belong simultaneously to many classes; it can be a red fruit, beginning with the letter *a*, that comes from a grocery store.

Multiplication of Series   During the final period of the Concrete Operations Stage in cognitive development, the child learns that an object can belong to two series at once.   The game Battleship, in which a square is designated by a number down and a letter across, is an example of this process.

Order of Succession   During the final period of the Concrete Operations Stage in cognitive development, the child learns that objects may be ordered by size, alphabetical order, how far they live away from school, and so on.

Preconceptual   The beginning phase of the preoperational period of the Concrete Operations Stage of cognitive development; in the preconceptual period of logical development, the child learns the basic use of language for simple communication and the rudiments of symbolism, although he remains tied to action rather than symbols in his everyday life.

Preoperational   Bridging the period between the sensory-motor stage and the first operations, the preoperational period is characterized by egocentric thinking.

Sensory-Motor Stage   The first of Piaget's three stages of cognitive development, Sensory-Motor is a prelanguage developmental stage devoted to mastery of sensory-motor responses.

Substitution   During the final period of the Concrete Operations Stage in cognitive development, the child learns that various combinations of numbers make the same total, and various combinations of coins add up to the same amount.

Symmetrical Relations During the final period of the Concrete Operations Stage in cognitive development, the child learns the reciprocity of relationships: two brothers are brothers to each other.

sensory-motor stage

The first eighteen to twenty-four months of a child's life are spent in mastery of physical responses: voluntary control of reflexive actions; selective attention and memory; and perceptual-motor actions that transform the environment. This sensory-motor period of intelligence may well set for life the child's attitudes, patterns, and styles of thinking as he learns to integrate his early childhood experiences.

Coordination of Secondary Schemas During the eighth to twelfth month, the development of logical thinking involves a progressively complex coordination of secondary schemas. It is characterized by a logical operation that involves the concept of detour. As is often the case in the development of new schemas, the principle of combination, detour, and intermediate steps is broadened into an across-the-board strategy to the point where the child now rearranges many of his schemas into these sequences; many rituals appear in the child's daily activities, rituals he is extremely fond of.

Invention of New Schemas Between eighteen and twenty-four months, a transition is made into Piaget's Stage II of cognitive development, Concrete Operations. The invention of new schemas consists of a mental tracing of sensory-motor actions that greatly increases the efficiency of the process. The child begins to make significant representations of the outside world in terms of eidetic or picture memories and symbols, with which he can operate without the necessity of making the related motor movements. This is the beginning of abstract reasoning and is a major step on the way to a functional language. The child spends less time in sensory-motor tasks and more time in reviewing, integrating, and reliving these sensory-motor memories: a period of great expansion of intellectual capacity; an almost explosive increase in the abstract ability of the human infant.

Primary Circular Schemas During the first to the fourth month, voluntary, coordinated movements become reliable. The child begins to develop some broad scanning strategies by which he effectively locates objects in his environment. He learns to look in specific quadrants of the visual field as a result of sounds. He has tandem use of a combination of sensory systems. Piaget refers to these sweeps of the environment as primary circular reactions, which clearly demonstrate the beginning of an effective memory, an effective sensory-motor cycle, and the rudiments of causality.

Reflex Exercises During the first few months after birth, the ability to release and to bind a reflex voluntarily is observed in the human infant: the reflex of sucking at stimulation of the mouth is restrained when the child places an unpleasant object into his mouth. By a motor manipulation, the child has learned to alter the sensory input from his environment; the first schema goes into operation. The child has the ability to control voluntarily some motor responses to some sensory inputs; and this can be a rather complex sensory-motor processing.

Secondary Circular Schemas During the fourth to eighth month, the circular reactions stabilize into reliable, repeated operations that produce an effect on the environment. Imitations become not only deliberate and systematic, but more functional. The child also seems to use cause-and-effect reasoning: he calls, and often cackles when he hears his mother answer. Thus he is not only effective in manipulating his environment, but enjoys the new-found power of control and anticipation. Fundamental to secondary circular schemas are a sense of time delay, a sense of permanence in an object's occupation of space, and some sense of physical causality. This is a period of the building up of a vast repertoire of perceptual-motor concepts that involve objects, relations, cause and effect. It is a time of development of basic strategies, and the true origin of intelligent behavior. This play period is probably one of the most important building periods of basic intellectual strategy.

Tertiary Circular Schemas Between twelve and eighteen months, cognitive development involves the testing of schemas. The child develops long chains of rituals with slight variations, and seems delighted with the effects of these variations. A concept of physical causality is evident. This is a stage of great concentration in child's play, and a period in which the adult may find playing with the child difficult. Ritualistic, solitary, and/or parallel play is the essential characteristic of this period. The child neither needs nor appreciates anything except an audience or a puppet; he does not want any "help." This is a period of significant development in nonverbal concepts that will serve as a foundation for the later verbal conceptualizations.

Implications

The senses form the basis for intelligence. To enhance and nurture the child's use of his senses is prerequisite to normal adult intellectual functioning. Obviously reasonable diligence regarding sensory deficiencies is demanded, but also a broad range of sensory stimulation as well as discrimination training. A child should be encouraged to listen, to feel, to taste, to smell, to see, to sense differences and similarities: guided experience provides optimal encouragement of his innate potential and assures that opportunities are not missed.

Summary

Piaget feels that a maturational clock controls intellectual and emotional development, that logical thinking follows a critical-period schedule just as do the motor activities upon which it is based. Just as a child cannot be taught to walk until the neurological development necessary for walking is complete, so a child cannot learn to perform mental combinations until a similar development in the brain is complete. On the other hand, evidence from studies of environmental deprivation suggests that age and the accompanying neurological development in the brain provide a necessary but not a sufficient condition for the development of logical thinking. It is probably true that intellectual ability, particularly in the middle range of intelligence, can be significantly manipulated by the heightening of experience in childhood.

NAMES TO KNOW

Sensory Acuity of the Infant

touch

ASHLEY MONTAGU Montagu has emphasized the importance of touch to the human infant. In the normal course of human development, throughout the critical period of formation of human personality, the first two years of life, the child receives a great deal of his emotional contact through the skin. Breast feeding, bathing, fondling, kissing, stroking, rocking, brushing, swaddling, holding, bouncing, all of which are the normal experiences of most infants, convey to the child security, warmth, affection, and love. Once the child is born, he depends upon his sense of touch for the development of his emotional ties.

HARRY HARLOW Harlow has studied the dimensions of mother love as it is expressed by monkeys. He has concluded skin contact, the sense of touch, to be the most critical aspect of monkey mothering. Lack of tactile stimulation in early infancy leaves monkeys socially and sexually aberrant. The emotional security provided by contact with the mother allows the infant to explore strange situations and to play with his peers. The movement and warmth of the mother add to the infant's security. The model provided by the mother guides the infant as he matures.

Sensory Processing of the Child

JEAN PIAGET That thinking develops in logical stages is fundamental to Piaget's theory of cognitive development. Also that biological maturational unfolding precedes specific stages is fundamental to Piaget: until the hereditary sequence of readiness is passed, specific development is not possible; conversely, if the hereditary stage arrives and is not used, the opportunity is lost almost irretrievably.

The development of logical thinking represents, according to Piaget, the application of a set of operations that either are used or not used; but once they are placed in use, the whole cognitive style of the child is altered permanently.

Piaget's stages of cognitive development are discrete and orderly; the sequence never varies; genetic factors predominate: Sensory-Motor—(0–18 months) a prelanguage developmental stage devoted to mastery of sensory-motor responses; Concrete Operations—(18 months–12 years) the preconceptual and intuitive stages of the child's development; Formal Operations—(12–15 years) the development of mature, logical thinking.

Summary

JEAN-MARC ITARD In 1800, Jean-Marc Itard took over the education of the Wild Boy of Aveyron. Itard felt that the Wild Boy had to be taught to see, to hear, to touch, to attend, to remember, to judge. Itard was extremely skilled and ingenious at his self-appointed task. Yet he was unsatisfied with his results. It has been suggested that Itard's error was the error of many pedagogues—that education provides all and the child nothing. The child is no more a pristine receptacle for society's wisdom than he is simply a biological unfolding of behavior. Yet there are those today who would agree with James Mill, "if education cannot do everything, there is hardly anything it cannot do."

Intelligence

The focus of the text thus far has been on the child as a biological organism, on the study of the interaction between a rather simple set of maturational, genetic codes and the environment in producing the sensory-motor activities of the child. During the maturation-dominated period of life, beginning at conception and extending through prenatal life, birth, and on into the second year, the higher-order animal species are remarkably similar. During the second year, during the formation of the sensory-motor schemas, the rapid utilization of sensory input and motor output reveals the human child to be a very special animal, special indeed in the way he codes his environment and cross-relates his experiences.

Good evidence suggests that many of the higher animals are also clever in their use of perceptual-motor skills. Chimps, porpoises, foxes, dogs, cats, and horses all give evidence of complex and clever sensory-motor learning. To demonstrate in many animals mental ability equal to or superior to that of the average eighteen-month-old child is relatively easy.

At the end of the sensory-motor period, however, between eighteen months and two years, something remarkable happens to the child: he develops functional language, what we refer to as the beginning of true intelligence. The present chapter is concerned with the development, enhancement, utilization, measurement, and predictive utility of intelligence.

THE CONCEPT OF MEASURED INTELLIGENCE

The development of instruments to measure intelligence first provided utility for the fledgling field of child psychology. Parallel to the exploration of the concepts of learning and memory, the developing concept of intelligence contributed greatly to the scientific maturity of the field.

Ironically, however, this concept of an operational definition of intelligence, one of the most significant statements concerning the nature of man made by psychologists and probably one of the most significant advances made by the field in the twentieth century, has become today one of the most controversial areas in psychology. There are many reasons for this controversy, and relevant arguments on both sides, but pressing social issues concerning the use of the concept outside the clinical setting, particularly with regard to school tracking and employment selection, have taken the concept of measured intelligence out of the hands of the psychologist and placed it, often as not, in the newspapers, in politics, in business, and in the courts. The question seems to be real: whether the concept of intelligence is to become the stone over which public confidence in psychology stumbles, or, as it first appeared to be, the foundation rock for a science of human behavior.

This concept of measured intelligence has been brought into sharp focus by the vituperative controversy regarding the heritability of intelligence and the relationship between intelligence and race, a painful controversy that is an unfortunate detour from the honorable effort of some early, distinguished psychologists to provide a satisfactory method for the measurement of an age-old concept.

In our Brief History, we reviewed the classic efforts of man to deal with the dimension of intelligence. That there was such a dimension, with the genius outstanding by his breadth and height of knowledge, understanding, and ability to reason, and the idiot outstanding by his narrowness and limited understanding, has always been obvious to mankind. From the beginning of recorded history, the wise man and the idiot have been authentic characters in story, tradition, and law. The child prodigy has long been taken as a sign for greatness in the future; man has always put a premium upon giftedness, wisdom, and astuteness.

Oracles, seers, and sages have had their place in the histories of all peoples. Geniuses in mathematics, music, art, architecture, literature, and leadership always have been readily identified and held in awe and wonder. Similarly, the village idiot, with his dull, glazed look, his thick tongue, his grunting animal sounds, and his lack of words, his lumbering gait and whimpering insensitivity, also has been readily identified and to some extent understood by mankind. What is more, some presumed continuity has existed between these two extremes, some mystical pecking order in which we all can locate ourselves, smarter than some and duller than others. This concept of continuity, if not linearity, is a historical if not scientifically proven dimension that has always been part of the concept of intelligence.

EARLY CONCEPTS OF INTELLIGENCE

Note that before the beginning of the current century, no valid distinction was made between insanity and idiocy. The terms *idiot* and *dementia* were almost synonymous, referring to all subnormal mental performance. No taxonomy, no classification of mental diseases, no definition of levels of mental retardation existed. Idiocy or dementia was considered to be a condition, much as, for instance, Down's syndrome or mongolian idiocy is considered today as an all-or-none state.

Emil Kraepelin

As late as the end of the nineteenth century, one of the great taxono-mers, Kraepelin (1896), defined a whole class of mental disorders, today known as the schizophrenias and accounting for over 60 percent of all long-term patients in mental hospitals, as dementia praecox, or premature dementia, premature senility: senility, the final stage of man, was con-sidered to be a form of idiocy. Kraepelin assumed that for some reason these patients had arrived prematurely in the childlike, demented state characterized by the very old; their brain had deteriorated, either because of a gradual failure in blood supply or because of a natural process of degeneration.

Jean-Etienne Esquirol

The publication of a classic book on mental maladies by Esquirol (1838) dates the beginning of a conceptual distinction between mental retardation and insanity. The logic of his critical distinction is interesting.

> Idiocy is not a disease but a condition in which the intellectual faculties are never manifested or have never been developed sufficiently to enable the idiot to acquire such amount of knowledge as persons of his own age reared in similar circum-stances are capable of receiving. Idiocy begins with life or at that age which precedes the development of the intellectual and affective faculties, which are from the first what they are doomed to be during the whole period of their existence. Up to the present time no way has been found of altering this condition.
>
> The mentally deranged person has been bereft of the good things which he once enjoyed; he is the poor man who once was rich; the idiot has always lived in misfortune and poverty. A state of abnormality may possibly be changed but the idiot remains always the same. The one has many childish features; the other retains for the most part the physiognomy of an adult. Although both have little or no understanding, the abnormal show in their organization and even in their intelligence something of what they had previously attained; the idiot, on the con-trary is all that he ever was, he is all that, in consideration of his primitive organiza-tion, he ever could have been [Esquirol as quoted by Goodenough, 1949, p. 3].

Esquirol carried his idea one step further and distinguished between levels of deficiency, clearly implying that mental retardation is not an all-or-none proposition, but that intelligence has dimension. Initially, Es-quirol hoped to distinguish between levels of intelligence on the basis of some type of physical measurement. He thought that perhaps the size, shape, or dimensions of the skull might provide the missing yardstick. Ultimately he abandoned this idea and chose instead a tool which remains today the mainstay of intellectual assessment: *the quantity and quality of language facility.*

Jean-Marc Itard

Esquirol was a taxonomist rather than an activist. He was convinced that little could be done to alter mental retardation, or genius for that matter. His view followed closely that of Itard (1801, 1807), who had become utterly discouraged by what he considered the colossal failure of his attempt to rehabilitate the famous Wild Boy of Aveyron, a severely retarded youth found running wild in the woods outside of Paris in 1798. Itard had tried to train the boy, despite medical opinion that the child was an idiot and uneducable. Although the boy made some progress in speech, he failed to develop adequate self-control or to adapt himself socially and emotionally to civilized living.

After years of dedicated effort uncrowned by success, Itard threw up his hands and cried:

> Unfortunate one! Since my pains are lost and my efforts fruitless, take yourself back to your forest and primitive tastes; or if your new wants make you dependent on society, suffer the penalty of being useless and go to Bicetre there to die in wretchedness [Itard as quoted by Goodenough, 1949, p. 6].

Although Itard was bitterly disappointed in the outcome, other members of the French Academy of Science were not nearly so pessimistic. They drew virtually opposite conclusions from Itard. It was not the boy's lack of normalcy that was impressive, but the great improvement Itard had wrought in his performance. Itard had demonstrated that a change in behavior could be effected by environmental control.

Edward Seguin

A student of both, Seguin (1866) combined the taxonomy of Esquirol and the methodology of Itard. More than any other person in the nineteenth century, he pressed for optimism regarding the alteration of intelligence. He insisted that the feebleminded could be educated and that success or failure could be judged only in terms of improvement made by the learner.

Charles Darwin

While Seguin was stressing the importance of schools to teach the mentally retarded, Charles Darwin and Francis Galton were producing theories that were to have a profound influence on our modern conception of intelligence. Darwin (1859) formalized the theory of the origin of species, or the survival of the fittest. Although his data were related to the adaptive mechanisms of plants and animals, Darwin had the wisdom and temerity to state, for the first time, that the continuity between man and animals was not merely coincidental or analogous—thus bringing down upon his head the wrath of the Anglican church and fundamentalists around the world. As Darwin became more convinced of the operation of the phenomena of survival, he began to believe that man too had characteristics that enabled him to adapt, and so to survive. These characteristics, these functional behavior patterns developed by man in the course of his evolution, Darwin came to view as intelligence. Darwin believed that brighter people had a higher probability of survival and reproduction.

Francis Galton

However, it was not Darwin who spelled out the full implication of his theory for mankind, but rather his eminent and long-lived cousin. Galton (1870) began his study of intelligence with a survey of inheritance in which he traced the family trees of eminent men in English history, science, and letters. He then began to develop a systematic, formal, and objective technique by which to measure intelligence.

A laboratory scientist, Galton took a vast spectrum of anthropometric measures: reaction time, auditory range, tactile discrimination, the number of taps an individual can make in a minute, speed of reflexes, speed of dilation of pupils, speed of reaction to light, sound, and touch, vocabulary, memory for numbers and letters, and a whole host of mechanical measures of reactions. In his enthusiasm, Galton opened his laboratory to the general public, taking individual measurements of over nine-thousand people.

Although his sensory-motor tasks failed to discriminate between the successful and the unsuccessful, Galton became convinced of a biological, physically based intelligence with great significance for survival. Following up his hypothesis with action, Galton formed the Eugenics Society, dedicated to the proposition that only by selective breeding could man ultimately rid himself of his inferior tendencies and develop a true superrace. As J. Hunt sums up Galton's reasoning, "if human characteristics are inherited, the way to improve man's lot is to breed better men" (1961, p. 12). Here, Galton himself seems to have forgotten his law of filial regression.

G. Stanley Hall

While Galton's British laboratory was cranking out measurements of the performance of his nine-thousand subjects on various sensory and motor tasks, in America G. Stanley Hall (1883, 1891a) and Stanford E. Chaille (1887) had become interested in the problem of assessment of intelligence. Twenty-one years before Binet's scale, Chaille published a series of tests for infants arranged in order of age of accomplishment. Although he did not use the term mental age, Chaille certainly understood the concept.

Hall was particularly interested in intelligence as it related to schoolchildren. In 1883, with the publication of "The Contents of Children's Minds," and in 1891, "The Contents of Children's Minds on Entering School," Hall developed the questionnaire method with children, a technique discovered but abandoned by Galton. Hall undertook his questionnaire "with the advantages of many suggestions and not a few warnings" from the author of a Berlin study prompted by the Pedagogical Society of Berlin in October, 1869. The Berlin study, "to determine the individuality of the children so far as conditioned by the concepts arising from their immediate environment," involved 138 questions to ascertain "how many children who entered the primary classes that fall had seen and could name certain common animals, insects, and plants, had taken certain walks, visited specific parks, museums, etc." (Hall, 1883, p. 255).

Although his questionnaire lacked much in technique, as compared to modern scales, its content had great validity, sampling the kind of information that, by everyone's standards, children ought to know. The importance of Hall's questionnaire was not so much in the quality of the questions, however, as in the development of a method that tapped information storage, language facility, and experience far more closely related to school work than did Galton's sensory-motor tasks.

Also, by combining the correct answers into a total numerical score, Hall for the first time defined intelligence in truly objective terms. A child who scored 25 on Hall's questionnaire was brighter than a child who scored 15. The more questions a child could answer, the more intelligent he was inferred to be. By ordering the questions in terms of difficulty, Hall developed a reasonably formal, quickly administered, interesting test that on a commonsense basis got at the business of measuring intelligence.

Although Hall, like Chaille, understood the concept of mental age, an error in logic occurred as he developed his test of intelligence: Hall's definition of intelligence did not take into account the effect of normal intellectual growth with increasing chronological age. Hall was concerned with first-graders. He was dealing in absolute terms along a single dimension related to the child's ability to answer questions about his environment. Thus for Hall, a five-year-old child who was able to answer twenty-five questions was considered as bright as but no brighter than a seven-year-old child who answered the same number of questions. Hall had developed a functional measure of mental age along essentially the same dimensions as those in general use today, but he had not understood the concept of IQ (Intelligence Quotient)—the relationship between chronological age and mental age that allows comparison of children of different age levels.

The most extraordinary aspect of Hall's work, however, was the depth and intensity of his questioning of children, which enabled him to penetrate, as perhaps only one other person in modern times has penetrated, into the development of the logical thinking of children. Only Hall and Piaget (1929, 1931) have demonstrated the rare ability to understand the conceptual world of the child.

An example of Hall's sharp insight is his description of the curious logic of children.

> Words, in connection with rhyme, rhythm, alliteration, cadence, etc., or even without these, simply as sound-pictures, often absorb the attention of children and yield them a really aesthetic pleasure either quite independently of their meaning or to the utter bewilderment of it. They hear fancied words in noises and sounds of nature and animals, and are persistent punners. As butterflys make butter, . . . grasshoppers give grass, bees give beads, . . . kittens grow on the pussy-willows, and all honey is from honeysuckles, and even a poplin dress is made of poplar-trees. . . . They wonder what kind of a bear was the consecrated cross-eyed bear as they understood the hymn "The Consecrated Cross I'd Bear" [1891a, p. 157].

Hall, of course, was maintaining a global conception of intelligence that tied it closely to language and information. He correctly perceived that his definition of intelligence was dependent, at least to some extent, upon the cultural background of the children, for he cites in his study the differences between rural and urban children and between black and white children. As early as the 1890s, Hall recognized that the cultural background of children must be considered in any adequate diagnosis of intelligence.

His molar definition of intelligence did not, however, excite much practical interest, because it did not discriminate between successful and unsuccessful students in a classroom. The items in Hall's questionnaire (see Table 6) objectified the kind of information skillful teachers had

Table 6

Contents of Children's Minds as Sampled by
G. Stanley Hall's Questionnaire

Name of the Object of Conception	Percentage of Children Ignorant of It in Boston	Name of the Object of Conception	Percentage of Children Ignorant of It in Boston
Seen sunset	53.5	That leather things come from animals	93.4
Seen clouds	35.0	Maxim or proverb	91.5
Seen stars	14.0	Origin of cotton things	90.0
Seen moon	7.0	What flour is made of	89.0
Conception of an island	87.5	Ability to knit	88.0
Conception of a beach	55.5	What bricks are made of	81.1
Conception of woods	53.5	Shape of the world	70.3
Conception of river	48.0	Origin of woolen things	69.0
Conception of pond	40.0	Never attended kindergarten	67.5
Conception of hill	28.0	Never been in bathing	64.5
Conception of brook	15.0	Can tell no rudiments of a story	58.0
Conception of triangle	92.0	Not know wooden things are from trees	55.0
Conception of square	56.0	Origin of butter	50.5
Conception of circle	35.0	Origin of meat (from animals)	48.0
The number five	28.5	Cannot sew	47.5
The number four	17.0	Cannot strike a given musical tone	40.0
The number three	8.0	Cannot beat time regularly	39.0
Seen watchmaker at work	68.0	Have never saved cents at home	36.0
Seen file	65.0	Never been in the country	35.5
Seen plough	64.5	Can repeat no verse	28.0
Seen spade	62.0	Source of milk	20.5
Seen hoe	61.0		
Seen bricklayer at work	44.5		
Seen shoemaker at work	25.0		
Seen axe	12.0		
Knows green by name	15.0		
Knows blue by name	14.0		
Knows yellow by name	13.5		
Knows red by name	9.0		

Reprinted, by permission of the publisher, from G. Stanley Hall, The contents of children's minds on entering school, *Pedagogical Seminary*, 1891, 1, 150.

known for some time, but did not carry the problem the additional step: they did not discriminate items pertinent to success in school. Whether a child knows that milk comes from cows makes little difference to a teacher, unless his knowing or not knowing this fact will in some way affect his academic performance.

William Stern

In 1912, as Frederick Rowe, Chairman of the Psychology Department at Randolph-Macon Woman's College, pointed out to me, Stern corrected Hall's logical error in measuring intelligence. Writes Stern:

> The full significance of [mental age] is disclosed only when we consider it in relation to other circumstances. It can evidently be related to other quantitative scales, like chronological age, school grade and school standing, or we can find out how it varies with certain qualitative conditions, like social level, type of school, nationality and the like.
>
> Doubtless most significant is the relation of mental age to the actual *chronological age* of the subject, for . . . a certain mental level goes normally with a certain age, so that the relationship of mental to chronological age indicates the amount of discrepancy between the intelligence present and that required (in the sense of a norm to be expected), and in this way affords an expression for the degree of the child's intellectual endowment.
>
> Up to now this discrepancy has always been computed in the simple form of the difference between the two ages, which, when negative gave the absolute *mental retardation,* when positive the absolute *mental advance* of the child in terms of years. Thus, if mental retardation = -2, the child's mental development is two years behind the normal level of his age.
>
> It is perfectly clear how valuable the measurement of mental retardation is, particularly in the investigation of abnormal children. It has, however, been shown recently that the simple computation of the absolute difference between the two ages is not entirely adequate for this purpose, because the difference does not mean the same thing at different ages. Only when children of approximately equal age-levels are under investigation can this value suffice: for all other cases the introduction of the *mental quotient* [is] recommended. This value expresses not the difference, but the ratio of mental to chronological age and is thus partially independent of the absolute magnitude of chronological age. The formula is, then: mental quotient = mental age $\div$ chronological age. With children who are just at their normal level, the value is 1; with those who are advanced, the value is greater than unity; with those mentally retarded, a proper fraction. The more pronounced the feeble-mindedness, the smaller the value of the fraction [Stern, 1912, pp. 41–42].

Thus in 1912, Stern had conceptualized the Intelligence Quotient, the IQ. Intelligence could now be measured and compared across age ranges. The stage was set for the monumental work of Alfred Binet and Lewis Terman.

Alfred Binet

Predictive measurement of intelligence was still an open question in October of 1904, when the Minister of Public Instruction in Paris charged a Commission with insuring the benefits of instruction to defective children. Alfred Binet and Theophile Simon (1905, 1905–1908) were given the responsibility of furnishing a guide for the Commission to use in discriminating between feebleminded children who were incapable of learning by ordinary methods and children who were simply poorly motivated.

Binet and Simon identified three methods for assessing the intelligence of children: medical, pedagogical, and psychological. The medical method, following medical tradition, was designed to discover the anatomical, physiological, and pathological signs of an inferior intelligence: the conventional medical examination. The pedagogical method, following academic tradition, was designed to judge intelligence by the sum of acquired knowledge: nothing more or less than a conventional, informal achievement test. The psychological method, developed by Binet and Simon, made direct observations and measurements of degrees of intelligence, which Binet identified as *aptitude for academic achievement*.

Binet and Simon addressed themselves to the Commission's problem by first carefully exploring with teachers the skills required for success in school. They then tied their definition of intelligence directly to these capacities. The fundamental assumption of the *Binet-Simon Test* was that, given equal opportunity, those children who had developed certain skill, certain knowledge, and certain ability at a given age were brighter than those who had not. Omitting the even-numbered years, the items used on the 1905 Binet-Simon Test were:

Three Years

> Show eyes, nose, mouth
> Name objects in a picture
> Repeat 2 figures
> Repeat a sentence of 6 syllables
> Give last name

Five Years

> Compare 2 boxes of different weights
> Copy a square
> Repeat a sentence of 10 syllables
> Count 4 sous
> Put together 2 pieces in a game of "patience"

Seven Years

> Indicate omissions in drawings
> Give the number of fingers
> Copy a written sentence
> Copy a triangle and a diamond
> Repeat 5 figures
> Describe a picture
> Count 13 single sous
> Name 4 pieces of money

Nine Years

> Give the date complete (day, month, day of the month, year)
> Name the days of the week

Give definitions superior to use
Retain 6 memories after reading
Make change, 4 sous from 20 sous
Arrange 5 weights in order [Binet and Simon, 1905–1908, p. 420]

The direct relationship between this test of intelligence and school is obvious. Any child able to perform these tasks should be able to learn in school. This is true even though none of the items requires formal education; they all should be part of the child's normal repertoire learned at home in the preschool years.

By tying their test directly to academic skills, Binet and Simon were immensely successful in performing the task they had set out to perform— *predicting academic success.* Bearing this in mind throughout our discussion of intelligence will add considerable clarity. This initial definition of intelligence as the ability to respond effectively to academic training is defensible today.

James McKeen Cattell

While Binet was developing practical tests useful in predicting academic success, James McKeen Cattell (1890), the first to use the term *mental tests,* had completed his dissertation on individual differences under Wilhelm Wundt (but not with Wundt's blessing), and had returned to America with undiminished interest in measuring individual differences. Cattell's tests, a compromise between the psychophysical methods of Galton and the school-oriented tasks of Binet, were intended for use in predicting success in college. They emphasized keenness of vision and hearing, color sensitivity, reaction time, rote memory, mental imagery, and the like.

Although Cattell's tests were singularly ineffective in predicting academic success, they were important as a second line of test development that allowed itself to be challenged by an outside criterion. Instead of considering intelligence to be what intelligence tests measure, Cattell was willing to state that an intelligence test should be put to the trial of predictive validity—could it predict some useful and independent variable such as success in college?

Henry H. Goddard

Galton and Cattell both believed in generalized superiority—that superior people should be faster in reaction time, faster in perception, and so forth. The fact that quickness of perception and reaction are not a major part of adult intelligence was a hard lesson to learn. It was not the first time, nor the last, that psychology would go down the primrose path of simplicity in the hope that just around the corner would be some one-to-one relationship leading to perfect prediction. Intelligence, however, is an abstraction far more complex than any single instrument so far devised for its measurement.

Since the European educational system was based on past achievement, there was little pressure in Europe for intelligence tests to be developed; moreover, family and upper class opportunity made far more difference in Europe than did anything that we might call intelligence. Decisions regarding advanced academic opportunities were based largely on earlier achievement, judgment of teachers, and family prestige. The concepts of the self-made man and equal opportunity were American, and they led to far greater interest in individual intelligence in America than on the Continent.

Henry Goddard (1910), a student of G. Stanley Hall and founder of the Vineland Training School in Princeton, New Jersey—one of the early schools for the retarded in America—first brought the *Simon-Binet* to America. However, Goddard made no effort to Americanize the instrument. He made no allowances for the cultural differences between Parisian schoolchildren and the retarded children and adults to be found in New Jersey at that time. Goddard simply made a literal translation of the items of Simon and Binet.

Lewis Terman

Also a student of G. Stanley Hall, Lewis Terman began the Americanization of intelligence testing. In 1916, Terman, whose dissertation had been an in-depth study of a few geniuses, devised a standardized American version of the *Simon-Binet: the Stanford-Binet Revision of the Simon-Binet Test.* This 1916 revision represented an entirely new tack. Terman's selection of items most directly relevant to the American culture, his large-scale sampling, and his publication of a careful manual of detailed instructions about how the test was to be used and scored, made the more or less personalized instrument of Binet and Simon the basis for a tradition of nationally standardized intelligence tests—a tradition that has withstood the pressures of time and controversy and that still remains one of the milestones of psychology's contribution to the American way of life. For all its limitations, weaknesses, and problems of standardization, no better way is available to man for making predictions regarding future success, regardless of the area, than the IQ. Nothing short of an exhaustive achievement test, taking three to four times as long to administer, approximates the predictive power of the IQ.

The genius of Terman lay both in his selection of items that sampled significant variables in the lives of his subjects and in his selection of subjects who were most representative of the children with whom his instrument was to be used. The *Stanford-Binet* in America has gone through three major revisions (Terman, 1916; Terman and Merrill, 1937, 1960). The most recent, the *Stanford-Binet Intelligence Scale, Form L–M* probably has been used in more studies of achievement and intelligence and their relationship than any other instrument in the world. The 1960 revision represents a compilation of the best features of the 1937 Form L and Form M. Its major claim to validity is its fidelity to the previous instrument; therefore, the vast validating research done for the 1937 revision was not repeated.

Arnold Gesell

Another of Hall's eminent students, Arnold Gesell was concerned with the general neurological development of children. From a concept of infant morphology and a study of infant behavior, Gesell developed a scale for measuring infant maturation. His work obviously is based upon neurological development as it is reflected in overt behavior (Gesell and Ames, 1947; Gesell and Amatruda, 1962).

Gesell's test and all of its revisions lack the precision of measurement typical of the *Binet* and the *Wechsler*, but it provides an intensive study of young children on a systematic basis and is particularly helpful to the novice who lacks the experience to recognize what is normal or abnormal in growth and development. Gesell and Amatruda's *Developmental Diagnosis*, first published in 1941, is even today a standard reference for calibrating the growth rate of children. As expressed by Goodenough:

> Although Gesell's tests of mental development lack statistical refinement and his instructions for giving and scoring them leave so much to individual judgment as to render it highly unlikely that different examiners will obtain similar results for the same cases, his work nevertheless has been the chief source of ideas for others whose technical skill in test construction outruns their talent for observing the infinite minutiae of infantile behavior and for judging which aspects of the child's responses to specific stimuli are most significant as indicators of his mental progress [Goodenough, 1949, p. 308].

THEORIES OF INTELLIGENCE

Although an intelligence test such as the *Stanford-Binet* contains nearly fifty individual items, they group naturally into several types, or factors. The single most dominant factor is vocabulary, which includes both definition of terms and distinction between various abstract terms. Other factors are numerical skill, including counting, mental arithmetic, and qualitative reasoning; memory, such as immediate recall of a series of digits and the long-term recall in academic achievement; and perceptual-motor skill, as involved in writing, drawing, and copying. Not only are the test items logically related to each other in groups, but the groups appear as unified factors when subjected to statistical analysis, using a test of relatedness or correlation. This natural grouping into specific factors raises a question, then, which has considerable relevance. Has intelligence a single dimension, ranging along a continuum from smartness to dullness? Or, has intelligence many dimensions too subtle to be defined by a single curve?

EARLY THEORIES

Binet, Simon, Goddard, and Terman, as well as Galton and Gesell, seemed to believe that intelligence was a single dimension: you had it or you didn't. Intelligent individuals were those with a good sense of music and timing, great mathematical skills, manual dexterity, and verbal ability—in fact, they exhibited excellence in everything.

Edward L. Thorndike considered intelligence to be defined within three boundaries:

1. *Altitude.* "Other things being equal, the harder the task a person masters, the greater his intelligence."
2. *Breadth.* "Other things being equal, the greater number of tasks of equal difficulty the person masters, the greater his intelligence."
3. *Speed.* "Other things being equal, the more quickly a person produces a correct response, the greater his intelligence" [G. Thompson, 1962, p. 395].

E. Thorndike et al. (1927) and many of the theorists who believed in a general factor in intelligence considered altitude to be the most important of these three boundaries.

A second view of intelligence was advanced by Charles E. Spearman and L. L. Thurstone. Spearman (1927) proposed that intelligence had two factors: a *g*, or general factor, and an *s*, or specific factor. Thurstone (1946) spoke of primary mental abilities and suggested that we should not speak in terms of intelligence, but rather in terms of intelligences, which may or may not be closely related. Thurstone visualized an individual who could be verbally fluent and numerically stupid, or abstractly intelligent and mechanically moronic. The stereotype of the absent-minded professor who, in spite of his genius in understanding abstract mathematical equations, can't remember to take his briefcase to the office, forgets where he parks his car, and can't for the life of him tie a bowtie, lends credence to the notion that intelligence is multifaceted. Through factor analysis, Thurstone identified what he considered to be eight separate and more or less mutually exclusive components of intelligence: space, number, verbal comprehension, word fluency, memory, induction, deduction, and flexibility factors.

1. Space. The ability to visualize two- and three-dimensional objects; heavily weighted toward mechanical aptitude.
2. Number. The ability to perform rather simple numerical computations.
3. Verbal comprehension. The ability to reason verbally, to think conceptually, and to define vocabulary.
4. Word fluency. The ability to use words in context.
5. Memory. The ability to use both short- and long-term recall.
6. Induction. The ability to discover the principle that will solve a series of problems.
7. Deduction. The ability to apply a given principle to a series of problems.
8. Flexibility. Speed in interpreting instructions and sizing up a problem; the ability to disregard a solution that doesn't work for a more promising one.

Thurstone concluded that Spearman's *g* factor was less definitive and useful than his own primary factors. His most important contribution was the claim, fairly well documented, that these factors of intelligence could be identified in both children and adults and thus possessed longitudinal significance.

A third view is exemplified by David Wechsler, who writes:

It appears, therefore, that the entity or quantity which we are able to measure by intelligence tests is not a simple quantity. Certainly, it is not something which can be expressed by one single factor alone.... Intelligence is all this and something more. It is the ability to utilize this energy or to exercise this ability in contextual situations, situations that have content and purpose as well as form and meaning. To concede as much is to admit that any practical definition of intelligence must be fundamentally a biological one in the widest sense of the term [Wechsler, 1958, p. 14].

As Tyler sums up, "Wechsler has always maintained that intelligence is a manifestation of the personality as a whole and that emotional and motivational characteristics are among the ingredients out of which it is made" (L. Tyler, 1965, p. 98).

ESTABLISHED DEFINITIONS

Today at least three definitions of intelligence are well established and virtually noncontroversial among psychologists and educators: definitions based on theoretical, operational, and empirical dimensions of intelligence.

Theoretical

The theoretical definition of intelligence addresses itself to some underlying dimensions inferred from the behavior of the subject. Intelligence is defined theoretically as *the ability to profit from experience*. This ability has been assumed to depend upon three primary abilities: memory, abstraction, and synthesization.

The rather uncomplicated memory factor refers to the ability of the individual to store experience in a manner that provides for efficient recall. The recall efficiency, however, is a function of the ability to abstract, since eidetic recall, visual or photographic memory, is not considered a function of intelligence per se. Thus the idiot savant, who has an uncanny ability to remember instantly the day of the week on which each date in history falls, is considered just that—an idiot. He is probably not an idiot—usually simply a person of borderline intelligence; the point is that we have never confused rote memory with intelligence.

Abstraction is the ability to classify information and experience in such a way that it is linked into interlocking concepts. This unifying ability helps us to organize the world of experience into a world of concepts. It is the factor in intelligence that enables us to interpret the complex stimuli around us, and to recall information in the correct context. Thus the child remembers that tomorrow is Sunday, that Aunt Martha comes on Sunday, and that Aunt Martha usually rewards nice behavior with something from her coin purse. So on Saturday, the child begins to lay the groundwork for Aunt Martha's Sunday visit by doing some obvious good deeds.

Obviously, this child has learned more than a series of unrelated facts about his life. He has learned to put things together. And the more concepts he can master, the more complex the concepts, the greater is his ability to synthesize. Synthesization is the process of creating new information on the basis of logical induction. Creativity, the ability to go be-

yond the immediate conclusions derived from experience, always has been
regarded as an underlying factor of intelligence.

The true genius is a person who spends much of his effort in the synthesizing process, since memorization and abstraction are so easy for him. In summary, then, agreement is general that the greater the memory span, the faster the acquisition and manipulation of facts, the broader and the more interrelated the abstractions, the more capable a person is to perform at the highest level of intelligence, the more able he is to create.

Operational

Intelligence is defined operationally through measurement; the IQ is the operational definition of intelligence. Operationally, intelligence is *that which an intelligence test measures.*

Initially, intelligence and achievement were confounded, inseparably bound together. The most intelligent persons in the land were those who had mastered the most tasks, be they the great poets, the great playwrights, the great historians, the great teachers. The achievement tests were mostly informal, but they were there: the tutor, the headmaster, the teacher, who graded, ranked, and rated the young child. And the more the child achieved, the greater his knowledge, the greater his intelligence.

The first operational measures of intelligence were the sensory-motor tests of Galton. The basis for these early measurements was the belief in a biological or genetic intelligence reflected in the speed and sensitivity of basic sensory-motor performance: the faster the reflexes, the wider the digit-recall range, the smaller the differences detected between musical tones, the greater the intelligence.

With the development of the *Binet-Simon Test* and the Americanization of the concept by Terman and Wechsler, the operational definition of intelligence came into its own. So great was the influence of this definition of intelligence, that the IQ became, for awhile, completely synonymous with intelligence. Not until the environmental manipulation studies of Beth Wellman and the Iowa group in the late 1930s and early 1940s did the operational definition of intelligence lose some of its significance. Yet it remains today one of the most useful definitions of intelligence because of its objectivity and its lack of implied but unsubstantiated meaning.

Empirical

Beyond the theoretical and operational definitions of intelligence is the empirical definition, which refers to the ability of the individual to cope with his environment, his ability to adjust to the problems he encounters, his ability to solve most of his problems, and his ability to achieve generally agreed-upon goals. *The more intelligent a person is, the better adjusted he is, the more successful he is and, in the broadest terms, the more he achieves.*

Many studies have related the IQ of these three empirical measures of intelligence and, in general, the correlation is positive: the best adjustment, the highest level of success, and the greatest achievement is obtained by those whose IQs fall in the higher ranges of bright normal to superior. However, as Hollingworth (1942) has pointed out, the very superior person often has tremendous difficulty adjusting to the social demands of his peers of normal intelligence; but high-order geniuses are extremely rare and are by definition abnormal, since all of their performance falls so far from the normal.

The appropriateness of the empirical definition of intelligence is supported by data from a longitudinal study of giftedness by Terman and Oden (1959). During their growing years, the physical development of their subjects, children with IQs of 140 or above, was consistently superior. Their academic achievement was also significantly above average. Their social development was generally superior, although they often sought out older companions. Their personal integrity was greater and their moral development was consistently superior. Parents and teachers alike rated them superior in emotional maturity and in personal motivation and drive, as well as in social and physical development. As adults they maintained their superior physiques and health, and their vocational achievement was greater than that of the average college graduate. Their childhood superiority was maintained at every level throughout their adult years.

ECONOMICS OF INTELLIGENCE

So far, we have presented a straightforward history of the development of an instrument with great utility, because it performed the useful function of isolating particularly pernicious aspects of perceptual-motor and cognitive skills that are the essential prerequisite for academic success. The test was used in a largely homogeneous population within a largely homogeneous school setting, where the overlap between the home environment and the school environment was great.

By the mid-twenties, the conviction that intelligence tests measured an underlying, genetically determined capacity had become so strongly ingrained that the influence of the early environment was considered trivial by comparison. At this point, two types of studies began to appear in the literature: the first tended to point out the generally low intellectual performance of culturally isolated minorities; the second dealt with the question of modifiability of intelligence through environmental manipulation.

STUDIES OF IMPOVERISHMENT

As early as 1932, Sherman and Key conducted a now classic, detailed study of the longitudinal picture of intelligence of isolated, deprived, impoverished mountain children from four isolated hollows in the Blue Ridge Mountains some hundred miles west of Washington, D.C. They made a comparison of the intelligence of these children with that of a similar group of children from a small village the same distance from the city, but with ready access to the outside world. These five groups of children had essentially the same genetic backgrounds.

Even though the four hollows districts were all impoverished, some were more so than others. In fact, Sherman and Key were able to classify these four hollows villages in order of overall deprivation. The single outlying village was further advanced, socioeconomically and in terms of cultural enrichment, than any of the four hollows. All the children had uniformly low IQs; their mean IQ on the *Stanford-Binet* was 61. They were slow and cautious, and had a slow tempo of response.

One of the most interesting findings of Sherman and Key was a direct relationship between the IQ and the level of deprivation. The further removed from cultural advantages, the more isolated the hollow, the lower the IQ. Also, the older the child, the lower the IQ.

Sherman and Key concluded that the measured IQs of these isolated mountain children support the contention that:

> performance on intelligence tests depends in a large measure upon the opportunities to gather information and upon the requirements made upon the individual by his environment. . . . Furthermore, as has been shown in this paper, the young children of the various Hollows do not differ greatly in intelligence, whereas great differences are found between the older children of the different Hollows. The only plausible explanation of the increasing difference with increasing age is that children develop only as the environment demands development [1932, p. 289].

The study by Sherman and Key is strongly supported by Gordon's (1923) study of English canal-boat children; by Asher's (1935) study of the children of a mining community in Harlan County, Kentucky; by Skeels and Fillmore's (1937) study, which found that the longer children remained in deprived home environments, the lower their IQs; and by Wheeler's (1932, 1942) studies of isolated mountain children in Tennessee. After these studies made their way into the literature, the question of causation versus correlation was still unanswered, and interest in the problem generally was tragically minimal.

STUDIES OF RACE

Other significant evidence of an alarming problem in the interpretation of intelligence tests had inserted itself into the American scene. In the mid-fifties, totally independent of the testing movement, a significant attack was made upon the grouping practices of the public schools system—grouping upon the basis of racial origin, with or without equal opportunity. As the country ponderously responded to the holding of the Supreme Court that racial segregation of schools was unconstitutional, and made valid efforts to begin the process of integration, large-scale studies of the functioning of impoverished and deprived children who were also black were undertaken.

Kennedy, Van De Riet, and White

Convincing evidence began to appear in the literature that the IQ is related to cultural enrichment. A study by Kennedy, Van De Riet, and White (1963) demonstrated the effect of environmental influence on individual IQs and illustrated the general cultural deprivation of the black schoolchild in the southeastern United States, who thus far has encountered generally low socioeconomic and cultural advantages within his home and poor educational opportunities at school.

The *Stanford-Binet Intelligence Scale* is designed to obtain an average, or mean, IQ of 100, with the scores distributed in a bell-shaped curve such

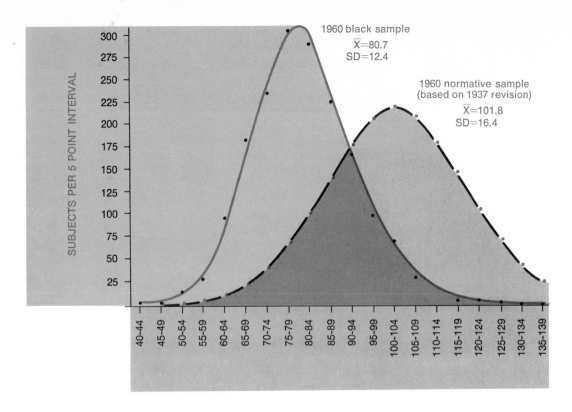

Figure 15

IQ distribution for Stanford-Binet normative sample and 1,800 black elementary school children in the Southeast. Reprinted, with permission of the authors and the publisher, from Wallace A. Kennedy, Vernon Van De Riet, and James C. White, Jr., A normative sample of intelligence and achievement of Negro elementary schoolchildren in the southeastern United States, *Monographs of the Society for Research in Child Development*, 1963, 28 (6), No. 90, Figure 2, p. 68. Copyright © 1963 by the Society for Research in Child Development, Inc.

that 68 percent fall within 16 points of the mean. This 16-point range above and below the mean, the standard deviation, is a measure of the scatter of the scores and therefore one test of the representativeness of the mean. Black elementary schoolchildren in the Southeast tested by Kennedy, Van De Riet, and White had a mean IQ of 80.7, with a standard deviation of 12.4. Figure 15 shows the IQ distribution for the sample used in standardizing the *Stanford-Binet* and for the sample of eighteen hundred black elementary school children. The standard deviation is a measure of the curve's peak: the smaller the standard deviation, the higher the peak. The smaller standard deviation for the black children indicates that more black children fall beneath the white mean than would be the case if the standard deviations were the same.

No appreciable difference in IQ between grades is noticeable in Table 7; the mean IQ remains constant across grade level. However,

223

Table 7

IQ Mean and SD for 1,800 Black Elementary
Schoolchildren, by Grade and Sex

Grade	Number	Mean	SD
First			
Male	160	81.28	11.76
Female	140	82.43	13.12
Total	300	81.81	12.43
Second			
Male	160	81.50	12.51
Female	140	79.10	12.99
Total	300	80.38	12.79
Third			
Male	144	81.00	11.16
Female	156	79.57	12.51
Total	300	80.25	11.90
Fourth			
Male	151	80.25	12.00
Female	149	79.05	11.63
Total	300	79.65	11.83
Fifth			
Male	137	81.00	13.16
Female	163	81.36	12.11
Total	300	81.20	12.60
Sixth			
Male	151	80.68	12.67
Female	149	80.85	13.07
Total	300	80.77	12.87
Grand total	1,800	80.71	12.48

Reprinted, by permission of the authors and the publisher, from Wallace A. Kennedy, Vernon Van De Riet, and James C. White, Jr., A normative sample of the intelligence and achievement of Negro elementary school-children in the southeastern United States, *Monographs of the Society for Research in Child Development*, 1963, 28 (6), No. 90, Table 41, p. 80. Copyright © 1963 by the Society for Research in Child Development, Inc.

Table 8 reveals an intriguing problem: the IQ was negatively correlated with chronological age. That is, the oldest children had the lowest IQ; the youngest children, the highest. This finding was due to the perennial problem encountered in the study of elementary schoolchildren: the difficulty in obtaining a sample representative of both age and grade. Because dull children tend to be retained, the duller, older children are grouped in the upper grades.

A five-year follow-up of a portion of this sample—subjects from one state—indicated that the bias in age did indeed account for the discrepancy. The original trend remained constant as these children grew older, both in terms of grade and age. The mean IQ of the follow-up sample was 79.4, with an SD of 14.3 (Kennedy, 1969).

Table 8

IQ Mean and SD for 1,800 Black Elementary
Schoolchildren, by Age

Age (in Years)	Number	Mean	SD
5	19	86.00	6.40
6	227	84.43	12.48
7	243	81.71	11.80
8	302	80.88	12.04
9	281	80.10	12.08
10	299	80.10	12.68
11	279	80.63	11.98
12	109	75.48	11.34
13	30	65.23	10.45
14	9	66.11	7.35
15	1	58.00	
16	1	51.00	
Total	1,800	80.71	12.48

This normative study of black children found a relationship between community size and mean IQ: the metropolitan children were brighter than the urban, the urban brighter than the rural (Kennedy, Van De Riet, and White, 1963, Table 43, p. 81).

Community Size	Mean IQ
Metropolitan	83.97
Urban	79.37
Rural	78.70

The most pronounced trend in the normative data, however, was the relationship between socioeconomic level and mean IQ: the higher the socioeconomic level, the higher the mean IQ. The range was from 105.00, for the highest level, to 78.43 for the lowest (Kennedy, Van De Riet, and White, 1963, Table 42, p. 80).

The Collaborative Study

A second study of far greater significance than the Kennedy, Van De Riet, and White study is still underway at the National Institute of Neurological Diseases and Stroke. This study, referred to as the Collaborative Study because it was carried out in collaboration with some thirteen medical schools across the country, is one of the largest and best controlled

225

studies ever undertaken. Beginning with the identification of a stratified sample of about fifty thousand women in their first trimester of pregnancy, the study to date has followed a residual sample of twenty-six thousand children through eight years of life, and recently has published the findings at year four, when all of the children were given the *Stanford-Binet Intelligence Scale*.

In any such longitudinal sample, children are lost for various reasons—disinterest of the mother, movement of the mother, miscarriage, stillborn, infant death, and so on—but the stability of this huge sample is remarkable, making certain trends quite clear. One of the major goals of the study was the prediction of outcome; and one of the most significant outcomes was the intelligence of the child predicted on the basis of medical, familial, social, and cultural factors.

Table 9 contains a brief look at the major variables that aid in the prediction of intelligence.

Table 9

Prediction of Four-Year IQ, the Collaborative Study (26,000 children)*

Variable	
Family Socioeconomic Index	.43
Race of Mother	.40
IQ of Mother	.36
Education of Mother	.35
Number of Prenatal Appointments Kept by Mother	.25
Infant Bayley Mental Score, Eight Months	.24
Infant Bayley Motor Score, Eight Months	.22
Lowest Hematocrit of Mother	.22
Lowest Hemoglobin of Mother	.21
Length of Gestation at First Medical Examination	−.19
Mother Married	.19
Father of Baby Living at Home	.19
Mother, History of X-Ray of Abdomino-Pelvic Area	.19
Four-Month Weight of Infant	.19
Eight-Month Height of Infant	.18
Birth Weight of Newborn	.17
Four-Month Height of Infant	.16
Eight-Month Weight of Infant	.16
One-Year Weight of Infant	.16
One-Year Height of Infant	.16
Mother, Anemia	.16
Forceps Delivery	.15
Length of Newborn	.15
Head Circumference of Newborn	.15
Four-Month Head Circumference of Infant	.15

*Unpublished data.

The first variable, the Socioeconomic Index, based upon the general economic level of the family determined by combining measures of employment, income, and education of the status parent, provides the best predictive information. Significantly, within this sample, race and socioeconomic status have a high degree of overlap, as is true for the country as a whole, with the black mothers being poor and the white mothers, nonpoor. Of course there were exceptions, but within this sample, the poverty variable was dominant.

Even such variables as number of appointments kept and gestation at the first medical exam were related closely to the socioeconomic variable. A poverty mother, even when offered taxi service, frequently does not have the free energy to go to the hospital for her examination.

The difference is vast between the response to a first pregnancy by a middle-class mother and by an impoverished mother, in terms of the energy free to invest in the pregnancy. When a middle-class mother becomes pregnant, her whole family is excited and concerned, often including great excitement on the part of the grandparents-to-be, neighbors, and friends. Her pregnancy is a time of great happiness; days before the first examination everyone is atwitter over the event. Not so with a tired, physically run-down working girl, whose life may be going on in the absence of the father of the child, for such is the way of poverty.

THEORIES OF THE RELATIONSHIP BETWEEN POVERTY AND INTELLIGENCE

The evidence from the Collaborative Study clearly demonstrates poverty to be the principal enemy to intellectual functioning of children. Obviously in the United States today, the correlation between the socioeconomic level of the parents and the IQ of the child is high. This well-established finding has led to three opinions of the primary cause of the relationship.

Heritability Group

In the first place, many sound investigators still follow the suggestions of Galton, Binet, and Goddard, holding that the primary cause of the relationship between economics and intelligence is the first principle of social evolution, "Them that has, gits!" Thus according to the interpretation of the heritability group, represented today by Cyril Burt (1958, 1968, 1972), Arthur Jensen (1969 a,b), William Shockley (1969), and Richard Herrnstein (1971), the effect of high intelligence in children is that they are more competitive, more successful, more dominant, such that over the long run, they accrue more of the world's resources at their disposal, provide better opportunities for their children, who in turn are brighter and accrue more of the resources, until the major resources of the country are in the hands of a few families with both high intelligence and high socioeconomic position. On the other hand, children of the poor begin life with less intellectual drive, accrue little in the way of family resources, and have children who face both low socioeconomic position and low ability.

This highly unpopular view has led to considerable harassment of its current defenders. The harassment is all the more vituperative because of the present confounding of economics and race in the United States, so that statements about the relationship between IQ and economics often take on racial significance. The effect of the controversy has been to radicalize the positions of the proponents, but perhaps it would be helpful to look briefly at the central proponents and their data.

Cyril Burt

Out of the tradition and the laboratories of Francis Galton, Cyril Burt, who died recently at the age of eighty-eight, for more than fifty years conducted research in England on the relationship between family similarities in academic and vocational achievement, intelligence, and physcial growth patterns. His principal vehicle was the study of identical and nonidentical twins. His principal concern was to identify the percentage of a child's IQ that can be predicted on the basis of what Burt called genetic factors.

In his pursuit of the heritability of intelligence, Burt studied the similarity of IQs of identical and nonidentical twins living together and apart and unrelated children living together. Over a period of time, he collected data on thirty cases of identical twins reared apart; his data are illustrated in Table 10.

Table 10

Familial and Nonfamilial Correlations between Mental and
Scholastic Assessments

Assessments	Identical twins reared together	Identical twins reared apart	Nonidentical twins reared together	Siblings reared together	Siblings reared apart	Unrelated children reared together
Mental "Intelligence"						
Group Test	.944	.771	.542	.515	.441	.281
Individual Test	.921	.843	.526	.491	.463	.252
Final Assessment	.925	.876	.551	.538	.517	.269
Scholastic						
General Attainments	.898	.681	.831	.814	.526	.535
Reading and Spelling	.944	.647	.915	.853	.490	.548
Arithmetic	.862	.723	.748	.769	.563	.476

Reprinted, by permission of the publisher, from Cyril Burt, The inheritance of mental ability, *American Psychologist*, 1958, 13, Table 1, p. 6. Copyright © 1958 by the American Psychological Association.

From these and related data gathered in America, Burt (1972) derived heritability equations that led him to conclude that some 88 percent of the variance in IQ could be predicted upon the basis of genetic factors. He restricted himself to the use of the operational definition of intelligence, the IQ, and always insisted that probability estimates apply only to groups, not to individuals.

With typical British detachment, Burt thought of himself as a pure scientist, not a meddler, and insisted that he had no social recommendations. Considering himself an advocate of the Mendelian principles of genetics, he was astounded that the operation of genetics in human intelligence would be questioned. He turned around the familiar environmental argument and asked:

> How, for example, do staunch environmentalists like Dr. Borstelmann account for the way in which children of exceptionally high ability not infrequently crop up in families where both parents appear relatively dull and the cultural circumstances of the home appallingly unfavorable? If our assessments of their ability are merely an "index of cultural achievement," how are these anomalous cases to be explained? On the Mendelian theory of "gene recombination," they are just what we should expect [Burt 1968, p. 16].

Burt contends that a child is born with a theoretical potential or upper limit. In the normal environment with adequate stimulation, this predisposition contributes to the individual differences among children. When the environmental conditions vary widely, these genetic predispositions may be overridden and obscured. In point of fact, the environmental conditions may be so strong, such as in lead poisoning in the slums, as totally to obscure the genetic picture.

In summarizing his years of research, Burt wrote:

> The two main conclusions we have reached seem clear and beyond all question. The hypothesis of a general factor entering into every type of cognitive process, tentatively suggested by speculations derived from neurology and biology, is fully borne out by the statistical evidence; and the contention that differences in this general factor depend largely on the individual's genetic constitution appears incontestable. The concept of an innate, general cognitive ability, which follows from these two assumptions, though admittedly a sheer abstraction, is thus wholly consistent with the empirical facts.
>
> ...A given genetic endowment is compatible with a whole range of developmental reactions and consequently of acquired attainments. All that a knowledge of a child's genetic endowment permits us to infer are the limits of that range, where "limit" is defined in terms of probability. The choice of a minimum probability will doubtless be decided in the main by financial considerations. Were more lavish funds available for the compensatory education of the dull and for the special education of the gifted, both would attain a higher level of achievement [1972, pp. 188–189].

From a strictly scientific point of view, Burt deplores the mixing of behaviorism and social conscience, which, according to him, has led to bad science and confused social theory. With his impeccable academic credentials, Burt enjoyed the detachment of the laboratory man of science. He remains in good standing today in both the professional and social domains, having been little affected by the nature-nurture controversy in the United States.

William Shockley

The center of the storm surrounding the heritability of intelligence is a highly unlikely character, William Shockley, a nobel laureate in solid-state physics, distinguished professor at Stanford, and member of the National Academy of Science. Shockley, who readily admits to being a layman in genetics, is nevertheless a strong proponent of the concept of the heritability of intelligence. Typical of the many speeches on the subject given by Shockley was the one delivered to the Academy in 1966.

> I evaluate the marrow of the city's slum problem to be our uncertainty about its genetic aspects and our fear to admit ignorance and to search openly for relevant facts.... Useful research in this area has been hampered by the fact that it will inevitably bear on intelligence distributions of minorities and American Negroes in particular.... My one and only recommendation today is that better studies can and should be attempted.... Can it be that our humanitarian welfare programs have already selectively emphasized high and irresponsible rates of reproduction to produce a socially, relatively unadaptable human strain [*New York Times,* October 18, 1966, p. 9.]?

Shockley uses as his primary data the many group studies of intelligence carried out in the United States, studies that consistently have indicated that the poor people of the country tend to score significantly lower than the middle class. He cites the fact that poverty tends to follow generation after generation and assumes that the major cause is quite possibly genetic. He does not understand the resistance to this point, since other blatant genetic differences in human beings are obvious. How could one question intellectual differences? Note that Shockley sees himself merely as a catalyst trying to encourage more research in this unpopular area because social and political pressures are restricting research and such pressures always tend to hide truth rather than solve problems.

Shockley frequently is prevented from speaking on university campuses by hostile audiences. He cites this harassment, and the harassment of two other researchers in the area, Jensen at Berkeley and Herrnstein at Harvard, as sufficient cause for great concern that out of a sense of fear or distrust, eminent scientists will withdraw from the field of human genetics and thereby fail to provide society with much needed guidance. Because Shockley is a solid-state physicist and not a geneticist, and because the data Shockley quotes have racial implications, he has had a poor press. His effectiveness in encouraging the kind of studies he feels are needed may not be sufficient for the task. Shockley wants multivariate studies performed to isolate the heritability of intelligence, and he wants to propose some social action out of the result of these studies.

Arthur Jensen*

Shockley, as a layman in the area of genetics and psychometrics, often has been dismissed by serious students of heritability, but Jensen, who

*Parts of the discussion of Jensen and Herrnstein are reprinted, by permission, from Wallace A. Kennedy, *Intelligence and Economics: A Confounded Relationship* (Morristown, N.J.: General Learning Press, 1973). Copyright © 1973 by the General Learning Corporation.

wrote an extensive and scholarly article on IQ and scholastic achievement in the *Harvard Educational Review* (Winter 1969), wrote from the vantage point of a senior researcher in the area of individual differences. His 123-page article is temperate, literate, and in places profound. It reviews the relationship between IQ and scholastic achievement and presents a lucid, simplified mathematical equation now referred to as the heritability quotient.

During his discourse on the heritability of intelligence, Jensen reviews several errors typically made in the application of genetics to a phenomenon such as intelligence.

> Heritability is a technical term in genetics meaning specifically the proportion of phenotypic variance due to variance in genotypes. When psychologists speak of heritability they almost invariably define it as:
>
> $$H = (V_G + V_{AM}) + V_D + V_i/V_p - V_e \text{ [Jensen, 1969a, p. 42]}$$
>
> where:
>
> V_G = genic (or additive) variance.
> V_{AM} = variance due to assortative mating.
> V_{AM} = 0 under random mating (panmixia).
> V_D = dominance deviation variance.
> V_i = epistatis (interaction among genes at 2 or more loci).
> V_p = phenotypic variance in the population.
> V_e = error of measurement (unreliability).
>
> [1969a, p. 34]

HEREDITY VERSUS ENVIRONMENT. The first misconception about heritability is the *all-or-none* phenomenon, where the fact that environmental and hereditary factors are additive, not opposites, fails to be taken into account.

> Any observable characteristic, physical or behavioral, is a phenotype, the very existence of which depends upon both genetic and environmental conditions. The legitimate question is not whether the characteristic is due to heredity or environment, but what proportion of the population variation in the characteristic is attributable to genotypic variation (which is H, the heritability) and what proportion is attributable to non-genetic or environmental variation in the population (which is 1.0 − H) [1969a, p. 42].

These are not all-or-none propositions; H can range in value between 0 and 1.

INDIVIDUAL VERSUS POPULATION. The second misconception is what he calls the *individual-versus-the-population* misconception.

> Heritability is a population statistic, describing the relative magnitude of the genetic component (or set of genetic components) in the population variance of the characteristic in question. It has no sensible meaning with reference to a measurement or characteristic in an individual. A single measurement, by definition, has no variance. There is no way of partitioning a given individual's IQ into hereditary and environmental components.... *The square root of the heritability ($\sqrt{H}$), how-*

ever, tells us the correlation between genotypes and phenotypes in the population, and this permits a probabilistic inference concerning the average amount of difference between individuals' obtained IQs and the "genotypic value" of their intelligence. (The average correlation between phenotypes and genotypes for IQ is about .90 in European and North American Caucasian populations.... The square of this value is known as the heritability—the proportion of phenotypic variance due to genetic variation) [1969a, pp. 42–43].

CONSTANCY. The third misconception about heritability refers to its *constancy:* heritability is an estimate of percentage of variance and is not a constant like the speed of light or π.

Estimates of H [heritability] are specific to the population sampled, the point in time, how the measurements were made, and the particular test used to obtain the measurements [1969a, p. 43].

MEASUREMENT VERSUS REALITY. The fourth error is *measurement versus reality.* His point is simply that there is no such thing as a variable independent of measurement. There can be no culture-free or culture-fair test any more than there can be, as he says, a nutrition-free scale of weight.

It makes no more sense to say that intelligence tests do not really measure intelligence but only developed intelligence than to say that scales do not really measure a person's weight but only the weight he has acquired by eating. An "environment-free" test of intelligence makes as much sense as a "nutrition-free" scale for weight [1969a, p. 44].

KNOW ALL VERSUS KNOW NOTHING. The fifth variable Jensen discusses with regard to misconception of heritability is the *know-all versus know-nothing* error: the assertion that, since we yet know little about the basic mechanism of causality and genetic transmittal, therefore we know nothing. Jensen's point is that we know how much we know on the basis of how accurate our predictions can be.

The science of quantitative genetics upon which the estimation of heritability depends has proven its value independently of advances in biochemical and physiological genetics [1969a, p. 44].

ACQUIRED VERSUS INHERITED. Sixth is the *acquired versus the inherited* definition of intelligence. In this he refers to the fact that one inherits a basic capacity that with specific training enables excellence. He gives the example of the difference that shows up when a Mozart and an average child are both given music lessons of equal quality.

IMMUTABILITY. The seventh error is the *immutability* error. The fact that a given individual has a tendency in a certain direction does not necessarily imply unmodifiability of the trait in question. Jensen gives the example of the PKU child with a recessive genetic defect in metabolism that invariably leads to brain damage unless environmental controls are put into effect to avoid certain proteins containing phenylalanine.

After this rather sophisticated review of the problems in making statements about genetics, Jensen proceeds to point out what conclusions can be drawn from a heritability quotient. First, and obviously, in some areas of academic performance, properly focused remedial programs can demonstrate significant improvements, even when the genetically based measurements would not encourage such a prediction.

However, Jensen notes that when dealing with cognitive tasks of an abstract nature, few studies have demonstrated any significant change, and fewer still have demonstrated long-term gain. He notes that most of the intervention programs have been attempted after the child already has established a way of abstracting; that we know little about the effect of early cognitive training. Jensen concludes that, if the effectiveness of early school intervention programs and the usual compensatory educational program is evaluated on the basis of changes in cognitive style and IQ, the evidence demonstrates them to be quite ineffective.

> If diversity of mental abilities, as of most other human characteristics, is a basic fact of nature, as the evidence indicates, and if the ideal of universal education is to be successfully pursued, it seems a reasonable conclusion that schools and society must provide a range and diversity of educational methods, programs, and goals, and of occupational opportunities, just as wide as the range of human abilities. Accordingly, the ideal of equality of educational opportunity should not be interpreted as uniformity of facilities, instructional techniques, and educational aims for all children. Diversity rather than uniformity of approaches and aims would seem to be the key to making education rewarding for children of different patterns of ability. The reality of individual differences thus need not mean educational rewards for some children and frustration and defeat for others [1969a, p. 117].

Now it so happens that the above statement, temperate as it is, has embedded in it a fundamental concept of genetic differences between individuals that account for differences in performance, styles of learning, and program needs. It also has embedded in it the statement that there are genetic differences between groups of people.

One might well ask, why so much vituperation to such a modest proposal as presented by Jensen? The answer is the nature of the subjects of the studies to which Jensen points. Most of the studies on the question of compensatory education are based not only upon economic and cultural differences, but also upon racial differences. The typical study has attempted, with mixed success, to remediate the presumed deficits of groups of black children through various remedial efforts. Also, the studies typically have used the IQ test as the major measure of the success of the remedial effort, because, taken as a whole, the IQ is remarkably stable over a long-range period.

What provides the irritation, then, is both the anger over the initial assumption that black children are somehow inferior in intelligence, and the poor success of current techniques in demonstrating permanent IQ changes. Thus Jensen's severest critics do not deal at all with the substance of his remarks, that poverty children have qualitative differences in learning skills that handicap them in certain abstract cognitive areas; instead they leap on the implication of racial inferiority or superiority as unacceptable, and as leading to unacceptable actions on the part of society.

It seems that no one really criticizes what Jensen has done, what he intends to do, or what he proposes others should do. Instead, his critics are alarmed at what they feel others might do, or say, or propose, on the basis of the genetic implications of Jensen's remarks. They fear that his remarks might be taken as supportive of Shockley's view that we should by some means limit the birth rate of the poor and thus enrich the gene pool of the country; they find in the application of such a suggestion the seeds of outrageous behavior.

Richard Herrnstein

At a time when neither Shockley nor Jensen could give a public speech because they faced being shouted down, harangued, harassed, or canceled, Richard Herrnstein, a Harvard professor, wrote a literate review of the problem of genetics and intelligence and group differences as a defense of Jensen's position. He did not, or course, address himself to the question of the possible misconduct of readers of Jensen, but instead addressed himself to the operation of human genetics regarding the problem of social grouping, after first mentioning that the extrapolation of the genetics findings to blacks is unwarranted, since the data regarding heritability of intelligence were gathered on white subjects. The estimate of the heritability of IQ, which is .85, or about 85 percent, is not relevant to cross-race comparisons, nor does it provide specific information about the heritability of intelligence in black children. He also cautions that heritability applies to populations as a whole, not to individual children.

> All we could say is that the differences between people, on the average and without regard to color, are 80 percent inherited. But within this broad generality, particular differences could and would be more or less inherited [Herrnstein, 1971, p. 57].

SYLLOGISM. Herrnstein summarizes his major point with a syllogism:

1. If differences in mental abilities are inherited, and
2. If success requires those abilities, and
3. If earnings and prestige depend on success,
4. Then social standing (which reflects earnings and prestige) will be based to some extent on inherited differences among people [1971, pp. 62–63].

COROLLARIES. Herrnstein cites five corollaries of this syllogism.

(a) As the environment becomes more favorable for the development of intelligence, its heritability will increase. That is, as you remove environmental differences, genetic differences will predominate.

(b) All modern political credos preach social mobility. Such social mobility, though, is a two-way street. Actual social mobility is blocked by innate human differences after the social and legal impediments are removed.

(c) When a country gains new wealth, it will tend to be gathered in the hands of the natively endowed. The growth of wealth will recruit for the upper classes precisely those from the lower classes who have the edge in native ability. Whatever else this accomplishes, it will also increase the IQ gap between upper and lower classes, making the social ladder even steeper for those left at the bottom.

(d) Technological advance changes the marketplace for I.Q. . . . . Technological un-employment is not just a matter of "dislocation" or "retraining" if the jobs created are beyond the native capacity of the newly unemployed. . . . And the ones who stay out of work are most likely the ones with the low I.Q.'s. The syllogism implies that in times to come, as technology advances, the tendency to be unemployed may run in the genes of a family about as certainly as bad teeth do now.

(e) The syllogism deals manifestly with intelligence . . . . However, there may be other inherited traits that differ among people and contribute to their success in life. Although the argument has been made on the basis of intelligence, because of its operational definition, it may well be that equal arguments could be made on the basis of temperament, personality, appearance, perhaps even physical strength or endurance, [which] may enter into our strivings for achievement and are to varying degrees inherited [1971, p. 63].

SUMMARY. The horror story Herrnstein predicts is a society in which the rich get richer and the poor get poorer to the point where there is an ever broadening gap between the life styles of the people with high IQs and those with low IQs. He differs with Shockley principally in regard to the percentage of blacks who will remain at the poverty level. Herrnstein is equally as sure as Shockley of the genetic cause of social class and the problems of an increasing lower class; he simply feels that the interaction is between economics and genetics instead of race and genetics.

Summary

The heritability group, then, is in essential agreement on the following points.

1. IQ has a high heritability quotient. The general estimate is that about 80 percent of the variance in IQ is due to heredity.
2. IQ has a high constancy quotient. Once the IQ is established at about six years of age, the test-retest reliability is high, and agreement across instruments is high.
3. IQ is extremely difficult to manipulate by conventional enrichment techniques, once the IQ is established by school age.
4. IQ is highly correlated with scholastic achievement, once the IQ is established.
5. IQ is highly correlated with socioeconomic status, once the IQ is established.
6. Therefore, IQ, scholastic achievement, and socioeconomic status operate under a common cause, which is inherited ability.

The major criticism of the group has been made in the area of the "Therefore." And the "Therefore" is in fact a minor point with Jensen, only slightly more important to Burt, and only a signal observation to Shockley and Herrnstein. The public response and course of action resulting from this conclusion has generated the concern. Selective population control on the basis of IQ has an unacceptable quality to it in the United States today, as does "benign neglect" as a public policy.

Language Deficit Group

Presently in America, a second group of investigators, examining the same data, have come to a different conclusion. This language deficit group, noticing that lower-class children frequently show no IQ deficit until about eighteen to twenty-four months of age, suggests that the difference may be accounted for by the change in intellectual measurement during this period, from nonlanguage to language. They assume that the functional explanation of the difference in mean intelligence test scores between middle- and lower-class children is in the failure of lower-class children to develop language ability during the critical period from eighteen to thirty-six months, a deficit that casts them into a mold of thinking and reasoning that severely handicaps them in developing the particular skills tapped by intelligence tests during the kindergarten and elementary school years, skills essential for academic achievement as schools presently are constituted.

Thus the language deficit group believes that a lack of cognitive skills related to speaking and reading and abstract thinking accounts for the deficit. The environment, not the genes, is presumed to account for the majority of the difference between children during early and middle childhood. Palmer (1971), R. Hess and Shipman (1965*a,b*), Deutsch, Katz, and Jensen (1968), and Zigler and Butterfield (1968) will serve as examples of the many careful investigators in this area.

Robert Hess

Robert Hess was one of the first to call attention to the specific environmental determinants of the language problem experienced by lower-class children upon entering school. He and his associates began to define cultural deprivation as deprivation of language training and usage that resulted from nonlanguage mother-child interaction.

> The picture that is beginning to emerge is that the meaning of deprivation is a deprivation of meaning—a cognitive environment in which behavior is controlled by status rules rather than by attention to the individual characteristics of a specific situation and one in which behavior is not mediated by verbal cues or by teaching that relates events to one another and the present to the future. This environment produces a child who relates to authority rather than to rationale, who, although often compliant, is not reflective in his behavior, and for whom the consequences of an act are largely considered in terms of immediate punishment or reward rather than future effects and long-range goals [R. Hess and Shipman, 1965*b*, p. 885].

Hess found that lower-class mothers not only do not play elaborate language games with their children, but, in fact, are incapable of doing so. The lower-class mothers in Hess's study communicated with their children simply and concretely, both verbally and nonverbally, using a few indefinite words to carry all their meaning; such as *thing, it, dude,* and *get, do, make.* The problem with such language vagueness is that context becomes all-important; the nonverbal communication becomes essential for meaning, with the result that language itself carries little meaning.

While the middle-class child is learning many combinations of linguistic subtleties in an exponential growth of vocabulary between the ages of eighteen and thirty-six months, the lower-class child's attention is directed away from syntax and cognitive variations of meaning toward the affective mood of the parent, the situational context, and rather subtle nonverbal cues. The average middle-class child is estimated to bring to bear some twenty thousand concepts during the beginning months of kindergarten, with all the verbal permutations and combinations he can use or comprehend. Meanwhile the deprived child is living in an environment in which linguistic variations are given an extremely low priority.

This nonverbal style, according to Hess, makes for the marked difference in measured intelligence between social classes. The lower-class child is learning a different style of communication. He has a rich affective life, a rich nonverbal, expressive life, and rather broad social experience, but he has not acquired the basic skills required for academic performance.

Hess concludes, then, that some type of language facilitation program is needed to deal with the problem of intellectual and scholastic deficit presented by poverty children at the beginning of school, a problem that seems pernicious as far as academic progress is concerned. He did not propose such a program, but allied himself firmly with the group contending that the deficit in intellectual and academic skills is environmentally produced: by environmental manipulation the problem is to be resolved. Hess further believes environmental manipulation to be essential in order for these children to break out of the poverty cycle of low verbal skills, low academic achievement, low intellectual functioning, low job entry points, low vitality, and low motivation, and, therefore, poverty.

Recognize also that Hess suggests a critical period in the life of a child, when this transition from nonverbal to verbal communication must occur, or the child will find great difficulty in acquiring verbal skills. He implies that the compensatory education programs so far have been too little too late. If they are an elementary school phenomenon, they are faced with making a 180-degree change in the language style of children, a communication style already solidly established. Hess finds considerable support from the work of Engelmann (1970), and Karnes (Karnes, Teska, and Hodgins, 1970a,b), both of whom identify language facilitation as the essential problem of the preschool poverty child.

Siegfried Engelmann

Taking a hard-line approach to the problem, Siegfried Engelmann was one of the first to apply behavioral objectives to the preschool child. He proposed that preschool programs should begin with identifiable objectives regarding the building of behaviors essential to the beginning schoolchild. He asked, "What are the essential behavioral tools, and what curriculum could be expected to produce such behaviors?"

Engelmann believes in try-out, analysis programming and evaluation directly related to the behavioral objectives. He calls for and demonstrates that one should analyze the tasks a child is expected to master, say at the entry point of kindergarten, and then design a curriculum that proceeds step by step to build these skills. The program should take the disadvantaged child where he is and proceed to move him through a series of developmental tasks to the point where he is ready for kindergarten.

Engelmann believes that the adoption of the traditional program used in university developmental kindergartens, programs associated with child development institutes for fifty years, is the problem of most preschool programs supposedly designed to help the underprivileged. These child development programs, highly successful with the children of middle- and upper-class faculty, represented a decompression atmosphere where children, too tense because of the achievement motivation of their parents, could learn to enjoy education instead of being so intense about achievement.

Giving these highly verbal, high-drive, tense children an unstructured fun experience with multimedia, allowing them to "mess" with paints, clay, and finger paints was a highly successful formula for them, but it is a formula totally inappropriate for the child who has spent much of the preschool life in "messing." This child needs a structured learning experience that teaches him skills and a behavioral repertoire that will enable him to attend to the right cues in the preschool environment and to develop the language skills required as a vehicle for education.

Engelmann also contends that the disadvantaged child needs to be helped to develop intrinsic motivation through the experience of extrinsic motivation. The disadvantaged child needs a firm, active stand on the part of the teacher; he needs structure, remediation, and language training. Engelmann believes that to adjust the child to a verbal, structured society is essential, instead of trying to adjust society to the child.

Merle Karnes

While Hess and Engelmann were making theoretical recommendations to offset the differences between deprived and middle-class children, Merle B. Karnes was principally responsible for the development and large-scale application of a preschool program that put these concepts to the test. Karnes, along with several colleagues at the University of Illinois at Urbana, first reported in 1968 on a long-range preschool program for disadvantaged children (Karnes, Hodgins, and Teska, 1968). They observed a strong placebo effect from the attention given a child in any preschool program. Thus, at least on a temporary basis, anything beats nothing; but a structured program designed to meet specific educational behavioral objectives produces a more obvious accommodation by the children to kindergarten, and a more lasting educational effect.

Her basic strategy used a baseline period as the control, which made optimal use of the children in the study by having both groups essentially experimental groups. The baseline-control technique measures the children for a period of time before the intervention program, and then observes any differences between the groups. The design assumes some placebo-based improvement on the basis of expectancy, excitement, and attention, but measures the difference between the improvement of the two groups.

Karnes's first group was treated to a replication of the traditional child development, nursery school program with low pressure and unstructured experiences emphasizing personal, social, and general motor development, with a great deal of free play, doll play, show and tell, rest periods, and so forth, a program with less high drive than middle-class children normally have at home, but a program bewildering to lower-class children in its lack of structure and its strangeness.

The second group followed the theoretical formulations of Engelmann, emphasizing developmental tasks as educational objectives. The fundamental concept was the development of the prerequisite skills of language, memory abstraction, and mental manipulations: the structured program covered the language arts, reading readiness, mathematical manipulations, social skills, and basic Piagetian science programming. Karnes found that the children in the highly specific, focused, structured training program displayed considerably more improvement in the development of those skills, reflected both in intelligence test scores and in kindergarten academic performance.

Francis Palmer

Palmer's program, making more use of parental involvement and focusing primarily on the development of logical thinking, gave children early experience in concept training and concept development. Using a game format similar to that of Karnes, Palmer focused on concept training rather than general school readiness in a study design that involved the labeling and demonstration of a concept by a model, and then performance by the child of a task that demonstrated the concept.

Palmer had more than the usual difficulty associated with long-term research with children, because his study was located in East Harlem; follow-up was difficult with many subjects lost: but on the basis of seven years on the project, he was able to reach tentative conclusions. The most obvious was the expected finding that the earlier a child is exposed to an intervention program, the greater the success of the program and the more lasting the effects. Palmer found no significant differences between children from the upper lower-class and the lower lower-class. And he found that the major result of the concept training was children who became more verbal.

Martin Deutsch

A related program developed by Martin Deutsch involved preschool language enrichment. Deutsch found that by early intervention and massive language training he could make significant improvement in the intellectual performance of the children, and that these differences had long-range implications.

Compensatory Education Group

In the United States evidence has been found to suggest that the ability of deprived children, even children with presumed genetic predispositions toward low IQ, that is, children from third- and fourth-generation poverty families, after early equal-learning opportunities, varies little from that of lower middle-class children from the same area. This has led another group of investigators, although subscribing to the concept of language training as an essential dimension of any remedial program, to feel that remedial programs in kindergarten and elementary school do not come too late to make significant contributions. This group, which in a sense preceded the Head Start Program, is referred to as the compensatory education group. Comprised of Susan Gray (Gray and Klaus, 1965, 1970; Klaus and Gray, 1968), Herbert Sprigle, and Vernon Van De Riet (Van De Riet, Van De Riet, and Sprigle, 1968–1969; Van De Riet and Resnick, 1973) as examples, this group has concerned itself with perfecting a school curriculum that will compensate children for language deficits resulting from their early home experiences.

Their program focuses upon making up developmental lags in behavioral tasks, behaviors middle-class children normally bring to the school situation, by pitching the behavioral objectives of the remedial class at mastery of these basic skills. Such programs have been successful in making significant gains in the children's performance, but the gains are less impressive than those achieved through early intervention.

Both the language deficit group and the compensatory education group tend to minimize genetic differences, yet they propose a program of remediation similar to one that would be proposed by a group who believe in genetic differences: a program that carefully identifies language and other scholastic weaknesses and proposes remedial steps to alter the condition. Each believes that the problem presented by the deprived children reflects a serious defect, and each is cautiously optimistic about the probability of the remedial steps affecting some or all of the deficit, regardless of the cause. Each would recommend a highly structured, language-behavior modification and concept-training program that focuses upon the prerequisite skills.

Psycholinguistic Group

Perhaps worth mentioning is a fourth group of psychologists, representing the psycholinguistic group, who propose a totally different cause, and remedy. This group has identified the problem as a lack of acceptance of a cultural difference that does not represent a cultural deficit. By logic and examples that are sketchy at best, Labov (1970, 1972), as the senior spokesman, indicates his belief that the language of poverty, although different than the language of middle class, is an authentic dialect with rich meaning and power; the problem is in middle-class teachers, middle-class books, middle-class examinations, and middle-class entry points into jobs. Labov proposes course texts written in black English, which he feels would provide adequate evidence of the intellectual power of the ghetto child.

The psycholinguist, by his analysis of the content of the poverty child's speech, has convinced himself that the communication of the ghetto child is as good as that of his middle-class peer. However, the psycholinguist is far from convincing the average teacher, employer, or supervisor of the logic of his position; but he has gotten the attention of the professional educator.

Labov argues that teaching poverty children middle-class words to replace black English words for identities is absurd, frustrating, and a waste of time: *commode* for *pot, gentleman* for *dude,* and so forth. Labov argues that "properness" should take second place to directness, bluntness, and, most importantly, to familiarity. Middle-class problems with directness, argues

Labov, are no concern of the ghetto child. But Labov, too, would argue for a structured, bare-boned program concentrating on language for the training of the preschool and elementary school child.

Labov seems to see language only as a means of communication, not as an integral part of man's thinking, cognitive system. According to Labov, complicated reasoning does not require complicated language: directness, bluntness, and simplicity—that's the thing.

The kernel of Labov's argument is that the words used to teach reading to the poverty child should be the words, expressions, and phrases of the speaking vocabulary of the ghetto child. To expect a five-year-old to learn simultaneously both the symbol and the word is too much, according to Labov. He proposes, then, black English primers that deal with the content of the ghetto in the words of the ghetto. Labov believes that once the ghetto child has learned to read, then adding vocabulary is possible.

Summary

The English sociologist Basil Bernstein (1961a,b) proposes that substandard dialects are inferior, that they handicap those who speak them. Speculating as to "why grossly different social environments affect verbal aspects of intelligence more than nonverbal aspects," Bernstein detected two fundamentally different forms of communication: formal and restricted. The one deals with abstractions and ideas: sentences are organized carefully to make meaning explicitly clear; formal communication is careful, highly structured speech, analytic and descriptive.

By contrast, the restricted communication of poverty is distinguished by limited syntax and clarity of meaning. Restricted communication concerns concrete matters, opinions, and feelings, with little motivation to make meaning clear. In restricted speech, concerned mainly with description, to state analytical arguments and abstractions is difficult.

> These two modes occur, according to Bernstein, in any society in which there is a sharp division between those individuals who are motivated to communicate ideas and those who regard such activity as marginal and unimportant. The middle- and upper-class child lives in both worlds, of course [Deese, 1970, pp. 78, 79].

The middle-class child easily copes with the conceptual problems of verbal tests of intelligence because he has an appreciation for and an understanding of abstractions. The middle-class child has learned that ideas are important and worth talking about.

MEASUREMENT OF INTELLIGENCE

Having discussed the concept of measured intelligence, early concepts of intelligence, theories of intelligence, and the relation economics has to intelligence, we should examine the intelligence test itself. Does motivation play a role? How is the intelligence test used? Abused? What makes a good intelligence test? What is its purpose? Its future?

We have discussed cultural variables that affect intellectual performance in general, but some variables directly affect performance on intelligence tests, one of the more obvious being the intrinsic motivation of the test itself. What does taking the test mean to the child? Why does he respond to the intelligence test? How does he respond?

The middle-class child, who has grown up with competitive games, who has derived pleasure from the mental stimulation of puzzles, riddles, and guessing games, obviously would have a different attitude toward the intelligence test than the poverty child who comes from a nonverbal environment where the question often is used only to establish guilt or innocence. In an insightful study of the motivational aspect of the changes in measured intelligence of culturally deprived children, Zigler and Butterfield (1968) demonstrated that the usual improvement found in the intellectual performance of poverty children after a year of nursery school was not due to improved cognitive achievement factors or improved reading readiness, but rather to an improvement in the motivation of the child. Attitudinal changes, not academic changes, made the difference.

For older children, motivation is not so clearly understood or demonstrated; no clear-cut pattern has emerged, in spite of many studies on the relative effectiveness of extrinsic motivation. Tiber and Kennedy (1964), in a study of lower-class white and black children, found no reliable differences in performance on the *Stanford-Binet* under four testing situations: verbal praise, verbal reproof, candy reward, and no reinforcement. In a review of the literature on the effectiveness of praise and blame in motivating children, Kennedy and Willcutt (1964) reported varying results, depending upon many factors, such as grade level, sex, and age. Nor are these differences reliable or stable; thus incentive seems to be a small factor in performance. Attempts to study the race and social class of the examiner in relation to that of the subject also have been inconclusive, indicating that these also are minor factors in performance on intelligence tests (Kennedy and Vega, 1965).

UTILITY

An intelligence test's usefulness rests solely on its ability to predict. It was designed to predict academic achievement, and hence, job success.

The status and acceptance of intelligence tests varies almost from decade to decade. The present trend leans toward emphasizing the achievement test, the skill test, or task test over the intelligence test. But we shall examine the usefulness of the intelligence test in light of its traditional purpose—the prediction of academic achievement.

Academic Achievement

The intelligence test was developed to sample the kinds of knowledge, information, and skill learned in school, without relating specifically to classroom content. And the intelligence test competently predicts academic success.

The first and foremost use of the intelligence test, then, is to predict academic success. No other test can better predict how a preschool child will do in school. The concept of mental age has added to our ability to predict, to understand, and to explain school readiness. Children whose mental growth is slow, regardless of the reason, can be expected to have a difficult time in school.

Admittedly, the earlier the test is given the child, the less accurate the prediction will be. However, decisions often have to be made—as, for instance, in adoptive placement of young children—and the IQ provides the best available estimate of the future intellectual or academic performance of the child. Even today, with the advances in school-readiness tests, an IQ test administered during the kindergarten year will be extremely helpful in preparing parents and teachers for the child's most probable level of work.

Achievement Discrepancy

Locating underachievement is a second contribution of the intelligence test. Regular administration of an intelligence test in kindergarten and in the fourth grade will aid in locating children who, in spite of superior ability, have not performed in the classroom at the level of their capability. Some children can learn more than they do. Their very identification will facilitate the provision of added attention and encouragement necessary to improve their performance.

Just so, some children have been perceived incorrectly by their parents as having more ability than they actually possess; they are pushed to the outer limit of emotional health in order to perform at an unrealistic level. Often, unrealistic demands are made of children of average ability from upper middle-class homes; they and their parents suffer a constant state of frustration over the child's failure to live up to the parents' expectations. When the parents adjust their expectations to the child's ability, everyone is happier and the child's performance even improves as tension drops in the home.

Intellectual Weaknesses

A third contribution of the intelligence test is the pinpointing of weaknesses in the intellectual ability of children. Particularly the subtest scores of individually administered intelligence tests, such as the Binet and WISC, help to point out areas in the child's performance needing attention.

For example, some children, particularly male children in the lower grades, lag developmentally in perceptual ability; special training is required to help the child make normal progress. Reversals, mirror writing, rotations of perception, distortions, all can be located on the intelligence test and helped by special training; consequently, the child's performance increases markedly. True, the alert teacher could discover these deficits in other ways, but the regularly scheduled intelligence test increases the likelihood of their discovery.

Academic Placement

The multiple-tracking academic placement of schoolchildren is enhanced by the regular use of the intelligence test. Even in the first years of school, children are unalike in ability. Although the best way to group children is open to discussion, sufficient evidence indicates that children learn more efficiently when allowed to move at their own pace. Such flexibility is aided by the administration of intelligence tests supplemented by achievement scores.

Homogeneous small groups, within the larger classroom setting, allow for the presentation of instructional materials especially appropriate for those specific children, materials with which they can deal effectively. In the early grades, the use of reading-readiness tests along with intelligence tests provides a stable and meaningful basis upon which to group children. No instrument is more powerful in determining the intellectual ability level of children than individually administered intelligence tests.

Exceptional Talent

The final contribution of intelligence tests is the identification of exceptionally talented youths to be given exceptional opportunities to develop their unique potential. The early identification of children of extraordinary ability provides an opportunity for the encouragement of their talents over long periods of time. Some of the most remarkable contributions made by man have resulted from the early encouragement of child prodigies at a critical period in their development. The longitudinal studies by Terman (Terman and Oden, 1947, 1959) are adequate proof that gifted children, without proper identification and stimulation, can live out mediocre and relatively unproductive lives; although most of his childhood geniuses went on to highly productive lives, a few fell by the wayside in spite of their superior intelligence.

ABUSE

As we examine the major contributions of the intelligence test, we should speak to its detraction, because the misuse of the concept of intelligence and intelligence testing has done some harm.

Defense of Genetic Intelligence

The foremost harm perpetrated by the misuse of the intelligence test has been the defense of the concept of genetically determined intellectual ability unchanged by environmental nurture or starvation. The IQ has been used as an explanation for failure: "Johnny can't be expected to do better because his IQ shows he is retarded." Conversely, good grades just come to a child tagged "genius" by his IQ; instead of always pushing him to do his best, teachers tend to reward little effort with good grades.

This elevation of the IQ as a measure of capacity, rather than as the prediction it is intended to be, has had anything but a positive effect on the modern American. Rather than promoting effort on the part of students, teachers, administrators, and parents to encourage every child to achieve at the highest possible level, misuse of the IQ has encouraged dead-end academic tracking, fatalism, and an overwhelming feeling of helplessness and frustration.

Unreliability of Infant Tests

A second abuse of the intelligence test has been the placement of too much emphasis upon infant tests of intelligence as predictors of adult intelligence. Many studies, from Anderson (1939) to Bayley (1965), have demonstrated that what we measure as intelligence in the young child is dissimilar to what we measure as intelligence in the schoolchild or the adult.

The behavior repertoire of young children is limited. Intelligence tests, which have to confine themselves to these few patterns of motor and prelingual behavior, necessarily fail to evaluate the major portion of what is called intelligence in the adult. Infant intelligence tests probably never will

Table 11

Correlations between Intelligence Test Scores Obtained at Different Age Levels, from Several Studies

Age in years	Hirsch[a] (1930) 8	13	Bayley[b] (1933) 3	Honzik[c] (1938) 7	Dearborn, Rothney, and Shuttleworth[d] (1938) 7	16	Honzik, MacFarlane, and Allen[e] (1948) 6	18	Bayley[f] (1955) 18
½			.10						.09
1			.45						.30
2			.80	.46			.47	.31	
3				.56			.57	.35	
4				.66			.62	.42	
5				.73			.71	.56	
6				.81				.61	
7						.58	.82	.71	
8		.80			.74	.64	.77	.70	
9	.87	.77			.70	.58	.80	.76	
10	.82	.77			.73	.74	.71	.70	
11	.79	.83			.67	.75			
12	.84	.90			.64	.79	.74	.76	
13	.80				.66	.78	.74	.78	
14					.65	.83	.67	.73	
15					.61	.90			
16					.58				
18							.61		

Table 12

Correlations between Intelligence Test Scores Obtained
at Different School Ages, from Bayley (1949)

Age at test	1916 7	L 8	Stanford-Binet Form L 9	M 10	L 11	M 12	Terman-McNemar Form C 13	Stanford-Binet Form L 14	Terman-McNemar Form D 15	Wechsler-Bellevue 16	Stanford-Binet Form M 17	Wechsler-Bellevue 18
6	.86	.85	.84	.90	.78	.81	.82	.74	.72	.79	.78	.77
7		.88	.83	.87	.82	.83	.88	.79	.75	.83	.83	.80
8			.91	.89	.89	.91	.88	.91	.85	.88	.84	.85
9				.88	.90	.82	.87	.86	.82	.87	.85	.87
10					.92	.90	.88	.92	.83	.88	.86	.86
11						.93	.91	.93	.89	.89	.92	.93
12							.87	.94	.85	.88	.90	.89
13								.89	.95	.90	.94	.93
14									.87	.92	.89	.89
15										.88	.89	.88
16											.89	.94
17												.90

Reprinted, by permission of the author and the publisher, from Nancy Bayley, Consistency and variability in the growth of intelligence from birth to eighteen years, Journal of Genetic Psychology, 1949, 75, Table 5, p. 183.

be refined to the point where they can provide reliable predictions of adult intelligence. The irregularity of growth patterns in young children, together with the many factors identified in adult intelligence that do not appear in the very young, make the task perhaps an impossible one.

It is made even more difficult by the great variability in the environments of young children, both in terms of basic cultural differences and differences in child rearing. In the brief span of the twentieth century, wave after wave of child-rearing practices has resulted in eras of permissiveness, when children were allowed all kinds of experiences, and eras of restrictiveness, when the environment of the child was tightly controlled and contained. Furthermore, longitudinal studies of physical growth, such as that of Bayley and Harold Jones (1937), have shown enormous variability in the growth pattern of children from one age to another. Starts, spurts, and plateaus, sharp increases and decreases are all evidently a part of the normal variation in growth rate. Whether intelligence was measured during a period of fast or slow growth would have a major effect upon the estimate of IQ. Honzik, MacFarlane, and Allen (1948) found, in a longitudinal study, great variation in one child's IQ over a sixteen-year span—the result of the interaction of various environmental and physical factors with his intellectual development.

Test-retest reliability over an age span, one measure of the IQ's predictive power, depends to a great extent upon the initial age of the child and how great the age span between the two testings. An IQ measured at two years of age has a correlation of only .46 with the IQ of the same child at seven; by five years of age, the correlation has increased to .73. The correlation between a child's IQ measured at eleven and sixteen years of age is .75; between fifteen and sixteen it is .90. Table 11 indicates the relationship between these measures.

The younger the child, the less reliably his intelligence test score can predict later performance. The longer the prediction is extended, the less useful it is. Bayley's (1949) study gives a clear, overall picture of the test-retest reliability of intelligence tests of schoolchildren (see Table 12).

Any use of infant intelligence tests, particularly before the age of two, must be accompanied with the utmost caution. Regarding an IQ obtained at six months as equivalent to an IQ obtained at twelve years cannot be justified on the basis of the exhaustive studies available at the present time. The use of the concept of IQ at these early ages only tends to confuse parents and other concerned individuals.

The concept of mental age can be used appropriately, however: a mental age of two months means that the infant exhibits the kind of behavior normally seen in a two-month-old infant. To speak, then, of mental age, of developmental age, of an advanced child versus a slow child, is appropriate—but the use of an IQ at this early age implies a stability that does not exist.

Branding of Children

A third misuse of the intelligence test is connected with one of its greatest strengths: although an intelligence test is extremely useful in the homogeneous grouping of children, labels have a tendency to stick. Children tend to remain in the slow track long after their relative ability has undergone significant change. And the tracking, or homogeneous grouping, is known to all concerned no matter what subterfuge is attempted. We are all aware of a number of track descriptions varying from the straight numerical one, two, three, through the nominal description, advanced, career, basic, to a description as far removed as the red birds, the green birds, and the blue birds. But when you ask a child in the second grade which birds are the dummies, he quickly responds, "the blue birds." Once a child visualizes himself as a dummy, breaking him out of the pattern is very difficult. And IQs have been one of the vehicles by which the branding process has taken place.

QUALITY

What qualities of an intelligence test determine whether or not it will have great utility, whether or not it will be successful in predicting a variable such as academic achievement, or job success, or even the ability to make money? Keys to this utility are the representativeness of the standardization sample, the validity of the test items, and the purpose for which it is to be used.

Representativeness

The sample of children selected for the initial standardization should be large and representative of the population on which the finished test is to be used. It should contain children from all socioeconomic levels in the population, from all ethnic subgroups, from all degrees of cultural opportunity and health, from both sexes and all races, from all relevant geographic locations, and from all ages. The sample should represent the entire range of variables pertinent to performance on an intelligence test.

Opinions about the proper way to obtain a representative sample differ rather markedly. And the manner in which this problem is resolved has considerable bearing on the use to which intelligence tests may be put. Terman and Merrill, in their monumental standardization of the 1937 *Stanford-Binet,* felt that with a few exceptions they could standardize their instrument with a sample of children that would be representative of the entire school population of the United States. First, they dealt with the problem of language by eliminating anyone who was foreign-born, whether he came from Czechoslovakia or England. Second, they eliminated all nonwhite children, since they believed that the cultural background of the nonwhite child was so incompatible with the background of the average child in the United States in 1937 as to consider him foreign-born: they regarded the experiences of the nonwhite child as foreign to the average middle-class and lower middle-class children who made up the majority of the children in the United States at the time.

The representation of geographic distribution and population density was attempted by selecting representative numbers of urban, rural, and metropolitan children. Because Terman and Merrill had a limited budget and had to work where they could obtain access to schools and adequate support from school administrators, a slight bias was introduced: the children in their sample came from a socioeconomic level higher than average. The sample also contained a disproportionately large number of urban and Northern children, and a smaller number of rural and Southern children than the total population of the United States. But Terman was able to make a good case for his sample being reasonably representative of American white, native-born children.

Obviously, in 1937, differences in the experiences of upper and lower socioeconomic children were large, as were differences between metropolitan and rural children. Below are two word lists that illustrate the discrepancy. Almost any normal twelve-year-old from rural America in 1937 could have defined easily the ten words on the left, and it is highly unlikely that any child from New York City could have answered any of them; on the other hand, most middle-class white children in New York City in 1937 could have identified all the items on the right.

Rural	Urban
hame	dumbwaiter
clevis	el
martingale	super
breeching	token
c-link	starter
5-7-5 mix	subway
joist	ferry
six-up	escalator
draw-bar	downtown vs. uptown
separator	walk-up

Sampling both urban and rural children leads to problems of incompatible backgrounds. Simply to eliminate the foreign-born and nonwhite children is not enough, then, to conclude that a homogeneous population remains. The differences between rural, lower-class, white children and metropolitan, middle-class, white children are probably more extreme than the differences between rural, lower-class, white and black children, or between white and black metropolitan children. Although Terman and Merrill are to be commended for their outstanding success in representing the white, middle-class children of America in their sample, three thousand is a small sampling of forty million and poses serious questions about the validity of the test items.

An alternate solution would be to have several samples and sets of norms. Thus a set of norms appropriate for predicting the intelligence of white, metropolitan, middle-class, suburban children would be developed; another for ghetto-dwelling, lower-class, recently migrated black children; and so forth. Far more representativeness in sampling could be achieved, even though it would be cumbersome and expensive.

The problem lies in the utility of the predictions made on the basis of instruments so standardized. For instance, the *Stanford-Binet* is most useful in predicting academic success. Academic success in a metropolitan ghetto school for blacks may well be related to passivity and compliance. The children who pass are the polite ones who give teachers their due, while their sassy, aggressive friends may spend all day in the principal's office, perhaps ultimately to be expelled as incorrigible because they are not polite and deferential to the ghetto teacher. In designing a test to predict academic success in a ghetto school, one might very well load the test in such a way as to predict conformity, passivity, and submission. But are these ultimately the characteristics of the intelligent person, even in the ghetto?

Standardization

When translating and Americanizing the *Binet-Simon Test*, Lewis Terman had in mind a specific definition of intelligence: the ability to think abstractly, to use abstract symbols in solving problems. This definition is reflected in the *Stanford-Binet,* the 1937 revision of which is an outstanding example of the standardization of an intelligence test. The 1937 Binet was developed with two equivalent forms, each with 192 subtests. Each item was selected on the basis of the precision with which it discriminated be-

Table 13

IQ Distribution of the 1937 Standardization of the Stanford-Binet

IQ	Percentage	Classification
160–169	0.03	Very superior
150–159	0.20	Very superior
140–149	1.10	Very superior
130–139	3.10	Superior
120–129	8.20	Superior
110–119	18.10	High average
100–109	23.50	Normal or average
90– 99	23.00	Normal or average
80– 89	14.50	Low average
70– 79	5.60	Borderline defective
60– 69	2.00	Mentally defective
50– 59	0.40	Mentally defective
40– 49	0.20	Mentally defective
30– 39	0.03	Mentally defective

Reprinted, by permission of Maud Merrill and the publisher, from Lewis M. Terman and Maud A. Merrill, *Stanford-Binet Intelligence Scale* (Boston: Houghton Mifflin, 1960), Table 1, p. 18.

tween high and low scorers in a total range of children. Items were eliminated if they contributed little or nothing to the total score: those items which everyone passed, or which no one passed, or which did not correlate with the bulk of the test items, were discarded on the assumption that they were not measuring intelligence as it was defined by Terman.

The subjects were 3,184 native-born, white children, including approximately 100 subjects at each half-year interval from one-and-one-half to five-and-one-half, 200 at each age level from six to fourteen, and 100 at each age level from fifteen to eighteen. Every group was equally divided as to sex, and in each group the subjects were within one month of a birthday (or half-year birthday).

Every effort was made to secure an adequate geographic distribution. Seventeen different communities representative of urban, suburban, and rural populations in eleven widely separated states were used. Despite these efforts to obtain a representative sample, census data proved it to be slightly higher in socioeconomic level than the country as a whole and slightly disproportionate in number of urban subjects. A statistical adjustment of the mean IQ was made to offset these inadequacies in the sample.

In terms of representing the mass of children in school in the United States at the time, and of presenting a broad spectrum of items relevant to academic performance, the 1937 revision of the *Stanford-Binet* was an exceptionally well-standardized instrument. The distribution of IQs of the 1937 standardization group is shown in Table 13.

Table 14 shows the classification of mental deficiency by the diagnostic manual of the American Psychiatric Association.

Table 14

Definition of mental retardation related to IQ*

Mental Retardation	IQ Range
Borderline	68–83
Mild	52–67
Moderate	36–51
Severe	20–35
Profound	<20

*Adapted from *Diagnostic and Statistical Manual of Mental Disorders*, 2d ed. (DSM-II) (Washington, D.C.: American Psychiatric Association, 1968), p. 14.

Validity

The validity, or representativeness, of the items themselves is as important as the representativeness of the sample. Validity can be measured in several ways.

251
INTELLIGENCE

Face

Face validity is the overlap between the test items and the predicted variable. An example of nearly complete overlapping is the employment test for secretaries, which usually involves recorded dictation, the usual stumbling, mumbling caterwauling so typical of average executive dictation. The prospective secretary is required to transcribe the record into a sensible letter. The overlapping can be maximized by using the last four or five tapes dictated by the executive for whom the secretary will work.

Face validity of intelligence tests, then, would involve maximizing the overlapping of achievement measures and intelligence measures. Face validity accounts for the extraordinary success of the *Binet-Simon*, for Binet and Simon invaded the school itself, peeked over the shoulders of teachers, and asked questions regarding basic skills.

Modern intelligence tests have maintained this concern for high face validity. Remembering that 1 represents a perfect correlation, notice the high correlations between the *Stanford-Binet Form L-M* and the *California Achievement Test,* reported by Kennedy, Van De Riet, and White (1963, Table 71, p. 106).

CAT Reading	.68
CAT Arithmetic	.64
CAT Language	.70
CAT Battery	.69

Predictive

The second criterion is predictive validity: the degree to which the items on the test predict future performance. Predictive validity depends upon the test items sampling the behaviors requisite for future learning. If, before a child can write, he must be able to draw a circle, and before he can draw a circle, he must be able to draw a straight line with a crayon, then testing this ability is relevant for predicting future academic success.

The greatest utility of intelligence test items stems from their predictive validity. Face validity, or content validity, does not have nearly as much utility, because face validity is an after-the-fact measurement. A test of shorthand and typing skills does not come soon enough to determine whether or not a nineteen-year-old girl should be given an expensive two-year business course. The test does not tell us whether she can learn the skills, only whether she has learned them. Just so, a vocabulary test based on abstract words does not predict whether a person will be able to master complex abstractions, but rather measures, after the fact, whether he has. A test with predictive validity brings us as close as we can come at present to measuring true potential or capacity. The assumption is made that given equal opportunity and equal exposure to experience, those individuals who have achieved the most in early childhood will continue to achieve in adulthood at the rate of acceleration they already have established.

One other form of validity we should consider is construct validity: a definition of the variable, in this case intelligence, which is internally consistent within the instrument. To have construct validity, the test items must be selected to be consistent with some underlying theory of intelligence and must correlate highly with each other. Construct validity is particularly important when there is, as with intelligence, no rigorous way to verify the definition externally. Intelligence is a hypothetical variable. There is no way, other than by using intelligence tests, to measure intelligence—unless you use the judgments of presumed experts or have more than one definition of intelligence so that you can verify one definition with another.

From the concept of construct validity arises the major difficulty in interpreting intelligence tests, a difficulty that stems from the early success of the intelligence test in predicting achievement. Because of the relatively high correlation between intelligence tests given at the beginning of the school year and achievement tests given at the end of the school year, intelligence gradually became synonymous with the Stanford-Binet IQ. As more and more people became aware of the IQ, their children's IQs, their students' IQs, more and more individuals began to act consistently with their own IQs. A child, identified on an intelligence test as being dull, and therefore excused by his teachers for poor performance, poor attention span, and poor level of cooperation, did in fact behave more and more consistently with his dull score. And children who scored as geniuses on intelligence tests began to take heart, to enjoy their high status, and to behave more consistently like whiz kids. Like the Emperor's new clothes, teachers began to see in the extra-test performance of these children evidence of their brightness.

This, then, perpetuated a vicious cycle of accepting the IQ as a measure of capacity or potential. The once useful test became a rather strong force in its own right. The intelligence test was propelled into an absolute criterion of intelligence, a position for which it was neither theoretically designed nor practically able to respond. The high correlation between low intelligence, low achievement, and minority-group status was consistent with the hereditary point of view of Terman, Galton, and Goddard. When a conflicting view was presented by Wellman, Skeels, and Skodak (Wellman, 1932–1933, 1945; Skeels and Fillmore, 1937; Skodak and Skeels, 1949; Skeels, 1966), it was profoundly unpopular.

The problem of representativeness of items relates specifically to the purpose for which the intelligence test is being administered. Herein lies a bitter controversy indeed. It is bitter because the intelligence test is no longer a trivial academic exercise or a wouldn't-it-be-interesting-to-know phenomenon. An intelligence test has become a gate, a gate that opens or closes, allows or denies entrance. Binet's job was simple. Given a relatively homogeneous population of Paris schoolchildren, he asked the question: Which of these children has developed the skills required for beginning academic performance? He assumed that the children had been exposed to experiences required to master the skills tested by his tasks. The fact that some did not accomplish the tasks was ample reason to suspect that they could not.

But now we have a quite different problem. If we were merely concerned with the adaptation of the child to his immediate environment, our job would be relatively simple. We could, as did Binet and Simon, take notebook in hand and, for instance, invade the ghetto and ask questions as they did. How do you stay alive in a ghetto? What makes the difference between being chewed up by the viciousness and grimy poverty of ghetto existence and escaping its tenacious clutches? What is it that causes some children to pop up, like a cork released from a bottle, and float along the top and escape? Is it wiliness? Is it dogged determination? Is it the ability to tolerate ridicule passively, cynically? Is it playing the game? And what is success? Is success moving up in the numbers racket with a small dry-cleaning business as a front, a big black car, a Brooks Brothers suit, flashy jewelry, paying off the proper people, staying alive? Is that success? Or is success escape, getting out, fleeing to or invading the middle-class world, going to college, working for IBM?

To develop a satisfactory intelligence test for the ghetto child, you have to decide what smart is. You have to decide how smart people think and act; how they handle their tensions, fears, resentments; what they have to know to be considered smart. And then you can make a test that is suitable for the ghetto—today, not tomorrow; here and now. Many argue for this point of view—that intelligence tests developed for middle-class children are irrelevant to existence in the ghetto.

A completely dissimilar view says that intelligence should be considered a measure of the ability to adapt to the culture at large, that the only items relevant for a test of intelligence are those that predict those children who will escape from the ghetto, those children who will move outward and upward, who will adjust to standards to which the country as a whole aspires. This kind of instrument is much easier to develop. It is easier to define what it takes to get out of the ghetto. To get out of the ghetto you've got to get an education. You've got to pass entrance exams and employment exams and merit exams and promotion exams. And that is predictable. Since we know what constitutes those exams, building items into the intelligence test that will lead to the ultimate prediction of exam-taking success is simple.

Thus one can make a reasonable argument for Terman and Merrill's decision to eliminate and ignore minority groups, to assume that the rules will be the same for any child, and to stick to the question: How does the average child get to the top? That is a harsh argument, and punitive. But if one reads correctly the history of the United States in the last fifty years, and perhaps the last one hundred fifty years, it is the realistic point of view. That is the way the game is played. But even granting all this, the magnitude and intensity of feeling surrounding the meaning of intelligence is surprising.

PURPOSE

The concept that man is born with a fixed quantity of intelligence dies hard. It is the bone of contention between environmentalists and geneticists. The problem is that the abstraction *intelligence* has to be defined in operational terms that are not physiological. Every attempt thus far to define intelligence physiologically or neurologically has been a failure. Only when they have invaded the culture have intelligence tests been effective.

An inherent fact of intelligence tests is that they cannot avoid a cultural bias, in spite of the desirability for a culture-free test that would not give any advantage to one cultural subgroup over another. Although theoretically desirable, such a test is probably impossible in practice.

What characteristics of the intelligence test make a culture-free test unlikely? Tests that were presumably culture-free, those constructed on the assumption of some type of biological intelligence—that is, measures of absolute reaction time, hearing acuity, color sensitivity, pitch sensitivity, spatial judgment, and so forth—were largely ineffective in predicting the kind of adaptation now referred to as intelligence: the ability to deal effectively with one's environment, to do well academically, to perform well on the job, and to be a social success. Intelligence tests became effective, became valid, only when they began to increase their content or face validity. And the validity of a test's content, by its very nature, is culture-bound. No intelligence test yet perfected does not relate directly to the degree to which a person has been able to absorb the culture to which he has been exposed. Attempts have been made, however, more or less successfully, to minimize the effect of culture on intelligence tests. The two most outstanding examples are the *Goodenough Draw-a-Man Test* and the *Raven Progressive Matrices Test*.

The *Goodenough Draw-a-Man Test* is based on the simple assumption that everyone has been exposed to the human form. Therefore, to ask a child to draw a man, the best man that he can draw, is presumably not totally outside any culture. There is evidence that the *Goodenough* is less influenced by cultural background that the *Stanford-Binet*. For instance, Kennedy and Lindner (1964), in their study of eighteen hundred black children in the southeastern United States, found that these children obtained a substantially higher IQ on the *Goodenough* than on the *Stanford-Binet,* with the scores distributed much more symmetrically.

The Raven Progressive Matrices Test consists of a series of abstract designs from which a part has been removed or cut out. With no time limit imposed, the subject is asked to select, from six to eight samples, the correct insert to complete the design. The administration requires little explanation and a rather passive cooperation from the subject.

However, the use to which these two tests can be put limits their effectiveness. Intelligence tests mainly have been used for, and are effective in, predicting academic success. And academic success is certainly not culture-free. School curricula are related to success in middle-class environments, and the middle-class child has a decided advantage. The utilization of intelligence tests depends upon the purpose of the examination. This was the missing consideration that gave rise to the heated debates during the Iowa controversy. Once intelligence tests had been accepted as a measure of potential for academic success, many accepted with difficulty the fact that this potential could be altered by lack of requisite experience. So, although the Goodenough and the Raven Progressive Matrices Test are both less affected by cultural variables, they are, in turn, less effective in predicting academic success.

What, then, does the future hold for intelligence testing? Intelligence testing undoubtedly has moved beyond its peak of importance. Achievement tests that directly measure ability seem much more useful today. The questions being asked by today's educators are much more likely to relate to the best strategy for aiding a particular child at a particular time. So a child has an IQ of 75 and is not progressing in the classroom. You don't need a psychological test to tell you this. The classroom teacher knows that the child is slow. She also is very much aware of the fact that she is not teaching the child. Teachers today are far less mystified by or impressed with IQs. The increasing precision of a wide range of group-administered tests has removed much of the mystery from the IQ. Teachers want far more from the school psychologist than a psychological report that elaborates on the statistical aspects of a child's performance. Strategies for efficient learning related to different levels of ability are far more important to the teacher than a specific IQ used as an explanation for success or failure.

Intelligence tests have weathered the first three quarters of the twentieth century and no doubt will weather the last, because they serve a useful and probably irreplaceable function. But never again will they rise to the position of omnipotence they enjoyed in the 1920s and 1930s. Intelligence measures are put to the same test as any scientific discovery: the test of utility. And thus far, intelligence tests have fulfilled this criterion.

PRACTICAL IMPLICATIONS

And now we are ready to derive some practical implications from the concept of intellectual development. Are there, for example, ways in which parents or teachers can increase the likelihood that children will perform at their highest intellectual capacity? Granted that intellectual development is only one aspect of adjustment to life and that intelligence tests are only one definition of this development, intellectual functioning is nevertheless a real and significant aspect of that development, which we as parents and teachers would do well to cultivate.

The general strategy I suggest for optimizing intellectual development has been gleaned from several theories of intellectual development and is intended to serve as a broad outline for a process that can be used by parents and teachers alike. To aid in recall, the acrostic STRENGTH has been employed to stand for the dimensions of the strategy:

Sense
Try
Relate
Experience
Name
Grapple
Talk
Haggle

Sense

The development of the earliest concepts depends upon eidetic recall: the representation of past experiences through sensations, often visual, but sometimes tactile, auditory, and olfactory. It follows, then, that early pre-conceptual development would be aided by enriching the child's environment, stimulating him through all sense modalities, and allowing him many exposures to such stimuli. Exposing the child to bright colors, varying textures, music, odors, sights, and sounds, all would tend to enrich the eidetic-recall bank of the child and to extend the foundations of early memory and conceptual units. *Enriched sensory exposure* is the first step in the development of intelligence.

Try

Passivity is the great enemy of intelligence. Initiative and drive both seem to develop from a basic exploratory drive that can be cultivated at a very early age. Children should be given the experience of trying to do things, trying to master tasks, trying to help themselves and depend upon themselves. The concept of learning-by-doing, though an old one, is one easily forgotten in the modern world where so many tasks are done for children and so few reserved for their own efforts. Much of the tenacity that becomes so important in adolescence and later life, particularly for males, is developed in early infancy through the process of trying. *Freedom to try* is the second major step in developing intelligence.

Relate

A variation of the old see-and-tell routine, by expanding the concept to include all of the senses, serves as one of the major underpinnings of intelligence. The oral process of relating experience, of putting action into words, of describing both the sensations of the child and his attempts to cope, needs to be encouraged at every turn. Parents who spend time with their children, allowing them the privilege or perhaps the right of verbal self-expression of their daily experiences, are developing in their children one of the key skills of intellectual development: verbal abstraction. Like no other experience, the slowly developing confidence in the power of expression brings forth the critical symbolic language of man, which is, after all, the fundamental basis of intelligence.

Language development, discussed in greater detail in Chapter 8, is a long process that cannot be started too early. Its impetus comes from trying to make someone understand sensory experience and coping effort. The act of relating is the first that sets a child apart from all other creatures on earth. Slow, patient listening, encouraging, suggesting words, and providing good models of simple communication all serve to optimize the process of intellectual development through facilitation of the skill of relating. *Learning to relate experience and feeling* is the third step in intellectual development.

Experience

As the child becomes more sophisticated in the process of sensing, trying, and relating, he begins to have the ability to integrate these activites into meaningful wholes that can be referred to as experiences. At this point the parent or teacher can involve the child in events and activities that will give him a feeling of the drama of life. An example might be a guided walk through a dairy. Here the child can see and smell and touch and taste and listen to the complicated process by which grass becomes milk and gets into the store. Here it becomes possible for the child to sense things, try things, relate things and, in a much broader sense, experience things that provide a whole general framework on which to hang knowledge—knowledge that would remain simply rote without the benefit of experience. *Freedom to experience* is the fourth step in intellectual development.

In the process of developing intellectual power, direct symbolic representation through language is one of the major tasks of the child. The parent and teacher can greatly facilitate the process by providing a name for all the familiar and unfamiliar objects, actions, and feelings in the child's world. Obviously these names should be arranged in an expanding sequence. Young Waldo learns the name *Tigger,* then *kitty,* then *cat,* then *pet,* then *animal,* and then *domestic animal,* all names relating to a ball of fur and fluff he has sensed, some long white whiskers he has tried to pull, a frustration to relate both to Tigger and to mother, as well as an experience of scratches across his stomach where Tigger explained his side of the frustration. All of this can become more meaningful if the parent will provide the words to tie it all together; that is, if the parent will name the experience piece by piece and then pull it all together into a meaningful whole. *Conscious and deliberate naming of objects, actions, and feelings* is the fifth step in development of intelligence.

Grapple

Ego mastery, or the belief by the child that he can deal effectively with frustration, solve problems, and approximate solutions, is indeed a significant aspect of intellectual development. Children who quit easily, who turn to their parents or teachers for the right answer, who constantly ask for reassurance that they are right, are not going to develop the divergent thought patterns essential to intellectual productivity. Teaching the child to grapple with problems and issues, to make a sustained effort in the absence of a quick solution or easy certainty that he is right, is more difficult for the average parent than providing the previous five experiences. We parents have a strong drive to help our child, to take life out of his hands.

The neat, carpenter-built, painter-painted, low-level tree house with fitted door and screens, lights, and a safety rail is one answer to coming

home and finding a few rickety boards nailed on some high branches in a not too steady tree, but it effectively eliminates the three-year program of grappling with carpentry, painting, engineering, aerodynamics, and acrobatics, and teaches nothing about territorial imperative because soon such a neat little house is abandoned by the fellows to build their own further in the woods where they won't be bothered. *Freedom to grapple* is the sixth step in the development of intelligence.

Talk

After the child learns the rudiments of speech, accompanied by great enthusiasm from his parents, a time comes when he just wants to talk. He doesn't seem to have anything really important to say. He just wants the floor. He talks freely and easily, except that he has to stop sometimes to catch his breath, and sometimes he stalls a little to try to think of another topic, because even he realizes that he is in a rut and has said the same thing five times. This process of talking and developing confidence in the power of oral communication provides the foundation for later writing and speaking, and serves as a model of complex thinking. It is not by accident that exposure to books and reading should come at this stage; reading is only an extension of the talking process. Reading to the child and having the child read to you are part of talking, and a major underpinning of intellectual growth. Step seven in the development of intellectual power is *freedom to talk, to read, and to be read to.*

Haggle

A hybrid somewhere between grappling and talking is the concept of haggling, often overlooked as an area in which the power of intellect comes into play. In a sense, haggling is informed disobedience. It is argument, harassment, tenacity, garrulousness, and is easily one of the most important dimensions of intellectual development. Should the child just do what is demanded of him, whether or not he understands? Or should he keep up the pressure on the environment, on authority, until he understands the reason or perhaps effects a change?

In the twentieth century one of the greatest problems of children is that they have not learned to deal effectively with authority. They respond in an all-or-none way: either by complete submission or complete rebellion. Much serious adolescent rebellion can be avoided if children early develop confidence in their power to haggle. Many adolescents can go on to a quiet, productive, and related life instead of to an angry, alienated one. When this much anger develops and there is a lack of confidence in the process of argument, the child drifts away from intellectual productivity and develops instead a quiet fury that saps all his creative energy. Step eight in developing intellectual power is *freedom to haggle.*

STRENGTH

We have, then, a guide for developing the child's intellectual strength to its fullest capacity through the process of **Sensing**, **Trying**, **Relating**, **Experiencing**, **Naming**, **Grappling**, **Talking**, and **Haggling**.

Theories of Intelligence

Factors of Intelligence Tests The most dominant factor of an intelligence test is vocabulary, which includes both definition of terms and distinction between abstract terms. Other factors of an intelligence test include numerical skill, memory, and perceptual-motor skill.

early theories

Multiple-dimensional Intelligence L. L. Thurstone conceived intelligence as primary mental abilities: space, number, verbal comprehension, word fluency, memory, induction, deduction, and flexibility.

Single-dimensional Intelligence Binet, Simon, Goddard, and Terman, as well as Galton and Gesell, believed intelligence to be a single dimension: you had it or you didn't. Intelligent individuals exhibit excellence in everything.

Three-dimensional Intelligence Edward Thorndike considered three dimensions of intelligence—altitude, breadth, and speed—with altitude being the most important.

Two-dimensional Intelligence Charles Spearman proposed intelligence to consist of two factors: *g*, general intelligence, and *s*, specific intelligence.

established definitions

Abstraction Under the theoretical definition of intelligence, abstraction organizes the world of experience into a world of concepts to enable interpretation of the complex stimuli in our environment.

Empirical Definition of Intelligence Empirically, intelligence is the ability to cope with one's environment, to adjust to the problems one encounters, to solve most of those problems, and to achieve generally agreed-upon goals. Data from the longitudinal study of giftedness by Terman and Oden support this empirical definition of intelligence. The more intelligent you are, the better adjusted you are, the more successful you are, and, in the broadest sense, the more you achieve.

Memory Under the theoretical definition of intelligence, efficient recall is a function of the ability to abstract; rote memory is not a function of intelligence.

Operational Definition of Intelligence Operationally, intelligence is that which intelligence tests measure. This operational definition of intelligence was so influential, that for a while, IQ became synonymous with intelligence.

Synthesization Under the theoretical definition of intelligence, synthesization is creativity, the ability to go beyond the immediate conclusions derived from experience; synthesization is the highest level of intelligence. The greater the memory span, the faster the acquisition and manipulation of facts, the broader and the more interrelated the abstractions, the more capable is a person to perform at the highest level of intelligence: the more able he is to create.

Theoretical Definition of Intelligence Theoretically, intelligence is the ability to profit from experience. This ability depends upon memory, the ability to store experience such that recall is efficient; abstraction, the ability to classify information and experience such that it is held together in interlocking concepts; and synthesization, the ability to create new information on the basis of logical induction.

Theories of the Relationship Between Poverty and Intelligence

Compensatory Education Group The compensatory education group believes that remedial programs in kindergarten and elementary school do not come too late for the poverty child, although agreeing that language training is an essential ingredient. Their efforts have been turned toward providing a school curriculum to compensate children for the language deficiencies of their early home environments. Their efforts have produced gains, but have not been as successful as early intervention.

Both the language deficit and compensatory education groups minimize genetic differences, yet all three groups agree on the seriousness of the problem and recommend a highly structured language and concept training program that focuses on prerequisite skills.

Heritability Group Represented by Cyril Burt, Arthur Jensen, William Shockley, and Richard Herrnstein, the heritability group, following the theory of Francis Galton and Alfred Binet, believe that high intelligence produces high drive, a competitive spirit, dominance, such that the highly intelligent achieve more and acquire more of the world's resources; thus they provide better opportunities for their children to achieve. Those with less intellectual drive, fewer resources, can provide less for their children who, therefore, begin life at an even greater disadvantage than their parents. The heritability group agrees that: (1) IQ has a high heritability quotient; about 80 percent; (2) IQ has a high constancy quotient; it doesn't change much after age six; (3) IQ doesn't change much under current intervention programs because ways of thinking are pretty well set by age four; (4) IQ correlates highly with academic achievement; (5) IQ correlates highly with socioeconomic status; and (6) therefore, IQ, scholastic achievement, and socioeconomic status operate under a common cause, inherited ability.

Language Deficit Group   The difference in lower- and middle-class children in scholastic achievement and measured intelligence is accounted for by the language deficit group as the failure of lower-class children to develop language during the critical period from 18 to 36 months; the lack of cognitive skills related to speaking and reading and abstract thinking accounts for the deficit: the environment is credited as the cause of the deficit.

The language deficit group agrees that: (1) IQ correlates highly with academic achievement; (2) IQ correlates highly with socioeconomic status; (3) the difference in IQ in lower- and middle-class children is caused by the former's lack of verbal ability; (4) this lack of verbal ability is due to environmental deprivation that causes these children to miss the critical period for language development; (5) early and intense language and concept training can remedy the defect.

Psycholinguistic Group   The psycholinguistic group does not recognize the problem as serious; the psycholinguistic group sees only a cultural difference, not a deficit. The problem, they say, is in middle-class teachers, middle-class books, middle-class examinations, and middle-class entry points into jobs. They see language as communication, not as an integral part of man's thinking, cognitive system: complicated reasoning does not require complicated language, they say.

Measurement of Intelligence

motivation

The suggestion has been made that the results of preschool programs have been brought about by attitudinal changes in the children, rather than by real academic changes. Certainly there is a placebo effect from the attention the children receive in the intervention programs. But for older children, studies of motivation show no reliable difference in performance under various extrinsic incentives. Motivation of the individual is difficult to analyze; perhaps by school age, the intrinsic motivational level of the individual is set and unaffected by extrinsic rewards.

utility

An intelligence test has utility when it can predict successfully a variable such as academic achievement or job success. However, the earlier an intelligence test is given to a child, the less accurate will be the prediction; in other words, it is easier to predict how a five-year-old will do in the first grade than whether a six-month-old infant will be an A-student in college.

Academic Achievement   The intelligence test was developed to sample the kinds of knowledge, information, and skill learned in school, without relating specifically to classroom content. The first and foremost use of the intelligence test, then, is to predict academic success. No other test can better predict how a preschool child will do in school. The concept of mental age has added to our ability to predict, to understand, and to explain school readiness. Children whose mental growth is slow, regardless of the reason, can be expected to have a difficult time in school.

Academic Discrepancy   An intelligence test has utility in locating achievement discrepancies, in finding those children who are underachieving in the classroom and those children under undue pressure to overachieve. Both of these groups of children, through proper identification of their abilities and consequent appropriate attention from the teacher, can better benefit from the classroom experience.

Academic Placement   An intelligence test has utility in placing schoolchildren, because children are unalike in their abilities and in their readiness to learn. Homogeneous small groups, within the larger classroom setting, allow for the presentation of instructional materials especially appropriate for those specific children, materials with which they can deal effectively.

Exceptional Talent   An intelligence test has utility in locating exceptional talent. The early identification of exceptional youth to benefit from exceptional opportunity more readily assures that they will be able to develop their unique potential. The longitudinal studies of Terman give adequate proof that potential alone does not guarantee performance; stimulation, encouragement, and, above all, opportunity are also necessary.

Intellectual Weaknesses An intelligence test has utility in locating specific weaknesses, thereby enabling the teacher to give appropriate remediation and encouragement. Locating weaknesses early can forestall long-term academic difficulties due to a poor beginning, which often results in a poor attitude.

abuse

Branding of Children As is often the case, one of the greatest strengths of the intelligence test— its ability to group children homogeneously according to their readiness level—is closely associated with one of its greatest misuses: the branding of children. Homogeneous grouping of children is appropriate only when the grouping is flexible enough to remain homogeneous; the relative ability of children fluctuates according to their maturational level, their health, their emotional stresses and strains.

Defense of Genetic Intelligence In spite of the major contributions of the intelligence test, the concept of intelligence and intelligence testing has done some harm. The foremost misuse of the intelligence test has been as a defense for the concept of genetically determined intelligence: the IQ is not a measure of capacity.

Unreliability of Infant Tests Infant tests, even the most sophisticated, are unreliable predictors of adult intelligence due to the differences between superior adult intelligence and that which marks a superior infant; the behavior repertoire of even a superior infant is extremely limited. Irregular growth patterns in the very young, together with the absence in infants of many factors present in adult intelligence, perhaps make reliable predictions about the adult intelligence of the very young an impossible task. Test-retest reliability over an age span depends upon the initial age of the child and how great the age span between testings: the younger the child, the less reliable is his intelligence score; the longer the prediction is extended, the less useful it is. The concept of MA is more appropriate for children under two years of age than is the concept of IQ.

quality

The quality of an intelligence test determines its usefulness; a test's quality is determined by three factors: representativeness, standardization, and validity.

Construct Validity Construct validity refers to a definition of the variable to be measured that is internally consistent within the test. Construct validity demands that the test items be selected to be consistent with some underlying theory of intelligence and be correlated highly with each other. The construct validity of the *Stanford-Binet* unintentionally propelled the intelligence test into an absolute criterion of intelligence, a position for which it was neither theoretically designed nor practically able to respond.

Face Validity Face validity refers to the overlap between the test items and the predicted variable. Face validity for an intelligence test would involve maximizing the overlapping of achievement measures and intelligence measures. Face validity accounted for the extraordinary success of the *Simon-Binet*.

Predictive Validity Predictive validity refers to the degree to which the items on the test predict future performance. Predictive validity depends upon the sampling of behaviors requisite for future learning. A test with reliable predictive ability comes as close as we can at present to measuring true potential.

Representativeness Without a large, representative standardization sample, an intelligence test is appropriate only for a small segment of the population; its general usefulness is nil. Representativeness refers to the populations on which the test is to be used: all socioeconomic levels, all ethnic subgroups, all degrees of cultural opportunity and health, both sexes, all races, all relevant geographic locations, and, of course, all ages; to be representative, the sample should represent the entire range of variables pertinent to performance on an intelligence test.

Standardization A well-standardized test represents the population on which it is to be used and presents a broad spectrum of items relevant to that variable it is designed to predict. The 1937 *Stanford-Binet Intelligence Scale* was designed by Terman to predict academic achievement; intelligence was defined by him as the ability to think abstractly, to use abstract symbols in solving problems; the 1937 *Stanford-Binet* was an exceptionally well-standardized instrument because it represented the mass of children in school at the time and because its items were carefully chosen according to the use to which the test was to be put and according to the definition of intelligence on which the test was based.

purpose

The main purpose of an intelligence test is to predict academic achievement. This purpose necessarily has given the intelligence test a cultural bias; academic success is not culture-free. Tests that claim to have less cultural bias are less able to predict academic achievement.

future

Intelligence testing undoubtedly has moved beyond its peak of importance; achievement tests that directly measure ability seem more useful today. Much more is needed by teachers today than a simple elaboration of where a child is; strategies for efficient learning where he is are more to the point. Nevertheless, intelligence tests serve a useful and so far irreplaceable function; they have passed successfully the test of utility.

Practical Implications

Granted that intellectual development is only one aspect of adjustment to life and that the intelligence tests are only one definition of this development, intellectual functioning is nevertheless a real and significant aspect of that development we as parents and teachers would do well to cultivate.

STRENGTH for optimizing intellectual development:

Sense **T** **R** **E** **N** **G** **T** **H**	Early preconceptual development is aided by enriching the child's environment through stimulation and experience for all his senses: visual, tactile, auditory, olfactory, and taste. Enriched sensory exposure is the first step in the development of intellectual power.
S **T**ry **R** **E** **N** **G** **T** **H**	Passivity is the great enemy of intelligence. Initiative and drive can be cultivated from a basic exploratory drive at an early age through the age-old concept of learning-by-doing. Freedom to try is the second major step in the development of intellectual power.
S **T** **R**elate **E** **N** **G** **T** **H**	The parents' habit of relating experience, of putting action into words, of describing both the sensations of the child and his attempts to cope, needs to be encouraged at every turn. The child's right of verbal self-expression of daily experiences develops the key skill of intellectual development: verbal abstraction. The critical symbolic language of man—the very foundation of intelligence—is brought forth through the slowly developing confidence in the power of expression. Learning to relate experience and feeling is a third step in the development of intellectual power.
S **T** **R** **E**xperience **N** **G** **T** **H**	The growing processes of sensing, trying, relating give the child an ability to integrate experiences into a meaningful whole. Now he can begin to build a framework on which to hang knowledge—knowledge that would remain simply rote without experience. Freedom to experience is the fourth step in the development of intellectual power.
S **T** **R** **E** **N**ame **G** **T** **H**	In developing intellectual power, one of the major tasks of the child is direct symbolic representation through language. Parents greatly facilitate the process by providing names for all the objects, actions, and feelings in the child's world. Conscious and deliberate naming of objects, actions, and feelings is the fifth step in the development of intellectual power.
S **T** **R** **E** **N** **G**rapple **T** **H**	Ego mastery, the child's belief that he can deal effectively with frustration, that he can approximate solutions to problems, is a significant aspect of intellectual development. The divergent thought patterns essential to intellectual productivity are developed only by the child who is taught to grapple with problems and issues, to make a sustained effort in the absence of a quick solution or easy certainty that he is right. Freedom to grapple is the sixth step in the development of intellectual power.
S **T** **R** **E** **N** **G** **T**alk **H**	The process of talking and developing confidence in the power of oral communication provides the foundation for complex thinking. And reading is only an extension of talking. Freedom to talk, to read, and to be read to are step seven in the development of intellectual power.

264

A hybrid between grappling and talking, haggling is informed disobedience. It is argument, harassment, tenacity, garrulousness, and is easily one of the most important dimensions of intellectual development. Confidence in the power of argument enables a youngster to better understand his environment, and in appropriate instances to effect changes. Freedom to haggle is step eight in the development of intellectual power.

NAMES TO KNOW

Early Concepts of Intelligence

EMIL KRAEPELIN At the end of the 19th century, Kraepelin defined a whole class of mental disorders as dementia praecox—premature senility. The final stage of man, senility, was considered to be a form of idiocy.

JEAN-ETIENNE ESQUIROL Jean-Etienne Esquirol dated the beginning of a conceptual distinction between mental retardation and insanity. Esquirol implied that intelligence has dimensions; it is not an all-or-none proposition. He chose as a measurement of intelligence a tool that remains the mainstay of intellectual assessment today: the quantity and quality of language facility. A taxonomist rather than an activist, Esquirol did not believe that the intelligence of individuals could be modified.

JEAN-MARC ITARD Through his attempt to rehabilitate the Wild Boy of Aveyron, Jean-Marc Itard demonstrated that a change in behavior and intellectual performance can be effected by environmental control.

EDWARD SEGUIN Edward Seguin insisted that the feebleminded could be educated, and that success or failure could be judged only in terms of improvement or nonimprovement made by the learner.

CHARLES DARWIN Charles Darwin propounded the theory of survival of the fittest. Darwin believed intelligence to be those characteristics, those functional behavior patterns that enabled man to adapt to his environment and, therefore, to survive.

FRANCIS GALTON Francis Galton, Darwin's cousin, believed in generalized superiority—superior people should be faster in reaction time, faster in perception, and so forth. With the enthusiasm of genius, Galton developed anthropometric sensory-motor tasks for measuring intelligence and became convinced of a biological, physically based intelligence with great significance for survival, even though his measures failed to discriminate between the successful and unsuccessful.

G. STANLEY HALL Interested in intelligence as it related to schoolchildren, G. Stanley Hall developed the questionnaire method with children, which was not important because of the quality of the questions, but because it tapped information storage, language facility, and experience far more closely related to school work than did Galton's sensory-motor tasks. Hall defined intelligence in objective terms for the first time, by combining correct answers in a total numerical score. Failing to understand the concept of IQ—the relationship between chronological age and mental age that allows comparison of children of different ages, Hall did demonstrate a rare ability to understand the development of logical thinking in children, the conceptual world of the child. Hall maintained a global conception of intelligence that tied it closely to language and information, and perceived that the cultural background of the child related to his intelligence; that is, his intelligence depended, at least to some extent, upon his cultural background. Hall failed to discriminate, however, those items pertinent to success in school; he could not predict success or failure in school.

WILLIAM STERN In Germany, William Stern conceived the Intelligence Quotient, which made measurement across ages possible: mental quotient equals mental age divided by chronological age.

ALFRED BINET Assigned the task of discriminating between children who were feebleminded and children who were simply poorly motivated, Alfred Binet defined intelligence, which was to be measured by the psychological method, as aptitude for academic achievement. Binet attacked the problem first by finding out from classroom teachers what skills were required for success in school; then, he tied the definition of intelligence directly to these skills. Binet's fundamental assumption was that given equal opportunity, those children who had developed certain skill, certain knowledge, and certain ability at a given age were brighter than those who had not. He was immensely successful in predicting academic success, because he had tied his test di-

265

rectly to academic skills: this initial definition of intelligence, as the ability to respond effectively to academic training, is defensible today.

JAMES MCKEEN CATTELL   James McKeen Cattell believed, as did Galton, in generalized superiority that could be measured by quickness of perception and reaction. The term *mental tests* was initiated by Cattell, who was interested in measuring individual differences. He constructed tests emphasizing keenness of vision and hearing, color sensitivity, reaction time, rote memory, mental imagery, and so forth, a compromise between Galton's psychophysical methods and Binet's school-oriented tasks, to predict success in college, but was singularly ineffective in predicting academic success. Cattell did initiate a second line of test development that allowed itself to be challenged by an outside criterion, however.

HENRY H. GODDARD   Henry H. Goddard, founder of the Vineland Training School—one of America's earliest schools for the retarded—brought the *Simon-Binet* test to America; making no allowances for differences between Paris and Princeton, he made a literal translation.

LEWIS TERMAN   Lewis Terman Americanized the *Simon-Binet* test; in 1916 he devised a standardized American version—the *Stanford-Binet Revision of the Simon-Binet Test*.   Terman instituted an entirely new tack: selection of items most directly relevant to the American culture, large-scale sampling, and publication of a careful manual of detailed instructions on how correctly to use and score the test.   The basis for a tradition of nationally standardized intelligence tests, a tradition that has withstood pressures of time and controversy, was laid by Lewis Terman.

ARNOLD GESELL   Arnold Gesell, concerned with the general neurological development of children, developed a scale for measuring infant maturation based upon neurological development as reflected in overt behavior.

Theories of Intelligence

early theories

EDWARD L. THORNDIKE   Edward L. Thorndike defined intelligence on three dimensions and considered the first to be the most important—altitude, breadth, and speed: (1) Altitude—other things being equal, the harder the task you master, the greater your intelligence; (2) Breadth—other things being equal, the more tasks you master, the greater your intelligence; (3) Speed—other things being equal, the faster you produce a correct response, the greater your intelligence.

CHARLES E. SPEARMAN   Charles E. Spearman defined intelligence within two factors: (1) *g*, a general factor, and (2) *s*, a specific factor.

L. L. THURSTONE   L. L. Thurstone defined intelligence as primary mental abilities.   Thurstone considered it quite possible for one to be abstractly intelligent and mechanically moronic. He identified eight separate and more or less mutually exclusive components of intelligence: space, number, verbal comprehension, word fluency, memory, induction, deduction, and flexibility.

DAVID WECHSLER   David Wechsler defined intelligence as fundamentally biological, maintaining that "intelligence is a manifestation of the personality as a whole," that "emotional and motivational characteristics are among the ingredients out of which it is made."

Economics of Intelligence

studies of impoverishment

SHERMAN AND KEY   Sherman and Key, in a classic environmental study of intelligence using isolated and deprived mountain children, concluded that performance or achievement depends upon opportunities to gather information, that children develop only as the environment demands development.

studies of race

KENNEDY, VAN DE RIET, AND WHITE   A normative study of 1,800 black elementary school children in the Southeast found a mean IQ on the *Stanford-Binet* of 80.7, with a standard deviation of 12.4, as contrasted with the mean IQ of 100 and standard deviation of 16 for the standardization sample.   This mean IQ was found to be constant across grade levels.   The most pronounced trend in the normative data, however, was the relationship between socioeconomic level and mean IQ: the higher the socioeconomic level, the higher the mean IQ.   The Collaborative Study of 26,000 children also found a high correlation between socioeconomic status and measured intelligence.

Theories of the Relationship Between Poverty and Intelligence

heritability group

CYRIL BURT   After years of research, Cyril Burt concluded that 88 percent of the variance in IQ could be predicted on the basis of genetic factors, insisting that probability estimates apply to groups, not individuals. Burt contended that children are born with a theoretical potential or upper limit: their environment can enhance or limit that potential, or, in some cases, environmental influences can obscure genetic potential.

WILLIAM SHOCKLEY   William Shockley, a solid-state physicist, has called for more research on the heritability of intelligence.

ARTHUR JENSEN   Jensen believes that intervention educational programs generally have been too little, too late. Jensen suggests that at least some portion of intelligence is inherited and he suggests different inherited abilities.

RICHARD HERRNSTEIN   Richard Herrnstein pointed out that heritability quotients for IQ are not relevant for cross-race comparisons, since the research so far has been conducted on white populations, adding, as did Burt, that heritability applies to populations, not individuals.

language deficit group

ROBERT HESS   Robert Hess was one of the first to call attention to the language problem of lower-class children, the nonverbal style under which they operated. His obvious suggestion was to provide programs of language facilitation; but he also points out a critical period in the child's development after which intervention programs have little impact.

SIEGFRIED ENGELMANN   Behavioral objectives were applied to the preschool child by Siegfried Engelmann, who believed structure, firm control, and guidance were needed to adjust the nonverbal child to a verbal, structured society.

MERLE KARNES   Merle Karnes developed a structured preschool program with highly specific, focused training that demonstrated greater improvement in skills than the traditional kindergarten programs produced.

Summary

BASIL BERNSTEIN   Basil Bernstein proposes that substandard language handicaps seriously, restricting the user mainly to description and making analytical arguments and abstractions quite difficult. Bernstein points out that the middle-class child has learned that ideas are important.

Achievement

As psychologists established a successful pattern of measurement of intelligence to supplement their understanding of children gained from studies of genetics and maturation, a new problem arose on the horizon—the problem of a systematic description of achievement. Not achievement in the classic sense of the apprentice who finally becomes a master and acquires his own apprentice, but achievement in a relative sense, a comparative sense, achievement of the masses.

HISTORY OF ACHIEVEMENT MEASUREMENT

Scholars long have been held in high esteem by their fellow men. When the masses were illiterate, achievement in letters was considered an almost magical accomplishment, far beyond the reach of the average man. The gulf separating the educated man of letters from the masses was in and of itself so wide that little consideration was given to making judgments of the relative education or achievement of scholars. Early achievement examinations were admission rites into a secret society.

Greene, Jorgensen, and Gerberich (1953) begin their classic review of achievement testing with an example from the Old Testament. The Gileadites separated the Ephraimites, their enemy, from friendly tribes at the fords of the Jordan by requiring the suspects to pass an objective language test by pronouncing the word *shibboleth*. The Ephraimites, who lacked the "sh" sound, would answer "sibboleth," and some forty-two thousand imposters were thus put to the sword (Judges 12:4–6). Plainly, foreign language competency examinations always have been rather trying.

In the pre-Christian era, oral achievement tests were mainly for the examination of priests. Socrates raised the oral examination for scholars to a peak of importance from which it has never descended: the oral examination remains today one of the most useful methods of assessing scholarly competence. However, as education shifted from the tutoring of the individual to the teaching of the masses, some type of objective test suitable for group administration became essential. The poles of the distribution pre-

270

sented no problem: just as the genius was readily identifiable and easily contrasted with the idiot, so the scholar was easy to separate from the illiterate. The middle distribution caused the difficulty.

Boston, Massachusetts, had the first large-scale public school program in America. Here the necessity for written achievement tests first became evident. Before 1845, the school board itself was charged with the annual examination; each child was examined individually and orally. As the number of students increased, the school board restricted the examination to the better students in each grade. Finally the task became too exhausting, and in 1845 the committee decided to use annual written examinations for grammar, astronomy, geography, history, mathematics, and natural philosophy. The students from the entire system were ranked according to their ability, and for the first time students and teachers alike were given some outside judgment of the quality of education.

A prominent educator and secretary of the Massachusetts Board of Education, Horace Mann (1845) encouraged the use of the new written examination. He believed it superior in every way to the committee's old oral examination: it (1) was impartial; (2) was just to the pupils; (3) was more thorough; (4) was free of "officious interference" from the teacher; (5) gave evidence "beyond appeal or gainsaying whether the pupils have been faithfully and competently taught"; (6) was free of "all possibility of favoritism"; (7) was scored such that the information obtained was available to all; and (8) was easily appraisable as to the ease or difficulty of the questions (quotations from Mann, 1845, as cited by Greene, Jorgensen, and Gerberich, 1953, p. 23). More than a commentary on the accomplishments of the first written public-school examination, Mann's list serves as a model for the attributes of any good examination.

In 1904, Edward L. Thorndike published his monumental volume, *An Introduction to the Theory of Mental and Social Measurement*. More than any other, this book and its author popularized the concept of the standardized achievement test. Thorndike (1910) and his student, Cliff W. Stone (1908), published the first two standardized achievement tests: the first was Stone's test of arithmetic abilities; the second, Thorndike's *Scale for Handwriting of Children*. The latter is important not only because it represents a pioneering effort to standardize an achievement variable; but more than this, it represents a pioneering effort to objectify judgment that had been purely subjective. When progress in handwriting could be graded by an objective criterion, agreement among testers and teachers about what constituted bad or good handwriting became possible.

Obviously, the primary force behind the development of achievement tests was the greatly increasing numbers of students in educational systems and the concomitant need for some efficient way to grade their achievement. Moreover, a growing number of psychologists and educators had become disenchanted with the accuracy of school marks. A number of studies had demonstrated a high degree of variability in the standards of different school systems, and even among teachers in the same school system. These studies clearly revealed that grades were subject to prejudice and bias, and often were inaccurate. Large school systems began to organize educational research bureaus with specific responsibility for developing instruments to assess intelligence and achievement in the massive educational systems developing around the country.

The transition from the unique classroom test, developed and used by a single teacher, or from the more general departmental examination developed by a group of compatible teachers, to the big-battery, nationally standardized achievement test required a technology not available to psychology at the turn of the century. The identification of achievement variables, and their systematization into a meaningful whole, to say nothing of the development of national standards, required new mathematical techniques. Quantitative measurement in psychology had not advanced to the point where such use of numbers was even possible, much less practical. A new system of descriptive mathematics was needed to relate the science of psychology, which deals mainly in probabilities, to the task of measuring and predicting the achievement of the individual child or the group to which he belongs.

The development of correlational analysis and sampling statistics at the turn of the century constituted the initial breakthrough. After correlational analysis came factor analysis, then analysis of variance, and trend analysis, and, today, multivariate analysis. The wide use of achievement tests today is in no small way dependent upon the basic statistical contributions of Francis Galton, R. A. Fisher, Karl Pearson, Charles Spearman, Cyril Burt, L. L. Thurstone, J. P. Guilford, and Raymond B. Cattell. Wrote E. Chadwick in 1864:

> Much of the scepticism prevalent as to the power and value of popular education arises from the inability of the educationist, or of the school teacher, to adduce satisfactory statistical evidence of the moral or of the intellectual results from any special courses of instruction or training, as manifested in after life [(1913), p. 551].

Francis Galton (1888) laid the groundwork for probability statistics, and R. A. Fisher (1932), a British statistician, made the first practical applications of the theory. But Karl Pearson (1896), through his correlational theory, made possible the prediction of variability in psychology. The probability model was born and, having been born, quickly became the new standard for the measurement of achievement. Pearson's most significant contribution, the product-moment coefficient of correlation (Pearson's r), made possible a numerical specification for the degree of relatedness between two variables.

Charles Spearman (1904, 1927) made the next significant step in the use of correlational theory. As early as 1904, he began to conceptualize multiple intelligence, or multiple factors of intelligence. He was responsible for the two-factor theory of intelligence in which he identified a g, or general, factor, and an s, or specific, factor. His (1904) original discovery that abilities of all kinds are correlated positively still stands. Spearman paved the way for the multiple measures of achievement contained in modern achievement batteries.

Factor analysis, which simplifies the description of data by reducing the variables into meaningful groups or clusters, was developed in the 1930s under the leadership of Cyril Burt (1941) in London and L. L. Thurstone (1927, 1947) in Chicago. Thurstone came to be known as the developer of paper-and-pencil tests of intelligence and aptitude. In 1927, his classic article on psychophysical theory laid the rational basis for quantifying data obtained from comparative judgments. In 1947 he published a method for analyzing a set of variables into common factors; and he developed tests of intelligence and temperament (the *Thurstone Tests of Primary Mental Abilities* and the *Thurstone Temperament Schedule*).

J. P. Guilford, in addition to making major contributions in the area of psychological statistics (1965), introduced the concept of aptitude, a measure of potential for achievement in the absence of opportunity. Guilford has conducted factorial research in many areas. He concludes, for instance, that there are probably 120 different varieties of intelligence (1959). In a comprehensive reexamination of his own research, and that of other factorial studies, he has proposed a revised and expanded definition of intelligence (1956, 1967*b*).

Most recently, through the method of factor analysis, Raymond B. Cattell has developed a series of personality factors related to achievement (Hundleby and Cattell, 1968). Cattell has made an ambitious attempt to integrate the results of statistical measurements, through ratings, questionnaires, and objective tests, with nonmathematical classifications of personality (1946, 1950). He also had a major responsibility in the development of Univac, one of the first large-capacity digital computers that made large-scale factor–analytic studies possible.

VARIABILITY OF ACHIEVEMENT

Before we look at those variables that seem to influence achievement, let us examine a few of the studies that point up the great variability in achievement. Teachers and students have always been aware of differences, but only since the development of standardized achievement tests have we realized how great they are. Tremendous differences among children can be found in any classroom or grade. There are also sexual differences: in the elementary grades, girls are usually better in reading comprehension, vocabulary, and basic language skills; boys are usually superior in arithmetic.

Learned and Wood (1938) conducted an early and exhaustive investigation of school accomplishment in Pennsylvania high schools and colleges from 1928 to 1932. Figure 16 shows their findings on a portion of their total examination.

This graph shows two things very plainly. First, there is a wide spread of scores within each of these groups of students who had spent the same amount of time in school. Second, there is a large amount of overlapping *between* groups.... In general we can say that the median for each of the higher groups falls at about the 75th percentile of the group below it. But this means that roughly a quarter of the lower group of students is made up of persons who already know more than the average person with two years more of schooling. Learned and Wood theorized that if individuals had been awarded diplomas on the basis of tested knowledge rather than hours and credits, ... the group would have consisted of 28 percent of the senior class, 21 percent of the juniors, 19 percent of the sophomores, and 15 percent of the freshmen [L. Tyler, 1965, pp. 104, 107].

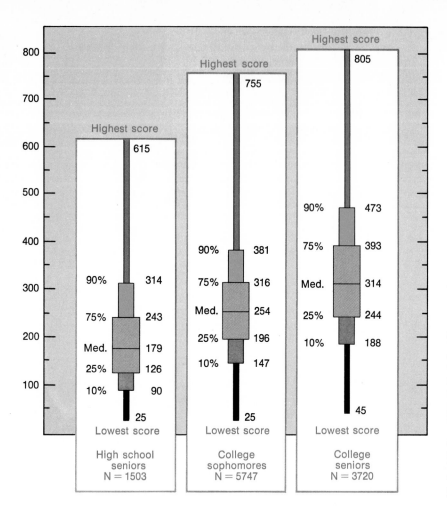

Figure 16

Distribution of scores for Pennsylvania students on a general culture test. Adapted from William S. Learned and B. D. Wood, *The Student and His Knowledge* (New York: The Carnegie Foundation for the Advancement of Teaching, Bulletin Number Twenty-Nine, 1938), by Leona E. Tyler. Reprinted, by permission of both publishers, from Leona E. Tyler, *The Psychology of Human Differences*, 3d ed. (New York: Appleton-Century-Crofts, 1965), Figure 20, p. 105.

Table 15
Correlations between Achievements and Other Variables, from Kagan and Moss (1962)

Variables	Boys	Girls
Intellectual achievement at ages 10 to 14 and general achievement at ages 3 to 6	.39	.68
Intellectual achievement at ages 10 to 14 and general achievement at ages 6 to 10	.81	.76
Intellectual achievement at ages 6 to 10 and adult achievement	.46	.38
Intellectual achievement at ages 10 to 14 and father's educational level	.71	.09

Although great variability in achievement is demonstrated between individuals, stability of achievement can be found within individuals and among individuals in the same family. From the Fels Institute data, Kagan and Moss (1962) concluded that achievement in later childhood or pre-adolescence does not correlate highly with achievement in the first three years. However, they found that from three to fourteen, general achievement, intellectual striving, competitiveness, expectancy of success or failure, and striving for recognition all were fairly stable, the correlations ranging from .39 to .81 (see Table 15).

Table 16
Sibling Resemblances in Intelligence and Achievement,
from Schoonover (1956)

Measure	Coefficients of Correlation (*r*) for Pairs of Siblings	Average Difference between Siblings (in Months)	Average Difference between Unrelated Pairs (in Months)	Percentage Reduction of Difference for Siblings
Mental Age	.71	9.9	18.3	46
Arithmetic Age	.49	10.7	15.1	29
Educational Age	.59	12.6	19.3	35
Language Age	.40	20.7	30.1	31
Literature Age	.41	14.3	20.7	31
Reading Age	.51	16.4	25.9	37
Science Age	.39	16.0	20.5	22
Social Studies Age	.64	13.6	19.7	31
Spelling Age	.53	14.7	21.5	35

Adapted from Sarah M. Schoonover. A longitudinal study of sibling resemblances in intelligence and achievement, *Journal of Educational Psychology*, 1956, 47, 440–441, Tables 1–3, by Willard C. Olson. Reprinted by permission of the author, from Willard C. Olson, *Child Development*, 2d ed. (Lexington, Mass. Heath, 1959), Table 6.3, p. 154.

Schoonover (1956) reported on resemblances in intelligence and achievement among siblings. In her longitudinal study, she compared the siblings at the same chronological ages. Table 16 shows that the average difference between siblings, in months, varies from 9.9 months in mental age to 20.7 months in language age. The spelling age of one child in a family at a given chronological age can be predicted by a knowledge of what an older child achieved at the same age. The difference between their performance will be 35 percent less than between random pairs of children of the same age.

Reading achievement in families is illustrated in Figure 17. Olson (1959) reports on brothers Tom and Tim, and brothers Billy and Bobby. Each pair of brothers differs three years in age. All four are sons of pro-

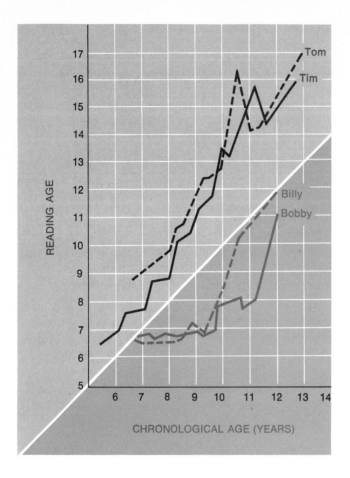

Figure 17

Familial resemblances in reading patterns. Reprinted, by permission of the author, from Willard C. Olson, *Child Development,* 2d ed. (Lexington, Mass.: D. C. Heath, 1959), Figure 6.3, p. 149.

fessional parents with above average cultural advantages. Tim and Bobby, the elder of each pair of brothers, were classmates, as were Tom and Billy.

INFLUENCES ON ACHIEVEMENT

Obviously, many variables affect the achievement of individuals, or even groups. We shall look at some of the more obvious.

PUPIL CHARACTERISTICS

Remember, academic achievement refers to particular learning in a particular setting. The American school system, modeled on the general, middle-class learning style, has great uniformity today. For this reason, those pupil characteristics most middle-class in nature tend to be the best predictors of academic success.

Academic achievement is defined by achievement test scores and teacher-given grades and percentiles in academic subjects. School success depends upon the ability of the student to perform the operations measured by these techniques. To argue that achievement scores and grades are not good or adequate measures of achievement is futile, because they are the present definition; they are in wide use and have serious implications for students, parents, and teachers.

Gough and Fink, after a series of studies using operational definitions of achievement and objective personality measures, described the high achiever within the American elementary school as a child who can rapidly code information. He can break down incoming stimuli, cues, perceptions, ideas, and data such that they can easily be recalled and cross-related to other information previously recorded. He has a high activity rate, high drive, and is mentally efficient. He is observant of stimuli and expends little time and energy in other than the productive task of cross-relating concepts.

> The pattern is one of positive personal effectiveness coupled with diligence, perseverance, and restraint. It is not a pattern of creativity or innovation, but rather that of constructive adaptation to a world in which one's circumstances are modest and one's destiny is limited [1964, p. 380].

Thus, the high-achieving child early understands the educational demands of society and placidly solves the developmental tasks called for by the school setting. The proper frame of mind is passive and receptive, with little divergent thinking.

Certain dimensions of these pupil characteristics are predictive and fall into the convenient acrostic,

MASTERED:

Maturation

Ability

Self-concept

Temperament

Experience

Reinforcement

Expectancy

Drive

Maturation

Physical maturation and mental readiness for achievement, which in turn affect the degree of success in school, are correlated highly. At an early age, maturational speed seems to have little permanent significance; in fact, Kagan and Moss (1962) found almost zero correlation between early growth patterns and later academic success. But with the middle-childhood growth sequence, this is no longer the case.

Research in underachievement in the first grade has centered about the question of maturity. Lowell Carter (1956) found that the classroom performance of 87 percent of underaged first graders did not measure up to that of children of normal age. Failing students were found to be less mature by Maria Simon (1959). And Klausmeier and Check (1959) found physical development to be related to boys' achievement in reading and arithmetic, but not girls'. However, Medinnus (1961) suggested that chronological age may affect first-grade achievement earlier in the year, but not by the end of the school year.

Strong evidence indicates that those children who enter the academic arena with greater maturation, greater physical size, bone structure, and body weight, with the presumed underlying neurological development, operate at a distinct advantage during the elementary-school period. This is true regardless of social class, sex, or ethnic background, and may in part be accounted for by an expectancy phenomenon; parents, peers, and teachers may all expect and demand better performance from "such a big boy."

Ability

The higher the ability demonstrated on tests of intelligence, the greater the probability of high achievement. Some of this correlation is, of course, a function of the overlap between the instruments, but the explanation goes beyond that. Regardless of the cause of high performance on an IQ test, whether social advantage, environmental stimulation, or genetic endowment, IQ and achievement tests both measure a dimension of acculturation required for academic performance. The factors of attention, ability to make figure-ground distinctions, ability to use and transform number concepts, vocabulary recognition and utilization, abstract reasoning, short- and long-term memory, all are important on both assessment devices and in the general life adjustment of the child, and all are predictive of academic performance during the elementary school years. Those children who succeed in preschool, both nursery school and kindergarten, achieve because they have mastered certain developmental tasks upon which basic literacy, reading, spelling, and writing are built. Thus, the IQ tests tap a particular kind of ability, itself an achievement and predictive of long-range school success.

Intelligence "is related to academic achievement but not synonymous with it" (Leona Tyler, 1965, p. 109), but is, of course, a highly significant factor in achievement as measured by achievement tests: other things being equal, the more intelligent the child, the greater will be his achievement in school. Yet Thurstone (1951) emphasizes that creative talent is not synonymous with superior academic achievement.

Intelligence tests were designed originally for the sole purpose of predicting achievement. Thus it comes as no surprise that the correlation between performance on the 1960 *Stanford-Binet Form L-M* and the *California Achievement Test* is about .69 (from Kennedy, Van De Riet, and White, 1963, Table 71, p. 106), an optimal correlation. If it were much higher, an intelligence test would have no use whatsoever outside of achievement measurement; in fact, it would be an achievement test.

Generally, intelligence test scores correlate more highly with scores on achievement tests than with grades given by teachers, thus reflecting the subjectivity of teachers' grades as well as the fact that scores on verbal intelligence tests are based to some extent on schooling. Achievement tests constructed on different philosophies of the aims and methods of education

correlate about equally well with verbal intelligence, a point made by
Lorge (1949), who summarized several studies of differences among
achievement tests.

Kennedy (1969, Table 7) compared the predictive power of the
L–M Binet IQ and the scores on the individual *California Achievement Test*
subtests for the different elementary grade levels over a five-year span. The
best predictor at each grade level was the *Binet* IQ predicting itself five
years later: the correlations were .60, grade 1; .86, grades 2 and 3; .74,
grade 4; and .76, grades 5 and 6. The *CAT* Reading Vocabulary subtest
was the second best predictor at all grade levels, but, interestingly enough,
its best prediction was for different subtests for different grade levels: for
grade 1, the *CAT* Reading Vocabulary subtest correlated .44 with itself five
years later; for grade 2, it correlated .47 with the *CAT* Mechanics of
English subtest administered five years later; for grade 3, .78 with *CAT*
Mechanics of English; for grade 4, .50 with itself; for grade 5, .57 with the
L–M Binet IQ; and for grade 6, .49 with the *L–M Binet* IQ. Kennedy found
that the highest correlations between the *L–M Binet* and the *CAT*, when
both were administered at five-year intervals, were for the children initially
in the third grade: the third grade seemed to be the optimum age for predicting later achievement.

Just how does intelligence affect children's learning? Do the bright
learn more rapidly, do they keep on learning longer, do they learn in a
different way, or do they learn different things? Studies by Woodrow
(1946) and Simrall (1947) produced no evidence that practice on the kinds
of material used in an intelligence test was related significantly to scores
obtained on the tests. Stolurow (1961), in a thorough discussion of programmed learning, concluded that the amount of information gained and
the rate at which it was acquired showed no consistent relationship to
measured intelligence. A child with an IQ of 80 is hampered throughout
school, not only because he is slower to learn, but also because he is never
ready to grasp new and more complex ideas. If a child must learn more
complex things in order to improve his score on a test, then there is a high
correlation between intelligence and academic achievement.

Intelligence seems to be related also to different ways of learning new
concepts and principles. In a study of concept formation in children of
six, ten, and fourteen, Osler and Fivel (1961) found more sudden learners
in the highest intelligence group. They interpreted this as a difference
in attack by children at the different intellectual levels. The very intelligent children gave evidence of proceeding through hypothesis formation
and testing. The less intelligent simply accumulated information. To test
this interpretation, Osler and Trautman (1961) presented the children
with tasks designed to throw hypothesis testers off the track with irrelevant
characteristics. As they had predicted, the bright children then made more
errors.

The correlation between intelligence and achievement is as optimal at
the first grade as it is at the sixth. Since the intelligence test in the main
represents the degree of acculturation—that is, the degree to which a person has mastered the developmental tasks with which he has been provided—and since achievement tests represent similar mastery, a child who

scores high on intelligence tests should also score high on achievement tests. It is safe to say that one of the major factors determining achievement in elementary school is intelligence.

We have discussed in some detail the variables that affect intelligence. It follows that all of these in turn affect achievement. Hundleby and R. Cattell (1968) conducted a factor analysis on the prediction of academic achievement of twelve-year-old children. Although the study is extraordinarily complex, the objectivity of the analysis permits some important observations. One is that general achievement is much more prevalent in children than specific achievement: that is, there is much greater support for good students and poor students than there is for students good in mathematics but poor in English. They also found that socioeconomic factors and the stability of the family are significant factors in academic success.

Self-Concept

Over the years, numerous studies have demonstrated the relationship between a positive self-concept and scholastic achievement. Anxiety is known to be detrimental to performance (Sarason, Hill, and Zimbardo, 1964; Hill and Sarason, 1966). Walsh (1956) reported the underachievement of bright boys to be directly related to their perception of themselves as restricted in pursuing their own interests, isolated, criticized, and rejected. Wattenberg and Clifford (1964) found measures taken of self-concept in kindergarten predictive of reading achievement two-and-a-half years later.

Children who believe in themselves, in their worth as individuals, in their ability to do what is expected of them obviously more easily achieve at a level commensurate with their ability than those children who do not believe in themselves, who expect to fail, who spend their energies in resentment, anxiety, and hostility. Achievement requires energy. A positive self-concept allows the child to focus his emotional energy on attending to the content of the school curriculum. Needless to say, the child's first concept of himself is derived from those significant adults in his early environment.

Attitude

Molded by his social interactions in early childhood, a child's self-concept is dependent upon his attitude toward himself, toward life in general, toward school, toward authority. His socioeconomic level affects his attitudes; his ethnicity affects his attitudes.

Recently, attention has been turned toward the self-concept differences between boys and girls regarding achievement. At the ages covered by the scope of this text, through elementary school, these attitudes do not seem to be strong determinants of long-range achievement. During elementary school, girls tend to be superior to boys in general achievement, particularly in reading (see Table 17).

Table 17

Mean and SD of Reading Age of Boys and Girls at Successive Ages, in Months

Chronological Age	Boys		Girls	
	Mean Reading Age	Standard Deviation	Mean Reading Age	Standard Deviation
84	86	7	90	7
96	97	10	103	10
108	110	15	118	14
120	127	19	135	19
132	147	23	154	23
144	167	32	173	31

Reprinted, by permission of the author, from Willard C. Olson, *Child Development*, 2d ed. (Lexington, Mass., Heath, 1959). Table 6.1, p. 146.

Some observers, however, are concerned that latent attitude factors may arise as a result of the content of some of the reading texts that make up the elementary-school curriculum, texts that tend to emphasize higher terminal achievement for men than for women; that is, men seen as physicians, pilots, engineers, lawyers, and judges, and women seen as maids, housewives, mothers, and nurses. These observers feel that although the effect of such exposure is not significant regarding achievement at the elementary-school level, its long-range effect may account for the drop in achievement motive in women during adolescence and early adulthood.

More apparent is the fact that with a positive attitude toward school and success in school comes a more sustained effort, which brings about more success. A circle of cause-and-effect is produced: effort achieves success, which prompts effort, which achieves success. But, another circle is just as effective: failure produces poor effort, which produces failure, which produces poor effort. Both circles evidence distinct attitudes: the first positive, the second negative. The question: what starts the circle? To separate cause and effect is difficult: does truancy cause a lack of success, or does a lack of success cause truancy and an inclination toward delinquency?

The interactions are obviously complex. But the results also are obvious. For years I have been a consultant to detention centers in which delinquent and predelinquent children are evaluated for the courts. By the time the delinquent child has reached the end of elementary school, he is usually two or more years behind in achievement, his IQ has dropped significantly as more abstract and less motor-oriented behaviors are required. His ability to cope with school is so low that turning to the streets is one of the few ways in which he can, at least for a time, experience success. For a short time, he can be the only child he knows who has stolen a hundred tape decks from cars, and who has unplayed tapes piled in his closet as a symbol of some form of success.

The answer or answers are not clear. But surely some aspects of the problem are. If an individual's self-concept, his attitude toward life, himself, and school, affects his adult achievement, and experience of success or failure in childhood affects his self-concept, then schools must provide an opportunity for success to all children, if all children are to continue to be expected to experience school.

If the state sees as its responsibility the education of the masses, then the state must take into consideration what psychologists and educators know about children, about learning, about intelligence and achievement. The state must early provide for all children an opportunity to take advantage of the critical periods of growth in perception, in cognition, in verbalization. Preschool early-childhood education should be available to every child, regardless of who his parents happen to be, just as first grade is available. Then maybe the state will have provided an opportunity for every child to have a positive self-concept, to experience success in his efforts, to have free energy to attend to the business at hand—learning.

Socioeconomic Level

Just as attitude is a significant aspect of self-concept, so is socioeconomic level. The models the child encounters as a result of his socioeconomic class directly affect his concept of himself and his attitude toward achievement. As early as 1927, Spearman called attention to group differences in achievement. After intelligence, socioeconomic status is probably the most critical variable in the determination of achievement; researchers have attempted to analyze why that is so.

For one thing, they have found that socioeconomic level carries with it differential emphasis upon academic achievement, which is extremely important at the upper socioeconomic levels and relatively unimportant at the lower. Opportunities to learn, days present in school, availability of special help at home, such as reference books and tutors when necessary, motivation for academic effort, and general energy level, which reflects nutrition, all are related to achievement, and each, in turn, is directly related to socioeconomic class.

Because the American school system is divided into districts, lower-class children tend to attend lower-class schools—that is, schools with poorer facilities, poorer equipment, more poorly trained and more poorly motivated teachers. Often the relationship between teacher and pupil is poorest in lower-class school districts, because of the teachers' difficulty in understanding the motivational problems of the children.

Early studies of social class and achievement in school emphasized the middle-class nature of schools and the great discrepancies among the social classes. Some authors (Eels, A. Davis, Havighurst, Herrick, and R. Tyler, 1951; Kennedy, Van De Riet, and White, 1963) have suggested, like Riessman, that "the greatest block to the realization of the deprived individual's creative potential seems to be his verbal inadequacies" (1962, p. 74), rather than differing attitudes toward school. Other researchers

(Havighurst and Janke, 1944; Havighurst and Breese, 1947) join Mussen, Conger, and Kagan in asserting:

> Upper-middle-class parents are great believers in education as the solution to many problems—economic, social, and personal. Lower-middle- and upper-lower-class parents tend to look upon school more as a way of getting children ready for adulthood. They are not great believers in education per se, but see it as necessary for vocational success. . . . Lower-class children, particularly . . . those suffering the double jeopardy of ethnic group segregation and discrimination as well, are likely to be far less highly motivated and to have lower aspirations for academic achievement. . . . These children have much less opportunity than middle-class ones to perceive relationships between academic achievement and success in life; consequently they are likely to adopt a "so what" attitude toward school. Their parents frequently feel isolated from, fearful of, or indifferent or antagonistic to the school as an institution, often viewing it simply as another extension of the middle-class "establishment" from which they have been excluded [Mussen, Conger, and Kagan, 1969, pp. 561, 562].

Another obvious aspect of socioeconomic level interacting with achievement is the effect of deprivation of opportunities to learn concepts and abstract thought processes. In speaking of the effects of cultural deprivation upon the developing intellect, J. McV. Hunt emphasizes the probable seriousness of continued deprivation in the necessary environmental stimulation for healthy maturation and development:

> The longer these conditions continue, the more likely the effects are to be lasting. . . . Tadpoles immobilized with chlorotone for 8 days are not greatly hampered in the development of their swimming patterns, but immobilization for 13 days leaves their swimming patterns permanently impaired; chicks kept in darkness for as many as 5 days show no apparent defects in their pecking responses, but keeping them in darkness for 8 or more days results in chicks which never learn to peck at all [1964, p. 89].

Piaget (1952b) has said the more a child has seen and heard, the more he wants to see and hear. The more environmental stimuli he encounters as he begins to grow, the more he will recognize and encounter as he continues to develop and mature. Relationships with adults, which enable him to continue his intellectual as well as his physical maturation, are necessary supports during a child's preschool years.

The problem, however, may be more complex than simple traditional nursery school enrichment. The quality of enrichment may well be crucial, as R. Hess and Shipman suggest: "enrichment for the sake of enrichment may miss the point—that it is not additional, or even more varied, stimulation that is needed, but experiences which give stimuli a pattern of sequential meaning" (1965a, p. 194). The relatedness of ideas and events must be shown to children at an early age to enable them to grasp the more and more difficult concepts presented in education at school.

Ethnicity

A third variable affecting self-concept, one strongly affecting attitude, is ethnicity. The ethnic subgroup to which the child belongs is intrinsically related to socioeconomic status and easily confused with it. Although a high correlation has been demonstrated between ethnic and socioeconomic grouping, within the last century in the United States a number of children from particular ethnic groupings have become outstanding examples of high mobility in achievement. In one generation they have been able to move from grinding poverty in the lowest socioeconomic level, and from the lowest level of achievement, to the highest levels of success.

Probably no one has more skillfully articulated this upward-bound movement than Harry Golden, the proverbial Carolina Israelite who, in *Only in America* (1958), described his childhood on the Lower East Side of New York at the turn of the century. His is a vivid account of the rather high percentage of Jewish children, living under austere ghetto conditions and facing harsh ethnic prejudice, who were driven to the point of obsession by their aspirations for high academic accomplishment. Thus an unprecedented number of young men and women, whose mothers and fathers were employed in the most marginal and undesirable jobs, broke out of the cycle. Children whose parents could not speak English, nor read, nor write, nevertheless were driven by an ethnic tradition that venerated achievement. Zborowski (1955, p. 123) quotes a Jewish lullaby:

> The Law shall baby learn,
> Great books shall my Yankele write.

In one generation these children went from the lowest socioeconomic level to nearly the highest, from the lowest educational attainment to the most advanced professionalism. Golden, in his inimitable fashion, describes a Jewish mother, herself dressed in shabby clothes, speaking broken English, and existing on a day-to-day budget, scornfully asking another, "But is your son a doctor doctor or a dentist doctor?"

This, of course, is the American dream—a dream obtained by few from the lowest socioeconomic level. But certain ethnic groups have exhibited a disproportionate amount of drive and achievement in the face of what would appear to be insurmountable obstacles. Because of a long tradition that instilled ambition, the probability of achievement on the part of a Jewish child of a poor immigrant family at the turn of the century in New York was different from that of a Puerto Rican child of the same socioeconomic level now living in the same neighborhood.

Although socioeconomic standing and ethnic subgrouping during any given period in the history of the country are highly correlated, ethnicity may be more important in determining the achievement level of the children. A major factor in the child's motivation to succeed is the existence of viable models and of attainable, albeit mind-stretching, goals. Opportunity becomes plausible to the child only when he sees upward-bound mobility. Without hope there is no ambition.

When making predictions about a child's ultimate level of achievement, then, his ethnic subgrouping must be kept in mind. Lesser, Fifer, and Clark (1965) suggest that individual ethnic groups have unique mental-ability score profiles (see Figure 18). "In summary, the findings lend selective support to Anastasi's premise [1958, p. 563] that groups dif-

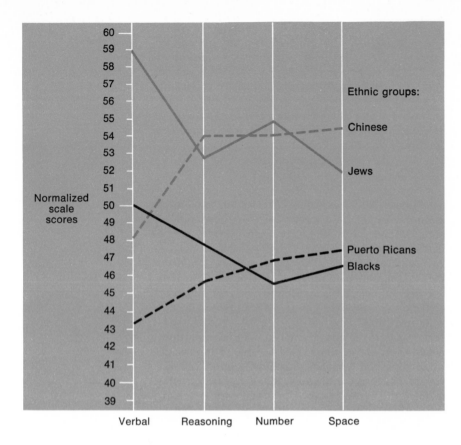

Figure 18
Pattern of normalized
mental ability scores for
four ethnic groups. Re-
printed, by permission of
the senior author and
the publisher, from
Gerald S. Lesser, Gor-
don Fifer, and Donald
H. Clark, Mental abilities
of children from different
social class and cultural
groups, *Monographs of
the Society for Research
in Child Development*,
1965, 30 (4), No. 102,
Figure 2, p. 64. Copy-
right © 1965 by the
Society for Research in
Child Development, Inc.

fer in their relative standing on different functions. Each … fosters the
development of a different *pattern* of abilities" (Lesser, Fifer, and Clark,
1965, p. 83), as well as different self-concepts and different motivation for
achievement.

Temperament

Earlier we made a distinction between personality and temperament.
Temperament refers to some dominant trends in behavior, which are more
or less independent of interpersonal interaction and which appear to have
strong physiological predetermination, probably on the basis of heredity as
well as the prenatal biochemical environment. These temperamental dimensions relate to mood swings, activity rate, exploratory drive, and
affective needs.

Mood Swings

Even in early childhood, children with strong mood swings are identified easily, those who are high one moment and low the next. If these
mood swings are within normal limits, they interfere little with classroom
performance, except that they produce inconsistency. Progress notes re-

peatedly come from the teacher, even as early as nursery school, mentioning unevenness of work, a general lack of predictability, and periods of aloofness, all of which seem to be characteristic of children with such mood swings. As we learn more about the cause and management of wide mood swings in adults, and begin to understand the manic-depressive syndrome in adults, quite possibly some of these lessons can be applied to the child. In any event, capitalizing on the highs and ignoring the lows is the best way for the teacher of the young child with wide mood swings to achieve optimal performance from him.

Hyperkinesis

Hyperactivity or hyperkinesis, which is probably related to some mild and diffuse brain irritation or damage, is a condition closely related to temperament. Hyperkinetic children frequently have severe learning problems because they lack sufficient attention span or self-control to master the passive-receptive dimensions of school. The problem these children present to the school is twofold: not only do they not receive much benefit from group instructions or environmental manipulations, but they disrupt the school environment to the point where the children around them do not receive sufficient stability for learning.

Several successful techniques have been devised to help the situation, each with some drawbacks. For about fifteen years now, hyperkinetic children have been known to respond paradoxically to amphetamines; these drugs, which normally cause an individual to be hyperalert and hyperactive, tend to calm down the hyperkinetic child. And certain schedules of reinforcement applied through behavior-modification are known to program the child to the point where he is more manageable and educable. The problem with both of these techniques is the possibility of misidentifying a child who is actually a high-drive, highly intelligent child simply being obnoxious and creative—in that order—as hyperactive, and thereby placing him on either of the above regimens, both of which tend to stifle creativity. The conservative use of amphetamines by physicians and reinforcement schedules by behavior modifiers, however, have enabled many hyperactive children, who ordinarily would be expelled from their group or their school, to do well in the school setting and to move through middle childhood into the more stable growth period of the brain, where they no longer require external control.

Exploratory Drive

Closely related to activity rate, exploratory drive or curiosity may be influenced socially but certainly has some hereditary predisposition that can be demonstrated both in children and in animals. Some children simply begin life with a strong exploratory drive. They are constantly probing, picking, touching, tasting, manipulating, and examining their environment, practically from birth, and tend to gain a great deal of information from their surroundings. Their early development of skills that enable them more effectively to cope with their environment contrasts them sharply with more placid, passive, and dependent children. These children

with a strong exploratory drive tend to maintain such a level of exploration
and to do extremely well in school, particularly with a teacher who allows
for individual differences. They are creative and confident, and, with their
high fund of information, quite easily become leaders in the classroom and
on the playground.

Affective Needs

A final dimension of temperament concerns affective needs. Again,
this tendency can be identified early in children's lives and continues to be
a significant dimension of their makeup. Some children almost from birth
show a strong desire and need for emotional contact with others. They
enjoy being held, cuddled, caressed, and fondled. They seek out others
and spend little time alone. They develop into drag-around children who
have an infectious friendliness that makes them easy to get along with and
content within groups. They contrast with children who are aloof, af-
fectively distant, and quiet, children who tend to be lonely in childhood, to
have few friends, and frequently to remain alone in school settings. Because these latter children lack social interaction, they frequently are isolated in the school setting, which often as not has a poor effect on their
learning. So much learning in the elementary school years is dependent
upon group teaching and group interaction that they tend to miss considerable instruction in large classes.

This is not always the case, however, because some lonely, aloof, and
distant children throw themselves into the world of reading and achievement, becoming outstanding students in spite of their lack of social skills.
These children probably account for the good student's frequently being
cast as the distant, detached, aloof bookworm. Such is not the usual case,
but the contrast in expectancy is so great that this is the child so frequently
remembered. Most good students are outgoing, with rich affective lives,
rather than being introspective or introverted.

Affective isolation becomes increasingly identifiable in adult life and
not simply academic achievement is affected. Early in the life of an introverted child efforts should be made to draw him out and to teach him the
basic social skills required for group life.

Experience

A fifth dimension of individual differences affecting achievement is
the experience of the child. Achievement is a pyramid phenomenon; the
more complex the conceptual repertoire, the more easily new information
can be processed. Children from grossly impoverished backgrounds have
difficulty in kindergarten and elementary school because their limited experience in the kinds of concepts and information carried in the subject
matter of the school curriculum makes school and education a bewildering
experience. Math, for instance, frequently is cast in contextual constructs
indecipherable to the poverty child. For the average adult to understand
the meaning of weightlessness, with all of its complexity, is probably no
more difficult than for the grossly deprived child to understand the relationship between "matching" clothes or clothes appropriate for certain oc-

casions. Obviously, the more the child's experience overlaps with the
learning environment, the more easily achievement is effected.

Reinforcement

Psychologists and educators frequently make allusions to the difference between intrinsic and extrinsic motivation of educational tasks as
though the distinction were obvious. Intrinsic motivation refers to conditions within which a child receives pleasure or reinforcement as a function
of performance or mastery. Building a tower of blocks and watching them
fall over is an example. The child appears to enjoy this "work" in spite
of not being given any external reward for the performance.

On the other hand, a child learns to show clean hands to his mother
prior to supper, because she rewards such behavior with a smile, a comment, a gold star, or perhaps an extra dessert. The child has learned, then,
to expect to be rewarded for performing tasks that in themselves are not
very rewarding or satisfying initially. Scrubbing one's hands is not the way
the average four-year-old would propose to spend an afternoon.

The middle-class child frequently is subjected to a reinforcement history such that by kindergarten age, he "loves" to stay in the lines when
coloring, because he "expects" to be rewarded for doing it. He "loves" to
get 100s on his papers, because he "expects" good things to happen to him
for bringing home such papers. Lower-class children, on the other hand,
have not developed such "love" or "expectancy" because their reinforcement history is not compatible with the achievement tasks of school. The
lack of intrinsic motivation, then, is actually a function of a lack of experience of reward for related performance, rather then any built-in difference
between the children.

Expectancy

In 1968, Robert Rosenthal and Jacobson came out with an appealing
theory, with reported results to support it, that teacher expectancy affected
pupil achievement, regardless of pupil ability. That is, bright children did
poorly when teachers expected them to do poorly, and vice versa. But
Rosenthal's self-fulfilling prophesy argument has turned out to be an often-
quoted (Labov, 1972) but unreplicated (Claiborn, 1969), statistically challenged (R. L. Thorndike, 1968; Snow, 1969) and unverified (Fleming and
Anttonen, 1971*a,b*) piece of research. Writes Thorndike:

> In spite of anything I can say, I am sure it [*Pygmalion in the Classroom*] will become
> a classic—widely referred to and rarely examined critically.... The indications are
> that the basic data upon which this structure has been raised are so untrustworthy
> that any conclusions based upon them must be suspect. The conclusions may be cor-
> rect, but if so it must be considered a fortunate coincidence [1968, pp. 708, 711].

A similar conclusion is reached by Snow:

> It is the considered opinion of this reviewer that the research would have been
> judged unacceptable if submitted to an APA journal in its present form....

Teacher expectancy may be a powerful phenomenon which, if understood, could be used to gain much of positive value in education. Rosenthal and Jacobson will have made an important contribution if their work prompts others to do sound research in this area. But their study has not come close to providing adequate demonstration of the phenomenon or understanding of its process. *Pygmaglion,* inadequately and prematurely reported in book and magazine form, has performed a disservice to teachers and schools, to users and developers of mental tests, and perhaps worst of all, to parents and children whose newly gained expectations may not prove quite so self-fulfilling [1969, pp. 197, 199].

Barber and Silver (1968*a,b*) have not only reviewed previous research on experimenter bias effect, but have made efforts at replication, which forced them "to raise serious questions about the conditions under which the experimenter bias effect occurs, if, in fact, it occurs at all" (Fleming and Anttonen, 1971*b*, p. 2). They report that "the experimenter bias effect appears to be more difficult to demonstrate and less pervasive than was implied in previous reviews in this journal [*Psychological Bulletin*]" (1968*a*, p. 1).

Other efforts have been made to sustain Robert Rosenthal's theory, but they have not proved successful (Jacob, 1968; Wessler and Strauss, 1968; Levy, 1969). More recently, Fleming and Anttonen conducted a study of 1,087 second-graders in thirty-nine classrooms. They found that the teachers recognized the inflated IQ group as inaccurate (1971*a*) and concluded:

Obviously the present study failed to find support for the widespread belief that the self-fulfilling prophecy generalizes over all educational practice. It is clear that the way in which teachers influence pupil behavior is a far more subtle and complex phenomenon than some have suggested. The body of knowledge and attitudes of teachers about testing and their personal characteristics and ways of dealing with children appear to be far more critical for bringing about pupil growth than external intervention per se....

It is abundantly clear that teachers do, in fact, exert a tremendous influence over the learning potential of children. While experimental procedure demands analysis by groups, inspection of individual classrooms in the present study revealed instances in which teachers, irrespective of testing-information conditions or socio-economic level, were bringing about dramatic increases and decreases in pupil performance....

While something does happen in classrooms, it is apparent that in the real world of the teacher using IQ-test information, the self-fulfilling prophecy does not operate as Rosenthal hypothesizes. Teachers, are, in fact, more sensitive to the functioning level of students....

However, a pattern of significant differences not related to testing-information-treatment condition did, in fact, emerge and centered on the teacher-opinion dimension. Here, higher-achievement performance and subject-matter grades were attained in the classes of teachers who valued IQ tests highly. In contrast, the classes of low-opinion teachers tended to have lower IQs, academic-achievement scores, and subject-matter grades [1971*b*, pp. 27, 26].

Obviously, what is expected of children affects their performance, to some degree at least. Palardy (1969) found first-grade boys whose teachers expected them to read as well as the girls did in fact read better than those

first-grade boys whose teachers expected poorer performance from them.
Part of the reason could be that the first group of teachers demanded that
the boys read as well as the girls, whereas the second group was content
with less effort. Most of us seem to do about as well as we must.

But when parents, teachers, and children all expect low performance,
a situation highly unfavorable for achievement is produced. And when
children are categorized on some group basis, such as ethnicity or race,
rather than on individual potential, the harm is doubled.

Children who experience failure tend to lower their level of aspiration; those who experience success tend to raise their aspirations. None
of us likes to fail, and most of us can sympathize with the feeling, why try
the impossible. To make the impossible possible should be a goal of education.

Drive

Closely related to temperament, drive level is a major determinant of
achievement. Frequently referred to as motivation, drive level refers to the
amount of creative free energy an individual has at his disposal. It goes
without saying that to perform with great enthusiasm, intensity, and determination produces a better student, but the question is, what are the
determinants of drive?

Drive level probably relates to several environmental factors in addition to physiological underpinnings. Part of drive level relates to models
around the child, obviously; one can learn to adopt a high drive level.
Second, drive level seems to relate to the pattern of reward for effort. The
greater the reward history for sustained effort, the more likely high drive
will be sustained. In the child, secondary or acquired drive is far more important than is basic physiological drive. Third and obviously, a child's
health will enter into his capacity to produce high drive performance. His
health will affect his attitude and his physical energy; his attitude will affect his emotional energy; his free energy will affect his drive.

MASTERED

Over the years, the American school system has molded its curriculum to produce graduates with specific middle-class characteristics. A certain type of student has best fit this mold; families that shaped their children into these school-desired characteristics produced successful graduates.

So long as our educational system was applied to this relatively
homogenous group of children, so-called public education succeeded
reasonably well. But appropriate social concerns, overdue civil-rights
legislation, and ill-thought-out attitudes about homogenous educational
requirements for all changed the nature of the educational system's mission, and public schools began to experience frustration and failure on a
large scale. The importance of individual differences was forsaken for
herculean attempts to mass produce a single-model high-school graduate.

As they were constituted, the schools were unprepared to provide
meaningful education to large numbers of lower-class students with
characteristics different from those of the middle-class mold. As the pupil

characteristics changed, the schools failed to respond: alienation between the children and the system became increasingly apparent.

What is needed urgently, what the frustration and failure demand, is a complete overhaul of our public educational system to make it appropriate to the needs of all our children, with all their significant differences, all their various goals, all their diverse strengths and weaknesses. Appropriate and competent educational objectives (what a tired, old phrase these days) require some courageous decisions on the part of responsible and creative parent groups, school boards, and school administrators. Our failure rate under the present system is so high, so wasteful of human potential, that to defend it is to delude ourselves in the belief that public education exists. To step out of the traditional model; to examine the characteristics, both the strengths and weaknesses, of all our children, lower-, middle-, and upper-class, their needs, their motives, their dreams; to tailor a multidimensional curriculum that will produce liberated, competent, self-reliant high-school graduates who can live independent, productive lives, unsupported by a humiliating dole system, able to make real choices in their lifestyles: all this is required.

Our present educational system produces, for all those children who differ from the middle-class mold, failure and alienation, in that order. When economic uncertainty looms ahead, when reading is difficult, spelling and calculating painful chores, and when success is thwarted every hour of the school day, then frustrated idleness is enforced, passive-aggressive hostility flourishes, and relevance becomes a passion, not a trite expression of the successful.

TEACHER CHARACTERISTICS

Another variable inherently connected with academic achievement is the quality of instruction—teacher characteristics. Children given better instruction obviously achieve at a higher level than those given poor instruction: to examine the essential qualities of good instruction might be helpful.

Teachers should be personally attractive to the students, in the broad sense of the word. Teachers who are models of achievement because of their own academic success can influence profoundly the attitudes of children toward academic progress. Teachers who are dull, drab, disinterested, and uninspiring fail to arouse the quality of response that greets the curious, serious, interested, and exciting teacher.

Heil, Powell, and Feifer (1960), studying teaching competency in grades 4, 5, and 6, assessed several qualities of the teacher, the child, and the school. The children were classified as conformers (26 percent), opposers (22 percent), waverers (10 percent), and strivers (17 percent), or unclassified (25 percent); the teachers, as turbulent (24 percent), self-controlling (31 percent), and fearful (45 percent).

The authors described the turbulent teachers as having frequent clashes with authority, as preferring to plan their work independently, and as thinking in an uninhibited and unconventional fashion. The self-controlling teachers were described as methodical, as submissive to authority but authoritarian toward those under them, and as reliable second-in-commands. The teachers exhibiting fearfulness suffered a constriction in thinking, were dependent and helpless, and very much preferred a "safe" atmosphere bounded by specific rules to which everyone adhered.

The children's personality characteristics were also defined by the authors. Conforming children incorporated and conformed to adult standards, were highly social, maintained strict control of their impulses, particularly their hostility, and emphasized mature behavior. Opposing children suffered from disturbed relationships with authority, were contrary, were pervasively pessimistic, and were intolerant of ambiguity. Frustration and disappointment in themselves and others was a central dynamic of the opposers. The wavering children demonstrated a high level of anxiety, ambivalence, fearfulness, floundering, and indecisiveness. The striving children were exhibitionistic and had a strong drive for recognition and academic achievement.

Heil, Powell, and Feifer concluded that as a total group the children learned best under the self-controlling teachers and least from the fearful ones (correlation .24). The academic achievement of the wavering and striving children was unaffected by the teacher's personality (correlations —.05 and .09, respectively). The conforming children were significantly affected by the teacher's personality in the same manner as the total group of children (correlation .19). The opposing children learned significantly more from self-controlling teachers, least under the turbulent teachers (correlation .40). When the children were classified by personality, significant differences were noted. As would be expected, the strivers made the greatest gains, the waverers the least: strivers, opposers, conformers, waverers. Achievement was unaffected by the sex of the children or the teachers.

When the effects of the particular school as well as the IQ were taken into account, the authors found that the self-controlling teachers, to a significantly higher degree, were obtaining achievement commensurate with their students' intelligence. Correlations between the mean class achievement and various characteristics of the teacher other than personality were nonsignificant, except for the teacher's professional education score (correlation .40). The authors report that "it seems fairly evident that not only is teacher knowledge an *unimportant* variable as a criterion of teacher effectiveness but also observer ratings, per se, are next to worthless in this respect" (1960, p. 66). But teacher interest does significantly affect pupil achievement. Teachers interested, excited, and enthusiastic about their subject matter arouse an answering spark of enthusiasm in their students.

In general, the turbulent teacher, except in the teaching of science and mathematics, came out second-best to the self-controlling teacher, who obtained uniform gains from all the children. The fearful teacher came out a poor third. Figure 19 shows the relative achievement of children under teachers with different personalities.

In addition to personal characteristics, which are in and of themselves sometimes difficult to define, teacher preparation also is an important factor in the achievement of children. Those teachers who have adequate preparation in their subject matter, who are competent as well as

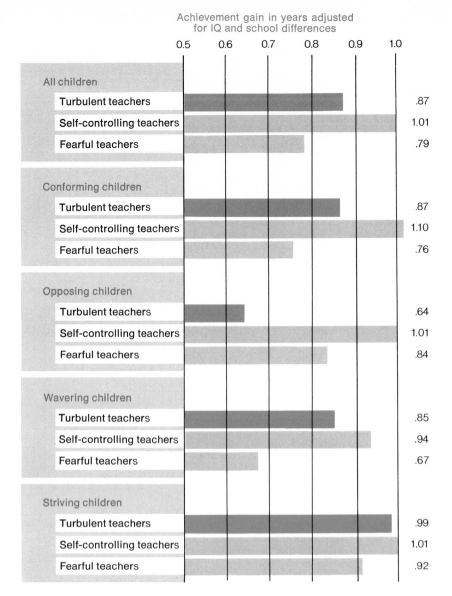

Achievement gain in years adjusted for IQ and school differences

	0.5	0.6	0.7	0.8	0.9	1.0	
All children							
Turbulent teachers							.87
Self-controlling teachers							1.01
Fearful teachers							.79
Conforming children							
Turbulent teachers							.87
Self-controlling teachers							1.10
Fearful teachers							.76
Opposing children							
Turbulent teachers							.64
Self-controlling teachers							1.01
Fearful teachers							.84
Wavering children							
Turbulent teachers							.85
Self-controlling teachers							.94
Fearful teachers							.67
Striving children							
Turbulent teachers							.99
Self-controlling teachers							1.01
Fearful teachers							.92

Figure 19
Relative achievement of children under teachers of different personality, from Heil, Powell, and Feifer (1960).

personable, and who have mastered techniques and strategies that lead to efficient presentation of concepts, ideas, and skills, tend to increase the general level of learning throughout the class and the specific level of particular children. In a detailed and careful study of how the personality of students interacts with the teaching of reading, Grimes and Allinsmith (1961) concluded that anxious or compulsive children are helped by structured teaching.

Other variables—the ratio between students and teachers, the quality of instructional material, and the adequacy of support personnel, particularly in reading, mathematics, and language—all help to determine whether children develop positive attitudes toward achievement or self-defeating patterns of adjustment.

PARENTAL CHARACTERISTICS

Obviously relevant to the achievement of children, parental characteristics have been studied enthusiastically. Training boys early for independence enhances their achievement; warm, affectionate mothers enhance their sons' achievement; fathers who dominate their sons less, who are more accepting, enhance their sons' achievement; parents who expect and demand the best of their children enhance achievement; parents with positive attitudes toward school and education enhance achievement; parents who discipline their children in accord, with love and reasonableness, enhance achievement; parents who treat their children as children, needing guidance and supervision, rather than as young adults ready to fly alone—that is, parents who are authoritarian and restrictive—enhance achievement; parents who encourage self-expression and reward curiosity enhance achievement; parents who are interested in and encourage their children's efforts enhance achievement.

MODELS FOR ACHIEVEMENT

Thus far we have considered the individual's immediate environment and the unique personal characteristics that affect his academic achievement. Now we should consider a general cultural problem that directly affects the individual: the question of models. Models affect not only academic achievement but general growth of personal competency.

The protracted academic program is, in a very real sense, an apprenticeship for life. Let us compare this apprenticeship with apprenticeships that have proved successful over the past few hundred years. Let's look at the essential elements of an apprenticeship—elements that turn the apprentice into the journeyman, the artist, the craftsman. A good apprenticeship program would seem to consist of seven essential characteristics. Perhaps they can best be remembered with the acrostic **EMULATE**, since the success of an apprenticeship depends primarily upon emulation.

> Employment
> Model
> Understanding
> Lability
> Access
> Termination
> Exaltation

Employment

The first essential characteristic of an apprenticeship is employment. The first day the apprentice goes on the job, he is put to work. He is assigned specific tasks relevant to the productive mission of the organization to which he is apprenticed. Tools are put in his hand. He is given a job. At the end of the day, he has little question about what he did during the day and its utility.

Model

The second critical element of the apprenticeship is the model. The first day on the job, the apprentice is introduced to many journeymen, men who are accomplished artists and craftsmen. They are fully trained and fully competent individuals capable of performing any task required in their profession. He sees them at work. He sees what they do and what they don't do. He talks with them. They discuss with him in some detail the nature of their work. But more important, he sees them in operation.

Understanding

The third aspect of an apprenticeship is understanding. An apprentice is accepted as an apprentice. Those around him are well able to judge his level of skill and understand that he is not yet an accomplished artist. He is, then, understood and accepted at the level he enters. He is not expected to do things for which he has not been prepared. No man in the group has not experienced the same problems as the apprentice.

Lability

Fourth is lability, the ability of the apprentice to move at different rates of speed depending upon his ability or growth. If a particular facet of the training requires more time, he is given more time. If he has mastered a task early and is ready to move on, he is allowed to move on. Flexibility within the program allows for individual rates of growth, for advancement and progression based upon mastery as the sole criterion. But always there is movement toward the day of becoming a journeyman.

Access

The fifth facet of the apprenticeship is access. The apprentice has access to the models at all times. He can inquire of the masters. At any moment during the day when he has questions, he has ready access to the information. He need only turn from his machine and ask for help. Instantly the journeyman moves in, answers his questions, and most often shows him what to do, taking the knowledge from the abstract, as contained in books and manuals, and putting it into the concrete, a show-you-how-to-do-it.

Termination

Next comes termination. One of the most important aspects of an apprenticeship is the tangible goal of termination at the end of the training program, the arrival of the promised day when the apprentice is no longer a learner, when he is no longer a novice, when he is no longer an apprentice, but, rather, he is graduated as a full-fledged member of the group. His apprentice days are terminated. In their place comes a future of professional standing as a craftsman.

Exaltation

Which brings us to the last part of the apprentice program, exaltation. Exaltation means joy on the part of all concerned when this day of graduation comes. There is an actual, formal annointment. There is an announcement to the entire world that says, "It is done, it is finished!" And the apprentice, now a journeyman, and his professional colleagues, the other journeymen, take great pleasure in this annunciation, the exaltation. The long task is complete and the day of reward is at hand.

EMULATE

Thus we see that the apprentice has moved logically, consistently, and honestly through a succession of events that take him, the unskilled apprentice, to the skilled journeyman in a scheduled, productive sequence that involves Employment, Model, Understanding, Lability, Access, Termination, and Exaltation. This apprentice program has been around for thousands of years in essentially the same form and has been extremely successful in carrying out its goal of faithful reproduction of craftsmen from generation to generation.

Now, let's compare, for a moment, the difficulties encountered when the task becomes an apprenticeship for life and the goal becomes mastery or achievement of both academic material and personal competency.

From the very beginning, we have inordinate difficulty in trying to employ our children. Relating the academic program of personal competency and skills training to the outside world perplexes parents and teachers alike. Few children are given employment early in life. Few children are given responsibilities, tasks that must be done by the child or will not be done at all. Learning to read, or learning to count, or learning to follow directions is extremely difficult for us to relate to any immediate and practical consequence. Education and achievement tests are performed in an absolute vacuum in the school. Few children have the opportunity to use their knowledge. The implication is that the world is so complex that it is better to have children spectators than employed; they might get hurt; life seems too complex and too difficult; children need to grow up first and then perhaps they will get a job, then perhaps they will be able to use their skills in some practical way. Employment is something dangled in front of children as a prospect for the far-off future. Knowledge for knowledge's sake now; employment later.

The second aspect of our achievement apprenticeship is the model. Carl Jung, in his treatise on education, said that we should, if we ever expect to raise man to the level for which he has the potential, select from all the land the healthiest, most productive, most energetic, most sensible, most responsive, and most mature people, people who have the potential and capacity for being models of health in the broadest sense. We should put these people in the most conspicuous place; and for Jung there was no

doubt where this conspicuous place was: they should be teachers! And most particularly, they should be teachers of the young! Children should be exposed constantly to viable models. On every hand they should have pointed out to them the alternative of workable models and, furthermore, they should have the opportunity of seeing these models in operation.

> It is important that the teacher should be conscious of the role he is playing. He must not be satisfied with merely pounding the curriculum into the child; he must also influence him through his personality. This latter function is at least as important as the actual teaching.... The teacher, as a personality, is then faced with the delicate task of avoiding repressive authority, while at the same time exercising that just degree of authority which is appropriate to the adult in his dealings with children. This attitude cannot be produced artificially; it can only come about in a natural way when the teacher does his duty as a man and a citizen. He must be an upright and healthy man himself, for good example still remains the best pedagogic method. But it is also true that the very best method avails nothing if its practitioner does not hold his position on his personal merits. It would be different if the only thing that mattered in school life were the methodical teaching of the curriculum. But that is at most only half the meaning of school. The other half is the real psychological education made possible through the personality of the teacher [Jung, 1954, pp. 55–56].

Picture, if you will, the plight of the average second-grade boy. His teacher is a competent, but not very emotionally secure, fifty-five-year-old spinster—a teacher who sees her job very simply as moving the children forward in the basic skills of reading, arithmetic, and English fundamentals; who is herself somewhat of a depressive person, who has never had a particularly happy life; who teaches, not now because of any particular excitement, but out of habit; who is dedicated, responsible, competent, but not very exciting. She talks about test preparation. She talks about grades. She talks about having to have an education to get anywhere in this world, but she really does not believe she has gotten anywhere. She talks about discipline, about what she will and will not tolerate going on

in her classroom. Occasionally she provides the boys with the opportunity of seeing a male model: that is, she sends them to the principal. And the principal, trying to back his teacher and get the job over with, is quick with the paddle or with the admonishment, "Better straighten up, son. I don't want to have any more trouble out of you. I'd better not see you again."

And Waldo goes home. He takes a little dab of homework, a paper to be signed because it was done poorly. When he arrives home, mother is there. It is the low point of her day. She has to get supper ready. A number of things around the house still need catching up. After a quick question, such as "Have you any homework?" and a negative response, the child is left to his own devices, which consist largely of sprawling in front of the TV set.

A car door slams and in comes father. A quick peck on the cheek for mother and for the boy the same daily question, "How did school go today, son?" And then a quick stab at the evening paper. Down in his chair, father begins to unwind from a hard day at the office. Trying to beat the tension, trying to shake off the problems of the office, he lights a cigarette, puffs a while, has a before-dinner cocktail.

Finally dinner is served. Mother, noticing Waldo's dirty hands, sends him back twice to wash them. Father doesn't talk about the office. Mother makes a few comments about neighborhood affairs, or gossip. Waldo contributes little to the supper conversation. Everybody is tired, mentally and emotionally exhausted.

The news comes on at 6:00. The TV set is in the corner. Father watches an hour of news, moving from the dinner table back into his lounge chair, occasionally glancing at the sports page of the paper while watching the news. A show comes on TV. Staying on the floor until bedtime, Waldo watches TV.

On Saturdays the routine changes. Father usually gets to sleep in, then may have some catching up to do at the office. But he is home in the afternoon. Sometimes there is an afternoon football game on TV, some-

times the real thing. Saturday night Mom and Dad go out somewhere. A female babysitter copes with Waldo. Sundays present the hustle and bustle to get off to Sunday School and two more women teachers. And then church. That afternoon a nap, sometimes a ride.

But where is the model? Where is the journeyman? At this stage in his life Waldo sees males when they are in a resting state at the worst possible time. Instead of at work, he sees them unemployed, puffing and blowing from the rigors of their work, and in the fullest sense of the word, psychologically down, dissipating, void of progress. In the years that form his basic personality, he hardly ever encounters males at work. Life is implied to be too complex, too vague to comprehend.

This model problem was vividly brought home to me when, accompanied by my four-year-old son and a neighborhood boy the same age, I was raking leaves in the front yard. As a car of university students drove by, one leaned out the window and called, "Hi, there, Dr. Kennedy." As they drove on, the neighborhood boy, a little awed by the whole thing, turned to my son and said, "Say, is your daddy a doctor?" And was promptly reassured, "Nah, he's not the kind of doctor that can do you any good."

The message was quite clear. This boy's father, an unusually visible one, was, then, a leaf raker, a gutter cleaner, a camellia grafter, a fisherman, a hunter, a hamburger cooker, a tree-house builder, a clown, but the role of professor, clinical psychologist, community leader was blotted out completely with the words, "not the kind that can do you any good." Most particularly for boys, a critical model shortage exists. And many of the models presented to children are diametrically opposed to those we would hope a child would adopt.

The next facet of our apprenticeship is understanding, acceptance of the child in relation to what he can do or cannot do. We tend to fluctuate from harsh demands, such as being still and quiet during certain periods, to no demands at all at other times. Little concern is given to what the child's developmental level is able to tolerate. The clinical psychologist is constantly exposed to children who make the complaint, "they treat me like a baby," or, "they expect me to go to bed at eight o'clock, and I can never go to sleep until eleven, so for years I have just laid there in bed, just thinking, just thinking how mad they make me." Although knowledge of growth rate in an industrial training program is well understood and well defined, the growth rate of children in terms of psychological growth and social maturity is little understood and has marginal influence upon the rules and restrictions placed on children.

Lability, the ability to advance at his own rate, is one of the greatest shortcomings of our childhood achievement program. We are not looking for opportunities to advance our children. As parents we very seldom seek out specific ways to permit advancement. The privilege of crossing the street is a typical example of this failure. When Waldo is a toddler, efforts are made to keep him out of the street. He is admonished for going in the street and sometimes spanked for going across the street.

Occasionally, however, when mother, looking out of her window, sees Waldo start into the street, she also sees that no cars are coming in either direction and that Mrs. Johnson across the way is watering her flowers.

She knows that Mrs. Johnson will be very pleased to have Waldo waddle up to her. And so mother ignores the fact that Waldo is now violating the rules. On other occasions when Waldo is playing near the street, mother hears the roar of a big truck and begins to scream at the top of her lungs for him to get out of the street, when in fact he isn't in it.

Gradually, however, Waldo grows older and the number of occasions when he surreptitiously crosses the street increases, and the number of times that mother, responding to truck noises, punishes him for being in the street decreases, until one day mother finally decides to just quit bothering. No systematic advance was made, no promotion, no decision made, just simply an eroding away of a rule.

The example can be multiplied hundreds of times and indicates a major problem in the apprenticeship for life. No provision is made for lability. No provision is made for advancement. No yardsticks or indices are available. Oh, there are some. You have to be sixteen to get a driver's license. You have to be five-and-one-half to go to school. These are rigid and make no allowances for added maturity, growth, sensitivity, or responsibility. These are absolutes. A well-developed system of labile advancement simply doesn't exist.

As far as access is concerned, it is virtually nonexistent. A child has no appeal system whatsoever. He has the utmost difficulty getting the appropriate resources at the right time. One cardinal rule in our families today, one rule well carried out by most families, is that mother and father should stick together. If mother says so, then that is the way it is going to be. You can't have disagreement between parents. "What did your mother say?" or "What did your father say?" is the usual response to appeal. The child is not encouraged to haggle with both parents.

Children are not encouraged to go to the expert. They are not encouraged to make the personal contact. They are encouraged to look it up in the encyclopedia, but generally the access is tightly restricted. You don't bother adults. Problem solving, then, is done very often in an ineffective, haphazard way because of a child's belief that he should stay out of contact with proprietors of information.

The termination problem of our society is unbelievable. One does not ever grow up. One never ceases to be a child. One escapes from childhood. There are no systematic terminal points. There are no benchmarks of achievement. The closest proximity is grade-level achievement in school, but even here there is a lack of termination. Some people in our society continue to be boys all their lives; they never really break out of childhood. This lack of termination provides one of the greatest frustrations for our young people and indeed causes considerable immaturity because of the hopelessness of it. Exaltation, then, the "I have-become-a-man," the great celebration, the puberty rites, are missing in Western society, and this lack encourages continuation of childhood immaturity.

TESTS OF ACHIEVEMENT

No discussion of achievement is complete without mention of its measurement. All sorts of yardsticks are available: subjective standards of social achievement, of financial achievement, or professional achievement; and objective measures of scholastic achievement on standardized tests, which we shall emphasize.

MEASUREMENT UNITS

Five units of measurement are used frequently. The first is grade equivalents, which relate to the average performance of the average child at a given grade level. The second is intelligence quotient (IQ), a standard score equivalent of the ratio between mental age and chronological age. The standard score, the third measure, translates raw scores of any given value into scores with a mean of 50 and a standard deviation of 10. The standard deviation is that distance, above and below the mean of a normal distribution, which defines a range that includes the midmost 68 percent of the population. Two standard deviations above and two below the mean define a range that will include about 95 percent of the population. The fourth measure, the familiar percentile, simply expresses an individual score in relation to all other scores on a percentile basis. The fifth, the stanine scale, developed by the US Air Force during World War II, is a single-digit scale from 1 to 9, with a mean of 5 and a standard deviation of approximately 2. Figure 20 and Tables 18 and 19 illustrate the relationships between these scores.

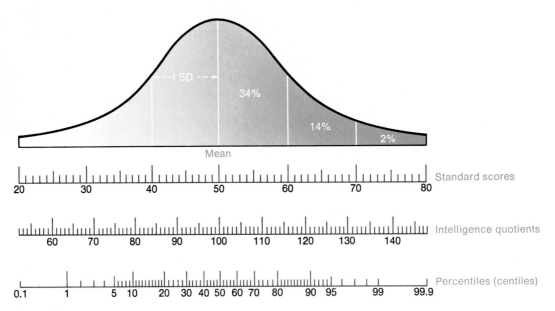

Figure 20

Relationship between standard scores, intelligence quotients, and percentiles. Reprinted, by permission of the publishers, from Lee J. Cronbach, *Educational Psychology*, 2d ed. (New York and London: Harcourt Brace Jovanovich and Rupert Hart-Davis, 1963), Figure 49, p. 217. Copyright © 1963 by Harcourt Brace Jovanovich, Inc. and Rupert Hart-Davis Ltd.

Table 18

Normal Curve Percentages for Use
in Stanine Conversion

Percentage	4	7	12	17	20	17	12	7	4
Stanine	1	2	3	4	5	6	7	8	9

Reprinted, by permission of the publisher, from Anne Anastasi, *Psychological Testing*, 3d ed. (New York: Macmillan, 1968), Table 5, p. 56. Copyright © 1968 by Anne Anastasi.

Table 19

Norms for Arithmetic Computation Test of Stanford
Achievement Test, Intermediate II Battery,
Form W, 1964 Edition

Raw Score	Grade Equivalent	Percentile Rank[a]	Stanine[a]	Raw Score	Grade Equivalent	Percentile Rank[a]	Stanine[a]
39	12.9			19	6.0	58	
38	12.6			18	5.9	50	
37	12.2			17	5.8	46	5
36	11.7			16	5.6	42	
35	11.2						
34	10.5		9	15	5.4	36	
33	9.9			14	5.2	30	4
32	9.4			13	5.0	24	
31	8.8	99+		12	4.8	20	
30	8.5	99		11	4.6	16	3
29	8.2	96		10	4.4	11	
28	7.9	94		9	4.1	8	
27	7.7	92	8	8	3.8	6	
26	7.4	90		7	3.7	6	2
				6	3.5	4	
25	7.1	88					
24	6.8	84	7	5	3.3	2	
23	6.6	80		4	2.9	1	
				3	2.6	1−	1
22	6.5	76		2	2.2		
21	6.3	70	6	1	2.0−		
20	6.2	64					

Reprinted by special permission of the publisher from Stanford Achievement Test. Copyright © 1964 by Harcourt Brace Jovanovich, Inc.

[a] End of grade 5: May—June

Test reliability refers to its consistency of measurement. This may be internal consistency of items within a test, but is more generally external consistency as measured by the same test over a time span or over equivalent forms of the test.

Internal Consistency

Internal consistency of a test refers to the degree to which the items at each level on the test are of equal difficulty. Thus a student who fails one item presuming to test long-division skill at a specific grade level should miss the other items measuring the same skill at the same grade level. The *Stanford Achievement Test* reports an internal consistency correlation of about .90 (Bryan, 1965, p. 121). This estimate was obtained by randomly dividing all of the test items and comparing the scores obtained on each half. This split-half reliability coefficient is the best measure of the internal consistency of an instrument.

External Consistency

Probably of more importance in measuring reliability of achievement tests are measures taken on the same child at different time intervals on the same test, or on equivalent forms of the same test. Two possible explanations can be projected for the lower correlations obtained by this method. First, a child could improve his classroom achievement level or achievement standing by a sudden spurt of activity, by a breakthrough in his understanding of certain concepts, which have kept him blocked for some time, by a better relationship with his teacher, or by changes in the home. Thus what appears to be an error in measurement may reflect a genuine change in the relative standing of the child. Second, as the child grows older, the achievement test measures different things—the curriculum changes. Thus, what a child is expected to know at the beginning of the fifth grade is not what he is expected to know at the end of the fifth grade— the test itself could contain different emphases.

The reliability of standardized achievement tests is superior to any other present measure of achievement. The standardized achievement test is less subject to bias than is teacher assessment, which is often colored by what psychologists call the "halo effect," a positive or negative distortion of judgment or grading resulting from personal interaction between the teacher and the child. Children can receive better grades because they are polite, compliant, and sweet, or lower grades because they are rebellious and recalcitrant. Their deportment thus affects their achievement grade even though it may be unrelated to what they actually learn. Children who are charming, pleasant, and helpful most often are overrated by classroom teachers; children who are negative, quarrelsome, and hostile often are underrated.

VALIDITY

An achievement test's validity, or the degree to which it predicts true achievement, is not as easy to establish as its reliability. The final criterion of the validity of an achievement test is the degree to which it samples the present curriculum in the school. The clear implication is that items on an achievement test must be truly representative of the content of the curriculum and must be phrased in such a way that a student who has mastered the curriculum content will be able to grasp the question's significance and to answer it correctly. The validity of achievement tests is assessed in various ways.

Academic

One criterion is academic validity: an achievement test should reflect a full nine months of academic growth across each grade level. That is, nine months of academic growth should be reflected on equivalent forms of the examination given to a large group of children at the beginning and at the end of the third grade. Heil, Powell, and Feifer (1960), however, have noted that children achieved more as grade level increased. In the fourth grade the mean achievement was .75 years; in the fifth grade, .89 years; in the sixth grade, .95 years.

Empirical

A second, similar criterion of validity for achievement tests, empirical validity, one of the most widely accepted, is the degree to which the mean achievement test grade placement reflects the mean actual grade placement in large samples of children. Although wide variations are noted, both among individuals and among small groups, the mean actual grade level and the mean test grade level should be similar. When the test is given to large numbers of children at the end of the third grade, the mean achievement score for the group as a whole should be third grade, ninth month. If it is not, this achievement test is not a valid instrument for sampling the achievement of children finishing up the third grade.

Now one might argue that the test is really correct and the problem is that the children are not learning enough. This is not an acceptable argument, however, because achievement tests are not designed to grade children's achievement at any given grade, but rather to compare individual children or small groups of children with a standardized norm. The achievement test should reflect what is normal for the entire population of third graders in the country, rather than set its own standards for achievement.

Concurrent

A third form of validity for achievement tests, concurrent validity, is the degree to which the achievement test agrees with another generally accepted measure of achievement.

Teachers' Grades

Teachers' grades, or ratings, or rankings, are the usual outside criterion against which the achievement test is checked. When a teacher is called upon to rate students in her class, she simply assigns them grades, such as A, B, C, D, or numbers, such as 100, 90, 80, 70. She might judge all the children to be superior and give every child an A. Or she might judge them all to be extremely poor students and give all of them an F. Generally, this is not the case: grades tend to be more or less normally distributed, with a slight tendency toward more As than Fs and more Bs than Ds. In any event, once a criterion for rating is established (i.e., A for excellent, outstanding performance; B for good performance, well above the mean; C for average performance; D for poor performance, below average; and F for failing performance), the teacher goes down her class roll and assigns grades.

Ranking is more complex and gives much more useful information. The teacher is required to rank her students from highest to lowest on the basis of some criterion for rating overall academic performance. She assigns the number 1 to the top student in her class of 35, and the number 35 to the bottom student, and then slowly and meticulously fills in the numbers between, until she has assigned all the students a rank. This forced choice actually sharpens considerably the teacher's grading, because she is forced to spend more time in the process.

To assess the concurrent validity of an achievement test by the degree to which it predicts teacher grades has an obvious limitation: one cannot improve either the test or the teacher grades without deciding which of the measurements is superior. If one merely wants the achievement test to reflect accurately the grade that the teacher would assign anyway, then administering an achievement test is a clumsy and expensive way of deriving grades. It would be much simpler merely to let the teacher assign the grades.

Although this criterion is not a satisfactory way of assessing the true worth of a test, it may predict whether or not the test is going to be commercially successful. Teachers obviously will not tolerate scores that differ too widely from what they consider to be the child's performance.

Other Achievement Tests

Another measure of concurrent validity is the degree to which scores on two achievement tests agree. A new test coming on the market—a test that is cheaper, because it is less expensive either to buy or to administer—can be compared with a test already generally accepted. This technique often is used to assess the utility of abbreviated tests. The *Wide Range Achievement Test* can be given to an individual in about twenty minutes, requires little time to score, and yields basic literacy scores in reading, spelling, and arithmetic. The concurrent validity of this abbreviated scale obviously is important.

Construct

Construct validity, as the word implies, refers to the definition of achievement contained in the instrument itself. The assumption is made that achievement can be defined in terms of tasks, accomplishments, abilities—that independently of any external criterion, achievement can be defined in terms of actual test performance. Construct validity requires the most persuasive arguments from the test constructor, since he is not relying on the rather convincing argument that the test is representative of what children are being taught; he is saying, rather, that it is representative of what achievement really is, regardless of what children are being taught. No major tests on the market rely solely on construct validity for their sales.

However, let us examine for a moment the concept of construct validity as it might apply to achievement tests. A basic assumption might be that achievement, in its most critical dimension, reflects vocabulary power —that only the utilization of complex language, the manipulation of concepts, the grasping of intricate relationships, ultimately determines academic progress. An achievement test based on this assumption must be directed toward the assessment of concept mastery. The test constructors might carefully analyze the language of science, of math, of geography, of history, and then develop a concept test to assess the language power developed by the child at a given level. Through this form of measurement, one might at the same time assess the progress of the child and the school: on the same assumption that through the building of concept mastery, progress takes place in school. Should the test scores not correlate well with the teachers' assigned grades or with other measures of achievement, the assigned grades and other achievement tests are incorrect: they measure the wrong variables in achievement and should be modified in order to become more appropriate for their tasks.

Such a test—flying in the face of the power hierarchy in the public school, flying in the face of experience accumulated over the years, experience that has developed ways of measuring achievement by sampling classroom activity, by following, not leading classroom achievement—would most likely be doomed. Merely an educational revolution would be required to permit test constructors this kind of liberty to define achievement. A slight undercurrent of hostility always exists between the test constructors and the teachers and school administrators, because, in a sense, the teacher is always under attack by the achievement test. Every year this instrument is used not only to grade her children, but is often misused to grade the teacher herself. Further to remove an instrument from the realities of the teacher-dominated curriculum would probably be insufferable.

A nationally standardized test frequently does not take into account the starting point of the children. Thus teachers in classes where the ability level is high and the achievement placement at the beginning of the year is high often are given acclaim by the administrators at the end of the year because their children have done so well. Teachers in classes serving the low-ability group, particularly the disadvantaged group, may find that although their children made some progress during the year on a relative basis, on an absolute basis they are one more month behind where they should be. For example, children who have a mean IQ of 80 at the beginning of the fourth grade and who are reading at the same percentile, will be about seven months behind their grade placement, or at about third-grade second-month. At the end of the school year, they will be about nine months behind even though they have improved their reading by seven months during the nine-month school year.

Predictive

One final criterion of the validity of achievement tests is predictive validity, or the degree to which the current achievement test scores predict future performance, either performance on a similar achievement test given at a later date, or in later grades, or on other generally accepted assessments of achievement. One might be interested in assessing the degree to which achievement in the second grade predicts achievement in the sixth grade. Extending this even further, one might want to assess the degree to which achievement in elementary school predicts achievement in high school, or predicts college boards, or predicts academic success in college, or predicts job success. The permanent, long-range utility of achievement tests is the question raised with predictive validity, which, as would be expected, is not nearly as high as reliability scores based either on the split-half method or equivalent forms of the test administered at the same time.

UTILITY

Achievement tests are useful to teachers, school administrators, and diagnosticians. Their competent use provides for teachers an adequate profile of each pupil and thus an objective basis for planning individualized instruction, for comparing present and past achievement, as well as for evaluating each pupil in terms of age and measured mental ability. Their competent use provides for school administrators an objective basis for analyzing strengths and weaknesses of individual subjects, grades, schools, and the system as a whole, a continuous record reflecting changes in curriculum and pupil population characteristics, and a source of information on which to base major curriculum changes.

Diagnosticians such as psychologists use the achievement battery as part of an extensive, individualized psychological study of the child. Frequently children experiencing academic difficulty are referred by the school to psychological service centers. Underachievement, when the child exhibits lower academic achievement than would seem indicated by formal or informal intellectual assessment, is a constant concern of academic personnel.

Within the clinical setting, then, to derive a plan of action whereby remediation would be effective, the psychological diagnostician administers the achievement battery to locate particular areas of difficulty and to compare these areas with weaknesses found on an individual intelligence test. Not infrequently, when the achievement test is administered in the individual setting, with the clinician watching every move of the child, contributing artifacts can be identified.

The major problem with the use of a large achievement battery in the clinical setting is its relative expense. When an achievement test is administered individually, the total time required is in excess of three hours. Clinic time now exceeds twenty dollars an hour and is in heavy demand. However, individually administered achievement tests often are necessary for a precise diagnosis; they frequently represent time well spent. The clinician, knowing the test is administered under ideal conditions, and having clinical notes of the problems the child encounters as he takes the test, is enabled to determine the relationship between the child's performance on the achievement test, his measured intelligence, and his usual academic performance.

One further use of achievement tests is in the evaluation of the effectiveness of new methods of teaching. In today's school systems, one hears a great deal about criterion-based instruction, or instruction specifically designed to produce certain information, techniques, or skills. Specialized achievement tests provide an excellent outside criterion against which to judge the success or failure of the methods designed to produce such changes.

SUMMARY

What, then, is to be learned from our examination of the variable, achievement?

The past twenty-five years have seen great improvement in the measurement of achievement. Competition for the national market has forced great strides in achievement test packaging and standardization, along with greater dissemination of information about these tests. This same pressure has forced rapid revision of tests to keep pace with the rapid changes taking place in the educational program.

Confidence in the assessment of achievement has improved greatly for the general public as well as for educators and psychologists alike. Particularly at the upper end of the achievement testing program, the College Entrance Examination Boards, an awareness that approaches fanaticism has developed in the minds of the general public. In the face of the baby boom, the pressure to get into better schools has made achievement tests assume a frightening importance in middle-class society. We now see developing in this country the same aura around achievement tests as developed in the 1920s around intelligence tests.

Achievement tests have become, then, the yardstick by which students, teachers, and school systems alike are judged, and woe be unto the student, teacher, or school system that does not make sufficient advance during the course of the year. Academic progress is now synonymous with achievement test performance. Academic excellence is to a large extent a function of test excellence.

This trend has been caused by the large numbers of students involved in the educational system. Under this pressure, the individualized grading system and the confidence of an individual teacher's grade standard have been eroded away by group standards based upon a total population at any given grade level.

This is the way it is today.

But it is not to say that this is the way it should be, or the way it will be. However, any look at the future requires us to face the obvious fact that the utilization of the computer on a system-wide basis will probably tend to standardize achievement testing further. The use of departmental tests in the elementary school is a new but fast-growing phenomenon. The availability of computers to do automatic item analysis and item rating, the production of a great deal of information about the distribution of scores and how they compare to other schools and to other classes in specific schools, will, in the long run, turn every class test into a standardized test. The pressure to live up to the standards of the nationally recognized test constructors will move ever downward into the individual schools, and soon small desk-top computers will be as common as the school mimeograph today. Achievement tests are here to stay. Regardless of their disclaimers, achievement tests will have an even more powerful influence upon the American school system.

The best aspect of standardized achievement tests is the accuracy of the data they provide about the distribution of information, knowledge, and power of an individual child and of groups of children. The worst aspect is the rigidity built into the system and the overwhelming confidence that is placed on the scores.

Few schools in the megalopolis make any exception for the child who does excellent classroom work, communicates well, and is creative, but who seems to fall apart on tests. Until the problem of individual differences in test-taking performance is mastered, a risk exists that slightly nonconforming students will be severely penalized. In present achievement test usage, there is little room for the child who is creative in his own right, but not conforming; the child who has read over a hundred books this year in rather esoteric areas, but who has not read that which everybody has read. Of course there are systems of appeal. But these require a great deal of initiative by the parents. Usually no appeal is made, or, if it is, then it is not readily effective in securing an exception. The child who is unable to perform on a standardized achievement test is indeed a child in serious academic difficulty.

And so, let us point up some broad, inescapable conclusions regarding individual levels of achievement. These conclusions have been supported now by countless studies across all areas of the country and for all types of school systems.

First, there is a well-defined and expected high correlation between achievement test performance and intelligence test performance. This is due, to a great degree, to the fact that the intelligence test was designed to predict academic achievement. If this correlation had not been high, the intelligence test most certainly would have been discarded as useless. Part of this relationship between achievement and intelligence, then, is an artifact of the construction of the two instruments. However, this should not obscure the point that there is a dimension called intelligence, which intelligence tests measure. The higher one rates on this dimension, the more likely he is to perform well in the school setting. This is in keeping with the old folk saying "Them that has, gits."

Dull children, then, tend to progress slower in school and to test lower on achievement tests. One of the major tasks of special education designed to deal with dull children should be to provide a foundation upon which job training can be laid by developing a curriculum that will deal effectively with simple literacy tasks. Any effort to prepare these children for adequate performance on achievement tests of the conventional variety would be an error in planning.

Second, there is a well-defined and expected high correlation between achievement test performance and socioeconomic class. Middle- and upper-class children have many cultural advantages that provide readiness for academic success. Their home environment provides rich stimulation in conceptual development, which eases the transfer from home to school. In addition, middle- and upper-class children enjoy nursery school and kindergarten experience, which again gives the child an added advantage in the educational system. And the parents of middle- and upper-class children remain in close communication with the school system: they provide extra resources when they are needed; they provide glasses or other corrective devices when they are appropriate. In the middle- and upper-class home, the role of education is appreciated—more correctly, worshiped—such that there is never any doubt in the child's mind that academic achievement is a major life task.

Also, there is a relationship between socioeconomic class and intelligence, which means that the first and second variables affecting achievement are interrelated.

Third, there is a well-defined and expected high correlation between achievement test performance and quality of schooling. The more resources possessed by a school, the more competent its teachers, the more efficient its administration, the higher its per-pupil budget, the greater the level of achievement of its children. Schools with extra resource personnel, special instruction, and low teacher-pupil ratios give the child advantages that are not present in poorer school systems.

There is a tendency in America for the better schools, the better teachers, and the better resources to be in the higher socioeconomic areas of any given school system. Thus children from lower socioeconomic families in lower socioeconomic areas of the city attend inferior schools. True, some brilliant children come from some very poor school systems. And it is possible, of course, for children from low socioeconomic families to make excellent students. But the general picture, which always allows for exception, is that the better the socioeconomic area, the better the school system.

Fourth, there is a well-defined and expected high correlation between achievement and a high drive level for parents and children alike. Children who come from families with a high level of aspiration, a high expectancy, a high drive, tend to have a broad exposure to and a generally positive attitude toward the learning process. This strong motivation provides them with an intense and broad learning experience. There are the exceptions—the backlash effect in which a rebellious child, pushed too far and too hard by parents with too high levels of aspiration, drags his heels and fails to achieve. But this is the exception. A higher drive level almost always leads to higher achievement.

The conclusion is inescapable. The most important single achievement predictor variable, one highly related to each of the others, is the socioeconomic variable. Whether this is a cause or an effect cannot, of course, be determined by the correlational measure. But the opportunity, encouragement, and facility, which in America accompany the middle class, as compared with the lower class, go a long way in accounting for the variability in individual achievement.

REVIEW

Influences on Achievement

Pupil Characteristics

The American school system is based on the middle-class model; those pupils with middle-class characteristics achieve better academic success. The high achiever can rapidly code information; has a high drive to organize his world and to cross-relate information; is efficient; has diligence, perseverance, and restraint; has not only intelligence, but a drive to succeed and all-around social adjustment. The low achiever is more immature than his peers; has a poor self-concept; is unduly anxious;

and is usually expected to do poorly. In the early grades, sex makes a difference in achievement level, girls being, for the time being at least, better pupils.

Certain dimensions of pupil characteristics are predictive and fall into the convenient acrostic **MASTERED.**

Maturation
A
S
T
E
R
E
D

Academic success is affected by maturation, both physical maturation and mental readiness. The low achiever is more immature than his peers, physically, socially, and emotionally.

M
Ability
S
T
E
R
E
D

Academic success is affected by ability, as measured by intelligence tests. Other things being equal, the more intelligent the child, the greater will be his achievement in school.

M
A
Self-concept
T
E
R
E
D

Academic success is affected by a positive self-concept, which is itself affected by attitude, socioeconomic level, and ethnicity.

M
A
S
Temperament
E
R
E
D

Academic success is affected by temperament, which includes mood swings, hyperkinesis, exploratory drive, and affective needs.

M
A
S
T
Experience
R
E
D

Academic success is affected by experience that includes opportunity to learn, to perceive, to conceptualize.

M
A
S
T
E
Reinforcement
E
D

Academic success is affected by reinforcement experience that teaches the value of achievement, academically and socially.

M
A
S
T
E
R
Expectancy
D

Academic success is affected by expectancy, both of the child and of significant adults, although perhaps not as Robert Rosenthal and Jacobson have claimed.

M
A
S
T
E
R
E
D

Academic success is affected by drive, the amount of creative energy a child has at his disposal.

M
A
S
T
E
R
E
D

The child who has **MASTERED** academic achievement is **m**ature, has **a**bility, a positive **s**elf-concept, a **t**emperament appropriate to learning effectively, **e**xperience that has taught him to perceive, to discriminate, and to generalize, **r**einforcement for his academic achievement, an **e**xpectancy for achievement, and **d**rive to achieve. Children nurtured in the lower socioeconomic levels of our society lack both the opportunity and the stimulation necessary for their full intellectual growth, which consequently affects their ability to achieve.

Teacher Characteristics

Children who are given better instruction will achieve at a higher level. Teachers who are viable, attractive, excited models for achievement will more profoundly influence their pupils to learn than the drab, dull, disinterested teacher. The personality characteristics of teachers and pupils interact in affecting pupil achievement; teacher personality, in fact, has more effect on pupil achievement than does teacher knowledge per se.

Parental Characteristics

Boys' achievement is affected positively by their training for independence, by the warmth of the mother-son relationship, and by accepting, less dominant fathers. Children's achievement is fairly stable over time, is affected positively by positive parental attitudes toward school and by consistent parental discipline. High achievers are more responsible to the socializing pressures of their parents, but also more hostile toward adults. The high achievers have more authoritarian and restrictive mothers, and parents who encourage self-expression and experimentation.

Models for Achievement

Viable, visible models affect not only academic achievement, but general growth of personal competency. Childhood is in a real sense an apprenticeship for competent adulthood.

Employment M U L A T E	An apprentice is employed, given specific tasks that have utility and purpose.
E Model U L A T E	He is assigned to a skilled workman, whom he can observe at work and of whom he can ask questions.
E M Understanding L A T E	He is understood and accepted at his own level of development, not expected to perform that for which he has not been prepared.
E M U Lability A T E	He is allowed lability in moving through the achievement-learning sequence at his own pace, taking more or less time to move forward as he requires.
E M U L Access T E	He has ready access to viable models for explanation and demonstration.
E M U L A Termination E	He is terminated when he has achieved mastery of specified skills; he becomes an accepted, full-fledged member of the skilled corps.
E M U L A T Exaltation	And when this termination day finally arrives, everyone rejoices and celebrates the formal annointment: "Today you are one of us, a master craftsman."

Tests of Achievement

measurement units

Grade Equivalents Grade equivalent refers to the average performance of the average child at a given grade level.

Intelligence Quotient (IQ) The IQ is a standard score equivalent of the ratio between mental age (MA) and chronological age (CA).

Percentile A percentile is the expression of an individual score in relationship to all other scores on a percentile basis.

Standard Deviation (SD) The standard deviation is that distance above and below the mean of a normal distribution that defines a range that includes the midmost 68 percent of the population. Two standard deviations above and below the mean define a range that will include about 95 percent of the population.

Standard Score A standard score is the translation of raw scores of any given value into scores that have a mean of 50 and a standard deviation of 10.

Stanine Scale A stanine scale is a single-digit scale from 1 to 9 with a mean of 5 and a standard deviation of approximately 2.

Units of Measurement All units of measurement relate specific performance to general performance: one child's performance to all children's performance.

313

External Consistency External consistency refers to the reliability of measures taken on the same child at different time intervals, using the same test or equivalent forms of the same test.

Internal Consistency Internal consistency refers to the degree to which items at each level on the test are of equal difficulty.

Test Reliability Achievement test reliability refers to consistency of measurement, both in terms of the items within the test and in terms of comparisons with other tests.

Academic Validity An achievement test should reflect a full nine months of academic growth across each grade level to have academic validity.

Concurrent Validity An achievement test should agree with other generally accepted measures of achievement to have concurrent validity.

Construct Validity An achievement test should be constructed on a definition of achievement that is reflected in the instrument to have construct validity. The assumption is made that achievement can be defined in terms of tasks, accomplishments, abilities that can be measured by actual test performance. And explicit is the implication that achievement can be defined outside of what is taught in schools, that school curriculums do not necessarily reflect what should be taught.

Empirical Validity Mean achievement test grade placement should reflect the mean actual grade placement in large samples of children for an achievement test to have empirical validity.

Predictive Validity For predictive validity, an achievement test should be able to predict future performance.

Test Validity Achievement test validity refers to the degree to which it predicts true achievement. The final criterion of achievement test validity is the degree to which it samples the present curriculum in the school.

Validity Other Achievement Tests Testing the concurrent validity of achievement tests with other achievement tests is often used to assess the utility of abbreviated tests.

Validity/Teachers' Grades Testing the concurrent validity of achievement tests against teachers' grades is a poor criterion with which to judge the achievement test because of the subjectivity of teachers' grades, no matter how carefully they are assigned.

Achievement tests have utility for teachers, school administrators, and diagnosticians. For teachers, achievement tests provide an adequate profile of each pupil; provide an objective basis for planning individualized instruction; compare present and past achievement; and evaluate each child in terms of age and measured mental ability. For school administrators, achievement tests provide an objective basis for analyzing strengths and weaknesses of individual subjects, grades, schools, the system as a whole; provide a continuous record reflecting changes in curriculum and pupil population characteristics; provide a source on which to base major curriculum changes; and provide an evaluation of the effectiveness of new methods of teaching. For diagnosticians, achievement tests locate particular areas of difficulty; provide comparisons between performance and measured intelligence; and identify artifacts contributing to the child's performance level.

Summary

Achievement Drive Level There is a well-defined and expected high correlation between achievement and high drive in both parents and children: that which is valued is striven for.

Achievement Intelligence There is a well-defined and expected high correlation between achievement and intelligence: that which encourages a child's intellectual growth encourages his achievement, both in personal competency and in academic performance.

Achievement/Quality of Education There is a well-defined and expected high correlation between achievement and education quality: the necessity for encouragement, opportunity, facility, viable models, and obtainable goals is emphasized in the school as well as in the home.

Achievement/Socioeconomic Status There is a well-defined and expected high correlation between achievement and socioeconomic class: encouragement, opportunity, facility, viable models, and obtainable goals are essential for achievement, both in personal competency and in academic performance.

NAMES TO KNOW

History of Achievement Measurement

HORACE MANN Horace Mann first encouraged the use of written examinations in 1845. His list of the qualities of the written examination: impartial, just to the pupils, thorough, free of "officious interference" from the teacher, evidences how well the pupils were taught, free of favoritism, results available to all, and easily appraised as to difficulty of the questions.

EDWARD L. THORNDIKE Edward L. Thorndike popularized the concept of standardized achievement tests. He pioneered in the effort to objectify judgment that had been purely subjective.

CLIFF W. STONE Stone, Thorndike's student, published the first standardized achievement test.

FRANCIS GALTON Francis Galton laid the groundwork for probability statistics. For him, statistics and anthropometry were inseparable.

> Sir Francis Galton, . . . fired by the ambition to unravel the problems of human heredity, undertook to measure individuals on a large scale. . . . Not finding the normal curve and its simpler applications adequate, he invented a number of additional statistical tools, among them the methods of corrlelation, the use of standard scores, the median, and such psychological scaling methods as the order-of-merit and the rating-scale method [Guilford, 1936, p. 7].

R. A. FISHER R. A. Fisher made the first practical application of statistical theory. He succeeded Karl Pearson in the Galton Professorship of Eugenics in the Francis Galton Laboratory at University College in London. He developed techniques for the analysis of variance and for the use and validation of small samples.

KARL PEARSON Through his product-moment coefficient of correlation (Pearson's r), Karl Pearson, a student of Francis Galton, made possible the prediction of variability in psychology. He developed and systematized what until recently constituted nearly the whole field of statistics.

CHARLES SPEARMAN Charles E. Spearman's two-factor theory of mental organization introduced a statistical technique that paved the way for factor analysis. His application of mathematical correlation to testing and his foundation for factor analysis in psychology, especially in the study of intelligence, carve for him a permanent niche among psychology greats.

CYRIL BURT Working in England with factor analysis, Cyril Burt helped to simplify the description of data by reducing the variables into meaningful clusters.

L. L. THURSTONE L. L. Thurstone developed factor analytic methodology in the United States. He came to be known as the developer of paper-and-pencil tests of intelligence and aptitude, and he laid the rational basis for quantifying data obtained from comparative judgments.

J. P. GUILFORD Particularly interested in the assessment of the individual, J. P. Guilford led an explosion of research into creativity. His factor analyses have led him to suggest the possibility of 120 factors in intelligence. He found Thurstone's "generalized, multiple-factor theory and methods" more promising than Spearman's "emphasis on his g factor. . . . As rapidly as Thurstone developed his methods, I applied them" (Guilford, 1967a, p. 181). Guilford introduced the concept of aptitude, a measure of potential for achievement in the absence of opportunity.

RAYMOND B. CATELL Raymond Cattell isolated a series of personality factors related to achievement. As a research associate under E. L. Thorndike, he began his vigorous research into various aspects of personality and objective measurement.

Variability in Achievement

LEARNED AND WOOD In a study of achievement in Pennsylvania, Learned and Wood found great variability within groups of students and great overlapping between groups of students: the median for each higher group fell at about the 75th percentile of the group below it.

KAGAN AND MOSS Although great variability in achievement is demonstrated between individuals, within individuals and within families can be found stability of achievement. Kagan and Moss found that achievement in the first three years does not correlate highly with later achievement. After three, general achievement is fairly stable and correlated with intellectual striving, competitiveness, expectancy of success or failure, and striving for recognition.

SCHOONOVER Schoonover, studying resemblances in intelligence and achievement among siblings, found 35 percent less difference between siblings than between random pairs of children.

Classical conditioning

In this chapter and the next a distinction is made between two rather basic kinds of learning on the part of the child. The first of these is classical or respondent conditioning; the second, operant or instrumental conditioning. The distinction between the two at first glance appears to be simple and meaningful.

Classical conditioning is reflexive, unconscious learning. In classical conditioning the child responds to a stimulus on the basis of a built-in, automatic reflex that is almost out of his control. This stimulus or signal can become associated with an increasing array of stimuli, any one of which can produce this same automatic response. Such conditioning implies a helplessness on the part of the child and accounts for most early learning and perhaps all emotional learning during childhood. Most of our emotions, particularly our negative emotions, are derived during states of helplessness experienced in the early years of our lives.

On the other hand, operant conditioning refers to learning that takes place in situations where the child is not helpless, but is able to manipulate his environment in such a way that he himself controls reinforcement. His world is arranged, naturally or socially, such that his behavior has a determining effect on what happens next. Most early learning that does not involve emotions is some variation of operant or instrumental conditioning.

Would that it were so simple! Unfortunately in the seventy years since the basic discovery of the conditioning process, the definitions have endured considerable tinkering. No group of scholars anywhere seems to enjoy controversy and argument with such utter abandon as the learning theorists. An advanced student or instructor will not be able to read through this and the following chapter without finding some statement or definition that does not disagree to some extent with some previous statement in the literature with at least equal merit. What is important, however, is to understand the behavior of the child—behavior that is now often predictable. So, aware of the potential overlapping between the two chapters, we shall continue without expending a great deal of effort on maintaining a purity between operant and classical conditioning.

Even before that great Russian experimentalist, Pavlov, considerable track laid in philosophy made the conceptual discovery of conditioning inevitable. The germ of conditioning certainly rested in the concept of associationism.

BRITISH ASSOCIATIONISM

Noticing that apparently disconnected ideas are related in men's minds, the concept of associationism arose from man's theoretical efforts to explain this phenomenon. A systematic theory, associationism explains mental phenomena in terms of primary mental processes, chiefly association, which manipulate the simple and complex data of experience. James Mill thought of it as mental mechanics; John Stuart Mill, as mental chemistry; and Alexander Bain, as the substructure for physiological psychology.

James Mill

Since the beginning of the nineteenth century and the writings of James Mill (1829), John Stuart Mill (1843), and Alexander Bain (1855), the concept of associationism has played an important role in our understanding of human learning. British associationism theorizes that ideas become associated or fused in a kind of mental chemistry. It is grounded in James Mill's principle of fusion. To illustrate his point, Mill used the color wheel. When rotated, first very slowly and then more rapidly, a color wheel with seven distinct spectral colors quickly becomes one uniform color, white. "The several sensations cease to be distinguishable; they run, as it were together, and a new sensation, compounded of all seven, but apparently a simple one, is the result" (Mill, as quoted in Boring, 1950, p. 225).

Now, Mill was concerned with the association of ideas and not the association of sensations, and he recognized colors as sensations, not ideas. But he was convinced, all the same, that the color wheel was a convenient model for understanding the mysterious bond between ideas presented simultaneously or in association with each other. According to James Mill, then, ideas come together to form more complex ideas: sand and lime together make mortar, and clay and pitch together make brick, and brick and mortar together make a wall. It is a thin analogue, but it spoke well for the beginning of a concept of the mind that gives at least a post hoc explanation of how apparently disconnected ideas are related.

John Stuart Mill

James Mill's son, John Stuart Mill, carried the concept much further and, in 1843, laid down three laws of association: similarity, contiguity, and intensity. In 1865, he added frequency and inseparability, and discarded intensity. The concept of mental chemistry became important, and with his laws some formal description of the elements of association was achieved.

The association laws imply that the more similar are the stimuli in the environment, the more likely they are to be associated. The closer they are temporally, the more likely they are to be associated. The more frequently they are experienced together, the more likely they are to be associated. The more difficult they are to separate, the more likely they are to be associated. And the more intense the stimuli, the more likely they are to be associated.

Inseparability is literal in associationism. For example, father-son and mother-daughter relationships are recognizable instantly. Older people in a community hardly ever encounter a grown son without verbalizing the association, "How is your father?"

In commenting on his father's use of the color wheel as an example of associationism, Mill said,

> it is correct to say that the seven colors when they rapidly follow one another *generate* white, but not that they actually *are* white; so it appears to me that the Complex Idea, formed by the blending together of several simpler ones, should, when it really appears simple, (that is when the separate elements are not consciously distinguishable in it) be said to *result from,* or be *generated by,* the simple ideas, not to *consist* of them.... These are cases of mental chemistry: in which it is possible to say that the simple ideas generate, rather than that they compose, the complex ones [Mill, as quoted in Boring, 1950, p. 230].

Alexander Bain

For Alexander Bain (1855) there were only two fundamental laws of association: contiguity and similarity. For its strength, the law of contiguity depended upon repetition of contiguous experience and also upon attention to this repetition. Bain believed that the conscious awareness of contiguity was important.

Bain's psychophysical parallelism laid the groundwork for physiological psychology. Although he was not the originator of either the term or the concept, which probably is a contribution of Leibnitz, he emphasized the structure and content of the brain, or mind, more than the early associationists. Simply, psychophysical parallelism says that mental events taking place in the brain parallel the events in the outside world: that is, some type of change, probably neurological, takes place in the brain, allowing the brain to represent the events in the external world. This dualism of mind and body gave some implied strength, at least, to associationism.

THE CONDITIONED RESPONSE

An infant invariably startles when he hears a sudden loud noise. The startle is an unconditioned response to an unconditioned stimulus, the loud noise. He did not learn to startle; he did it automatically, involuntarily. But he can learn to startle at an open umbrella simply by the open umbrella being paired with the loud noise. He has been conditioned: his startle is now a conditioned response.

Associationism was entrenched in the literature and in the thinking of psychologists when the first report of a conditioned reflex appeared. Edwin Twitmyer, in 1905, viewed his conditioned knee jerk in the light of associationism, and his report produced no ripple on the surface of psychology. Although Ivan Pavlov also interpreted the conditioned reflex in terms of associationism, he studied it carefully and carried the concept further into classical conditioning.

> It is clear that the phenomenon of conditional reflexes had been observed several times during the nineteenth century. Furthermore, it had been given an explicit associationistic interpretation by Erasmus Darwin a century before Pavlov offered a similar interpretation.... Since they did not attempt to establish new associations, the earlier workers did not produce any information about the actual process of the formation of conditioned responses. Only a thoroughgoing program of investigation, such as that begun by Pavlov, could show how fertile this field could become [Rosenzweig, 1959, p. 633].

Edwin B. Twitmyer

The contributions of the two Mills and Bain, which had been established in the literature, were followed by the 1902 doctoral dissertation of Edwin Twitmyer (1905) at the University of Pennsylvania, on the patellar reflex, or knee jerk. This reflex, a common measure of neurological symmetry, is elicited by striking the patellar tendon just below the knee while the lower leg is hanging free. In his study, Twitmyer tapped a bell once, to signal, and a half-second later gave his subjects a sharp tap with the percussion hammer. After one subject had received 125 trials, he responded at the sound of the bell before the hammer tap.

Twitmyer followed up this peculiar reaction in all of his subjects. He intermittently omitted the hammer tap and found the anticipatory response universal. The most surprising aspect of the experiment was that even when called sharply to their attention, the subjects could not inhibit the conditioned responses, which they claimed were entirely involuntary.

> Twitmyer's interpretation assumed that every incoming sensory impulse diffuses itself over the entire nervous system and that, after many repetitions of bell followed by knee jerk, a "habit of interaction between the two involved centers" is developed. "The connecting pathway of discharge has become well worn so that the sound of the bell alone is an adequate stimulus to the movement" [Woodworth, 1938, p. 115].

This is the first publicized account of a conditioned response and, except for its timing, Twitmyer might well have been credited with the discovery of one of the most important methods in all of psychology, since much of modern psychological theory and practice is based upon the conditioned response. However, when Twitmyer presented his study to the American Psychological Association, the psychological community was so steeped in the principles of associationism that Twitmyer's findings were dismissed on the grounds that they represented no new discovery, but were simply another example of associationism. That is, an association had been set up between the bell and the hammer blow and, by the simple process of elementary chemistry, the two had become fused into one contiguous event with great intensity.

William James, then president of APA, chaired the meeting in which Twitmyer presented his research. No discussion followed the presentation. "Twitmyer's own recollections of this occasion were always mingled with feelings of disappointment at the failure of his auditors to express interest in his results" (Irwin, 1943, p. 452).

That Twitmyer had developed a technology that made possible the overt measurement of association was not obvious to the leaders of the psychological community at the time. That is, the strength and magnitude of the knee jerk in relation to the loudness and pitch of the bell made it possible to remove the elements of association from the dark recesses of the mind and put them into the external world where they could be observed, measured, and controlled.

Dallenbach places the blame for letting "one of the most, if not the most, important experimental discoveries of his day and generation" slip through his fingers squarely on Twitmyer's shoulders.

> Had he "christened" his discovery, given it an intriguing name, such as "conditioned reflex" instead of calling it simply a "new phenomenon," had he published his reports in a periodical with world-wide circulation whose papers were listed in bibliographical indexes, had his dissertation come to Pavlov's attention, and had he, despite discouragement, pushed his investigations forward and effectively reported them, the history of this experiment would have been very different [1959, pp. 635, 637].

Influenced as he was by the tradition of associationism, Twitmyer failed to see the implications of his serendipitous discovery of the conditioned response. He and his professional colleagues thought it simply another example of an association, this time between the sound of a bell and a hammer blow just below the knee. The possibility of observing, measuring, and controlling the elements of association by controlling the stimulus just didn't occur to him or his peers.

Ivan P. Pavlov

Pavlov (1927), on the other hand, recognized the potential. Through his manipulations of the conditioned response, Pavlov laid the groundwork for much of modern psychological theory and practice. He deserves credit not so much, then, for his discovery, which had been made before, but because he recognized the significance of this serendipitous event and proclaimed its significance to the scientific community. Pavlov, an eminent Russian physiologist, discovered what he called the conditioned reflex while investigating the properties of salivation. He became intrigued with what he called "psychic secretion" of saliva. Noting that salivation increased dramatically when a hungry animal was shown food, Pavlov found that the salivary response could become conditioned to almost any stimulus. Any event that signaled the advent of feeding—the ticking of a metronome, the flashing of an electric light, a thermal or vibratory stimulus to the skin, a sequence of musical notes, a visual pattern—any such stimulus would produce salivation.

Pavlov studied intensively the elements of this basic experiment. He began to manipulate not only the nature of the stimulus, but also the relationship of the time interval between the conditioned stimulus and the unconditioned stimulus, food, that invariably produced salivation. He discovered extinction: over a period of time, initially conditioned stimuli lost their capacity to produce the response. He also noticed spontaneous recovery: after a lapse of time a conditioned response, extinguished due to lack of reinforcement over a period of time, suddenly reoccurs in the presence of "one set of stimuli in whose presence the response was previously reinforced" (Reynolds, 1968, p. 35).

CLASSICAL CONDITIONING DEFINITIONS

It might be well at this point to review some basic definitions in classical conditioning.

Conditioned Stimulus and Unconditioned Stimulus

Classical conditioning itself is the procedure whereby an organism is subjected to a pair of stimuli. The first stimulus is a neutral one. It does not provoke any reaction on the part of the organism. It does not provoke a reflex; it has no particular significance. It becomes a conditioned stimulus through pairing with a response-producing event a sufficient number of times such that the organism responds to the once neutral stimulus.

The second stimulus, the unconditioned stimulus, is one which invariably results in a response from the organism without any prior learning. The simplest unconditioned stimulus is a reflex-producing stimulus, such as an electric shock, which causes a reflexive jerking of the muscle fibers without any information whatsoever on the part of the subject as to what this stimulus means.

The unconditioned stimulus in Pavlov's experiment was the food, which, when tasted by the hungry dog, produced a salivary response. Even in this simple experiment, the food, the unconditioned stimulus, had certain learned qualities. The animal had learned something about the nature of the food, at least from a visual point of view, and thus the food had learned or conditioned qualities.

In Pavlov's experiment, the click of the metronome, or the buzz of the buzzer, did not initially cause salivation. Only by becoming associated or paired with food did the signal gain significance. The conditioned response in classical conditioning is the same as the unconditioned response: the metronome, when paired with food, also produces anticipatory salivation.

Classical Conditioning

Conditioning, then, in the classical sense refers to the process whereby a neutral stimulus becomes conditioned to the point where a specific response is invariably associated with its presentation to the subject. In classical conditioning, the conditioned stimulus always is followed by the unconditioned stimulus during the learning phase of the experiment, regardless of the behavior exhibited by the child. Thus, for example, in experiments involving conditioning of a knee jerk reaction to a tone, the shock always follows the tone regardless of whether or not the child gives a knee jerk prior to the shock. Operant conditioning, in which the child by his own actions determines the appearance of the unconditioned stimulus, is discussed in Chapter 8.

Extinction and Forgetting

In classical conditioning literature, forgetting refers to the extinguishing of a response due to lack of practice. Forgetting is the decay in response associated with lapsed time after the last exposure to the conditioned stimulus: without frequent exposure to the metronome, the animal forgets its significance.

Extinction, on the other hand, refers to repeated exposure to the conditioned stimulus, the metronome, in the absence of the unconditioned stimulus, the food. The conditioned response breaks down because of no reinforcement.

Spontaneous Recovery

Spontaneous recovery is a peculiar event that follows extinction. In the usual case, after extinction has occurred (following a series of presentations of the conditioned stimulus, the metronome, not followed by the unconditioned stimulus, food) and a time interval has passed with no presentation of the conditioned stimulus, a re-presentation will frequently evoke the conditioned response in the absence of any reinforcement. This spontaneous recovery is usually temporary, but there are some specific conditions that greatly increase its likelihood and magnitude.

Reinforcement

In classical literature, reinforcement usually describes the unconditioned stimulus, which can be positive, such as food, or negative, such as electric shock.

Secondary Reinforcement

Secondary reinforcement is "assumed to occur when a stimulus, through its association with a reinforcer [an unconditioned stimulus], acquires the capacity to influence behavior in a manner similar to that of the original reinforcer" (Stevenson, 1970, p. 865). It is a reduction in drive—for example, an actual reduction in hunger—that can occur when the organism is presented with a stimulus repeatedly paired with the unconditioned stimulus. For example, a mother about to nurse her baby makes preparations: she unbuttons her blouse, unsnaps her brassiere, bathes her breasts. These events, closely associated with the unconditioned stimulus of the breast in the mouth, have a pacifying effect on the youngster. He stops crying and begins to make sucking, smacking responses, in anticipation of the feeding. The cues that feeding is about to begin have taken on secondary-reinforcement properties.

Facilitation and Inhibition

Facilitation is a temporary increase in the likelihood and magnitude of the response, associated with the presentation of a second stimulus not previously associated with the response. Suppose a child is being conditioned to respond to a high-frequency sound paired with a mild shock to the bottom of the foot. The possibility of his responding is fairly small, because the frequency range is high and the shock level is low. Then a strobe light is introduced. The effect of the strobe light flashing on the wall will be to increase or facilitate the probability that the infant will respond to the high-frequency sound.

Inhibition, on the other hand, is a temporary decrease in the strength of the response because of the presentation of the second stimulus. In the usual case, inhibition is nothing more than a distraction that causes the organism to pay less attention to the conditioned stimulus. A response can be inhibited, however, due to nonreinforcement.

Stimulus Generalization and Stimulus Discrimination

Stimulus generalization is the spread of effect that occurs once a simple conditioned response is established. If the child has been conditioned to respond to a bell with a knee jerk, similar stimuli, the sounding of a gong, a sudden beating on a tin pan, will in all likelihood induce the response. "Reinforcement of a response in the presence of one stimulus increases the probability of responding not only in the presence of that stimulus, but also in the presence of other stimuli" (Reynolds, 1968, p. 37).

Stimulus discrimination refers to the ability of the child to isolate the essential characteristic of the stimulus. If the child is being conditioned to respond to high-frequency sound and not to low-frequency sound, discrimination would involve learning how low a high-frequency sound can be and still be likely to lead to reinforcement.

EARLY THEORETICAL EXPERIMENTS

Although Pavlov's experiments were begun in 1902, the full impact of classical conditioning trickled slowly into the mainstream of American psychology. In 1915, the presidential address of John B. Watson to the American Psychological Association brought the concept of the conditioned reflex to the attention of American psychologists (Watson, 1916). His research with Rosalie Rayner (Watson and Rayner, 1920), the "experiment with the boy Albert, whose fear of a loud sound was conditioned to a white rat and then to other furry objects, probably provides the most famous single case in the conditioning literature" (Kimble, 1961, p. 24).

At Clark University, William H. Burnham followed the work of Pavlov and Krasnogorskii before it was published in English, and encouraged his student, Florence Mateer, to modify the research of Krasnogorskii (Burnham, 1917; Mateer, 1918). Then, in 1927, Anrep's translation of Pavlov's work strengthened the growing interest in experimentation with the conditioned reflex (Pavlov, 1927). And in 1936, in his presidential address to the American Psychological Association, Clark L. Hull of Yale, following a provocative series of articles beginning in 1929 in the *Psychological Review*, illustrated the changes that had developed since Watson's presidential address (Hull, 1929, 1937).

To add to our understanding of and to demonstrate the importance of classical conditioning as a research tool in child psychology, let us review a few classic experiments in conditioning that have contributed greatly to our understanding of the behavior of children.

PHYSICAL RESPONSES

Heinrich Bogen

Shortly after Pavlov presented his findings on conditioned digestive secretions in dogs, a three-and-a-half-year-old child with a blocked esophagus, a result of his drinking a teaspoon of lye, was referred to Dr. Heinrich Bogen of the University Children's Clinic in Heidelberg, Germany. While attempts were being made to open the esophagus, the child was fed through a stomach fistula, which enabled Dr. Bogen not only to feed the child, but also to monitor the stomach secretions.

The esophagus was so narrowed that no food could pass into the child's stomach. His sole source of nutrition was predigested food put directly into his stomach cavity. In spite of his adequate nutritional level, the child was acutely concerned about eating and therefore was allowed to eat small quantities of food, which remained only a short time in the esophagus before being regurgitated.

The relationship between the secretion of stomach juices and the eating of this food was noted by Dr. Bogen, and in a short time the same observation made by Pavlov on the dog was confirmed by Bogen on the child. The phantom feeding process—simply showing the child food, talking about food, going through any of the preparatory rituals of getting out the food—tended to start the production of stomach juices. Bogen conditioned the child to secrete stomach juices at the sound of a trumpet by sequentially pairing the blowing of the trumpet forty times with the feeding of small amounts of meat. Thus, a smooth transition was demonstrated between the findings on dogs to those on human subjects (Bogen, 1907).

Nickolai I. Krasnogorskii

Although Bogen's study demonstrated conclusively that Pavlov's findings do apply to young children, some more ordinary way to study the relationship between conditioned and unconditioned responses was needed. An innovative study by Krasnogorskii provided such a method. Krasnogorskii determined that children swallow with a most insignificant accumulation of saliva in their mouth, about .5 cc, thus establishing that the externally observable swallowing reflex is an adequate measure of the production of saliva by a child.

Krasnogorskii first conditioned a fourteen-month-old child to respond to the sight of milk in a glass. Then he obtained a higher order of conditioning by pairing the sight of the milk with the sound of a bell. The measured response was the number of swallows during a three-minute period up to and during the sound of the bell. The sound of the bell stimulated salivation. Krasnogorskii declared: "there is no doubt whatsoever that the ringing of the bell after its combination with the unconditioned stimulus became a conditioned stimulus, nor that I observed in the child an artificially formed conditioned reflex" (1907, p. 239).

Florence Mateer

Before the English publication (1925) of Krasnogorskii's continued research on classical conditioning, his work came to the attention of W. H. Burnham, a former student of G. Stanley Hall at Hopkins and head of Clark University's Department of Pedagogy, "which in the Clark atmosphere was almost synonymous with educational psychology" (Boring, 1950, p. 520). Clark University became the entry point not only for classical conditioning research with children, but also for the dynamic viewpoint with Freud's first American lectures. In September, 1909, Clark's psychologist president, G. Stanley Hall, invited Freud to deliver his now famous lectures, "The Origin and Development of Psychoanalysis" (Freud, 1910*a*). More recently it has become the fount of much of the research following Piagetian theory.

Burnham encouraged one of his students at Clark, Florence Mateer (1918), to modify and repeat Krasnogorskii's experiments with children. Her work furthered Burnham's case for the place of the conditioned reflex in mental hygiene.

In a carefully controlled experiment with fifty normal and fourteen subnormal children between twelve and ninety months old, she associated, by the classical conditioning technique, a swallowing, chewing response to the stimulus of pulling a bandage over the child's eyes. The unconditioned stimuli were sugar water and sweet chocolate. Krasnogorskii's technique of observing the conditioned response of swallowing and chewing made possible the study of normal children without the surgery required by Pavlovian methods. Mateer found that conditioning took only "from 3 to 9 trials in normal children. This is a narrower range than that found by Krasnogorskii" (1918, p. 201). From three to eighteen trials were required for conditioning the defective children. Her results also suggested that susceptibility to conditioning increased with chronological age.

EMOTIONAL RESPONSES

John B. Watson

In 1920 John B. Watson and his graduate student and later wife, Rosalie Rayner, conducted the first conditioning experiment with emotions. Watson began his experiment when his subject, a healthy male child named Albert, was nine months old. Albert was confronted suddenly and for the first time with a white rat, a white rabbit, a dog, a monkey, masks with and without hair, cotton wool, and burning newspaper. He at no time showed any fear.

Then Albert was exposed to a loud sound made by striking a hammer upon a suspended steel bar four feet in length and three-quarters of an inch in diameter. Upon first hearing this sharp noise, the child:

> ... started violently, his breathing was checked and the arms were raised in a characteristic manner. On the second stimulation the same thing occurred, and in addition the lips began to pucker and tremble. On the third stimulation the child broke into a sudden crying fit [Watson and Rayner, 1920, p. 2].

Watson had at his disposal, then, an unconditioned stimulus for fear and crying and a wide range of neutral stimuli to test in a laboratory setting. He concluded that fear is conditioned or learned except in response to a few primitive stimuli such as falling and loud noises.

When Albert was eleven months old, the conditioning began. When the white rat initially was shown to Albert, he reached out for it with his left hand. Just as he touched the rat, the bar was struck immediately behind his head. He started violently and fell forward, burying his face in the mattress, although not crying. Shortly afterward he recovered his composure, reached again for the rat, this time with his right hand, and again the bar was struck. He started violently, fell forward, and began to whimper. (Notice that by pairing Albert's reaching toward the rat with the loud sound, Watson was confounding operant conditioning into his study.)

Seven days passed in which no pairing of the conditioned stimulus, the white rat, and the unconditioned stimulus, the loud noise, occurred. At the end of the week the white rat was presented without the noise. Although Albert reached toward it, he did not touch the rat. The rat was removed and he was allowed to play with his blocks. Then the rat and noise were presented simultaneously three times. Each time Albert started and fell over, but did not cry. The fifth time the rat was presented alone. Albert withdrew and whimpered. The sixth and seventh presentations again were simultaneous; Albert withdrew and whimpered, actually crying on the seventh presentation. On the eighth presentation, when the rat was presented alone, Albert began to cry and "to crawl away so rapidly that he was caught with difficulty before reaching the edge of the table" (Watson and Rayner, 1920, p. 5). Thus, on the second day of learning and with a week's interval between the two days, an emotional response of fear had been conditioned to the white rat.

This conditioned emotional response was studied five days later for generalization or transfer effect. After first determining that Albert still feared the white rat, he was tested with a white rabbit, a dog, a sealskin fur coat, cotton wool, and a Santa Claus mask. To all of these, Albert presented varying degrees of negative emotional affect. A month later all of the responses were found to be still intact, although much less extreme than they had been.

Watson demonstrated, then, that reasonably permanent conditioned emotional responses can be established.

These experiments would seem to show conclusively that directly conditioned emotional responses as well as those conditioned by transfer persist, although with a certain loss in the intensity of the reaction, for a longer period than one month. Our view is that they persist and modify personality throughout life. It should be recalled again that Albert was of an extremely phlegmatic type. Had he been emotionally unstable probably both the directly conditioned response and those transferred would have persisted throughout the month unchanged in form [Watson and Rayner, 1920, p. 12].

To comprehend the full implication of Watson and Rayner's findings, we need to be reminded of a protracted dialogue in the literature regarding emotional behavior. Watson's work was received with general hostility by the physicians, psychiatrists, and psychologists who dominated the mental-health scene at the time. To the psychoanalysts, who considered anxiety to be the major cause of all neuroses and psychoses, the consequence of inducing anxiety or fear was grave indeed. The distinction between anxiety and fear was merely one of degree of consciousness, fear involving a conscious awareness of the nature of the stimulus and anxiety being fear in the absence of any known stimulus.

The experiment became an ethical issue of some magnitude. The analysts believed that after Watson's little experiment, Albert was unquestionably neurotic: that is, he had a disproportionate fear of a neutral and perhaps necessary stimulus. The thought that Albert had been made afraid, by the process of generalization, of not only white rats and rabbits, but people in white lab coats, like doctors, and perhaps even blondes, presented a disruptive influence on his life of such magnitude as was horrifying. In fact, the whole psychoanalytic movement and all of its strategies were based upon attempts to relieve anxiety through the process of psychoanalysis. Anxiety was considered to be a tenacious enemy with deep roots extending into the unconscious.

Watson inadvertently had challenged a major tenet of mental health by proposing and demonstrating a simplified model for the development of anxiety and fear. He demonstrated rather conclusively that full-blown, terrifying anxiety could be developed by simple classical conditioning. The question remained, however, as to whether the same strategies could be employed to break down the conditioned response which had been established.

Mary Cover Jones

Following Watson's work at the Johns Hopkins laboratory on analyzing the process by which fears are acquired in infancy, Mary Cover Jones (1924a) undertook a study of how children's fears could be reduced or eradicated. Using seventy children from three months to seven years of age, she studied several possible methods of eliminating children's fears under laboratory conditions. When the children reacted fearfully to such situations as being left alone, being in a dark room, being with other children who showed fear, or being presented suddenly with a snake, rat, rabbit, frog, or loud sound, she made attempts to remove their fear.

Not all of the methods tested were successful. She found children's fears could not be eliminated through disuse or by ignoring them, through verbal appeal or explanation, through repeated presentations of the feared object without some auxiliary support, through ridicule or teasing, or through distraction.

On the other hand, two methods proved distinctly successful in eliminating children's fears: direct conditioning and social imitation. To condition the child's response, Mary Cover Jones associated with the feared object a stimulus capable of arousing a positive reaction: in her laboratory experiments, she found feeding to be the most effective. By associating the feared object with the pleasurable activity of eating, she was able to eliminate the fear completely. Also she could eliminate children's fears through social imitation. By placing the frightened child in a group of youngsters who were not afraid, he learned that the feared object was not so fearful after all.

In her laboratory, Dr. Jones had found Peter, a thirty-four-month-old, healthy, normal, and interesting child who was well adjusted except for his exaggerated fear reactions. His fear of a white rat extended to a rabbit, a fur coat, a feather, and cotton wool, but he was not afraid of wooden blocks and similar toys. The child seemed an ideal subject for a study of conditioning as a technique for eliminating fear. And thus the stage was set for Mary Cover Jones (1924*b*) to present the sequel to Watson's Albert, a case to demonstrate deconditioning and extinction.

> Peter was put in a crib in a play room and immediately became absorbed in his toys. A white rat was introduced into the crib from behind. (The experimenter was behind a screen.) At the sight of the rat, Peter screamed and fell flat on his back in a paroxysm of fear. The stimulus was removed, and Peter was taken out of the crib and put into a chair. Barbara [a child without fear of the white rat] was brought to the crib and the white rat was introduced as before. She exhibited no fear but picked the rat up in her hand. Peter sat quietly watching Barbara and the rat. A string of beads belonging to Peter had been left in the crib. Whenever the rat touched a part of the string he would say "my beads" in a complaining voice, although he made no objections when Barbara touched them. Invited to get down from the chair, he shook his head, fear not yet subsided. Twenty-five minutes elapsed before he was ready to play about freely [M. C. Jones, 1924*b*, p. 309].

As Peter exhibited more fear of a white rabbit than he did of the white rat, the rabbit was used in the deconditioning process. Peter, along with three children carefully selected because of their complete lack of fear of the rabbit, was brought into the playroom daily for a play period. The rabbit was always present during part of this period. As Peter was desensitized, or deconditioned, the following progressive steps in toleration were observed:

A. Rabbit anywhere in the room in a cage causes fear reaction.
B. Rabbit 12 feet away in cage tolerated.
C. Rabbit 4 feet away in cage tolerated.
D. Rabbit 3 feet away in cage tolerated.

E. Rabbit close in cage tolerated.

F. Rabbit free in room tolerated.

G. Rabbit touched when experimenter holds it.

H. Rabbit touched when free in room.

 I. Rabbit defied by spitting at it, throwing things at it, imitating it.

 J. Rabbit allowed on tray of high chair.

K. Squats in defenseless position beside rabbit.

L. Helps experimenter to carry rabbit to its cage.

M. Holds rabbit on lap.

N. Stays alone in room with rabbit.

O. Allows rabbit in play pen with him.

P. Fondles rabbit affectionately.

Q. Lets rabbit nibble his fingers [M. C. Jones, 1924*b*, pp. 310–311].

Thus the experiment, terminated by Watson because of his subject's removal from the hospital, was continued by Mary Cover Jones through its logical sequence. Clearly, a child can be made afraid by simple conditioning—and fear can be removed by the same process.

Harold E. Jones

For a study similar to that of Watson and Rayner, Harold Jones chose Robert, "a child fifteen months of age, of a markedly stolid and apathetic disposition, able to walk, and possessing a speaking vocabulary limited to fewer than five words" (1931, p. 127). The laboratory situation involved an electric bell as the auditory stimulus to be conditioned and a mild electric shock as the unconditioned stimulus. Robert's initial reaction to the bell alone was indifference. After three repetitions of bell and shock simultaneously, however, five presentations of the bell alone produced a startle reflex such that an observer concluded that the shock had been administered all eight times.

After seventy-two hours, the sound of the bell resulted in momentary crying. "It should be noted that the conditioning was distinctly to the bell and not to the platform" on which the baby played during the experiment. "There was no conditioning against the total situation (of entering and playing in the room) and no indication that the experiment produced any harmful carry-over in the child's normal play activities" (p. 129). Thus Harold Jones, like Watson and Rayner, had demonstrated a conditioned emotional response to a neutral object.

Elsie O. Bregman

The startling success of Watson and Rayner and Mary Cover Jones depended to no small degree upon their fortunate choice of unconditioned stimuli—both the negative, the very loud noise, and the positive, social interaction. These two powerful unconditioned stimuli, together with a more or less neutral but somewhat positive conditioned stimulus, the white rabbit or white rat, made a sharp and clear presentation. To demonstrate how fortuitous this was, one need only examine the elaborate and careful study of Elsie O. Bregman, of the Institute of Educational Research at Teachers College of Columbia University.

Bregman had fifteen subjects, aged eleven to sixteen months. She used two positive stimuli, a baby's dumb-bell rattle and a music box; six neutral stimuli, geometric forms in three pairs; and one negative stimulus, a loud, electric, cowbell mounted on a small board hung on the back of the child's chair. Half the neutral stimuli were paired with a positive stimulus, half with a negative. Bregman reported that "comparison of the responses . . . before and after training fails to prove any evidence of the effect of joint stimulation" (1934, p. 196). Unable to get reliable conditioning of either a negative or a positive affect to the neutral stimuli, Bregman concluded:

> . . . changes in emotional behavior, in attitude and interest, are not as a general rule, at least, readily brought about by joint stimulation in early life, and that conditioning *per se* cannot be accepted as the cover-all explanation of the emotional modifications which take place during that period [Bregman, 1934, p. 196].

Bregman had failed to replicate the work of Watson and Rayner. Other investigators have determined since that pilot work needs to determine specifically whether the positive and negative unconditioned stimuli are of sufficient magnitude to produce conditioning, and also whether the neutral stimuli are readily perceived by the child. Harold Jones was able to replicate the results of Watson and Rayner by using a mild electric shock and an electric bell.

Arthur T. Jersild

Studying methods of overcoming children's fears, Arthur Jersild and Frances Holmes utilized data gathered from parents, school-age children, and adults, as well as from their experimental study of 105 children. Like Mary Cover Jones before them, they found unsupported verbal explanation and reassurance to be ineffective. They found the "most effective techniques in overcoming fears are those that help the child to become more competent and skillful and that encourage him to undertake active dealings with the thing that he fears" (Jersild and Holmes, 1935b, p. 102). They list three helpful techniques which, along with those of Mary Cover Jones, are forerunners of Wolpe's technique of systematic desensitization or reciprocal inhibition:

1. Prompt the child to acquire skills that may be of specific aid to him in coping with the feared situation.
2. Lead the child by degrees into active contact with and participation in the situation that he fears: presenting the stimulus at first in a less intense form, or without some of its most frightening features, or in conjunction with reassuring features, and then gradually introducing all of the conditions that initially evoked fear.
3. Give the child an opportunity to become acquainted with the feared stimulus on his own accord, by making it readily accessible to him in his normal environment, but under circumstances that permit him to inspect or ignore it, approach or avoid it, as he sees fit [Jersild and Holmes, 1935b, pp. 102–103].

Dorothy Marquis

Watson's experiment with Albert aroused the interest of Dorothy Marquis, who was impressed by the considerable argument in the literature. Since the cortex of the newborn infant was inactive, if not inoperative, and since Pavlov asserted that no new nervous connections can be formed except in the cerebral hemispheres, conditioning in the newborn theoretically was impossible. Marquis reasoned, however, that although the cerebral cortex is in maturity the dominant part, or the pace setter, of the central nervous system, it is not necessarily the dominant center during the early months of life. Just as the lower centers—the thalamus, midbrain, and medulla—are important to early reflexive behavior concerned with elimination, swallowing, sneezing, and so on, they might also serve as the locale for conditioned responses.

To test this hypothesis, Marquis used eight newborn children as experimental subjects in an extremely simple plan: their bottles always were preceded or accompanied by the sound of a buzzer. The experiment lasted the first ten days of the children's lives. During the experiment, in a small compartment controlled for temperature and lighting, the children were placed on a stabilimeter, which graphically recorded their movement. In addition, clinical notes were taken by the same observer throughout the period.

Two experiments served as controls. First, a flashlight projecting into the child's eyes and a hammer striking the end of a tin can were used to determine if, in the absence of conditioning, they would elicit the same general response as the buzzer. A second control was a group of four children, of about the same age, who were stimulated by the buzzer at feeding time without being permitted to feed immediately after.

Seven of the eight infants, after a period of three to six days, showed significant changes in reaction following the buzzer, while other stimulation produced no change in general activity or crying. The one child who failed to exhibit food-taking reactions to the buzzer was in generally poor physiological condition. He never seemed hungry, and was not as responsive to stimuli as the other infants.

In the control groups, stimulation unassociated with feeding failed to produce any change in general activity. And the four infants stimulated by the buzzer at feeding time without being fed immediately afterwards responded with increased general activity and crying throughout the nine-day period.

On the basis of these findings, Marquis concluded that:

1. A conditioned response of foodtaking reactions to the sound of a buzzer was established in seven out of eight newborn infants during the first ten days of life.
2. Conditioned responses can be formed in newborn infants, at least, by subcortical correlation.
3. Individual differences in learning ability are present even at this early age.

4. Systematic training of human infants along social and hygienic lines can be started at birth.
5. Since habit formation may begin so early, the sharp lines drawn by some writers in their classifications of some acts as instinctive and some acts as learned must be viewed with some hesitation [Marquis, 1931, pp. 488, 490].

Delos D. Wickens

Some years later, in the same laboratory, Delos and Carol Wickens (1940) studied the conditioning of children less than ten days old. Their subjects were divided into three groups of twelve infants each, one experimental and two control. All of the infants were initially tested to determine whether or not the sound of a buzzer produced an unconditioned response. The thirty-six infants chosen did not move their feet in response to the buzzer.

This carefully controlled study indicated that the experimental group did indeed show evidence of conditioning, extinction, and spontaneous recovery, but one of the control groups showed almost identical evidence. The authors concluded that a major portion of the apparent conditioning was the result not of stimulus pairing but of the sensitivity of the subjects. They concluded that the neonate is not readily conditioned, that maturational factors and attentional factors are so critical to the primitive nervous system of the newborn that learning at best is an unstable, overdetermined response.

Hanus Papousek

Although Wickens and Wickens's study raised some serious questions about the stability of conditioning in the newborn, a number of Russian and Czechoslovakian investigators continued to pursue the problem. One of the most precise and definitive studies was conducted by Papousek (1967), who reasoned, from the tradition of a cephalocaudal developmental pattern, that the head movement should be the most stable and well-developed movement at birth. More particularly, infant "rooting behavior," a wobbling and searching action of the head as he seeks the breast, is prevalent in a stable form during the first twenty-four hours after birth.

Papousek developed an ingenious experimental apparatus capable of measuring the slightest movement of the baby's head. The baby's trunk was contained on an inclined plane with the head resting on a separate cradle constructed from thermoplastic styrene for extreme lightness and lined with soft styrene foam padding. This separate cradle for the head was balanced in perfect alignment with the rotational axis of the child's neck to provide minimum resistance to his head movements. This sensitive balance provided a near-perfect vehicle for studying the particular type of head movement common in newborns (see Figure 21).

The children in Papousek's study were in a carefully controlled nursery setting in which extraneous stimulation was minimized during the course of the research. Under these circumstances, Papousek was able to demonstrate conditioning, extinction, spontaneous recovery, and re-extinction in all of his subjects. Papousek's study suggests that the in-

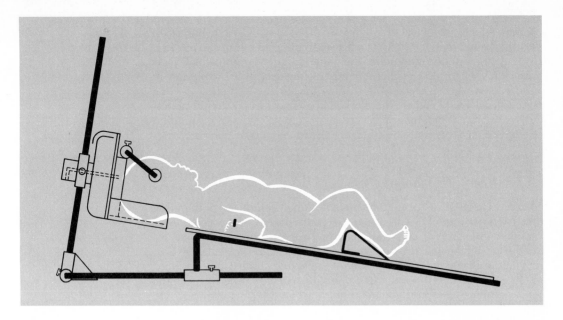

Figure 21

Experimental apparatus for studying conditioned head turning in infants. Reprinted, by permission of the publisher, from Hanus Papousek, Conditioning during early postnatal development, in Yvonne Brackbill and George G. Thompson (eds.), *Behavior in Infancy and Early Childhood* (New York: The Free Press, 1967), Figure 1, p. 265. Copyright © 1967 by Crowell-Collier and Macmillan, Inc.

stability of conditioning in the newborn may be due principally to interference from maturational and environmental changes.

FETUS RESPONSES

With a reasonably straightforward technique, Spelt (1948) attempted to demonstrate that the human fetus can be conditioned experimentally during the last two months of pregnancy. Applying pressure-sensitive tambour receivers to the mother's abdomen, Spelt used a loud clapper for the unconditioned stimulus and a mild vibrator for the conditioned stimulus. Using five fetuses between seven and nine months gestation age, he reported that with as few as sixteen paired stimulations he could produce a conditioned response to the vibrator alone. He also suggested that one of the fetuses retained the conditioning over an eighteen-day period.

He had three control groups. With the first, six subjects in the late eighth and ninth month of pregnancy, he tested the conditioned stimulus alone and found that the fetuses did not respond to the vibrator. With the second, a nonpregnant control of three subjects, he demonstrated that the mother's uterus did not become sensitized. Results from the third group of two subjects indicated that the clapper was an ineffective stimulus before the eighth calendar month of gestation.

A major methodological defect of Spelt's study was his failure to establish that it was not the mother who was conditioned. Imagine that the fetus's response to the loud noise, the unconditioned stimulus, is a jerking movement. The mother's uterus tends to constrict, to control, and to contain the fetus when it engages in sudden movements. If these jerking movements are aversive to her, the mother might well make accommodating movements in anticipation of the fetus's reaction. Thus the apparent conditioning of the fetus could be simply conditioned uterine contractions.

EARLY EMOTIONAL DEVELOPMENT

A major portion of the significant emotional responses dominating the affective repertoire of children is but a continuation of the generalization and discrimination of classically conditioned primitive emotional responses during infancy. Let us review some of the early speculation and research on the development of emotionality in young children.

J. B. Watson (1919) concluded that the natural repertoire of the newborn contained only three primary emotions: love, fear, and anger. He contended that the stimulus for the love response was tactile stimulation, stroking, caressing, fondling; that the fear response was produced principally by loud noises or sudden loss of support; and that anger was the reflexive response to firm physical restraint.

Two problems were almost immediately apparent in Watson's interpretation. Both of these were demonstrated clearly by Sherman (1927*a,b*). The first is that descriptions of fear, love, and hate are anthropomorphic when applied to infants. These terms have excess meaning in the adult world, and when applied to very young children, they have considerable excess meaning. The primitive responses of children are related much more directly to reflexes than to emotions: for instance, the fear response Watson described in great detail is more precisely the Moro reflex.

Second, the anger response is difficult to distinguish from the fear response and both seem to result from any sudden or intense stimulation. Sherman demonstrated that distinguishing the specific emotional response caused by a wide variety of stimuli is extremely difficult, even for trained judges. He found that both graduate and undergraduate students of psychology, medicine, and nursing failed to distinguish the cause of an infant's emotion, and failed to agree upon which emotion was being displayed. George G. Thompson summed up Sherman's findings as follows:

> As a result of his investigations, Sherman proposed a genetic theory of emotional development. He concluded that emotional behavior in the newborn infant is not differentiated beyond the simple feelings of "pleasant" and "unpleasant.".... With increasing maturation and experience the infant learns to make those responses that are more likely to attract and retain pleasant situations, and to avoid or resist unpleasant circumstances.... Sherman's theory of emotional development does not assume the presence of adult-like emotions in the newborn infant, thus avoids the fallacy of Watson's reasoning [G. Thompson, 1962, p. 282].

In his attack on Watson, Sherman laid the groundwork for Bridges's more plausible concept that emotional behavior develops along a single line. According to Bridges's theory (1930, 1932), a child's only emotion at birth is generalized excitement. The infant's emotions range from the tranquilized state of deep sleep to the extreme excitement, agitation, and discomfort associated with colic. Gradually, excitement becomes bifurcated into pleasure and displeasure. All positive emotions are further delineations of this positive state, which Bridges calls "delight," and all negative emotions arise from the negative state of "distress."

Her major thesis is that emotional responses are primitive and generalized in early infancy, and that they result principally from some large-scale physiological stimulation that induces a large-scale physiological response. Almost any strong stimulation is noxious to the infant. Thus, the Moro reflex, the unconditioned startle response to any large-scale stimulation, is the foundation upon which early unpleasant emotional responses are built. On the other hand, tactile stimulation, cuddling, holding, rocking, even feeding, tend to induce a relaxed state that provides the necessary basis for the development of pleasant emotional responses. The importance of tactile stimulation in the development of emotionality is shown clearly in the classic work of Harlow and Zimmerman (1959) and Montagu (1971).

The major portion of complex, adult-like emotional responses occurring in later childhood are assumed to stem from repeated conditioning. Personality theorists have suggested that part of the difficulty in the remediation of anxiety in adults is due to the long chain of conditioning that is difficult, if not impossible, to trace. The beginnings of emotional responses are obscured in early childhood, and the clinician is dealing with far-removed sequences of events. Most of our emotional responses result from classical conditioning, which perhaps explains their great tenacity.

THE BEGINNINGS OF BEHAVIOR THERAPY

After the rather clear demonstrations, by Watson and the Joneses, of the application of classical conditioning to the conditioning and desensitization of a child's emotional response to neutral objects, thirty years passed before the knowledge was put to practical use. Two reasons for this long delay were outstanding: one technical, the other philosophical.

On the technical side, positive and negative unconditioned stimuli for emotional responses are rather difficult to identify clearly and sharply. The complex array of human emotions does not result from one, or even several simple stimuli. Although Watson (1925) identified two negative unconditioned stimuli—loud noise and loss of support—that inevitably produced the fear response, positive unconditioned stimuli that tended to induce the opposite of a fear response, or what one might call a comfort response, were more difficult to identify. Generally, some type of verbal or tactile reassuring had been used: holding, cooing, talking, singing, rocking, cuddling. And the desensitization process, of course, depends upon some type of positive unconditioned stimulus. Experimental extinction, in and of itself, was slow and the undesired response was subject to spontaneous recovery. Although the negative emotional response of fear seemed to be under the control of the experimental investigator, other, more difficult to define emotions, such as apprehension or anxiety, were not as easily manipulated. Moreover, classical psychotherapists considered anxiety to be the basis of most emotional problems.

The second issue that delayed the application of learning theory techniques to mental health was philosophical. The mental health field was dominated, in the 1920s, 1930s, and 1940s, by the psychoanalytic movement, which was based on the fundamental tenet that most visible neurotic behavior, including fear, is not meaningful per se, but is merely symptomatic of an underlying problem. The symptoms are considered defense mechanisms, the individual's attempts to defend himself against anxiety. Neurotic behavior, such as a phobia, was considered analogous to fever in the physically ill: the fever is only symptomatic of some hidden, internal disorder that is the real problem.

The psychoanalytic concept held that the elimination of one symptom, or one specific fear or phobia, would simply cause a shift in symptoms. Suppose a child has an hysterical paralysis of his right hand because of an internal fear of failing an important examination. Psychoanalytic theory would hold that if you merely eliminated the paralysis of the right hand without dealing with the underlying fear of failure and inability to cope with competitive situations, the child might very well become hysterically blind. His hands might function, but he still would be unable to take the examination because he could not see.

The theory, which arose from Freud's experience with symptom transformation or symptom shift in the treatment of hysteria, was generalized to all kinds of emotional problems, and thus prevented behavioristic experimentation with emotional problems from proceeding. Learning theory was not applied to children's problems, then, until the 1950s, when three important developments considerably changed the emphasis in the mental health field.

Within a four-year span beginning in 1950, three critical events signaled the awakening of learning theory application in the field of mental health. The first of these was a classic translation of psychotherapeutic theory into learning theory language by two Yale professors, John Dollard and Neal Miller, colleagues of Clark Hull, the father of formal learning theory in America. The second was a controversial attack by Hans Eysenck on the outcome claims of psychotherapy. And the third was the discovery of thorazine, a psychologically effective drug. These three developments in the early 1950s resulted in a renaissance in the application of behavior theory and classical conditioning to the mental-health field.

Dollard and Miller

In *Personality and Psychotherapy*, Dollard and Miller (1950) examined the process of psychotherapy in terms of personality development from the point of view of social learning theory. Their contribution was immense, not so much because practical applications followed their text, but rather for their literate, imaginative translation of language, which gave convincing testimony that even so complex a process as psychotherapy could be translated into modern, definable, measurable terms. Part 4 of this classic text, "How Neurosis Is Learned," is a masterpiece of translation. In enlightened, operational terms, it struck at the core of the traditional terminology of psychoanalytic and classical psychiatry.

Very little research in fact resulted directly from Dollard and Miller's work, but their text provided the theoretical basis for much of the behavioristically oriented research of the late fifties. Out of Dollard and Miller's framework arose assumptions on which a behavioristic approach to psychotherapy could be based. Psychotherapy came to be defined as a set of procedures designed to eliminate undesirable responses, whether these responses be external, maladaptive behavior or internal tension. Psychotherapy was conceptualized as a learning process in which new learning or unlearning was used to remedy deficiencies.

Dollard and Miller identified four critical training situations in which the social learning that takes place affects the personality development of young children. First is feeding, where conflicts and attitudes arise as a result of the kind of learning that occurs. The second is cleanliness and toilet training, where again critical learning takes place and attitudes develop that affect adult behavior. Early sex training, which ranges from the masturbation taboo through sex modeling by personality to general attitudes toward sexual expression, is the third critical training situation. And the last is the anger-anxiety conflict, which concerns the relationship between anger and fear and frustration.

Thus the modern, behavioristically oriented theorist regards neurotic behavior the same as any other behavior: a learned set of responses. He emphasizes that this behavior resulted initially from various external events —through reinforcement, generalization, and contiguity—rather than from some internal, psychic phenomenon that cannot be observed. This model of neurosis rejects the disease model of mental illness, and instead speaks of neurosis as learned, maladaptive behavior. The objective of behavior therapy is, thus, to change overt, maladaptive emotional behavior.

Hans J. Eysenck

In his study of the effectiveness of various methods of psychotherapy available in the 1950s, Eysenck concluded that no one method was more effective than any other and, in fact, that the rate of spontaneous remission was nearly as high as remissions obtained by any method then in use. "Roughly two-thirds of a group of neurotic patients will recover or improve to a marked extent within about two years of the onset of their illness, whether they are treated by means of psychotherapy or not" (Eysenck, 1952, p. 322). Eysenck indicated that no one group in the mental-health field was justified in claiming an absolute answer or cure-all, and that psychoanalysts were not in a position to say that research using other techniques for dealing with emotional problems should not be undertaken, since psychoanalysis had not been demonstrated sufficiently superior to justify its maintaining control over treatment.

Eysenck was taken to task by several authors, most notably Hans Strupp, who reviewed "Eysenck's (1952) widely quoted survey, which capitalized upon and added considerably to the existing confusion" over the outcome problem in psychotherapy.

Furthermore, if two-thirds of all people who suffer from a "neurosis" "recovered" within two years "after onset," emotional disorder would scarcely be the serious problem which manifestly it is.... There is no doubt that Eysenck's zeal has led him to place the worst possible interpretation upon the results [Strupp, 1963, p. 3].

Eysenck responded to Strupp in kind:

In reply I would like to suggest that Strupp's review is, in the lawyer's phrase, irrelevant, incompetent, and immaterial.... Strupp clouds the issue by lengthy argument but fails to adduce a single study disproving my original conclusion, much strengthened since then by numerous more recent and better executed studies [Eysenck, 1964, p. 97].

Even so, "the questions raised by Eysenck (1952) ten years ago regarding the effectiveness of psychotherapy when compared with the effects of nontreatment can be rephrased today in much more sophisticated and scientific terminology, but they are still questions" (Bergin, 1963, p. 244), despite Eysenck's depressing view expressed in his quotation of Galen: "All who drink this remedy recover in a short time, except those whom it does not help, who all die and have no relief from any other medicine. Therefore it is obvious that it fails only in incurable cases" (Eysenck, 1960, p. 697).

Thorazine

The third major development in the 1950s was the discovery by pharmaceutical researchers of psychologically effective drugs. These drugs, which operate on the emotional centers in the brain and commonly are referred to as tranquilizers, antidepressants, and mood stabilizers, demonstrated that a considerable portion of the emotional problems prevalent today can be ameliorated through biochemistry. This discovery enabled physicians to manage a great many patients formerly referred to psychiatry. Alternate explanations of emotional problems became possible.

THE TECHNIQUES OF BEHAVIOR THERAPY

Joseph Wolpe

The most systematic account of behavior theory conditioning techniques for therapeutic purposes has been presented by Wolpe (1948, 1958), who uses various combinations of anxiety-reducing procedures to achieve counterconditioning, his technique of reciprocal inhibition. An incompatible emotional pattern, relaxation, is induced and then paired with gradually more intense emotional stimuli, until they induce no emotional disturbance.

In 1961, Wolpe culminated a dozen years of research following his 1948 doctoral dissertation on the application of behavior-oriented therapy to emotional problems:

The general idea of overcoming phobias or other neurotic habits by means of systematic "gradual approaches" is not new. It has long been known that increasing measures of exposure to a feared object may lead to a gradual disappearance of fear.... What is new in the present contribution is (1) the provision of a theoretical explanation for the success of such gradual approaches and (2) the description of a method in which the therapist has complete control of the degree of approach that the patient makes to the feared object at any particular time [Wolpe, 1961, pp. 200–201].

Wolpe named his therapy reciprocal inhibition after Sherrington's (1906) original description of the phenomenon. The essence of the treatment is nearly identical to Mary Cover Jones's desensitization process involving the presentation of two conflicting stimuli. The first is the anxiety-provoking stimulus, generally a conditioned stimulus that causes a rather extensive physiological and emotional reaction or response; the second is a relaxation-producing stimulus. The theory of reciprocal inhibition implies that the simultaneous presentation of these stimuli will cause a reciprocal inhibition process whereby the anxiety response is inhibited by the comfort response: "The framing of the reciprocal inhibition principle of psychotherapy . . . is that if a response inhibitory of anxiety can be made to occur in the presence of anxiety-evoking stimuli it will weaken the bond between the stimuli and the anxiety" (Wolpe, 1964, p. 10).

For a simple example, take a child afraid of dogs. Waldo has been knocked over and badly frightened by a puppy. The anxiety-provoking stimulus, then, is a jumping, dancing, bouncing puppy, which causes Waldo to show all manner of signs of tension and anxiety: sweating, crying, whimpering, retreating. The comfort stimulus on the other hand is his mother—holding, talking, caressing, rocking, reassuring. Now, if the mother, while providing the comfort stimulus, walks slowly toward the puppy, now confined in a box, Waldo will show no signs of anxiety until she gets fairly close to the box. The mother then stops, again comforts Waldo, maybe backs off a few feet, talks about the puppy, provides more comfort, and again moves forward. The mother is able, through the process of desensitization or reciprocal inhibition, to break down the conditioned anxiety response, the fear of the playful puppy.

Wolpe's major contribution was his recognition that the stimuli also could be manipulated mentally. In the security of the therapist's office, the patient can conjure up the anxiety-producing stimulus. His technique was to teach progressive physical relaxation, a strategy developed by Edmund Jacobson (1938) whereby one consciously relaxes to almost a hypnotic state. The assumption is that you cannot be both relaxed and anxious simultaneously. The subject is taught to relax, progressively, various parts of his body, starting with his toes and his legs, until he is relaxed totally and completely. The relaxed state is usually monitored by some type of physiological measure, often a heart-rate indicator. When he has reached a stable, relaxed condition, the therapist suggests that the subject now imagine a specific level in a preconceived anxiety hierarchy.

This anxiety hierarchy is established with the client's assistance. If one is afraid of dogs, the lowest level in the hierarchy might be finding dog hairs on the floor or seeing a dog's picture. Succeeding levels might be standing in the house and seeing a dog through a window or screen door, then standing outside while a dog is nearby on a leash or completely un-

fettered. One can actually imagine these experiences. Through the process of reciprocal inhibition, while very relaxed, tranquil, and secure, the patient can induce and defeat each succeeding level of the anxiety hierarchy.

The success of this vicarious experience in dealing with phobias has been demonstrated in numerous cases, most particularly with adults, but also with children. The crux of Wolpe's technique is the confrontation of an anxiety-provoking stimulus under circumstances in which the child can tolerate the anxiety. The more pairings of an anxiety situation under tolerable conditions, the less the fear. However, the further one moves from the simple laboratory situation, the more complex the problem becomes. Yet, more and more research is moving in this direction.

Wallace A. Kennedy

An example is a technique developed for the elimination of school phobia—a massive emotional and physiological reaction to school such that the child refuses to attend. The unconditioned, anxiety-producing stimulus is either the process of going to school or the process of being left there by the mother. The conditioned comfort reaction is firmness on the part of the parents. The child has learned that his parents are capable of protecting him from danger. When they are firm and sure in their actions, he feels secure. During the twelve years that the school phobia project (Kennedy, 1965) has continued, some sixty cases have been successfully treated by the desensitization method recommended by Mary Cover Jones and similar to Wolpe's.

THE PRACTICE OF BEHAVIOR THERAPY

The fact of conditioned responses in early childhood has been established. Classical conditioned responses are part of the early training of children; much of the learning that occurs in the first few months is a result

342

of classical conditioning. Thus far, our discussion has been confined to the nature of the classical conditioned response in young children: when it occurs, how stable it is, and the conditions under which it can be produced or eliminated. Let's shift from these important theoretical aspects of classical conditioning to a brief study of the practical applications of this technique as it affects the lives of children today.

What difference does it make, from a psychological point of view, that even in the first few weeks of life one can establish a conditioned response to a stimulus in the environment? Watson has demonstrated that classical conditioning can be used to establish both positive and negative emotional responses toward a neutral stimulus. The application of that finding is particularly important in clinical psychology. Let us look at some studies of the practical utility of a classical conditioned response during infancy and early childhood.

HEARING IN CHILDREN

Maternal diseases, such as rubella, frequently produce serious hearing losses in the newborn, especially when the mother is affected during the critical first three months of pregnancy, and certain hereditary patterns of deafness are identifiable. If a child is suffering from a serious hearing loss, particularly in certain tonal ranges, his speech development will be awkward and slow, and sometimes nonexistent. Therefore, hearing examinations are critical not only to test the gross hearing of a child, but also to determine his specific hearing range. A classical conditioning technique has been developed to determine the complete hearing range of newborn infants.

C. Anderson Aldrich

One of the first practical applications of classical conditioning was made by C. Anderson Aldrich (1928), a pediatrician at the Mayo Clinic, who showed that classical conditioning could be used to refine an old technique for determining if a very young child can hear. The pediatric examination previously had used a small dinner bell as the stimulus. The baby's visible response, the movement of his head or eyes, indicated that he could hear.

This, of course, depended upon the mood of the child, his cooperativeness, and especially the development of visual-motor coordination, which is independent of hearing itself. A child might be able to hear the dinner bell but might not be attending to it, or he simply might not tend to turn his head or move his eyes toward the sound. At best the old dinner bell was an imprecise instrument for determining gross hearing loss. But it was the preferred technique until the 1920s.

Aldrich set up a classical conditioned response to the old dinner bell. First he rang the bell, and then followed, a half-second later, with a pin scratch on the sole of the foot. He found that as few as twelve to fifteen combinations of the bell and pin were enough to elicit a reflexive withdrawal of the leg. "By mid-morning, after perhaps twelve or fifteen applications, the infant cried and drew up the leg when the bell was rung and the foot was not touched. No one could see the experiment without being perfectly sure that the child heard" (Aldrich, 1928, p. 37).

William G. Hardy

However, the old dinner bell is a very simple sound. Often, the major question of the audiologist is not whether or not a child can hear some tonal range from a dinner bell, but whether he hears the critical tonal range of the inflections in the human voice. Further refinement was therefore required in order to measure the full range of auditory insufficiencies in young children. A conditioned stimulus much more precise than a dinner bell was needed.

That precision was provided by William G. Hardy, an otolaryngologist and Director of the Hearing and Speech Center at Johns Hopkins University and Hospital, and his associates, beginning in 1947. Not only did Hardy refine the conditioned stimulus or sound source by utilizing a standard audiometer, but he made its use possible with very young children by developing the use of the psychogalvanic skin response:

> The idea is that, with the use of a pure tone as a warning signal a few seconds before the shock is given, a child can be conditioned so that significant skin-resistance changes are developed following the tone in anticipation of the shock.... In short, the child is conditioned to respond to the test-tone in anticipation of the shock. The shock annoys but it does not hurt; it startles but it does not traumatize [Hardy and Bordley, 1951, pp. 125, 128].

The psychogalvanic skin response, first demonstrated by Féré in 1888, is a change in electrical conduction of the skin due to sweating. This change can be detected by a sensitive amplifier and recorder and can be interpreted as a response to the stimulus. Mild emotional stimulation—such as mild shock, loss of support, or loud noises—produces a psychogalvanic skin response, called the GSR, which is usually measured on the palms of the hands or the ends of the fingers, where response to stress is highest. The technique involves the linking of an unconditioned stimulus (shock) to a conditioned stimulus (a tone from the audiometer) measured through response to the GSR.

By the process of stimulus generalization and reconditioning at various pitch and volume levels, a complete audiometric study of the infant can be performed. Hardy and his associates developed the technique for very young children who could not follow complex directions, and then demonstrated how the technique could be used to study the hearing of older children who were unable to respond because of handicaps such as palsy and mental retardation.

Bernard B. Schlanger

Some writers have challenged the utility of the GSR technique for handicapped children, indicating they have found it to be unreliable with very young children and most mental retardates. Nevertheless, in a careful study of the GSR technique with mentally retarded children, Schlanger (1961) achieved good results. His technique established the hearing loss of retarded children in spite of minimum cooperation from the subjects.

PHOBIAS IN CHILDREN

Lazarus and Rachman (1957) used Wolpe's desensitization technique with a fourteen-year-old boy who for four years had suffered from an intense phobia of hospitals and ambulances. The authors first constructed an anxiety-hierarchy scale for their subject's reaction to hospitals and ambulances. The hierarchy consisted of descriptions of disturbing situations, ranging from a relatively unthreatening one, such as "imagine an old ambulance in a junk yard," through increasingly higher and higher steps, such as "sitting beside the driver in a moving ambulance," up through "riding in an ambulance as a patient." At the same time, the boy was trained in deep-muscle relaxation, a kind of hypnotic technique in which the person learns a response antagonistic to the anxiety response. The experimenter and his subject moved progressively up the scale until, after just three sessions, the boy experienced little anxiety when he walked past an ambulance. After ten sessions he was able to visit a hospital. A four-month follow-up showed that the boy experienced little anxiety over either hospitals or ambulances.

Lazarus and Abramovitz (1962) reported successful desensitization of seven out of nine phobic children ranging in age from seven to fourteen years. Their method grew from Mary Cover Jones's "pleasant stimulus," through Jersild and Holmes's "gradual habituation," and Wolpe's "reciprocal inhibition," to their "emotional imagery" technique. Their study explored the possibility "of inducing anxiety-inhibiting *emotive* images, without specific training in relaxation." By emotive imagery, they refer to "those classes of imagery which are assumed to arouse feelings of self-assertion, pride, affection, mirth, and similar anxiety-inhibiting responses" (Lazarus and Abramovitz, 1962, p. 191).

The procedure is similar to that used with relaxation. A hierarchy of fear situations is made up as before. But instead of using relaxation to counterbalance the feared situation, the child is urged to imagine an anxiety-inhibiting response by thinking of his "heroes from radio, cinema, fiction, and sports." This systematic procedure, as in ordinary systematic desensitization, is repeated until the highest item in the hierarchy is tolerated without distress. Follow-up twelve months later revealed no relapses or symptom substitution.

ENURESIS IN CHILDREN

Nocturnal enuresis, or bed wetting, is probably the most common behavioral disorder now treated by a classical conditioning technique, although the most effective technique is a hybrid between classical and operant conditioning. Morgan (1938), Morgan and Witmer (1939), and Mowrer and Mowrer (1938), developed an efficient technique, using a classical conditioned-response procedure.

Bed wetting, except when there are kidney or bladder troubles, is usually caused by faulty training in the management of bladder tension. Ordinarily, pressure from his full bladder awakens the child during the night and he gets out of bed and goes to the bathroom. The enuretic child has learned to reduce the internal pressure by voiding in bed. This inappropriate learning usually occurred at an early age; the child never really learned adequate bladder control.

The Mowrers used water-sensitive paper placed on the bed under the sheet, a battery, and a bell. When the child began to urinate, the sensitized paper completed the circuit and rang a large bell, which immediately awakened the child. The bell is the unconditioned stimulus that elicits awakening. The conditioned stimulus is bladder tension; that is, the subtle internal cues enabling the child to detect that his bladder is filling. The pairing of the conditioned stimulus with the bell teaches the child to awaken when his bladder is full.

The picture is complicated somewhat, however, by the fact that the child's behavior causes the bell to ring. Technically, this is operant conditioning; it is considered classical conditioning because the child has no control over the filling of his bladder. The Mowrers believe that the few drops of urine that precede actual voiding are incidental, from the child's point of view, to the larger conditioned stimulus of bladder tension.

The point is not critical. The argument can go either way. Many of the more effective conditioning strategies described later in the text could be designed to be either classical or operant in format. The classical design is effective in the treatment of enuresis because the child does not have to awaken completely in order to avoid the conditioned stimulus. By partially awakening, he can maintain bladder tension and avoid ringing the bell entirely.

The inexpensive conditioning apparatus, complete with clear instructions, is available through several commercial catalogs. The success rate for the cure of enuresis through this strategy is high. Beforehand, of course, the child should be seen by a pediatrician to determine whether or not a urological examination is indicated. Although most bed wetting is not a medical problem, a routine consultation with a pediatrician is still very much in order.

SUMMARY

The present chapter represents a presentation of the complex role of classical conditioning in the understanding, prediction, control, and modification of the behavior of the child. Classical conditioning joined intelligence and achievement testing as a major methodological advance in the development of a scientific child psychology, which was removed from the cloud of mentalism and the mind-body duality of the nineteenth century. With the advent of classical conditioning, the mind became the brain that stored stimulus-response connections and registered probabilities. Thus the mind became merely a behavior-probability register that accumulated information about the environment and its significance to the individual. Free will, a concept related to dualism and said to separate man from the animal kingdom, was greatly reduced as an explanatory principle, and the parallel between the behavior of animals and that of humans became abundantly clear.

The major limitation of the method seemed to be the lack of opportunity to establish conditioned responses to meaningful stimuli because of the lack of their simultaneous occurrence. Much of the complex behavior in the repertoire of children does not occur in natural sequence, but must be built up out of small pieces of behavior. Some method of establishing these connections needed to be developed; some method that provided a greater range of response than the simple unconditioned response. With very young children, most particularly in the assessment of sensory response and the development and restructuring of basic physiological responses, classical conditioning had made its contribution, but a new technique was required if we were to apply our developing knowledge of learning to higher human responses.

Because psychology in the 1970s is so concerned about behavior, particularly adaptive behavior, there is a general reluctance to pursue, to consider, or even to be concerned today about classical conditioning. The early contribution of classical conditioning to the diagnosis of sensory deficit has been replaced with instrumental conditioning. With our interest in changing behavior or behavior modification, response discrimination and response generalization are the main thrust in psychology.

Why, then, a chapter entitled classical conditioning when classical conditioning does not change responses? It changes only signals that produce responses. Is not, after all, the instinctive repertoire of the child too narrow to be of much consequence?

Were we interested merely in externally obvious behavior, interest in classical conditioning long since would have waned into oblivion. But man is not simply a creature of habit. He is also a creature of emotions. He feels. He hates. He loves. He quakes. And these represent stimulus substitution, or classical conditioning.

We don't learn emotions—or, when we do, they are superficial, stylized, with a dramatic, false quality. What we learn are stimuli that evoke emotion; and we learn these early in life as we react instinctively to stimuli in our environment. Terror is not learned. Terror stalks from within. Terror is a reflex, a response built in from antiquity. The signal is learned and generalized and discriminated. The emotion can only be suppressed or acerbated. As a response, it is altered very little.

Classical conditioning is the acme of passive learning. Implied is an inability to cope, the necessity of enduring a lock-step certainty that some emotion-producing stimulus is on the way, its appearance signaled by some cue in the environment. What makes for problems is the often haphazard, unplanned, and unobserved pairing of the unconditioned stimulus for an emotion and a conditioned stimulus that brings forth the emotional responses. The child who buckles in a confrontation with the man up the street who yells at him, "Get out of my yard!" is tracing steps laid down in antiquity, using part of man's basic reflexive repertoire.

So long as the cause of positive and negative emotions is of concern to child psychology, the study of classically induced responses to conditioned stimuli will go on. It will not be as easy as research in operant conditioning, because the associations are early and the cues often trivial. But the search will go on. And the possibility exists that man, through his understanding of classical conditioning, can learn to live better with himself as he really is, to live a more happy, contented, rich emotional life avoiding the plague of unnecessary anguish in the face of a nonhostile environment.

REVIEW

British Associationism

The concept of associationism arose from man's theoretical efforts to explain the fact that apparently disconnected ideas are related in men's minds. James Mill felt that simple ideas become associated into more complex ideas. His son, John Stuart Mill, felt that simple ideas, which become associated due to contiguity, similarity, intensity, frequency, and inseparability, generated the more complex ideas. Alexander Bain felt that some neurological phenomena in the brain allowed the brain to parallel events in the world. The ever widening concepts of these three men laid the groundwork for Pavlov's classical conditioning.

The Conditioned Response

Conditioned/Unconditioned Response The invariable startle of an infant in response to a loud noise is an unconditioned response. He did not learn to startle; the behavior was automatic. But he can learn to startle to other stimuli simply by their being paired or associated with a loud noise: then his response has been conditioned.

Classical Conditioning Definitions

Classical Conditioning The process whereby a

neutral stimulus becomes conditioned to the point where a specific response is invariably associated with its presentation to the subject is classical conditioning. It is conditioning that implies a helplessness of the child and that accounts for perhaps all emotional learning during early childhood.

Conditioned Response The conditioned response in classical conditioning is always the same as the unconditioned response.

Conditioned Stimulus The conditioned stimulus has no particular significance for the organism until it is paired with a response-producing stimulus a sufficient number of times for the organism to perceive the connection between the two.

Extinction The breakdown of the conditioned response due to a lack of reinforcement is extinction.

Facilitation The temporary increase in the likelihood and magnitude of the conditioned response due to the addition of a second stimulus not previously associated with the response is facilitation.

Forgetting Forgetting is the extinguishing of a conditioned response due to a lack of practice.

Inhibition Inhibition is a temporary decrease in the strength of the conditioned response due to the presentation of a second stimulus that distracts from the conditioned stimulus.

Reinforcement In classical conditioning, reinforcement refers to the unconditioned stimulus, which can be positive or negative.

Respondent A respondent is "innate behavior regularly elicited by specific stimuli" (Reynolds, 1968, p. 8). A respondent is an unconditioned response.

Secondary Reinforcement A conditioned stimulus that signals the advent of an unconditioned stimulus can, in and of itself, provide secondary reinforcement. If turning on a light over the stove indicates that mother is preparing the meal, the child is willing to wait patiently after the light is turned on, i.e., the turning on of the light itself brings satisfaction.

Spontaneous Recovery The reappearance of an extinguished conditioned response upon the reappearance of the conditioned stimulus, in the absence of any reinforcement, is spontaneous recovery.

Stimulus Discrimination The ability to isolate the essential characteristics of the conditioned stimulus is stimulus discrimination.

Stimulus Generalization Stimulus generalization is the spread of effect once a simple conditioned response is established. When a stimulus is generalized, any stimulus similar to the original conditioned stimulus will induce the conditioned response.

Unconditioned Response The unlearned response invariably made by the organism when presented with an unconditioned stimulus is an unconditioned response. An infant invariably startles when he hears a sudden loud noise: the startle is the unconditioned response; the loud noise is the unconditioned stimulus.

Unconditioned Stimulus The stimulus that invariably results in an unlearned response from the organism is an unconditioned stimulus. It can be positive, such as food, or negative, such as shock.

Early Emotional Development

A major portion of the significant emotional responses dominating the affective repertoire of children is but a continuation of the generalization and discrimination of classically conditioned primitive emotional responses during infancy. Coupled with this, remember that early social deprivation is most damaging to the affective responses. That most of our emotional responses result from classical conditioning early in childhood perhaps explains their great tenacity.

The Beginnings of Behavior Therapy

Even after the clear demonstrations by John B. Watson and Mary Cover Jones of the application of classical conditioning to the conditioning and desensitization of a child's emotional response to neutral objects, thirty years passed before the knowledge was put to practical use. Two reasons for this delay were outstanding: one technical, one philosophical. Technically, positive and negative unconditioned stimuli for emotional responses are difficult to define clearly and sharply; complex human emotions do not result solely from several simple stimuli; the problem was a complex one indeed. Philosophically, the mental health field was dominated by psychoanalytic theory, which held that most visible neurotic behavior, including fear, is not meaningful per se, but is merely symptomatic of an underlying problem; curing the symptom did not cure the problem.

Thirty years later, the discovery of psychologically effective drugs, such as thorazine, demonstrated that a considerable portion of the emotional problems prevalent today can be ameliorated through biochemistry. Physicians could now manage many patients previously referred to psychiatry. Alternate explanations of emotional problems became possible.

The Techniques of Behavior Therapy

Anxiety Hierarchy An anxiety hierarchy is made up of various levels of stimuli for a specific phobic response, ranging from the least anxiety-producing to the greatest anxiety-producing.

Reciprocal Inhibition Reciprocal inhibition is a counterconditioning technique in behavior therapy, developed by Wolpe, whereby an incompatible emotional pattern, relaxation, is induced and then paired with gradually more intense emotional stimuli until no emotional disturbance is elicited. The assumption is that you cannot be both relaxed and anxious at the same time.

NAMES TO KNOW

British Associationism

JAMES MILL James Mill, grounding associationism in the principle of fusion, used the color wheel to demonstrate how distinct colors blend into one when the wheel is rotated rapidly. Interested in ideas rather than sensations, James Mill, English philosopher, historian, diplomatist, and economist, believed the color wheel served as a convenient model for understanding the mysterious bond between ideas presented simultaneously or in association with each other.

JOHN STUART MILL John Stuart Mill carried his father's concept further and laid down laws of association: similarity, contiguity, intensity (later discarded), frequency, and inseparability. John Stuart Mill, English philosopher, logician, and political economist, felt that complex ideas are generated by simple ideas, rather than that complex ideas consist of simple ideas; that, the colors of the wheel generate white when the wheel is spun, but they are not white.

ALEXANDER BAIN Alexander Bain, Scottish philosopher and psychologist, believed only two laws were fundamental to associationism: contiguity and similarity. Bain believed that conscious attention to

contiguity was necessary. And he believed in psychophysical parallelism: that mental events in the brain parallel the events in the outside world.

The Conditioned Response

EDWIN B. TWITMYER Influenced by the tradition of associationism, Edwin Twitmyer failed to see the implications of his serendipitous discovery of the conditioned response. He and his professional colleagues thought it simply another example of an association, this time between the sound of a bell and a hammer blow just below the knee. The possibility of observing, measuring, and controlling the elements of association by controlling the stimulus just didn't occur to him or to his peers.

IVAN P. PAVLOV When Ivan Pavlov, Russian physiologist and father of classical conditioning, made his now famous serendipitous discovery of the conditioned reflex, he recognized its potential. He began to manipulate not only the nature of the stimulus, but also the effect of the time interval between the presentation of the conditioned stimulus and the unconditioned stimulus, food, which invariably produced salivation, the unconditioned response. He laid the groundwork for much of modern psychological theory and practice.

Early Theoretical Experiments

JOHN B. WATSON In his presidential address to the American Psychological Association, John B. Watson called the attention of American psychologists to the conditioned reflex. He and Rosalie Rayner conducted the famous experiment with Albert and the white rat. They demonstrated that fear could be conditioned to a previously neutral stimulus and that reasonably permanent conditioned emotional responses could be established.

WILLIAM H. BURNHAM William Burnham studied at Johns Hopkins under G. Stanley Hall and was appointed chairman of the Department of Pedagogy at Clark University while Hall was President. Burnham's was perhaps the first systematic attempt to base a theory of the prevention and treatment of psychopathology on learning principles (1924). He encouraged Florence Mateer to modify Krasnogorskii's research on the conditioned response.

CLARK HULL The study of conditioned reflexes and learning was the chief interest of Clark L. Hull, although he did research in many areas. Hull (1943) offered a deductive theory accounting for the major phenomena of classical and operant conditioning. He hypothesized that learning was a gradual process, rather than a sudden or insightful one. His learning theory dominated early research in learning and influences it even today.

physical responses

HEINRICH BOGEN Heinrich Bogen confirmed on a child Pavlov's observations on the dog—conditioned salivation in response to stimuli signaling feeding.

NICKOLAI I. KRASNOGORSKII N. I. Krasnogorskii, Russian pediatrician and physiologist who studied under Pavlov, provided a more reasonable method for studying conditioning in children through salivation: the swallowing reflex.

FLORENCE MATEER Florence Mateer modified and repeated Krasnogorskii's experiments, suggesting that susceptibility to conditioning increased with age.

emotional responses

JOHN B. WATSON John B. Watson conducted the first experiment with emotions using nine-month-old Albert, whose fear of a loud sound was conditioned to a white rat and then to other furry objects; he demonstrated that reasonably permanent conditioned emotional responses can be established. Watson's experiment produced an ethical issue of some magnitude because mental health tradition held that anxiety was the major cause of all neuroses and psychoses, and that the difference between anxiety and fear was only in degree of consciousness; Watson demonstrated rather conclusively that full-blown, terrifying anxiety could be developed by simple classical conditioning.

MARY COVER JONES Mary Cover Jones, following Watson's work, undertook to reduce children's fears under laboratory conditions. She found that children's fears could not be eliminated through disuse or by ignoring them, through verbal appeal or explanation, through repeated presentations of the feared object without some auxiliary support, through ridicule or teasing, or through distraction. By deconditioning three-year-old Peter's fear of a white rabbit, she found that children's fears could be eliminated through direct conditioning and through social imitation.

HAROLD E. JONES Harold Jones conducted an experiment similar to Watson's; he demonstrated a conditioned emotional response to a neutral object.

ELSIE O. BREGMAN Elsie Bregman demonstrated that the startling success of Watson and Mary Cover Jones was due to their fortunate choice of unconditioned stimuli—both the negative, the very loud noise, and the positive, social interaction; for conditioning to take place, the child must be able to perceive the stimuli.

ARTHUR T. JERSILD Arthur Jersild found verbal explanation and reassurance to be ineffective in reducing children's fears. He found the most effective techniques for reducing fears to be those "that help the child to become more competent and skillful and that encourage him to take active dealings with the thing that he fears." His research, along with Watson's and Mary Cover Jones's, was the forerunner of Wolpe's technique of systematic desensitization or reciprocal inhibition.

newborn responses

DOROTHY MARQUIS Dorothy Marquis demonstrated that conditioned responses can be established in newborn infants, and concluded that individual differences in learning are evident even at this age.

DELOS D. WICKENS Delos Wickens concluded that a major portion of the apparent conditioning in the newborn was the result not of stimulus pairing but of the sensitivity of the subjects. Wickens concluded that the neonate is not readily conditioned, that maturational and attentional factors are so critical to the primitive nervous system of the newborn that learning at best is an unstable, overdetermined response.

HANUS PAPOUSEK Hanus Papousek demonstrated conditioning in the newborn in a carefully controlled study, suggesting that instability of learning or conditioning in the newborn may be due principally to interference from maturational and environmental changes.

fetus responses

DAVID SPELT Although he seemed to have demonstrated conditioning in the fetus, David Spelt did not have controls that established clearly whether the mother was conditioned rather than the fetus.

Early Emotional Development

JOHN B. WATSON John B. Watson, the founder of behaviorism, concluded that infants are born with three primary emotions: love, fear, and anger. Love is generated by tactile stimulation; the stimulus for love is cuddling, caressing, fondling. Fear is generated by loud noises or sudden loss of support. Anger is generated by firm physical restraint.

MANDEL SHERMAN Mandel Sherman pointed out that infantile emotions are not that distinguishable; that fear, love, anger are anthropomorphic when applied to infants; that both "fear" and "anger" responses are aroused by any intense or sudden stimulation. Sherman felt that the primitive responses of young children are related more to reflexes than to emotions; Watson's fear is more precisely the Moro reflex. He concluded that "emotional behavior in the newborn infant is not differentiated beyond 'pleasant' and 'unpleasant'"; that as an infant matures, he "learns to makes those responses that are more likely to attract and retain pleasant situations and to avoid or resist unpleasant circumstances."

KATHARINE BRIDGES Katharine Bridges theorized that an infant's only emotion at birth is generalized excitement; the other extreme being deep sleep, or a tranquilized state. Gradually excitement becomes differentiated into pleasure and displeasure: all positive emotions grow out of this primitive pleasure state—delight; all negative, out of displeasure—distress. She theorized that emotional responses are primitive and generalized in early infancy, that they result principally from some large-scale physiological stimulation that induces a large-scale physiological response. Almost any strong stimulation is noxious to an infant; thus the Moro reflex, the unconditioned startle response, is the foundation upon which early unpleasant emotional responses are built. Conversely, tactile stimulation, cuddling, holding, rocking, feeding, tend to induce a relaxed state, which provides the necessary basis for positive, pleasant emotional responses.

The Beginnings of Behavior Therapy

JOHN DOLLARD and NEAL MILLER In 1950, Dollard and Miller translated psychotherapy in terms of personality development from the point of view of social learning theory. Psychotherapy came to be defined as a set of procedures designed to eliminate undesirable responses; psychotherapy was conceptualized as a learning process in which new learning or unlearning was used to remedy deficiencies. Dollard and Miller identified four critical training situations in which the social learning that takes place affects the personality development of young children: feeding, cleanliness and toilet training, early sex training, and anger-anxiety conflict. For Dollard and Miller, neurotic behavior is the same as any other behavior—a learned set of responses.

HANS J. EYSENCK Hans Eysenck concluded that no one method of psychotherapy was more effective than any other, thus freeing the field to experiment on therapy techniques.

The Techniques of Behavior Therapy

JOSEPH WOLPE Joseph Wolpe developed the technique of reciprocal inhibition: a counterconditioning technique whereby an incompatible emotional pattern, relaxation, is induced and then paired with gradually more intense emotional stimuli until no emotional disturbance is elicited. The assumption is that you cannot be both relaxed and anxious at the same time. Wolpe demonstrated that stimuli could be manipulated mentally by using an anxiety hierarchy to enable patients to defeat succeeding levels of anxiety. The crux of Wolpe's technique is the confrontation of an anxiety-provoking stimulus under circumstances in which the child can tolerate the anxiety.

WALLACE A. KENNEDY Wallace Kennedy used a behavior therapy technique to eliminate school phobia. Instead of relaxation, Kennedy used firmness on the part of the parents; the child has learned that when his parents are firm and sure in their actions, he feels secure.

The Practice of Behavior Therapy

hearing in children

C. ANDERSON ALDRICH Hearing in young children

is extremely important in developing speech and language; therefore hearing examinations are critical not only to test gross hearing, but to test specific hearing range. C. Anderson Aldrich, a pediatrician, used classical conditioning techniques to refine sharply the hearing examination of a very young child.

WILLIAM G. HARDY William Hardy used the psychogalvanic skin response and classical conditioning techniques to refine further the audiological examination of a young child.

BERNARD B. SCHLANGER Bernard Schlanger used the GSR technique successfully to test the hearing of retarded children in spite of minimum cooperation from the children.

phobias in children

ARNOLD LAZARUS Arnold Lazarus and Arnold Abramovitz reported the successful desensitization of phobic patients by their emotive imagery technique. Instead of training their subjects to relax, they trained them to imagine emotional images—such as their heroes in sports or entertainment—that would inhibit anxiety. Lazarus and Rachman used Wolpe's desensitization technique successfully in the treatment of an ambulance-and-hospital phobia.

enuresis in children

O. HOBART MOWRER O. Hobart Mowrer developed a successful technique, a hybrid between classical and operant conditioning, to help enuretic children.

Operant conditioning and language acquisition

D iscussion in Chapter 7 centered around the development of simple responses associated with reflexes, or innate responses to specific environmental stimulation. Generally these are automatic, self-protective responses, which may or may not currently have utility for the child. They are the type of response required for survival in a primitive environment and, more often than not, also are required in the first few hours of life. The palmar, plantar, patellar, and Babinski reflexes are all of this quality. A sudden loud noise elicits the Moro embrace reflex. The stroking of an infant's palm elicits a grasping reflex. These responses, part of the natural repertoire of all normal children, are unlearned and highly stylized. Through learning, they can be associated with more complex stimuli, but the initial responses are uniform throughout the species.

Conditioning occurs through the contiguous association of a neutral stimulus, the conditioned stimulus, with an unconditioned stimulus that evokes a natural reflex. This highly stylized, universal, reflexive response is called, in operant terms, a respondent. Thus a stimulus can become conditioned as a result of close temporal proximity to the unconditioned stimulus, which is invariably followed by a respondent.

The present chapter is concerned with operant conditioning—or, as it is sometimes called, instrumental conditioning—and its application to language acquisition. Operant conditioning differs from classical conditioning on one major point. In the strictest sense, in classical conditioning the unconditioned response, the respondent, invariably follows immediately the unconditioned stimulus and is, for the most part, a basic reflex or a basic physiological response that may not now have any adaptive significance and may not now change the environment in any way.

Operant conditioning is a learning process in which the behavior of the subject is modified as a consequence of the results from his own behavior. A child learns that when he smiles his environment changes in a gratifying way. A smile causes parents to do pleasant things such as picking him up, or hugging him, or giving him a cookie, or bouncing him on their knees. In a sense, then, the child has operated on his environment such that he receives a reward as a result of his behavior. In another sense, the child's smiling is regulated by its consequence: smiling increases because it produces gratification.

Although the distinction is slight, a highly significant, practical difference exists between the two techniques of conditioning. In classical conditioning the responses induced are, for the most part, reflexive and rather simple, and must be in the natural repertoire of the subject. In operant or instrumental conditioning, the responses may be built step by step in successive approximations to the point where highly complex behavior may be introduced. The child learns that certain behavior of his becomes effective in modifying his environment. The acquisition of language may be understood and, in fact, may be greatly stimulated by using the operant model.

OPERANT CONDITIONING DEFINITIONS

The language of operant conditioning must be understood clearly, because it is a precise language with special meaning. Here, then, are operational definitions of operant conditioning terminology, often called Skinnerian terminology because of the pioneering work in the field by B. F. Skinner and his associates.

Operant

An operant is any behavior that modifies the environment in which the child lives. It is not, strictly speaking, a response to a stimulus on its first occurrence. In fact the operant may precede the stimulus, and frequently does, and is, often as not, a random response in the child's repertoire. It is, however, most importantly a response that does in fact change the environment in some noticeable way. The change may be subtle and the child may take some time to learn that the operant has potency, but nevertheless it has.

The infant, for example, has a normal repertoire of babbling, cooing, clucking, sucking, and blowing sounds—all part of his preverbal behavior. Poets, and perhaps some psychologists, have waxed eloquent about the evolutionary significance of language, but electromagnetic recordings of thousands of hours of children's babbling seem to indicate that their sounds, within certain limits, are nearly random.

> Actual transcription of infant vocalizations . . . was used by the writer in a study on the development of vocalization in a single infant during the first year of life. . . . The first observation of note was that within the data for the first two months of life may be found all of the speech sounds that the human vocal system can produce, including French vowels and trills, German umlaut and guttural sounds, and many that are only describable in phonetic symbols. This is in flat contradiction to the notion that the infant gradually "becomes capable" of making various sounds. A more accurate statement would be that the comparative *frequencies* of various speech sounds change as development proceeds; owing to a number of anatomical factors, there is variation in the *probability* of given combination of jaw, lip, and tongue positions being assumed (and hence the probability of various sounds being produced) [Osgood, 1953, pp. 684–685].

Two sounds, however, begin to surface rather early in the response repertoire of the child. Both are vowel sounds: *ma, da.* Now, when Waldo first emits the sound "dada," wonderful things begin to happen. Mother picks him up with a great deal of joy and rushes to father: "Listen to what Waldo can say!" With a little bit of luck, it comes again: "dada." Father beams proudly, picks up Waldo, and talks to him, saying over and over again, "dada, dada." From Waldo's point of view the environment has been changed radically as a result of a little lever he stuck in the crevice of life. He has found that a random sound "dada" has tremendous power to affect his world for the better. "Dada," then, is an operant, and Waldo has taken his first step toward building the powerful tool called language.

This is a two-way street. The child operates on his environment by saying "dada" and having his parents do tricks; and the parents manipulate the child into saying "dada" by their reinforcement.

Reinforcer

A reinforcer, then, is any event, any stimulus in the environment that affects the rate of a given operant. If the operant becomes more frequent following the occurrence of a stimulus, this stimulus is a positive reinforcement stimulus, or a positive reinforcer. If, on the other hand, the disappearance of the stimulus results in an increase in the probability of the operant occurring, it is an aversive stimulus, or negative reinforcer. Note that a reinforcer always is defined in terms of its effect on the subsequent frequency of the response immediately preceding it.

In the example above, the response of the parents is a positive reinforcing stimulus for the child if the child says "dada" more often because of it. From the Skinnerian point of view, the definition of a stimulus as being positively or negatively reinforcing depends upon its actual effect in controlling the rate of the response with which it is associated. One does not, for example, assume that candy is a reinforcer for children unless one demonstrates that feeding or not feeding children candy can increase certain responses on their part. Will children work for candy? Will they work to avoid candy? In either case, candy is a reinforcer, either positive or negative. "In any case of reinforcement, an operant occurs, has an effect on the environment, and, because of the effect, occurs more frequently in the future" (Reynolds, 1968, p. 9).

Certain behaviors of parents have been demonstrated to be positive reinforcers for children's talking. Almost any social activity on the part of the parents that involves talking to the child and playing with him serves as a positive reinforcer. Almost any low-level background noise serves as a positive reinforcer for children's talking.

Discriminative Stimulus

In addition to positively and negatively reinforcing stimuli, discriminative stimuli in the environment provide cues as to when a given reinforcer is likely to occur—or, more particularly, when a given response is likely to be reinforced. Thus, on a long winter's day, when the parents begin to put on their coats and hats and go to get baby's coat and hat, the likelihood of the child being picked up if he extends his arms is great. Thus the dressing-to-go-outdoors behavior of the parents becomes a discriminative stimulus for the operant of lifting one's hands. This operant is positively reinforced by the parent's picking up the child. The infant also learns that when he is placed in the high chair with a bowl of food before him and all the family members are seated around the dinner table, his raising his arms is unlikely to be reinforced by his being picked up. He learns to discriminate through cues when reinforcement is likely to occur.

The discriminative stimulus can also be manipulated in such a way as to control behavior. For instance, one can lower one's voice, settle into a favorite chair, and behave in the mysterious fashion that indicates the story hour is about to begin, and a group of children will quiet down quickly, gather in a small circle, and prepare to give sustained and intense concentration to the words of the adult. This is called stimulus control.

Discriminative stimuli tell the child when talking is an operant. He learns to discriminate when the parent is listening, when he is apt to respond to verbal communication. Parents often hamper language growth in children because of their hurried manner indicating that they will not respond to verbal operants on a low key, but will respond only to high-key vocalization such as crying or angry outbursts.

Conditioned Reinforcer

Although some stimuli in our environment have intrinsic power of reinforcement without any learning—food, water, certain tactile qualities of cloth, and certain rocking motions, for example—these stimuli, called primary or unconditioned reinforcers, are rare indeed. The overwhelming majority of the stimuli that regulate the behavior of children acquire reinforcing properties early in the child's life through learning and experience. These are called secondary or conditioned reinforcers.

An example of a conditioned reinforcer in the early life of a child is the magical dime placed under his pillow when he has performed an exceptionally good deed during the day. Because of its shiny quality, a dime perhaps has some intrinsic value, some primary reinforcing quality. But when a child first goes into a store with a dime in his hand and learns the magical properties of a dime turned over to the store clerk, the dime begins to have secondary, or conditioned reinforcing qualities. The dime now has control over the rate of occurrence of some desirable behavior on the part of the child.

Language too becomes a powerful conditioned reinforcer. The words "thank you" from a parent are perhaps intrinsically reinforcing because of the animation, sparkle, and warmth with which they are said, but their real reinforcing power comes when the child begins to understand that several thank you's will probably lead to a more tangible reward, such as a caress or a cookie. Children then will work for a thank you.

Partial Reinforcement

Partial reinforcement, an important concept in operant conditioning, refers to situations in which the response is followed by reinforcement less than 100 percent of the time. On occasion the child engages in an act with an expectancy of reinforcement that does not occur. Learning acquired and maintained under conditions of partial reinforcement differs from learning acquired under conditions of 100 percent reinforcement. The most noticeable difference is resistance to extinction.

Verbal practice in the absence of reinforcement is an example of partial reinforcement. The child makes a sound, such as "dada," over and over again, and only occasionally, after the first excitement, does the parent reinforce the child. This partial reinforcement, however, encourages the steady stream of language.

Extinction

The extinction of a response in operant terminology, as in classical terminology, is the discontinuance of the response from the child's repertoire. Resistance to extinction refers to how long the response continues in the absence of reinforcement.

In early language development, the application of extinction principles comes into play when children curse. Young children, experimenting with sounds or imitating their illustrious father, tend to pick up certain Anglo-Saxon phrases that are recognized if not completely understood by Aunt Martha when she visits. These little words can be eliminated by the process of ignoring or not reinforcing them, and they will go away. The parents' attempts at punishment for these "naughty" terms are so fraught with ambivalence that inadvertent partial reinforcement probably occurs, which in turn gives rise to the problem of resistance to extinction and to spontaneous recovery. These two developments, the reader may remember, will most likely occur when there is some added excitement in the environment, such as a birthday party.

Accidental Chaining, or Superstitious Behavior

A reinforced response is often part of a series of actions chained together by some temporal or logical continuity with the result that the entire chain or sequence of behavior is reinforced.

Most parents are familiar with the I'm-sorry routine. The operant in this case is the child's apology for doing something wrong. The parent reinforces the apology, cuddles the child, and forgives him, "Oh, that's all right." The parent is then dumbfounded when the child does the same naughty thing again: he kicks the puppy, then runs over to the parent, smiles brightly, and says, "I'm sorry." An accidental chaining of responses—kicking the family dog, running to the parent, smiling, and saying "I'm sorry"—has been forged.

A second example, one which provides an explanation for another rather strange behavior pattern of children, is the working-up-to-a-spanking routine. Parents often report that when things have not been going very well between parent and child for some time, when hostility has been in the air, the child will suddenly become extremely provocative and pushy, with the result that the parent loses control and spanks the child.

When the spanking is over and the child is punished, tension in the home is reduced considerably. The child is now accepted, and the parent, often as not acting out of a sense of guilt, is especially kind to the child. Peace and harmony reign.

The child has learned to step up his badness and provoke a spanking, all without any logical understanding of what is taking place. The better learning would be for him to accept his responsibility for doing ugly things and to apologize for his misdeeds. Instead, he has developed a pattern of superstitious behavior that will follow through into a very poor, fight-and-make-up adjustment in marriage. Much of the undesirable behavior of children can be explained on the basis of this accidental chaining.

Let us examine one other example of how pathology develops as a result of accidental chaining. Mother is off in the bedroom doing a little mending, and Waldo has been on his own for a few minutes. He is entertaining himself rather well when he notices a jar of candy on top of the piano. He goes to the piano and carefully closes the cover over the keys. He then slides the piano bench out from under the piano, climbs first on the bench, then on the closed key box, and very carefully stands up and opens the candy jar, takes out two pieces of candy, one for himself and one for his baby brother playing in another room.

He then carefully closes the candy jar, turns, and is about to step down from the piano when his elbow inadvertently brushes against the very small and, to him, somewhat ugly clay vase. Unbeknown to Waldo, this vase is an expensive porcelain gift from his mother's favorite aunt and it has great sentimental value for her. At the crash, mother comes rushing into the room and upon seeing the shattered vase, is absolutely overwhelmed with rage and grief and shock and finally, with all this welling up in her, she decides not to discipline Waldo for fear that she will "kill him," and says instead, "you just wait 'til your father comes home."

Waldo, somewhat traumatized by all this, decides to make up. All afternoon he proceeds to do a number of helpful things around the house. He picks up all the toys in the toyroom, he cleans off the table, he straightens up the kitchen. All afternoon he engages in a number of highly desirable behaviors. Each time he does one of these excellent tasks, he runs to his mother to show her what a good boy he has been and she merely snarls.

Finally father, who has had a bad day at the office and who is most anxious to get out of the car and into the den, after pausing briefly at a certain cabinet, is met instead by a wife who has again welled up into a tirade and, like a banshee, is wailing and shrieking through the story of the agony of the broken vase and is insisting that father immediately lay waste to Waldo. Sizing up the situation very quickly, recognizing that it is not to be delayed, that he must "back up" his wife, father yells at Waldo, takes him into the bedroom, and gives him a spanking.

Now in the mother's eyes Waldo has been spanked for breaking the vase. But let's look at what Waldo has actually been spanked for. In the first place, Waldo has been spanked for using extremely good judgment, engineering, and great care in climbing on the piano without harming the keys, by getting the piano bench located carefully in the center so that he wouldn't fall. For this he has been punished. Waldo has opened the candy

jar very carefully and taken out only two pieces of candy, one for himself and one to share with his baby brother. For this he has been punished. Waldo has closed the candy jar and very carefully climbed down to make sure he didn't hurt himself. For this he has been punished. Without even realizing he did it, Waldo brushed against what in his eyes was a very ugly vase. For this he has been punished. Waldo has done a number of very mature tasks all afternoon, helping his mother clean the house, being very pleasant and easy to get along with. He has demonstrated some new and mature language growth. For all this, he has been punished. Waldo has seen his father come home and get out of the car. And for this he has been punished.

The whole chain of events has been punished and at no point was the essential message relayed to Waldo that certain valuable, fragile pieces of furniture and accessories should be very, very carefully avoided lest he damage them. All the emotion and yelling and screaming has been associated with an event much more easy to detect, father's coming home. Furthermore, he has learned that there is no way to appease a harried mother when he has an accident. These are the seeds of adult neuroses.

Aversive Stimulus

In Skinnerian terms, an aversive stimulus acts as a reinforcer when its disappearance increases the probability of occurrence of a specific response. Loud noises, either intermittent or continuous, are generally viewed by children as aversive stimuli. Children will work in order to turn them off. A vacuum cleaner run in another room causes interference with TV cartoon-viewing on Saturday morning. This induces the children to perform tasks in order to get the vacuum cleaner turned off. It is amazing how quickly children can clean up a living room under such a stimulus.

Contingency

Contingency refers to the chaining of an environmental event with a behavior such that it does in fact follow the behavior but need not. If a child holds up his hands to be picked up, his parents may pick him up. The contingency is extremely likely or probable, but it does not necessarily occur. Being picked up is contingent upon raising one's hands. In a broad sense, contingency is responsible for determining or shaping behavior.

Shaping

In operant conditioning, shaping is the process by which a given response is refined and made more precise by regulating the reinforcement so that it occurs when the subject is engaging most precisely in the behavior desired. Remember the childhood game "hotter, hotter"? One child is supposed to perform a specific act: for instance, he is supposed to sit in a chair, fold his arms, and rock back and forth. The group, as he tries different things, tells him whether he is getting hotter or colder. As the child learns the rules of the game, he will first locate the correct position in the room, by moving around the room and listening to cues from the group, "hotter, hotter," or "colder, colder," until he finds himself in front of the chair. Finally he sits in the chair and begins to go through various postures and positions, all of which are responded to by the group, until finally, through a series of successive approximations, he arrives at the point at which he has performed the desired act.

The shaping process is continuous in language development as the child comes closer and closer to correct enunciation and use. In shaping language the reinforcement must lead the child into the best approximation he can make. The baby talk in which many parents indulge is a sure method of delaying the shaping process and of adding confusion to language acquisition.

Dependency

In Skinnerian terms, dependency refers to the fact that a specific event, by the nature of the situation, must follow upon specific behavior. If a child puts his hand on a hot stove, he will be burned. In language development, dependency does not play as important a role as contingency. The contingent behavior of parents reinforces the child's use of particular words and phrases.

Spontaneous Recovery

Following extinction, that is, after the subject no longer engages in the unreinforced behavior, a rather peculiar phenomenon, called spontaneous recovery, occurs. After a period of time, the extinguished response will reoccur in the absence of reinforcement, and although it will rather quickly extinguish again without reinforcement, for some time this response will remain in the repertoire of the subject and occasionally surface.

Spontaneous recovery is under the control of some cue variables, the most obvious of which is some sudden change in the environment. For example, a child who has learned not to cry, whose crying behavior has been extinguished by nonreinforcement or by punishment, particularly in the case of a male child, will cry again as a result of some generally exciting or traumatic event in the environment. Children who are ill and generally feel bad can resort to crying behavior that had been extinguished for months or even years. Changes in the environment can also result in a child returning to old, extinguished behavior that once was reinforced by primary and then secondary reinforcement.

In more precise terms, spontaneous recovery refers to the subject's response to a set of environmental variables or cues initially associated with reinforcement. Previously, the child cried in any distressing situation and was comforted. He is now exposed to a new and unusually traumatic set of cues, which resembles the infantile situation, and he again cries.

Stimulus Discrimination

Stimulus discrimination is the process by which the subject increases his rate of response in the presence of one stimulus and decreases it in the presence of a similar one. The distinction is made regarding the stimulus that is reinforced. An example is a young child's response to his bottle.

Occasionally, because the room is hot and the bottle has been lying undetected in the corner of his bed, the milk sours. As a result, the milk forms an observable, irregular pattern on the inside of the bottle. The child learns that a milk bottle with an irregular coating on the inside tastes bad, and rejects this bottle although he eagerly accepts one that does not have the irregular pattern on the inside. He has learned, then, to discriminate successfully a cue that determines whether or not he will receive reinforcement.

The child learns to discriminate his "dada" from that of other children. He learns not to toddle up to strange men in the grocery store, grab them by the leg, and say "dada." This particular discrimination is greatly encouraged both by his mother and by the somewhat hasty withdrawal of the strange man.

Stimulus Generalization

Stimulus generalization, on the other hand, refers to the ability to recognize a commonality among cues that indicates that apparently dissimilar objects have some common quality. An example is the ability of the child, after very few experiences, to recognize candy in a wide variety of forms and colors and shapes and wrappings. He recognizes the commonality of sweetness in all its forms.

Schedule of Reinforcement

A term with special meaning in operant conditioning is schedule of reinforcement. One of the major contributions of operant conditioning was the discovery that the relationship between the response of the organism and the frequency of reinforcement affects the speed with which the response is learned and the length of time it will persist in the absence of reinforcement, i.e., its resistance to extinction. In the main, schedules of reinforcement are significant under conditions of partial reinforcement. When reinforcement is 100 percent, there is, of course, little room for variety. There are two kinds of schedules: those based on ratios, and those based on intervals.

Fixed-Ratio

In a fixed-ratio schedule of reinforcement the subject is not reinforced for every response, but on the basis of a fixed number of responses, such as every fifth trial. Usually the subject is not introduced to a fixed-ratio schedule immediately, but only after the initial shaping, usually done on a 100 percent schedule, has taken place. The general effect of a fixed-ratio schedule is that a subject works hard, produces many responses during a short period of time on a stable basis, and that the response is highly resistant to extinction, particularly when the schedule is very lean. The fixed-ratio schedule of reinforcement is the familiar piecework schedule: the child is paid for so much work, given a dime for each basket of leaves he rakes up, taken to the movies after he has read three books. The reward is proportional to the amount of work done: the more work, the greater the reward.

Fixed-Interval

In the fixed-interval schedule of reinforcement the subject again is not reinforced for every response, but only after certain intervals of time. The result of such a schedule is a highly variable work rate. The individual tends to slow down immediately after reinforcement and to speed up just prior to the time for the payoff. If the paymaster comes out every half hour to pay those who are raking leaves, he will soon discover that there is a great flurry of activity just before he enters the yard.

Variable-Ratio

In the variable-ratio schedule of reinforcement, the ratio between responses and payoff is different from time to time. On some occasions the subject is paid off every third trial, and on some occasions he is paid off on every twentieth trial. This is typical of the "one-armed bandit," or slot machine. Another example is a child's asking to stay up later. The parents usually say no and give a long explanation about the need for sleep for growing bodies and how sleep helps the disposition. But every now and then parents get worn down, they relent, and let Waldo stay up. This kind of parental behavior leads to behavior from Waldo that is highly resistant to extinction and prone to a great deal of superstitious behavior or accidental chaining. The child comes to believe, rightly or wrongly, but mostly wrongly, that something he is doing is affecting the likelihood that the payoff will come on the next trial.

Such a schedule, then, generates a wide variation in the type and intensity of the response. To return to the leaf-raking project, in the variable-ratio schedule the children do not really know how many basketloads of leaves they must rake in order to be paid off, as it varies from time to time. The lack of knowledge of the circumstance that produces the variability is the factor responsible for the increase in superstitious behavior, such as piling the leaves up in a high stack rather than a wide stack, filling the baskets very full rather than even, raking leaves in one section of the yard rather than in another.

Variable-Interval

In the variable-interval schedule of reinforcement, the payoff comes after a certain interval of time, but the subject does not know when. The reinforcement is also independent of the amount of work done, but this is not explicit. In the case of the leaf-raking, the children do not know when father will come out and reward or punish them, and thus they tend to keep up a stable work schedule of raking leaves. The superstitious behavior still exists, except now it is related to time expectancy.

Punishment

Punishment is used in an attempt to reduce the rate of responding. It is the "technical term for the presentation of an aversive stimulus following and dependent upon the occurrence of an operant" (Reynolds, 1968, p. 111). The effect of punishment depends upon many variables.

The application of operant conditioning principles to the acquisition of most complex motor responses and habits is rather easy to comprehend, but one behavior of man separates him uniquely from all other species. Although, undoubtedly, some communication exists among all animals, and although, undoubtedly, some animals have a rather complex communications system, no other species has a complex, symbolic language facility. The uniqueness of speech in man always has separated him from his closest cousins in the animal kingdom, but the magnitude of the gap has often been overlooked by those anthropological scientists who have been overawed by man's prehensile development which led to tools. MacDougall, as early as 1913, put the problem in bold relief:

> The beginning of speech is the most momentous event in the history of the child. Its understanding is a key to the whole storehouse of knowledge, and upon its use all human fellowship depends. As the means of social intercourse, the repository of learning and the general instrument of intelligence, the invention of language constitutes the greatest single achievement of human evolution [MacDougall, 1913, p. 29].

THEORIES OF LANGUAGE DEVELOPMENT

Such complex language requires a complex system of acquisition. Social-learning theory, based on operant conditioning, has the greatest likelihood of offering an acceptable explanation for this human phenomenon, although other explanations are offered in the literature.

Mowrer's theory originated from his work with talking birds. A bird learns to talk, according to Mowrer, through the process of associating the sounds the trainer makes with the satisfaction received from food, water, and attention. "In terms of learning theory, what has happened is that initially neutral sounds, by virtue of their occurrence in temporal contiguity with primary reinforcements, have acquired secondary reinforcing properties" (Mowrer, 1952, p. 264). He concludes that birds copy human sounds because they derive satisfaction from so doing; they do so on an autistic basis, for self-satisfaction.

Mowrer suggests that the same sequence holds also for human language acquisition. Up to the time the child learns to put words together to make original language, Mowrer believes, birds and babies learn the same way. He feels that the autistic aspect of language learning is a necessary, built-in mechanism. "When one considers how unlikely it is that a baby or a bird would ever, in the course of purely random behavior, produce word-like noises which could then be specifically rewarded, it becomes apparent how necessary is some mechanism of the kind just described" (1952, p. 266).

The example of deaf children is used by Mowrer to drive home his point.

> The fact that congenitally deaf babies babble very little, if any, and do not, without highly specialized instruction, learn to talk at all indicates how crucial is the capacity to hear and inwardly enjoy first the pleasant, reassuring voices of

others and then one's own somewhat similar sounds. Although congenitally deaf children usually have completely normal voice organs and although their parents would only too gladly reward them for using these organs to make word-like noises, the fact that such responses, because of the deafness, are not autistically satisfying to the child is a crucial handicap [1952, p. 268].

N. Miller and Dollard place more emphasis on the part the mother plays:

Since the mother talks to the child while administering primary rewards such as food, the sound of the human voice should acquire secondary reward value. Because the child's voice produces sounds similar to that of his mother's, some of this acquired reward value generalizes to it.... From this hypothesis it may be deduced that children talked to while being fed and otherwise cared for should exhibit more iterative and imitative babbling than children not talked to while being rewarded [1941, p. 277].

Still another theory is produced by Lenneberg, who proposes that "the ability to acquire language is a biological development. The basis for language capacity might well be transmitted genetically.... It seems as if language is due to as yet unknown species-specific biological capacities" (1964a, pp. 78–85). He does not believe that language development affects intelligence, and cites studies of congenitally deaf children to show that the absence of language neither affects nor depresses their cognitive skills (Furth, 1961; Rosenstein, 1960). Dollard and N. Miller, on the other hand, state that "without language and adequate labeling the higher mental processes cannot function" (1950, p. 15).

Actually, both of these supposedly different views could be accurate. One does not have to speak a word to understand its meaning; one does not have to read aloud to be able to read. Lenneberg uses the word *language* to mean "spoken language"; Dollard and Miller use *language* to refer to the symbolic presentation of ideas and abstractions. In normal usage, language is spoken, as well as written and read.

Although social-learning theory based on operant conditioning offers the greatest likelihood of an acceptable explanation for language acquisition, this explanation is not completely satisfactory either. Something about the human child's cortical organization causes him to be different from all other animals. We do not know just what this structural difference is, but it is a factor that cannot be explained by any theory of learning. As Hymes has said.

There must be some kind of distinctive mechanism, peculiar to the human brain, which is appropriate to the processing of speech. One must somehow account for the fact that, when children have heard a lot of speech, they start to talk; whereas, if apes hear the same noises, they do not talk. A "language generator" must be built into the brain and set to operate independent of any natural language. The character of possible language, or the set of possible grammars, must somehow be represented in the brain. In the broadest sense, the language generator must contain the information processing procedures which any human organism will use when exposed to some speech community. The language generator is either initially or through maturational processes primed to go off when suitable samples of speech are presented to it, and this has little to do with learning. This is not to say that man has *a priori* knowledge of any particular language. The particular language, particular grammar and phonological system, are *learned*. When we talk of language acquisition, it is often in the sense of the child's internalization of the particular grammar to which he has been exposed [Hymes, 1964, pp. 113–114].

Our discussion keeps this limitation in view. Obviously some unique language generator accounts for the functional difference between the language utilization of a very young child and that of any of the language imitators. For example, the myna bird, with great effort, can learn all the speech qualities of human language and can even recite short but complex paragraphs beyond the capacity of a three-year-old child. W. M. Mann, Director of the National Zoological Park of the Smithsonian Institute, trained a myna bird to say, "How about the appropriation?" "These verbal sound patterns were made by the bird on a signal from Dr. Mann when he was entertaining the Director of the Bureau of the Budget at the Zoo" (Carmichael, 1964, p. 4).

But when the chips are down, when his life depends upon it, the myna cannot attract the attention of his caretaker by reaching into his memory bank and pulling out a simple operant, the simple word *water*. And thus he dies. Not because of any problem in articulation, but because he lacks the operant function of language. He cannot move from speech imitation into language.

We must understand the abstract nature of language and differentiate it from communication, which is part of the repertoire of most animals. No one will dispute that a bird can be taught to say "water," or make his needs known in the normal course of things by vigorously pecking on his water dish. The functional use of language, the combination of abstractions involved in the use of a noun as an imperative or as an operant, differentiates language from vocalization.

> Language is not only our chief means of understanding things not in our immediate environment but also our chief vehicle for thinking and reasoning. Development of reasoning is directly related to development of language abilities; reasoning is, in fact, considered an inner language [Garrison, Kingston, and H. Bernard, 1967, p. 177].

> Both learning and maturation are necessary conditions for the development of language, but neither is sufficient [McNeil, 1970, p. 1062].

STAGES IN LANGUAGE DEVELOPMENT

How language is acquired has interested researchers of many generations. Most recently, learning principles as defined by Skinner, bridging the gap between Pavlov's conditioned responses and Thorndike's puzzle boxes, have provided an impetus for language acquisition research.

Many investigators have studied the acquisition of language by children, and all have concluded that speech develops in definite stages. Myklebust (1954) describes three stages in language development: inner, receptive, and expressive. Language is used autistically as described by Mowrer during the inner stage. Language is used to understand others during the receptive stage. And language is used to make others understand during the expressive stage.

Earliest Vocalization

The earliest vocalization of the human infant is unlearned and organically based. Studies of the vocalization of infants born to deaf and hearing parents and of deaf and hearing children have found essentially no differences in the language patterns of the two groups during the first three months of life. During the first thirteen weeks, fussing sounds, crying, whimpering, and cooing were the most prevalent. These related to the physical comfort of the child, his drive (measured in terms of hours since feeding, minutes since being changed, and so forth), and seemed completely independent of any social reinforcement.

Mandel Sherman's early research on emotional development in infants demonstrated that the cry of an infant per se provided little information about its cause to even skilled observers. Thus the mother who knows her infant's voice, and what he is "saying," also knows her infant's schedule and knows that it is time for him to be hungry, or wet, or both. Hearing the voice out of context is quite another matter.

The most effective way to manipulate vocalization during the first thirteen weeks is by meeting the infant's physical needs. Social reinforcement of a differential nature seems to have little effect upon the actual quality of the vocalization. The evidence supports the contention that verbal behavior of children up to the age of three months is controlled by maturation. The only social modification is in the amount, not the quality, of vocalization.

Babbling

At three months, infants begin to make social responses. An important study that sets the stage for our discussion of the operant nature of early vocalization was performed by Weisberg (1963), following one by Rheingold, Gewirtz, and H. Ross (1959). The question was whether social reinforcement influences the rate at which three-month-old infants vocalize. The first age at which the rate of infant vocalization can be influenced by an adult, not through primary reinforcement but rather through his presence, would set a beginning point for our study of language training.

No one will deny that rate of vocalization can be influenced by primary reinforcement from birth on via classical conditioning and social modeling. A pin prick, a pinch, or the withholding of food will bring about a massive increase in vocalization. But what about the presence of the adult? Rheingold demonstrated that "the social vocalizing of infants, and, more generally, their social responsiveness may be modified by the responses adults make to them" (Rheingold, Gewirtz, and Ross, 1959, p. 73). Rheingold concluded that an infant's vocal behavior in the third month could be brought under stimulus control; that is, it can be increased by social stimulation. This led her to the conclusion that the everyday caretaking of mothers is a reinforcing stimulus by the third month.

Weisberg found that once the child had become familiar with the experimental surroundings, a responding adult could increase the child's rate of vocalization, while a nonresponding adult could not. Social stimulation noncontingent upon vocalizing by the infant tended to have little effect, as did the nonsocial stimulus, a door chime; neither seemed to reinforce vocalization in three-month-old infants. Dodd (1972), studying older infants, nine to twelve months, concluded that social and vocal elements were necessary to stimulate vocalization: social-vocal behavior from adults increased the number of vocal utterances, and their length, but did not yet produce imitation.

Shortly after thirteen weeks, the voice pattern of the young child begins to change and take on the babbling quality, which, to naive observers seems to resemble adult speech. At this stage, the parents begin to "recognize" words and phrases as they listen to and talk to their children. Actually, according to acoustical studies, the natural babbling that begins in the third month bears little resemblance to adult speech. But what the parent thinks he hears can make a great deal of difference in the life of the child. Regardless of whether or not a three-month-old infant actually can speak, the parent begins the slow process of differential reinforcement on the basis of what he thinks he hears. Once the parents begin to "understand" what the child is "saying," they begin to reinforce certain patterns of babbling.

Thus the expelling sound "dada" does not have to have the pure tone qualities of the vowel sound in the adult repertoire. This particular babble is given instant and strong reinforcement every time it appears. Thus, the potential of babbling is evident. It becomes the first step in the development of an operant.

At the babbling stage a significant difference develops between the vocalization of children whose parents are deaf and those whose parents can hear, and between deaf and hearing children. In the babbling stage, environmental stimulation begins to affect the language development of young children.

In his study of speech disorders in deaf children, Lenneberg notes that the practiced observer can detect differences between hearing and deaf children as early as the sixth month, when they are well into the babbling stage. The first differences are more in quantity than in quality, however. "A hearing child at this age will constantly run through a large repertoire of sounds whereas deaf children will be making the same sounds sometimes for weeks on end and then, suddenly change to some other set of sounds and 'specialize' in these for a while" (1964b, p. 154).

He notes that no sound preference is typical of the deaf child. Not until much later does the typical abnormally pitched voice characteristic of deaf children make its appearance. When the voice comes under cortical control, audition is the major guide to speech. When the vocalizing is in response to some strong emotion, control returns to the subcortical centers, and the emotionally upset, hearing child sounds very much like the unemotional deaf child.

Osgood (1953) reports that the first control achieved over sound is volume. During the second month, a child produces the same sound repeatedly but at differing volumes. The second control is over pitch, which begins during the third and fourth months. During the fifth month, control of sequence begins to appear. This is when the babbling stage begins. All of these different stages in sound control seem to be "practiced" by the child purely for his own pleasure. "The baby's discovery that he can produce a sound is sufficient reason for its practice" (Krech and Crutchfield, 1958, p. 461).

The babbling stage is all-important in the development of language. "The enjoyment of the patterns of speech in themselves and the enhanced skill in producing these patterns will contribute to a child's language. In particular, they open the way to the intervention of others" (Lewis, 1963, p. 21).

Imitation

Thus far we have discussed several related facts. First, between three and six months of age, the average parent begins to feel that the vocal behavior of the child has meaning: that is, that the child is saying words. Second, social reinforcement tends to increase the rate of vocalization. What remains to complete the package is to demonstrate that social reinforcement in the early months affects not only the quantity, but the quality of vocalization. Imitation begins to come into effect here.

Imitation is a process parallel to operant conditioning, but not independent of it. Some confusion and lack of clarity exists in the literature regarding the relationship between imitation and reinforcement. Children, and most social animals, seem to derive some pleasure, or intrinsic reinforcement, from the act of imitation itself, regardless of any external reward. The remarkable amount of repetition and imitation in which young children engage is sufficient evidence to suggest that not all of it is operant: that is, not all imitation can be accounted for by immediate external reinforcement. Watching a baby with a mirror for a while is sufficiently convincing that imitation does occur in the absence of reinforcement.

In the final stage of beginning language, social reinforcement becomes essential. This is when the difference between deaf and hearing children, and children with deaf and hearing parents, becomes evident. From babbling, the child turns to imitation. From imitation comes the growth of meaning in language.

VARIABLES IN LANGUAGE DEVELOPMENT

A child is born a speaker.... From birth he vocalizes and responds to sounds.... The child utters sounds and responds to the human voice, his mother responds to his sounds and speaks to him. If any of these four necessary conditions is impaired, the child's linguistic growth may suffer [Lewis, 1963, pp. 13, 14].

Two basic assumptions have been made regarding the acquisition of language: first, that a language activator in the human brain, at a certain level of maturation, motivates the human child to develop language and accounts for the wide range of sound production unique to humans. This language activation is instinctive, probably biochemical, and is independent of early experience though perhaps not independent of such environmental factors as nutrition; second, that language quickly becomes an operant for the child. The development of language is very much dependent upon circumstances that provide for the child's developing confidence in the power of this operant. Let us examine some of the factors that affect the development of language.

Stimulation

Stimulation has been shown by many researchers to exert a necessary influence upon language acquisition. Studies of maturational deficiencies in institutionalized children have pointed up the language deficits in these understimulated children. Reading to children has been demonstrated to increase their vocalization. Language training obviously increases performance, and, as obviously, is stimulation. Children who receive little verbal stimulation for language during their first three years suffer what seems to be a permanent deficit in language ability.

Socioeconomic Status

In all comparisons, children of parents in professional groups are superior in their rate of acquiring the sounds characteristic of adult speech, in the extent of their vocabularies, in the length, completeness, and complexity of sentences they use, and in the number of informative statements they make and questions they ask [Landreth, 1967, p. 192].

Cultural differences in the acquisition and utilization of language make for a high correlation between socioeconomic status and language development. This high correlation may well depend upon many interrelated variables. Such cultural dimensions as nutrition, medical care, and exposure to disease in both prenatal and postnatal life play a role in the development of the underlying dimension of intelligence that affects language acquisition.

A second aspect of cultural differences in the acquisition and utilization of language is the effect of the language skills of the model. R. Hess and Shipman (1965a,b) ingeniously demonstrated the cultural dimension of language use by engaging mothers from four socioeconomic levels and their four-year-old children in simple tasks. The mothers were taught three simple tasks and then required to teach these tasks to their children. Correct performance required the mother to verbalize the task to the child, who had to understand what to do from the mother's verbal communication.

The study results indicated that lower-class mothers lacked the basic vocabulary to explain simple tasks and thus required nonlanguage cues for communication. This lack of language utilization in the home, as demonstrated by these tasks, is one of the most obvious causes of the lack of verbal facility in culturally deprived children. Cultural deprivation includes language deprivation. Many studies have demonstrated the superiority of the language environment in upper socioeconomic homes. Language is the predominant operant in upper-class homes, whereas in lower-class homes nonverbal communication is the primary operant.

Bernstein (1961a,b), like R. Hess and Shipman, found that working-class families use words mainly to denote objects and action. Middle-class families use them more often to indicate relationships. This difference is responsible for the differences in speech patterns and thinking processes.

The same problem that exists in making racial comparison on intellectual factors exists to an even more complex degree in making racial comparisons in language facility. The confounding of socioeconomic variables and the problem of dialects and general social enrichment make comparisons based on race alone impossible. There is no convincing evidence of any differences in language facility due to race per se. But the black child in America enters grade school with a serious language deficit. Evidence indicates that this language deficit begins to occur between the ages of two and four. One of the strongest arguments for the establishment of public early-childhood education is that language training can make a substantial difference in the performance of disadvantaged children.

Sex

American girls usually develop language faster than boys. The female in the American culture is encouraged to make use of language in all areas. Doll play, table games, staying in close proximity to mother, all tend to give the girl more experience with language. In addition, several studies have suggested that in the early years, at about the time language acquisition is becoming the primary task of childhood, girls have a far greater capacity for concentration. Boys are more apt to be superior in physical activites, to be playing nonverbal games, or games that do not emphasize verbal facility. Two boys can spend the morning in a sandbox, in great concentration, making a tremendous variety of exquisite vocalizations of hundreds of truck and tractor sounds, and never say a single word of conversation. In the meantime, their younger sister talks herself nearly hoarse, trying vainly to reassure her doll that she will somehow get over the serious physical affliction that has struck her down. These sex differences in language acquisition and utilization have been demonstrated across cultural lines in every subculture in America.

Family Constellation

A long series of studies describes the relationship between birth order and family constellation to language development. At this point, after over one hundred years of observation, no reliable data suggest any differences, at least up to the age of school entrance, in the language development of only children, first-born children, and children with many siblings. However, consistent evidence indicates that twins are retarded in language development through the preschool years and, furthermore, that triplets are even more retarded in language development than are twins. The evidence indicates that the major problem arises from the increased nonverbal communication among these children. The nonverbal operants become dominant in early life and this habit is not broken easily.

CHARACTERISTICS OF LANGUAGE DEVELOPMENT

The characteristics of language development have been stated most succinctly by Catherine Landreth (1967, pp. 184–188). A child learns simultaneously the phonology, morphology, syntax, and prosody of language. His first words are concerned with here and now. Gradually they begin to deal with the past and the future, the unseen and the imagined. His first words have a telegraphic quality and are dominated by nouns and verbs. He understands phonemic contrasts before he is able to produce them. He uses words concretely before he can use them abstractly. His learning requires him to be creative. He induces grammatical rules from the sentences he hears. He progressively adds adjectives and adverbs to his vocabulary. He uses correct tense when he understands time relationships. He gradually adds nested sentences. His speech contains fewer tangles as he grows older.

Taine, a French literary critic and historian, in reporting on personal observations of one infant girl "whose development was ordinary, neither precocious nor slow" (1876, p. 252), observed the developmental characteristics outlined by Landreth. In commenting on his granddaughter's creativity, he said:

> In short, example and education were only of use in calling her attention to the sounds that she had already found out for herself, in calling forth their repetition and perfection, in directing her preference to them and in making them emerge and survive amid the crowd of similar sounds. But all initiative belongs to her [1876, p. 253].

Taine viewed the development of speech as inevitable:

> In short, a child learns a ready-made language as a true musician learns counterpoint or a true poet prosody; it is an original genius adapting itself to a form constructed bit by bit by a succession of original geniuses; if language were wanting, the child would recover it little by little or would discover an equivalent [1876, pp. 257–258].

Robert MacDougall characterizes children as being able to master language quite easily. However, there are a few rough spots on the road: "Resemblance to other words leads to wholesale misconception. 'Lava,' wrote one child, 'is what the barber puts on your face'; 'the equator,' said another, 'is a menagerie lion running around the middle of the earth'" (MacDougall, 1913, p. 35).

Another characteristic of the child's use of language is his delight in sound and imagery. Hall and Piaget both point this up in sensitive studies of the intelligence of children.

REINFORCEMENT OF LANGUAGE SKILLS

Several studies of language skills have concluded with suggestions for improving children's language development. One such was Liyamina (1960), who ended his report with six suggestions.

1. Begin early the use of audible models. Talk with the child even before he can talk with you.
2. Name objects for the child and encourage him to repeat the names.
3. Encourage him often to use the words he knows.

4. Don't rush him. Give him adequate time to say what he wants to say.
5. Encourage him to pronounce correctly the words he uses.
6. Encourage him to use his vocabulary in the correct grammatical context. Teach him the correct way from the very beginning.

Landreth (1967, pp. 209–212) also listed several aids to language development.

1. Improve the parental model.
2. Encourage communication and expression.
3. Give the child experiences he can talk about.
4. Encourage him to listen.
5. Encourage speech as a substitute for action.
6. Use exact terminology.

Speech develops through reinforcement of specific sounds. Once the child's sounds begin to be understandable, parental reinforcement becomes even greater. Through successive approximations, the child's speech gradually is shaped by the parents' reinforcement. Language development can be greatly simplified if the parents will but follow several rules easily identified in terms of operant psychology.

SPEAK CLEARLY. The more care the parent takes in enunciating, the slower and more distinctly he speaks, the easier imitation becomes.

SPEAK CORRECTLY. The rule of successive approximation makes it essential that the parent does not downgrade his speaking to imitation, but rather lets the child adjust. For example, the child, in trying to imitate the word *water*, in the early stages will double the first sound and say "wawa." Parents, who think this is cute and downshift to the babytalk of "wawa," do two things immediately. First, they shift the cue word, so now the child is no longer hearing *water* to imitate. Second, they are setting a precedent for a pidgin English or babytalk that has all the demands of a second language that will have to be learned and unlearned.

SPEAK PROGRESSIVELY. The parent needs to stretch language imitation through the process of successive approximation such that the operant becomes more and more complex. That is, the parent can sustain a mild level of frustration to maintain the drive level of the child. In the example above, the child can for a time get water by using the operant "wa." Then he gets water after doubling the sound, "wawa." And then he has to get the final sound, "wa-ter." After a very short period of time, the model begins to repeat the word *please* after the word *water*, and the operant now becomes "water, please." It is, then, a short step to "I water, please" and "I want water, please." All this can be accomplished while other parents are stamping in the pidgin word *wawa*, and sharing Waldo's "funny little word" with all the assorted neighbors, relatives, and friends.

SPEAK OFTEN. The parent can take on the task of verbalizing everything that the child does. When the baby is being put to bed, the parent can say so. "Let's put Waldo to bed." "Let's find Waldo's rabbit." "Let's cover up Waldo." "Let's cover Mr. Rabbit." "Let's turn out the light." "Now, let's tell a little story." Short, concise sentences are all potential operants for the child. These are the kinds of words that the child should hear over and over again.

SPEAK GRAMMATICALLY. The parent can correct errors in pronunciation, diction, and sentence construction by providing correct models and by encouraging imitation, rather than by direct frustration of the child. Although some neurological problems can produce stammering, most stammering seems to result from problems of tension when the frustration level in language is too high and when the child's attention has been called too often to his tendency to repeat. Stammering is a normal process in language development during the time that parents and children are encountering discipline problems that lead to hostile interchange. For four- and five-year-old children, whose behavior problems are rather high, stammering is also rather high. Most authorities feel that if the parent will keep providing a simple model of communication, give the child time, and ignore the stammering, it will be merely a developmental phase that will spontaneously disappear.

LISTEN ATTENTIVELY. The child needs opportunity to practice. In the modern home the parents are so frantic in their activities and generally so hurried that they do not have the time to listen. Under such circumstances no wonder children develop little confidence in language as an operant and consequently shift to behavior, and often problem behavior, as operants. Confidence in the operant quality of language comes only with repeated experience. Confidence that subtle distinctions in language make one form more potent than another is perhaps one of the most important messages of childhood. The ancient game "May I?" which can be multiplied a hundred times and provides continuous delight, is an example of this kind of distinction.

READ REGULARLY. The child needs experience in listening. Reading to children as little as fifteen minutes a day helps even very young children in basic phoneme development. Reading to children should be an active process in which pictures, examples, and elaborations are used, as well as the fill-in-the-blank kind of questioning.

The importance of the written word is nowhere more clearly presented than in the delightful expressions contained in some of Kipling's *Just So Stories*. The musical quality of the words, the enthusiasm with which each expression is presented, give the child an exposure to the great interest and pleasure contained in language.

> Then the Kolokolo Bird said, with a mournful cry, "Go to the banks of the great grey-green, greasy Limpopo River, all set about with fever-trees, and find out."
>
> That very next morning, when there was nothing left of the Equinoxes, because the Procession had preceded according to precedent, this 'satiable Elephant's Child took a hundred pounds of bananas (the little short red kind), and a hundred pounds of sugar-cane (the long purple kind), and seventeen melons (the green-crackly kind), and said to all his dear families, "Goodbye. I am going to the great grey-green, greasy Limpopo River, all set about with fever-trees, to find out what the Crocodile has for dinner." And they all spanked him once more for luck, though he asked them most politely to stop.
>
> Then he went away, a little warm, but not at all astonished, eating melons, and throwing the rind about, because he could not pick it up.
>
> He went from Graham's Town to Kimberley, and from Kimberley to Khama's Country, and from Khama's Country he went east by north, eating melons all the

time, till at last he came to the banks of the great grey-green, greasy Limpopo River, all set about with fever-trees, precisely as Kolokolo Bird had said.

Now you must know and understand, O Best Beloved, that till that very week, and day, and hour, and minute, this 'satiable Elephant's Child had never seen a Crocodile, and did not know what one was like. It was all his 'satiable curiosity.

The first thing that he found was a Bi-Coloured-Python-Rock-Snake curled round a rock.

"'Scuse me," said the Elephant's Child most politely, "but have you seen such a thing as a Crocodile in these promiscuous parts?"

"Have I seen a Crocodile?" said the Bi-Coloured-Python-Rock-Snake, in a voice of dretful scorn. "What will you ask me next?"

"'Scuse me," said the Elephant's Child, "but could you kindly tell me what he has for dinner?"

Then the Bi-Coloured-Python-Rock-Snake uncoiled himself very quickly from the rock, and spanked the Elephant's Child with his scalesome, flailsome tail.

"That is odd," said the Elephant's Child, "because my father and my mother, and my uncle and my aunt, not to mention my other aunt, the Hippopotamus, and my other uncle, the Baboon, have all spanked me for my 'satiable curiosity—and I suppose this is the same thing."

So he said good-bye very politely to the Bi-Coloured-Python-Rock-Snake, and helped to coil him up on the rock again, and went on, a little warm, but not at all astonished, eating melons, and throwing the rind about, because he could not pick it up, till he trod on what he thought was a log of wood at the very edge of the great grey-green, greasy Limpopo River, all set about with fever-trees.

But it was really the Crocodile, O Best Beloved, and the Crocodile winked one eye—like this!

"'Scuse me," said the Elephant's Child most politely, "but do you happen to have seen a Crocodile in these promiscuous parts?"

Then the Crocodile winked the other eye, and lifted half his tail out of the mud; and the Elephant's Child stepped back most politely, because he did not wish to be spanked again.

"Come hither, Little One," said the Crocodile. "Why do you ask such things?"*

NAME DESCRIPTIVELY. The parent can present new words to the child's vocabulary. He can do this most easily by exposing the child to simple nouns together with the objects or referents. Picture books and picture blocks with illustrated action verbs are a great assistance. So is putting into words the everyday activities around the home. The parent can add synonyms to the child's vocabulary by repeating and expanding the child's sentences and phrases, suggesting alternative expressions. The parent can add adjectives and adverbs by defining and describing specifically: "Please bring me the big blue book with the black and white dog on the front cover."

STIMULATE OFTEN. Parents can provide the child with an enriched environment to give him something to talk about. The more stimulation the child receives, providing it is verbalized, the more he is able to develop his language. Having experience with new concepts and having them simultaneously verbalized is in and of itself the key to building language

*Reprinted by permission of the publisher, from Rudyard Kipling, "The Elephant's Child," in *Just So Stories* (New York: Schocken Books, 1965), pp. 65–67.

power. The word *fuzzy* can be remembered more easily and can be used more effectively when associated with the feel of a cattail in the wind, a loose-weave comforter, or a caterpillar.

REWARD COMMUNICATION. Language can become a substitute for behavior. The child can learn that language is a more effective operant than behavior. The child can learn to substitute angry words for blows, and to use direct communication, instead of direct action, to get what he wants. Children should be rewarded as often as possible for using language to communicate.

As has been pointed out, some children lack the models they need for full language development. Substitute models can be provided. The culturally deprived child suffers most from a failure of the language model. The placement of good verbal models in early childhood education centers for these children during their preschool years will do much to offset their severe problems. An active language environment with improved models can help reduce the tendency of lower-class children to develop poor, incorrect, and often fragmented language patterns.

REVIEW

Operant Conditioning Definitions

Accidental Chaining Accidental chaining is the unintentional reinforcement of behavior because of its association with another behavior.

Aversive Stimulus See Negative reinforcer.

Chaining "A chain is composed of a series of responses joined together by stimuli that act both as conditioned reinforcers and as discriminative stimuli" (Reynolds, 1968, p. 53).

Conditioned Reinforcer Conditioned reinforcers are those stimuli that, through experience, acquire power to reinforce behavior; a conditioned reinforcer is a secondary reinforcer.

Contingency Contingency is the association of an environmental event with behavior such that the event does in fact follow the behavior but need not do so; thus the environmental event is contingent upon the behavior.

Dependency Dependency is the association of an environmental event with a behavior because the event must follow the behavior, i.e., the environmental event is dependent upon the behavior.

Discriminative Stimulus A discriminative stimulus in the environment cues the probability of a given reinforcer; a discriminative stimulus cues when a given operant is going to be reinforced.

Extinction Those operants no longer in the child's repertoire are extinct. "Extinction refers to a procedure in which an operant that has previously been reinforced is no longer reinforced" (Reynolds, 1968, p. 28).

Fixed-interval Schedule of Reinforcement The reinforcement of behavior at fixed time intervals— say every fifteen minutes or every three hours or every week—is a fixed-interval schedule. Such a schedule results in a highly variable work rate that slows down after the payoff and speeds up just before.

Fixed-ratio Schedule of Reinforcement The reinforcement of behavior on a fixed ratio—say every third or every fifth or every tenth response— is on a fixed-ratio schedule. Such schedule results in a high rate of response and behavior highly resistant to extinction.

Negative Reinforcer A negative reinforcer is a stimulus that by its disappearance increases the rate of a given operant.

Operant An operant is any behavior that modifies the environment in which the child lives.

Operant Conditioning "Operant conditioning is an experimental science of behavior. Strictly speaking, the term *operant conditioning* refers to a process in which the frequency of occurrence of a bit of behavior is modified by the consequence of the behavior" (Reynolds, 1968, p. 1).

Partial Reinforcement Partial reinforcement covers those situations in which the operant is reinforced less than 100 percent of the time. Partial reinforcement produces great resistance to extinction.

Positive Reinforcer   A stimulus that by its occurrence increases the rate of a given operant is a positive reinforcer.

Primary Reinforcer   See Unconditioned reinforcer.

Punishment . An aversive stimulus following and dependent upon the occurrence of an operant is punishment.

Reinforcement Schedule   Operant conditioning has discovered the important relationship between the frequency of reinforcement and the frequency of occurrence of an operant behavior and its resistance to extinction. Partial reinforcement is the basis for schedules of reinforcement that can be based on ratios or intervals.

Reinforcer   Any stimulus that affects the rate of a given operant is a reinforcer.

Resistance to Extinction   The tendency of an operant to continue in the absence of reinforcement is its resistance to extinction.

Respondent   A respondent is a response elicited by a stimulus "because of the inherited structure of the organism and not because the organism has had any specific previous experience with the stimulus. The same stimulus elicits the same response from all normal organisms of the same species" (Reynolds, 1968, p. 7). How often a respondent occurs depends upon how often the stimulus occurs. A respondent's frequency is not affected by the environmental events that follow it.

Schedule of Reinforcement   See Reinforcement schedule.

Secondary Reinforcer   See Conditioned reinforcer.

Shaping   Shaping is the process of changing existing responses into new and more complex responses by reinforcement control, usually on a 100 percent schedule of reinforcement.

Spontaneous Recovery   Spontaneous recovery is the spontaneous reappearance of an operant during or after extinction.

Stimulus Control   Stimulus control refers to environmental events that control the operant; you don't turn a radio off unless it is on.

Stimulus Discrimination   Stimulus discrimination refers to the ability to discriminate which situation is more likely to be reinforced.

Stimulus Generalization   Stimulus generalization refers to the ability to recognize a commonality among stimuli.

Superstitious Behavior   Superstitious behavior attributes reinforcement to some behavior that actually is irrelevant. Because of chaining, the child cannot distinguish which behavior is being reinforced.

Unconditioned Reinforcer   Those stimuli that without experience are able to reinforce behavior are unconditioned reinforcers.

Variable-interval Schedule of Reinforcement The reinforcement of behavior at time intervals unknown to the subject is on a variable-interval schedule. This schedule of reinforcement produces a more stable work rate but still leads to superstitious behavior.

Variable-ratio Schedule of Reinforcement   The reinforcement of behavior at a different ratio of responses each time—say on the third response, then the eighth, then the second—is a variable-ratio schedule. This schedule leads to ineffective learning on the child's part and produces superstitious behavior, since he cannot distinguish what is triggering the reinforcement.

Language as an Operant

One behavior of man separates him uniquely from all other species. Although, undoubtedly, some communication exists among all animals, and although, undoubtedly, some animals have a rather complex communications system, no other species has a symbolic language facility. The uniqueness of speech in man always has separated him from his closest cousins in the animal kingdom.

theories of language development

Autistic Theory   Originated by O. Hobart Mowrer from his work with talking birds, the autistic theory holds that language sounds are copied because self-satisfaction is derived from so doing. "In terms of learning theory, what has happened is that initially neutral sounds, by virtue of their occurrence in temporal contiguity with primary reinforcements, have acquired secondary reinforcing properties." Mowrer uses the example of deaf children to drive home his point: without being able to hear and to enjoy the voices of others, deaf children rarely babble and with only the greatest difficulty and special training do they learn to talk.

Biological Theory Eric Lenneberg theorizes that "the ability to acquire language is a biological development. The basis for language capacity might well be transmitted genetically." Something about the human child's cortical organization causes him to be different from all other animals.

Mother-reward Theory Neal Miller and John Dollard emphasize the role of the mother. ". . . Children talked to while being fed and otherwise cared for should exhibit more iterative and imitative babbling than children not talked to while being rewarded."

Social Learning Theory Based on operant conditioning, the social learning theory of language development has the greatest likelihood of offering an acceptable explanation for the human phenomenon, language—a complex, symbolic facility that "constitutes the greatest single achievement of human evolution."

stages in language development

All researchers into the acquisition of language agree that language develops in stages. However, the conceptualization of these stages differs. Helmer Myklebust conceptualized language development in terms of use: inner stage—language used autistically as described by Mowrer; receptive stage—language used to understand others; and expressive stage—language used to make others understand.

Babbling Vocalization During the babbling stage, parents begin to reinforce differentially the sounds the child makes. Differences begin to develop between the vocalizations of deaf and hearing children and between children of deaf and hearing parents. The babbling stage begins when the child learns to control sequence and is all-important in the development of language. The baby's discovery that he can produce a sound is sufficient reason for its practice. During the second month, the child produces the same sound repeatedly but at different volumes. During the third and fourth months, he learns to control pitch. During the fifth month, control of sequence begins to appear.

Earliest Vocalization The earliest vocalization of the human infant is unlearned and organically based. During the first three months of life, the vocalization is virtually no different between deaf and hearing children, or between children with deaf and hearing parents. The most effective way to manipulate vocalization during an infant's first thirteen weeks is by meeting his physical needs.

Verbal behavior of children up to three months of age is controlled by maturation. The only social modification is in the amount, not the quality, of vocalization.

Imitative Vocalization In imitation, the infant's verbalization is altered in evident response to an adult who makes a sound within the repertoire of the child; social reinforcement increases the rate of vocalization, and, in the final stages, along with modeling, social reinforcement becomes essential. Out of imitation grows true language.

Social Vocalization At three months, infants begin to make social responses; their vocalization can now be brought under social control; that is, it can be increased by social stimulation; the everyday caretaking of mothers is a reinforcing stimulus. But social stimulation not contingent upon vocalizing by the infant has little effect on the rate of vocalization.

variables in language development

A child utters sounds and responds to the human voice; his mother speaks to him and responds to his sounds: all four ingredients are required for linguistic growth. In the human brain, a language activator, instinctive and probably biochemical, at a certain level of maturation motivates or allows the human child to develop language, which quickly becomes an operant for the child—a behavior that modifies his environment: the development of language very much depends upon circumstances that allow the child to develop confidence in the power of language as an operant.

Family Constellation Multiple-birth children develop language much more slowly than single-birth children. The cause seems to be the nonverbal communication that develops between these youngsters.

Sex Earlier studies reported differences in the language facility of boys and girls, but more recently these differences have been less pronounced.

Socioeconomic Status In all comparisons of language quantity and quality, upper socioeconomic groups are superior. All those aspects of socioeconomic status that affect intellectual development and achievement also affect the acquisition of language. As pointed out by Robert Hess and Shipman, as well as others, modeling has a great effect on language development: language is the predominant operant in upper-class homes, whereas in lower-class homes, nonverbal communication is the primary operant. Bernstein, like Hess and Shipman, found words used in lower-class families mainly to denote objects and actions, rarely to indicate relationships. A strong argument for the establishment of early childhood education centers for deprived children is that language training can make a substantial difference in the performance of disadvantaged children.

Stimulation Stimulation exerts a necessary influence upon language acquisition. Did not Sherman and Key find that children tend to develop only as the environment demands development? Did not the studies of institutionalized children point out language deficits? Did not studies of the stages in language development point out the necessity of social reinforcement? Obviously early stimulation is necessary for language to develop adequately, and some studies have indicated that a deficit in early language acquisition may permanently impair language development.

reinforcement of language skills

Speak clearly, correctly, progressively, grammatically, and often!

Listen attentively!

Read regularly!

Name descriptively!

Stimulate often!

REWARD COMMUNICATION!

Teach your child the power of language!

Anxiety

Dread is the possibility of freedom. Only this dread is by the aid of faith absolutely educative, consuming as it does all finite aims and discovering all their deceptions. And no Grand Inquisitor has in readiness such terrible tortures as has dread, and no spy knows how to attack more artfully the man he suspects, choosing the instant when he is weakest, nor knows how to lay traps where he will be caught and ensnared, as dread knows how, and no sharpwitted judge knows how to interrogate, to examine the accused, as dread does, which never lets him escape, neither by diversion nor by noise, neither at work nor at play, neither by day nor by night.

He who is educated by dread is educated by possibility, and only the man who is educated by possibility is educated in accordance with his infinity [Kierkegaard, 1844, pp. 139–140].

AN OLD ENEMY: DREAD

Søren Kierkegaard was not the first man to be schooled by the Grand Inquisitor, anxiety, but, being filled with both dread and literary brilliance, he has given us one of the earliest and perhaps most succinct statements of the power of anxiety over the life and destiny of mankind. Writing in the middle of the nineteenth century, Kierkegaard recognized a significant distinction between fear and anxiety; fear was related to some objective danger wherein the emotions were appropriate to the magnitude of the risk. Thus, a child who has been stung by a honeybee is appropriately afraid upon finding a bumblebee sitting on his nose. He has felt the sting and hurt inflicted by a small honeybee, and now, with this large, yellow and black monster sitting dead center of his line of vision, it is little wonder that he is fearful.

Anxiety, however, is not so easily understood, because anxiety often has no object, or, if it has, the object is difficult to detect and, furthermore, is not appropriate for the magnitude of the effect. Thus, a child has some reason to fear elevators. One, after all, is held many stories up in the air by a one-inch cable, and cables do break, and stories are told about elevators falling. Besides that, the child is absolutely helpless, locked in a cage, riding up and down as a result of adults pushing buttons above his reach. But that would not account for terror. The risk of falling in an elevator is extraordinarily low, and children who are paralyzed with dread over getting into an elevator are said to be anxious because, although there is an appropriate level of fear associated with mechanical contrivances, terror is a response out of all proportion to the risk involved.

Aristotle, as early as 350 B.C., recognized that like all other emotions, both fear and anxiety have their roots in a physiological process.

> Now all the soul's modifications do seem to involve the body—anger, meekness, fear, compassion, and joy and love and hate. For along with these the body also is to some degree affected. An indication of this is that sometimes violent and unmistakable occurrences arouse no excitement or alarm; while at other times one is moved by slight and trifling matters, when the physical system is stimulated to the condition appropriate to anger. This is still more evident when, nothing fearful being present, feelings occur as in one who is frightened. If this is the case, it is evident that the passions are material principles; hence such terms as "becoming angry" mean a motion of such and such a body, or of a part or power proceeding from and existing for the body [Aristotle, *De anima*, I. k. 403ab].

Aristotle recognized, then, that in describing any emotion, one must describe both the object and the affect in order to obtain a complete definition.

Even in antiquity, the physiological basis of anxiety was obvious. Children, aware of their own sweat and trembling and pallor and shortness of breath, say, "My stomach feels funny." They recognize anxiety in themselves and they recognize it in others. Clearly, it is an action of the body. Since the time of Aristotle we have made enormous progress in our ability to understand and measure the physiological processes that accompany anxiety. But, to believe that the task is complete would be an error. Even today, no adequate physiological test differentiates anxiety from generalized excitement.

Let us assume that we have placed two young women subjects, identical twins, in two separate rooms in the best-equipped physiological laboratory available today. Each twin is completely wired for the most advanced telemetry and the most sophisticated physiological measures known today. In one cubicle the young woman is experiencing an acute anxiety attack. She is in abject terror of the most excruciating kind, such as that which accompanies some of the most serious neurotic states. The other woman is experiencing a totally successful orgasm. All of the recordings are transmitted into a third room with a duplicate set of dials on each of two walls, where the world's leading physiological experts are asked to look at the two panels and answer the single question "Which of the twins is having the anxiety attack?" Even today it would be pure chance as to whether they were right or wrong.

To measure levels of excitement is easy today, but to determine the object of this excitement is difficult to the point of impossibility. Thus Watson's failure, as demonstrated by Sherman, to identify fear, love, and rage as primary emotions in infants on the basis of casual, superficial observation of facial expression is not so difficult to understand.

The difficulty in assessing anxiety through physiological measurement was made abundantly clear by Sternbach (1962), who placed ten eight-year-old children in a standardized, emotion-inducing situation while they were being monitored by a large number of physiological sensors. The children were first accustomed to the room and equipment, and then, once the telemetric equipment was in place, they were shown a film—Walt Disney's *Bambi*, which, you will remember, has many highly emotional scenes ranging from joy to grief. Children watching the movie frequently go through a wide range of visible emotions.

After viewing the film, the children were asked to report which parts were the saddest, scariest, nicest, happiest, and funniest. Six major physiological measurements of emotion were scored for each of these parts of the film for each of the ten children. In the main there was little agreement between the instruments and the stated emotions. Only eye blinking and sweating seemed to make any differentiation at all between the emotions and that was consistent only in the scene where Bambi's mother dies. And as anyone who has been in a theater with a group of children, most of whom are crying buckets of tears and holding on to their seats for dear life, knows, this is no great accomplishment for $500,000 worth of monitoring equipment.

All this is by way of saying that although anxiety is an old enemy, the subject of countless treatises, novels, short stories, and autobiographies, and although it is a demon assiduously studied by the modern, physiologically oriented psychologist, it is still beyond our grasp. That which we know about anxiety, we know by inference. And unfortunately, we probably know more about anxiety from personal experience than from science. The present chapter will review the concept of dread—most particularly, the ways in which it is understood by child psychologists today and the strategies by which we attempt to reduce its power. Anxiety reduction is one of the noblest and most significant research topics in psychology.

ANXIETY: PSYCHOANALYTIC THEORY

Among the psychic functions there is something which should be differentiated (an amount of affect, a sum of excitation), something having all the attributes of a quantity—although we possess no means of measuring it—a something which is capable of increase, decrease, displacement and discharge, and which extends itself over the memory-traces of an idea like an electric charge over the surface of the body [Freud, 1894, p. 75].

SIGMUND FREUD

Because of the delay in translating Kierkegaard's work, Freud was not influenced by his remarkable writings. Independently, in the course of his clinical work, Freud noticed the universal power and influence of anxiety over the lives of his patients.

Freud noted also the remarkable resemblance between the behavior associated with extreme anxiety and the behavior that accompanies orgasm. With this in mind, and noting the rather extreme repressive nature of sexual morality, together with the general fear of pregnancy that dominated his female patients, Freud reasoned that perhaps anxiety was simply dammed-up sexual energy being displaced into another context. Since his patients could not describe any object of their anxiety, and since they were all victims of severe sexual frustration and fear, this plausible argument served as the sexual basis of Freud's theory. Moreover, Freud was struck by the uniformity with which his adult female patients described seductions in early childhood by fathers, uncles, or other "dirty old men." Thus Freud was forced to conclude further that the real cause for the damming up of the sexual drive, which he called libido, was sexual trauma experienced during childhood.

As Freud continued to increase his caseload and delve more deeply into the sexual fantasies of his patients and himself, he soon noted a peculiar aspect of childhood memories. Apparently the adult could make no distinction between those events that actually occurred in childhood and those merely daydreamed. Since early childhood memories are composed exclusively of vivid pictures rather than verbal abstractions from pictures, their eidetic nature allows for considerable distortion. And even when the event can be demonstrated to have occurred, there can be massive distortions of its actual nature. Children can construct vivid memories of events that never transpired.

For example, when Waldo was twenty-two months old, he was knocked off the back steps by a dog. One of the oft-repeated family stories was how Old Spot knocked Waldo off the steps and Waldo had to have seven stitches in his head. Everybody remembers how sorrowful Old Spot was, and, as Waldo grows up, he has a vivid memory of Old Spot, with his big black patch over one eye and his tongue hanging out, looking mournfully at his master who has fallen off the steps. In fact, this memory is the anchor point of Waldo's early memories.

Then, Aunt Susie comes to visit and, as is often the case, everyone, sitting at ease around the living room, is talking about the old days. Finally someone says, "Why, Aunt Susie, you haven't been here for ten years. The last time you were here Old Spot knocked Waldo off the back porch." Everyone smiles and nods in agreement. However, Aunt Susie suddenly says, "Spot? It wasn't Spot. Don't you remember? Old Spot was at the vet's. It was that old red hound of the Andersons' up the street."

And everybody begins to remember and say, "Oh, yes, I remember. And how concerned old Mrs. Anderson was about whether or not we would sue." Everybody quickly gets his thinking straight—except Waldo. Waldo is stuck with a vivid memory picture of Old Spot with his tongue hanging out, his black patch, and his mournful expression. It is not so easy to straighten out a memory picture, or eidetic memory, and Waldo never really believes the family, even though they now unanimously agree that it was the Andersons' dog.

Anxiety Basis of Abnormal Behavior

As a result of his discovery that the childhood seductions reported by his patients probably never occurred, Freud realized the unlikelihood that these events were the cause of anxiety. Anxiety did not represent dammed-up libido resulting from repression of sexual feelings as he had originally thought. Rather, the repression of sexual feelings was one way in which the individual was trying to deal with anxiety.

In a sense, then, the repression of sexual feelings was a defense against anxiety. And thus came about the origin of the basic concept that most abnormal behavior is an attempt to deal with anxiety by means of some mental exercise the individual believes will ward off dread. The similarity between the two states of arousal, panic and orgasm, caused the psychoanalytic movement to begin on the long, circular route by which all behavior was thought to have a basic sexual origin.

Anxiety as a Danger Signal

To Freud, anxiety signaled danger. Mowrer writes: "Freud repeatedly referred to anxiety as a kind of 'signal,' a premonition of impending danger, an indicator that something is not going well in the life of the affected individual" (1950, p. 535).*
Freud also distinguished between anxiety and fear:

> Anxiety is undeniably related to expectation; one feels anxiety *lest* something occur. It is endowed with a certain character of indefiniteness and objectlessness; correct usage even changes its name when it has found an object, and in that case speaks

*This and following passages reprinted, by permission of the author and the publisher, from O. Hobart Mowrer, "The Problem of Anxiety," in O. Hobart Mowrer (ed.), *Learning Theory and Personality Dynamics: Selected Papers* (New York: Ronald Press, 1950). Copyright © 1950 by the Ronald Press Company.

instead of *dread.* Anxiety has, moreover, in addition to its relation to danger, a relation to neurosis [Freud, 1936, p. 112].

We then started from the distinction between objective anxiety (fear) and neurotic anxiety (anxiety proper), the former being what seems to us an intelligible reaction to danger—that is, to anticipated injury from without—and the latter altogether puzzling and, as it were, purposeless [Freud, 1933, p. 114].

Anxiety Basis of Neurosis

Freud viewed all neurotic symptoms as an attempt by the individual to either control or avoid anxiety. Mowrer writes:

The neurotic is thus a person who attempts, knowingly or unknowingly, to neutralize this signal, this indicator, without finding out what it means or taking realistic steps to eliminate the objective danger which it represents.... This definition of neurosis as any type of behavior which serves to reduce anxiety without affecting its fundamental causation has the important theoretical advantage of explaining why it is that such a "symptom" is at one and the same time both self-perpetuating and self-defeating. It is self-perpetuating because it is reinforced by the satisfaction provided through the resulting anxiety reduction; and it is self-destructive in that it prevents the individual from experiencing the full force of his anxiety and being modified by it in such a direction as to eliminate the occasion for the anxiety [Mowrer, 1950, p. 535].

Initially, Freud conceived of anxiety as being dammed-up libido that transformed sexual energy into anxiety when both voluntary and involuntary repression prevented discharge of sexual tension. Ultimately, Freud began to see anxiety as a much more complex phenomenon stemming both from internal and external threats: internal, in terms of a flooding of internal physical stimulation, and external, in terms of revenge or retaliation from significant others provoked by the internal impulses. Freud was approaching the position of recognizing anxiety as a response to a signal in the environment indicating some real or imagined threat.

391

Freud ultimately identified three forms of anxiety: objective anxiety, what we identified earlier as fear, an appropriate response to a dangerous stimulus; neurotic anxiety, an irrational dread of being overwhelmed by one's internal drives or of being retaliated against as a consequence of having these drives; and moral anxiety, an overwhelming sense of guilt experienced as feelings of depression. Defense mechanisms are used in response to any of the three. The appropriateness of the response is measured in terms of how much energy it consumes and whether it prevents the person from engaging in some adaptive mechanism that might have great utility. If a child in a hospital terminal ward faces certain death from leukemia, flying away from all reality with a denial mechanism, though psychotic, is nevertheless entirely appropriate and effective, because it is not draining his energy, it is not preventing him from making adaptive moves, and it is making him comfortable.

Anxiety Defense Mechanisms

In his final position, Freud surmised that anxiety represented a psychological reaction in the face of some threat. The primary threat, as envisioned by Freud, was becoming overwhelmed by a flood of internal physical stimulation. There is some reason to believe that at birth most stimulation is experienced as noxious, that the newborn is most comfortable when he is unstimulated, contented, or in what one might call a homeostatic balance. The goal in life, then, is to reduce this internal physical stimulation to the point of tranquility. The terror in life is to be overwhelmed with stimulation.

Take the childish game of tickling a peer. If he is unusually sensitive to tickling, the game quickly disintegrates into his moving into a state of panic. True, the object of stimulation is known—fingers probing the rib cage. But there is an unknown quality, since the child does not know how long the tickling will continue and whether it will increase in intensity. The anxiety component is caused by his fear of internal stimulation in response to the tickling.

In addition to this internal threat, there is the external threat: the anxiety over what those significant people in the outside environment may do in response to his behavior. The possibility exists that society will for some unknown reason attack the child, stimulate him if you will, and he will not be able to cope with the stimulation. This feeling is what the modern existential philosophers, following Kierkegaard, call existential anxiety, or, fear of the possibility of what might be.

According to Freud, the basic problem of mankind is how to deal with anxiety. All behavior, both normal and abnormal, is an effort to slay the demon, dread. He viewed man's strategies for dealing with dread as falling into four response categories: normal or sublimated responses, neurotic responses, psychotic responses, and character responses.

Sublimated

A sublimated response is an adaptive and socially accepted way of dealing with anxiety. For example, a person who is anxious about his insignificance, or is suffering from what the Adlerians refer to as an inferiority complex, may compensate for this feeling by overachievement in some area to the point where he has so many merit badges on his chest that he no longer feels inferior. He has dealt with anxiety and at the same time has performed tasks that are socially applauded and generally adaptive both for himself and for the good of all mankind. The more sublimated the response, the less it is identifiable as a defense against anxiety, the less a person is aware of being anxious.

Neurotic

Neurotic anxiety defenses, however, according to psychoanalytic theory, are not adaptive in the realistic sense. Neurotic behaviors simply make a person feel more secure without really helping him adapt to the environment. For example, superstitious behaviors, such as carrying a rabbit's foot, knocking on wood, or crossing one's fingers, are harmless neurotic defenses. They are harmless because they take up little of the free energy of the person involved, offer little distraction from the business at hand, and contribute to the ability of the person to overcome his feelings of anxiety.

Neurotic defenses are not always so benign. The nine-year-old boy who, in order to feel safe going to sleep, must count from 1 to 1,000,000 and then count backward from 1,000,000 to 1, will soon be tired, irritable, upset, and nonproductive in the fourth grade, with the result that his general well being will suffer a greater and greater deficit, until he becomes exhausted and unable to cope with the demands of his world. Unbending compulsivity is a neurotic behavior that can disrupt, rather than smooth, a person's day-to-day existence in the real world. Thus a neurotic defense can become so expensive, in terms of time and energy, that it wears the person down and collapses of its own weight.

Psychotic

Psychotic defenses, on the other hand, deal with anxiety in a completely different way. These defenses escape into a dream world and in a sense deny the existence of anxiety. Again, there are degrees. Daydreams are a kind of psychotic defense—as Freud says, a consciously willed, temporary psychosis. Here is a way of turning off reality and escaping from stress through a mechanism that never deals with reality.

The severity of the psychotic defense mechanism depends upon the difficulty of turning it off—the power the conscious will has over the state, upon the amount of energy that it requires, and upon the degree to which society can tolerate the behavior. Thus, some forms of psychotic behavior, such as daydreaming, are allowed by society, while other kinds, such as verbalized hallucinations, are not accepted. Society will tolerate nicely the five-year-old's imaginary playmate, even when it comes to a rather marked extreme. But it will not tolerate the same child turning in a fire alarm because he thinks he sees a sheet of fire running up a wall that is not actually there.

A character defense—a systematic, acquired, or learned pattern of dealing with anxiety—is not superimposed upon a more or less normal personality, as is the psychotic defense. The character response to anxiety typically emerges in early childhood. A set of superstitious behaviors, though extremely maladaptive, nevertheless is acquired by an individual who for some reason believes them to be adaptive.

The sociopathic or psychopathic character, readily identifiable in late childhood, is an example of such a defense. The psychopath deals with anxiety by behaving in an omnipotent manner, as though he were somehow above the reaches of rules and laws that govern normal human behavior. The psychopath, then, fails to learn from experience because he fails to integrate experience in any causative fashion. When he is punished for behavior, he looks upon the punishment as a stupid, irrational act performed by a significant person in his environment and does not consider even remotely possible that it is a signal regarding a relationship he should learn. In all societies psychopaths are unacceptable by the very definition of a society.

The character disorder mechanism deals with anxiety by denying a causal relationship and by completely exonerating one from any sense of guilt or responsibility. The world is looked upon, then, as a perfidious place where misfortune strikes down unlucky people, not because of any action of theirs, but simply on the basis of chance. The world is characterized as being made up of smart people and stupid people—the smart people agreeing with, supporting, and yielding to the whims and caprices of the psychopath, and the stupid people blocking his immediate gratification. This lack of ability to postpone gratification serves as one of the major identifying marks of the psychopath.

The Child

Throughout the early psychoanalytic explanation of anxiety runs the concept that a part of the human personality is the core self, the real me, or the ego, which views the world as either hostile or benign, and which sees the need for dealing with reality in a prescribed way that falls into these neat categories: character, psychotic, neurotic, or normal. The problem is that people, and most particularly children, don't really fall into such neat categories. It is not at all unlikely to find a healthy youngster, doing excellent work in the fourth grade, who has a "super-dooper" good-luck charm in his left shoe, who has a ready dislike of anyone "messing with his stuff" jumbled in careful disarray on his bedroom desk, and who has often been seen, alone in the side yard, conducting a shoot-out at the OK Corral accompanied by a wide variety of loud sound effects.

Obviously this lad, representing a neat balance between normal, neurotic, and psychotic defenses blending into a highly satisfactory adjustment for a middle-class, nine-year-old male who lives in a fairly dull neighborhood, presents a severe challenge to Freud's classification system. There may be whole afternoons in which this child remains completely submerged in his daydreams and imaginary play. He may, on another day, stay in a veritable rage because his sister has straightened up his desk. And again, he may sit down and do his homework three weeks in advance. The question remains, "What kind of child is he?"

Subsystem Theory of Personality

To understand the nature of defense against anxiety, it is important to grasp the personality subsystems as conceptualized by Freud. Freud conceived of three major systems, which either coexist at birth or grow from a primitive beginning with little structure. His theory stresses that at birth the child is equipped with well-functioning primitive reflexes and responses, the purpose of which is the reduction of tension. The child is delicately balanced between states of sleep and states of extreme discomfort associated with hunger, cold, wetness, or stomach distress. He has a drive system that is constantly attempting to reduce this tension. The primitive drive system, which is not governed by rational thought, is considered to be the id and would seem to be a universal system in mankind.

As the child learns to deal with his environment in a rational way, as he learns to delay gratification and tolerate or bind tension, one sees evidence of the development of a primitive ego, or self, that will provide mostly rational, reality-oriented, adaptive reactions to the environment.

At the same time the ego is developing strength, the child is made aware of a series of *ought nots,* usually by a parent, or nurse, or older child. An awareness of potential for doing something one should not, the sense of guilt, begins to develop through a recognition of the guilt feelings produced in relationship to a significant person in one's environment. This sense of failure, of guilt, of sin, is evidence of the development of the third system, the ego ideal, or the superego. However, not all guilt is a function of the superego. Rational guilt, rational conscience, is a function of the ego, because it is realistic, appropriate, and in the broadest sense, adaptive to the problems of the world. Guilt that is part of the superego is irrational, unrelated to actual environmental conditions.

One further point that should be made is that adaptive drives—such as hunger, thirst, and a need for warmth—are considered by Freud to be ego instincts, not id instincts, for reasons of theoretical consistency. Apparently Freud viewed the drive of the id as a tension-reducing drive arising in the body unrelated to mere survival instincts. He finally decided that these drives were a part of the basic, internal clock mechanism that regulated the life sequence of mankind.

Two basic, competitive, internal drives arising from the id were responsible for a concept of homeostasis in the broadest possible terms. The two drives were called eros and thanatos. *Eros* refers to life instincts, the creative, fixed, aggressive drives. *Thanatos* refers to death instincts, or instincts that tend to reduce man to an inactive state. According to Freud, then, the chief aim of all mankind is to live out his brief span on earth and die in his own way in his own time. Child psychology usually does not involve the functioning of the death instinct, and little will be said about it other than that this theory is one of the least accepted and least productive of the psychoanalytic conceptions.

Before we leave the discussion of the three personality subsystems, perhaps it would be well to offer an analogy of their operations such that their relationship to each other can be fully understood. Imagine, for the moment, a primeval existence in which a hunter lives in a stone hut with his mother. This hunter lives in a hostile environment that provides only meat for him and his mother to eat. But he himself is unable to catch any animals and must depend instead on the hunting powers of a pack of wild cats, which he keeps in the cellar and which he has trained to hunt for him. The hunter is the ego, the mother is the superego, and the cats are the id.

A healthy hunter is able to control most of his cats, is able to keep them sleek and healthy and well disciplined to the point where he can catch a surplus of food and enjoy the chase. His mother, who does not enjoy living with these vicious animals, nevertheless is usually quiet, except when the hunter gets a little overconfident and tries to add to the hunt one or two giant cats that have never been fully domesticated. At this point she becomes most uneasy and warns her son repeatedly about the great dangers that will occur if the cats get out of control. The hunter under these circumstances would be, in Freudian terms, a normal person, or even a supernormal one.

The neurotic hunter, however, is so badgered by his mother that he has lost his nerve and seldom goes hunting at all. When he goes, he takes only a few cats, and these he keeps on a tight cord, constantly afraid they will get out of control, constantly worried about the strength of the cord, and whether or not he should really be hunting at all. His mother constantly hovers over his shoulder and badgers him, further depleting his energy and nerve. Such a hunter is neurotic in psychoanalytic theory.

Another hunter has lost the key to the cellar door, with the result that the cats have all escaped into the hut. The poor confused hunter is hanging from the ceiling while the cats jump and snap and mill around the room. All the while, his mother, hanging with him, is screaming invectives: "You've really done it now! We're going to die! It's all your fault!" Obviously, such a hunter is or soon will be mad. This is the analytic conception of the psychotic.

The character disorder, or psychopath, however, has let all of the cats out of the cellar, fed mama to them, and is now going hell for leather down the road, right in the middle of the pack of cats, having joined them in a wild chase across the country, killing and destroying everything in their way.

ANNA FREUD

We may conjecture that a defence is proof against attack, only if it is built up on this twofold basis—on the one hand the ego and, on the other, the essential nature of instinctual processes. . . . But the ego is victorious when its defensive measures effect their purpose, i.e., when they enable it to restrict the development of anxiety and "pain" and so to transform the instincts that, even in difficult circumstances, some measure of gratification is secured, thereby establishing the most harmonious relations possible between the id, the super-ego and the forces of the outside world [Anna Freud, 1946, pp. 192–193].

A problem in evaluating a treatment program for youngsters is that almost anything works; the aging process itself is often sufficient to get a child through a crisis. However, the child-guidance movement, arising out of the theories of Freud and his daughter, Anna Freud, has given a reasonable account of itself operating within the concept of neurotic defense mechanisms. Anna Freud has outlined anxiety defenses as they apply to children who meet the clinical criterion of being neurotic; that is, children who themselves feel the need of help, or who are viewed by the significant adults in their life—teachers, parents, physicians—as being in need of help because their adjustment to the demands of society is inadequate or because they appear to be in great distress.

Phobia

A common emotional problem bringing children into mental health clinics and guidance centers is the rapid development of, or at least an acceleration of, a phobic reaction. At first glance a phobia would appear to be an example of fear, not of anxiety. The complete lack of justification for a fear of the object, however, gives a phobia its abnormal or anxiety component.

Fear of the dark is a rather common phobia. The child cannot stay in an unlighted room; he is frightened by dark hallways. This fear of darkness is rather obvious. But according to analytic theory, the darkness is not what the child is afraid of; the darkness makes it possible for his mind to wander to other topics of which he is really afraid. The darkness is, in a sense, the focal point of his expressed fear, but he is much more afraid, perhaps, of being punished for misdeeds. He is afraid of what has been called since antiquity, "the evil eye," that all-seeing, revengeful one who pays back evil with evil.

A child has a sense of what Piaget (1932) called immanent justice. A child believes you get what you deserve. And most parents have participated in this belief. Take the instance of a youngster jumping up and down on the sofa until he loses his balance and hits the wall or falls off. Immediately, older children and sometimes parents react: "You see there. You see what you get when you act that way?" The message is clear. There is a punisher, an evil eye that sees that you "get what you have coming." According to analytic theory, then, the child who has a fear of darkness has a fear of either his own impulses, or more likely, a fear of the lashing-back punishment that is part of immanent justice.

The phobic reaction has the double effect of keeping the child away from objects that stir up emotional trauma and at the same time offering to the child an explanation for his basic anxiety. Obviously the problem with a phobic response is twofold. First, the phobia prevents the child from functioning normally, from going about the business of life, be it getting a good night's rest, going through a darkened hall, or walking down the street in a dog-infested neighborhood. A phobia is debilitating. Second, unless there is an objective quality to the phobic response, it represents totally wasted energy. The child's energy is drained away and his whole creative potential becomes frozen. He becomes more and more quiescent, sedentary, and disabled.

Phobias have the added potential of becoming self-perpetuating. A child responds in a phobic manner to what he considers to be a threat, and he survives. That, in and of itself, is proof enough for the child that the phobia is valid. If he had not cringed and stayed out of dark corners and put his head under the sheet, who knows what might have happened.

So long as the phobic child is immobilized by his phobia, he can never test its validity. Obviously a child who is terrified of elevators and therefore will not get into one continues to believe that if he did, he would certainly die. He owes his life to his good sense in staying off the infernal contraptions. His phobia becomes, in effect, his best friend who has saved his life.

Repression

A second reaction to anxiety, also considered to be a neurotic defense by the Freudians, is the repressive response. In the psychoanalytic sense, repression is a response blocking off all feeling, or at least all feeling in some significant area. The classic example of repression is a hysterical disorder that has its origin in the child's failure to respond emotionally. The child dams up his feelings, which then fail to grow into mature, "full-bloom" emotional responses. Children who resort to the repressive defense mechanism are, then, superficial children, chronically immature, continuing through childhood to behave in a fragile manner, giving the impression of naiveté and helplessness.

A major problem with this defense mechanism is that it fails to allow the individual to face the stresses of the world realistically, to address himself to problem solving, because he never tunes into the affective or feeling nature of the world. A second problem is that the repressive defense mechanism tends to consume all of the child's free energy—or perhaps a better description would be, tends to bind all the free energy—so that the child does not have any ability to solve problems. Children who use this mechanism tend to be chronically tired, energyless, incapable, and inadequate, living in a passive, dependent manner.

Obsessive Compulsion

A third response to basic anxiety seen in children is the obsessive compulsive mechanism. The basis of obsessive compulsion is organization and activity that keep the child from having time to become panicked. In milder form, compulsive acts range from such childhood games as "step on a crack, break your mother's back," wherein children walking on sidewalks become preoccupied with not stepping on the cracks, to carrying a rabbit's foot or four-leaf clover, to not taking any risks on Friday the 13th.

Nighttime rituals, common enough as a part of the process of getting the child ready for bed, can be stepped up to the point where they become an obsession. A parent who is asked to put all three dolls in their proper order on the bed, and finds that this helps the child to sleep, will not identify this as a compulsion. But the parent who finds himself asked to check all windows to see if they are locked, repeat five different childhood prayers, kiss each of fifteen toys, the dolls on each cheek, then each hand, and then on each toe, will soon realize that the ritual has gotten out of hand. Here is a child who is showing neurotic signs because his defense against anxiety has crossed both the bounds of the common and the bounds of excess that mark the rather loosely defined difference in Freudian terms between normality and neurosis.

Obsessive-compulsive defense mechanisms are most often observed in bright, middle-class children, for whom a place-for-everything-and-every-thing-in-its-place neatness compulsion is a vivid part of the cultural milieu. Within middle-class society certain underlying obsessional ideas are part of the overorganization typical of a home in which specific activities are planned for almost every hour in the day for all the children in the family, not to mention the parents.

Consider the typical family with four children. Mother starts the week Monday morning chauffering the children to four different schools: senior high, junior high, elementary, and nursery school; Monday afternoon the seventh-grader has an orthodontist appointment at 2:30; the four-year-old goes to the library story hour at 3:00; the fourth-grader to Brownies at 3:30; at 4:00 are dancing lessons for the seventh-grader; at 5:00 the four-year-old has been picked up and the fourth- and seventh-graders must be picked up; supper must be on the table by 6:00 because junior high play practice starts at 6:30; the high school football player must be picked up at 6:45 and get his supper and be back at school by 7:00 for orchestra practice. Tuesday afternoon is dancing for the fourth-grader; baton lessons for the seventh-grader; that evening Explorer Scouts for the high school junior; and choir practice for the seventh-grader. Wednesday, horseback riding lessons and piano lessons and junior high band. Thursday, dancing lessons, play practice, Future Homemakers meeting, and Girl Scouts, junior high football game, and a birthday party. Friday is guitar lessons, horseback lessons, art lessons, high school football game, and a slumber party. Mother chauffeurs the children in car pools to and from school, to guitar lessons, piano lessons, orchestra practice, Cub Scouts, Brownies, Boy Scouts, Girl Scouts, Little League, dancing lessons, baton twirling lessons, tumbling lessons, horseback riding lessons, orthodontist appointments, choir practice at a different time for each child, art lessons, birthday parties, slumber parties, football games, basketball games, play practice, football, basketball, track practice, ad infinitum. If the reader is still following, he's obviously been raised in an obsessive middle-class home and knows what it's like.

What should be abundantly clear is that a little organization is great. It makes for efficiency and effectiveness in everyday activity. But, the more organization is used to alleviate anxiety, the greater is the likelihood that it will break down, that the adjustment process will become literally frozen, and the child will become so obsessed with details, so worried about whether he has thought of everything, that he will become immobile.

Take the bright eight-year-old boy who had a tendency toward obsessive compulsive defense mechanisms and had decided on his own, start-

ing from analysis of the child's prayer, "If I should die before I wake," that
maybe before he went to sleep, he should tell God that he was sorry for all
the bad things he had done. Now in and of itself this is not a bad idea, and,
as we will later elaborate, Mowrer thinks it's splendid.

But after the child had elaborated the fifteen or twenty sins of the
day, it occurred to him that maybe he should tell God that he was sorry
twice. And then it occurred to him that he might die before he got through
with the list, and then would God forgive him? So he began to speed up
the two lists so he couldn't die in between.

It also occurred to him that God might have other things to do and
might not be listening just then. Perhaps he should list his sins on paper
and leave the list on the nightstand, so that if God came when he was
asleep, He would see that he had said that he was sorry, but He hadn't
been listening. Following this he remembered the classroom punishment
of writing "I will not talk in class" twenty times, and it occurred to him
that maybe he should write his apologies for his sins twenty times each.

Well, there's more. But obviously our little fellow was getting very
little sleep and was becoming increasingly worried about the possibility
of dying in a state of unconfessed sinfulness. His obsessive compulsion
had totally debilitated him.

Rationalization

A defense mechanism common in our society, but nevertheless
neurotic, is rationalization. The essence of the rationalization defense is
the avoidance of anxiety-producing feelings of inadequacy and failure by
means of somewhat elaborate justifications, excuses, and dismissals such
as that characterized by the sour-grapes response of Aesop's fable fame.
The child who is bewildered by the complexity of fourth-grade modern
math has a teacher who is "dumb," who "can't explain things," and whom
"everyone hates." The boy, an hour late for supper because he was completely lost in a sandlot football game, thought "what with the longer eve-
nings that supper was going to be later."

These defense mechanisms, which tend to reduce the risk of retaliation by society, or the guilt and anxiety related to impotency, become
defined as neurotic when they consume a significant portion of the person's
time and energy and when they fail to allow time and energy for actually
solving the problem producing the anxiety. Most of these defense mechanisms are acquired from adult models in the child's environment. A child
who, when asked why he went to Joey's house after being told not to, responds, "Well, I just started up there and then went on up," receives so
much abuse for such a "stupid" answer that he does better next time for
both his parents' benefit and for his own: "Well, I couldn't remember what
the arithmetic homework was, and I thought you would want me to get it,
so I went up and asked Joey."

Reaction Formation

A fifth neurotic defense mechanism defined by the Freudians is reaction formation, often called counterphobic behavior in childhood. The

essence of this defense mechanism is the complete submerging of an anxiety-producing impulse with the surfacing of diametrically opposed behavior. In the classic analytic sense, a child is engaged in reaction formation when, while leaving for summer camp, he giggles, cracks jokes, and talks a great deal about the fun he will have. His feelings of wanting to cling to his mother, to cry, and to otherwise be a baby are controlled by behavior minimizing the importance of the situation, by acting as if he couldn't care less. He is dealing with separation anxiety by using a neurotic defense mechanism that, through bravado, prevents him from becoming overwhelmed by his emotions.

In analytic literature one finds suggestions that just at the time in the child's life when he is experiencing his strongest homosexual urges, during the period of latency in the early grammar school years, he is acting very masculine and is most apt to be amused by crude, derogatory humor about homosexuality. He deals with his subconscious fantasy by acting the role of the super male gunslinger in his play.

Psychotic Defense Mechanisms

In addition to the neurotic defense mechanisms, which operate in varying degrees in all people, even those considered quite healthy by their peers, there are psychotic defense mechanisms that differ only qualitatively from the neurotic ones.

Denial

One of these, usually considered rather benign because of its transitory nature, is the defense mechanism of denial. Consider the youngster who, with stringent instructions about the power tools, has been allowed by his father to use the family basement workshop. He has been told not to use the jointer, a high-speed plane used to prepare surfaces of wood for gluing. The father has explained that the jointer, an extremely dangerous piece of machinery, accounts for most of the accidents in woodworking shops. Waldo has been promised that when he is older, he will be taught to use the tool. At the same time, as an added precaution, an understanding father casually has mentioned that under no circumstances should a piece of wood smaller than twenty-four inches be planed.

Well, one rainy day Waldo is down in the basement, repairing his favorite wooden rubber-band gun, which, through heavy use, has arrived at a state of somewhat dirty ill repair. Suddenly it occurs to him that he can greatly improve its looks by running the frame of the gun through the jointer, even though it is only about fourteen inches long. He flicks on the switch and begins to feed the wood through the jointer when a knot suddenly catches in the jointer and his hand is sucked into the blade with a blinding flash of pain and numbness.

Waldo stands there, his hand behind his back, the jointer humming. "I couldn't have! I wouldn't have! Surely I didn't put a little block of wood in the jointer and have it grab.... No! Perhaps it just tipped my hand a bit."

As the jointer slows to a stop and the roar in his ears subsides, a drip, drip, drip is heard on the floor behind, and the pain returns to the thumb. Finally, peeking with one eye over his shoulder, the child looks at his hand. Sure enough, there is a sizeable portion of the thumb left on his hand, although he has lost perhaps a bit more than a tip.

The denial mechanism, then, is a short-term reaction that lets Waldo get ready for the possible shock of finding no thumb. The mechanism becomes a psychosis when there is a long or permanent delay in the return to reality. An example of a severe loss of reality is the child who continues to ask "When will mother be back home?" after he has been told many times that his mother has died, after he has attended the funeral, and after he has made half a dozen trips to the cemetery. Such a situation often does not return to a benign state without professional help. Once a denial state lasts beyond a day or two, it is indeed a serious condition and is considered by the analysts to be a full-blown psychosis.

Regression

A second psychotic defense mechanism, regression, is seen in most children when they become physically sick or experience severe disappointment or stress. They cry, often suck their thumbs, and want to be held. In severe states, however, a massive across-the-board regression occurs: the child talks, acts, and responds emotionally like an infant. Such a condition can last for long periods of time. Again, it is a psychotic mechanism regardless of the degree, but we do not diagnose it as such unless it begins to have a long-term significance for the child. In childhood schizophrenia, now thought by most investigators to have a biochemical basis, the major observable symptom is massive regression that even takes the appearance of hovering in a fetal position in a chair or corner.

Withdrawal

Withdrawal, a third psychotic defense mechanism, in its extreme forms represents a complete escape from reality by moving into a dream

world. *Harvey* and *The Secret Lives of Walter Mitty* represent this phenomenon in an adult. In children it is generally regarded as somewhat less severe, and only becomes a serious consequence when it greatly reduces the child's ability to cope with reality and to respond effectively to the demands of the environment.

Some children find the real world such a threatening place, and their dream world such a pleasant place, that they withdraw further and further from reality, spend more and more of their waking hours in dreams and reveries, with the result that they become less and less efficient and effective in dealing with the demands of reality, and thus become further tempted to withdraw. Life outside their dream world becomes unbearable and they become recognizable as truly psychotic. One of the problems of this particular defense mechanism is that it is initially so innocuous and inoffensive that it fails to come to the attention of competent authorities soon enough. Children can become deeply immersed in their psychotic state without ever being identified as being in difficulty.

THE DIFFICULTY IN REFUTING PSYCHOANALYTIC THEORY

In the first half of the twentieth century, the psychoanalytic theory of personality—based as it is upon the three subsystems of the ego, the super-ego, and the id, and a series of interlocking defense mechanisms used by the ego to defend itself from attack by overwhelming stimulation coming from either the impulses of the id, the moral threat of the superego, or the anticipated retaliation of society—has been an appealing theory. What has made it even more appealing is its global explanation, its ability to handle anything in retrospect, and its lack of refutation. Psychoanalytic theory, however, finds it difficult to refute other more parsimonious explanations that are also post hoc. The demise of psychoanalytic theory came about principally through the ineffectiveness of psychoanalytic therapy and the system of generating unilateral predictions. The concept of reaction formation allows for any behavior to be predictable unilaterally.

403

To test the adequacy of the reaction formation concept, let's take a typical example requiring prediction. Suppose a male child is raised exclusively under the domination of an indulgent, quarrelsome, querulous, bickering mother, who frequently derides, abuses, and carps at her ex-husband, the child's father. Suppose he is raised in this environment and finds that so long as he complies with his mother's wishes and agrees with her perception of most men, his life is pleasant, but if he asserts himself, or attempts to gain independence, she is punitive, abusive, derisive, and sarcastic. What kind of basic personality will this child develop?

According to psychoanalytic theory, the child will be a passive, dependent male with a strong propensity toward homosexuality. This is, then, a pathogenic mother who produces ineffective, impotent, dependent, immature males.

But sometimes this is not the case. Instead the boy is hostile, aggressive, and a natural leader in the school setting. He is independent and assertive, and is picked as the most popular boy in the fourth grade. One says that the psychoanalytic theory is in error. "Not so," says the psychoanalyst. "This is a classic example of reaction formation. The child indeed has strong dependency needs, has grave fear of impotence, but these are so frightening to him that he is dealing with these impulses through the mechanism of reaction formation. He is behaving in the exact opposite manner from that in which he would really like to behave."

Now even fourth-grade science won't accept that explanation. If psychoanalytic theory would stick to a probability model and report that under the conditions mentioned above, the odds are three to one that the child will be passive-dependent, its acceptance in the general field of science would be much higher. This circular definition, which allows for the theory to be correct no matter which way the data run, is insufferable. Although the psychoanalytic theory is still considered a helpful, global approximation of the nature of personality development, and although it gives a convincing description of anxiety reduction, it nevertheless has failed to gain scientific acceptance because of its definition of terms.

PSYCHOANALYTIC TREATMENT

Certainly psychoanalysis has developed out of magical therapeutic methods. But it has eliminated the magical background of its forerunners.... Scientific psychology explains mental phenomena as a result of the interplay of primitive physical needs—rooted in the biological structure of man and developed in the course of biological history (and therefore changeable in the course of further biological history)—and the influences of the environment on these needs.... That the mind is to be explained in terms of constitution and milieu is a very old conception [Fenichel, 1945, p. 5].

Development of Insight

The basic strategy for the alleviation of moral and neurotic anxiety in psychoanalytic theory is the development of insight. Insight in the child refers to his acceptance of his parents' statement that his anxiety is irrational. This acceptance, of course, must be more than just lip service.

Thus the distinction is often made in psychoanalytic literature between emotional and intellectual insight.

Intellectual insight is illustrated by sentences divided with a but. "Well, I know I don't need a light on to go to sleep. Mommie and daddy are here. The world is not really a very dangerous place. Even having the light on wouldn't make much difference in my safety, but . . . if I could have the light on tonight, I'll be a good boy and turn it off tomorrow night." In analytic terminology the child is repeating verbatim the reassurance provided by the significant adults in his environment, but . . . it doesn't do the job of dealing with his anxiety. Thus psychoanalytic treatment of children consists in efforts to uncover the basis of the anxiety, whether external or internal.

Mechanisms of Treatment

The mechanisms of the psychoanalytic therapists are talk and play. In play therapy, the child is given a toy world. The usual stimuli in the child's normal environment are reduced to miniature and are represented by dolls, doll houses, sand boxes, and assorted toys. The child is allowed to dramatize his world, his fears, his feelings. The therapist functions as an interpreter, a recorder, a sounding board. Through this dramatization process the child is able to comprehend and accept the unrealistic nature of his anxiety.

In the talking relationship in child therapy, emphasis is placed on what the psychoanalyst calls transference. The assumption is that the most likely cause of a child's anxiety is some form of disturbed interaction between this child and the significant adults in his environment. And thus, if the child can derive an anxiety-reduced relationship with another significant individual, namely his therapist, then he can have what Franz Alexander calls a corrective emotional experience (Alexander and French, 1946, p. 22): that is, he can sort out healthy aspects of his relationship with adults and begin to see himself more realistically.

The analogy is that of a child who has grown up in a house where there are only terribly warped mirrors. If he has viewed himself in these mirrors and combed his hair in these mirrors, he no doubt has developed a horribly distorted self-image and has probably been combing his hair in a grotesque fashion. Such a child would be markedly moved and inestimably aided by being handed a perfectly reflecting mirror and allowed to see himself without distortion for the first time. Even though he had to return to the same old room with the same old mirrors all about, there is little reason to question that he would ever be the same. Having once seen himself correctly, he is never again so vulnerable to the distortions of the reflecting mirrors.

In analytic theory, the major cause of anxiety is a distorted self-image resulting from a pathological interaction between a child and his parents. In analytic literature, normal parents do not have disturbed youngsters and disturbed youngsters do not have normal parents. So the parent who brings his child to an analyst obviously encounters a person who believes that the child's problems are caused in the home in the relationship with the very person who is making the complaint.

Medical Model of Disease

The psychoanalytic theory of personality is based upon the medical model of disease. In the medical model, the human mind is like the human body; its natural state is a healthy balance of many complex, interacting systems. Because of some internal disruption, or more likely because of some external infecting agent, this balance can be tipped, and the mind is then considered to be ill. When the mind is ill, it displays certain symptoms that point to the cause of the illness—symptoms that, with few exceptions, are by themselves insignificant and are treated only to reduce the discomfort. The major treatment is internal and directed toward the cause of the infection or the infectious agent. There are tremendous regenerative powers within the mind, and quite often mere rest is sufficient to allow these powers to restore it to its original healthy condition.

Case of Sara

Perhaps before we leave the psychoanalytic or medical model of anxiety, we should discuss in some detail a case illustrating both the theoretical rationale and the treatment program for an acute anxiety state in a child. Sara was a nine-year-old raised in a family that bred horses. She had been an extremely warm, happy, bright, outgoing girl, who was alert, productive, and successful. Sara lived in a household where there was little concern about modesty. Suddenly, one summer, just before the beginning of school, she began to show considerable evidence of being anxious. She was restless, jumpy, blushed frequently, sweated, and stayed in her room. Books and magazines began to have missing pages. When retrieved from the trashcan, they were found to have advertisements for ladies' undergarments.

She began to show other strange behavior. She was no longer affectionate; in fact, she wouldn't allow anyone to touch her and was most fearful of being around her father. She began to wear several sets of underclothes and two or three blouses, which she tied at the sleeves. It soon became apparent that she was also wearing shorts under her dresses and had the legs of these shorts tied with string.

Her mother noticed that she was voiding into towels instead of the commode. And when she took a bath, which she did seldom, she was using a great many towels. When school began, she was unable to stay at school for more than a two-hour period. She was spending a great deal of time in her room with the shades drawn. She became ferocious about personal modesty and would panic if any member of the family was seen in even the slightest stage of undress. Within a short time, she was in a state of complete panic and did not seem to derive any satisfaction from any of the behaviors she employed in trying to reduce her anxiety.

The family history contained several clues for the therapist as to the cause of Sara's panic. First was the family bedtime ritual. Because the father rose at about 3:00 A.M. to go to work, he went to bed at about 8:00. The mother generally stayed up, watched TV, and did household chores. She went to bed at about 10:00. From an early date, the girls, Sara and her older sister had gone to bed with their daddy. When she came to bed, mother would move the girls to their room. The older sibling had terminated this pattern about two years earlier, when she reached nine, mostly because she did not want to go to bed until 10:00 or so, when her mother went to bed.

Second, during the summer Sara made the acquaintance of a girl who was a year older chronologically and many years older in terms of worldly wisdom. The two girls had been very close through August, and then had abruptly broken off their friendship.

Third, in spite of the rural setting, neither Sara nor her older sister had ever spoken with their mother about any aspect of sex and the mother had never offered any instruction.

Fourth, the older sister had begun to menstruate in the early part of the summer but had not talked to Sara about it, even though the necessary paraphernalia was now left in the girls' room.

Fifth, although Sara had been somewhat anxious before the beginning of school, her real state of free-floating anxiety did not begin until about the second week of school.

Sixth, concern was obviously being expressed by Sara about exposure of the genital area, since she seemed to be less concerned about her blouse being tied at the sleeves than she was about her shorts being tied.

Seventh, she was much more concerned about her father's physical presence than she was about her mother's.

Eighth, she had abruptly left her father's bed and did not even go into the parents' bedroom anymore.

Ninth, she seemed to be placing undue stress on efforts to keep her stomach flat.

The complex treatment program followed psychoanalytic theory. Through use of a sand table, a doll house, a play telephone set, and various doll clothes, the therapist established communication with Sara. Initially, to remove the dialogue from reality, he communicated by calling Sara on the play phone and using the animated voice of a cartoon character. Gradually, play themes were introduced into the doll house and descriptions were made of the dolls. Finally, doll clothes were discussed, and ultimately the relationship between the daddy doll and the mamma doll was stressed. Prior to this, the sand table with its animals, particularly the horses, was used to lay the groundwork.

From analytic theory several possibilities were derived regarding the cause of the anxiety producing the symptoms. First, some kind of sexual event could have occurred to arouse the anxiety. The event could have been of three types. It was theoretically possible that there had been some kind of actual sexual play initiated by the father. It was theoretically possible that the child had been subjected to some other sexual trauma, such as assault or threat of assault. It was more likely that some information or misinformation had caused her to misinterpret the significance of the relationship with her father.

In any event, it was abundantly clear that she considered herself to be either seriously damaged, or pregnant, or both; that her inability to stay at school was caused by the fact that she could not allow herself to void in a public bathroom and her anxiety was causing frequent voiding; that the use of towels and curtains was an attempt to prevent anyone, even herself, from having a view of her genitals; and that one of the triggering events had been her discovery of the sister's menstruation paraphernalia and her inability to account for this in any way other than that her sister was pregnant.

The actual sequence of events that led up to Sara's illness was as follows. The family had a long history of utilization of the repressive defense mechanism. They never talked about unpleasant things and never had unpleasant feelings. They never argued or yelled or cursed or fought, but lived in a benevolent, pretty little world that walled out all evil. Thus Sara really believed that hospitals were adoptive agencies where you went to get babies. Although she had seen pregnant women, she had never really paid any attention.

So it was a naive, immature, repressive little girl who encountered an earthy new friend. In the course of their conversations, Patty told all and summarized her lesson in biology with the profound statement, "Well, I'll tell you how you get pregnant. You get pregnant by sleeping with men."

Initially Sara was panicked by the thought, but she quickly rallied with two major counterarguments to herself. One, "That isn't true. That is simply not how you get pregnant. You get pregnant by going to the doctor and having a baby put in." And two, "If it were true, my sister would be pregnant."

Upon starting school in the fall, Sara noticed for the first time the decorations on the bathroom wall with its drawings and specific terminology. She decided to ask her really best friend, having dismissed her summer friend as being nasty. Her best friend, in a slightly humorous, not unkind, but superior manner, confirmed Sara's worst fears by using the euphemism, "sleeping with men." She said, "Of course, that's how you get pregnant."

Sara observed her older sister preparing for bed and noted a suspicious bulge, which was actually a sanitary pad. This drove the final nail into the coffin. Her sister was indeed pregnant. And now Sara began to look frantically in magazines and noticed everywhere about her sex, sex, sex. She began to examine her own body and since she was just prepubertal, began to note changes that she quickly confirmed as symptoms of pregnancy. She then began to engage in a frantic effort to conceal the fact from others and herself, to try to deny the obvious fact that she would soon be giving birth to a child.

The therapy program first involved the confirmation of these facts through the use of play, telephone talk, and ultimately, protracted dialogue involving some reassurance, some confirmation, and a considerable amount of factual information and interpretation. As Sara became more aware of the truth and falsity of her conceptions, impulses, and fears, her anxiety subsided and her symptoms began to disappear. She returned to her original state of health. In terms of the medical model, she was cured of her disease.

Sara's case illustrates the psychoanalytic conception of paralyzing anxiety stemming from fear of impulses and fear of retribution by society. This nine-year-old girl was beginning to be stirred by an increased awareness of her own body, her own drives, which made her sensitive to events in the world she had previously successfully ignored. She was thus being stimulated by internal drive mechanisms. At the same time, she was also threatened by the prospect of retaliation. What if the world became aware of her pregnancy? What would people say and do if they could see what had happened? According, then, to the Freudian view, anxiety stems from a fear of impulse, or as Mowrer has said, in his summary of Freud's position: "In essence, Freud's theory holds that anxiety comes from evil wishes, from acts which the individual would commit if he dared" (Mowrer, 1950, p. 537).

ANXIETY: GUILT THEORY

"The alternative view is that anxiety comes, not from acts which the individual would commit but dares not, but from acts which he has committed but wishes that he had not" (Mowrer, 1950, p. 537).

O. HOBART MOWRER

Mowrer, in contrast to Freud, has developed a guilt theory of anxiety. This form of anxiety closely approximates Freud's moral anxiety and is akin to what the orthodox analyst would call agitated depression. According to Mowrer, the emotional disturbance observed in children is "the lawful, well-earned, and eminently normal result of abnormal (in the sense of socially and morally deviant) behavior" (1965, p. 243).*

Mowrer has the therapist saying, "the reason you have all these feelings of guilt is because, By God! you're guilty." He thus sees anxiety as a distinctly normal phenomenon that signals misbehavior. To put it in Mowrer's terms:

> It will instead be our thesis that in psychopathology the primary, basic cause is deliberate, choice-mediated behavior of a socially disapproved, reprehensible nature which *results* in emotional disturbance and insecurity (because the individual is now objectively guilty, socially vulnerable, and, if caught, subject to criticism and punishment). The symptoms which then ensue, represent ways in which the individual is trying to defend himself against and *hide* his disturbing and suspicion-arousing emotions (of moral fear and guilt) [1965, p. 243].

Mowrer's explanation of Sara's case would be that Sara knew better than to sleep with her father, knew that some of her thoughts were evil, and, thus, when she was caught by her friend, she panicked and tried to hide her guilt. Thus, according to Mowrer, it was not that she had impulses and was afraid of them, but rather that she had "sinned" and had been caught.

In discussing his theoretical view of anxiety Mowrer points out differences in his theory from that of earlier psychologists.

*This and other passages reprinted, by permission of the author and the publisher, from O. Hobart Mowrer, "Learning Theory and Behavior Therapy," in Benjamin B. Wolman (ed.), *Handbook of Clinical Psychology* (New York: McGraw-Hill, 1965). Copyright © 1965 by McGraw-Hill Book Company.

Writing in 1890, William James stoutly supported the then current supposition that anxiety was an *instinctive* ("idiopathic") reaction to certain objects or situations, which might or might not represent real danger. To the extent that the instinctively given, predetermined objects of anxiety were indeed dangerous, anxiety reactions had biological utility and could be accounted for as an evolutionary product of the struggle for existence. On the other hand, there were, James assumed, also anxiety reactions that were altogether senseless and which, conjecturally, came about through Nature's imperfect wisdom. But in all cases, an anxiety reaction was regarded as phylogenetically fixed and unlearned [Mowrer, 1939, p. 554].

"Some years later John B. Watson demonstrated experimentally that, contrary to the Jamesian view, most human fears are specifically relatable to and dependent upon individual experience" (Mowrer, 1939, p. 554).

Learned Anxiety

Mowrer believes that anxiety is learned:

In contrast to the older view, which held that anxiety (fear) was an instinctive reaction to phylogenetically predetermined objects or situations, the position here taken is that anxiety is a learned response, occurring to "signals" (conditioned stimuli) that are premonitory of (i.e., have in the past been followed by) situations of injury or pain (unconditioned stimuli). Anxiety is thus basically anticipatory in nature and has great biological utility in that it adaptively motivates living organisms to deal with (prepare for or flee from) traumatic events in advance of their occurrence, thereby diminishing their harmful effects. However, experienced anxiety does not always vary in direct proportion to the objective danger in a given situation, with the result that living organisms, and human beings in particular, show tendencies to behave "irrationally," i.e., to have anxiety in situations that are not dangerous or to have no anxiety in situations that are dangerous [1939, p. 564].

Positive Concept of Anxiety

Mowrer makes extensive use of the Judeo-Christian concept of guilt, sin, and atonement and their relationship to anxiety, and obviously takes the view that anxiety is a positive, adaptive mechanism absolutely essential to the adequate functioning of mankind. Mowrer talks about Yom Kippur, the Day of Atonement where in orthodox Judaism,

... one appears before God (on the Day of Atonement) only after having spent a month making right one's transgressions against one's fellow men during the preceding year. And in the New Testament we read: "Therefore if thou bring thy gift to the altar, and there rememberest that thy brother hath ought against three, leave there thy gift [to God] before the altar, and go thy way; *first be reconciled to thy brother, and then come and offer thy gift*" (Matthew, 5:23–24, italics added) [1965, p. 249].

Mowrer's whole approach to dealing with psychological problems is a direct effort toward changing behavior, toward accepting guilt, and toward public confession.

One is reminded of the description of the early childhood experiences of Jane Addams, when she went through periods of habitual lying:

> She records how, after telling a lie, she would stay awake for hours torn by a double dread: that she might die herself "in sin" and go straight to hell; or that her father would die before she told him of her lapse from grace. Finally, she would screw up her courage for the perilous journey down dark stairs, past the street door kept unlocked on principle, and across an empty room to reach the confessional of her father's bedside. His reply was always the same: "If he had a little girl who told lies, he was very glad that she felt too bad to go to sleep afterwards" [Tims, 1961, p. 19].

This statement was sufficient to allow her to return to bed comforted.

In the analytic sense, that kind of abuse coming from a parent would be almost the epitome of a poor mental-health practice, but in Mowrer's terms it is dead center of therapy. She had lied, and it was necessary to get her to accept the fact that she had lied and to help her publicly acknowledge it.

GUILT THEORY TREATMENT

According to Mowrer, then, the only really appropriate therapy is a "*behavior therapy,* in the sense of (1) changing the behavior which originally got the individual into trouble and (2) changing what the individual has since been trying to do about his trouble" (1965, p. 243). This is quite different from the Freudian view that the neurotic's problem is troubling emotions rather than troubling behavior. In the Mowrer framework, "the 'sick' individual's problem lies not in how he is feeling, but in what he has been, and perhaps still is, doing" (1965, pp. 243–244). Neurotic children "do not act irresponsibly because they are sick; instead, they are sick because they act irresponsibly" (1965, p. 244).

It is interesting to note that following such a tough line in explaining anxiety, Mowrer then goes on to suggest a therapy that involves a concept of public confession. For Mowrer,

> a rational and effective therapy must be a behavior therapy, which involves (1) admission rather than denial, to the significant others in one's life, of who one genuinely is and (2) rectification of, and restitution for, past deviations and errors. Thus one must again traverse the same path which led him into neurosis in the first place, but now in the reverse direction. If it is by sinning and then trying to conceal the sinning that one progressively destroys his social relatedness (i.e., his identity), the only possibility of recovering it is to move back in the opposite direction, toward openness, cooperation, community, and fellowship [1965, p. 247].

Group psychotherapy, involving public confession and atonement, is the method suggested by Mowrer.

ANXIETY: SOCIAL-LEARNING THEORY

> If a neurosis is functional (i.e., a product of experience rather than of organic damage or instinct), it must be learned. If it is learned, it must be learned according to

already known, experimentally verified laws of learning or according to new, and as yet undiscovered, laws of learning [Dollard and N. Miller, 1950, pp. 8–9].

If a child lives with criticism, he learns to condemn.
If a child lives with security, he learns to have faith in himself.
If a child lives with hostility, he learns to fight.
If a child lives with acceptance, he learns to love.
If a child lives with fear, he learns to be apprehensive.
If a child lives with recognition, he learns to have a goal.
If a child lives with pity, he learns to be sorry for himself.
If a child lives with approval, he learns to like himself.
If a child lives with jealousy, he learns to feel guilty.*

JOHN DOLLARD AND NEAL MILLER

In formulating a social learning theory of behavior, Dollard and Miller's ultimate goal was "to combine the vitality of psychoanalysis, the rigor of the natural-science laboratory, and the facts of the culture" (1950, p. 3). They postulated that anxiety and the responses to it are acquired in a social context under rather simple learning conditions. Anxiety is a complex emotion, but is, in the main, under control of social reinforcement.

Socially Derived Anxiety

Dollard and Miller point out that one of the child's earliest anxieties, fear of being alone, related to an expansion of Freud's concept of stimulus flooding. Because the child is absolutely dependent upon his mother, or mother substitute, for his basic needs, which are fierce in their intensity, he learns that if he's experiencing the pain of an empty stomach, the need to burp, or other gastric distress, his only chance of reducing the tension is through proximity to his mother. Thus a kind of existential anxiety arises: What if she doesn't return? Dollard and Miller postulate that the fear of being alone does indeed have its origin in awareness of possible consequences of abandonment. Thus, anxiety is a generalized fear arising from a specific set of stimuli and is generally a socially derived phenomenon.

Dollard and Miller also suggest that a child can learn to fear retaliation for certain psychological responses if he has been punished directly or indirectly for their expression. Children, for example, can be punished for belching, regurgitating, or evacuating. Thus the combination of the extreme discomfort associated with colic and the obvious displeasure, rejection, or punishment of parents can contribute to early anxiety states. Social contagion, that is, subtle communication through gestures, hesitancy, and other affective responses, communicates displeasure in such areas as sexual behavior, where there is no spoken comment, but merely subtle withdrawal and an apprehensive affect.

*Reprinted from Dorothy Law Nolte, *Children Learn What They Live,* with the permission of John Philip Company, 91 Lost Lake Lane, Campbell, California 95008.

The beauty of Dollard and Miller's approach is the overt, behavioristic explanation of anxiety. And even though a concept such as contagion makes for extreme difficulty in measurement through the use of rating scales and objective tests, it is still possible. One is dealing with an independent variable rather than an intervening one.

This is not to say that Dollard and Miller do not imply more than they can measure. They are firmly convinced that one can introspectively sense what they call "anxiety-protected" areas:

> If any normal person wishes to verify the fact that there are anxiety-protected areas in his own mental life he need only attempt self-study. He will find that mysterious forces arise to stop his work. He will find himself welcoming distractions and thinking of interesting plans for other things to do. Persons whom he would ordinarily shun are surprisingly welcome when they drop in. Hopeless thoughts easily come to mind. If the person persists, he will find himself facing the vague terror of anxiety. He will find indeed that the effect of past punishments will rise again when he contemplates the course of action that was punished. Such a normal person will then understand better the value of the reassuring presence of the therapist to the neurotic person and what resolution is required to carry on self-study outside the supportive context of the psychotherapeutic situation [1950, pp. 440–441].

SOCIAL-LEARNING TREATMENT

What Dollard and Miller suggest, then, is, after all, a rather simpleminded approach to anxiety. Anxiety is learned following the laws of learning; therapy involves unlearning—a conditioning, extinction, deconditioning theory of anxiety. They suggest that the therapist needs certain role expectancies associated with being a doctor or priest in order effectively to carry out the therapy program, which is the kind of caution carried in the ancient rabbit stew recipe that begins with the suggestion "First, you catch a rabbit." It was abundantly clear to Dollard and Miller that one has to begin a therapy approach after having caught a patient; that is, having established a relationship that will carry a rather simple, but highly charged, and somewhat lengthy process of deconditioning.

Dollard and Miller's approach did not by itself generate a large number of studies following their conceptions. In fact, R. Sears (Sears, Maccoby, and Levin, 1957), by making comparisons of the effects on children's personalities of various child-rearing practices, is one of the few investigators who has attempted to verify within the family setting the basic social-learning-theory approach of Dollard and Miller.

Both a strength and a weakness of Dollard and Miller's approach to anxiety reduction is that it makes so few assumptions and its methodology is so simplistic. Reducing complex human emotions, interactions, and dynamics to stimulus-response terms is a neat semantic trick, but the clinician in the field soon recognizes that calling a hairbrush a stimulus and the wailing of a child a response does not account for all of the variability in child-rearing practices.

The net effect of this simplicity is that practically Dollar and Miller's approach to psychotherapy as related to anxiety has had little effect on mental-health practices. When it comes to concrete application of learning theory to clinical practice, most clinicians who pay lip service to a behavioristic approach are hardly more sophisticated than Thorndike's law of effect. Behaviorism, then, became active in the therapy process not as a result of the word games of Dollard and Miller, but rather from the practical application of Wolpe (1958), Bijou and Baer (1961, 1965, 1966), and Ullmann and Krasner (1965).

ANXIETY: BEHAVIOR THEORY

A habit is a consistent way of responding to defined stimulus conditions. Ordinarily, a habit declines—undergoes extinction—when its consequences become unadaptive, i.e., when it fails either to subserve the needs of the organism or to avoid injury, pain or fatigue. Neurotic habits are distinguished by their resistance to extinction in the face of their unadaptiveness. Behavior therapy is the application of experimentally established principles of learning to the overcoming of these persistent habits [Wolpe and Lazarus, 1966, p. 1].

JOSEPH WOLPE

During the last twenty years, behavior modification, a simplified application of reinforcement theory to the prediction and control of emotional and behavioral problems of children, has been greatly on the increase. This application of classical and operant conditioning techniques has been reviewed in Chapters 7 and 8, but at this point it is appropriate to relate these techniques to the specific problem of anxiety.

At present, two main thrusts are emerging from the body of learning theory in efforts to solve the problem of anxiety. One thrust, generally referred to as reciprocal inhibition and desensitization, arose out of a relaxation technique developed in the 1930s by Jacobson and supported and defended in the late 1950s by Wolpe. As described in Chapter 7, this technique involves the concepts of progressive relaxation, assertive training, and systematic desensitization developed into a treatment strategy under the direction of Wolpe.

BEHAVIOR TREATMENT

The practice of behavior therapy may thus be viewed as a "double-barrelled" means of alleviating neurotic distress. As in most systems of psychotherapy, the patient enjoys the nonjudgmental acceptance of a person whom he perceives as possessing the necessary skills and desire to be of service, but, in behavior therapy he receives, in addition, the benefits of special conditioning procedures which have independent validity [Wolpe and Lazarus, 1966, p. 10].

Progressive Relaxation

Jacobson (1938) noted the possibility of inducing a relaxed state through a rather brief schedule of mental and physical exercises closely

resembling the induction procedure for a hypnotic trance. He found that
for a person in this relaxed state to be aware of anxiety was highly unlikely;
as he became progressively more relaxed, his anxiety diminished in a
reciprocal process.

Reciprocal Inhibition

Wolpe (1958), who conceived of using Jacobson's technique in actual
clinical treatment of anxiety, coined the phrase *reciprocal inhibition*. He
affirms that all conditioning therapies, including reciprocal inhibition, are
predicated upon the fundamental conception that all neuroses, including
anxiety states and phobias, are merely "persistent unadaptive habits that
have been conditioned (that is, learned)" (Wolpe, 1964, p. 9).

Furthermore, the treatment programs proposed to remedy these disorders are specific examples of deconditioning, or unlearning of these maladaptive responses. According to Wolpe, the central problem of all neuroses is the persistent habit of "reacting with anxiety to situations that,
objectively, are not dangerous" (1964, p. 16). Because neurotic anxiety
responses are overlearned, both theoretically and practically, they are
highly resistive to extinction or cure.

The basic premise of the Wolpean treatment strategy is that "if a
response inhibitory to anxiety can be made to occur in the presence of
anxiety-evoking stimuli so that it is accompanied by a complete or partial
suppression of the anxiety response, the bond between these stimuli and
the anxiety response will be weakened" (Wolpe, 1961, p. 189). In contrast
to Mowrer, Wolpe and Lazarus state that "the behavior therapist does not
moralize to his patient, but on the contrary goes out of his way to nullify
the self-blame that social conditioning may have engendered" (1966,
p. 16).

The Wolpean strategy, then, is to lead the child into a state of almost
total relaxation and then to introduce, on the periphery of awareness, the
anxiety-producing stimulus in its mildest form. "The method involves
three separate sets of operations: (1) training in deep muscle relaxation;
(2) the construction of anxiety hierarchies; and (3) counterposing relaxation and anxiety-evoking stimuli from the hierarchies" (Wolpe, 1961,
p. 191).

Case of Thaddeus

For example, let's take a child who has a terror of birds, a bird
phobia. The problem has become so severe that the child can no longer
leave the house. Thaddeus spends a great deal of time checking the screens
and is made very anxious by the door being opened. He has taken down
the curtains in his room so that there will be no place for a bird to hide.
And he carries a tennis racket to protect himself. This nine-year-old boy
has become paralyzed by his bird phobia. He is out of school and is in a
constant state of high anxiety.

The treatment program developed by Wolpe would begin by the
establishment of a hierarchy of terror. Thaddeus and his therapist would
work out a list of degrees of terror, beginning, for example, with a black-

and-white, simplified line drawing of a parakeet and moving up through color photographs, a feather of a real bird, a bird in a cage outside the window, a bird in a cage inside the house, and on upward to the ultimate of a description of a screaming eagle with talons outstretched flying toward his face when his arms are tied behind his back.

The second stage of the treatment program would be to introduce a state of relaxation to the point where the child is almost unconscious, and then introduce to him the lowest stimulus on the hierarchy list. If the child demonstrates any anxiety, he is brought back to the state of relaxation and the stimulus re-presented until he shows no anxiety at this level of the hierarchy. Once this is accomplished, the therapist introduces the next item on the hierarchy list. And so on up through the situations that produce great anxiety in the child.

By the way, in case the reader is now curious, one never works up to the screaming eagle, which simply acts as an upper anchor of the hierarchy. The stages would be terminated at the upper limits of a reasonably expected encounter in the child's normal life situation.

However, the effectiveness of the treatment program depends to a great extent upon the ability of the therapist to re-create the anxiety-producing stimuli causing the problem. This ability to bridge the gap between the office and the real world makes for maximum generalization, which is a problem in office-type therapies. Some stimuli must be established through the imagination of the child, such as having a mockingbird attack him during the nesting season. This can best be done when the stimulus is as realistic as possible through either color slides, movies, or tape recorders. Such a treatment program, to be effective, makes severe demands on the therapist and the child alike.

Case of Margaret

An application of reciprocal inhibition outside the therapist's office was used by Bentler to treat eleven-month-old Margaret's fear of water. "Distraction, affective responses towards attractive toys, and body-contact with the mother as well as other mother-related stimuli, were used to elicit responses incompatible with anxiety" (1962, p. 186). By thirteen months Margaret was thoroughly recovered, and follow up at eighteen months indicated the behavior changes were quite permanent.

Assertive Training

In addition to the strategies of progressive relaxation and reciprocal inhibition, Wolpe used a technique called assertive training. The essence of assertive training is the conception that if the child can behave for a period of time in a brave manner, he becomes less fearful as a result. This process, which Wolpe calls assertive training, the psychoanalysts call ego mastery. "Each act of assertion to some extent reciprocally inhibits the anxiety response habit. The assertion required is not necessarily aggressive, and behavior in accordance with affectionate and other feelings may need to be instigated" (Wolpe, 1964, p. 11).

Assertive training is a fundamental part of the rapid-treatment program for school phobia mentioned in Chapter 7. In school phobia treatment, the child is forced to act as though he and his parents believe that of course he is able to survive in school and that of course he is expected to go. The very act of attending school is, then, anxiety-reductive. The child in this case is trained to assert himself in the face of the anxiety and to go on to school; or he is forced to mingle with other children on the playground in a crowd phobia; or he is forced to remain in his bedroom with the light off in a darkness phobia.

The term *forced* is used in its broadest context: he is coerced, encouraged, convinced, brain-washed to the point where he undertakes an activity that normally produces anxiety and that tends to produce increased anxiety the longer it is postponed. We often play games in parent and popular magazines and make transparent references. Perhaps it would have been more palatable to say that the child is encouraged and convinced, rather than forced, but from a realistic prospective, when a 47-pound child with a mental age of six, an emotional age of five, and an ego maturity age of two, encounters a 170-pound, college-educated, life-educated, logically sophisticated, intelligent adult with a professional behavior therapist as a consultant, the term *forced* carries the true meaning.

The combination of assertive training—which can involve positive emotional acts, such as smiling and speaking to another child in the group, as well as aggressive ones—and reciprocal inhibition is the most successful strategy in the repertoire of the behavior therapist, and, when combined with purer forms of operant and classical conditioning, provides an effective technique for the amelioration of certain kinds of anxiety states in children.

ANXIETY: OPERANT MODEL THEORY

An emotion is a complex response elicited and occasioned by environmental conditions and composed of both operants and respondents.... Fear and anxiety are produced by aversive and conditioned aversive stimuli. Everyone knows from experience the manifestations of these two emotions in internal feelings, although probably no two individuals experience them in exactly the same way [Reynolds, 1968, pp. 118, 122].

B. F. SKINNER

The second thrust in the application of learning theory to the problem of anxiety, termed conditioned emotional response (CER), developed out of a research program of Estes and Skinner (1941). In operant language, anxiety, or the CER, is defined as a change, either an increase or decrease, in operant behavior maintained by a schedule of reinforcement in the presence of a conditioned aversive stimulus: that is, anxiety is the change in performance that occurs in the presence of a stimulus that has acquired negative reinforcement properties. In the simplest terms, then, anxiety is a response to a stimulus, but the response is generally measured not directly, as an act, but indirectly, as the increase or decrease of another act.

Let us take as an example a mother who has the ability to produce a CER. For reasons of her own, this mother is an erratic person who frequently has outbursts toward her children that are, in operant language, noncontingent; that is, they are independent of what Waldo is doing at the time. She simply appears, with a stern facial expression, her hands on her hips, and shortly becomes enraged at Waldo and lashes out. The only cue that signals to Waldo that some form of punishment is imminent is "that look."

Let us further suppose that at this period in his life Waldo is engaged generally in a positively reinforced schedule of investigation, such as opening camellia buds and finding pretty petals inside—what we will call curiosity behavior. His curiosity behavior has become rather stable, as is the general nature of children provided with stimulation and reinforcement for this pattern. He is on a high work rate, a stable schedule, and the best guess is that he will continue this behavior and become a good student.

However, in the midst of this activity, and all other activities that in some way represent a curiosity drive, the mother periodically arrives with "that look," and regardless of what Waldo is doing at the time, she "belts him one," and yells at him to stop it. His rate of exploring behavior is, in this case, drastically curtailed and the operant theorists would report that he is now anxious because of the presence of the conditioned aversive stimulus. "That look" has indeed inhibited his rate of response and he has demonstrated a conditioned emotional response.

Measurement of Anxiety

It is important to note that the rather marked distinction between fear and anxiety, made both in the psychoanalytic and Wolpean tradition, is disregarded in the operant model. If any distinction is to be made at all, it is made on the basis of the sharpness or vividness of the stimulus, the

amount of anxiety it arouses. But this is a between-the-lines assessment and is of little practical significance.

The essence of the formulation is that a conditioned stimulus appears and has an effect on the rate of performance. Generally, the CER has a negative effect on the child's adaptive performance; that is, it decreases the rate. But anxious children sometimes engage in a flurry of activity when in the presence of the CER stimulus. For example, in the case of the curious boy mentioned earlier, he might engage in a high rate of "helping tasks" in the presence of his mother, who periodically hits and yells, scowls and yowls.

The CER stimulus is assumed to be a learned or conditioned stimulus; the stimulus was originally neutral. Thus, the first time Waldo encountered the stern face, "that look," the folded arms, and the banshee-like screaming, he did not change his rate of performance. But once the CER stimulus becomes conditioned, the child is said to have become anxious.

The anxiety is measured by a change in the rate of performance, usually in the direction of a lower rate. This follows logically, if simplistically: a person whom the analyst calls anxious reduces his rate of performance of some act. This operant concept gives a more parsimonious and operational definition of the critical concept of anxiety.

OPERANT TREATMENT

Two interlocking strategies are employed to reduce the CER in the operant model. The first of these involves the use of avoidance training and the second involves competing positive reinforcement that overrides the CER. Their use in combination, together with the modification of the conditioned stimulus itself, would seem to provide the optimal strategy for the elimination of the anxiety response.

Avoidance Training

In avoidance training, the child is placed in a situation in which he learns to avoid the aversive stimulus. The retraining is carried out in a different environment from the one in which the conditioned stimulus for the CER is located. This provides the dual function of minimizing the generalization of the anxiety response, which can be held place-specific for the time being, and controlling the appearance of the conditioned stimulus, which in turn effectively reduces the CER, with the result that the response rate returns to normal or near normal.

Let us return to the mother who has produced an anxiety response in her child. Her presence with "that look" has become the conditioned stimulus for the CER of a large reduction of all behavior, but most particularly the exploratory and creative acts that are essential for mental and emotional growth in childhood. The mother's periodic appearance with "that look" has made Waldo so anxious that he is not learning from experience because his exploratory and creative responses have been suppressed. He is an anxious child in need of professional help; he is suffering from paralyzing anxiety.

In the operant treatment strategy, to remove this anxiety or suppression, one does three things in combination. First, the child is removed from the home environment and the presence of his arm-folded, scowling mother, with her history of yowling and scowling and punishment following "that look." In operant language, he is removed from the presence of the aversive or suppressive conditioned stimulus. Waldo is placed, instead, in a nursery school setting where his exploratory behavior is not terminated by the appearance of the arm-folded, scowling, yowling mother. He is encouraged to explore in the presence of a warm, friendly, responsive, accepting nursery school teacher who does not fold her arms or scowl, but instead smiles and encourages when Waldo engages in exploratory or creative behavior. She continues to smile and be accepting even in the presence of such behavior by Waldo as taking a flower apart to see what is inside, or, for that matter, taking a lizard apart for the same reason. Gradually the exploratory behavior returns and Waldo is no longer anxious in performing creative, exploratory learning tasks.

Competing Positive Reinforcement

At the same time the child is removed from the presence of the conditioned suppressive stimulus, he is being rewarded for his exploratory behavior. This reward can be social, as discussed above, or in the form of candy, stars, checkmarks, or the self-reinforcement that comes from seeing the insides of a lizard when you are four. With removal from the presence of the scowling, yowling, arms-folded mother, and with unpunished and/or reinforced exploratory behavior, the child is now able to return to a high rate of exploratory or creative behavior and is thus now cured of his anxiety.

Modification of Conditioned Stimulus

The third leg of the operant treatment program would be an attempt to reschedule the mother's behavior such that it does not appear to be so aversive to exploratory behavior. The mother may be encouraged to stay away from the child when she is in one of those black moods brought on by migraine headaches or periodic depression. Or she herself might be reinforced for reinforcing her child's exploratory behavior. Obviously this is more difficult to accomplish practically than is the work with the child.

Test of Effectiveness

Assuming now that the nursery-school teacher has been successful in her program of reestablishing exploratory and creative behavior, the child may indeed be considered cured of his anxiety. But the acid test will be whether, when he returns home, he is able to continue to respond with his exploratory and creative behavior in the presence of the aversive stimulus of the scowling, yowling, arms-folded mother, if she has not made any change. Will he be able to distinguish that it is only when "that look" is present that his behavior is likely to bring on punishment? In operant theory such a cure is possible, and assuming some change by the mother, even if only to the point of her being relied upon never to strike out except when emitting "that look," a cure is highly likely.

The appeal of the operant explanation of behavior therapy is that the few assumptions and the operational definitions for all of the variables make a prescription therapy program possible. This model is a long way from the medical model of the traditional mental-health worker, but its simplicity may yet make it the leading treatment therapy in use.

ANXIETY: PUNISHMENT THEORY

Phobias which are complex to unravel often have simple beginnings as conditioned emotional reactions [Bentler, 1962, p. 185].

The procedures used in avoidance training give rise to conditioned emotional responses that influence the course of future learning.... Conditioned emotional responses may, in fact, be elicited simply by the presence of an adult who has been the agent of punishment [Bandura and Walters, 1963, p. 13].

ALBERT BANDURA AND RICHARD WALTERS

The conditioned emotional response was accepted as the best operational definition of anxiety by Bandura and Walters, who then applied the general notion to the problem of anxiety transmission in children. They pointed out that with children, most conditioned emotional responses are the result of punishment used in avoidance training. Some of the most important training in early childhood is related to avoidance—not eating certain unedibles, not climbing too high, not touching hot things, not going into the street—and in each case the teaching agent is the same, mother. It follows then that "conditioned emotional responses may, in fact, be elicited simply by the presence of an adult who has been the agent of punishment."

Modeling

One of the major strengths of the approach suggested by Bandura and Walters is their emphasis on vicarious training. They point out that not

only can various social-training procedures be employed in the modification of a single child's behavior, but that they also have a predictable effect on other children who watch. In the area of social imitation and modeling Bandura and Walters have made their greatest contribution to the prediction and control of group behavior of children in situations typical of the classroom, where so much of a child's training takes place today.

They begin their presentation with the notation that the effectiveness of modeling depends upon the ability of the observer to identify the emotion and to identify the cues that produce the emotion. The more vivid the encounter, the easier the vicarious learning is.

Spider Phobia

Take the example of a spider phobia that most girls develop and keep throughout their lives. Father and four-year-old Waldo are in the living room looking at the Sunday afternoon ball game while mother and three-year-old daughter are in the bedroom changing the baby's diapers. Suddenly, as mother leans over the crib to put the baby down, she finds herself eyeball to eyeball with a great gray house spider. With one hand she grabs up baby, with the other she snatches her daughter. Backing into the corner, she lets out a piercing scream that would wake the dead in the next county.

Father, hearing the scream, flies right out of his chair, leaves a can of beer in midair, and rushes into the bedroom brandishing the only club he could find, a rolled up sports page. Once in the room, he looks where his quivering wife is pointing and gradually takes in the situation. "Good Lord, Alice! Scare a man to death, why don't you! That little speck?" And then deftly, with a flick of the sports page, he does in the house spider, and shaking his head, he returns to the living room to mop up the beer, after first hugging his grateful wife and patting his daughter on the head. Waldo, whose heart has stopped pounding, has regained his calm, and he too is shaking his head in disgust at those women.

422

Later, of course, the situation is repeated in the children's play, with the little girl finding a spider and being afraid and the little boy killing the spider with a newspaper and being disgusted at the weakness and scareyness of women. The fear reaction by the girl and the counterphobic behavior by the boy, then, are learned through the modeling effect of being in the home with mothers and fathers who have in turn learned their role by watching other models.

And of course, fair is fair. The little girl, who models on her father instead and chases little boys around the yard with a snake in her hand, is not playing fair and usually is punished for such infraction of the rules of the game by social isolation from her peers who recognize that she is breaking a "sacrament" by such behavior.

Dog Phobia

Let us look at two studies by Bandura (Bandura, Grusec, and Menlove, 1967; Bandura and Menlove, 1968) that are related to the extinction of fear of dogs. These studies utilize the concept of vicarious extinction.

In the first study parental interviews identified children with a general tendency toward a lack of confidence in or actual fear of situations in which a dog was present. This group was selected further through a test situation that required an increasing exposure to a dog in a pen. A series of fourteen performance tasks required the children to engage in increasingly intimate interactions with a dog. The tasks ranged in difficulty from walking up to the pen in which the dog was securely fastened, through walking the dog on a leash, to the final and most difficult task requiring the children to climb into the playpen with the dog and pet her while she was loose from any leash and no one else was in the room. The intensity of the dog phobia was established, then, both on the rating of the parents and on the number of the tasks that the children could perform.

The children were then exposed to four different conditions. Group 1, in the highly positive context of a birthday party, participated in a series

423

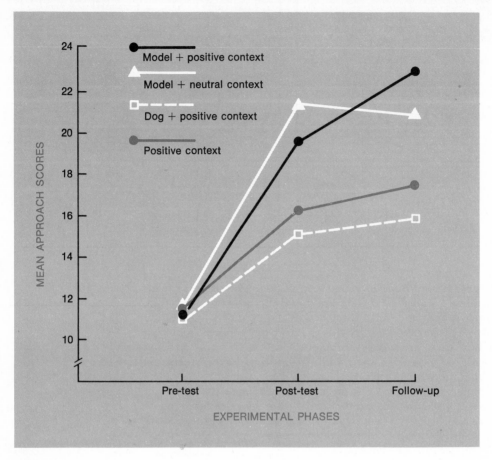

Figure 22

Mean approach scores of dog-phobic children under
different live-model treatment conditions. Reprinted,
by permission of Albert Bandura and the American
Psychological Association, from Albert Bandura, Joan
E. Grusec, and Frances L. Menlove, Vicarious extinction
of avoidance behavior, *Journal of Personality and
Social Psychology*, 1967, 5, Figure 1, p. 21.

of modeling sessions in which they observed a fearless peer model exhibit
progressively stronger approach responses to a dog. Group 2 went through
the same modeling situation except that the party atmosphere was missing.
Group 3 observed the dog in the party atmosphere in the absence of a
model. And Group 4 experienced the party atmosphere with no dog and
no model.

Following the procedure of treatment or nontreatment, depending on
the group, the children were retested to determine the effectiveness of the
procedures in decreasing the dog phobia. Those children who were exposed to a model exhibiting a fearless encounter with a dog reduced their
avoidance behavior in the post-test regardless of whether or not the context
was a party atmosphere.

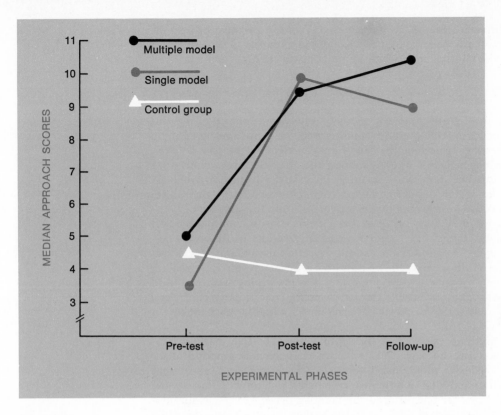

Figure 23

Mean approach scores of dog-phobic children under different movie-model treatment conditions. Reprinted, by permission of Albert Bandura and the American Psychological Association, from Albert Bandura and

Frances L. Menlove, Factors determining vicarious extinction of avoidance behavior through symbolic modeling, *Journal of Personality and Social Psychology*, 1968, 8, Figure 1, p. 102.

Figure 22 shows the relationship between the four treatment procedures. Clearly the two model procedures are superior. In the long-term follow up, the modeling in the positive context continued to be effective, although the difference was not great.

The second study represents an extension of the study, which mechanized the modeling process by having the children observe a movie comprised of eight three-minute sections shown to the children two per day on four days. The first group observed a fearless five-year-old male model display progressively bolder approach responses toward a cocker spaniel. The child went through essentially the same process as the live model in the previous study. The second group was exposed to a film sequence essentially the same as the first, except that there were several models and several dogs, with the familiarity and the apparent ferociousness of the dogs increasing from sequence to sequence. The same pre- and postmeasures were taken and performance was compared with a control group that saw no movies. Figure 23 illustrates the results. Notice again that both model methods were equally effective in reducing the dog phobia and further, that the multiple model had a greater lasting effect.

PUNISHMENT THEORY TREATMENT

Bandura and Walters make a distinction between removal of positive reward, nonreward, and aversive conditioning, or punishment. In the removal procedure, something the child has been given in the past is taken away. In an experimental situation, the child may be given candy in a cup for performance, and candy may be taken away from him when he misses. In the social situation, the parents may take away their love. Pained expressions or frowning by the parents fall into this category.

The major difference between the effectiveness of nonreward and aversive conditioning is that "nonreward usually results in the extinction of responses, aversive conditioning suppresses rather than eliminates them" (Bandura and Walters, 1963, p. 14), and may in fact result in a general decrease in performance. More important when working with children, "emotional responses established through aversive conditioning may motivate socially undesirable behavior patterns that are highly resistant to extinction" (1963, p. 13).

In the previous example of the child whose creative drive is suppressed by the CER, he may well develop a tic during this period of inactivity, or a reflexive motor habit, such as a neck jerk or a gasp, that becomes so habitual that it remains even after the intervention of the nursery-school teacher has restored the creative drive. Aversive stimulation should be used with children only in circumstances wherein desirable behaviors are being elicited and rewarded at the same time, such that the direction of change is under the control of the therapist and not left to chance.

ANXIETY: CLIENT-CENTERED THEORY

"In the typical neurosis, the organism is satisfying a need which is not recognized in consciousness, by behavioral means which are consistent with the concept of self and hence can be consciously accepted" (Rogers, 1951, p. 508).

CARL ROGERS

At this point, it would seem important to review both the theory and practice of a somewhat different view of anxiety held by the client-centered psychotherapists such as Rogers (1951), Axline (1947), and Ginott (1961). The client-centered psychologists view the major cause of anxiety in children as a feeling of loneliness and isolation, together with a lack of understanding of the emotions of one's self and others. The anxious child, then, is a child who is very much wrapped up in himself and who has great difficulty in expressing, or even recognizing his feelings. The system generally accepts the Freudian notion that the difference between conscious and unconscious feelings is the degree to which the person has the ability to turn these feelings into logically consistent verbal statements that he himself can accept as being valid. Self-acceptance, then, of one's true feelings and understanding the feelings of others, as well as the relationship between the two, is what the client-centered therapist would call insight.

CLIENT-CENTERED TREATMENT

Under these terms, the responsibility of the therapist is to correctly reflect the true feelings of the child in a setting in which the child can accept these reflections. Such a task requires a great deal of empathy from the therapist and considerable experience with the child in a setting wherein his personality can be expressed with little threat. The contention of the nondirective, client-centered therapist is that the playroom is the ideal place for such communication to occur.

Playroom

The child is introduced into the playroom equipped as a miniature world resembling that in which the child lives. Sand tables and doll houses, as well as puppets, dolls, and toys, lend themselves to more or less plastic use by the child. The child is introduced into this play world with as few rules as possible, such as "You can do anything or say anything you like here, so long as you do not hurt yourself or me, and so long as you do not deface the room."

With this the child is turned loose. The therapist serves the role of commentator and describer, often using a third-person explanation of what is going on. Statements, such as "Now the little boy is angry at his mother and is hitting her," accompany the activity of the child. The major goal of the therapist is the development of empathy such that the child will begin to understand himself, what kind of stresses he is under, and, what is more, will come to recognize that someone else understands.

Release Therapy

A part of the client-centered approach is release therapy, in which the child is permitted to express a considerable degree of raw emotion without any evaluation or criticism so long as he confines himself to the rules. Under these circumstances the therapist may be simply verbalizing the flow of emotions that result from the surge of feelings. His whole task at the moment may be to convince the child that another human being is able to comprehend his feelings and, furthermore, express them in a way that makes some sense.

Assumptions

The success of the method is predicated upon the assumption that there is within all children a drive for understanding and psychological growth. The act of being understood and accepted for what one is, in and of itself, is sufficient to loosen the growth impulse within the individual and enable him to mature emotionally. The client-centered approach is more like the traditional medical model than like Mowrer's, in that anxiety is believed to be the result of an improper perception and the resulting accumulation of guilt feelings regarding natural impulses and feelings, whereas Mowrer feels that the cause of anxiety is mainly correctly perceived feelings of guilt.

The underlying assumption, then, is that as the child is accepted and understood by his therapist, his behavior will become more socially acceptable and he will become a more fully functioning individual because his creative energy will be released. He will not spend so much of his energy holding himself down for fear of retaliation by society. Rather, he will be able to use this energy to cope with the real stresses of society. The purpose of the therapist is not simply to reassure, because he recognizes that there is a real world out there, but rather, his role is to empathize with the child and to help him understand the nature of the demands of society.

Basic Conformity Goal

One of the goals of nondirective therapy is to help the child understand that, in order to be free of the threat of society, he must come to terms with it and correctly perceive the nature of the minimum demands by which freedom is gained. This acceptance of the basic structure of society is an essential part of the maturing process that enables a person to develop his own freedom within the constraints of our society.

HARRY STACK SULLIVAN

The basic assumption underlying the nondirective or client-centered approach is also carried in the theory of Sullivan: "The tension of anxiety, when present in the mothering one, induces anxiety in the infant" (1953, p. 41). "For Sullivan, anxiety is a product of education and living among significant people and is social and human" (Sarason, Davidson, Lighthall, Waite, and Ruebush, 1960, p. 36).

The assumption is that the root cause of anxiety is isolation or the fear of isolation. Whether this is derived from the experience of being temporarily alone when a small child and having pressing, unmet needs, as suggested by Dollard and Miller, or instinctive, as suggested by Freud and Jung, is really of little concern to the nondirective therapists. Their goal is to break down the barriers of communication, reduce the feelings of isolation, which have stunted psychological growth, and thus free the child to resume his development into a fully functioning individual.

OBJECTIVE MEASUREMENT

To leave a discussion of the client-centered approach without applying the same yardstick to this movement as was applied to the psychoanalytic movement would not be fair. And again the objective measurement of client improvement has been a problem. The client-centered

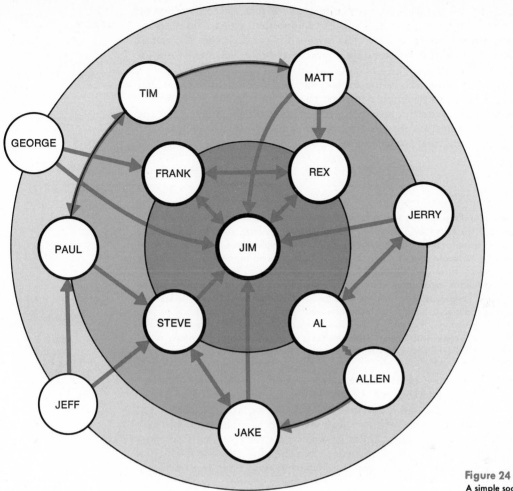

Figure 24
A simple sociogram.

therapists are much concerned about internal emotional events, which admittedly are difficult to measure. They have been forced to resort to evaluations of a relatively objective scoring technique of self-descriptive statements by the client.

Discomfort Relief Quotient

The discomfort relief quotient (DRQ) is a technique developed to score specific words as having discomfort or relief qualities on a semantic rating. These are formed into a ratio or quotient to show the affective state of the child. The PNAVQ is essentially the same technique, scoring positive, negative, ambivalent verbalizations in self-describing statements.

Sociogram

Another technique evaluates the social movement of a child within the group. Each child in the classroom chooses the classmate he would most like to play with, study with, take home with him after school, or go home with. The relative position of each child is then charted in a sociogram, as illustrated in Figure 24. The farther the child is from the center of the picture, the less he is chosen for any activity. The double arrows indicate a mutual choice.

One of the most interesting aspects of the isolation problem is the choice of the isolate. Presumably his best chance for mutual choice would be with someone else on the periphery, but, in point of fact, such is not the case. He buys right into the system and tends to choose a leader, or the only leader, and in effect verifies his own isolation.

ANXIETY: TRAIT THEORY

Research findings suggest that it is meaningful to distinguish between anxiety as a transitory state and as a relatively stable personality trait, and to differentiate between anxiety states, the stimulus conditions that evoke them, and the defenses that serve to avoid them. There is considerable general agreement that anxiety states are characterized by subjective, consciously perceived feelings of apprehension and tension, accompanied by or associated with activation or arousal of the autonomic nervous system. Anxiety as a personality trait would seem to imply a motive or acquired behavioral disposition that predisposes an individual to perceive a wide range of objectively nondangerous circumstances as threatening, and to respond to these with anxiety state reactions disproportionate in intensity to the magnitude of the objective danger [Spielberger, 1966, pp. 16–17].

Thus far we have been talking about anxiety in a pretty subjective manner. Aristotle, Kierkegaard, Freud, Mowrer, and Dollard and Miller all had felt anxiety and had made inferences regarding anxiety in all men. Thus, anxiety arose in the psychological literature as what we could call today an intervening variable. That is, we can measure, at least to some degree, the probable expression of anxiety, but the internal state itself is an inference, an inference based on input and output, it is true, but nevertheless an inference.

The whole psychoanalytic movement is based upon the assumption that there is a quality, called anxiety, of which some people have more than others and with which some people deal more effectively than others. The assumption is that the therapist's role is to reduce anxiety and to help the individual to develop strategies that make him more effective in anxiety control. Anxiety, however, is experienced as arousal, and little distinction can be made between pleasant and unpleasant arousal. Thus, the need clearly existed for more objectification of the subjective experience of anxiety.

A different tack to the problem of anxiety, one related to a covertly measured variable of anxiety, is a measurement approach to manifest anxiety as determined through a trait scale. The *Taylor Manifest Anxiety Scale* (Taylor, 1953) assumes that anxiety has a dimension of quantity that can be measured by a questionnaire.

Manifest anxiety was derived as a description of the verbalized expression of the psychic experience of anxiety. Examples of manifest anxiety would be: "I can hear my heart pounding"; "My hands are sweaty most of the time"; "I have a tight feeling in my chest as though I'm going to explode"; "I have this feeling that something terrible is going to happen"; "My tummy has butterflies"; "I am anxious." By developing a number of such statements, and by scaling them in order of their subjective severity as agreed upon by a large number of people, a manifest anxiety scale was possible; that is, a series of statements, to be answered yes or no or to varying degrees by an individual, which would place this person in the dimension we call manifest anxiety. Such a procedure is represented in the *Children's Manifest Anxiety Scale* and the half dozen or so scales that closely resemble it.

Children's Manifest Anxiety Scale

The *Children's Manifest Anxiety Scale* was developed in 1956 by Castaneda, McCandless, and Palermo. This test represented a translation of the *Taylor Manifest Anxiety Scale,* which in turn was a selection of items from the *Minnesota Multiphasic Personality Inventory,* a large test of some 560 yes or no items. The *Children's Manifest Anxiety Scale* carefully rephrased these statements such that they were appropriate for children and reduced the number of questions to 53 to be answered yes or no by the child. Some of the scale represents filler questions and some of the scale represents validity questions to determine whether a person is giving careful and honest consideration to the questions being asked. They are questions that anyone being at all faithful to the task at hand would answer true, such as "I sometimes get mad." Obviously anyone, even a child, who emphatically denies ever having been mad, widens the credibility gap to a chasm.

The effectiveness of the *Children's Manifest Anxiety Scale* depends upon the ability of the child to verbalize the degree to which he is anxious. There are obvious problems related to a child's expression of anxiety. His use of vocabulary expressing affective state is still rather primitive. But the utilization of simplified language, carefully selected to be in their repertoire, enables such an instrument to be used with schoolchildren. The test was standardized initially on fourth-, fifth-, and sixth-grade children, after going through several stages of pretesting to translate the adult scale, or *Taylor Manifest Anxiety Scale,* into language geared for the upper elementary-school level.

There is bound to be some disagreement among experts as to whether or not a given statement actually describes anxiety. The face validity of a manifest anxiety scale will always be open to question. Consensual validation, although providing an impelling argument, is open to question because a simple majority may be mistaken. But even if one questions the construct validity of the *Children's Manifest Anxiety Scale,* one still must deal with the fact that it obviously measures something, that it measures in an objective, and, as it turns out, reliable fashion, and that a manifest anxiety score can be used to make predictions about behavior logically related to anxiety.

The importance of the *Children's Manifest Anxiety Scale* is not its general acceptance, even though it is broadly accepted, or its utility, even though it is effective in making predictions. The importance is that the *Children's Manifest Anxiety Scale* represents a break from the tradition of subjective ap-

praisal of anxiety—how the analyst feels that the patient feels. And any
move away from that technique is a step toward the light. The discussion
of manifest anxiety scales for children, then, is a two-thrust presentation:
first, to demonstrate the relationship between the anxiety scales and other
variables presumed to be affected by anxiety; and, second, to look at
methods and procedures by which children's anxiety can be modified.

Manifest Anxiety Related to Children's Behavior

Studies of children's behavior as it relates to manifest anxiety have
covered the usual variables: age, sex, rate of performance, verbal performance, test-taking ability, etc. Let us look at a few of these behaviors
that demonstrate the relationship between the manifest anxiety scales and
other variables presumed to be affected by anxiety.

Task Performance

The task performance of children high in manifest anxiety has been
found to surpass that of those children low in anxiety for simple tasks, but
has proven to be inferior for complex ones. Using the *Children's Manifest
Anxiety Scale,* Castaneda, Palermo, and McCandless (1956) found that
anxious children appear to have high drive, which enables them to do well
on simple tasks where the need to achieve gives the child an added advantage. However, when the task becomes more complex, with abstract
reasoning required, high-anxiety children do not perform as well as low-
anxiety children.

An inverted U-shaped relationship between anxiety and performance
has been fairly well established (Malmo, 1966). As anxiety, or alertness, or
sensitivity increases, performance increases, until one reaches an optimal
point, and then performance begins to decrease as sharply as it increased.
High-anxiety children appear to peak out sooner than low-anxiety children.

Thus, alertness is useful in the solution of complex tasks only up to a
certain point. Then one becomes too excited, too alert, and the performance disintegrates. Stage fright is an excellent example of this dis-
integrating effect of high drive. In school plays performance can be so
pushed that after hours of practice and successful repetition of the part, the
child becomes unglued during the actual performance and can't say anything. In effect he has peaked out and his performance declines rapidly.

Test Performance

One of the most frequent explanations of low academic test performance in spite of high intellectual potential is the concept of anxiety as
an inhibitor, the thought being that the net result of anxiousness is mental
inefficiency. Sarason, Davidson, Lighthall, Waite, and Ruebush (1960),
however, point out in their extended research on the subject that such a
statement is often incorrect since the effect of anxiety on performance is
much more complex and depends upon such variables as the amount of
anxiety and the complexity of the task. After first demonstrating that their
instruments, the *Test Anxiety Scale for Children* and the *General Anxiety Scale*

for Children, seem to be good predictors of general difficulty in test performance, they then investigated the relationship between anxiety scores and performance.

They found that test anxiety is not related to social class—that is, it is not the attitude of the parent toward academic achievement that determines test anxiety, but rather the whole relationship between parent and child. They found that girls have higher anxiety scores than do boys. And they noted with interest that in predicting anxiety scores for their own children, only fathers could make a reliable distinction between low-anxiety sons, whom they viewed as more mature and responsible, and high-anxiety sons; and fathers could also identify low-anxiety daughters, whom they saw as more optimistic, responsible, and less generous than their anxious sisters.

Verbal Performance

Not only, then, does anxiety interfere with performance on tests, but it also interferes with general verbal performance, both written and oral. Stevenson and Odom (1965) demonstrated clearly that high-anxiety children, as measured by the *Test Anxiety Scale for Children,* do increasingly poorly as the tasks move from concrete, rote problems to verbal, abstract problems.

One can carry this conclusion over into the realm of social interaction, as did Haggard in studying the relationship between anxiety and social performance in gifted children. He found that the more complex the social interaction, the greater the inhibitory effect of anxiety. In essence, high-anxiety states critically interfere with verbal performance and, as Haggard says, "the best way to produce 'clear thinkers' is to help children develop into anxiety-free, emotionally healthy individuals who are also trained to master a variety of intellectual tasks" (1957, p. 409).

Distractibility

Highly anxious boys in classroom observations show less orientation toward tasks than boys of low anxiety. In a classroom situation, anxious boys show a higher degree of distractibility, a proneness to wander from the task at hand, to a much greater degree than non-anxious boys. Why the same is not also true for girls is not at all clear. But highly anxious girls are less distractible (Sarason, Davidson, Lighthall, and Waite, 1958, 1960). Taken as a whole, a high-anxiety scale indicates a high degree of conditionability: the higher the anxiety, up to a point, the more rapidly a student learns, the more easily his behavior is modified by conditioning. But above a certain point anxiety seems to produce irritability and random, unproductive, anxiety-reducing behavior.

The research of Sarason et al. has been related to children's anxiety as measured by the *Test Anxiety Scale for Children* and the *General Anxiety Scale for Children.* The *Test Anxiety Scale,* highly structured and with high face validity, requires the child to answer yes or no to a list of thirty questions about a variety of test situations. The *General Anxiety Scale* is intended as a measure of general, chronic anxiety, and as such, resembles somewhat the *Children's Manifest Anxiety Scale*.

Popularity

High-anxious children are less popular with their peers than low-anxious children (McCandless, Castaneda, and Palermo, 1956). Children who experience a great deal of subjective anxiety have very little free energy and thus are incapable of giving themselves in a relationship. The effect of the manifest anxiety causes them to be wrapped up in themselves, to pay little attention to other people's needs. And this does not make for popularity. It makes instead for a lonely, solitary existence.

Self-Estimate

Highly anxious children have less positive self-concepts (F. Horowitz, 1962; Lipsitt, 1958). Children with high anxiety—children who are fearful, apprehensive, and psychologically uncomfortable—take a poor view of themselves, hold themselves in low esteem, and rate themselves in an inferior position within a group.

The corollary is also true. Not only do such children express less positive feelings toward themselves, but they also express more negative feelings than less anxious children (J. Bernard, Zimbardo, and Sarason, 1961). Both of these evaluations are taken from personal assessments, self-estimate statements rated by independent observers as being negative, positive, or ambivalent in nature.

THE TOPOGRAPHY OF CHILDREN'S FEARS

As early as 1935, interest was focused on the general frequency, nature, and characteristics of children's fears. The first detailed mapping of children's fears was the work of Jersild and his associates (Jersild, 1954; Jersild and Holmes, 1935a,b). Watson had already pretty well established, through the study of the Moro reflex, that very young children have an unlearned fear of probably only two stimuli—loud noises and falling. The Moro primitive startle reflex responds to either of these signals even when given at low levels of intensity.

Through the use of questionnaires administered to parents and children, Jersild began a systematic investigation of the development of children's fears. These studies stand as a monumental effort. In spite of great improvement in the sophistication of child research methods and, even more significantly, the change history has made in the lives of children today, not a single later study, even the most recent, fails to confirm the basic conclusions of Jersild and his associates.

Children's fears have been studied as a function of age, social class, sex, education, and race by many investigators throughout the years. Our discussion represents the essential agreement in all of the studies. What, then, is the basic course of the development of fears in children, and how is this course affected by sex, social class, education, and race?

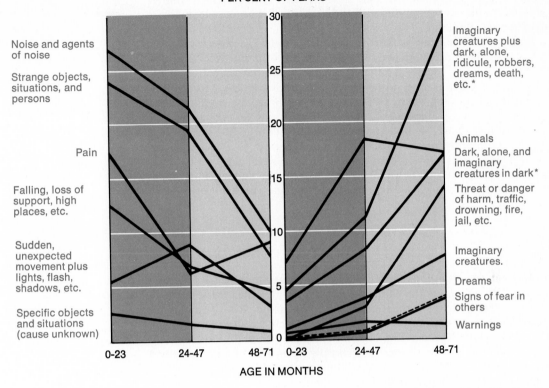

PER CENT OF FEARS

Noise and agents of noise

Strange objects, situations, and persons

Pain

Falling, loss of support, high places, etc.

Sudden, unexpected movement plus lights, flash, shadows, etc.

Specific objects and situations (cause unknown)

Imaginary creatures plus dark, alone, ridicule, robbers, dreams, death, etc.*

Animals

Dark, alone, and imaginary creatures in dark*

Threat or danger of harm, traffic, drowning, fire, jail, etc.

Imaginary creatures.

Dreams

Signs of fear in others

Warnings

0-23   24-47   48-71   0-23   24-47   48-71

AGE IN MONTHS

*Starred items represent a cumulative tally of two or more categories that also are depicted separately.

Figure 25

Relative frequency of various fear responses. Reprinted, by permission of Arthur T. Jersild and the publisher, from Arthur T. Jersild and Frances B. Holmes, Children's fears, *Teachers College Child Development Monographs* (New York: Teachers College Press, Columbia University), 1935, 20, Figure A, p. 54.

UNCONDITIONED FEARS

Beginning with the two unconditioned fear stimuli of loud noises and falling, Jersild and his associates quickly noted a third stimulus. This one represents a whole class of stimuli, which could be called change variables. Jersild called it a fear of strange objects, situations, and persons, but one could just as well classify it as a strange or change variable; it is easily analogous to loss of support, as it represents a sudden change in the status quo of the background.

Evidently, children accommodate to their environment and become secure with a consistent background or noise level. Sudden changes in this background or sudden new stimuli with significance for the child tend to frighten him—as many an aunt, with her bright coat, strange new voice, and different odor, has discovered as the smiling baby begins to wail when she leans over his crib to speak to him. Not what she does, but what she is, causes the fear. New, sudden, and strange, she produces the primitive startle reflex and mother, in a rather embarrassing scene, has to reassure baby and aunt simultaneously.

Figure 25 indicates a fourth variable, surely overlooked by the Watsonians, which produces fear—the occurrence of pain. Now it is true that babies do have a poorly developed sense of pain, but they are not oblivious to it. Sudden pain is quite effective in producing the Moro reflex, as any mother finds out when, at three in the morning, she shuffles over a nylon rug in her wool slippers and the small static charge jerks baby wide awake, first fearful and then angry, and costs her two hours' sleep. It is amazing how quickly mother learns to ground herself on the bed spring before she picks up a drowsy youngster. Pain can cause fear, particularly when it is unexpected. Figure 25 indicates that any sudden movement, flashing light, or moving shadow, also tends to cause the fear response to blast off.

CONDITIONED FEARS

It is apparent that these reflexive, unconditioned stimuli for fear tend to become less potent as the child grows older, while other fears begin to increase in frequency as a function of age. Thus the fear of imaginary creatures, darkness, dreams, and death tends to increase sharply with age, as does fear of harm through fire, drowning, traffic, jail, and so forth.

Specific fear of animals increases sharply during the second and third years, but begins to decline during the kindergarten and school years. This specific animal fear begins to decline at about six, when fears take on a more abstract and sophisticated nature with increasing age and knowledge. Yet some concrete fears continue to remain powerful determinants of behavior throughout one's life.

We all know that an indigo snake is harmless, has a pleasant disposition, and is in fact beautiful and even a little friendly. But, let an absent-minded professor of biology pick up a box on the lectern, gaze into it in a perplexed fashion, and mutter, "Hmmmmm, that's strange, my snake was here just a minute ago," while he begins looking under the seats of the first row, and one will quickly find an unsolicited testimonial to the residual effect of snake phobias and "the devil take the hindmost." Now it goes without saying that this snake phobia is reinforced by experience and is perhaps maintained by social reinforcement, but it is an exception to the trend in the development of fearful behavior.

A number of studies have compared the fear reactions of children from different social classes. Several conclusions seem to be warranted. Lower-class children tend to report more fear of animals, robbers, failure, scolding, starvation, punishment, and divorce, whereas upper-class children tend to be more afraid of being hurt, alone, in darkness, and in physical danger (Angelino, Dollins, and Mech, 1956). In the United States there is a significant correlation between social class and measured intelligence; thus, when one is making a socioeconomic comparison, one is also making an intellectual comparison. Almost identical findings are demonstrated when one compares children with high intelligence and low intelligence, and with high mental age and low mental age for the same degree of intelligence.

Throughout the literature, a significant relationship is reported between the parents' fears and those of their children. The great majority of children's fears are learned from experiences in the home. Parents have in their power the development of most of the fears of childhood. Failure of communication is one of the greatest causes of anxiety and fear in the child. Parents fail to specify the characteristic of the object that needs to be feared and thus tend to develop a generalized fear reaction when a simple avoidance reaction is all that is required.

Take the case of the five-year-old child referred to a child development clinic because of evidence of great anxiety. The child was clingy, tearful, hyperactive, had a poor appetite, and was unable to sleep.

The parents were in the midst of a financial crisis and had become completely wrapped up in the problem, looking more and more worried each day, and carrying on long and somber-toned conversations far into the night. The child, picking up the anxiety from the parents' tone and expressions, became more and more concerned about what was happening. Finally one night he heard the mother say, "We have got to consider the expense of the children." The poor child, raised as he was on what we laughingly call children's stories such as "Hansel and Gretel," immediately got the picture. He was up for sale.

You have never seen a happier child when he learned that the worst that the family would have to deal with was a day in court and father having to go back to work for a salary. They would keep the home, the family car, have plenty to eat, each other, and not sell the children. So why was everybody so terribly unhappy about that little thing?

The parents, of course, had not wanted to worry the children, so instead had inadvertently subjected them to abject terror. The communication of fears to children is often done in just such a way, with no intention on the part of the parent to cause the children any worry, but rather to make them safe.

Society, too, has a role in provoking fears in children. Black children, as a group, tend to have more fears and to have more intense fears. This is perhaps a function of the insecure position in which they find themselves, as well as the fact that fear is so often used for both internal (within the family) and external (by society) means of control.

SUMMARY

A child comes into the world with two, perhaps three, well-established fears: loud noises, falling, and pain. All of the theorists take this beginning point and, to varying degrees, suggest that fear increases both as a function of the increasing complexity of the child's sensory and cognitive systems and of the increasingly complex social situations he encounters. All theories indicate that the primary relationship, that between the child and his mother, is the most important one in the development of anxiety, the term usually given for nonspecific fears. The more anxiety-free the mother and father are, and the more objective they are in their socializing of the child, the less apt he is to develop anxiety. Once outside the immediate influence of his parents, the child is profoundly affected by other models in his environment. He suffers the most anxiety in those ambiguous and inconsistent situations where he has less experience with models who cope effectively.

The major disagreement among the theorists is in regard to the role internal drives play in the promotion of anxiety. Freud and the psychoanalysts are struck with the flooding concept of anxiety, which relates to the trauma of birth—a newborn child, fresh from a nearly stimulus-free environment where he rests in a liquid medium, generally insulated from sounds, chemical irritants, light, falling, or some other form of stimulation, is thrust into a somewhat hostile world filled with stimulation, while simultaneously confronted with massive stimulation from his insides, in terms of stomach cramps, hunger, thirst, muscle spasms, and the like. This sensation of being overwhelmed with stimulation is the real source of anxiety according to the Freudian's viewpoint, and the social situation simply serves as a reminder of this possibility.

Modern social and learning theorists, on the other hand, are convinced that this flooding occurs at a time when the cortical area of the brain is not functioning. They claim that such a theory, to account for the nature of anxiety, requires a nervous system and memory much more elaborate than those of the newborn. They contend that anxiety is a contagious phenomenon that is "caught" from significant others and is both learned in terms of social reinforcement and imitated in terms of social models.

No one, however, doubts its real significance, nor doubts that anxiety reduction is a necessary condition for effective living. The inverted U-shaped function hypothesized by Malmo is indeed an effective description of the results of anxiety. As anxiety increases, mental efficiency increases in a steep curve up to a critical point, and then just as sharply, the mental efficiency deteriorates under further increase of anxiety. Anxiety, then, or alertness, or high-drive state, is perhaps a necessary condition for the child to function effectively in today's world, but beyond a certain level, it becomes a decrement, and beyond that, a paralyzing agent.

The teacher or parent will do well to bear in mind that there is a real world out there, and that sometime the child must deal with it. In our world some things are worth being anxious about, and anxiety is the correct word. A certain level of tolerance for ambiguity, tolerance for prolonged indecisiveness, and even danger, is required in our world today. There are uncertainties, and there is danger. And not all danger is objective. Some is subjective, and part of the private destiny of man is to be a creature of existential anxiety, but that will come soon enough.

Reduction of anxiety in children through the use of proper models, objective instruction about real danger, reassurance when it is appropriate, empathy when it is not, tend generally to reduce the level of anxiety in children and to make them better able to cope with the realities of their daily life. The high level of anxiety noted in objective and subjective testing and the increase in ulcers and other somatic evidences of anxiety during the past twenty years indicate that we are a long way from making childhood an experience in which the child is free to get on with the business of growing up.

We seem bent on further penetration of the child's world with demands for increased performance. Reading can now be taught by new technology to three-year-olds. Perhaps we do not yet have such high levels of technology in the elimination of anxiety, but one thing is sure: we know a great deal more about the avoidance of anxiety than we know about its remediation, and we know more about its remediation than we tend to put into practice. With the exception of psychotic anxiety in children, which may yet prove to be organic or genetic in nature, not a single child caught up in the ravishes of chronic or acute anxiety could not be greatly aided with kindness, empathy, and a little counterconditioning to undo the learning that produced this state.

REVIEW

Anxiety: Psychoanalytic Theory

Character Defense Mechanism   A character defense mechanism is a systematic, learned pattern of dealing with anxiety; a pattern acquired in early childhood and extremely maladaptive because it deals with anxiety by denying any causal relationship or personal responsibility or sense of guilt: the world is looked upon as a perfidious place where misfortune strikes the unlucky, not because of any action of theirs, but purely by chance. In all societies a sociopath or psychopath is unacceptable by the very definition of a society.

Denial   Denial, a psychotic defense mechanism, is a short-term reaction that allows a person time to adjust; it becomes psychotic when the reaction is long-term.

Ego   The ego is that portion of the personality that is rational, reality-oriented, and adaptive in its reactions to the environment.

Id   The id is that portion of the personality that is primitive, with a reflexive drive system not governed by conscious thought.

Insight   Insight is a profound understanding of causal relationships in one's life; implied is far more than lip service: a full emotional acceptance. A child, who understands that his clinging to people causes them to pull back and that he clings because he fears people will pull back, is said to have developed insight. In the analytic sense, great care is taken to differentiate between intellectual insight, merely saying the words, and true insight, acceptance of the full consequences of the words.

Medical Model of Disease   In analytic theory, the mind is viewed as the body is viewed in medicine: when the mind is ill, it displays symptoms that point to the cause of the illness. The symptoms themselves are insignificant and are treated only incidentally to reduce discomfort. The major treatment is internal and directed toward the cause of the illness or infection.

Moral Anxiety   Moral anxiety is defined by Freud as an overwhelming sense of guilt experienced as feelings of depression.

Neurotic   Freud saw all neurotic symptoms as attempts to control or avoid anxiety. A neurotic was defined as someone who attempted to neutralize the danger signal without trying to find out why it went off or to take realistic steps to eliminate the danger that set it off. Thus, neurosis is self-perpetuating and self-defeating.

Neurotic Anxiety   Neurotic anxiety is defined by Freud as an irrational dread of being overwhelmed by one's own internal drives or of being retaliated against as a consequence of having these drives.

Neurotic Defense Mechanism   Neurotic defense mechanisms are nonadaptive responses to anxiety that make a person feel more secure without helping him to adapt to his environment. As further defined by Anna Freud, neurotic defense mechanisms include: phobia, repression, obsessive compulsion, rationalization, and reaction formation.

Objective Anxiety   Objective anxiety is defined by Freud as an appropriate response to a dangerous stimulus.

Obsessive Compulsion A neurotic defense mechanism, an obsessive compulsion is organized activity that keeps the child from having time to be panicked.

Phobia A neurotic defense mechanism, a phobia is an irrational fear of a specific object or situation.

Play Play is a mechanism of psychoanalytic treatment. The child is given a toy world that replicates his own, wherein he can dramatize his fears and his feelings.

Psychoanalytic Treatment Freud's method of treatment, following the medical model of illness, is the development of insight through two mechanisms—talk and play. In play therapy the child dramatizes his world, his fears, his feelings in miniature while the therapist provides an anxiety-reduced relationship in which the child can be reflected as he really is. Thus, for Freud, anxiety in the child is caused by a distorted self-image resulting from a pathological relationship between the child and his parents.

Psychotic Defense Mechanism Psychotic defense mechanisms are escape responses to anxiety that deny its existence. As further defined by Anna Freud, psychotic defense mechanisms include denial, regression, and withdrawal.

Rationalization A neurotic defense mechanism, rationalization avoids anxiety-producing feelings by elaborate justifications and excuses.

Reaction Formation A neurotic defense mechanism, reaction formation completely submerges the anxiety-producing impulse, with diametrically opposed behavior surfacing.

Regression A psychotic defense mechanism, regression is a rather usual reaction when children are ill or under stress. It becomes psychotic when it becomes a massive across-the-board reaction.

Repression A neurotic defense mechanism, repression blocks off all feeling in some significant area.

Sublimated Defense Mechanism Sublimated defenses are adaptive and socially accepted ways of dealing with anxiety.

Superego The superego is that portion of the personality that is aware of a potential for doing something one should not; a sense of guilt.

Talk Talk is a mechanism of psychoanalytic treatment. The therapist functions as an interpreter, recorder, sounding board to reflect a true picture of the child to himself.

Transference In analytic theory, the assumption is made that the likely cause of the child's anxiety is some form of disturbed interaction between the child and significant adults in his environment. Thus, if he can derive an anxiety-reduced relationship with his therapist, he can see himself more realistically. The major cause of anxiety is seen as a distorted self-image resulting from a pathological interaction between the child and his parents; in analytic theory, normal parents do not have disturbed children, and disturbed youngsters do not have normal parents.

Withdrawal A psychotic defense mechanism, withdrawal, in extreme form, represents complete escape from reality.

Anxiety: Behavior Theory

Assertive Training Assertive training is based on the assumption that behaving bravely for a period of time can help the child to become less fearful.

Behavior Therapy A habit is a consistent way of responding to defined stimulus conditions. Neurotic habits are distinguished by their resistance to extinction in the face of their unadaptiveness. Behavior therapy is the application of experimentally established principles of learning to the overcoming of these persistent habits.

Desensitization Desensitization is a technique used by Wolpe "when the immediate objective is to eliminate conditioned emotional responses and their behavioral by-products" (Reyna, 1964, p. 174).

Progressive Relaxation First used by Jacobson, progressive relaxation induces a relaxed state through a brief set of mental and physical exercises.

Reciprocal Inhibition Based on the assumption that one cannot be both anxious and relaxed, reciprocal inhibition pairs relaxation and anxiety-provoking stimuli until anxiety is no longer felt.

Anxiety: Operant Model Theory

Avoidance Training Avoidance training is an operant treatment strategy that places the child in a situation in which he learns to avoid the aversive stimulus.

Conditioned Emotional Response (CER) Conditioned emotional response is the operant definition for anxiety, an emotion produced by aversive and conditioned aversive stimuli. A conditioned emotional response is defined as a change in behavior, usually a decrease in some behavior.

Anxiety: Trait Theory

Manifest Anxiety Manifest anxiety is a verbal expression, which can be measured on a scale, of the psychic experience of anxiety. The *Children's Manifest Anxiety Scale* was developed by Castaneda, McCandless, and Palermo from the *Taylor Manifest Anxiety Scale*. Its effectiveness depends upon the child's ability to verbalize his anxiety. It is important because it represents a break from the tradition of subjective appraisal of anxiety. Manifest anxiety is related to children's behavior.

Implications

All theories of anxiety indicate that the primary relationship, that between the child and his mother, is the most important in the development of anxiety. The more anxiety-free are the parents, the more objective are they in socializing the child, the less apt he is to develop anxiety.

Once outside the immediate influence of his parents, the child is profoundly affected by other models in his environment, where he suffers the most anxiety in ambiguous and inconsistent situations.

Anxiety is a contagious phenomenon caught from significant others. It is learned in terms of social reinforcement and imitated in terms of social models. Some anxiety may be natural and necessary, but beyond a certain level, it becomes a decrement, and beyond that, a paralyzing agent.

Some things in our world are worth being anxious about; a certain level of tolerance for ambiguity, tolerance for prolonged indecisiveness, and even danger, is required today. But anxiety in children can be reduced, enabling them to cope better with the realities of their daily lives, through the use of proper models, objective instruction about real danger, reassurance when it is appropriate and empathy when it is not.

NAMES TO KNOW

An Old Enemy: Dread

SØREN KIERKEGAARD Kierkegaard defined anxiety as the possibility of freedom. He recognized a significant distinction between fear and anxiety, with fear being related to some objective danger wherein the emotions were appropriate for the magnitude of the risk; anxiety is not so easily understood.

ARISTOTLE Aristotle recognized that anxiety and fear, like all emotions, have their roots in physiological processes. In describing any emotion, one must describe both the object and the affect.

Anxiety: Psychoanalytic Theory

SIGMUND FREUD Noticing the resemblance between behavior associated with anxiety and behavior associated with orgasm, Sigmund Freud at first supposed anxiety to be dammed-up sexual drive, which he called libido. Later Freud saw repression of sexual feelings as one defense against anxiety. Thus, all abnormal behavior was seen as an attempt to ward off anxiety. Finally, Freud regarded anxiety as a danger signal, a premonition of impending disaster, whether real or imagined. Like Kierkegaard, he distinguished between anxiety (indefinite and objectless, altogether puzzling and purposeless) and fear (an intelligent reaction to danger).

Freud saw all neurotic symptoms as unrealistic attempts to control or to avoid anxiety, which he ultimately defined under three categories: objective anxiety, neurotic anxiety, and moral anxiety. Defense mechanisms are used against any of the three. The appropriateness of the response is measured in terms of how much energy it consumes and whether it prevents some adaptive mechanism that might have great utility in coping with reality. Freud divided defense mechanisms into four categories: sublimated, neurotic, psychotic, and character.

Freud conceptualized man's personality as three subsystems: the id, the ego, and the superego. He viewed rational guilt, rational conscience, as a function of the ego because it is realistic, appropriate, and adaptive; superego guilt is irrational and unrelated to actual environmental conditions.

Freud saw the purpose of psychoanalytic treatment as aiding the child to develop insight. In analytic theory, the mind is viewed as the body is viewed in medicine: when the mind is ill, it displays symptoms that point to the cause of the illness. The major treatment is internal and directed toward the cause of the illness.

ANNA FREUD Anna Freud further defined neurotic

defense mechanisms as: phobia, repression, obsessive compulsion, rationalization, and reaction formation. Psychotic defense mechanisms she defined as: denial, regression, and withdrawal.

Anxiety: Guilt Theory

O. HOBART MOWRER Freud believed that anxiety arises from evil wishes, from acts that the individual would commit, if he dared. O. Hobart Mowrer believed that anxiety arises from acts that the individual did commit, but wishes he had not. Thus, Mowrer sees anxiety as a normal phenomenon that signals misbehavior.

Mowrer believes that anxiety is learned, basically anticipatory in nature, and has great utility when it motivates individuals to adapt realistically to their environment. He sees a positive relationship between the concept of sin, guilt, and atonement and the concept of anxiety. He views anxiety as a positive, adaptive mechanism essential to the adequate functioning of mankind.

Mowrer's approach to dealing with anxiety is a direct effort toward changing behavior, toward accepting guilt, toward public confession. His view of appropriate therapy requires changing the behavior that originally got the individual into trouble, and changing what the individual has since been trying to do about his trouble.

Freud saw the neurotic's problem as troubling emotions; Mowrer, as troubling behavior. For Mowrer, children do not act irresponsibly because they are sick, but they are sick because they act irresponsibly.

WILLIAM JAMES William James saw anxiety as an instinctive, phylogenetically fixed and unlearned reaction to certain objects or situations.

JOHN B. WATSON John Watson demonstrated that, contrary to the Jamesian view, anxiety is learned through individual experience.

Anxiety: Social-Learning Theory

JOHN DOLLARD and NEAL MILLER A complex emotion, anxiety nevertheless is learned in a social context under rather simple learning conditions, according to John Dollard and Neal Miller. Anxiety initially arises from a fear of being alone, of being abandoned, because the infant is absolutely dependent upon his mother or mother substitute for his basic needs, which are fierce in their intensity. Later, anxiety arises from a fear of retaliation for certain psychological responses that elicit punishment from significant adults: a social contagion derived from parents' dis-

pleasure. If anxiety is learned, then treatment involves unlearning: a conditioning-deconditioning theory of anxiety.

Anxiety: Behavior Theory

JOSEPH WOLPE Joseph Wolpe defined anxiety as learned behavior exhibited as maladaptive neurotic habits that must be unlearned. Unlike Mowrer, Wolpe believes one of the roles of the therapist is "to nullify the self-blame that social conditioning may have engendered."

Anxiety: Operant Model Theory

B. F. SKINNER Defined by the operant model of B. F. Skinner, an emotion is "a complex response elicited and occasioned by environmental conditions and composed of both operants and respondents. Fear and anxiety are produced by aversive stimuli." Under the operant model, anxiety is termed a conditioned emotional response (CER), which is a change, either an increase or decrease, in operant behavior maintained by a schedule of reinforcement in the presence of a conditioned aversive stimulus: anxiety is a response to a stimulus, but anxiety is not measured directly as an act, but indirectly as the increase or decrease of an act. No distinction is made between fear and anxiety.

In operant treatment, the child is first removed from the presence of the conditioned aversive stimulus. At the same time, he is rewarded for performing that behavior which his anxiety had decreased. And thirdly, an attempt is made to modify the behavior of the significant adult who was the conditioned aversive stimulus for the child. The appeal of the operant explanation of behavior therapy is that the few assumptions and the operational definitions for all of the variables make a prescription therapy program possible.

Anxiety: Punishment Theory

ALBERT BANDURA and RICHARD WALTERS The punishment theorists, Albert Bandura and Richard Walters also see anxiety as a conditioned emotional response, one that can be elicited "simply by the presence of an adult who has been the agent of punishment." Bandura and Walters point out that with children, most conditioned emotional responses are the result of punishment used in avoidance training, and important training in early childhood is related to avoidance: don't eat this, don't go in the street, don't touch that.

One of the major strengths of the punishment approach is the emphasis on vicarious training: not only can various social-training procedures be employed to modify a single child's behavior, but they also have a predictable effect on other children who watch. In the area of social imitation and modeling, Bandura and Walters have made a great contribution to the prediction and control of group behavior in children. However, the effectiveness of their approach depends upon the ability of the observer to identify the emotion and to identify the cues that produce the emotion. Bandura and Walters make an important distinction between nonreward and aversive conditioning: "nonreward usually results in extinction of responses, aversive conditioning suppresses rather than eliminates them."

Anxiety: Client-Centered Theory

CARL ROGERS Carl Rogers sees anxiety in children as a feeling of loneliness and isolation, together with a lack of understanding of their own emotions and the emotions of others. Insight is defined by the client-centered theorist as self-acceptance of one's true feelings and understanding of the feelings of others, as well as an understanding of the relationship between the two.

The responsibility of a client-centered therapist is to reflect correctly the true feelings of the child in a setting where the child can accept these reflections. Necessary, then, are a great deal of empathy on the part of the therapist, and considerable experience with the child in a setting where his personality can be expressed with little threat.

A goal of nondirective client-centered therapy is to enable the child to understand himself, what kinds of stresses he is under, and to realize that someone else not only understands how he feels but can express his feelings in a way that makes sense.

Another goal is to help the child understand that, in order to be free of the threat of society, he must come to terms with it and correctly perceive the nature of the minimum demands by which freedom is gained. The purpose of the therapist is not simply to reassure, because he recognizes there is a real world out there, but rather, his role is to empathize with the child and to help him understand the nature of the demands of society.

An assumption underlying this approach to therapy is that children have a drive to understand and to grow psychologically; they desire maturity naturally.

The client-centered approach is more similar to Freud than Mowrer in that anxiety is felt to be the result of an improper perception and the resulting accumulation of guilt feelings regarding natural impulses and feelings.

The goal of nondirective therapists is to break down the barriers of communication, reduce the feelings of isolation that have stunted psychological growth, and thus free the child to resume his development into a fully functioning individual.

HARRY STACK SULLIVAN For Harry Stack Sullivan, "the tension of anxiety, when present in the mothering one, induces anxiety in the infant." For Sullivan, "anxiety is a product of education and living among significant people and is social and human." The assumption is that the root cause of anxiety is isolation or the fear of isolation.

The Topography of Children's Fears

ARTHUR JERSILD Arthur Jersild added a third fear, fear of strangeness or change, to Watson's two unconditioned fears of infants, fear of falling and fear of loud noises. Children evidently can adjust to their environment and become secure with a consistent background or noise level, but sudden changes and new stimuli frighten them. Another cause of infant fear overlooked by Watson is fear of pain; sudden and unexpected pain can cause the Moro fear response to blast off.

Conditioned fears of children change as they grow and mature, according to their models and environment. Parents' fears relate significantly to the fears of their children; the great majority of children's fears are learned at home. Society also has its effects on the fears of children: blacks have more fears and more intense fears than their white counterparts; and pressures put upon children in the learning situation have grown greater rather than less.

The clinician's notebook on child-rearing

A child psychologist frequently is with groups of teachers and parents in discussions focusing on problems that arise during the course of child rearing, training, and education. That certain problems surface in almost any such session has become obvious through some twenty years of participation as a clinician, teacher, and parent. These problems are in part characteristic of the times in which we live, in part characteristic of the demands of socialization, which come extremely early in Western society, and in part represent inherent weaknesses in our system of raising children.

Some general principles of behavioral management of children apply to most problems; a few particular problems have more subtle dimensions. The purpose of The Clinician's Notebook is to share the results of over two decades of these group meetings and to provide a systematic review of behavioral techniques for parents and teachers, the consistent application of which will prevent or eliminate harmful and wasteful expenditure of energy on the part of parents, teachers, and children.

First, we will go over some general principles of child management, principles that seem to hold regardless of the nature of the particular problem the child is encountering during the sometimes painful process of growing to maturity. Second, we will review some specific problems with high frequency, in addition to those already discussed, such as phobic responses, toilet training, and enuresis. Certain general problems emerge as a result of our children's growing up in a relatively dense social environment with relatively constant and high-level demands, problems that fall into one of four categories: active defiance, passive defiance, fixation and regression, or anxiety. Most of the problems parents encounter with their children can be categorized within one of those four areas.

Active defiance includes such things as tantrums, running away, deliberate property destruction, deliberate lying, stealing, or hurting of others. Passive defiance includes poor memory, self-serving hearing defects, failure to respond, having a wide variety of convenient accidents that include nondeliberate destruction of property, nondeliberate hurting of others, nondeliberate theft, and nondeliberate conveying of erroneous information. Regression or fixation refers to the holding onto or going back to behaviors more appropriate for a much younger age, such things as thumb-sucking, excessive rocking, crying, hiding, clutching, clinging, and whimpering. And the final general problem, which has been discussed rather thoroughly in the previous chapter, is the broad anxiety response that includes night terrors, phobic reactions, and a whole host of anxiety symptoms that indicate great distress on the part of the child.

BEHAVIOR CHANGE TECHNIQUES

Parents have at their disposal, as a function of biological and social forces that impinge upon the child, ten powerful behavioral tools with which to prevent or to eliminate the problems frequently encountered in our society. The ultimate goal from the utilization of these ten devices is freedom and independence for the child, self-direction and self-motivation under the broad umbrella of minimal social conformity. With the advent of the rather powerful behavioral techniques of the 1960s, for parents to deal effectively with these four classes of common problems of children is not only possible, but the parent can overkill, thereby sapping the initiative and ultimate independence of the child.

A primary focus will be to illustrate the development of a minimum conformity contract between the child and his parents and between the teacher and the child, a contract that evolves into a situation of independence and mutual respect. The process, admittedly and actively parent-centered in the preschool years, should lead to a gradual decrease in parental heavy-handedness during elementary school, with the aim of ultimate independence emerging in early adolescence.

These ten devices with great utility for leading the child to productive independence and for eliminating common developmental problems of early childhood are:

1. Modeling
2. Companionship
3. Consistency
4. Consequenting
5. Minimum conformity
6. Discrimination training
7. Fading
8. Contingent reinforcement
9. Punishment
10. Extinction

Many of these devices have been discussed in isolation throughout the text, but to review these concepts and to demonstrate their application to general developmental problems should be helpful.

MODELING

Probably as a result of both his almost total dependency upon his parents for nurture and his biological predisposition toward imprinting, which is characteristic of most animals, in the early stages of Waldo's life, his attention is almost irresistibly drawn toward his parents. Therefore, the parents have at their disposal the extraordinarily powerful technique of simply acting out those tasks, behaviors, and values they most desire in Waldo. That such important characteristics as moral values, conscience, and ethics can hardly be taught any other way has been demonstrated time and time again.

Development of Conscience

Innumerable studies have shown that church school attendance or lectures and stories about morals and ethics have little effect, because children can always add what Freud calls the *but* that separates words from deeds. Waldo can easily say, "I know I shouldn't take that, *but,*" and then go ahead and take it. He is much more likely to do just that when he has not had a long series of experiences with his parents as models, where they have verbalized their own desires to take things and have added, "But, we don't do that, Waldo. We will find a different way, a way to earn it." And of course, that the parents not take something, but make other arrangements and thereby act out their honesty is essential. Because, if we don't . . .

Temper Tantrums

Parents who wish to combat temper tantrums in Waldo must recognize that they must give up the luxury of tantrums themselves, even when these tantrums take the form of self-righteous indignation over bad behavior on Waldo's part. Parents who wish Waldo to give up lying must themselves tell Waldo the truth, even when that truth is embarrassing or compromising.

Trust

If the model makes promises, and then goes to considerable sacrifice to make good on those promises, he provides a much more plausible means

for Waldo to learn honesty than any fable indicating the importance of promises. How many fathers have promised Waldo to go kite-flying on Saturday and then failed to do so with the feeble excuse "I *have* to go back to the office"? In point of fact, to go back to the office is convenient, to go back to the office is self-serving, but to go back to the office is not necessary. The parent may learn from Waldo's raised-eyebrow expression of disbelief that he is not so easily fooled by a little white lie. Not only is he not fooled, but Waldo learns that his father is not to be trusted.

Regression

Parents who themselves are regressive, in that they eat too much, or drink too much, or act grossly immature, will find it difficult to lecture and advise Waldo on his problems with regression or fixation. Nothing a parent can do in socializing Waldo's behavior is more effective than good, high exposure of adjustive behavior.

COMPANIONSHIP

A second technique, extraordinarily important and grossly underused by parents, is companionship. Unfortunately, when behavioral scientists have examined the interaction between parents and children and between teachers and children, they have found a high density of negative evaluative comments as the dominant interaction feature of the relationship. A vast percentage of the eyeball-to-eyeball interaction offered to Waldo is filled with admonishments, criticisms, complaints, a general tidying up of the ends of Waldo's behavior. Thus Waldo never learns to enjoy the companionship of his parents and teachers. An outward-focused relationship of mutual enjoyment, pleasure, and activity is never formed, a relationship that makes a parent's or a teacher's approval or disapproval important to Waldo.

When Waldo has a high regard for another human being, this person has an inordinate capacity to influence his life. Parents often are shocked

at the ease with which another adult can take Waldo away from them simply by offering him some form of companionship. A neighbor down the street, often as not a retiree, who offers Waldo nothing but conversation and companionship, suddenly becomes the most dominant feature in Waldo's life. Parents are driven mad by the constant phrases that drip from Waldo's lips: "Well, Mr. Anderson doesn't like getting up early, and I don't think it is very good either"; "Mr. Anderson likes going to the fair and I think that's what we should do"; "Mr. Anderson eats raw squash"; "Mr. Anderson drinks papaya juice"; "Mr. Anderson likes CBS news on TV."

Parents are infuriated because some other person has such control over Waldo. What they fail to recognize is the indication of Waldo's desperate need for companionship, a need met by another person because the parents failed to provide it, which puts considerable influence into the hands of this other person. A parent, then, who offers Waldo companionship, a teacher who gives of himself in companionship, has enormous power for good in influencing Waldo to give up defiance and immaturity and to feel comfortable about himself.

CONSISTENCY

A third technique grossly underused by parents and teachers alike is consistency. Picture the dilemma of a blind person who has to use a room in which the furniture constantly is moved about. This dilemma produces two kinds of behavior on his part. First, it produces fumbling, hesitant, groping behavior in which the blind person feels for, taps for, and finally finds a chair in which to sit. Second, it produces an inattentiveness on his part. He quickly learns that the furniture is in constant disarray and therefore to pay attention to the organization is useless. His blindness becomes gaudily obvious; he becomes increasingly helpless-appearing.

On the other hand, most of us have observed a blind person in a familiar, consistently laid-out environment, such as a room where the chairs are always in approximately the same place, the doors are always opened or closed, and other people using the room generally sit in the same area. The blind person quickly learns where people are; he learns where his seat is. He walks briskly into the room. Hearing rustling sounds, he turns, "Good morning, Ann." He walks over, flips his seat around, drops in it, and turns to his left, where he has heard a nasal breathing. "Charlie, how are you doing this morning?" He proceeds to have a good old time because he is dealing with a consistent environment in which he can learn. He is himself at ease and he is able to put others at ease.

Waldo is similarly blind socially. He does not see with the same social vision as an adult; he needs every break he can get. Therefore parents should set consistent, stable, and reliable routines: mealtimes, naptimes, storytimes, bedtimes; routines for the weekends, for dressing, for putting up one's clothes; routines for tidying up one's room. With such consistency, Waldo quickly masters these essential but highly distracting activities and therefore is freed for creative activities in which he can launch out on his own.

Waldo is a product of his routines. He probably is biologically pro-grammed to enjoy routines. Notice the ritualistic routine games he plays with such great enthusiasm, games that drive his parents mad, and you recognize the ease with which children can learn routinized behavior.

If Waldo knows from day to day what his parents expect, he can fit into this expectancy and thereby remove a great deal of the uncertainty and probing that results from inconsistent parental behavior. When Waldo does not know what to expect from his environment, he is con-stantly sending out probes, testing the limits, pushing and pushing, and is, then, provoking an inordinate amount of negative responses from his par-ents, responses that do neither Waldo nor his parents any good. Many of the problems related to defiance, regression, and anxiety can be attributed directly to a lack of stability in the demands of the home environment, a lack that results in Waldo's need to probe just how far the limits can be extended.

Obviously, flexibility is needed. Routines do need to be broken for holidays, special events, and unexpected occasions, but belligerence and passive resistance most often occur in the face of inconsistent demands from the parents, from Waldo's not knowing the rules of the game because they are forever changing.

CONSEQUENTING

Probably no single device at the disposal of the parents in their strug-gle to develop independence and autonomy on Waldo's part ranks with consequenting, with allowing Waldo to experience the full consequences, good and bad, of his actions and failures to act. If Waldo develops a deter-ministic philosophy toward the world around him, if he learns that his actions are a powerful influence that can cause real changes that affect his comfort, happiness, security, and opportunity, he is encouraged to develop an attitude of personal accountability that is extremely important in later life.

Treatment of Animals

This does not mean a home should be filled with land mines into which Waldo is constantly stumbling. Rather, in the mini-world of early childhood, the opportunity for taking actions and feeling consequences can convey a sharp lesson without great danger. Young Waldo should be told not to jump on an animal when he is asleep. But, having said that such behavior is a no-no, his parents should stand back, fully confident that sooner or later Waldo is going to jump on old Tom basking in the sun on the rug under the window. A two-year-old toddler who sneaks up to fall full force on top of an old Tom will have to reckon with a howling-mad cat determined to put some stripes on somebody.

Now, cat claws can cause rather infectious and painful scratches, and I suppose, be mildly dangerous, but even when awakened from a sound sleep, house toms tend to make more noise than damage and to disengage rapidly. A strange Doberman pinscher, however, asleep in his burrow under the shrubs in the front yard, lunged at by a three-year-old, may very well take out Waldo's face in one snarling, snapping reflex.

Neatness

Waldo can be told that if he picks up his toys and keeps his room a little orderly, mother and daddy will have more time. But only by his parents noticing that his room is cleaned up and flopping down to take that extra time with Waldo in a special game, while pointing out this special game is possible because the toys are picked up and they have time to play, does Waldo learn the message that he has power for good and evil in his own life, that he can make good things happen and he can make bad things happen; and this of course is the rudiment of high ego strength and a high sense of moral consciousness.

Responsibility

Waldo soon learns that from this power comes responsibility. The reason daddy didn't go for a walk with him this evening and stop by the neighborhood store for an ice cream is because daddy and he had to spend the better part of an hour sorting out the tool box and getting it back in order from Waldo's having spent the afternoon scattering the tools across the garage. Knowing that the consequence of this act is displeasure on the part of the father and denial of an important part of the day's fun is far more likely to keep Waldo from tearing up the tool box than is a lecture on the importance of neatness.

MINIMUM CONFORMITY

Another important dimension of adult-child interaction is the setting of priorities regarding conformity behavior. As mentioned earlier, a rather high percentage of interaction between parents, teachers, and children has a negative, harping, nagging, scolding quality in which Waldo constantly is being corrected; each encounter with Waldo affords the opportunity for the adult to do a little more tidying up.

Even in the absence of all other conversation, parents say to Waldo: "I wish you would wash your hands a little better"; "Why don't you comb your hair?"; "Go back and wipe your feet"; "Please sit up straight, you are ruining your back." The back problem is probably closer to the truth than the parents realize: not until adolescence does the back-ruining come into the forefront, when the plaintive cry or the snarl of the adolescent emphasizes the get-off-my-back concern that Waldo has about adults.

The concept of minimum conformity is a superb guideline for adults to adopt for their interaction with children. Minimum conformity is the setting of priorities for how much of Waldo's behavior needs to be under control. By these priorities, Waldo learns that some behaviors are more important than other behaviors. Under these conditions, the parents have more power to influence Waldo's behavior for good.

Occasionally unusual circumstances, such as bone curvature, make the posture of Waldo as he watches television important. Orthopedic surgeons disagree; pediatricians often as not have no opinion; but parents are adamant, fully confident that sprawling on the floor with feet on the coffee table will inflict permanent injury upon Waldo, either through his bone structure or his character. Few parents can walk through the living

room and see a ten-year-old girl in an unladylike position, with her feet up in the air in a squirming position on the floor, watching her favorite TV show, without picking away: "Why don't you get in a chair?"; "Why don't you sit up straight?"; "Why don't you get your feet down?"

Hairstyles in boys change from time to time, but all parents can be sure that with maturity their boys will probably spend more time on their hair then any parent could ever believe. However, during the sixes, sevens, and eights, Waldo does not need constantly to be told to comb his hair, to get his hair out of his eyes, to wash his hair, etc.

Perhaps parents are annoyed, particularly those raised in leaner times, to see Waldo waste food, leaving a plate that has to be scraped into the garbage. The problem, however, in American children is more often overweight than underweight; few children, if presented day in and day out with nourishing food and a limited supply of sweets, will fail to eat a balanced diet. Constantly harping, "Finish your eggs, your peas, your beans," diverts the parent's attention from the essential areas of conformity.

Waldo's failure to stay out from under cars parked on an inclined driveway produces a high likelihood of his being killed. The parent who sees three-year-old Waldo under the wheels of a car, as he picks bugs for his collection out of the cowling, is remiss if he doesn't fly out of the house with great animation, great irritation, and abject horror to drag Waldo from under the car, all the time telling him how easily an absent-minded adult could come out of the house and let the car roll backward as he starts it, completely squishing an innocent three-year-old who wants only to find some bugs under the radiator. This is followed with the promise that if Waldo wants to get dragonflies out of the car radiator, the wheels will be properly blocked, an adult will stand by, and Waldo will then be allowed a nearly exhaustive amount of time to collect every single bug in the radiator, even to the point of opening up the hood and getting those special giant-sized dragonflies that seem only to be at the top.

Waldo is learning that in some areas there is no give, there is no

casualness. Without the principle of minimum conformity, without setting a few highly essential no-no's and ignoring the overwhelming majority of Waldo's behavior that is self-corrective with age, the parent loses entirely his power to influence Waldo's behavior for good. A minimum conformity contract with Waldo frees the parents to engage in friendly and warm conversation, companionship, and modeling without the static and disruption of becoming the nag that the child simply braces for and learns to ignore.

A minimum conformity contract, then, sets few rules, sets these rules in specific language with high consequenting. There are consistent rules, followed by the model as well, and interspersed with long periods of companionship. Each dimension of the minimum conformity contract has a direct consequence. Every effort is made to give a high density of rewards and punishments related to this contract.

If a child's responsibility is a single chore, which in the preschool years is probably appropriate, such as taking out the trash and putting it in the garbage can or dumpster, the routine should be spelled out carefully, the purpose carefully explained, the importance properly highlighted. Then, when the parent comes into the kitchen, long after the child has gone to bed, and finds the garbage was not taken out, an attitude of outrage on the part of the parent is required, an outrage that has him march into Waldo's bedroom in feigned if not real indignation, which conveys to Waldo that the entire family was counting on him to do his chore and he has gone off to bed and ignored his responsibility and one cannot run a family like that. One sleepy, mildly confused, somewhat cold tour into the back yard with the garbage at midnight beats a hundred naggings and pickings, "When are you going to do your chores?" or "When I was a boy," which make chores such a chore in the average household.

DISCRIMINATION TRAINING

Evidence seems good, for both boys and girls in the preschool and early elementary school years, that roughhousing in the form of wrestling,

rolling in the grass, tumbling, and contests of physical strength are quite useful in developing ego-mastery, confidence, self-control, and strength. On the other hand, few coffee tables or sofas are designed to tolerate the tumbling of two healthy nine-year-olds, particularly when both are wearing shoes that are somewhat less than clean and when the coffee table contains a considerable layer of bric-a-brac. Discrimination training, then, is the delicate balance of preventing destructive roughhousing without disrupting this developmentally important task of laying on of hands: a difficult task for parents, who most often come in after the damage has been done and who, extremely angry over that, punish the activity of roughhousing for breaking the vase, without attending at all to discrimination training that where the roughhousing occurred broke the vase, not the roughhousing per se, which is not bad. Training Waldo not to be rough with younger children is far more important than training Waldo not to be rough.

Teaching Waldo to observe the subtle distinctions between being hustled by a malevolent stranger and being smiled at by a warm-hearted, open person whom he has never seen is part of this delicate balance. Broad, undiscriminated admonishments regarding behavior break down at a critical moment due to their own absurdity, leaving Waldo, at the very time he should not do something, to elect to do it because he doesn't see how this time differs from any other time.

Parents should be very conscious of the necessity of constantly making discriminating comments, such as "Let's not pick the flowers now, let's pick them when they are in full bloom," rather than "Keep your hands off the flowers, you've ruined those blossoms" or "I think you should stay out of Mr. Anderson's yard because it upsets him to have noisy children around," rather than "Stay in your own yard and stay off of other people's property." Efforts spent by the parents in discrimination training regarding appropriate versus inappropriate timing, places, and actions aid Waldo in the socialization process so that he becomes able to have open experiences without danger.

My experience indicates that one of the great failures of parent education, whether that be sex education, education concerning property of others, education concerning rules, laws, and ethics, is due to the parents' tendency to generalize the principles; later, Waldo begins to find the exceptions. The danger from not having the exceptions pointed out to him through discrimination learning is that Waldo may throw out the baby with the bath, so to speak, and reject the entire principle. Waldo, told that all strangers are inherently evil, out to do him great bodily harm, then discovering inadvertently and with considerable trepidation that some strangers are very nice, warm people, is apt to lose the entire message and fall fully into the hands of the stranger, in a context in which it was abundantly clear that this was the stranger his parents were really talking about. Waldo, taught that all laws are equally important and to be obeyed to the letter, is apt, upon finding that some laws are ridiculous, inconsistent, antiquated, and absurd, to decide that all laws are stupid and he should be immune to them.

FADING

The use of fading by parents, an old technique with a new name, adds considerable precision to the process of Waldo's learning new behaviors and dropping old ones. The fading technique originated from Skinner's observation that errorless learning is enormously efficient compared with trial-and-error learning. In the early stages of learning, Waldo, under the concept of errorless learning, is prevented from making an erroneous trial. The cues, instructions, structure, and reward are set up with such high intensity that Waldo clearly understands the correct move.

With such vivid structure, to set up rewards that actually reward the correct performance and punishments that actually punish incorrect responses, when they are possible, is easy. Take the example of training Waldo as a toddler to stay out of the street in front of his house. The parent takes Waldo out to the street, where with brightly colored chalk, he

draws on the sidewalk a line a foot from the edge of the street and labori-
ously writes the word *stop*. Of course, Waldo cannot read the word; he
doesn't exactly understand the chalk mark; but the vividness of the situation is electrifying. With great solemnity and gravity he traces with his
finger as the parent goes through the magical incantation, "stop." After
Waldo has been shown the cars moving up and down the street, he is taken
farther back into the yard and encouraged to run toward the sidewalk until
he comes to the line where daddy is standing with a big smile, his hand
pointing down at the line, and saying, "stop." In doing so, the parent prevents Waldo from going across the line and into the street, which affords
the opportunity for much smiling, hugging, and encouraging: "Good boy,
Waldo. Waldo stopped."

Now, this quickly becomes a routine in which Waldo goes back to the
porch and runs full tilt down to the sidewalk, comes to a complete halt,
points to the line and says, "stop," at which point, gales of laughter come
from the adult, who is jumping up and down with excitement, and who
with a great deal of animation and vividness and encouragement picks
Waldo up, swings him around, and starts him again toward the porch.
And again Waldo runs down to the sidewalk, comes to the mark, and says
"stop," and is gaudily complimented on his excellent behavior.

After Waldo has done this many, many times, another mark is made
on the sidewalk with two arrows, one pointing up the street, one pointing
down the street. Waldo is encouraged to take one step forward from the
line and look to the left and look to the right. Again the process is repeated, running down the sidewalk, coming to a stop, smiling, cackling,
giggling, stepping one foot forward, looking to the left, then looking to
the right. After this is mastered and cars pointed out, "Look at that car,
see the car, look at that car, now look at the street, no cars," Waldo is encouraged to trot across the road—not to run, not to walk, but to trot. He
trots to the other side to receive much praise and encouragement, and then
back to the porch and another run-through.

Over and over again, each trial absolutely perfect because of the omnipresent, intense parent who prevents an error; and then, the fading. Gradually the animation and the intensity are reduced. The child is encouraged to go through the act, but more and more in a functionally autonomous fashion, as opposed to high-density encouragement, with the parent ever alert, ever watching, until this behavior becomes absolutely second nature to Waldo. Waldo may not now be absolutely accident proof in crossing the street, but he is as much so as a behaviorist can make him; only the random, occasional, spontaneous behavior of childhood would lead to trouble.

The advantage of the fading technique is that Waldo can learn behavior in situations that provide great risk and that must be done perfectly the first time. Another example would be an attitude toward toxins. Simply to child-proof one's own home is not enough, to take away Drano, Lysol, alcohol, isotox, and tranquilizers, because one cannot count on one's neighbors and friends to child-proof their homes. Thus, Waldo has to go through errorless learning. These areas obviously demand errorless learning, but the fading technique can be extended to all kinds of behaviors, such as putting the toys back in the toy box. Again with great animation, great verbalization, great physical, social, and emotional enhancement, and rewards, such as candy or juice or piggyback rides around the living room, Waldo can learn to stop on leaving his room, to go back and to put up the toys, and to come out knowing that good things happen to boys who put up their toys. The fading technique makes the connection between the behavior and the reinforcement easy for Waldo to track; it guarantees tenacious learning of routines.

CONTINGENT REINFORCEMENT

According to behavioral technologists, one of the most powerful devices, which is least understood and least carried out by parents and teachers, is the principle of contingent reinforcement. In the average household, children are so satiated with reinforcement during early childhood that they are somewhat difficult to control and manage. Since parents routinely shower their children with reinforcement when they, the parents, feel good and deny reinforcement when they feel bad, from Waldo's point of view, little is to be learned from reinforcement. In a correctly managed home, however, good things follow good deeds and bad things follow bad deeds. A set of rules applies to high-priority learning; Waldo can learn quickly that performance of these behaviors leads to strong reinforcement.

Reinforcement should be positive on almost all occasions. Praise, candy, juice, social interaction, all tend to be better forms of reinforcement than any form of punishment. Reinforcement focused on consequences of behavior removes confusion and ambiguity, sharpens learning, and gives Waldo considerable freedom of action because he learns to develop a degree of control over whether good things or bad things happen to him.

In contingent reinforcement, Waldo is rewarded only when he performs a given behavior. He works for rewards and suffers from lack of work and incorrect behavior. This provides for efficient learning. Waldo has daily experience in which he not only faces consequences but immediately is rewarded for adaptive behavior: he easily learns from his experiences whether he is correct or incorrect.

Parents and teachers recognize that they cannot always be with children at critical moments when performance is demanded; they frequently ask, "What is the best way to insure that desirable behavior will continue in the absence of direct supervision?" The principle of partial reinforcement long has been known to have a potent influence on behavior; this influence can be for the good or it can make maladaptive behavior persist.

Partial Reinforcement of Maladaptive Behavior

Partial reinforcement refers to the fact that behaviors rewarded after five or six trials tend to have a high degree of resistance to extinction; they become tenacious modes of behavior. Begging is an example of an undesirable and rather annoying behavior on the part of young children. Waldo, for instance, has been told he cannot go swimming because he has a slight cold, the water is cold, the air somewhat damp. Then begins the following sequence.

Beg 1:   "Please, Mommy, let me go. I won't stay in long."

Answer: *"No, you have school tomorrow. We can't afford your getting sick."*

Beg 2:   "Oh please, couldn't I go in for just a little while?"

Answer: *"No, you cannot."*

Beg 3:   "If I went in with a towel and kept the towel around my shoulders and just waded up to my knees?"

Answer: *"No, you cannot get in the water."*

Beg 4:   "Well, how about if I go in with my clothes on and have a jacket and just wade up to my ankles?"

Answer: *"No, you absolutely cannot."*

Beg 5:   "Well, couldn't I go in just for a little while, if I promise to come in and take a hot bath?"

Answer: *"No, you cannot."*

Beg 6:   "Mommy, please let me go for just a little while."

Reward: *"Go on then. I don't care if you die with pneumonia. I am so sick of hearing about it. Just leave me alone."*

Reply: "Thank you Mommy, thank you. You're the goodest mommy," Splash!

Waldo has made an undesirable behavior, which we are calling begging—"please may I do something that I should not do?" He has made five consecutive probes, and each one has been resisted by the parent. Let's say, to keep the example clean, that the parent has resisted each one with the same degree of firmness and the same degree of negativism, although this is not usually the case. On the sixth trial, however, the parent relents. He rewards Waldo on what the Skinnerians call a fixed ratio of 1 to 6.

Now the odds are that in a few days, Waldo will come back and say to his father: "May I use this steak knife to whittle a sling shot?" The answer is, of course, "No! Steak knives are extremely difficult to sharpen.

They are not designed for wood carving. That knife is part of a matched set that goes on our dinner table. Absolutely not!''

Beg 2: "Could I just start the sling shot, just get the bark off? I will finish it up tomorrow when I can find another knife."

Answer: *"No, absolutely not. Working on the bark is the worst possible misuse of the knife."*

Until after six or seven trials, father, who is trying to look at TV with one eye while tending to baby sister Sally, says, "Well, go ahead. I don't guess it would hurt too much." Via the avenue of partial reinforcement and for obvious reasons, Waldo becomes firmly locked into negative behavior that is extremely tenacious behavior to break up.

Partial Reinforcement of Adaptive Behavior

Now, the purpose of The Clinician's Notebook is to point out how things can go wrong, but more to the point, to point out how things can be straightened out. Fortunately, partial reinforcement also can be used for socializing behavior, as well as in setting up undesirable behavior.

Work Ethic

Let's take a form of behavior that even today appears desirable, a work ethic. As parents, we would like for our children to throw themselves into some constructive effort with considerable vigor. To use a confusing term, we want our children to be motivated. And not only do we want them to be motivated when we are around to motivate them, but we want this motivation or drive for achievement to be functionally autonomous, that is, to last after our influence wanes into the background. The question, then, is how can one channel a child's energy into creative tasks and maintain it at a high level over a long period of time?

In answer, begin with a fairly high rate of reinforcement, which is decreased gradually over the years until a fairly lean schedule of partial reinforcement is effective. Let's say that Waldo's first chore is indeed to empty all the trash baskets in the house every day. Initially one begins with 100 percent reinforcement: Waldo is encouraged after he takes each basket out; his work is carefully monitored to see that it is done every day; a great deal of praise, direction, and attention are given for taking out the baskets.

After the behavior has been established, the rate of reinforcement is decreased. The reinforcement is still vivid, but Waldo does not get paid off after each trip to the dumpster. Sooner or later, the parents arrive at a point where approximately every seventh trial, plus or minus two—that is, about once a week, though not on the same day and unexpectedly—the father goes out into the back yard, allegedly for some other purpose, and notices that the area around the dumpster is relatively clean and neat. He goes back into the house and finds that the garbage cans are relatively empty. He waits until an auspicious moment, with a relatively large audience within the family, and then reaches into his pocket and pulls out a Kennedy half-dollar and says, "Hey, Waldo, I have just made my semi-

annual inspection tour of the trash cans and the dumpster and I find that everything is in fine shape. I thought maybe you would like to have this.''

Now, what happens, of course, is that immediately the next day Waldo is attentive to emptying all the trash and making sure the dumpster area is spic and span. But daddy does not inspect. And he doesn't inspect for a couple of days. But again he picks the right moment, with the right audience, and rewards Waldo.

Now, obviously he can continue to decrease this partial reinforcement schedule; Waldo's attention and responsibility become functionally autonomous on a thinner and thinner schedule, becoming more and more nearly self-sustaining. In addition, of course, positive feedback occurs from other sources, along with a sense of accomplishment, to aid in sustaining this behavior.

Jealousy of New Baby

Partial reinforcement can be used to sustain behavior competitive with or the reciprocal of undesirable behavior. When a new baby comes into the home, Waldo, in spite of good preparation about all the joy and excitement of having a new brother or new sister, probably correctly perceives that this baby poses considerable rivalry for attention, affection, and goodies, and is, in fact, going to represent a damn nuisance in the world of a three-year-old.

Now a three-year-old can engage in many activities that will bring accidental harm to the baby. For instance, Waldo can share his sack of blocks by throwing them in the crib on top of the baby. An alert parent, however, will anticipate that possibility. Upon finding Waldo sitting at the side of the crib, glaring at this new bundle of joy, and thinking evil thoughts as to how to eliminate this problem, while holding on to the crib and rocking it slightly, the mother will smile widely: "How nice, Waldo. Come look, Dad. Waldo is rocking the baby.'' The father will come in and also be very pleased with Waldo's rocking the baby. He talks about what a big boy Waldo is and how nice it is to have a son you can count on when you need him occasionally and in general pour attention and affection and encouragement upon Waldo, while ignoring the baby.

Now basking in the warmth of all this inordinate praise for his rocking the baby all on his own, Waldo forgets that he really was sitting there musing to himself about some way of dropping this bundle of joy in the commode; he begins to believe that he was indeed rocking the baby. And so he proceeds, over the next few days, to see if he can do other nice things for the baby because there seems to be some mysterious payoff in this.

An alert mother or father, not every time, but initially every other time or every three times, catches Waldo in the act of doing a positive, supportive, good thing for the baby and, while ignoring the baby, heaps rewards and praises on Waldo. As time passes, the reinforcement schedule is decreased, but a behavior is programmed that is a reciprocal to throwing a sack of blocks on top of the baby or pulling a blanket down over his head, which are much more natural to three-year-olds upon their first encounter with the new baby.

PUNISHMENT

Little needs to be said about punishment. In spite of its being the least effective, least stable, and slowest of all the techniques employed by parents, teachers, and counselors, punishment clearly is the most overused. Verbal punishment heads the list, followed by denial of privileges, particularly those the parents were reluctant to extend in the first place, both of which represent the grossest misuse of what can be, when properly discriminated, a precise, focused technique.

Punishment is a consequence that reduces the likelihood of a specific behavior reoccurring. Take the stirring example of punishment in the one-trial learning regarding wall sockets. When Waldo takes a bent paper clip, a hair pin, or pipe cleaner, and sticks the two ends in that funny little brown thing at the base of the wall, he immediately receives a jolting, burning, and sometimes odorous response from the wall socket that usually results in his not playing with wall sockets for the rest of his life. Electric stoves, with their invisible heat, cause Waldo immediate pain; Waldo tends not to put his hands on the top of the stove while trying to get into the brown sugar jar in the cupboard.

Some mothers have been known to go utterly berserk over their sewing basket. One occasion of having a normally sane, friendly nurturer turn into a screaming banshee is usually enough to make Waldo look somewhere else for scissors to cut tails for his kite. In its precise use, then, punishment should be like the fading technique, it should be used very occasionally and with great dramatic overplay, where the attention of the child is electrified beyond forgetting.

I still remember the evening my father, after listening to the cattle bawl for an hour or so, went down to the corral and found the water troughs empty. Now, of course penned cattle have no way to find water unless the responsible person, a nine-year-old boy, fills the troughs; the appearance that the cattle had been water-famished for forty-eight hours brought from a mild-mannered, calm, rational, old cattleman a cry of rage that could be heard the full three hundred yards to the house. The "Wallace (never Wally on such an occasion), get yourself down here!" certainly got my attention. Being restricted to the house without water for a day and a half, which seemed like three months, makes it extremely easy for me to note the fill level of water troughs, even today when they certainly are not mine.

Sparing, fierce, unrelenting, traumatic punishment has devastating effectiveness. Constant, low-level threatening, bickering, and unreliable punishment are useless harassments that separate children from their parents without modifying undesirable behavior.

EXTINCTION

The extinction technique can be illustrated by breath-holding. Most children on occasion, but some children in particular, display an extremely intense rage reaction at moments of frustration. Such a child, often as not when blocked in getting something he wants, will suddenly suck in a great deal of air, screw up his face in the most grotesque manner imaginable, clench his fists, draw up his knees, and fail to breathe. During this period, not a sound comes from Waldo, except a kind of a dry intake of air. Something terrible appears about to happen. Waldo first turns somewhat blue and then almost cyanotic or gray.

On the first occasion, this is a terrifying experience for parents. They feel that some dreadful thing has happened to Waldo, that he is suffocating, that he has swallowed something, that he has jammed his windpipe, that surely he is going to die. They grab him up and sometimes pound on his back, sometimes turn him upside down. Whatever they do makes little difference, because in a few moments, with an enormous exhalation of air, Waldo is functioning again.

Now most parents, whether or not they have read a child psychology book, are staggered by this first encounter. They rush to their pediatrician to tell him that they feel Waldo has some dreadful problem. I do not counsel against this, because there is the rare occasion when the child does have a spasmodic breathing problem or heart condition that bears looking into, but ninety-nine times out of one hundred, or really more often than that, the child is a spinal breath-holder who is using a particular strategy for a temper tantrum. Once correctly diagnosed—and obviously this is not a subtle diagnostic problem for the pediatrician—the parents need to recognize that this behavior is undesirable and can become tyrannical, if they scurry around meeting every whim and desire of Waldo in order to prevent one of these attacks.

So, obviously the best thing for the parents to do, within the limits of propriety, is to provoke the next one on their own terms: it is always more convincing to a parent that this is a deliberate act if they themselves provoke it. They might simply take some toy away from Waldo and put it on the shelf. And Waldo immediately has a tantrum. In which case, he is left absolutely alone.

Waldo goes through his full act, with all of its variations, almost losing consciousness, becoming very blue, and then ashen. When his normal color comes back, and he gets up, he notices father quietly reading the newspaper and mother arranging flowers on the table. They turn around pleasantly, and say, "Oh, hello, Waldo." They are subdued, calm, and unrewarding. After a few trials in which Waldo goes to all this effort without any apparent success, the spinal breath-holding is extinguished: he simply no longer uses this behavior.

Extinction works most effectively then against outrageous behavior that has occurred spontaneously. Waldo's use of some ear-shattering curse word he has picked up can best be dealt with by the extinction technique. In the usual case, masturbation and assorted scratching likewise disappear without attention or without external reinforcement. "Showing-off" is

another undesirable response that disappears under the vacuum of failure to draw attention.

Reinforcement comes in a positive sense when the child is rewarded directly for counter-tantrum behaviors: that is, when the child obviously starts to have a tantrum, but catches himself and does something more adaptive instead. A partial reinforcement technique simply recognizes that it is not necessary to deal with the reinforcement regimen on every occasion. A negative reinforcement occurs at the point where the child is confronted with the nature of the cost of the tantrum; that is, as a result of having the tantrum, he will not be able to enjoy some privilege to which he was entitled. When all ten of these techniques are brought fully to bear on tantrum behavior, it is usually eliminated in a single day, certainly within a few days.

BEHAVIOR PROBLEMS

We have reviewed ten powerful devices at the disposal of parents or teachers to bring to bear on problems presented by childhood. At this point, let's consider a few examples by which the parent can address himself to problems that typically cause concern.

ACTIVE DEFIANCE

Temper Tantrum

Contrary to folk opinion, fighting fire with fire is an extremely poor device for dealing with a temper tantrum. That is, the *modeling* by the parents of a tantrum themselves in response to Waldo's tantrum is certainly an inefficient way to deal with the child's tantrum. It would behoove the parent to model controlled, pleasant, polite, gentle behavior during the time Waldo is exhibiting his tantrum. Thus, in spite of Waldo's tantrum providing a frustration to his father nearly as great, or even more so, than was the frustration that provoked the tantrum on the part of the child, the parent, instead of having a tantrum himself, engages in what the psychoanalyst would call reaction formation. Calm, serene, quiet, peaceful, over-controlled, overly slow, subdued in voice, smiling, he maintains a posture of patiently waiting for Waldo to wind down.

Meanwhile the offer of *companionship* is held out to Waldo. The very posture and gesture of the model, the father, imply a willingness to discuss, to think through, to relate to this problem of the child, to be a friend and companion to hold Waldo's hand while he experiences some of the frustrations necessarily encountered in the world.

The parent can offer *consistency* by attempting to remove frustration through giving Waldo the ability to anticipate the nature of his world, so that frustrations are few and far between; and by making every effort to apply *extinction* consistently. Waldo learns that a tantrum is no more likely to work in a downtown restaurant with the most elaborate French cuisine than it is on the back porch with no one present but mother, that the visit of Aunt Suzy is no more a license to have a tantrum than is the visit of a neighbor who has three children in the same age range and who is perfectly comfortable around a child who is "showing himself."

The parent makes the *consequences* abundantly clear. During the tantrum, all good things that Waldo might be experiencing cease. The net result of the tantrum is far on the negative side, with no gain to feed the hedonistic principle, and an obvious loss of privilege with some expression of sorrow on the part of the parent.

Minimum conformity comes into play when children are allowed to mumble and grumble without being viewed as having a tantrum. While Waldo obviously is angry, making an awful face and mumbling to himself, the parent considers his controlled behavior as being within the bounds of propriety, of minimum conformity, and thus Waldo does not lose pleasures, privileges, companionship, or incur bad consequences as a result of just being vexed. Waldo learns, then, that a person has a right to be vexed when he doesn't get his way: one doesn't have to be deliriously happy when refused a Coke just because it is almost dinner time. To mumble and grumble and to make a face about that is permissible, so long as that is the end of it.

Waldo is taught that he is entitled to expressions of emotions and that when hurt, particularly when seriously hurt, he is entitled to a full-throttled, ear-shattering wail to express his grief, sadness, unhappiness, or pain. He learns to *discriminate* when a vast outpouring of emotions is appropriate and when it is inappropriate, and to develop a rich repertoire of emotional expressions. He has the capacity, then, when confronted with a situation that justifies self-righteous indignation, to climb upon his soap box and berate his tormenters at full volume. He learns to make a discrimination between a senseless, self-defeating tantrum and an open expression of true feelings.

He learns this best, of course, with the *fading technique,* which involves, often as not, a monologue on the part of the parent, who looks around the room and says something to the effect, "Gracious, everyone is smiling and being pleasant and happy and having a good time, and Waldo is having a fit." Companionship is offered with such comments as, "And while Waldo is having a fit, there is no one to play checkers with Daddy," or "no one to go out and feed the birds with Mother." And statements such as, "I wish Waldo would just say what it is he wants to say and not be so mad." With this followed by some discriminating statement such as, "Well, if Waldo had mashed his finger and was hurt, I would understand why he would be crying."

Fading makes the other techniques so obvious, Waldo easily picks up the message. With the passage of time, these messages become less obvious, less repetitious, and less verbose. Subtlety comes when Waldo gets the message without the excess baggage of the fading technique.

Fighting

Fortunately, the majority of fighting behavior among siblings occurs before Waldo has the capacity to inflict serious injury; also, a prevalent taboo leads to siblings pulling their punches when they become sufficiently strong to cause injury. On the other hand, many parents and teachers are concerned about siblings starting at the picking level, progressing to the poking level, and finally descending to the thumping level, and furthermore, seeming to stay at this task for a great deal of the time.

Several responses to sibling fighting behavior can be used with success by the parents. Of course the parents must always begin with the concept of modeling; if they themselves are using physical assault in their relationships, either in deed or in conversation—"I am going to spank you, if you don't do thus and so"; "I should have punched him"—they will be unsuccessful in stopping Waldo's aggression. In addition, evidence indicates that the modeling of TV violence between family, friends, and acquaintances tends to increase the amount and kind of fighting behavior on the part of youngsters.

Parents involved in a companionship role with Waldo have the advantage of being able to turn off these sequences, almost before they start, by the simple act of diversion. In addition, that the parents not shift in attitude from one day to another is important; they must be consistent. If Waldo is influenced not to fight his brother, but to look for other solutions on one day, he cannot be held up as "cowardly" and unwilling to stand up for himself on the next. Parents must decide what kind of response they expect from Waldo to interpersonal conflict and then try to influence that response across the board.

The most significant influence parents have over fighting behavior among siblings, back-yard friends, and casual acquaintances is consequenting. If parents would assume that "it takes two to tango" and therefore hand out group consequences, they would do two things: they would stop the fighting and they would excuse themselves from a tour of duty on the supreme court as they listen to elaborate dialogues.

"He hit me first."
"Yes, but she spit on me before I hit her."
"I wouldn't have spit on him, if he hadn't been yelling in my face."
"I wasn't yelling in her face; I was trying to get her to give me back my slingshot."
"He traded me his slingshot for . . ."

Now that may be an entertaining way to spend the morning, but it does not stop fighting. Fighting is stopped by aversive stimulation as a direct consequence.

The most effective punishment is one that relates to the ultimate cost of fighting, some type of direct loss of privileges: the TV goes off for an hour during prime time for the children; the fighters are to go to their rooms without their radios playing and sit on their beds (although sitting on one's bed is a total waste of time and should not be used for discipline often, it is so totally aversive to fighting-aged boys as to be one of the most effective punishments known); the fighters are to rake the entire yard to a midline, starting at each corner; they are to do some other useful task that atones for the abuse they have heaped on other members of the family. The important thing is that once the fighting has begun, there is no arbitration, there is no court appeal, there is only a bored, disinterested response to any justification. The only acceptable fighting is a limited rear-guard action of self-defense accompanied by retreat and an appeal to higher authority. If the consequence of sibling battles royal is nothing but abuse for both parties, it is amazing how quickly children can resolve their conflicts short of mayhem.

Minimum conformity allows for venting one's rage short of physical encounter by saying a few "uglies": it involves going outside and wrestling around on the ground, without harassing other people or complaining afterward; and it involves sublimated aggression in the form of athletics. Minimum conformity does not permit physical tyranny of another child, nor harassing other members of the family who have to put up with the distraction.

Obviously, discrimination training and the fading technique make the first two or three encounters extremely gaudy, almost to the point of being ridiculous. I am reminded of the fading technique used by the Washington, D.C., police, when a heated or inebriated or unthinking tourist shoves a policeman on his beat. The policeman, with his eyebrows raised in astonishment, says in a very loud voice, "Stop! Step back! Do not touch me! Do not put your hands about my body!" Not one citizen in a thousand, no matter how drunk or testy, fails to be awed by this technique and to be quickly brought to his senses. An arrest can be avoided and a somewhat contrite citizen can go on his way, sightseeing in the nation's capital, when he might have accelerated the situation into a catastrophe.

If parents, upon the first occasion of sibling aggressiveness, will issue such a mind-boggling, vehement denunciation, they will be amazed at how quickly the issue settles into the past. Extinction occurs as a result of the failure of the fighting to produce any desirable consequences.

Lying and Stealing

For problems with lying and stealing on the part of young children, the most important influence will be the modeling behavior of the adults in the family. If the parents themselves cut corners with the truth when it is self-serving, if they make a habit of white lies—"Tell him I am not in," "We can't afford that"—then the child has a more complicated problem. Of course, all children go through a self-serving dishonesty period, but most often they know they are doing wrong, they fairly exude guilt, they feel bad afterward, and they most often own up to it.

But those children confronted with a complex model who is adamant about the truth sometimes and slippery at others, depending upon a complex set of values, find it difficult to make these subtle discriminations. Parents who find that Waldo has walked out of the store with an extra candy bar and who fail to do anything other than yell at the child become accessories after the fact. Although this is a somewhat complex concept for Waldo, he can easily discriminate the difference between the parent who is too embarrassed, apprehensive, or busy to go back to the counter and the one who stops everything and accompanies him back to the store, approaches the cashier, aids the child in the proper return of the object, and accepts the sharp tongue of the cashier and the glare of other customers. This latter parent provides the model for honesty that will be followed by the child. Providing modeling behavior that is constantly trying to do the right thing, trying to stay honest, respecting the property of others, the privacy and dignity of others, has a profound effect on a child's behavior.

Of course, the more time parents spend with their children, the greater the opportunity to influence their behavior. To teach morals in vivo, in a low-key, informative, on-the-spot form of instruction, has a distinct advantage: undesirable behavior often is observed on its first occurrence, when it can be dealt with in a short, specific period of time without souring the relationship between parent and child. Parents who have little contact with their child, until the child is accused of lying or stealing by someone outside the family, are at a severe disadvantage. Such parents often do not know the true facts; they spend most of their contact hours in a defensive, after-the-fact reaction rather than in a forward-looking traumatic presentation of modeling behavior on the first instance of a child's undesirable behavior.

The dimension of consistency is perhaps obvious. Yet adolescents who get into trouble and look backward to their childhood most often react to the hypocrisy of their parents, whose Sunday set of morals and weekday set of morals do not match up: the child has turned away from his parents' values because of their lack of consistency and has done a poor job of setting his own.

Consequenting morality is important. One phrase that probably should be removed from the instruction of morality is "I am sorry." Not because one should not be sorry, or because apology is not a social courtesy, but because in the minds of children there is something magical about incantations. Children should learn that atonement, replacement, undoing, are far more meaningful to morality than the simple "Oh, I am sorry."

A child who breaks a neighbor's window should not say "I am sorry" from behind his father's pocketbook, but should take an active part in the replacement repairs and in payment. Waldo should rake leaves, dig weeds, clean windows, so that he can understand the importance of personal responsibility. A child should suffer the consequences for his actions; his parents should hold his hand in the process, but they should not get in the way.

In the case of lying and stealing, discrimination training is probably not appropriate in early childhood. Waldo can be helped to discriminate between good manners and consideration for the feelings of others and white lies. Waldo can be taught to say "Thank you for inviting me" instead of "I had a nice time," when the latter is not true. This distinction is difficult for children to understand, but it is worth the effort. The parent is trying to stay honest without abusing people who are well intentioned. At this point, minimum conformity enters the picture, since one does have a choice of saying nothing or saying something that is politely oblique, such as "Hello, Aunt Martha. Thanks for the stamps you sent me," instead of telling the truth, "Mamma, what a big, ugly nose Aunt Martha has," or a lie, "You look so pretty, Aunt Martha."

On the other hand, it is all too apparent that today there is too much justification for dishonesty per se, too little assertion that after all, lies are lies, cheating is cheating, stealing is stealing, all are dishonest, untrustworthy, and injurious. Rationalization about lies being "white" and thievery from corporations being merely equalization of property á la Robin Hood are just that, rationalization. Teaching children to cut corners regarding morality, whether by modeling or lack of consequenting, has a high cost not only for the child, but also for the community; these children develop a severe character defect that makes them incapable of distinguishing right from wrong.

The use of fading is critical, since in the early stages it is important that the child see all of the elements of morality. The parent should, in the case of sticky fingers at the supermarket, respond with wide-eyed amazement, a prompt, almost trotting return to the store, and an almost breathless explanation to the cashier. This focuses the child's attention on the elements of (1) picking up the candy when told he could not have any, (2) hiding the candy from the father, (3) hiding the candy from the cashier, (4) leaving the store with the candy not paid for. The emphasis upon the elements, the step by step walking through the correct way, including a discussion of the importance of discussion, make the morality of the situation clear to the child. The understanding that if the child needs very much to have a piece of candy when it has been forbidden, he has the right and responsibility to make a case for its being highly important, that a good case will be rewarded but most emphatically begging will not, emphasizes to the child the power of language and the lack of power of undesirable, selfish actions.

Refusal

Occasionally a child will be given direct or implied instruction to which he responds by eyeball-to-eyeball refusal to comply. This is particularly vexing in later childhood when the child's power to refuse is increasing. An example of a rather common refusal situation occurs in joint-custody issues following a divorce, a rapidly accelerating problem in America. One of the undesirable side effects of the no-fault divorce is the joint-custody-of-children problem. Time was when getting the divorce itself involved such an exhaustive battle that the ultimate custody of children was pushed aside as a fringe issue that usually involved major custody by the mother and visitation rights related to support payments on the part of the father. Now, since divorce itself does not necessarily involve grotesque infighting, parents have energy left over to focus on visitation.

The psychologist, or counselor, or teacher, encounters the complaint by the mother (or father) that Waldo does not want to visit his father (or mother); that Waldo is upset before the visit and upset and/or exhausted after the visit; that stopping or radically curtailing these visitations would make Waldo's life much more pleasant. And the mother (or father) is evidently being truthful: Waldo does cry, whimper, and beg not to have to go with the father (or mother, depending on the primary custody), and is upset, unhappy, and exhausted after the visit.

The problem is one of cause and effect. The psychoanalysts have an interesting concept, *acting-out through*. For instance, assume that the father has primary custody. He has been bruised severely in his relationship with his former wife and maintains an inordinate residual rage. At almost a preconscious level, he cannot imagine how that wretch, his former wife, could treat her daughter in other than a neurotic, hateful way. And so, when the daughter picks up his ambivalence about her visiting with her mother, the father is not at all surprised and may well be secretly gratified.

He then acts-out through the child his own anger toward his former wife. Under the guise of trying to understand the "problem," he proceeds to be highly suggestive. He asks such leading questions as "Is she mean to you?" "Does her boyfriend upset you?" "Does she leave you alone?" Ad nauseum. And the daughter, sensing the importance of this game to her father, begins working herself into a classic phobic response to going with her mother. The result, of course, is an utterly mystified mother, frightened and humiliated by her own child's fear of her and unwillingness to go with her. The situation quickly accelerates back into court, with an attempt to cut off the visitation privileges in the best interest of the child.

Now, this situation is both avoidable and correctable, requiring only common sense and interpersonal decency, but it can be helped by our ten steps. Obviously the parents are bruised by their marriage and subsequent divorce; they do have some bad feelings about each other in most cases; but they can be decent about it. They can be polite; they can be kind; they can be sincere; they can be helpful. They can model good interpersonal relationships, even though it takes an effort. They can allow sufficient time for each party to have extended companionship with Waldo to bridge the emotional gap.

They can introduce positive consequences of Waldo's going with the other parent and severe negative consequences for his refusing, so that Waldo's best interest obviously is served by his graciously visiting with the other parent. Minimum conformity requires Waldo's being held to the line of politeness, respect, obedience, and time-specific encounter. He is not told that he must love his other parent, but rather it is assumed he will. What he must do is go through the appropriate behaviors that permit love to flourish.

Discrimination training involves learning what the minimum conformity contract implies: on that special occasion when the Boy Scouts are having an overnight camping trip that coincides with the visit to daddy, that visit can be skipped; but one cannot make plans that habituate this. The fading technique involves making the first move on Waldo's part to resist a visit so utterly flabbergasting, so unacceptable, and so outrageous as to be inconceivable.

Obviously there are rare occasions in which the misconduct on the part of one or the other parent does require termination of visits except under strict supervision; alcoholism, serious mental illness, sexual aberrations, psychopathic irresponsibility do occasionally occur. Usually, however, such is not the case: Waldo's refusal to go results merely from his reaching into his bag of uglies and deciding, probably on the spur of the moment, to punish one or the other of his parents for the disruptive influence they have had on his life. The reinforcement of Waldo's positive behavior toward the other parent and the punishment of his negative behavior will result in the extinction of this seriously maladaptive response on Waldo's part.

PASSIVE DEFIANCE

Earlier we discussed the inappropriateness of rituals such as "I am sorry" taking the place of atonement or making up for destructive behavior. Let's look for a moment at the correct response to passive defiance, such as forgetting and self-serving accidents.

Forgetting

Preschool children particularly are plagued with the problem of poor memory. Waldo forgets to do his household chores, he forgets to come home on time, he forgets to deliver messages. And the usual response on the part of his parents is to be mildly aversive: they complain or fuss but do not seem to penetrate beyond Waldo's wide-eyed, innocent "Oh, my goodness, I forgot."

Now since this is a self-rewarding behavior on Waldo's part—that is, Waldo has profited by his forgetting—he is setting up poor behavior patterns for adulthood. A child who was due home at 5:00 P.M. but does not arrive until 6:30 because "I forgot" has engaged in self-rewarding behavior that is highly resistive to extinction and can set a pattern for later adulthood in which he uses poor memory as a device to get his own way. In its adult form, it is more likely to be confusion: "Oh, I thought we agreed to meet at the library."

But forgetting is a poor interpersonal behavioral response and is best extinguished fairly early in childhood. The device for extinction is quite clear. The parent should simply pay no mind whatsoever to the explanation "Oh, I forgot," but should respond as though the failure to perform, the failure to come home at five, the failure to do one's chores, the failure to share some treat with a younger sibling, was a deliberate, calculated, aggressive act and should be dealt with on those terms as though the concept of forgetting has no meaning with regard to human relationships.

Obviously the parent is trying to avoid the child's lacking personal responsiblity for his deeds. If parents will simply ignore the superstitious ritual of "the sorries," they can develop a sense of accountability within the child. Thus Waldo, exposed to models who make up for their errors and oversights and who take the consequences for forgetting, will assume responsibility for his actions. Parents who react strongly to having forgotten a promise made to a child by instant atonement—"Good heavens, I promised to take you fishing this Saturday and I've arranged to play golf with a foursome. I'll call them and try to get a substitute. If I can't, I'll take you tomorrow, and we'll go again next week too"—make more of an impression on the child than they ever realize.

For the parents to do this consistently is important, of course, and to bear the full consequences on themselves, just as they have Waldo suffer the consequences of his poor memory as if it were deliberate. For the parent to take the role of the "forgiver" is a poor policy, with the it's-all-right-this-time-but-don't-let-it-happen-again routine. He should, of course, forgive Waldo, but he should expect Waldo to make the amends himself, or to take the punishment.

The minimum conformity contract says one has the privilege of forgetting some trivia, but not self-serving trivia. Discrimination training involves the distinction between trivia and nontrivia. And fading again implies that the first time is the most important time; the parents' response to the first time should be gaudy to help Waldo identify the importance of the behavior.   Reinforcement of remembering and punishing forgetting leads to a lack of reinforcement for forgetting and subsequent extinction.

Passivity

Occasionally, more frequently with male than female children, one encounters extreme passivity. This passivity is pervasive, influencing all dimensions of the child's interaction with the world. Not only is the child easily intimidated by peers, he appears to be highly sensitive to any form of criticism, he prefers to avoid any situation with even the potential of conflict, unhappiness, or stress. He spends an inordinate amount of time in solitary preoccupation, perhaps musing and thinking, perhaps engaged in elaborate fantasy. He avoids the world, hides from social encounter, and has little drive, motivation, or initiative.

Of course, such passivity is an extreme of the continuum. Vast individual differences among children are perfectly normal. Parents and teachers need to accept these differences and not be constantly trying to tidy up the child's personality. Of all the behavior patterns of children, those related to temperament, such as activity level, sensitivity, and sleep cycles, are the most resistive to change. Generally speaking, parents should accept these large individual differences among children with good grace.

The case in point, however, is a child whose passivity is not only extreme but is grossly interfering with his healthy development. Passivity can affect all areas of social, emotional, intellectual, and academic growth. A child who is grossly introverted, grossly quiet, and grossly disinterested in people and activities is likely to become a lonely and often nonproductive adolescent and adult.

Granted, there are exceptions to this rule. People who have spent their early childhood as virtual recluses have turned out to be extremely talented, artistically significant writers or researchers. But by and large this response is maladaptive in our society; parents would do well to attempt to influence it.

Unfortunately, passivity frequently comes from modeling the parents, often the same-sex parent. If such is the case, the task of that parent, and of the other parent, is much more difficult. In any event, expressing to the child the joys of activity, the joys of interpersonal interaction, and the pleasures derived from ego-mastery in the social context should be conveyed by demonstration. Children who are solitary, who are passive, can still gain a great deal from companionship. If Waldo is not strong enough to enter the outside world, then one can quietly impinge upon his inside world through the vehicle of companionship.

Not only is companionship from the parents important during the child's sedentary activities, but also peer companionship is important. If Waldo is severely passive, a certain amount of pump-priming is necessary regarding peer companionship; younger children at about the same emotional age as Waldo often succeed in breaking through where other, more accomplished, and more mature children of the same chronological age cannot.

A thoroughly passive child, who is withdrawn and introverted, does not respond to consequenting: he knows the cost of his passivity and introversion is loneliness and seems fully capable of paying this price. In fact, he seems to enjoy certain dimensions of it far more than he enjoys interpersonal activities.

So, one puts a little reverse English on the situation and insists that Waldo earn the right to his quiet time, to his passivity and withdrawal; the consequences are set up so that if Waldo will invite over a friend, if he will engage in conversation at the dinner table, if he will tell the family a story, then he is allowed the utter bliss and peace of being by himself, alone and quiet.

By this process is accrued a secondary gain or secondary reinforcement; Waldo begins to get some pleasure from these social activities in which he so reluctantly engaged. That this be so is extremely important with a passive child. He does not need to be given the impression that he has to be a hale-fellow-well-met, backpounding extrovert in order to get people off his back; rather he must learn that he has certain social responsibilities to peers, family, and acquaintances. Discrimination training consists of helping the child to identify when it is appropriate to be sedentary, introspective, withdrawn, and passive, and when it is not.

The fading technique involves the efforts of the parents to make sure that the child is successful in his early probes in breaking his pattern of passivity. Every effort should be made to have the peer group receptive; socialization efforts should be manipulated somewhat so that the occasions, such as birthday parties, having a friend over, a pony ride, go well. The heavy hand of the parent used to manipulate the situation to cause success is extremely important in tolling the child out of passivity.

Reinforcement has good things happen in social contexts and punishment consists of causing the child to miss important, significant interpersonal activities as a result of failure to get into the social context.

Extreme cases of passivity, particularly in the male child, will often require some extra help from a psychologist, psychiatrist, or resource teacher; it is not something that is best left until later. The general experience is that although children grow out of many things, they do not grow out of passivity without considerable help on the part of supportive adults in their environment.

Somatic Preoccupation

One of the most insidious and pervasive behavioral problems of American children is an escape from life via the mechanism of psychosomatic complaints. We are a medically conscious nation, bombarded by television advice, counsel, and suggestions regarding our bodily functions. The typical American family has a medicine cabinet full of medication; we also have a tradition that makes illness a respectable way of ducking undesirable activities. It would appear, then, that flight into illness is a relatively serious behavior problem of young children.

Unfortunately, modeling makes this problem severe. Children who observe their parents escape unpleasant activities or work via headaches, via allergies, via "not feeling well," model this behavior and spend a substantial portion of their early childhood in the throes of some form of illness. In order to combat this, parents must first be convinced that the human body has tremendous resiliency and internal healing capacity; that constant preoccupation with bodily functions and how one feels is an escape rather than an alert surveillance in a preventive sense. This means, of course, that medicating and self-treating and introspecting about how one feels and what one's throat looks like and whether one's bowel movements are exactly normal and whether one's system is too acidic and whether one needs a tranquilizer, antidepressant, appetite suppressor, activity stimulator, or a laxative, is not a desirable preoccupation on which to spend one's life.

If parents can model extremely low-profile psychosomatic preoccupation, they will greatly improve their children's chances of escaping the scourge. If they will minimize this introspective, how-do-I-feel-this-morning behavior, if they will comment infrequently about their own body and their own aches and pains, they can expect that their children will likewise be able to adjust to life without this debilitating crutch.

As in all the previous situations, influencing one's children depends upon healthy companionship. Parents have an influence on the thinking, outlook, and attitudes of their children via the mechanism of long-standing interpersonal relationships. If parents do not spend considerable companionship time with their children, children are likely to be influenced by other people, who may well have one of these psychosomatic preoccupations and may be constantly filling the children's heads with fear, worry, and preoccupation with medical problems. The importance of consistency in handling emotional problems is probably obvious.

The most radical of the behavioral techniques regarding somatic complaints is consequenting. Unfortunately, many parents, if not all parents, operate with a certain level of guilt about their children at all times. They consider that they do not spend enough time with their children, that in some way they have shortchanged their children. When a child appears to be ill, then, the usual consequence in the American household is massive secondary gain. A child who wakes up feeling a little queasy in the morning and finds himself put into a freshly made bed with a fluffed-out pillow, and with the TV moved into his room, a cup of chicken soup with crackers at his disposal, and a mother or father who spends all day reading to him, talking with him, and feeling his brow, has little reason to want to reexamine the question of whether or not he really is ill.

Oftentimes, the only good interpersonal relationship between mother or father and Waldo occurs when Waldo is thowing up and everyone is suddenly concerned. Obviously from a commonsense point of view, parents should make every effort to give Waldo as much attention and affection and emotional support as possible on a daily basis, but during illness, they reduce as far as possible this secondary gain, this emotional profit that comes from being sick.

This does not say that the parents should be abusive or unconcerned. This does not say the physician should not be consulted. It says simply that the day Waldo throws up in the morning should not become a delight-ful holiday in which all good things come his way.

Sickness, missing school, being away from his peers, should be un-pleasant. Recovery, returning to school, getting back with his friends, should be something that he looks forward to with pleased anticipation. Sickness is an abnormal situation and should be regarded as that by every-one, not as a holiday.

Obviously, minimum conformity requires that children make valid reports of any medical problems they have, but that they learn to make these reports matter-of-factly and undemandingly. Children need to recog-nize the transient abnormality of feeling bad, that feeling bad is not a sub-ject for conversation, but a simple statement of a temporary condition. Discrimination training requires teaching children to pay attention to the few passing body sensations that are of any significance at all. Nausea, loss of color, fever, abdominal pains, muscle sprains, and cracked bones are all rare events in a child's life; he should have the ability to discrimi-nate these rare events and separate them from feeling a little queasy when one wakes up in the morning, having a sharp pain in one's colon prior to a bowel movement, everyday mild bruises, bangs, and strains from growing up in a healthy world.

Fading technique is simply the strategy by which the parents em-phasize recovery with great celebration and help the child to make the distinction between doing what he is supposed to do to get well and doing something merely to get attention. One reinforces children for low-profile washing and bandaging a cut and then getting on with life; and one punishes emphasis upon how much removing a splinter hurts. Under such conditions, Waldo develops a repertoire of other ways of handling stress; he extinguishes somatic complaints.

Now, in passing, there are children with chronic illnesses and here one walks a thin line. Rheumatic heart, extraordinary allergy, blood dis-ease, fragile bones demand special care for children. It is a matter of emphasis. In my experience of working on a terminal ward for children for over a year, I was amazed at the fresh, emotionally healthy outlook managed by many children, where the outcome of their disease was certain and known to them and their parents, yet their daily preoccupation was with things other than their disease; they lived out their lives with great courage, much to the betterment of themselves and all the people around them.

FIXATION AND REGRESSION

Thumb-Sucking

Thumb-sucking is a common behavior pattern in young children. Some children are born with deep indentures in their thumb from many hours in utero clamped between teethless gums. Throughout early child-hood, most children continue sucking, mouthing, tasting, and chewing on their environment, finally developing some sucking ritual that seems to be just right for them. Sometimes this sucking becomes a strong drive.

With the growth of teeth and permanent mouth shaping, this sucking and thrusting becomes a problem of concern to parents, dentists, and sometimes to children themselves, who become slightly ashamed of the looks the thumb-sucking generates in others. The problem is to prevent the child from sucking his thumb without further complicating his life. Again for the sake of demonstration, let's assume we are following the total-push program outlined above, having decided that this behavior is worth changing.

Perhaps the most difficult aspect of the thumb-sucking treatment is the first step or the modeling, because as adults we present poor models. Many adults chew their fingernails, suck on pipes or cigarettes, chew gum, eat excessively, and in general call considerable attention to oral gratification, and thus have a hard time convincing Waldo that to stop sucking his thumb is easy. If it turns out that Waldo needs to be asked to give up something important to him in terms of gratification, perhaps the adult should give up something himself as an example or model.

By friendly companionship with Waldo, the parent is able to use his presence as a diversion for the thumb-sucking child. The more table games, social interaction, encouragement, and interpersonal gratifications Waldo enjoys with his parents, the less important is this solitary gratification derived from his thumb. Because of what we know about partial reinforcement, once the regimen has been established to prevent the thumb-sucking, consistency is demanded.

In the dimensions of consequenting, Stumphauzer and Bishop (1969) performed an extremely slick experiment, which, like most good clinical research, was diabolically simple. On Saturday morning, when the cartoons come on TV with their full splendor of four hours of mayhem, violence, and toy commercials, the experienced thumb-sucker settles into his best thumb-sucking position and focuses on the center of that screen. If mother or father will struggle out of bed, come downstairs, and sit generally a cord's length away from the TV set (make that a long cord), and watch Waldo from the corner of his eye, he can see Waldo slowly curl into position and insert the thumb, at which point daddy pushes a remote cutoff switch and sets a timer, such as an egg timer or hourglass. The TV goes black; Waldo often as not goes black; and Daddy calmly tells Waldo that as soon as a minute is over, the TV will go back on, *if* his thumb is out of his mouth during that minute. Waldo complains, jumps up and down, glares at the television, whines, whimpers, and engages in subvocal cursing, all to no avail.

One minute later, the TV comes on, those fighting animals come back on the screen, and Waldo is back in business. But not for long. In a few moments, the thumb mysteriously reappears and on its own creeps slowly up, at first barely touches the lips, and then shoots home. Blank goes the television set.

Now comes a stream of Philadelphia lawyer's arguments as to how he cannot keep his thumb out of his mouth; how this is mean, unusual punishment; how other children do not have to endure this, et cetera, et cetera: all to no avail. One minute later, back comes the mayhem on the screen, where it remains for a considerable period of time, until, with great stealth, cunning, and mystery associated with slight turns of the body away from the parent, perhaps under a shawl, back in the mouth goes the thumb. And click, off goes the TV.

In as few as nine trials, children have done the impossible: they have traded their thumb, their good, old, dependable, reliable, faithful thumb, for cartoon shows. And as distressing as it is to see a child sell out that cheaply, it nevertheless is gratifying to a parent facing extended orthodontistry.

The minimum conformity allows Waldo to make some reasonable substitutions, such as chewing sugarless gum, eating cut-up apples, grapes, or popcorn, so that the violence of the loss is not so obvious. Discrimination training helps Waldo to learn techniques in which he can manage to obtain oral gratification without thrusting his tongue or sucking his thumb. And the fading technique simply comes in as the electrical setup is removed from the TV set, with the mere threat to turn it off substituted. Waldo is rewarded extensively by having the TV set on and by being given generous prizes as he succeeds. He is given punishment by the TV being turned off for substantial blocks of time. Extinction is the natural consequence when gratification is blocked and Waldo forgets how lovely that thumb really was.

Crying

Part of the general immaturity syndrome exhibited by children is excessive crying, whimpering, and whining. This excessive emotional expression is an operant: at least from Waldo's point of view, it is a productive behavior. In spite of the fact that it seems to be a nuisance to everyone around him, in spite of the fact that everyone claims to try to stop Waldo's whining, if you observe from the background, you will see that on a rather rich, partial reinforcement schedule, Waldo is indeed being reinforced for his crying, whining behavior.

Now, children should be encouraged to express emotions. For children to be in touch with their emotions is not only normal, but highly desirable. To laugh, to cry, to giggle, to feel happy, to feel sad, and to express these both physiologically and articulately is important. I am not talking about any effort to frustrate, dampen, or in any way interfere with the expression of emotional behavior. What I am talking about is abusive, manipulative, controlling behavior on the part of a child who has learned this maladaptive style of social control.

Obviously, if a parent himself is a whiner, if he spends a good deal of time moaning, groaning, and wailing over the misfortunes of life, he will have little influence on Waldo in attempting to stop this behavior. Parents too should display a rich variation of emotional behavior. They should likewise laugh when they are happy, cry when they are sad, and snarl when they are angry. But, a parent who wishes to develop a rich repertoire of responses on the part of the child cannot be a one-response person himself. If the mother and father spend a good deal of their waking hours in wailing, moaning, and groaning about the tough life, they well deserve a child who is a whimperer and whiner.

Children frequently whine to get attention; if this attention is contingent upon their whining—they are ignored when they are not whining—then of course the whining behavior becomes an important operant in the child's life. Thus, a parent needs to provide considerable companionship to the child, a mutual interchange of emotional feelings and expressions, long dialogues, a good deal of physical and emotional touching of the child in companionship. This must be done on a daily basis and not just when the child is in great distress.

Parents inadvertently set up conditions that maintain whining behavior because they are inconsistent in their responses to their own children. However, the most important dimension for modifying whining, crying, wailing behavior is consequenting. If the parent can make sure that Waldo does not gain from his whining and whimpering, if the parents are not under the control of this aversive behavior of Waldo, then Waldo drops this behavior in favor of other behaviors that work. The consequence of abusive whimpering and whining should be a net loss to Waldo, and this should be made quite clear. Phrases such as "As soon as you finish that, we will be able to do this" are powerful controllers of human behavior.

The minimum conformity contract allows Waldo to be unhappy and periodically to become maudlin in his expression of unhappiness; he does not have to be constantly smiling in a big toothy grin: rather, he can, on appropriate occasions, express the full range of emotional behavior. Most of the time, his emotional responses are a private, inner world that should be encouraged rather than discouraged.

Discrimination training requires that Waldo learn when it is appropriate and when it is inappropriate to give in to one's emotions. He learns public and private expressions of emotions. He learns when emotions are valid communication and when they are harassments. And this kind of discrimination training is done best in vivo, and it is done best with a fading technique in which vivid contrasts between correct emotional responses and incorrect emotional responses are made.

A child who has banged his finger and whose eyes are rimmed with tears is picked up by the adult and held close and has his finger kissed with great significance and preoccupation and is given fully to understand that this is the time and place to be emotional appropriately. But later, he is confronted fully with the fact that his whining, whimpering, crying, and temper tantrum is only costing him time and pleasure. This technique reduces to a minimum the number of trials that Waldo uses this immature response. Emphasis on errorless learning of appropriate discrimination makes the socialization of young Waldo a much simpler process for him. Reinforcing appropriate emotional responses in the full range and calmly punishing tantrum behavior results ultimately in elimination of this immature phase that most children go through.

Soiling

A problem more frequent with boys than with girls is soiling. Soiling, the result of unaccomplished, incomplete, or lost toilet training, is most frequent in three-year-olds who find themselves in need of extra attention. In spite of the displeasure of the adults in the home over these "accidents" of the child, the usual case results in Waldo's receiving extra attention, handling, bathing, powdering, washing, and stroking. The parent has a clear option to spend more time with Waldo, helping him to master his "job," while recognizing that this "problem" is a signal on Waldo's part that he is in need of more emotional support, or to endure the problem and let Waldo grow out of it, which in most cases he does. Since children who are soilers do seem to need more contact, the former option would seem to be the preferred one. Certainly both of the options above are vastly superior to a rage reaction on the part of the parent, with inconsistent threats, punishment, "campaigns," and so on.

Since most adults have established for themselves a comfortable routine with a low profile regarding their own bowel movements, they almost without exception make good models, if they themselves were not traumatized by their own childhood toilet training to the point of "privacy panic," which causes the child to assume something very secretive is going on behind that door.

Most children give subtle, and sometimes not so subtle, indications of being about to have a bowel movement. This is the time to give them attention, to take them to the correct-sized potty, and to require them to sit until they are finished. They should be promised a special treat when they have finished the task, and they should be required to remain until they do. They quickly become bored over the forced sitting, eager to do other things, and often as not eager to receive the special treat.

On the other hand, Waldo may indeed be somewhat recalcitrant, but firmness is required. Time on the seat will almost always do the trick. If given adequate but not excessive attention while sitting, and the promise of great pleasure, attention, and reward upon completion, few children will resist for more than a few minutes. Pediatric consulation is sometimes needed to make sure that the child does not become impacted, is not constipated, and has normal bowel function; and in very rare cases, psychological consultation is needed. But in the main, patience for a couple of days and a determined effort on the part of the parents to be consistent, firm, and encouraging is all that is needed.

RARE AND DIFFICULT PSYCHOLOGICAL PROBLEMS

Perhaps we should review some classical problems, which, though relatively infrequent, have sufficient seriousness to warrant active consideration on the part of parents when they occur.

Schizophrenia

Earlier we mentioned childhood schizophrenia or autistic behavior as probably caused by some genetically related metabolism problem that leads to malfunctioning of the emotional control centers and language control centers in the brain. Now the prognosis for a full recovery from childhood schizophrenia is virtually zero. After some fifty years of extensive literature on the subject, one would have to conclude that the majority of spectacular recoveries from childhood schizophrenia were not schizophrenia at all, were not spontaneous recoveries or sensory improvements related to schizophrenia, but were related to some neurological developmental lag, some major sensory deficit, or the like.

In childhood schizophrenia, the psychologist has little to offer other than behavioral programming via intensive behavior modification strategies that make the autistic child more tractable, manageable, and in general more pleasant to be around. The primary agent for treatment of the autistic child is now and probably will remain the family physician, or child psychiatrist, or pediatrician, who, via medication and institutionalization, tries in some way to alter the basic metabolic balance of the child.

Thus, parents with an autistic child are of course first of all advised to seek the advice and counsel of their pediatrician, who will probably make a referral to a child psychiatrist. The psychological assistance to the family comes after that. After the diagnosis is established and after chemotherapy has done whatever it can do, the behavioral technology of the psychologist comes into play to aid this child in becoming a more tractable member of the family. The specific technology of behavioral control of autistic children is extremely complex and should not be undertaken by teachers and parents without the direct consultation and supervision of a psychologist.

There is, of course, some controversy over whether the behavior of the parents has some causative relationship to the development of autistic children. But by and large, nearly overwhelming evidence seems to indicate that such is not the case; the behavior pattern of the parents is a result, not a cause, of living with an *enfant terrible* on a twenty-four-hour-a-day basis.

Anorexia

A second condition equal in severity and quite possibly also having an organic basis, anorexia is the failure to thrive syndrome. Anorexia typically does not occur until late childhood, although there are cases in early childhood. In its simplest form, anorexia is a failure to gain weight; in fact, a failure to maintain a critical weight. The prognosis in anorexia is not good. Anorectic children simply do not eat; they throw up food that they do eat. They seem to derive some bizarre satisfaction from their thinness.

A number of both behavioral and dynamic interpretations of the cause of anorexia have been made. These children, who are grossly emaciated, who have no interest in food, and who seem to be mildly depressed most of the time, represent a severe challenge to the pediatrician and the child psychologist. Both of them, working together, along with the parents, in a heroic team effort do, on occasion, turn the anorectic child around before he dies as a consequence of some secondary infection resulting from his low resistance.

The anorectic child needs to be put on a regimen that involves a great deal of affection and attention during the eating period. He needs to be around young children who are good models of eating behavior. And he seems to need to be on a reinforcement schedule that induces a stable eating pattern. Thus far the success in treating anorexia is not good. But the combination of medication and behavior modification, along with supportive emotional interaction and modeling, does seem to have the best chance of the technology available today.

Alopecia

A third syndrome in children, alopecia is either a change in hair color or the falling out of hair in small plug-sized bald spots. As far as we know, alopecia relates to a chronic stress reaction on the part of children. It sometimes occurs, particularly the sudden change of hair color, as a result of some single, traumatic event; but the usual case is a chronic stress reaction.

Treatment of alopecia is twofold. First is an attempt to remove the child from the stress-producing situation in which he finds himself; the second is a continuing relationship therapy, in which someone, probably a child psychologist, interacts with him on a twice-weekly basis to help him develop other avenues of expressing emotions. Evidently the child is highly constricted in his repertoire of emotional expression and needs the encouragement that can be derived from having a special friend who talks with him and interacts with him on several interpersonal dimensions.

Allergies

Earlier, the problem of allergies was mentioned briefly. To recognize that allergy treatment is the purview of the pediatrician is essential. But most pediatricians recognize the strong psychological mechanism regarding the secondary gain from the allergy. Thus, with an equal physical allergic reaction, two children may be entirely different in their psychological response to it. The general suggestion of the child psychologist working with the pediatrician is a concerted effort to reduce the secondary gain derived from the allergy: to provide the child with attention, emotional support, and success in behaviors at times when he is not in the midst of an allergic reaction. To minimize the secondary gains of asthma and other allergic reactions would seem to be well worth while. On the basis of what might be a transitory acute phase of the allergic reaction during childhood, a child can become psychologically severely crippled, afraid of the world, afraid to move, for fear he may touch off allergic reactions. Minimizing these responses on the part of the parents, downplaying their concern, even when they are extreme, seems to be the treatment of choice.

Depression

In a previous chapter, we discussed hospitalism, marasmus, or anaclitic depression, which seems to occur in children who at an early age are separated from their mothers. The prognosis for a child suffering from anaclitic depression is not good and requires expert counsel.

Even in normal home situations, children encounter losses, either actual or fantasized, and some react to these with considerable neurosis to the point of clinical depression. In our highly mobile society, this most frequently occurs when children are abruptly uprooted from their home and friends to move to a new neighborhood, school, and peer group. They grieve, become introspective and quiet; often they become picky eaters; their academic work falls off.

In the usual case, this depression is transitory. By encouraging new friendships, via open house for the neighborhood kids, a few get-together parties, and some joining, parents can help children to overcome their depression, as they can overcome the loss of a pet or the occasional death of a friend. The basic strategy is existential, helping the child to accept separation as one of the tragedies in life, as part of the whole life drama, and to recognize the transitory nature of most relationships.

A child who persists in morose preoccupation and depression for several weeks, however, probably should have consultation through a guidance center, pediatrician, or child psychologist. Having expert counsel during such a crisis period can be helpful both to the child and to the parents in their working with the child. As unusual as it is, childhood depression, although transitory, can be severe. The incidence of childhood suicide is on the increase in this country. Parents simply cannot afford to take an ignore-it-and-it-will-go-away attitude toward these tense feelings. Emotional support, diversion, and a significant gift, with its symbolic replacement of the lost object—a new pet, a new blanket, a painting set, or musical instrument—all represent to the child that recouping is possible.

Psychopathic Personality Disorders

Although fortunately rare, and still somewhat problematic as to cause, the psychopathic character, or the so-called primary or criminal psychopath, is a problem in our society. A considerable body of literature suggests that there may be some genetic or metabolic predisposition toward the development of psychopathic tendencies; however, the young psychopath seems to appear in a home in which he has been allowed to become personally irresponsible; his actions are almost always after-the-fact justified, excused, and minimized. He seldom faces consequences of his own behavior. He frequently is the violator of other persons' rights within the home, neighborhood, and community. He has a strong sense of situational ethics; with uncanny skill in the tradition of the Philadelphia lawyer, he can successfully justify anything. He has indulgent parents, who, often as not, overvalue him as a late child in their marriage, or an adopted child, or simply a child who meets the neurotic rather than the healthy needs of the parents. He thus develops a tyrannical use of his affection as leverage in getting his way. He grows up feeling that he is an exception to every rule. When he occasionally encounters consequences for his acts, he is indignant, surprised, and angry. He usually is so abrasive in such circumstances that the parents find themselves stirring around attempting to insure that people do not cross their son because it upsets him. Ultimately his tyranny moves out into the school, the neighborhood, and finally, in the late teens, begins to run afoul of the law.

At which point everyone is properly sorry, but never able to turn him around. The secret of successful treatment of psychopathic youngsters is early identification of the problem and extremely firm guidance of the parents by a professional therapist. Only through careful management of the child's environment, by providing good models for him and consistent consequenting of his behavior, can the budding young psychopath, with much squealing and outraged indignation, be molded into the minimum-conformity model. Only then will he make an acceptable member of society. He probably never will go out of his way for other people, but at least he can be prevented from throwing himself in the face of society, ultimately to be crushed.

Night Terrors

Nightmares are particularly common during the preschool years, when the child still has vivid, eidetic imagery and the capacity to replay with great vividness personal fantasies, fragments of movies, TV shows, and plays. The role of a nightmare is positive: a nightmare helps the child to discharge residual tension related to "scary" themes.

For the most part, then, parents need not be concerned with nightmares. Few children bring a nightmare across the consciousness barrier, so are, for the most part, completely amnesic about their nightmare when they wake up. Nightmares terminate themselves, do no damage to the child, and are best unmentioned, since even kidding the child about it the next day only causes additional triggering of the syndrome, which is neither helpful nor unhelpful.

The best policy for parents in responding to children's nightmares is to wake up the child, if the nightmare lasts beyond a few minutes, simply make sure the child is fully awake, and then put him straight back to bed, without any questioning or comments regarding the nightmare. Such questions and comments only add to the child's bewilderment as to why he is being waked up and what outrageous thing is going on in the middle of the night.

Very occasionally, a child with frequently occurring nightmares is showing signs of being temporarily incapable of dealing with some symbolic event. Not infrequently these symbolic events relate to sexual misinformation, as in the case of Sara mentioned in Chapter 9. Such nightmares indicate that some professional help on a short-term basis is probably advisable. Consultation with a guidance center, pediatrician, or child psychologist would be helpful both to the parents and to the child. However, even in these extreme cases, the nightmare itself should be regarded as adaptive. It is serving the need of the child to dissipate pent-up feelings; what Freud calls dream work, or the working through of the latent content of the dream, will usually take place even without treatment.

Pica and Self-Mutilation

Two relatively rare, related syndromes, pica and self-mutilation, are normal at a low level. Most children go through a stage of eating things, chewing on their sweaters, their hair, their pencils, or picking the paint off armchairs or bedposts. Most children will likewise pick at a sore; I hesitate to mention that so do college students. Such behavior usually is benign and best handled by mild admonishments.

Occasionally, however, because of metabolic disturbances more often than vitamin deficiencies, children become obsessed with one or the other of these behaviors. I have seen X-rays of four-year-olds with enough dirt in their stomachs to grow a small garden; any time these children are not watched, off they go with their little spoon into the dirt. Some children will flick the paint off all the way around their bed, and when the paint contains lead, the consequences can be severe and permanent. These cases of pica are best handled with pediatric consultation and with a radical behavioral approach similar to the thumb-sucking routine, but more intense. Self-mutilation, particularly the maintenance of open sores, likewise can be handled with such a regimen.

WILD-CARD OPTION

Thus far we have reviewed the relative ease with which parents can produce behavioral change in children through the massive use of behavioral technology, with the result that Waldo loses most of the battles. We emphasized earlier that parents should be highly selective in engaging Waldo in behavioral control and, within the minimum conformity controls, should allow Waldo a great deal of latitude within the limits of safety and tolerance of the family. One additional safeguard is suggested to insure the continuation of personal growth, the wild-card option.

Occasionally, for totally incomprehensible reasons, Waldo almost at random selects a particular desire as being extraordinarily important. Many times this desire, although incomprehensible and, on the face of it, absurd, meets the criterion of the wild-card option; that is, it is frightfully important to Waldo, does not represent an unreasonable risk to him or harassment to the rest of the family, and is possible. Now, of course the parents could exercise their full behavioral control and, within a few days, eliminate this strong desire; but the crunching effect on the child's imagination and intrapsychic growth is probably unjustified. So, even at a very young age and even in a small family, Waldo should understand that any member of the family has the right, on rare occasions, to exercise the option of the wild card, or the just-because-I-need-it card.

An example of a wild card with a preschooler would be the undesirable-pet desire. Occasionally in the suburbs, and even in the downtown areas, a door-to-door salesman suddenly appears with a small box in which a small, white, furry, red-eyed bunny rabbit resides. The rabbit is always young and eager and friendly and beautiful and utterly consumes the passions of a four-year-old girl. At that moment in time, this little girl would sell her soul in order to possess that rabbit.

Now even a half-asleep, dull-witted parent realizes that that teensy, weensy white ball of fluff is a Belgian Giant doe, that within six to eight weeks, she will weigh fourteen to sixteen pounds, will consume a cup of rabbit chow a day, will process that quickly, along with a half-pint of water, and will turn any bedroom into a stable; rabbit urine is almost toxic in its corrosiveness; it stinks abominably. In addition, rabbits gnaw and chew and scurry around and nibble on fingers and things in general. For the average household, an enormous white rabbit, with its constant demands to be fed and watered and changed, its tremendous odor problem, is an extremely undesirable pet made even more so by the fact that a healthy, well-fed rabbit can (sigh) live twelve years. Any parent also knows that within two or three years, this rabbit is going to become a family chore, that the little girl is going to be spending the night with her friends, that the family is going to want to travel, that taking care of this bunny rabbit is going to be a plague.

For some families, the bunny rabbit does not meet the criterion of the wild card. It simply affords too much harassment for the rest of the family, it is too expensive in terms of time, energy, and money, and consumes too much space. In such a case, the parent will just have to have it out with the child and bring to bear our ten steps to postpone, at least for the time being, the rabbit, with one final or eleventh step *substitution* or sublimation, which involves the purchase of a small hamster in an enclosed cage at a later date. In order to maintain the image that there are appropriate times and places to learn things for oneself, it is possible to allow Waldo to exercise the just-because-I-need-it option and have the family go into the rabbit business for a couple of years.

The key to the successful operation of the wild-card option is its occasional use. Waldo should understand that such an option is probably only successful once a year. He should also know that it represents a joint sacrifice on the part of all other members of the family in order to allow him his option and will demand that he pitch in to help other people get their wildest dreams.

Under the wild-card option, Waldo learns personal responsibility and he also learns the cost of doing his own thing, because he shares this with other members of his family. The wild-card option prevents one of the inherent weaknesses of democracy—tyranny of the majority: the masses can always outvote the individual; the individual alone does not have the capacity to engineer something for himself, unless he is given some exercise of personal freedom and the dignity to do some outrageous thing "just because."

SUMMARY

The model presented for child-rearing has as its fundamental premise the fact that vast individual differences in children should not only be tolerated, but encouraged. Even within one family, there are incredible differences in temperament, attitude, interests, and drive level. The role of the parent, teacher, and psychologist should be one of minimum interference in the establishment of these individual differences. The concept of minimum conformity is an act of gently shaping children's behavior into the realm of social acceptability. Children should be encouraged to test the limits, to put out probes, to feel the consequences of their behavior, for that is the stuff from which personal responsibility and personal integrity are made. Hardly any mistake parents make causes them more grief in the long run than the mistake of constantly tidying up their children. If parents would in general leave their children alone, provide them with good models of happy, productive adulthood, and reserve their energy for those few rough edges that the child's lack of conceptual strength produces in our complex society, both the children and the parents could live out healthy, interrelated lives.

Glossary

Adolescence   The transitional years between puberty and adulthood in human development; usually covers the teens.

Analysis of Variance   Analysis of variance is a statistical technique for discovering the significance of the differences between three or more groups. Its major use is to demonstrate which of several treatment procedures is superior.

Anoxia   An abnormally low amount of oxygen in the body tissues.

Anxiety   Anxiety is an emotional response in the absence of any clearly defined stimulus; a fear reaction altogether puzzling and purposeless, indefinite and objectless, wherein the emotions are inappropriate to the situation.

Associationism   A systematic theory explicating psychological phenomena in terms of primary mental processes, chiefly association, to which are attributed the simple and complex data and constructs of experience; associationism theorizes that ideas become associated or fused in a kind of mental chemistry.

Autogenous   Self-generated or self-generating.

Autonomic Nervous System   "The sympathetic and parasympathetic divisions of the nervous system that control the motor functions of the heart, lungs, intestines, glands, and other internal organs, and of the smooth muscles, blood vessels, and lymph vessels" (*Webster's New World Dictionary of the American Language,* 2d ed.).

Behavior Genetics   "Behavior genetics as an approach to the study of children combines the concepts and methods of genetic analysis, based on knowledge or control of ancestry, with the concepts and methods of behavioral analysis from psychology, based on knowledge or control of experience" (J. Hirsch, 1967, p. xv).

Behaviorism   Behaviorism stresses overt behavior, and the probability of a given behavior occurring, as the major avenue to understanding the mind, which, for the behaviorist, is simply a memory bank that integrates experience. For the behaviorist, "the only significant realities are events in the external world and *the behavior* that they elicit in living organisms. Mental states are 'by-products and not to be mistaken for causes' [p. 16]" (Mowrer, 1972, p. 469, quoting Skinner, 1971, p. 16).

Behavior Modification   An attempt to train individuals, to change behavior, using manipulations of contingent reinforcement schedules, behavior modification applies the techniques of operant conditioning to the treatment of a wide variety of behavior problems.

Child Psychology   Psychology is an empirical study of the measurement, prediction, and control of behavior. Child psychology includes the study of childhood development, in terms of behavior, personality, perception, and intelligence, and the application of findings to the prevention and management of childhood problems.

Chromosome   The chromosomes (Greek for "colored bodies"), stringlike bodies of chromatin in the cell nucleus, carry genes in a linear fashion. Humans normally have 46 chromosomes, "crowded with the genetic factors of inheritance. . . . The 46 chromosomes of the human complement consist of 22 homologous (identical) pairs

489

of autosomal chromosomes and a pair of sex chromosomes" (Reisman and Matheny, 1969, pp. 23, 24).

Classical Conditioning Classical conditioning refers to the response behavior of an organism. Response behavior changes "very little, if at all, throughout the organism's life" (Reynolds, 1968, p. 7). A thorn produces the same response in a puppy or an old dog.

Classical conditioning is reflexive, unconscious learning that implies a helplessness on the part of the child and accounts for most early learning and perhaps all emotional learning during childhood. The child responds to a stimulus on the basis of a built-in, automatic reflex that is almost out of his control. The initial stimulus can become associated with an increasing array of stimuli, any one of which can produce the same automatic response.

Classical conditioning refers to learning developed around simple, reflexive responses to specific environmental stimulation. These unconditioned responses, part of the natural repertoire of all normal children, are unlearned and highly stylized. Through learning, or classical conditioning, they can be associated with more complex stimuli; but the initial responses are uniform throughout the species.

Congenital Existing at or from birth.

Constitution The physical character of the body —strength, health, size, body build, etc.

Correlation A statistic used to describe the degree of relatedness between two scores. A perfect correlation is indicated by the whole number 1.

Correlational Analysis The transition from single-teacher classroom tests to nationally standardized achievement tests required new mathmatical techniques. With the correlational technique, the magnitude of the relationship between two variables can be precisely described in numerical form (Pearson's *r*).

Critical Period A critical period is a period of decisive importance; it is a concept developed in maturational theory that holds that, as a result of neurological or other genetic unfolding, for a short period of time a peculiar sensitivity develops that facilitates certain kinds of learning. A critical period is that period in a young child's life when social interaction with other humans is essential or he will be forever lacking in the ability to form relationships with his peers. Research on imprinting in animals first pointed up this critical period in development.

Cross-sectional The simultaneous sampling of children of all ages. In research on growth, a cross-sectional study uses different children for each age level, thereby showing a steady increase in height from birth to about eighteen years of age. Cross-sectional studies are easier to conduct than longitudinal ones, but have inherent problems difficult to overcome in some areas of research.

Defense Mechanism A defense mechanism is a strategy by which a child deals with anxiety, a mental exercise that causes the child to feel more comfortable. Sometimes defense mechanisms are discovered spontaneously, but more often they are modeled after the strategy of a significant adult in the child's environment. Typical of defense mechanisms is the superstitious behavior, knocking on wood after having made an optimistic statement: "I haven't had a cold all winter" (knock, knock).

Development The process of progressing, growing, unfolding, maturing; change that occurs through time. "Development is a process of maturation meeting a process of education" (Maier, 1969, p. 79). "The psychological development of a child is made up of progressive changes in the different ways of interacting with the environment. Progressive development is dependent upon opportunities and circumstances in the present and in the past. The circumstances are physical, chemical, organismic, and social" (Bijou and Baer, 1961, p. 25).

Dizygotic Twins developed from two fertilized ova; fraternal twins.

Dominant In a heterozygous state (when the two chromosomes of a pair are different, as in color blindness), a manifest character is dominant. Since both X chromosomes must carry the color-blind trait for a female to be color blind, color blindness is recessive.

Empirical Relying or based solely on experiment and observation rather than theory.

Environment The aggregate of things, people, conditions, and influences that surround an individual and that affect his development and existence.

Etiology The assignment of cause.

Factor Factor defines a group of highly correlated items that can be described conceptually; a factor is one of the elements contributing to a particular result or situation, such as factors in intelligence.

490

Factor Analysis The grouping of many variables into meaningful clusters is factor analysis. It is most useful in determining the dimensions of behavior that almost invariably appear together in the same person.

Fear Fear is an emotional response related to some objective danger where the emotions are appropriate to the magnitude of the risk.

Gene "Each cell in the body (including the original fertilized egg) contains 100,000 or so genes. These genes or minute units of deoxyribonucleic acid (DNA) are arranged in linear fashion on the chromosomes" (Reisman and Matheny, 1969, p. 21). Through metabolic reactions, these genes control the inherited characteristics of the individual.

Genetic Having specifically to do with the genes; a genetic disease is one in which the etiology clearly indicates the genes. A congenital disease, although manifest at birth, does not necessarily have a genetic etiology; prenatal environmental factors could have caused the problem.

Genetics The study of heredity dealing with characteristics of organisms resulting from the interaction of their genes and their environment.

Genotype The genetic constitution of an individual; the sum total of genes transmitted from parents to their offspring.

Growth The process of developing; gradually increasing in size or complexity.

Heredity The transmission of genetic characteristics from parents to offspring.

Heredity/Environment Interaction Heredity determines a child's potential; environment determines whether or not that potential will be fulfilled.

Imprinting Coined by Konrad Lorenz, imprinting defines learning that occurs rapidly early in life and that is characterized by resistance to extinction.

Intelligence An individual's ability to profit from past experience in solving present problems, to deal effectively with his environment, to do well academically, to perform well on the job, and to be a social success.

Intelligence Test An intelligence test is designed to measure intelligence, to predict academic success and future overall achievement. The most dominant factor in a test of intelligence is vocabulary, both definition and abstraction. Items on an intelligence test combine into several factors: vocabulary, numerical skill, immediate and long-term recall, and perceptual-motor skills. To insure maximum usefulness, an intelligence test should be standardized on a representative population; it should be valid for its purpose. An intelligence test is used in predicting academic achievement, locating achievement discrepancies, placing children in school, and locating exceptional talent. It has been abused to defend the concept of genetic intelligence and to brand children in rigid homogeneous groupings. It has yet to be refined to the point where infant intelligence tests can be used to predict adult intelligence.

IQ Intelligence quotient, arrived at by dividing the mental age by the chronological age and multiplying by 100. The concept of IQ made possible the measurement and comparison of intelligence across ages.

Karyotype A systematic arrangement of the chromosomes of a single cell in a drawing or photographic form.

Longitudinal The following of the same children year after year; a longitudinal study uses the same subjects at different age levels. Instead of studying five-, six-, and seven-year-olds simultaneously, the researcher studies the same children when they are five, again when they are six, and then again at seven. A longitudinal study of growth results in a truer picture of growth rate than is presented by a cross-sectional study.

Strengths of the longitudinal method are: (1) it shows the full trend; (2) it avoids retrospective error; (3) it allows for miscroscopic intensity; (4) it fits well the critical-period model; (5) it allows for long-range validation; and (6) it gives cause-and-effect relationships.

Weaknesses are: (1) the confounding of data with contemporary events; (2) data unmanageability; (3) staff turnover; (4) subject loss; (5) antiquation of measures; (6) post hoc theory reconstruction; and (7) inertia for replication.

Maturation The process, in human development, of maturing to a more or less predetermined adulthood through a programmed sequence under genetic control that involves changes in complexity, as well as size and function, to allow for the increasing capacity of the child-adolescent-adult to adjust to his environment.

Meiosis Cell division in which each gamete receives one of each pair of chromosomes.

Mental Age The objective measurement of intelligence began when an objective definition of mental age was developed. Mental age refers to the level of ability of one child compared to the average ability of all children. An MA of four indicates that the child can achieve on the same level as the average four-year-old.

Mitosis Cell division process for all body cells except germ cells; mitosis ensures a full complement of chromosomes for each gamete.

Monozygotic Twins developed from a single fertilized ovum; identical twins.

Morphology The form and structure of an organism as a whole.

Mutation Any gene change transmitted to a gamete.

Neurosis Neurosis is a psychologically disabling set of habits, responses, and typical reactions that is maladaptive or ineffectual.

Operant Conditioning Under operant conditioning, the child is able to manipulate his environment such that he himself controls reinforcement; his world is arranged, naturally or socially, such that his behavior has a determining effect on what happens next. Instrumental learning, or operant conditioning, grew out of the concept that the subject was instrumental in achieving his own reward; that is, by a set of rules called contingencies, his behavior triggered the delivery of a consequence or reward, which could be positive or negative. The behavior can be a single act or a long complex chain of acts. Operant conditioning requires the conscious attention of the child, rather than an unlearned, reflexive response. Operant conditioning is a learning process in which the child learns the power of a smile to change his environment for the better.

Operational An operational definition is functional; practical in the sense of applied. Intelligence is defined operationally in terms of its measurement: the IQ approximates intelligence; intelligence is what intelligence tests measure.

Parity The condition of having borne offspring.

Pearson's *r* See Correlational analysis.

Perception The act or faculty of apprehending

by means of the senses or of the mind; an awareness derived from sensory processes.

Perinatal Surrounding birth, before and after.

Personality A characteristic way of behaving that defines the uniqueness of an individual in a social setting.

Phenotype The expression of an individual's genotype as physical, biochemical, and physiological traits.

Prenatal Before birth.

Psychosis A psychosis is a characteristic set of responses that is bizarre and peculiar within the social organization in which the person resides. The legal definition of psychosis is insanity, which also includes incompetence.

Psychosomatic Describes a physical disorder originating from an emotional process.

Puberty The age at which an individual is first capable of sexual reproduction; the end of childhood and the beginning of adolescence.

Recessive See *Dominant.*

Reliability The reliability of a test refers to its consistency of measurement.

Respondent A respondent is the highly stylized, universal, reflexive response to an unconditioned stimulus; an unconditioned response.

Retrospective Study A study based on data gathered after the fact.

Schizophrenia "A group of disorders manifested by characteristic disturbances of thinking, mood and behavior. Disturbances in thinking are marked by alterations of concept formation which may lead to misinterpretation of reality and sometimes to delusions and hallucinations, which frequently appear psychologically self-protective. Corollary mood changes include ambivalent, constricted and inappropriate emotional responsiveness and loss of empathy with others. Behavior may be withdrawn, regressive and bizarre" (DSM-II, p. 33).

Standard Deviation The standard deviation (SD) is that distance above and below the mean of a normal distribution that defines a range that includes the middle 68 percent of the population. Two standard deviations above and two below the mean define a range that will include about 95 percent of the population.

Standardization The administration of a test to

a sufficiently large, representative group of children so that the published norms allow for the interpretation of an individual score in relation to the scores of many is to standardize the test.

Surrogate One who acts in place of another.

Syndrome A group of symptoms that together characterize a specific disease or condition.

Teratogene An agent that produces a malformation, or raises the incidence of malformation in a population. The best known human teratogenes are viruses, radiation, and drugs.

Theoretical Limited to and based on theory; not practical or applied.

Validity The validity of a test refers to its effectiveness in fulfilling its purpose.

Biographies

Bandura, Albert. b. 1925. *Psychologist:* modeling theory.

Albert Bandura studied clinical psychology at the University of Iowa, receiving his Ph.D. in 1952. The Hullian tradition was strong at Iowa under Kenneth Spence, Judson Brown, and Robert Sears, all of whom had studied at Yale and who themselves had extended Hull's theory. After a year's post-doctoral work, Bandura joined the faculty of Stanford University, where he has been ever since.

The importance of modeling, emphasized long ago by Aristotle, was again pointed out by Albert Bandura: the conditioning of Watson and Pavlov and the behavioral techniques of B. F. Skinner do not adequately explain all the behaviors of children. Bandura and Richard Walters based their social learning theory on the premise that most human behavior is acquired under the principles of learning. Previous learning theorists failed to take into account the social context in which behavior is acquired as well as the fact that much important learning takes place vicariously. Bandura demonstrated that classically conditioned emotional responses can be learned vicariously and can be extinguished vicariously (Bandura and T. Rosenthal, 1966).

In 1973, Bandura was elected President-Elect of the American Psychological Association.

Bayley, Nancy. b. 1899. *Psychologist:*children.

Nancy Bayley culminated a lifetime devoted to the study of children with the *Bayley Scales of Infant Development* (1969). In an early longitudinal study of children, she and Harold Jones pointed up the effects of early and late maturation. She was the President of the Society for Research in Child Development from 1961–1963, chief of the psychological laboratory in the child development section of the National Institute of Mental Health from 1954–1961, chief of the psychological laboratory in the early development section of NIMH from 1962–1964, and received the Distinguished Scientific Contribution award from the American Psychological Association in 1966.

Binet, Alfred. 1857–1911. *French psychologist:* developer of the first individual intelligence test, the *Binet-Simon Scale.*

In the mental testing field, the 1880s were Francis Galton's decade; the 1890s, James McKeen Cattell's; and the 1900s, Binet's. France's greatest psychologist of that generation, Binet was an experimentalist who stressed individual differences. He founded France's first psychological laboratory and first psychological journal. He was the first to produce a scale of age norms for the intellectual performance of children. The first successful constructor of a test to measure intelligence, defined as the ability to achieve, Alfred Binet carefully pinpointed the requirements for school performance and then constructed a test to predict these requirements. The high face validity of Binet's test made it an immediate success.

As early as 1896, Binet classified the areas of intelligence he wished to measure: memory, mental imagery, imagination, attention, comprehension, suggestibility, aesthetic appreciation, force of will as indicated by sustained effort in muscular tasks, moral sentiments, motor skill, and judgment of visual space. As his research on the measurement of intelligence developed, he began to discard the objective, average-speed, average-number-of-response measurements of Galton for an all-or-none measurement. The validity of his measure was determined not by an increase in a "quantitatively graded measure," but "in terms of an increase with age, school grade, or estimated intelligence in the percentage of children who solved a given task in a certain way" (Goodenough, 1949, p. 44).

Wrote Binet:

It seems to us that in the intelligence there is a fundamental faculty, the alteration or lack of which is of the utmost importance for practical life. This faculty is *judgment,* otherwise called good sense, practical sense, initiative, the faculty of adapting oneself to circumstances. To judge well, to comprehend well, to reason well, these are the essential activities of the intelligence.... Indeed the rest of the intellectual faculties seem to be of little importance in comparison with judgment [Binet and Simon, 1916, p. 42, as quoted by Hunt, 1961, p. 13].

Binet defined intelligence as the ability of an individual to direct his behavior toward a goal, to make adaptations in his goal-oriented behavior when necessary, to know when he had reached the goal. "Comprehension, invention, direction, and censorship: intelligence lies in these four words" [G. Thompson, 1962, p. 394].

By the beginning of the new century, he had accumulated a tremendous amount of data about the way children respond to a great number of different kinds of tasks. He had compared the responses of individual children with the quality of their schoolwork and with such other evidences of their abilities as he was able to secure. He knew which of his measures looked promising and which appeared to be worthless for his purpose. He had formed a pretty clear idea of what children of each age are able to do. He thus had the raw material for constructing a scale, but no one, thus far, had devised a way for putting such material together. Binet had to be his own architect [Goodenough, 1949, p. 46].

Charles Spearman, in discussing his two-factor theory of intelligence in which he showed that "the general factor could be measured ... simply by measuring promiscuously any large number of different abilities and pooling the results together," commented on Binet's acceptance of this "hotchpotch" system of measurement:

Binet theoretically continued to profess his old doctrine of faculties, but tacitly and practically adopted the hotchpotch procedure, utterly discordant though it was with his cherished faculties. He and Simon incorporated this hotchpotch procedure in their celebrated scale of tests published in 1905; this was composed of a great many promiscuous tests and was said to discover the subject's "level," which is only another name for his mean result at the different tests. The instant success of this scale overwhelmed all opposition [Spearman, 1930, pp. 324–325].

Burt, Cyril. 1883–1974. *English psychologist:* intelligence.

In England in the 1930s, Cyril Burt was pioneering work with factor analysis as L. L. Thurstone pursued it at Chicago. In 1931, Burt inherited at London the Chair as Professor of Psychology vacated by Charles Spearman. In 1946, he was knighted. Sir Cyril Burt's study of intelligence in twins led him to surmise that about 80 percent of intelligence is inherited; the environment

could enhance or deny that inheritance. Wrote Burt:

During the twenty years that I have occupied the Chair of Psychology at University College, my main aim has been to preserve its original traditions, and to make it a focus for that branch of psychology which was founded and developed there by Galton — "individual" or, as Stern used to call it, "differential psychology"—the study of the mental differences between individuals, sexes, social classes and other groups [1952, p. 72].

In discussing a definition of intelligence as "innate, general cognitive efficiency," Burt wrote:

This phrase ... seems to make explicit the idea in the minds of nearly all the earlier workers. First it seems clear that Binet and his predecessors (Galton for example) were seeking to measure a capacity that is "innate," "inborn," or "natural," as distinct from knowledge or skill that is acquired.... Secondly, they were attempting to measure a "cognitive" characteristic, and under cognitive we must include practical capacity, as well as intellectual capacity in the narrower sense. Finally, they were seeking to measure a general or all around ability, not a special ability confined to some limited group of tasks [1947, quoted by Horrocks, 1964, p. 111].

In 1972, Burt summarized his years of research on individual differences.

The two main conclusions we have reached seem clear and beyond all question. The hypothesis of a general factor entering into every type of cognitive process, tentatively suggested by speculations derived from neurology and biology, is fully borne out by the statistical evidence; and the contention that differences in this general factor depend largely on the individual's genetic constitution appears incontestable. The concept of an innate, general, cognitive ability, which follows from these two assumptions, though admittedly a sheer abstraction, is thus wholly consistent with the empirical facts [1972, p. 188].

Burt continued to define intelligence as "general cognitive ability" as he recommended further study of his, and others, theory of inheritance.

The recent cry that "the old issue of nature and nurture is out of date" is itself outdated. Modern genetics, besides its many profitable applications to agriculture and stock-breeding, has already made valuable contributions to human physiology, pathology, and medicine; it will assuredly prove yet more informative and fruitful in the field of psychology [1972, p. 189].

Carmichael, Leonard. 1898–1973. *Psychologist:* early development of behavior. Carmichael conducted the classic study on maturation (1926).

After obtaining his Ph.D. from Harvard, Carmichael went to Princeton to teach physiological psychology (1925–1927). During the summers he taught educational psychology at Harvard. In 1927 he went to

Brown University as a full professor and director of the laboratory (1927–1936). From Brown, Carmichael went to the University of Rochester to become Dean of the Faculty of Arts and Sciences and professor of psychology (1936–1938).

In 1938 Carmichael accepted the presidency of Tufts College, where he established a laboratory of sensory physiology and psychology (1938–1952). In his presidential address to the American Psychological Association (1941), Carmichael

... presented the view that the experimental embryology of behavior provides a basis for the understanding of some aspects of adult human behavior in a way that is comparable with the explanatory role of a knowledge of embryology in the study of adult anatomy.... In the years since this presidential address it has become even more clear to me on the basis of my study of fetal and newborn animals, that genetically determined maturation is of the utmost importance in understanding much behavior at the adult level as well as in the early stages of human and animal development.... It seems to me that my studies suggest that much more human and mammalian behavior change, even in adult life, is a result of genetic determination than has been thought to be true in recent decades by some students of learning and especially by some psychoanalytic theorists [Carmichael, 1967, pp. 47–48].

In 1953 Carmichael became the Secretary of the Smithsonian Institution in Washington, where he remained until his retirement in 1964 at 65; in 1970, he was still active as Vice-President for Research and Exploration of the National Geographic Society.

Carmichael considers the thread that has run most consistently throughout his career to be research: "I began a little investigation as an undergraduate at Tufts, and ever since that time my own research, or the administration and funding of the research of others, has been my central day-in and day-out interest" (1967, p. 52).

Cottell, James McKeen. 1860–1944. *Psychologist: developer of paper-and-pencil tests of intelligence.*

James McKeen Cattell's influence upon American psychology has been greater than his personal scientific output. For 26 years he represented psychology at Columbia. He was president of the American Psychological Association in 1895; became the editor of six important journals of psychology and general science; and was the first American to promote mental testing, a term coined by him. Thorndike's mentor and colleague at Columbia, Cattell was the world's first (1888) to be titled "professor of psychology."

Between 1891 and 1917 Cattell built the nation's largest Ph.D. program at Columbia, himself supervising some 50 dissertations. He was the first psychologist elected to the National Academy of Sciences, in 1901, preceding even William

James. Cattell was of that small group which established the American Psychological Association....

Cattell's importance rests ultimately upon his organizational zeal, publishing efforts, and administrative service to the whole of American science; he was the entrepreneur *non pareil* of the scientific community [Jonçich, 1968, p. 439].

In his choice of tests, Cattell shared Galton's view that a measure of intellectual functioning could be obtained through tests of sensory discrimination and reaction time. Cattell's preference for such tests was also strengthened by his belief that simple functions could be measured with precision, in contrast to more complex functions, whose objective measurement looked like a well-nigh hopeless task at the time [Anastasi, 1958, p. 14].

E. L. Thorndike, a student of Cattell's, became "America's most distinguished leader in the field of mental tests" (Boring, 1950, p. 540).

Cattell grew interested in scientific eminence when his paper-and-pencil tests failed to be as successful as Binet's test. He compiled the first edition of *American Men of Science*. At the beginning of World War I, Cattell was dismissed from Columbia because of his pacifist stand. He continued to be active in his editorships and in the Psychological Corporation, "which he promoted for the sale of expert psychological services to industry and to the public" (Boring, 1950, p. 535).

Many persons have tried to get Cattell to write autobiographically but he refused resolutely. He would reminisce about psychology but not in relation to his own affairs. He refused invitations to contribute to any of C. Murchison's three volumes of *Psychology in Autobiography*. He may have felt that description of achievement should come from without—as indeed it did, partly in his life-time and more after his death [Boring, 1950, p. 580].*

Darwin, Charles. 1809–1882. *English naturalist.*

The grandson of Erasmus Darwin, physician and poet, Charles Darwin provided a biography of his son as an infant, bringing to bear his great observational powers upon the emotional development of the child. Darwin was the first to bring genetic theory into the thinking of man, with his theory of the survival of the fittest, or natural selection, which he conceived as the principle that governed the development of variations in species: given an overproduction of offspring and a hostile environment where only a few survive to reproduce, those with the best adaptive characteristics survive. Darwin believed intelligence to be one of those characteristics of survival.

*This and following passages reprinted, by permission of the publisher, from Edwin G. Boring, *A History of Experimental Psychology*, 2nd ed. (New York: Appleton-Century-Crofts, 1950). Copyright © 1950 by Appleton-Century-Crofts, Educational Division, Meredith Corporation.

497

Doll, Edgar A. 1889–1968. *Psychologist:* special education.

Responsible for the *Vineland Social Maturity Scale,* a standard for the measurement of social competence, Edgar Doll worked with Henry Goddard at the Vineland Training School. The unique value of the *Vineland* is its measurement of habitual performance, rather than performance on a specific day. In 1967, both the American Psychological Association and the Association of Mental Deficiency awarded Doll Distinguished Service Certificates.

Freud, Sigmund. 1856–1939. *Austrian neurologist and physician;* founder of psychoanalysis.

Freud did his research and tested his hypotheses in his private practice. He was active for 60 years, which have been divided into decades by Boring (1950, pp. 710–713).

1. *The 1880s were a time of training and preparation in clinical neurology, hypnosis, and classical psychiatry.*
2. *The 1890s were a time of trial and error and of first maturation. During this time he recognized the collapse of his first theory of the origin of neurosis as an actual sexual assault.*
3. *The 1900s brought further maturity and the beginning of fame and notoriety with the publication of his work on dreams. The disciples began to gather (Alfred Adler, Otto Rank, Hans Sachs, Carl G. Jung, Sandor Ferenczi, Ernest Jones). "The decade ended with G. Stanley Hall's inviting Freud, Jung, Ferenczi, and Jones to Clark University's celebration of its vigentennium in 1909."*
4. *The 1910s brought conflict within the inner circle, resulting in three camps: Adler, Jung, and Freud. The concept of the death wish began to appear in his writings.*
5. *The 1920s contained final maturation and the spreading of fame. "Psychoanalysis was now far away from psychoneurosis and fast becoming the means of understanding all human motivation and personality." His work on the ego and the id appeared during this period.*
6. *The 1930s were the period of culmination for Freud and his work. He escaped the Nazi terror which burst upon Viennese Jews and died peacefully in London at 83.*

The founder of psychiatry and psychoanalysis, Sigmund Freud interpreted man's emotions as revealed to him in his private practice. Freud believed, as does Jean Piaget, that development or maturation occurs in distinct stages. Freud saw development as both psychological and neurophysiological.

Anxiety was defined by Freud as a psychological response to a signal in the environment indicating some real or imagined threat, internally in terms of flooding of internal physical stimulation or externally in terms of revenge or retaliation from significant others provoked by the internal impulses. He defined three forms of anxiety: objective, what we call fear—an appropriate response to a dangerous stimulus; neurotic—an irrational dread of being overwhelmed by one's internal drives or of being retaliated against as a consequence of these drives; and moral—an overwhelming sense of guilt experienced as depression.

Freud's most critical works are: *The Problem of Anxiety* (1936); *The Interpretation of Dreams* (1938); *The Ego and the Id* (1927); *A General Introduction to Psychoanalysis* (1922); and *New Introductory Lectures on Psychoanalysis* (1933). In 1931, in the Foreword to the third English edition of *The Interpretation of Dreams,* Freud says of the book, first published in 1900: "It contains, even according to my present-day judgment, the most valuable of all discoveries it has been my good fortune to make. Insight such as this falls to one's lot once in a lifetime" (1938, p. 181).

Galton, Francis. 1822–1911. *English scientist.*

The cousin of Charles Darwin, Francis Galton was a genius of great energy. With the strong conviction that intelligence was biologically determined, Galton set out to measure intelligence through sensory reaction time, and thus began the tradition of the psychometric method, which ultimately became one of psychology's great successes. Galton felt that man's innate tendencies needed to be encouraged by his environment; that a child's natural bent toward scientific endeavors, for example, could go to naught in an environment that did not encourage, enhance, and develop these natural tendencies. Galton believed in generalized superiority.

Galton was responsible for early research in human differences and was a proponent of the genetic determination of intelligence. The laboratory he founded became the forerunner of the Biometric Laboratory at University College, London. The first to work out the method of statistical correlation, Galton and Karl Pearson began quantitative analysis in psychology. "The correlation method, an essential tool in psychology and of several other fields of science, was first suggested in this paper [Galton, 1888]. It was later modified by Pearson to its present form (Pearson's r)" (Dennis, 1948, p. 336).

Galton's influence in psychology was not greater, according to Boring:

for the simple reason that, with attention dispersed in so many other directions, his psychological productivity was not greater. After all, Galton was but half a psychologist and that for only fifteen years.... His greatest contribution to introspective psychology was, however, his study of imagery and of individual differences in imagery.... Galton's other contributions to psychology consist for the most part in the invention of apparatus for mental tests.... Galton lost out to Binet in the matter of the kind of tests that were going to bring out the individual psychological resources most useful to a nation. The testers concentrated upon intelligence, Spearman's G, not on assessing the variety of capacities which were listed in Galton's inventory of human abilities [Boring, 1950, pp. 482, 485, 488].

Charles Spearman, in summarizing the important influences in his life, writes:

I am brought back to Wundt with his epoch-making introduction of the experimental method. To him and to Galton I certainly owe far more than to anyone else; so that I cannot end better than reiterating my grateful acknowledgements to these two great inspirers of modern mental science [1930, p. 333].

Gesell, Arnold.   1880–1961.   *Psychologist and physician:* measurement of infant development; embryology of human behavior.

A student of G. Stanley Hall and a contemporary of Lewis Terman, Gesell (1928), of Yale University, unquestionably made the chief early contribution to our knowledge of mental development during infancy. Gesell followed the testing line of Galton rather than Binet. As an M.D. as well as a Ph.D., Gesell was concerned about the physical development of infants. His was a long-time, dedicated study of the motor-sensory development of children. Gesell saw growth as a continuous development that involved only a shift in emphasis, rather than distinct and different stages.

The Gesell Developmental Schedules laid the foundation on which Bayley was to build her *Bayley Infant Scales of Development. The Gesell Schedules,* covering four major behavior areas—motor, adaptive, language, and personal-social—are less standardized than the usual psychological test, but with adequate training in their use, reliability can be maintained.

Gesell was one of the psychologists who believed in a fixed intelligence established by genetics (Gesell, 1945). His approach to infant study was concerned with:

describing what is characteristic of children at each age. The conceptual significance of this so-called normative approach is based upon the faith that development is inherently or genetically predetermined. In the light of this faith the description of forms constitutes also explanation [Hunt, 1961, p. 43].

Anastasi describes the *Gesell Schedules* as:

... a refinement and elaboration of the qualitative observations routinely made by pediatricians and other specialists concerned with infant development. They appear to be most useful as a supplement to medical examinations for the identification of neurological defect and organically caused behavioral abnormalities in early life [1968, p. 256].

Arnold Gesell was the eldest of five boys. He began his advanced education at Stevens Point Normal School in Wisconsin, where his psychology professor, a student of G. Stanley Hall, eventually directed him to Clark University. Before attending Clark, however, he studied for two years at the University of Wisconsin and served a year as principal of a large high school in Wisconsin. He received his Ph.D. in psychology from Clark in 1906. Not long after, he joined Lewis M. Terman, a fellow Clark student, as a professor of psychology in the Los Angeles State Normal School, where he was "overtaken by a strange, subdued kind of restlessness, a vague sense of unpreparedness for a task which was taking shape in my mind. I wished in some way to make a thorough–going study of the developmental stages of childhood" (Gesell, 1952, p. 128).

Five years later, in 1915, he received his medical degree from the School of Medicine at Yale University. While still a student, he began the Yale Clinic of Child Development and upon his graduation was appointed a full professor in the Yale graduate school.

I became increasingly interested in the normal developmental characteristics of the period of infancy and the pre-school years. From the standpoint of diagnosis, prevention and social control it seemed clear that there should be more concentration on the first years of life....

Our clinical service gave special attention to the youngest age groups; and with the aid of graduate students we made a systematic survey of the developmental patterning of behavior at ten age levels in the first five years of life. One purpose was to define normative criteria which could be used in the diagnostic appraisal of normal, deviant and defective infants. I was not specifically interested in the psychometry of intelligence, per se, but rather in the diagnosis of the total developmental status as expressed in motor, adaptive, language, and personal-social behavior patterns. The approach was and remains essentially comparative [1952, p. 130].

In summarizing his stand in psychology, Gesell writes:

In my own view the protection of mental health, beginning with infancy, should be primarily based on a science of normal human growth, and only secondarily on psychopathology, particularly a psychopathology conceptually derived from a study and theory of adult symptomatology. The relativities of the growth process are all pervasive. They influence even the morphology of emotions....

Pediatrics as the broadest speciality of general medicine is in a position to focus on the dynamics of growth with a minimum of ideology. It might in time bring into being a new type of child psychiatry and a genetic form of constitutional medicine. Cultural factors inflect but they do not generate the basic progressions and the ontogenetic patterning of behavior. There is a constitutional core of individuality which is manifested in growth characteristics [1952, pp. 137, 138].

The concluding paragraph of Gesell's autobiography sums up his concern for the direction psychological study of children should take.

With an achieved perspective on the first ten years of life, it is important to learn to what extent the mechanisms of early development continue into the years from ten to sixteen. What are the year by year transformations in maturity traits? And what are the developmental indices of individuality? Do such indices have a significance for constitutional medicine? These are primary questions on which we lack elementary knowledge to an amazing degree. They are important questions for child psychology and for a clinical science of child development. A clinical science of child development might eventually prove to be one cornerstone of a more comprehensive science of man. A science of man under the heightening pressures of the second half of this atomic century should help to define the mechanisms and principles which underlie child life and family life. This alone can enable man to act more consciously and more rationally as an agent in his own evolution [1952, p. 142].

Goddard, Henry. 1886–1957. *Psychologist:* systematic hereditary studies of feeblemindedness.

A founder of the Vineland Training School and a student of G. Stanley Hall, Henry Goddard considered intelligence to be an inherited trait. He translated Binet's test into English without taking into account the differences between his intended population and that of Binet's schoolchildren.

Guilford, Joy Paul. b. 1897. *Psychologist:* aptitudes; instructional research; psychological measurement; statistics.

In speaking of his undergraduate days at the University of Nebraska, Guilford concluded that "the choice of teacher is frequently more important for the student's development than the choice of course" (1967a, p. 175). His interest in the analytic assessment of the individual grew during his graduate days. From Nebraska, Guilford went to Cornell University with an assistantship under Edward B. Titchener. He began his teaching career at the University of Kansas, then returned to the University of Nebraska, and finally settled in 1940 at the University of Southern California, where he emphasized research.

Guilford found Thurstone's "generalized, multiple-factor theory and methods" more promising than Spearman's "emphasis on his *g* factor. . . . As rapidly

as Thurstone developed his methods, I applied them to the analysis of basic traits in the area of C. G. Jung's concept of introversion-extroversion" (1967a, p. 181).

Guilford's presidential address to the American Psychological Association (1950) was the forerunner of an explosion of research on creativity. Whereas about 25 intellectual abilities have been demonstrated by factor analysis, Guilford has isolated about 80 dimensions of ability, and his research has led him to redefine intelligence (Guilford, 1956, 1959).

Guilford has received several awards for his prodigious research efforts: the Legion of Merit of the National Academy of Science; and the Distinguished Service Award and the Richardson Creativity Award of the American Psychological Association.

Hall, G. Stanley. 1844–1924. *Psychologist:* the father of child psychology.

The father of child psychology, G. Stanley Hall is one of psychology's greats because of his catalytic influence upon his students. One of the first to recognize the value of the questionnaire in studying children, Hall was able to excite and to challenge his students to unprecedented creative efforts. He himself was one of the first to define intelligence in objective terms, although he did not have the concept of IQ—the relationship between chronological age and mental age.

Hall is noted as a pioneer in psychology. He established the first psychological laboratory in America at Johns Hopkins. His subsequent work had great influence on American psychology. He held various journal editorships, was a prolific writer himself, and many of his students went on to shape and direct the destiny of psychology in the United States: Gesell, Goddard, Kuhlmann, Mateer, and Terman, to name a few.

Hall took a degree in divinity and was for ten years a preacher in a country church, then tutor in a private family, before he earned his doctorate at Harvard. "Hall received at the hands of James what is presumably the first doctorate of philosophy in the new psychology to be granted in America" (Boring, 1950, p. 519). From Harvard he went to Germany as Wundt's first American student.

In 1881, Hall was invited to lecture at the new graduate university, Johns Hopkins, where in 1882 he was given a lectureship in psychology, and in 1884 a professorship. Here he founded the nucleus of young men later destined to shape psychology in the United States: John Dewey, J. McKeen Cattell, W. H. Burnham, and others. Like Binet in France, Hall in the United States founded the first psychological laboratory and the first psychological journal, the *American Journal of Psychology*, in 1887.

In 1888 he became the first president of the new Clark University at Worcester, Massachusetts. While at

Clark he founded, in 1891, *Pedagogical Seminary* (now the *Journal of Genetic Psychology*), and in 1915 he founded the *Journal of Applied Psychology*. He helped organize the American Psychological Association and was its first president in 1892. He was again president in 1924, but died at the age of 80, before the year was out.

Hall was a genetic psychologist, that is to say, a psychological evolutionist who was concerned with animal and human development and all the secondary problems of adaptation and development. When he died he left his money to Clark for founding a chair of genetic psychology—a chair now named after him [Boring, 1950, p. 522].

The importance of the stages in the autogenetic development of the individual, in Hall's thinking, is illustrated by his parable of the tadpole's tail. Adult frogs lack tails, but tadpoles have them. If the tail is not tampered with, it is absorbed and gradually disappears, but if it is cut off, the back legs fail to grow. Thus, the appearance and disappearance of the tail appears to be essential to morphological development. The parable was presumed to hold also for behavioral development. The behavior of each stage was conceived to be essential to the appropriate development of the behavioral patterns to come. This is the faith in a predetermined unfolding of behavioral patterns which Hall passed on to his students and to the common sense of America, for Hall was also a popular influence who was instrumental in starting the child-study associations that influenced ideas about human development very widely [Hunt, 1961, p. 44].

Hall had little interest in methodology for its own sake. He did not care for details; he wanted broad outlines, general principles, facts that could be applied at once to everyday life and the guidance of children. His questionnaire studies cover a wide range of topics and had a tremendous influence in stimulating interest in child development. That they violated practically every canon of questionnaire construction known to us today is of less importance than the fact that they dealt with such vitally fresh and interesting topics. Presented as they were against the background of Hall's encyclopedic knowledge of scientific facts and theories, the results of these studies attracted widespread attention and brought to Hall's laboratory for graduate study many of the most promising young men of the period [Goodenough, 1949, p. 32].

"Although Hall wrote much, it is likely that his influence endured more through the profound effect he had upon his students than through the effect of his writing" (Hunt, 1961, p. 43). A majority of those men associated with the early development of intelligence tests were students of Hall: H. H. Goddard, F. Kuhlmann, L. M. Terman, Arnold Gesell.

Remembering his Clark days, Arnold Gesell writes:

G. Stanley Hall was the acknowledged genius of the group at Clark. Although the term genius is often overused, we can safely apply it to his intellect. True genius may be regarded as a creative developmental thrust of the human action sys-

tem into the unknown. Hall embodied such thrusts, almost inverterately, in his thinking and in his teaching. He had, in addition, an empathic propensity to revive within himself the thought processes and the feelings of other thinkers. This same projective trait enabled him to penetrate into the mental life of children, of defectives, of primitive peoples, of animals, of extinct stages of evolution. What if he could not verify his prolific suggestive thrusts, what if he seemed unsystematic and self-contradictory, what if he exaggerated the doctrine of recapitulation—he nevertheless was a naturalist Darwin of the mind, whose outlook embraced the total phylum, and lifted psychology above the sterilities of excessive analysis and pedantry. In many ways, no doubt, he must now be considered outmoded. But as a teacher his so-called defects became virtues, and I still find in his writings a catalytic quality. Indeed if the young psychologist of today ever needs a little refreshment of spirit, perhaps he can read with profit some of the page-long sentences that issued from the ardent, exuberant mind of G. Stanley Hall [Gesell, 1952, pp. 126–127*].

Lewis M. Terman, a contemporary of Gesell's at Clark, writes:

The Clark of my day was a university different in important respects from any other that has ever existed in America, if not in the world—in spirit much akin to the German university yet differing from it because of the small student body. It enrolled in all its departments only about fifty full-time students, besides possibly a dozen whose attendance was limited to Saturday classes or special seminars. Possibly thirty of the fifty were there primarily for psychology, philosophy, and education. The informality and freedom from administrative red tape was unequalled. The student registered by merely giving his name and address to President Hall's secretary. He was not required to select formally a major or a minor subject. There was no appraisal of credentials for the purpose of deciding what courses he should take. *Lernfreiheit* was utterly unrestricted. There were professors who proposed to lecture and there were students who proposed to study; what more was necessary? The student could go to three or four lectures a day, or to none. No professor, so far as I could see, kept a class list. Attendance records were, of course, unheard of. No marks or grades of any kind were awarded at the end of the year or semester. One could attend a course of lectures all year without being required or necessarily expected to do the least reading in connection with it. There were no formalities about candidacy for a degree. The student was allowed to take his doctor's examination whenever the professor in charge of his thesis thought he was ready for it. No examination except the four-hour doctor's oral was ever given.... For me Clark University meant chiefly three things: freedom to work as I pleased, unlimited library facili-

*This and other passages are reprinted, by permission of the publisher, from Arnold Gesell's autobiographical chapter in Edwin G. Boring, Herbert S. Langfeld, Heinz Werner, and Robert M. Yerkes (eds.), *A History of Psychology in Autobiography*, Vol. IV (Worcester, Mass.: Clark University Press, 1952; New York: Russell & Russell, 1968). Copyright © 1952 by the trustees of Clark University.

ties, and Hall's Monday evening seminar. Any one of these outweighed all the lectures I attended.

When Clark students of the old days get together, their conversation invariably reverts to Hall's seminar. All agree that it was unique in character and about the most important single educational influence that ever entered their lives. No description could possibly do it justice; its atmosphere cannot be conveyed in words. It met every Monday evening at 7:15 and was attended by all the students in psychology, philosophy, and education; in my day about thirty in number. Each evening two students reported on work which had occupied the major part of their time for several months. Usually we knew in advance who would hold forth, and an air of expectancy was general. If the reporting student was one whose ability and scholarship commanded respect, we were prepared to listen and learn. If he was an unknown quantity or was regarded with suspicion, we were prepared to listen and criticize. The longer or more important report came first. It was always under way before 7:30 and might last an hour or longer. Ordinarily, though not always, it was read from manuscript. It might be either a summary and review of the literature in some field or an account of the student's own investigation. When the report was finished Dr. Hall usually started the discussion off with a few deceivingly generous comments on the importance of the material that had been presented, then hesitantly expressed just a shade of doubt about some of the conclusions drawn, and finally called for "reactions." Sometimes when we were most critically disposed Dr. Hall's initial praise of the report momentarily spiked our guns. Soon, however, a student bolder than the others would dare to disagree on some fundamental proposition; others would then follow suit, and the fat was in the fire. When the discussion had raged from thirty minutes to an hour, and was beginning to slacken, Hall would sum things up with an erudition and fertility of imagination that always amazed us and made us feel that his offhand insight into the problem went immeasurably beyond that of the student who had devoted months of slavish drudgery to it. Then we were herded into the dining room, where light refreshments were served, and by 9:30 or so we were in our chairs listening to another report. Sometimes the second half of the evening was even more exciting than the first half, and we rarely got away before eleven or twelve o'clock. I always went home dazed and intoxicated, took a hot bath to quiet my nerves, then lay awake for hours rehearsing the drama and formulating the clever things I should have said and did not. As for Dr. Hall, he, as I later learned, always went upstairs to his den and finished his day by reading or writing until 1:00 A.M. or later. So inexhaustible was his energy! [Terman, 1930, pp. 313, 315–316*].

Harlow, Harry F. b. 1905. *Psychologist:* experimental psychology with rhesus monkeys.

Born in Fairfield, Iowa, Harlow completed his university education at Stanford, receiving his Ph.D. in 1930. He immediately joined the faculty of the University of Wisconsin and has remained there ever since. Harlow's use of the rhesus monkey was serendipitous: Wisconsin's animal lab had been torn down the summer before he arrived, which forced him to the Vilas Park Zoo where he was converted from rats to monkeys, which were "so much more broadly able."

Harlow's long-term research on the various aspects of mothering in the monkey has provided us with many key insights. A woman's maternal instinct to cuddle and to rock and to caress her infant is necessary for his survival as a warm and loving adult, able to make and to maintain close and meaningful relationships with his peers. Harlow found that infant monkeys deprived of mothering were socially and sexually aberrant adults. And he felt that tactile stimulation was the most critical dimension of mothering.

Harlow was president of the American Psychological Association in 1958, and editor of the *Journal of Comparative and Physiological Psychology* from 1951 to 1963. In 35 years of research with rhesus monkeys he has offered new hypotheses in areas of neurophysiology, motivation, and love. He has shown that animal and human societies are based on a multiplicity of affectional bonds, rather than solely on sex, as previously assumed. Professor of psychology at the University of Wisconsin, he was awarded the National Medal of Science by the President of the United States, in 1967, for his outstanding contribution to biological science. In 1960, he was recognized by the APA Distinguished Scientific Contribution Award. He is one of the select few psychologists who are members of the National Academy of Science.

In 1973, Harry Harlow received the Gold Medal Award of the American Psychological Foundation, awarded each year "to a senior American psychologist in recognition of a distinguished and long-continued record of scientific and scholarly accomplishment."* A large share of Harlow's attention has been given to affective behavior—

especially to the affective relations between parents and offspring and to the pathologies of these relations. Although he would surely agree that "love is not enough," it is clear that he believes love is in first place, and that whatever is second is quite a few furlongs back.

Harlow's Gold Medal Award citation read:

to Harry F. Harlow—a creative scientist and dedicated in-

*This and other passages are reprinted, by permission of the publisher, from Lewis M. Terman's autobiographical chapter in Carl Murchison (ed.), *A History of Psychology in Autobiography,* Vol. II (Worcester, Mass.: Clark University Press, 1930; New York: Russell & Russell, 1961). Copyright © 1930 (renewed © 1958) by the trustees of Clark University.

*American Psychological Foundation Awards for 1973, *American Psychologist,* 1974, 29, 48–53.

502

vestigator, he has enlarged the science of man through artful experimentation with monkey.

Hull, Clark L. 1884–1952.   *Psychologist:* quantitative investigation of the conditioned reflex and basic learning mechanisms.

Clark Hull graduated from Wisconsin in 1918 and remained there until 1929, when he joined the faculty at Yale for a long period of effective work. Hull's interests were varied: statistical devices, the effects of tobacco on mental efficiency, aptitude tests, hypnosis and suggestibility, robots. His chief occupation with the problems of conditioned reflexes and learning began at Yale. Hull was president of the American Psychological Association in 1936, and was a member of the National Academy of Science.

Principles of Behavior (1943) was:

the highpoint of Hull's series of efforts at system building. . . . He presented a deductive system to account for the major phenomena of classical and instrumental conditioning. . . . A distinguishing feature of Hull's system was the hypothesis that learning is a gradual process rather than a sudden or insightful one. . . . Hull's theory directly or indirectly dominated research in the field of learning for the next decade. In a lesser degree it continues to do so [Kimble, 1961, p. 27].

In his autobiography Hull commented on the stormy atmosphere in psychology when the proponents of different theories clashed, in:

. . . a kind of warfare. It has always seemed to me that the efforts involved were to a large extent wasted. A view attributed to Edward L. Thorndike is to the effect that the time spent in replying to an attack could better be employed in doing a relevant experiment [1952, p. 154].

In outlining his concept of psychology, Hull wrote:

I came to the definite conclusion around 1930 that psychology is a true natural science; that its primary laws are expressible quantitatively by means of a moderate number of ordinary equations; that all the complex behavior of single individuals will ultimately be derivable as secondary laws from (1) those primary laws together with (2) the conditions under which behavior occurs; and that all the behavior of groups as a whole, i.e., strictly social behavior as such, may similarly be derived as quantitative laws from the same primary equations. With these and similar views as a background, the task of psychologists obviously is that of laying bare these laws as quickly and accurately as possible, particularly the primary laws. This belief was deepened by the influence of my seminar students, notably Kenneth W. Spence and Neal E. Miller. It has determined the most of my scientific activities ever since, and the longer I live the more convinced I am of its general soundness [1952, p. 155].

Hull's influence on the thinking of John Dollard and

Neal Miller is clearly shown in his description of his seminar:

The influence of these ideas [Hull's theoretical system which he was developing and teaching] was brought to bear on the Institute [of Human Relations at Yale] and related personnel quite definitely in 1936, when several of us, including Neal E. Miller, John Dollard, and O. H. Mowrer, ran an open seminar specifically concerned with the essential identities lying in conditioned reflexes and behavior laws generally on the one hand, and, on the other, in the phenomena considered by Freud and his psychoanalytic associates [1952, p. 156].

Hull truly believed that man's behavior could be synthesized into precise mathematical equations and formulas. He deplored subjectivity as "one of the greatest sources of international conflict and human misery." But his insistence on the "scientifically true and unmistakable definitions of all critical terms involved" (1952, p. 162) proved to be a giant step forward for psychology.

Itard, Jean-Marc. 1774–1838.   *French physician.*

Itard made a valiant attempt to educate and to socialize the Wild Boy of Aveyron and, although he considered his efforts to have failed, his methods predicted the successful efforts of today's special education.

Jensen, Arthur. b. 1923.   *Psychologist:* educational.

Receiving his Ph.D. from Columbia in 1956, Jensen has been on the Berkeley faculty since 1958. His research on individual differences in learning and the genetic basis of mental abilities has heaped undeserved coals of criticism upon his head. The 1960s and 1970s in the United States have not been characterized by academic freedom—"Freedom of a teacher to discuss any social, economic, or political problems without interference or penalty from officials, organized groups, etc." (*Random House Dictionary of the English Language*).

McGraw, Myrtle. b. 1899.   *Psychologist;* neuropsychology.

Theorizing that the human brain has two major divisions, the cerebral cortex and the subcortical nuclei, Myrtle McGraw believes that maturation is an essential component of the behavior of the child: until his brain has matured, certain behaviors are impossible; with maturation, certain behaviors are inevitable.

Mowrer, O. Hobart. b. 1907.   *Psychologist:* vestibular physiology; motivation; emotion; learning; conflict; personality.

Before he moved on to Harvard and the University of Illinois, Mowrer was a member of the Yale group under Clark Hull, which included John Dollard and Neal Miller. He was president of the American Psychological Association in 1954 and has authored or coauthored many books and articles on learning theory. Mowrer states that if man is:

... preeminently a social creature, rather than a "mere" animal, our conception of psychological efficiency and stamina is bound to change. We will not see mental hygiene as dominating personal and social values, but the other way around: we will see moral existence (interpersonal relationships, obligation, and loyalty) as setting the conditions for mental health [1965, p. 257].

Piaget, Jean. b. 1896. *Swiss psychologist:* originator of the concept of discrete stages in cognitive development.

Jean Piaget has suggested in his autobiography that there is:

... probably some truth in the statement by Bergson that a philosophic mind is generally dominated by a single personal idea which he strives to express in many ways in the course of his life, without ever succeeding fully.... My one idea, developed under various aspects in (alas!) twenty-two volumes, has been that intellectual operations proceed in terms of structures-of-the-whole. These structures denote the kinds of equilibrium toward which evolution in its entirety is striving; at once organic, psychological and social, their roots reach down as far as biological morphogenesis itself.... Now this law of evolution, which dominates all mental development corresponds no doubt to certain laws of structuration of the nervous system which it would be interesting to try to formulate in regard to qualitative mathematical structures.... I hope to be able some day to demonstrate relationships between mental structures and stages of nervous development, and thus to arrive at that general theory of structures to which my earlier studies constitute merely an introduction [1952a, pp. 237, 256*].

Jean Piaget early demonstrated a bent to be "serious." At the age of 10 he began, under the tutorship of a specialist, a study of mollusks that was to have him publishing in professional journals in his teens. Before he was 20 he had decided "to consecrate my life to the biological explanation of knowledge.... Between biology and the analysis of knowledge I needed something other than a philosophy. I believe it was at that moment that I discovered a need that could be satisfied only by psychology" (1952a, p. 240).

*This and other passages are reprinted, by permission of the publisher, from Jean Piaget's autobiographical chapter in Edwin G. Boring, Herbert S. Langfeld, Heinz Werner, and Robert M. Yerkes (eds.), *A History of Psychology in Autobiography*, Vol. IV (Worcester, Mass.: Clark University Press, 1952; New York: Russell & Russell, 1968). Copyright © 1952 by the trustees of Clark University.

By 1918 Piaget had outlined his theoretical concept organizing biology and philosophy:

I suddenly understood that at all levels (*viz.*, that of the living cell, organism, species, society, etc., but also with reference to states of conscience, to concepts, to logical principles, etc.) one finds the same problem of relationship between the parts and the whole; hence I was convinced that I had found the solution. There at last was the close union that I had dreamed of between biology and philosophy, there was an access to an epistemology which to me then seemed really scientific!
... My solution was very simple. In all fields of life (organic, mental, social) there exist "totalities" qualitatively distinct from their parts and imposing on them an organization. Therefore there exist no isolated "elements"; elementary reality is necessarily dependent on a whole which pervades it. But the relationships between the whole and the part vary from one structure to another, for it is necessary to distinguish four actions which are always present: the action of the whole on itself (preservation), the action of all the parts (alteration or preservation), the actions of the parts on themselves (preservation) and the action of the parts on the whole (alteration or preservation). These four actions balance one another in a total structure; but there are then three possible forms of equilibrium: (1) predominance of the whole with alteration of the parts; (2) predominance of the parts with alteration of the whole; and (3) reciprocal preservation of the parts and of the whole. To this a final fundamental law is added: Only the last form of equilibrium (3) is "stable" or "good," while the other two, (1) and (2), are less stable; though tending toward stability, it will depend on the obstacles to be overcome how closely (1) and (2) may approach a stable basis [1952a, pp. 241–242].

In 1919, Piaget went to Paris with a recommendation to see Dr. Simon:

... who had at his disposal Binet's laboratory at the grade school in Paris.... Dr. Simon received me in a very friendly manner and suggested that I should standardize Burt's reasoning tests on the Parisian children....
Now from the very first questioning I noticed that though Burt's tests certainly had their diagnostic merits, based on the number of successes and failures, it was much more interesting to try to find the reasons for the failures. Thus I engaged my subjects in conversations patterned after psychiatric questioning, with the aim of discovering something about the reasoning process underlying their right, but especially their wrong answers. I noted with amazement that the simplest reasoning task involving the inclusion of a part in the whole or the coordination of relations of the "multiplication" of classes (finding the part common to two wholes), presented for normal children up to the age of eleven or twelve difficulties unsuspected by the adult....
At last I had found my field of research.... It became clear to me that the theory of the relations between the whole and the part can be studied experimentally through analysis of the psychological processes underlying logical operations [1952a, pp. 244–245].

Along with his research on the logical operations of children, Piaget has been active in the Swiss Bureau of the International Office of Education, which is now sponsored jointly by UNESCO and the International Office of Education. In 1929 he became Director and worked with it throughout World War II. After Switzerland joined UNESCO, Piaget was appointed President of the Swiss Commission of UNESCO and headed the Swiss delegation to the conferences in Bayreuth, Paris, and Florence. In the 1950s he served on the Executive Council of UNESCO.

Writing more recently with his research assistant Bärbel Inhelder, Piaget sums up his theoretical point of view of child psychology. He writes:

Mental growth is inseparable from physical growth.... This implies that in order to understand mental growth it is not enough to start with birth.... It implies that child psychology must be regarded as the study of one aspect of embryogenesis, the embryogenesis of organic as well as mental growth, up to the beginning of the state of relative equilibrium which is the adult level.

Organically as well as mentally, however, environmental influences assume increasing importance after birth. Child psychology in its search for factors of development, cannot be limited to a study of biological maturation [Piaget and Inhelder, 1969, pp. vii–viii].

Piaget has been characterized by his close associate as "a zoologist by training, an epistemologist by vocation, and a logician by method" (Inhelder, 1953, p. 75). In 1969, he was awarded the APA Distinguished Scientific Contribution award.

Jean Piaget's long professional career was concerned with the development of logical thinking in children. Piaget was convinced of a specific developmental sequence of reasoning ability as well as a predictable pattern of development. Piaget felt that all development proceeds in a unitary direction; that there are five distinct, orderly developmental phases; that childhood and adulthood are distinctly different in all areas of human functioning; that all adult behavior has roots in infant behavior and develops sequentially; that all development is interrelated and interdependent. Piaget's stages of cognitive development are discrete and orderly; the sequence never varies; genetic factors predominate.

Rogers, Carl. b. 1902. *Psychologist*: originator of client-centered therapy.

Carl Rogers' intense interest and concern for psychotherapy and personality theory has led him to an interest and concern with "the basic assumptions and philosophy of the behavioral sciences, with the implications of the prediction and control of human behavior, with the potency of the intensive group experience, with

the development of a humanistically oriented psychology," interests and concerns which in 1970 he was pursuing as a Fellow of the Western Behavioral Sciences Institute at La Jolla, California (Rogers, 1967, p. 378). Rogers says of himself:

I am a psychologist; a clinical psychologist I believe, a humanistically oriented psychologist certainly; a psychotherapist, deeply interested in the dynamics of personality change; a scientist, to the limit of my ability investigating such change; an educator, challenged by the possibility of facilitating learning; a philosopher in a limited way, especially in relation to the philosophy of science and the philosophy and psychology of human values. As a person I see myself as fundamentally positive in my approach to life; somewhat of a lonewolf in my professional activities; socially rather shy but enjoying close relationships; capable of a deep sensitivity in human interaction though not always achieving this; often a poor judge of people, tending to overestimate them; possessed of a capacity for setting other people free, in a psychological sense; capable of a dogged determination in getting work done or in winning a fight; eager to have an influence on others but with very little desire to exercise power or authority over them [1967, p. 343].

Carl Rogers earned his undergraduate degree at the University of Wisconsin. While there he formulated an idea which has remained with him throughout his life: "Man's ultimate reliance is upon his own experience" (1967, p. 351). As a junior he was selected as one of ten students from the United States to attend a World Student Christian Federation Conference in Peking, China.

From Wisconsin he went on to Union Theological Seminary. While a student there, his interest changed to clinical and educational psychology and he moved into Teachers College, Columbia University. After graduation Rogers accepted a position in the Child Study Department of the Rochester New York Society for the Prevention of Cruelty to Children. He remained there for twelve fruitful years while he worked on his formulation of what therapy should be. "There was only one criterion in regard to any method of dealing with these children and their parents, and that was 'Does it work? Is it effective?'" (1967, p. 358). After a year as director of the Rochester Guidance Center, he moved on to Ohio State University where he wrote *Counseling and Psychotherapy* (1942).

From Ohio he moved to the University of Chicago where he established the Counseling Center. Of these years Rogers writes, "I learned more and contributed more during the twelve years at the Center (1945–1957) than at any other period" (1967, p. 364). In 1956, Rogers received the APA Award for Distinguished Scientific Contribution. After Chicago came Wisconsin, the Western Behavioral Sciences Institute, and, finally, the Center for Studies of the Person at La Jolla, California.

In summarizing the significant threads of his life, Rogers writes that he "never really belonged to any professional group." He was educated by and worked with "psychologists, psychoanalysts, psychiatrists, psychiatric social workers, social caseworkers, educators, and religious workers." Yet he never felt in a "total or committed sense" that he belonged to any of these groups. He writes that "whatever its disadvantages, this lack of belonging has left me free to deviate, to think independently" (1967, p. 375).

In his 1973 Distinguished Professional Contribution Award address to the annual meeting of the American Psychological Association in Montreal, Canada, Rogers accented communication as the central concern throughout his career.

I have wanted to understand, as profoundly as possible, the communication of the other, be he a client or friend or family member. I have wanted to be understood [1974, p. 121].

He states that his main idea, which he describes as "an idea whose time had come," is

the gradually formed and tested hypothesis that the individual has within himself vast resources for self-understanding, for altering his self-concept, his attitudes, and his self-directed behavior [1974, p. 116].

Rogers sees himself as a humanist, as opposed to a behaviorist.

My experience in therapy and in groups makes it impossible for me to deny the reality and significance of human choice. To me it is not an illusion that man is to some degree the architect of himself. I have presented evidence that the degree of self-understanding is perhaps the most important factor in predicting the individual's behavior. So for me the humanistic approach is the only possible one [1974, p. 118].

He goes on to say that the path you choose, humanistic or behavioristic, does have consequences. Choosing the humanistic philosophy

means an approach to social change based on the human desire and potentiality for change, not on conditioning [1974, p. 118].

Here, Rogers obviously is thinking of the adult. The young child is conditioned to many feelings before he has the cognitive ability to make decisions or even has a choice to make. Thus we recognize the all-importance of mothering and the setting of consistent values, priorities, and emphases early in the child's life for providing the child a basis from which to mature to an adult capable of understanding himself and those

around him, capable of desiring change, and able to work toward bringing it about.

As Carl Rogers has continued working with people, his interest in individual therapeutic learning has moved to a broader concern for the social implications of adequate communication and understanding. His work has had a great impact on therapy as it has moved from the individual to groups.

Skinner, B. F. b. 1904. *Psychologist:* developed techniques for experimental analysis of behavior, particularly operant conditioning; analysis of schedules of reinforcement and their effects.

B. F. Skinner earned his undergraduate degree at Hamilton College in Clinton, New York. His undergraduate activities pointed toward a career as a writer but, as Skinner puts it, "I had failed as a writer because I had had nothing important to say" (1967, p. 395). His interest turned toward psychology and he entered the Department of Psychology at Harvard. Skinner writes that Pavlov gave him a glimpse of experimental method: "Control the environment and you will see order in behavior" (1967, p. 399).

Skinner writes that he is not interested

. . . in psychological theories, in rational equations, in factor analyses, in mathematical models, in hypothetico-deductive systems, or in other verbal systems which must be *proved* right. . . . I am more interested in measures for the control of a subject matter. Some relevant measures are verbal, but even so they are not so much right or wrong as effective or ineffective, and arguments are of no avail [1967, p. 409].

Skinner distinguishes between observation and experimentation.

Observation overemphasizes stimuli; *experimentation* includes the rest of the contingencies which generate effective repertoires. . . . To me behaviorism is a special case of a philosophy of science. . . . Behaviorism is a formulation which makes possible an effective experimental approach to human behavior. It is a working hypothesis about the nature of a subject matter. It may need to be clarified, but it does not need to be argued. I have no doubt . . . but that it will provide the most direct route to a successful science of man [1967, pp. 409–410].

Skinner lists five principles of scientific practices (1956, pp. 223, 224, 225, 227):

1. *When you run onto something interesting, drop everything else and study it.*
2. *Some ways of doing research are easier than others.*
3. *Some people are lucky.*
4. *Apparatuses sometimes break down.*
5. *Serendipity: the art of finding one thing while looking for something else.*

Writes Skinner:

We are within reach of a science of the individual. This will be achieved, not by resorting to some special theory of knowledge in which intuition or understanding takes the place of observation and analysis, but through an increasing grasp of relevant conditions to produce order in the individual case. ... It is time to insist that science does not progress by carefully designed steps called "experiments" each of which has a well-defined beginning and end. Science is a continuous and often a disorderly and accidental process [1956, pp. 231, 232].

In 1958, Skinner's work was recognized by the APA Distinguished Scientific Contribution Award. In 1968, he was recipient of the National Medal of Science, the federal government's highest award for distinguished achievement in science, mathematics, and engineering, awarded the year before to Harry Harlow.

B. F. Skinner pleads eloquently for the democratic philosophy to apply the method of science to human affairs:

This is no time to abandon notions of progress, improvement or, indeed, human perfectibility. The simple fact is that man is able, and now as never before, to lift himself by his own bootstraps. In achieving control of the world of which he is a part, he may learn at last to control himself [1955–1956, p. 49].

Spearman, Charles E. 1863–1945. *English psychologist*; intelligence; correlation.

Spearman's "original article putting forth his two-factor theory of mental organization and introducing a statistical technique for investigating the problem" appeared in 1904. "With this publication, Spearman opened up the field on research on trait relationships and paved the way for current factor analysis" (Anastasi, 1958, p. 19):

The empirical study of trait organization was initiated by Spearman, who first developed a method for analyzing intercorrelations among test scores. On the basis of his research, Spearman proposed a two-factor theory, which described intellectual functions in terms of a single g factor and numerous s factors, although narrow group factors were subsequently included [Anastasi, 1958, p. 339].

Spearman was a member of numerous German, British, and American psychological organizations, and president of the British Psychological Society from 1923 to 1926. His application of mathematical correlation to testing and his foundation for factor analysis in psychology, especially in the study of intelligence, carve for him a permanent niche among psychology's greats.

Charles Spearman began his psychological studies under Wilhelm Wundt, "the originator of experimental psychology" (Spearman, 1930, p. 321). One of Spear-

man's first aims was to investigate the dogma that all thought consists essentially of images. He satisfied himself that imageless thought does exist and that "no excellence of images—either their vividness, or their steadiness, or their completeness—had any correlation with excellence of thought" (1930, p. 311*).

Spearman then set about to discover the laws of thought. He finally came up with three which he felt covered "every case of evoking any new item into the mind and every case of knowing anything with self evidence" (1930, p. 318).

1. *Perceiving relations.*
2. *Old relations applied to a new situation were capable of generating a new plan of behavior.*
3. *The mind tends to know its own experience.*

He called these qualitative laws and proceeded to add a set of quantitative laws:

1. *Constant output*
2. *Retentivity*
3. *Fatigue*
4. *Conation*
5. *Primordial potency*

Inspired by Francis Galton's *Human Faculty*, Spearman started experimenting in a nearby village school:

The aim was to find out whether, as Galton had indicated, the abilities commonly taken to be "intellectual" had any correlation either with each other or with sensory discrimination. The intellectual abilities I measured by the children's school marks in various subjects; the sensory discrimination, by a musical "dichord" of my own contrivance. The reply of the experiment was prompt and decisive; all the mental powers measured did obviously correlate with each other in considerable degree.

But hastily as I had embarked upon this investigation, I fell to brooding long over the results. Not satisfied with noting that the different abilities correlated considerably, I wanted to know *how much*. With great labor, I evolved an elaborate theory of "correlation coefficients" by which the degrees of correlation could be definitely measured [1930, p. 322].

Commenting on his two-factor theory, Spearman writes:

I was then faced by the problem of explaining it. And here another happy thought came to the rescue. Aided by the

*This and other passages are reprinted, by permission of the publisher, from Charles Spearman's autobiographical chapter in Carl Murchison (ed.), *A History of Psychology in Autobiography*, Vol. II (Worcester, Mass.: Clark University Press, 1930; New York: Russell & Russell, 1961). Copyright © 1930 (renewed © 1958) by the trustees of Clark University.

concept of attenuation—the correlational coefficient between two abilities (or other variables) suffers a spurious decrease of apparent size from the (random) errors of measurement involved—proof could be furnished that such a system must needs occur whenever each of the abilities at issue is the compound result of two factors, of which the one is common to all the abilities, whereas the other is specific to each different ability. Herewith was born into the world an extraordinary source of discord and labor, but also, let us hope, of progress. It has been called the "Theory of Two Factors." . . . The general factor could be measured . . . simply by measuring promiscuously any large number of different abilities and pooling the results together [1930, pp. 322, 323–324].

Lewis Terman has commented on Spearman's two-factor theory when discussing his own research.

Spearman's two notable contributions of 1904 came too late to have much influence on my thesis plans; and, even if they had come earlier, it is doubtful whether my equipment and point of view would have enabled me at the time to profit greatly from them. I shall never forget, however, the impression that those articles made on me—the dogmatic tone of the author, the finality with which he disposed of everyone else, and his one-hundred-per-cent faith in the verdict of his mathematical formulae [Terman, 1930, p. 319].

Commenting on the practicality of his own findings, Spearman wrote: "the practical application of tests necessitates their standardization; and standardization spells scientific stagnation" (1930, p. 326).

In closing his autobiography Charles Spearman reacted to his contemporaries. He wrote that he had a "complex" against "the doctrines of sensualism and associationism." He classified Thorndike as "still following in much the same lines" as Hartley, Hume, the Mills, and Bain:

For him [Thorndike], the mind—like the brain as he conceived it—was composed of infinitely numerous minute elements connected together by associations, now presented under the name of "bonds." Such a beginning seems to me to have hampered his psychology ever afterwards. That, in spite of this, he should have achieved such great work as he has done often made me wonder what services he might have rendered to psychology had his early conditions been more propitious. The reflexologists, as Bekhterev and Pavlov, disturbed me in less degree, since in them I had never expected to find psychology anyway [1930, pp. 330–331].

Spearman ends his autobiography with a tribute to Wundt and Galton as the "two great inspirers of modern mental science" (1930, p. 333).

Stern, William. 1871–1938. *German psychologist.*

In Germany, William Stern conceived the intelligence quotient, which allowed for the measurement of intelligence across ages: IQ = MA/CA. Stern, who studied at Berlin with Ebbinghaus and Stumpf, is noted for his differential psychology and educational psychology. Although he first conceptualized the IQ, it was first used by Terman in the 1916 form of the Stanford-Binet.

Terman, Lewis M. 1877–1956. *Psychologist:* mental and achievement tests; gifted children; personality.

"The practical validity of intelligence tests like the Stanford-Binet in identifying the intellectually gifted has been brilliantly demonstrated by Terman and his associates over a research period of almost four decades" (G. Thompson, 1962, p. 447). "Terman and his associates . . . issued the Stanford Revision of the Binet scale in 1916, the form that remained standard for more than twenty years" (Boring, 1950, p. 574).

Lewis Terman was born the twelfth of 14 children in an Indiana farm family. His earliest education was in a one-room school. At 15 he attended Central Normal College in Danville, Indiana, where he earned a B.S. in the scientific course, a B.Pd. in the pedagogy course, and an A.B. in the classical course. From there he entered the junior year at Indiana University, where he earned A.B. and M.A. degrees. And thence to a fellowship at Clark University. At both Central Normal College and Indiana University, Terman was taught by men trained at Clark University. He began his education in a rural school and ended it at Clark University under G. Stanley Hall. During his Clark days he says, "My own interest in mental tests at the time was more in their qualitative than in their quantitative aspects. I wanted to find out what types of mental processes are involved in this thing we are accustomed to call intelligence" (1930, p. 319).

Upon graduation Terman spent a year as principal of a high school in San Bernardino, California, before accepting a professorship in child study and pedagogy at the Los Angeles State Normal School. Here he remained four years before moving on to Stanford. Of these years Arnold Gesell, who joined him, writes:

With suddenness came a summons to join Lewis M. Terman as professor of psychology in the Los Angeles State Normal School. The double lure of California and my friendship for Terman sufficed. Soon he and I were in our respective citrus groves on opposite sides of Valley View Road, Casa Verdugo. It was a happy association. I had known Terman at Clark when he was engaged in his path-breaking study of Genius and Stupidity, a study which retains momentum in his hands to this day. At Los Angeles his interest in Binet and the measurement of intelligence was gathering strength, and came to notable fulfillment at Stanford University [1952, pp. 127–128].

Five years after leaving Clark, Terman went to Stanford University, where he remained the rest of his life. There he conducted his work on mental tests and giftedness; among his students were Arthur Otis, Maud Merrill, Florence Goodenough, Robert Bernreuter, and Harold Carter. Terman sums up his work in psychology as follows:

I am fully aware that my researches have not contributed very greatly to the theory of mental measurement. On the problems of less theoretical significance, but of importance for the usefulness of tests and for the psychology and pedagogy of individual differences I think I have made contributions of value. If I am remembered very long after my death, it will probably be in connection with my studies of gifted children, the construction of mental tests, and the psychology of sex differences. I think that I early saw more clearly than others the possibilities of mentality testing, have succeeded in devising tests that work better than their competitors, and, by the application of test methods, have added to the world's knowledge of exceptional children [1930, p. 328].

In 1930, writing a statement of his position on current psychological issues, Terman offered the following credos, "which range all the way from tentative beliefs to fairly positive convictions":

That mental testing is in its merest infancy and will develop to a lusty maturity within the next half century; that its developments will include improved tests of general intelligence (in the reality of which I believe), tests of many kinds of special ability, and tests of personality traits which no one has yet even thought of measuring;
That within a few score years school children from the kindergarten to the university will be subjected to several times as many hours of testing as would now be thought reasonable;
That educational and vocational guidance will be based chiefly on test ratings, and that Hull's proposal to measure every important ability and personality trait and to "grind out" a hundred or more occupational success predictions for every youth is practicable and will be realized; . . .
That it will some day be possible to identify, largely by means of tests, the pre-delinquent and the pre-psychotic, and that effective preventive measures will result from this advance; . . .
That mental testing is destined to exert a profound influence on economic theory, industrial methods, politics, and the administration of law; . . .
That the major differences between children of high and low IQ, and the major differences in the intelligence test scores of certain races, as Negroes and whites, will never be fully accounted for on the environmental hypothesis; . . .
That contrary to what would be suggested by an examination of the courses in teachers colleges and schools of education, psychology offers almost the sole basis for a science of education; . . .

That the Freudian concepts, even when their validity has been discounted about 90 per cent, nevertheless, constitute one of the two most important contributions to modern psychology, mental tests being the other. . . .
Of the founders of modern psychology, my greatest admiration is for Galton. My favorite of all psychologists is Binet; not because of his intelligence test, which was only a by-product of his life work, but because of his originality, insight, and open-mindedness, and because of the rare charm of personality that shines through all his writings [1930, pp. 329–331].

Thorndike, Edward L. 1874–1949. *Psychologist:* animal psychology; educational psychology; mental and social measurement; psychology of learning; measurement of intelligence; educational statistics.

Thorndike studied at Wesleyan, where William James's *Principles of Psychology* aroused his interest; at Harvard, where he studied under James and began his experiments on animal intelligence with chicks housed in the basement of James's home; and at Columbia, where James McKeen Cattell encouraged him to continue his work with animal intelligence, this time with cats and dogs. Thorndike's thesis (1898) is "the famous, the much cited, research of the *puzzle-box,* the study in which the *law of effect* in learning . . . was firmly established and got ready for the use of educational psychology" (Boring, 1950, p. 562).

After a brief interim at the College for Women of Western Reserve University, Thorndike moved to Teachers College, Columbia University, where he remained for the rest of his career. Of that appointment, Boring wrote: "James McKeen Cattell established the atmosphere for graduate study at Columbia. Thorndike carried it on at Teachers College and Robert Woodworth at Columbia proper. . . . In psychology the land of the free included Columbia under Cattell, Thorndike and Woodworth" (1950, p. 561). Cattell's encouragement of Thorndike to try to apply his animal techniques to children and young people resulted in the famous paper on the transfer of training (Thorndike and Woodworth, 1901).

Thorndike says that "perhaps the most general fact about my entire career as a psychologist" is "responsiveness to outer pressure or opportunity rather than to inner needs. Within certain limits set by capacity and interest I did in those early years and have done since what the occasion seemed to demand." He conducted research on mental inheritance, individual and sex differences, memory, work, fatigue, interest, the interrelations of abilities, the organization of intellect, and other topics in educational psychology, because in each case the matter seemed important for theory or practice or both. At Columbia, he annually prepared "an intelligence examination suitable for use in the selection and placement of freshmen." During his later years, Thorndike carried on two investigations of his own choosing, "one on the fundamentals of measurement of intellect and capacity, the other on the fundamentals of learning" (Thorndike, 1936, pp. 266, 267).

Thorndike pioneered a characteristically American psychology, and was president of the American Psychological Association in 1912. He was elected to the National Academy of Sciences in 1917, and was its President in 1934. Wechsler writes, of Thorndike's research on intelligence: "Professor Thorndike was the first to develop clearly the idea that the measurement of intelligence consists essentially of some qualitative and quantitative evaluation of mental productions in terms of their number, and the excellence or speed with which they are effected" (1944, p. 4).

Thorndike retired in 1940, after four prolific decades of service to Teachers College, to become the William James Lecturer at Harvard.

Watson, John B.   1878–1958. *Psychologist:* founder of behaviorism.

As an undergraduate, Watson attended Furman University, where his interest in psychology grew out of his interest in philosophy despite his disenchantment with college. For graduate work he chose the University of Chicago under John Dewey and James R. Angell, with a major in experimental psychology, a first minor in philosophy, and a second minor in neurology—all of which he accomplished in three years. After graduation he remained at the University of Chicago under Angell for several years before, in 1908, at 29, he joined the staff at Johns Hopkins as a professor at $3,500.

Watson was editor of *Psychological Review* from 1908 to 1915 and editor of *Journal of Experimental Psychology* from 1915 to 1927. He was president of the American Psychological Association in 1915. His writings contributed to neurology and to animal and infant psychology. Watson stressed that psychology should be an empirical study of man's behavior and not a study of his conscious and subconscious mind.

Watson's research with animals, begun at Chicago and continued at Johns Hopkins, led to his own point of view about behaviorism, which he founded "in the spring of 1913 with his paper entitled *Psychology as the Behaviorist Views It* (Watson, 1913)" (Boring,

1950, p. 643). "Watson, in addition to believing firmly that all behavior was learned by associationistic processes, also believed that only overt, observable behavioral concepts belonged in psychology" (Baldwin, 1968, p. 391).

After World War I, Watson began studying infants at Johns Hopkins, including the classical laboratory experiment of conditioning in which Albert, a year-old child, was conditioned to fear a white rat, as well as conducting "extensive work on learning—learning and performance under hypnosis, alcohol, and drugs. All of this work came abruptly to a close with my divorce in 1920. I was asked to resign" (1936, p. 270).

After his resignation, Watson left the academic world and joined the J. Walter Thompson Company, an advertising agency. But he found time to write for popular magazines as well as to publish a series of lectures. Watson, in 1936, wrote: "I believe as firmly as ever in the future of behaviorism—behaviorism as a companion of zoology, physiology, psychiatry, and physical chemistry" (p. 281).

Wellman, Beth. 1895–1952. *Psychologist:* modification of IQ.

Beth Wellman and the Iowa Child Welfare Station pioneered the research on the modifiability of the IQ, by demonstrating the effect of preschool educational experiences.

Wolpe, Joseph. b. 1915. *Psychiatrist:* research on behavior therapy based on learning principles.

Wolpe began his career as a general practitioner in South Africa. He then specialized in psychiatry. In 1960, after lecturing at the University of Witwatersrand in South Africa for 11 years, he joined the faculty of the University of Virginia School of Medicine. In 1965 he joined the faculty of Temple University Medical School.

Wolpe's reciprocal inhibition therapeutic technique has completed the full cycle begun by Freud some 75 years ago. Wolpe has defined a mental process in very specific terms, has utilized a form of hypnosis, and has reinstated the mind as the central battleground in mental health. The use of vicarious experience and visual imagery to desensitize a person to anxiety-provoking situations is an imaginative, creative step.

References

ALDRICH, C. ANDERSON. 1928. A new test for hearing in the new-born: The conditioned reflex. *American Journal of Diseases of Children*, 35, 36–37.

ALEXANDER, FRANZ, AND THOMAS MORTON FRENCH. 1946. *Psychoanalytic Therapy: Principles and Application.* New York: Ronald Press.

ALLPORT, GORDON W. 1961. *Pattern and Growth in Personality.* New York: Holt, Rinehart & Winston.

ANASTASI, ANNE. 1958. *Differential Psychology.* New York: Macmillan.

ANASTASI, ANNE. 1968. *Psychological Testing*, 3d ed. New York: Macmillan.

ANDERSON, JOHN E. 1939. The limitations of infant and preschool tests in the measurement of intelligence. *Journal of Psychology*, 8, 351–379.

ANGELINO, HENRY, JOSEPH DOLLINS, AND EDMUND V. MECH. 1956. Trends in the "fears and worries" of school children as related to socioeconomic status and age. *Journal of Genetic Psychology*, 89, 263–276.

APGAR, VIRGINIA, AND JOAN BECK. 1972. *Is My Baby All Right? A Guide to Birth Defects.* New York: Trident Press.

ARISTOTLE. 1912. *De generatione animalium.* Arthur Platt (trans.). In J. A. Smith and W. D. Ross (eds.), *The Works of Aristotle*, Vol. V. Oxford: Clarendon Press.

ARISTOTLE. 1951. *De anima: In the Version of William of Moerbeke, with the Commentary of St. Thomas Aquinas.* K. Foster and S. Humphries (trans.). New Haven, Conn.: Yale University Press.

ASHER, E. J. 1935. The inadequacy of current intelligence tests for testing Kentucky mountain children. *Pedagogical Seminary*, 46, 480–486.

AXLINE, VIRGINIA MAE. 1947. *Play Therapy: The Inner Dynamics of Childhood.* Boston: Houghton Mifflin.

BAIN, ALEXANDER. 1855. *The Senses and the Intellect*, 3d ed. London: Longmans, Green, 1868.

BALDWIN, ALFRED L. 1968. *Theories of Child Development.* New York: John Wiley & Sons.

BANDURA, ALBERT, JOAN E. GRUSEC, AND FRANCES L. MENLOVE. 1967. Vicarious extinction of avoidance behavior. *Journal of Personality and Social Psychology*, 5, 16–23.

BANDURA, ALBERT, AND FRANCES L. MENLOVE. 1968. Factors determining vicarious extinction of avoidance behavior through symbolic modeling. *Journal of Personality and Social Psychology*, 8, 99–108.

BANDURA, ALBERT, AND TED LEE ROSENTHAL. 1966. Vicarious classical conditioning as a function of arousal level. *Journal of Personality and Social Psychology*, 3, 54–62.

BANDURA, ALBERT, AND RICHARD H. WALTERS. 1963. *Social Learning and Personality Development.* New York: Holt, Rinehart & Winston.

1968a. Fact, fiction, and the experimenter bias effect. *Psychological Bulletin*, 70 (No. 6, Part 2), 1–29.

BARBER, THEODORE X., AND MAURICE J. SILVER. 1968b. Pitfalls in data analysis and interpretation: A reply to Rosenthal. *Psychological Bulletin*, 70 (No. 6, Part 2), 48–62.

BARNES, ALLAN C. 1964. Prevention of congenital anomalies from the point of view of the obstetrician. In *Congenital Malformations: Papers and Discussions at the Second International Conference on Congenital Malformations.* New York: International Medical Congress. Pp. 377–385.

BARROWS, C. H., JR., AND LOIS M. ROEDER. 1961. Effect of age on protein synthesis in rats. *Journal of Gerontology*, 16, 321.

BARROWS, C. H., JR., AND LOIS M. ROEDER. 1963. Effect of reduced dietary intake on the activities of various enzymes in the livers and kidneys of growing male rats. *Journal of Gerontology*, 18, 135.

BARTOSHUK, ALEXANDER K. 1962. Human neonatal cardiac acceleration to sound: Habituation and dishabituation. *Perceptual and Motor Skills*, 15, 15–27.

BAYLEY, NANCY. 1933. Mental growth during the first three years: A developmental study of sixty-one children by repeated tests. *Genetic Psychology Monographs*, 14, 1–92.

BAYLEY, NANCY. 1949. Consistency and variability in the growth of intelligence from birth to eighteen years. *Journal of Genetic Psychology*, 75, 165–196.

BAYLEY, NANCY. 1955. On the growth of intelligence. *American Psychologist*, 10, 805–818.

BAYLEY, NANCY. 1965. Comparisons of mental and motor test scores for ages 1–15 months by sex, birth order, race, geographic location, and education of parents. *Child Development*, 36, 379–412.

BAYLEY, NANCY. 1969. *Bayley Scales of Infant Development: Birth to Two Years*. New York: Psychological Corp.

BAYLEY, NANCY, AND HAROLD E. JONES. 1937. Environmental correlates of mental and motor development. *Child Development*, 8, 329–341.

BAYLEY, NANCY, AND EARL S. SCHAEFER. 1960. Maternal behavior and personality development: Data from the Berkeley Growth Study. *Psychiatric Research Reports*, 13, 155–173.

BAYLEY, NANCY, AND EARL S. SCHAEFER. 1964. Correlations of maternal and child behaviors with the development of mental abilities: Data from the Berkeley Growth Study. *Monographs of the Society for Research in Child Development*, 29 (6), No. 97.

BEACH, FRANK A., AND JULIAN JAYNES. 1954. Effects of early experience upon the behavior of animals. *Psychological Bulletin*, 51, 239–263.

BEARD, RUTH 1969. *An Outline of Piaget's Developmental Psychology for Students and Teachers*. New York: Basic Books.

BENDA, CLEMENS E. 1960. *The Child with Mongolism*. New York: Grune & Stratton.

BENDER, LAURETTA. 1947. Childhood schizophrenia: Clinical study of one hundred schizophrenic children. *American Journal of Orthopsychiatry*, 17, 4–56.

BENDER, LAURETTA. 1955. Twenty years of clinical research on schizophrenic children with special reference to those under six years of age. In Gerald Caplan (ed.), *Emotional Problems of Early Childhood*. New York: Basic Books. Pp. 503–515.

BENDER, LAURETTA. 1956. Schizophrenia in childhood: Its recognition, description, and treatment. *American Journal of Orthopsychiatry*, 26, 499–506.

BENTLER, PETER M. 1962. An infant's phobia treated with reciprocal inhibition therapy. *Journal of Child Psychology and Psychiatry*, 3, 185–189.

BERG, B. N., AND H. S. SIMMS. 1960. Nutrition and longevity in the rat. *Journal of Nutrition*, 71, 255.

BERGIN, ALLEN E. 1963. The effects of psychotherapy: Negative results revisited. *Journal of Counseling Psychology*, 10, 244–250.

BERNARD, HAROLD W. 1962. *Human Development in Western Culture*. Boston: Allyn & Bacon.

BERNARD, JAMES W., PHILIP G. ZIMBARDO, AND SEYMOUR B. SARASON. 1961. Anxiety and verbal behavior in children. *Child Development*, 32, 379–392.

BERNSTEIN, BASIL. 1961a. Aspects of language and learning in the genesis of social process. *Journal of Child Psychology and Psychiatry*, 1, 313–324.

BERNSTEIN, BASIL. 1961b. Social class and linguistic development: A theory of social learning. In A. H. Halsey et al., *Economy, Education, and Society*. New York: The Free Press. Pp. 288–314.

BETTELHEIM, BRUNO. 1959. Joey: A "mechanical boy." *Scientific American*, 200, 116–127.

BETTELHEIM, BRUNO. 1967. *The Empty Fortress*. New York: Macmillan.

BIJOU, SIDNEY W., AND DONALD M. BAER. 1961. *Child Development*. Vol. I: *A Systematic and Empirical Theory*. New York: Appleton-Century-Crofts.

BIJOU, SIDNEY W., AND DONALD M. BAER. 1965. *Child Development*. Vol. II: *Universal Stage of Infancy*. New York: Appleton-Century-Crofts.

BIJOU, SIDNEY W., AND DONALD M. BAER. 1966. Operant methods in child behavior and development. In Werner Honig (ed.), *Operant Behavior: Areas of Research and Application*. New York: Appleton-Century-Crofts. Pp. 718–789.

BINET, ALFRED, AND THEOPHILE SIMON. 1905. Upon the necessity of establishing a scientific diagnosis of inferior states of intelligence. In Wayne

Dennis (ed.), *Readings in the History of Psychology.* New York: Appleton-Century-Crofts, 1948. Pp. 407–411.

BINET, ALFRED, AND THEOPHILE SIMON. 1905–1908. The development of the Binet-Simon Scale: 1905–1908. In Wayne Dennis (ed.), *Readings in the History of Psychology.* New York: Appleton-Century-Crofts, 1948. Pp. 412–424.

BINET, ALFRED, AND THEOPHILE SIMON. 1916. *The Development of Intelligence in Children.* Elizabeth S. Kite (trans.). Baltimore, Md.: Williams & Wilkins.

BIRNS, BEVERLY, MARION BLANK, WALTER H. BRIDGER, AND SIBYLLE K. ESCALONA. 1965. Behavioral inhibition in neonates produced by auditory stimuli. *Child Development,* 36, 639–645.

BLACKWELL, BOON-NAM, R. QUENTIN BLACKWELL, THOMAS T. S. YEH, YIH-SHYONG WENG, AND BACON F. CHOW. 1969. Further studies on growth and feed utilization of progeny of underfed mother rats. *Journal of Nutrition,* 97, 79–84.

BOGEN, HEINRICH. 1907. Conditioning gastric secretions. In Yvonne Brackbill and George G. Thompson (eds.), *Behavior in Infancy and Early Childhood.* New York: The Free Press, 1967. Pp. 231–236.

BORING, EDWIN G. 1950. *A History of Experimental Psychology,* 2d ed. New York: Appleton-Century-Crofts.

BOWLBY, JOHN. 1951. Maternal care and mental health. *Bulletin of the World Health Organization,* 3, 355–384.

BOWLBY, JOHN. 1960. Separation anxiety. *International Journal of Psychoanalysis,* 41, 89–113.

BRACKBILL, YVONNE, GAIL ADAMS, DAVID H. CROWELL, AND M. LIBBIE GRAY. 1966. Arousal level in neonates and preschool children under continuous auditory stimulation. *Journal of Experimental Child Psychology,* 4, 178–188.

BRAINE, MARTIN, CARYL B. HEIMER, HELEN WORTIS, AND ALFRED M. FREEDMAN. 1966. Factors associated with impairment of the early development of prematures. *Monographs of the Society for Research in Child Development,* 31 (4), No. 106.

BREGMAN, ELSIE O. 1934. An attempt to modify the emotional attitudes of infants by the conditioned response technique. *Journal of Genetic Psychology,* 45, 169–196.

BRIAN, CLARA R., AND FLORENCE L. GOODENOUGH. 1929. The relative potency of color and form perception of various ages. *Journal of Experimental Psychology,* 12, 197–213.

BRIDGES, KATHARINE M. B. 1930. A genetic theory of the emotions. *Journal of Genetic Psychology,* 37, 514–527.

BRIDGES, KATHARINE M. B. 1932. Emotional development in early infancy. *Child Development,* 3, 324–341.

BROCKMAN, LOIS M., AND HENRY N. RICCIUTI. 1971. Severe protein-calorie malnutrition and cognitive development in infancy and early childhood. *Developmental Psychology,* 4, 312–319.

BRYAN, MIRIAM M. 1965. Stanford Achievement Test: 1964 Revision. In Oscar K. Buros (ed.), *The Sixth Mental Measurements Yearbook.* Highland Park, N.J.: Gryphon Press. Pp. 110–124, Test No. 26.

BURLINGHAM, DOROTHY, AND ANNA FREUD. 1942. *Young Children in War-time: A Year's Work in a Residential War Nursery.* London: Allen & Unwin.

BURNHAM, WILLIAM H. 1917. Mental hygiene and the conditioned reflex. *Journal of Genetic Psychology,* 24, 449–488.

BURNHAM, WILLIAM H. 1924. *The Normal Mind.* New York: Appleton-Century.

BURT, CYRIL. 1941. *The Factors of the Mind: An Introduction to Factor-Analysis in Psychology.* New York: Macmillan.

BURT, CYRIL. 1947. *Mental and Scholastic Tests.* London: Staples.

BURT, CYRIL. 1952. Cyril Burt. In Edwin G. Boring, Herbert S. Langfeld, Heinz Werner, and Robert M. Yerkes (eds.), *A History of Psychology in Autobiography,* Vol. IV. Worcester, Mass.: Clark University Press; New York: Russell & Russell, 1968. Pp. 53–73.

BURT, CYRIL. 1958. The inheritance of mental ability. *American Psychologist,* 13, 1–15.

BURT, CYRIL. 1968. Mental capacity and its critics. *Bulletin British Psychological Society,* 21, 11–18.

BURT, CYRIL. 1972. Inheritance of general intelligence. *American Psychologist,* 27, 175–190.

BUTTERFIELD, EARL C., AND EDWARD ZIGLER. 1970. Preinstitutional social deprivation and IQ changes among institutionalized retarded children. *Journal of Abnormal Psychology,* 75, 83–89.

CARMICHAEL, LEONARD. 1926. The development of behavior in vertebrates experimentally removed from the influence of external stimulation. *Psychological Review,* 33, 51–58.

CARMICHAEL, LEONARD. 1941. The experimental embryology of mind. *Psychological Bulletin,* 38, 1–28.

CARMICHAEL, LEONARD. 1954. The onset and early development of behavior. In Leonard Carmichael (ed.), *Manual of Child Psychology*, 2d ed. New York: John Wiley & Sons. Pp. 60–185.

CARMICHAEL, LEONARD. 1964. The early growth of language capacity in the individual. In Eric H. Lenneberg (ed.), *New Directions in the Study of Language*. Cambridge, Mass.: M.I.T. Press. Pp. 1–22.

CARMICHAEL, LEONARD. 1967. Leonard Carmichael. In Edwin G. Boring and Gardner Lindzey (eds.), *A History of Psychology in Autobiography*, Vol. V. New York: Appleton-Century-Crofts. Pp. 29–56.

CARTER, CEDRIC O. 1964. The genetics of common malformations. In *Congenital Malformations: Papers and Discussions Presented at the Second International Conference on Congenital Malformations*. New York: International Medical Congress. Pp. 306–313.

CARTER, CEDRIC O., AND D. MacCARTHY. 1951. Incidence of mongolism and its diagnosis in the newborn. *British Journal of Social Medicine*, 5, 83–90.

CARTER, HAROLD D. 1933. Twin similarities in personality traits. *Journal of Genetic Psychology*, 43, 312–321.

CARTER, HAROLD D. 1935. Twin similarities in emotional traits. *Character and Personality*, 4, 61–78.

CARTER, LOWELL B. 1956. The effect of early school entrance on the scholastic achievement of elementary school children in the Austin public schools. *Journal of Educational Research*, 50, 91–103.

CASLER, LAWRENCE R. 1961. Maternal deprivation: A critical review of the literature. *Monographs of the Society for Research in Child Development*, 26 (2), No. 80.

CASTANEDA, ALFRED, BOYD R. McCANDLESS, AND DAVID S. PALERMO. 1956. The children's form of the Manifest Anxiety Scale. *Child Development*, 27, 317–326.

CASTANEDA, ALFRED, DAVID S. PALERMO, AND BOYD R. McCANDLESS. 1956. Complex learning and performance as a function of anxiety in children and task difficulty. *Child Development*, 27, 327–332.

CATTELL, JAMES McKEEN. 1890. Mental tests and measurements. *Mind*, 15, 373–380.

CATTELL, PSYCHE. 1960. *The Measurement of Intelligence of Infants and Young Children*. New York: Psychological Corp.

CATTELL, RAYMOND B. 1946. *The Description and Measurement of Personality*. New York: Harcourt, Brace & World.

CATTELL, RAYMOND B. 1950. *Personality: A Systematic, Theoretical and Factual Study*. New York: McGraw-Hill.

CHADWICK, E. 1864. Statistics of educational results. *The Museum*, 3, 480–484. Partially reprinted in *Journal of Educational Psychology*, 1913, 4, 551–552.

CHAILLE, STANFORD E. 1887. Infants: Their chronological progress. *New Orleans Medical and Surgical Journal*, 14, 893–912.

CHAMPAKAM, S., S. G. SRIKANTIA, AND C. GOPALAN. 1968. Kwashiorkor and mental development. *American Journal of Clinical Nutrition*, 21, 844–852.

CHAMPNEYS, F. H. 1881. Notes on an infant. *Mind*, 6, 104–107.

CHASE, H. P., AND H. P. MARTIN. 1969. Undernutrition and child development. Paper presented at the Conference on Neuropsychological Methods for the Assessment of Impaired Brain Functioning in the Malnourished Child, Palo Alto, June.

CHILD, IRVIN L. 1950. The relation of somatotype to self-ratings on Sheldon's temperamental traits. *Journal of Personality*, 18, 440–453.

CHOW, BACON F., R. QUENTIN BLACKWELL, BOON-NAM BLACKWELL, T. Y. HOU, JANET K. ANILANE, AND ROGER W. SHERWIN. 1968. Maternal nutrition and metabolism of the offspring: Studies in rats and man. *American Journal of Public Health*, 58, 668–677.

CHOW, BACON F., AND AGATHA A. RIDER. 1973. Implications of the effects of maternal diets in various species. *Journal of Animal Science*, 36, 167–173.

CHOW, BACON F., MARIA SIMONSON, HARLEY M. HANSON, AND LOIS M. ROEDER. 1971. Behavioral measurements in nutritional studies. *Conditional Reflex*, 6, 36–40.

CHOW, BACON F., AND JOANNE K. STEPHAN. 1971. Fetal undernourishment and growth potential. *Nutrition Reports International*, 4, 245–255.

CLAIBORN, WILLIAM L. 1969. Expectancy effects in the classroom: A failure to replicate. *Journal of Educational Psychology*, 60, 377–383.

COFFEY, VIRGINIA P., AND W. J. E. JESSOP. 1959. Maternal influenza and congenital deformities. *The Lancet*, 2, 935–938.

CORNER, GEORGE W. 1961. Congenital malformations: The problem and the task. In *Con-*

genital *Malformations: Papers and Discussions Presented at the First International Conference on Congenital Malformations.* Philadelphia: J. B. Lippincott. Pp. 7–17.

CRAVIOTO, JOAQUIN, AND BEATRIZ ROBLES. 1965. Evolution of adaptive and motor behavior during rehabilitation from kwashiorkor. *American Journal of Orthopsychiatry,* 35, 449–464.

CRONBACH, LEE J. 1963. *Educational Psychology,* 2d ed. New York: Harcourt, Brace & World.

DALLENBACH, KARL M. 1959. Twitmyer and the conditioned response. *American Journal of Psychology,* 72, 633–638.

DARWIN, CHARLES. 1859. *Origin of Species.* London: John Murray.

DARWIN, CHARLES. 1877. A biographical sketch of an infant. *Mind,* 2, 286–294.

DAVIS, ROBERT L., SYLVIA M. HARGEN, AND BACON F. CHOW. 1972. The effect of maternal diet on the growth and metabolic patterns of progeny (mice). *Nutrition Reports International,* 6, 1–7.

DAYTON, GLEN O., JR., AND MARGARET H. JONES. 1964. Analysis of characteristics of fixation reflex in infants by use of direct current electrooculography. *Neurology,* 14, 1152–1156.

DEARBORN, WALTER F., JOHN W. M. ROTHNEY, AND FRANK K. SHUTTLEWORTH. 1938. Data on the growth of public school children from the materials of the Harvard Growth Study. *Monographs of the Society for Research in Child Development,* 3 (1), No. 14.

DEESE, JAMES. 1970. *Psycholinguistics.* Boston: Allyn & Bacon.

DENNIS, WAYNE. 1935. Laterality of function in early infancy under controlled developmental conditions. *Child Development,* 6, 242–252.

DENNIS, WAYNE. 1941. The significance of feral man. *American Journal of Psychology,* 54, 425–432.

DENNIS, WAYNE. 1948. *Readings in the History of Psychology.* New York: Appleton-Century-Crofts.

DENNIS, WAYNE. 1951. A further analysis of reports of wild children. *Child Development,* 22, 153–158.

DENNIS, WAYNE. 1960. Causes of retardation among institutionalized children: Iran. *Journal of Genetic Psychology,* 96, 47–59.

DENNIS, WAYNE, AND MARSENA G. DENNIS. 1940. The effect of cradling practices upon the onset of walking in Hopi children. *Journal of Genetic Psychology,* 56, 77–86.

DENNIS, WAYNE, AND MARSENA G. DENNIS. 1951. Development under controlled environmental conditions. In Wayne Dennis (ed.), *Readings in Child Psychology.* Englewood Cliffs, N.J.: Prentice-Hall. Pp. 104–131.

DENNIS, WAYNE, AND PERGROUHI NAJARIAN. 1957. Infant development under environmental handicap. *Psychological Monographs,* 71 (436).

DEUTSCH, MARTIN, IRWIN KATZ, AND ARTHUR R. JENSEN. 1968. *Social Class, Race, and Psychological Development.* New York: Holt, Rinehart & Winston.

Diagnostic and Statistical Manual of Mental Disorders, 2d ed. (DSM-II) 1968. Washington, D.C.: American Psychiatric Association.

DICKERSON, J. W. T., AND A. L. WALMSLEY. 1967. The effects of undernutrition and subsequent rehabilitation on the growth and composition of the central nervous system of the rat. *Brain,* 90, 897.

DODD, BARBARA J. 1972. Effects of social and vocal stimulation on infant babbling. *Developmental Psychology,* 7, 80–83.

DOLL, EDGAR A. 1953. *The Measurement of Social Competence: A Manual for the Vineland Social Maturity Scale.* Minneapolis, Minn.: Educational Test Bureau.

DOLLARD, JOHN, AND NEAL E. MILLER. 1950. *Personality and Psychotherapy: An Analysis in Terms of Learning, Thinking, and Culture.* New York: McGraw-Hill.

DORIS, JOHN, AND LOWELL COOPER. 1966. Brightness discrimination in infancy. *Journal of Experimental Child Psychology,* 3, 31–39.

DREGER, RALPH M., AND KENT S. MILLER. 1960. Comparative psychological studies of Negroes and whites in the United States. *Psychological Bulletin,* 57, 361–402.

DREGER, RALPH M., AND KENT S. J. MILLER. 1968. Comparative psychological studies of Negroes and whites in the United States: 1959–1965. *Psychological Bulletin Monograph Supplement,* 70 (No. 3, Part 2), 1–58.

EBBS, J. H., A. BROWN, F. F. TISDALL, W. J. MOYLE, AND M. BELL. 1942. The influence of improved prenatal nutrition upon the infant. *Canadian Medical Association Journal,* 46, 6–8.

EELS, KENNETH, ALLISON DAVIS, ROBERT J. HAVIGHURST, VIRGIL E. HERRICK, AND RALPH W. TYLER. 1951. *Intelligence and Cultural Differences.* Chicago: University of Chicago Press.

EMERY, ALAN E. H. 1968. *Heredity, Disease, and Man: Genetics in Medicine.* Berkeley: University of California Press.

ENGELMANN, SIEGFRIED. 1970. How to construct effective language programs for the poverty child. In Frederick Williams (ed.), *Language and Poverty.* Institute for Research on Poverty Monograph Series. Chicago: Markham. Pp. 102–122.

ERIKSEN, CHARLES W. 1957. Personality. *Annual Review of Psychology,* 8, 185–210.

ERLENMEYER-KIMLING, L., AND LISSY F. JARVIK. 1963. Genetics and intelligence: A review. *Science,* 142, 1477–1479.

ESQUIROL, JEAN-ETIENNE D. 1838. *Des Maladies Mentales Considerées sous les Rapports Médical, Hygiénique, et Médico-Légal.* Paris: J. B. Bailliere.

ESTES, WILLIAM K., AND B. F. SKINNER. 1941. Some quantitative properties of anxiety. *Journal of Experimental Psychology,* 29, 390–400.

EYSENCK, HANS J. 1952. The effects of psychotherapy: An evaluation. *Journal of Consulting Psychology,* 16, 319–324.

EYSENCK, HANS J. 1960. *Behavior Therapy and the Neuroses.* New York: Pergamon Press.

EYSENCK, HANS J. 1964. The outcome problem in psychotherapy: A reply. *Psychotherapy,* 1, 97–100.

FENICHEL, OTTO. 1945. *The Psychoanalytic Theory of Neuroses.* New York: W. W. Norton.

FISH, BARBARA. 1959. Longitudinal observations on biological deviation in a schizophrenic infant. *American Journal of Psychiatry,* 116, 25–31.

FISH, BARBARA. 1961. The study of motor development in infancy and its relationship to psychological functioning. *American Journal of Psychiatry,* 117, 1113–1118.

FISH, BARBARA, AND MURRAY ALPERT. 1962. Abnormal states of consciousness and muscle tone in infants born to schizophrenic mothers. *American Journal of Psychiatry,* 119, 439–445.

FISHER, R. A. 1932. *Statistical Methods for Research Workers,* 4th ed. Edinburgh: Oliver & Boyd.

FLAVELL, JOHN H. 1963. *The Developmental Psychology of Jean Piaget.* Princeton, N.J.: D. Van Nostrand.

FLEMING, ELYSE S., AND RALPH G. ANTTONEN. 1971a. Teacher expectancy or my fair lady. *American Educational Research Journal,* 8, 241–252.

FLEMING, ELYSE S., AND RALPH A. ANTTONEN. 1971b. Teacher expectancy as related to the academic and personal growth of primary-age children. *Monographs of the Society for Research in Child Development,* 36 (5), No. 145.

FRASER, F. CLARK. 1959. Causes of congenital malformations in human beings. *Journal of Chronic Disease,* 10, 97–110.

FRAZIER, TODD M., GEORGE H. DAVIS, HYMAN GOLDSTEIN, AND IRVING D. GOLDBERG. 1961. Cigarette smoking and prematurity: A prospective study. *American Journal of Obstetrics and Gynecology,* 81, 988–996.

FREEDMAN, DANIEL G. 1965. An ethnological approach to the genetical study of human behavior. In Steven G. Vandenberg (ed.), *Methods and Goals in Human Behavior Genetics.* New York: Academic Press. Pp. 141–161.

FREEDMAN, DANIEL G., AND BARBARA KELLER. 1963. Inheritance of behavior in infants. *Science,* 140, 196–198.

FREUD, ANNA. 1946. *The Ego and the Mechanisms of Defence.* Cecil Baines (trans.). New York: International Universities Press.

FREUD, SIGMUND. 1894. The defence neuropsychoses. John Rickman (trans.). In Sigmund Freud, *Collected Papers,* Vol. I. London: Hogarth Press, 1953. No. 4, pp. 59–75.

FREUD, SIGMUND. 1909. Analysis of a phobia in a five-year-old boy. In Sigmund Freud, *Collected Papers,* Vol. III. London: Hogarth Press, 1953. No. 2, pp. 149–289.

FREUD, SIGMUND. 1910a. The origin and development of psychoanalysis (five lectures delivered in September 1909, at Clark University). Harry W. Chase (trans.). *American Journal of Psychology,* 21, 181–218.

FREUD, SIGMUND. 1910b. *Three Contributions to the Theory of Sex.* New York: Nervous and Mental Disease Publishing Co.

FREUD, SIGMUND. 1933. *New Introductory Lectures on Psychoanalysis.* W. J. H. Sprott (trans.). New York: W. W. Norton.

FREUD, SIGMUND. 1936. *The Problem of Anxiety.* Henry A. Bunker (trans.). New York: W. W. Norton.

FREUD, SIGMUND. 1938. *The Interpretation of Dreams.* In A. A. Brill (trans. and ed.), *The Basic Writings of Sigmund Freud.* New York: The Modern Library, Random House, Pp. 180–549.

FULLER, JOHN L., AND WILLIAM R. THOMPSON. 1960. *Behavior Genetics.* New York: John Wiley & Sons.

FURTH, HANS G. 1961. The influence of language on the development of concept formation in deaf children. *Journal of Abnormal and Social Psychology*, 63, 386–389.

FURTH, HANS G. 1969. *Piaget and Knowledge*. Englewood Cliffs, N.J.: Prentice-Hall.

GALTON, FRANCIS. 1870. *Hereditary Genius: An Inquiry into Its Laws and Consequences*. New York: D. Appleton.

GALTON, FRANCIS. 1874. *English Men of Science: Their Nature and Nurture*. London: Macmillan.

GALTON, FRANCIS. 1888. Co-relations and their measurement, chiefly from anthropometric data. *Proceedings of the Royal Society of London*, 45, 135–145.

GARRISON, KARL C., ALBERT J. KINGSTON, AND HAROLD W. BERNARD. 1967. *The Psychology of Childhood: A Survey of Development and Socialization*. New York: Charles Scribner's Sons.

GARROD, ARCHIBALD E. 1909. *Inborn Errors of Metabolism*. London: Henry Frowde.

GESELL, ARNOLD. 1928. *Infancy and Human Growth*. New York: Macmillan.

GESELL, ARNOLD. 1934. *An Atlas of Infant Behavior*. New Haven, Conn.: Yale University Press.

GESELL, ARNOLD. 1941. *Wolf Child and Human Child*. New York: Harper.

GESELL, ARNOLD. 1945. *The Embryology of Behavior: The Beginnings of the Human Mind*. New York: Harper.

GESELL, ARNOLD. 1952. Arnold Gesell. In Edwin G. Boring, Herbert S. Langfeld, Heinz Werner, and Robert M. Yerkes (eds.), *A History of Psychology in Autobiography*, Vol. V. New York: Appleton-Century-Crofts. Pp. 168–191.

GESELL, ARNOLD. 1954. The ontogenesis of infant behavior. In Leonard Carmichael (ed.), *Manual of Child Psychology*, 2d ed. New York: John Wiley & Sons. Pp. 335–373.

GESELL, ARNOLD, AND CATHERINE S. AMATRUDA. 1962. *Developmental Diagnosis: Normal and Abnormal Child Development, Clinical Methods and Practical Applications*, 3d ed. New York: Harper.

GESELL, ARNOLD, AND LOUISE B. AMES. 1947. The development of handedness. *Journal of Genetic Psychology*, 70, 155–175.

GESELL, ARNOLD, HENRY M. HALVERSON, HELEN THOMPSON, FRANCES B. ILG, B. M. CASTNER, LOUISE B. AMES, AND CATHERINE S. AMATRUDA. 1940. *The First Five Years of Life: A Guide to the Study of the Preschool Child*. New York: Harper.

GIBSON, ELEANOR J., AND RICHARD D. WALK. 1960. The "visual cliff." *Scientific American*, 202, 64–71.

GINOTT, HAIM G. 1961. *Group Psychotherapy with Children: The Theory and Practice of Play-Therapy*. New York: McGraw-Hill.

GLUECK, SHELDON, AND ELEANOR GLUECK. 1950. *Unraveling Juvenile Delinquency*. New York: Commonwealth Fund.

GODDARD, HENRY H. 1910. A measuring scale for intelligence. *The Training School*, 6, 146–155.

GODDARD, HENRY H. 1912. *The Kallikak Family: A Study in the Heredity of Feeblemindedness*. New York: Macmillan.

GOLDEN, HARRY. 1958. *Only in America*. New York: World.

GOLDFARB, WILLIAM. 1945. Psychological privation in infancy and subsequent adjustment. *American Journal of Orthopsychiatry*, 15, 247–255.

GOLDFARB, WILLIAM. 1961. *Childhood Schizophrenia*. Cambridge, Mass.: Harvard University Press.

GOLDFARB, WILLIAM. 1970. Childhood psychosis. In Paul Mussen (ed.), *Carmichael's Manual of Child Psychology*, 3d ed., Vol. II. New York: John Wiley & Sons. Chapt. 29, pp. 765–830.

GOODENOUGH, FLORENCE L. 1949. *Mental Testing: Its History, Principles, and Applications*. New York: Rinehart.

GOODNIGHT, CLARENCE J., MARIE L. GOODNIGHT, AND PETER GRAY. 1964. *General Zoology*. New York: Rheinhold.

GORDON, H. 1923. *Mental and Scholastic Tests among Retarded Children*. Board of Education Pamphlet No. 44. London.

GOUGH, HARRISON G., AND MARTIN B. FINK. 1964. Scholastic achievement among students of average ability, as predicted from the California Psychological Inventory. *Psychology in the Schools*, 1, 375–380.

GRAY, SUSAN W., AND RUPERT A. KLAUS. 1965. An experimental preschool program for culturally deprived children. *Child Development*, 36, 887–898.

GRAY, SUSAN W., AND RUPERT A. KLAUS. 1970. The early training project: A seventh-year report. *Child Development*, 41, 909–924.

GREENE, HENRY A., ALBERT N. JORGENSEN, AND J. RAYMOND GERBERICH. 1953. *Measurement and Evaluation in the Elementary School*. New York: Longmans, Green.

GRIMES, JESSE W., AND WESLEY ALLINSMITH. 1961. Compulsivity, anxiety, and school achievement. *Merrill-Palmer Quarterly of Behavior and Development*, 7, 247–271.

GUILFORD, J. P. 1936. *Psychometric Methods.* New York: McGraw-Hill.

GUILFORD, J. P. 1950. Creativity. *American Psychologist*, 5, 444–454.

GUILFORD, J. P. 1956. The structure of intellect. *Psychological Bulletin*, 53, 267–293.

GUILFORD, J. P. 1959. Three faces of intellect. *American Psychologist*, 14, 469–479.

GUILFORD, J. P. 1965. *Fundamental Statistics in Psychology and Education*, 4th ed. New York: McGraw-Hill.

GUILFORD, J. P. 1967a. Joy Paul Guilford. In Edwin G. Boring and Gardner Lindzey (eds.), *A History of Psychology in Autobiography*, Vol. V. New York: Appleton-Century-Crofts. Pp. 168–191.

GUILFORD, J. P. 1967b. *The Nature of Human Intelligence.* New York: McGraw-Hill.

HAGGARD, ERNEST A. 1957. Socialization, personality, and academic achievement in gifted children. *School Review*, 65, 388–414.

HAIMOWITZ, MORRIS L., AND NATALIE R. HAIMOWITZ (eds.). 1966. *Human Development: Selected Readings*, 2d ed. New York: Thomas Y. Crowell.

HALL, CALVIN S., AND GARDNER LINDZEY. 1970. *Theories of Personality*, 2d ed. New York: John Wiley & Sons.

HALL, G. STANLEY. 1883. The contents of children's minds. *Princeton Review*, 11, 249–272.

HALL, G. STANLEY. 1891a. The contents of children's minds on entering school. *Pedagogical Seminary*, 1, 139–173.

HALL, G. STANLEY. 1891b. Notes on the study of infants. *Pedagogical Seminary*, 1, 127–138.

HANSON, HARLEY M., AND MARIA SIMONSON. 1971. Effects of fetal undernourishment on experimental anxiety. *Nutrition Reports International*, 4, 307–314.

HARDY, WILLIAM G., AND JOHN E. BORDLEY. 1951. Special techniques in testing the hearing of children. *Journal of Speech and Hearing Disorders*, 16, 122–131.

HARLOW, HARRY F. 1958. The nature of love. *American Psychologist*, 13, 673–685.

HARLOW, HARRY F., AND MARGARET K. HARLOW. 1962. Social deprivation in monkeys. *Scientific American*, 207, 136–146.

HARLOW, HARRY F., AND STEPHEN J. SUOMI.

1970. Nature of love—simplified. *American Psychologist*, 25, 161–168.

HARLOW, HARRY F., AND ROBERT R. ZIMMERMAN. 1959. Affectional responses in the infant monkey. *Science*, 130, 421–432.

HAVIGHURST, ROBERT J., AND FAY H. BREESE. 1947. Relation between ability and social status in a midwestern community. III. Primary mental abilities. *Journal of Educational Psychology*, 38, 241–247.

HAVIGHURST, ROBERT J., AND LEOTA L. JANKE. 1944. Relation between ability and social status in a midwestern community. I. Ten-year-old children. *Journal of Educational Psychology*, 35, 357–368.

HEIL, LOUIS M., MARION POWELL, AND IRWIN FEIFER. 1960. *Characteristics of Teacher Behavior and Competency Related to the Achievement of Different Kinds of Children in Several Elementary Grades.* U.S. Office of Education Cooperative Research Project No. SAE-7285.

HERRNSTEIN, RICHARD. 1971. I.Q. *The Atlantic*, 228, 43–58, 63–64.

HERSHENSON, MAURICE. 1964. Visual discrimination in the human newborn. *Journal of Comparative and Physiological Psychology*, 58, 270–276.

HESS, ECKHARD H. 1959. Imprinting. *Science*, 130, 133–141.

HESS, ROBERT D., AND VIRGINIA C. SHIPMAN. 1965a. Early blocks to children's learning. *Children*, 12, 189–194.

HESS, ROBERT D., AND VIRGINIA C. SHIPMAN. 1965b. Early experience and the socialization of cognitive modes in children. *Child Development*, 36, 869–886.

HILDRETH, GERTRUDE. 1948. Manual dominance in nursery school children. *Journal of Genetic Psychology*, 72, 29–45.

HILDRETH, GERTRUDE. 1949. The development and training of hand dominance: I, II, III. *Journal of Genetic Psychology*, 75, 197–275.

HILL, KENNEDY T., AND SEYMOUR B. SARASON. 1966. The relation of test anxiety and defensiveness to test and school performance over the elementary-school years: A further longitudinal study. *Monographs of the Society for Research in Child Development*, 31 (2), No. 104.

HIRSCH, JERRY. 1967. *Behavior-Genetic Analysis.* New York: McGraw-Hill.

HIRSCH, N. D. M. 1930. An experimental study upon three hundred school children over a six-year period. *Genetic Psychology Monographs*, 7, 487–548.

HOLLINGWORTH, LETA S. 1942. *Children above 180 IQ*. New York: World.

HONZIK, MARJORIE P. 1938. The constancy of mental test performance during the preschool period. *Journal of Genetic Psychology*, 52, 285–302.

HONZIK, MARJORIE P. 1963. A sex difference in the age of the parent-child resemblance in intelligence. *Journal of Educational Psychology*, 54, 231–237.

HONZIK, MARJORIE P., JEAN W. MACFARLANE, AND LUCILE ALLEN. 1948. The stability of mental test performance between two and eighteen years. *Journal of Experimental Education*, 17, 309–324.

HOROWITZ, FRANCIS D. 1962. The relationship of anxiety, self-concept, and sociometric status among fourth-, fifth-, and sixth-grade children. *Journal of Abnormal and Social Psychology*, 65, 212–214.

HOROWITZ, NORMAN H. 1956. The gene. *Scientific American*, 195, 78–90.

HORROCKS, JOHN E. 1964. *Assessment of Behavior*. Columbus, Ohio: Charles E. Merrill.

HSUEH, ANDIE M., CONRADO E. AGUSTIN, AND BACON F. CHOW. 1967. Growth of young rats after differential manipulation of maternal diet. *Journal of Nutrition*, 91, 195–200.

HSUEH, ANDIE M., R. QUENTIN BLACKWELL, AND BACON F. CHOW. 1970. Effect of maternal diet in rats on feed consumption of the offspring. *Journal of Nutrition*, 100, 1157–1163.

HUANG, I-NING. 1943. Children's conception of physical causality: A critical summary. *Pedagogical Seminary*, 63, 71–121.

HULL, CLARK L. 1929. A functional interpretation of the conditioned reflex. *Psychological Review*, 36, 498–511.

HULL, CLARK L. 1937. Mind, mechanism, and adaptive behavior. *Psychological Review*, 44, 1–32.

HULL, CLARK L. 1943. *Principles of Behavior*. New York: Appleton-Century-Crofts.

HULL, CLARK L. 1952. Clark L. Hull. In Edwin G. Boring, Herbert S. Langfeld, Heinz Werner, and Robert M. Yerkes (eds.), *A History of Psychology in Autobiography*, Vol. IV. Worcester, Mass.: Clark University Press; New York: Russell & Russell, 1968. Pp. 143–162.

HUNDLEBY, JOHN D., AND RAYMOND B. CATTELL. 1968. Personality structure in middle childhood and the prediction of school achievement and adjustment. *Monographs of the Society for Research in Child Development*, 33 (5), No. 121.

HUNT, J. MCVICKER. 1961. *Intelligence and Experience*. New York: Ronald Press.

HUNT, J. MCVICKER. 1964. How children develop intellectually. *Children*, 11, 83–91.

HYMES, DELL. 1964. Discussion. Following Margaret Bullowa, Lawrence G. Jones, and Thomas G. Bever, The development from vocal to verbal behavior in children. In Ursula Bellugi and Roger W. Brown, The acquisition of learning. *Monographs of the Society for Research in Child Development*, 29 (1), No. 92, pp. 107–114.

INHELDER, BARBEL. 1953. Criteria of the stages of mental development. In James M. Tanner and Barbel Inhelder (eds.), *Discussions on Child Development*, Vol. I. New York: International Universities Press.

IRETON, HAROLD, EDWARD THWING, AND HOWARD GRAVEM. 1970. Infant mental development and neurological status, family socioeconomic status, and intelligence at age four. *Child Development*, 41, 937–945.

IRWIN, F. W. 1943. Edwin Burket Twitmyer: 1873–1943. *American Journal of Psychology*, 56, 451–453.

ITARD, JEAN-MARC G. 1801, 1807. *The Wild Boy of Aveyron*. George and Muriel Humphrey (trans.). New York: Appleton-Century-Crofts, 1932.

JACOB, THEODORE. 1968. The experimenter bias effect: A failure to replicate. *Psychonomic Science*, 13, 239–240.

JACOBSON, EDMUND. 1938. *Progressive Relaxation*. Chicago: University of Chicago Press.

JAMES, WILLIAM. 1890. *The Principles of Psychology*. New York: Holt.

JENSEN, ARTHUR R. 1969a. How much can we boost IQ and scholastic achievement? In *Environment, Heredity, and Intelligence. Harvard Educational Review* Reprint Series, No. 2, pp. 1–123.

JENSEN, ARTHUR R. 1969b. Reducing the heredity-environment uncertainty. In *Environment, Heredity, and Intelligence. Harvard Educational Review* Reprint Series, No. 2, pp. 209–243.

JERSILD, ARTHUR T. 1954. Emotional development. In Leonard Carmichael (ed.), *Manual of Child Psychology*, 2d ed. New York: John Wiley & Sons. Chapt. 14, pp. 833–917.

JERSILD, ARTHUR T., AND FRANCES B. HOLMES. 1935a. *Children's Fears*. Teachers College Child Development Monographs, No. 20. New York: Teachers College Press.

JERSILD, ARTHUR T., AND FRANCES B. HOLMES. 1935b. Methods of overcoming children's fears. *Journal of Psychology*, 1, 75–104.

JONÇICH, GERALDINE. 1968. E. L. Thorndike: The psychologist as professional man of science. *American Psychologist*, 23, 434–446.

JONES, HAROLD E. 1931. The conditioning of overt emotional responses. *Journal of Educational Psychology*, 22, 127–130.

JONES, HAROLD E., AND NANCY BAYLEY. 1941. The Berkeley Growth Study. *Child Development*, 12, 167–173.

JONES, KENNETH L., DAVID W. SMITH, CHRISTY N. ULLELAND, AND ANN P. STREISSGUTH. 1973. Pattern of malformation in offspring of chronic alcoholic mothers. *The Lancet*, 1, 1267–1271.

JONES, MARY COVER. 1924a. The elimination of children's fears. *Journal of Experimental Psychology*, 7, 382–390.

JONES, MARY COVER. 1924b. A laboratory study of fear: The case of Peter. *Journal of Genetic Psychology*, 31, 308–315.

JONES, MARY COVER. 1957. The later careers of boys who were early- or late-maturing. *Child Development*, 28, 113–128.

JONES, MARY COVER, AND NANCY BAYLEY. 1950. Physical maturity of boys as related to behavior. *Journal of Educational Psychology*, 41, 129–148.

JOST, HUDSON, AND LESTER W. SONTAG. 1944. The genetic factor in autonomic nervous-system function. *Psychosomatic Medicine*, 6, 308–310.

JUNG, CARL G. 1954. *The Development of Personality*. R. F. C. Hull (trans.). New York: Pantheon.

KAGAN, JEROME, AND HOWARD A. MOSS. 1962. *Birth to Maturity*. New York: John Wiley & Sons.

KALLMANN, FRANZ J. 1946. The genetic theory of schizophrenia. *American Journal of Psychiatry*, 103, 309–322.

KALLMANN, FRANZ J., AND BERNARD ROTH. 1956. Genetic aspects of preadolescent schizophrenia. *American Journal of Psychiatry*, 112, 599–606.

KARNES, MERLE B., AUDREY HODGINS, AND JAMES A. TESKA. 1968. An evaluation of two preschool programs for disadvantaged children: A traditional and a highly structured experimental preschool. *Exceptional Children*, 34, 667–676.

KARNES, MERLE B., JAMES A. TESKA, AND AUDREY S. HODGINS. 1970a. The effects of four programs of classroom intervention on the intellectual and language development of 4-year-old disadvantaged children. *American Journal of Orthopsychiatry*, 40, 58–76.

KARNES, MERLE B., JAMES A. TESKA, AND AUDREY S. HODGINS. 1970b. The successful implementation of a highly specific preschool instructional program by paraprofessional teachers. *Journal of Special Education*, 4, 69–80.

KELLOGG, WINTHROP N. 1934. A further note on the "wolf children" of India. *American Journal of Psychology*, 46, 149–150.

KELLOGG, WINTHROP N., AND LUELLA A. KELLOGG. 1933. *The Ape and The Child: A Study of Environmental Influence upon Early Behavior*. New York: McGraw-Hill.

KENNEDY, WALLACE A. 1965. School phobia: Rapid treatment of fifty cases. *Journal of Abnormal Psychology*, 70, 285–289.

KENNEDY, WALLACE A. 1969. A follow-up normative study of Negro intelligence and achievement. *Monographs of the Society for Research in Child Development*, 34 (2), No. 126.

KENNEDY, WALLACE A. 1973. *Intelligence and Economics: A Confounded Relationship*. Morristown, N.J.: General Learning Corporation.

KENNEDY, WALLACE A., AND RONALD S. LINDNER. 1964. A normative study of the Goodenough Draw-A-Man Test on Southeastern elementary school children. *Child Development*, 35, 33–62.

KENNEDY, WALLACE A., VERNON VAN DE RIET, AND JAMES C. WHITE, JR. 1963. A normative sample of intelligence and achievement of Negro elementary school children in the Southeastern United States. *Monographs of the Society for Research in Child Development*, 28 (6), No. 90.

KENNEDY, WALLACE A., AND MANUEL VEGA. 1965. Negro children's performance on a discrimination task as a function of examiner race and verbal incentive. *Journal of Personality and Social Psychology*, 2, 839–843.

KENNEDY, WALLACE A., AND HERMAN C. WILLCUTT. 1964. Praise and blame as incentives. *Psychological Bulletin*, 62, 323–332.

KESSEN, WILLIAM. 1965. *The Child*. New York: John Wiley & Sons.

KESSEN, WILLIAM, MARSHALL M. HAITH, AND PHILIP H. SALAPATEK. 1970. Human infancy: A bibliography and guide. In Paul H. Mussen (ed.), *Carmichael's Manual of Child Psychology*, 3d ed. New York: John Wiley & Sons. Chapt. 5, pp. 287–445.

KIERKEGAARD, SØREN. 1844. *The Concept of*

Dread. Walter Lowrie (trans.). Princeton, N.J.: Princeton University Press, 1957.

KIMBER, DIANA C., CAROLYN E. GRAY, CAROLINE E. STACKPOLE, AND LUTIE C. LEAVELL. 1950. *Textbook of Anatomy and Physiology*, 12th ed. New York: Macmillan.

KIMBLE, GREGORY A. 1961. *Hilgard and Marquis' Conditioning and Learning*, 2d ed. New York: Appleton-Century-Crofts.

KLAUS, RUPERT A., AND SUSAN W. GRAY. 1968. The early training project for disadvantaged children: A report after five years. *Monographs of the Society for Research in Child Development*, 33 (4), No. 120.

KLAUSMEIER, HERBERT J., AND JOHN CHECK. 1959. Relationships among physical, mental, achievement, and personality measures in children of low, average, and high intelligence. *American Journal of Mental Deficiency*, 63, 647–656.

KNOBLOCH, HILDA, AND BENJAMIN PASAMANICK. 1966. Prospective studies on the epidemiology of reproductive casualty: Methods, findings, and some implications. *Merrill-Palmer Quarterly of Behavior and Development*, 12, 27–43.

KNUDSON, ALFRED G., JR. 1965. *Genetics and Disease.* New York: Blakiston, McGraw-Hill.

KRAEPELIN, EMIL. 1896. *Psychiatric.* Leipzig: Barth.

KRASNOGORSKII, NICKOLAI E. 1907. The formation of conditioned reflexes in the young child. In Yvonne Brackbill and George G. Thompson (eds.), *Behavior in Infancy and Early Childhood.* New York: The Free Press, 1967. Pp. 237–239.

KRASNOGORSKII, NICKOLAI E. 1925. The conditioned reflex and children's neuroses. *American Journal of Diseases in Childhood*, 30, 753–768.

KRECH, DAVID, AND RICHARD S. CRUTCHFIELD. 1958. *Elements of Psychology.* New York: Alfred A. Knopf.

KRETCHMER, NORMAN. 1964. Whither birth defects? *Perspectives in Biology and Medicine*, 8, 15–29.

KRETCHMER, NORMAN. 1972. Lactose and lactase. *Scientific American*, 227, 70–78.

LABOV, WILLIAM. 1970. The logic of nonstandard English. In Frederick Williams (ed.), *Language and Poverty.* Institute for Research on Poverty Monograph Series. Chicago: Markham. Pp. 153–189.

LABOV, WILLIAM. 1972. Academic ignorance and black intelligence. *The Atlantic*, 229, 59–67.

LANDRETH, CATHERINE. 1967. *Early Childhood Behavior and Learning.* New York: Alfred A. Knopf.

LANE, HARLAN. 1973. Dr. Itard and the Wild Boy of Aveyron Revisited. Invited Address, Rocky Mountain Psychological Association, May 10.

LAZARUS, ARNOLD A., AND ARNOLD ABRAMOVITZ. 1962. The use of "emotive imagery" in the treatment of children's phobias. *Journal of Mental Science*, 108, 191–195.

LAZARUS, ARNOLD A., AND S. RACHMAN. 1957. The use of systematic desensitization in psychotherapy. *South African Medical Journal*, 31, 934–937.

LEARNED, WILLIAM S., AND B. D. WOOD. 1938. *The Student and His Knowledge.* New York: Carnegie Foundation for the Advancement of Teaching.

LEE, CHI-JEN, AND BACON F. CHOW. 1968. Metabolism of proteins by progeny of underfed mother rats. *Journal of Nutrition*, 94, 20–26.

LENNEBERG, ERIC H. 1964a. A biological perspective of language. In Eric H. Lenneberg (ed.), *New Directions in the Study of Language.* Cambridge, Mass.: The M.I.T. Press. Pp. 65–88.

LENNEBERG, ERIC H. 1964b. Language disorders in childhood. *Harvard Education Review*, 34, 152–177.

LESSER, GERALD S., GORDON FIFER, AND DONALD H. CLARK. 1965. Mental abilities of children from different social class and cultural groups. *Monographs of the Society for Research in Child Development*, 30 (4), No. 102.

LEVY, LEON H. 1969. Reflections on replications and the experimenter bias effect. *Journal of Consulting and Clinical Psychology*, 33, 15–17.

LEWIS, M. M. 1963. *Language, Thought, and Personality in Infancy and Childhood.* New York: Basic Books.

LINDZEY, GARDNER. 1965. Morphology and behavior. In Gardner Lindzey and Calvin S. Hall (eds.), *Theories of Personality: Primary Sources and Research.* New York: John Wiley & Sons. Pp. 344–353.

LING, BING C. 1942. A genetic study of sustained visual fixation and associated behavior in the human infant from birth to six months. *Journal of Genetic Psychology*, 61, 227–277.

LIPSITT, LEWIS P. 1958. A Self-Concept Scale for Children and its relationship to the children's form of the Manifest Anxiety Scale. *Child Development*, 29, 463–472.

LIPSITT, LEWIS P. 1970. Pattern perception and information seeking. In Francis A. Young and

Donald B. Lindsley (eds.), *Early Experience and Visual Information Processing in Perceptual and Reading Disorders.* Washington, D.C.: National Academy of Sciences. Pp. 382–402.

LIYAMINA, L. M. 1960. Mechanism by which children master pronunciation during the second and the third year. In *The Central Nervous System and Behavior: Translations from the Russian Medical Literature.* Bethesda, Md.: Josiah Macy, Jr., Foundation, National Science Foundation, and U.S. Public Health Service.

LOCKE, JOHN. 1693. *Some Thoughts Concerning Education,* 4th ed. London: Churchill, 1969.

LORENZ, KONRAD Z. 1937. The companion in the bird's world. *Auk,* 54, 245–273.

LORGE, IRVING. 1949. Trends in the measurement of achievement. In Wilma T. Donahue, Clyde H. Coombs, and Robert M. W. Travers (eds.), *The Measurement of Student Adjustment and Achievement.* Ann Arbor: University of Michigan Press.

McCANDLESS, BOYD R. 1967. *Children: Behavior and Development,* 2d ed. New York: Holt, Rinehart & Winston.

McCANDLESS, BOYD R., ALFRED CASTANEDA, AND DAVID S. PALERMO. 1956. Anxiety in children and social status. *Child Development,* 27, 385–391.

MacDOUGALL, ROBERT. 1913. The child's speech. IV. Word and meaning. *Journal of Educational Psychology,* 4, 29–38.

McGRAW, MYRTLE. 1940. Neural maturation as exemplified by the achievement of bladder control. *Journal of Pediatrics,* 16, 580–590.

McGRAW, MYRTLE. 1943. Influence of cortical development upon early behavior patterns. In Myrtle McGraw, *The Neuromuscular Maturation of the Human Infant.* New York: Columbia University Press. Pp. 27–36.

McNEIL, DAVID. 1970. The development of language. In Paul H. Mussen (ed.), *Carmichael's Manual of Child Psychology,* 3d ed., Vol. I. New York: John Wiley & Sons. Chapt. 15, pp. 1061–1161.

MAIER, HENRY W. 1965. *Three Theories of Child Development.* New York: Harper & Row.

MAIER, HENRY W. 1969. *Three Theories of Child Development,* rev. ed. New York: Harper & Row.

MALMO, ROBERT B. 1966. Studies of anxiety: Some clinical origins of the activation concept. In Charles D. Spielberger (ed.), *Anxiety and Behavior.* New York: Academic Press. Chapt. 7, pp. 157–177.

MANN, HORACE. 1845. Boston grammar and writing schools. *Common School Journal,* 7 (19).

MANN, IDA CAROLINE. 1964. *The Development of the Human Eye,* 3d ed. New York: Grune & Stratton.

MARQUIS, DOROTHY P. 1931. Can conditioned responses be established in the newborn infant? *Journal of Genetic Psychology,* 39, 479–492.

MATEER, FLORENCE E. 1918. *Child Behavior: A Critical and Experimental Study of Young Children by the Method of Conditioned Reflexes.* Boston: Richard G. Badger, The Gorham Press.

MEDINNUS, GENE R. 1961. The development of a First-Grade Adjustment Scale. *Journal of Experimental Education,* 30, 243–248.

MENDEL, GREGOR. 1866. Experiment on hybrid plants. In Edmund W. Sinnott, L. C. Dunn, and Theodosius Dobzhansky, *Principles of Genetics,* 4th ed. New York: McGraw-Hill, 1950. Pp. 463–493.

MILL, JAMES. 1829. *Analysis of the Phenomena of the Human Mind.* New York: A. M. Kelley, 1967.

MILL, JOHN STUART. 1843. *System of Logic: Ratiocinative and Inductive.* In F. E. L. Priestly (ed.), *John Stuart Mill: Collected Works,* Vol. VIII. Toronto: University of Toronto Press, 1963.

MILLER, NEAL E., AND JOHN DOLLARD. 1941. *Social Learning and Imitation.* New Haven, Conn.: Yale University Press.

MONTAGU, M. F. ASHLEY. 1954. Constitutional and prenatal factors in infant and child health. In William E. Martin and Celia Burns Stendler (eds.), *Readings in Child Development.* New York: Harcourt, Brace. Pp. 15–29.

MONTAGU, M. F. ASHLEY. 1971. *Touching: The Human Significance of the Skin.* New York: Columbia University Press.

MORENO, JACOB L. 1953. *Who Shall Survive? Foundations of Sociometry, Group Psychotherapy, and Sociodrama,* 2d ed. Sociometry Monograph No. 29. New York: Beacon House.

MORGAN, JOHN J. B. 1938. Treatment of enuresis by the conditioned reaction technique. *Psychological Bulletin,* 35, 632–633.

MORGAN, JOHN J. B., AND FRANCES J. WITMER. 1939. The treatment of enuresis by the conditioned reaction technique. *Journal of Genetic Psychology,* 55, 59–65.

MOSS, HOWARD A., AND JEROME KAGAN. 1959. Maternal influences on early IQ scores. *Psychological Reports,* 14, 655–661.

MOWRER, O. HOBART. 1939. A stimulus-response analysis of anxiety and its role as a reinforcing agent. *Psychological Review*, 46, 553–565.

MOWRER, O. HOBART. 1950. The problem of anxiety. In O. Hobart Mowrer, *Learning Theory and Personality Dynamics: Selected Papers*. New York: Ronald Press. Chapt. 19, pp. 531–561.

MOWRER, O. HOBART. 1952. Speech development in the young child. I. The autism theory of speech development and some clinical applications. *Journal of Speech and Hearing Disorders*, 17, 263–268.

MOWRER, O. HOBART. 1965. Learning theory and behavior therapy. In Benjamin B. Wolman, *Handbook of Clinical Psychology*. New York: McGraw-Hill. Chapt. 12, pp. 242–276.

MOWRER, O. HOBART. 1972. Review of *Beyond Freedom and Dignity* by B. F. Skinner (Knopf 1971). *Contemporary Psychology*, 17, 469.

MOWRER, O. HOBART, AND WILLIE MAE MOWRER. 1938. Enuresis: A method for its study and treatment. *American Journal of Orthopsychiatry*, 8, 436–459.

MURCHISON, CARL, AND SUZANNE LANGER. 1927. Tiedemann's observations on the development of the mental faculties of children. *Pedagogical Seminary*, 34, 205–230.

MUSSEN, PAUL H., JOHN J. CONGER, AND JEROME KAGAN. 1969. *Child Development and Personality*, 3d ed. New York: Harper & Row.

MUSSEN, PAUL H., AND MARY COVER JONES. 1957. Self-conceptions, motivations, and interpersonal attitudes of late- and early-maturing boys. *Child Development*, 28, 243–256.

MYKLEBUST, HELMER R. 1954. *Auditory Disorders in Children*. New York: Grune & Stratton.

NEILL, ALEXANDER S. 1960. *Summerhill: A Radical Approach to Child Rearing*. New York: Hart.

NEILON, PATRICIA. 1948. Shirley's babies after fifteen years: A personality study. *Journal of Genetic Psychology*, 73, 175–186.

NELSON, K. B., AND DEUTSCHBERGER, J. 1970. Head size at one year as a predictor of four-year IQ. *Developmental Medicine and Child Neurology*, 12, 487–495.

NEWMAN, HORATIO H., FRANK N. FREEMAN, AND KARL J. HOLZINGER. 1937. *Twins: A Study of Heredity and Environment*. Chicago: University of Chicago Press.

NICHOLS, ROBERT C. 1965. The national merit twin study. In Steven G. Vandenberg (ed.), *Methods and Goals in Human Behavior Genetics*. New York: Academic Press. Pp. 231–243.

OAKES, MERVIN E. 1945. Explanations of natural phenomena by adults. *Science Foundation*, 29, 137–142.

OLSON, WILLARD C. 1959. *Child Development*, 2d ed. Boston: D. C. Heath.

OLSON, WILLARD C., AND ELIZABETH M. CUNNINGHAM. 1934. Time-sampling techniques. *Child Development*, 5, 41–58.

OSGOOD, CHARLES E. 1953. *Method and Theory in Experimental Psychology*. New York: Oxford University Press.

OSLER, SONIA F., AND MYRNA F. FIVEL. 1961. Concept attainment. I. The role of age and intelligence in concept attainment by induction. *Journal of Experimental Psychology*, 62, 1–8.

OSLER, SONIA F., AND GRACE E. TRAUTMAN. 1961. Concept attainment. II. Effect of stimulus complexity upon concept attainment at two levels of intelligence. *Journal of Experimental Psychology*, 62, 9–13.

PALARDY, J. N. 1969. What teachers believe, what children achieve. *Elementary School Journal*, 69, 370–374.

PALMER, FRANCIS. 1971. Minimal intervention and intellective change at two and three. In Ron K. Parker (ed.), *Conceptualization of Preschool Curricula*. Boston: Allyn & Bacon.

PAPOUSEK, HANUS. 1967. Conditioning during early postnatal development. In Yvonne Brackbill and George G. Thompson (eds.), *Behavior in Infancy and Early Childhood*. New York: The Free Press. Pp. 259–274.

PASAMANICK, BENJAMIN, AND HILDA KNOBLOCH. 1958. The contribution of some organic factors to school retardation in Negro children. *Journal of Negro Education*, 27, 4–9.

PASAMANICK, BENJAMIN, AND HILDA KNOBLOCH. 1966. Retrospective studies on the epidemiology of reproductive casualty: Old and new. *Merrill-Palmer Quarterly of Behavior and Development*, 12, 7–26.

PAVLOV, IVAN P. 1927. *Conditioned Reflexes: An Investigation of the Physiological Activity of the Cerebral Cortex*. G. V. Anrep (trans.). London: Humphrey Milford, Oxford University Press.

PEARSON, KARL. 1896. Mathematical contributions to the theory of evolution: Regression, heredity, and panmixia. *Philosophical Transactions*, 187A, 253–318.

PHILLIPS, JOHN L., JR. 1969. *The Origins of Intellect: Piaget's Theory.* San Francisco: W. H. Freeman.

PIAGET, JEAN. 1929. The origin of names. In Jean Piaget, *The Child's Conception of the World.* London: Routledge & Kegan Paul.

PIAGET, JEAN. 1931. Children's philosophies. In Carl Murchison (ed.), *Handbook of Child Psychology.* Worcester, Mass.: Clark University Press. Pp. 377–391.

PIAGET, JEAN. 1932. The idea of immanent justice. In Jean Piaget, *The Moral Judgment of the Child.* London: Routledge & Kegan Paul. Pp. 250–253.

PIAGET, JEAN. 1950. *The Psychology of Intelligence.* London: Routledge & Kegan Paul.

PIAGET, JEAN. 1952a. Jean Piaget. In Edwin G. Boring, Herbert S. Langfeld, Heinz Werner, and Robert M. Yerkes (eds.), *A History of Psychology in Autobiography*, Vol. IV. Worcester, Mass.: Clark University Press; New York: Russell & Russell, 1968. Pp. 237–256.

PIAGET, JEAN. 1952b. *The Origins of Intelligence in Children.* New York: International Universities Press.

PIAGET, JEAN. 1954. *The Construction of Reality in the Child.* New York: Basic Books.

PIAGET, JEAN. 1960. The general problems of the psychobiological development of the child. In James M. Tanner and Barbel Inhelder (eds.), *Discussions on Child Development*, Vol. IV. New York: International Universities Press. Pp. 3–27.

PIAGET, JEAN. 1961. The genetic approach to the psychology of thought. *Journal of Educational Psychology*, 52, 275–281.

PIAGET, JEAN, AND BARBEL INHELDER. 1969. *The Psychology of the Child.* New York: Basic Books.

PINNEAU, SAMUEL R. 1955. The infantile disorders of hospitalism and anaclitic depression. *Psychological Bulletin*, 52, 429–452.

PRATT, KARL C. 1934. The effects of repeated visual stimulation upon the activity of newborn infants. *Journal of Genetic Psychology*, 44, 117–126.

PRATT, KARL C. 1954. The neonate. In Leonard Carmichael (ed.), *Manual of Child Psychology*, 2d ed. New York: John Wiley & Sons. Chapt. 4, pp. 215–291.

PRATT, KARL C., AMALIE K. NELSON, AND KUO HUA SUN. 1930. *The Behavior of the Newborn Infant.* Columbus: Ohio State University Press.

PREYER, WILHELM. 1881. *The Mind of the Child.* H. W. Brown (trans.). New York: Appleton, 1888–1889.

RAMSAY, A. OGDEN, AND ECKHARD H. HESS. 1954. A study of imprinting. *Wilson Bulletin*, 66, 196–206.

REISMAN, LEONARD E., AND ADAM P. MATHENY, JR. 1969. *Genetics and Counseling in Medical Practice.* St. Louis: C. V. Mosby.

REYNA, L. J. 1964. Conditioning therapies, learning theory, and research. In Joseph Wolpe, Andrew Salter, and L. J. Reyna (eds.), *The Conditioning Therapies: The Challenge in Psychotherapy.* New York: Holt, Rinehart & Winston. Pp. 169–179.

REYNOLDS, G. S. 1968. *A Primer of Operant Conditioning.* Glenview, Ill.: Scott, Foresman.

RHEINGOLD, HARRIET L., JACOB L. GEWIRTZ, AND HELEN W. ROSS. 1959. Social conditioning of vocalizations in the infant. *Journal of Comparative and Physiological Psychology*, 52, 68–73.

RHODES, A. J. 1961. Virus infections and congenital malformations. In *Congenital Malformations: Papers and Discussions Presented at the First International Conference on Congenital Malformations.* Philadelphia: J. B. Lippincott. Pp. 106–116.

RIBBLE, MARGARET A. 1943. *The Rights of Infants: Early Psychological Needs and Their Satisfaction.* New York: Columbia University Press.

RICCIUTI, HENRY N. 1970. Malnutrition, learning, and intellectual development: Research and remediation. In *Psychology and the Problems of Society.* Washington, D.C.: American Psychological Association. Pp. 237–253.

RIESSMAN, FRANK. 1962. *The Culturally Deprived Child.* New York: Harper & Row.

ROEDER, LOIS M., AND BACON F. CHOW. 1972. Maternal undernutrition and its long-term effect on the offspring. *American Journal of Clinical Nutrition*, 25, 812–821.

ROGERS, CARL R. 1942. *Counseling and Psychotherapy.* Boston: Houghton Mifflin.

ROGERS, CARL R. 1951. *Client-Centered Therapy.* Boston: Houghton Mifflin.

ROGERS, CARL R. 1967. Carl R. Rogers. In Edwin G. Boring and Gardner Lindzey (eds.), *A History of Psychology in Autobiography*, Vol. V. New York: Appleton-Century-Crofts. Pp. 343–384.

ROGERS, CARL R. 1974. In retrospect: forty-six years. *American Psychologist*, 29, 115–123.

ROSENSTEIN, JOSEPH. 1960. Cognitive abilities

of deaf children. *Journal of Speech and Hearing Research*, 3, 108–119.

ROSENTHAL, ROBERT, AND LENORE JACOBSON. 1968. *Pygmalion in the Classroom: Teacher Expectation and Pupils' Intellectual Development.* New York: Holt, Rinehart & Winston.

ROSENZWEIG, MARK R. 1959. Salivary conditioning before Pavlov. *American Journal of Psychology*, 72, 628–633.

ROSS, M. H. 1959. Protein, calories, and life expectancy. *Federation Proceedings*, 18, 1190.

ROUSSEAU, JEAN-JACQUES. 1762. *Emile, or On Education.* Barbara Foxley (trans.). London: Dent, 1911.

RUCH, FLOYD L. 1963. *Psychology and Life*, 6th ed. Glenview, Ill.: Scott, Foresman.

SARASON, SEYMOUR B., KENNETH S. DAVIDSON, FREDERICK F. LIGHTHALL, AND RICHARD R. WAITE. 1958. Classroom observations of high and low anxious children. *Child Development*, 29, 287–295.

SARASON, SEYMOUR B., KENNETH S. DAVIDSON, FREDERICK F. LIGHTHALL, RICHARD R. WAITE, AND BRITTON K. RUEBUSH. 1960. *Anxiety in Elementary School Children.* New York: John Wiley & Sons.

SARASON, SEYMOUR B., KENNEDY T. HILL, AND PHILIP G. ZIMBARDO. 1964. A longitudinal study of the relation of test anxiety to performance on intelligence and achievement tests. *Monographs of the Society for Research in Child Development*, 29 (7), No. 98.

SAWIN, CLARK T. 1969. *The Hormones: Endocrine Physiology.* Boston: Little, Brown.

SCHLANGER, BERNARD B. 1961. *The Effects of Listening Training on the Auditory Thresholds of Mentally Retarded Children.* U.S. Office of Education Cooperative Research Project No. 973(8936).

SCHOONOVER, SARAH M. 1956. A longitudinal study of sibling resemblances in intelligence and achievement. *Journal of Educational Psychology*, 47, 436–442.

SEARS, ROBERT R., ELEANOR E. MACCOBY, AND HARRY LEVIN. 1957. *Patterns of Child Rearing.* New York: Harper & Row.

SEGUIN, EDWARD. 1866. *Idiocy: Its Treatment by the Physiological Method.* New York: Teachers College, Columbia University, 1907.

SHELDON, WILLIAM H., AND S. S. STEVENS. 1942. *The Varieties of Temperament: A Psychology of Constitutional Differences.* New York: Harper.

SHERMAN, MANDEL. 1927a. The differentiation of emotional responses in infants. I. Judgments of emotional responses from motion picture views and from actual observation. *Journal of Comparative Psychology*, 7, 265–284.

SHERMAN, MANDEL. 1927b. The differentiation of emotional responses in infants. II. The ability of observers to judge the emotional characteristics of the crying of infants, and of the voice of an adult. *Journal of Comparative Psychology*, 7, 335–351.

SHERMAN, MANDEL, AND CORA B. KEY. 1932. The intelligence of isolated mountain children. *Child Development*, 3, 279–290.

SHERRINGTON, CHARLES S. 1906. *Integrative Action of the Nervous System.* New York: Charles Scribner's Sons.

SHIELDS, JAMES. 1962. *Monozygotic Twins, Brought Up Apart and Brought Up Together.* London: Oxford University Press.

SHIRLEY, MARY M. 1933. *The First Two Years: A Study of Twenty-Five Babies*, Vol. III. Minneapolis: University of Minnesota Press.

SHOCKLEY, WILLIAM. 1969. Offset analysis description of racial differences. Paper prepared for presentation at Autumn meeting of the National Academy of Sciences, Dartmouth College, Hanover, New Hampshire.

SHUEY, AUDREY M. 1958. *The Testing of Negro Intelligence.* Lynchburg, Va.: J. P. Bell.

SHUEY, AUDREY M. 1966. *The Testing of Negro Intelligence*, 2d ed. New York: Social Science Press.

SHUTTLEWORTH, FRANK K. 1939. The physical and mental growth of girls and boys, age six to nineteen, in relation to age at maximum growth. *Monographs of the Society for Research in Child Development*, 4 (3), No. 22.

SIMON, MARIA D. 1959. Body configuration and school readiness. *Child Development*, 30, 493–512.

SIMONSON, MARIA, JOANNE K. STEPHAN, HARLEY M. HANSON, AND BACON F. CHOW. 1971. Open field studies in offspring of underfed mother rats. *Journal of Nutrition*, 101, 331–335.

SIMPSON, WINEA J. 1957. A preliminary report on cigarette smoking and the incidence of prematurity. *American Journal of Obstetrics and Gynecology*, 73, 808–815.

SIMRALL, DOROTHY. 1947. Intelligence and the ability to learn. *Journal of Psychology*, 23, 27–43.

SINGH, J. A. L., AND ROBERT M. ZINGG. 1942. *Wolf-Children and Feral Man.* New York: Harper.

SKEELS, HAROLD M. 1966. Adult status of children with contrasting early life experiences. *Monographs of the Society for Research in Child Development*, 31 (3), No. 105.

SKEELS, HAROLD M., AND EVA A. FILLMORE. 1937. The mental development of children from underprivileged homes. *Journal of Genetic Psychology*, 50, 427–439.

SKINNER, B. 1955–1956. Freedom and the control of men. *American Scholar*, 25, 47–65.

SKINNER, B. F. 1956. A case history in scientific method. *American Psychologist*, 11, 221–233.

SKINNER, B. F. 1959. Baby in a box. In B. F. Skinner, *Cumulative Record*. New York: Appleton-Century-Crofts. Pp. 419–427.

SKINNER, B. F. 1967. B. F. Skinner. In Edwin G. Boring and Gardner Lindzey (eds.), *A History of Psychology in Autobiography*, Vol. V. New York: Appleton-Century-Crofts. Pp. 385–413.

SKINNER, B. F. 1971. *Beyond Freedom and Dignity*. New York: Alfred A. Knopf.

SKODAK, MARIE, AND HAROLD M. SKEELS. 1949. A final follow-up study of one hundred adopted children. *Journal of Genetic Psychology*, 75, 85–125.

SMITH, A. 1960. A further note on mongolism in twins. *British Journal of Preventive and Social Medicine*, 14, 27.

SMITH, RICHARD T. 1965. A comparison of socioenvironmental factors in monozygotic and dizygotic twins: Testing an assumption. In Steven G. Vandenberg (ed.), *Methods and Goals in Human Behavior Genetics*. New York: Academic Press. Pp. 45–61.

SNOW, RICHARD E. 1969. Unfinished Pygmalion. *Contemporary Psychology*, 14, 197–199.

SPEARMAN, CHARLES E. 1904. "General intelligence" objectively determined and measured. *American Psychologist*, 15, 201–293.

SPEARMAN, CHARLES E. 1927. *The Abilities of Man*. New York: Macmillan.

SPEARMAN, CHARLES E. 1930. C. Spearman. In Carl Murchison (ed.), *A History of Psychology in Autobiography*, Vol. I. Worcester, Mass.: Clark University Press; New York: Russell & Russell, 1961. Pp. 299–333.

SPEARS, WILLIAM C., AND RAYMOND H. HOHLE. 1967. Sensory and perceptual processes in infants. In Yvonne Brackbill (ed.), *Infancy and Early Childhood: A Handbook and Guide to Human Development*. New York: The Free Press. Chapt. 2, pp. 49–121.

SPELT, DAVID K. 1948. The conditioning of the human fetus in utero. *Journal of Experimental Psychology*, 38, 338–346.

SPIELBERGER, CHARLES 1966. Theory and research on anxiety. In Charles D. Spielberger (ed.), *Anxiety and Behavior*. New York: Academic Press. Chapt. 1, pp. 3–20.

SPITZ, RENÉ A. 1949. Motherless infants. *Child Development*, 20, 145–155.

SPITZ, RENÉ A. 1955. Reply to Dr. Pinneau. *Psychological Bulletin*, 52, 453–458.

SPITZ, RENÉ A., AND KATHERINE M. WOLF. 1946. Anaclitic depression. *Psychoanalytic Study of the Child*, 2, 313–342.

SQUIRES, PAUL C. 1927. "Wolf children" of India. *American Journal of Psychology*, 38, 313–315.

STEINSCHNEIDER, ALFRED. 1972. Prolonged apnea and the sudden infant death syndrome: Clinical and laboratory observations. *Pediatrics*, 50, 646–654.

STEPHAN, JOANNE K. 1971. The permanent effect of prenatal dietary restriction on the brain of the progeny. *Nutrition Reports International*, 4, 257–268.

STERN, WILLIAM. 1912. *The Psychological Methods of Testing Intelligence*. Guy Montrose Whipple (trans.). Educational Psychology Monographs No. 13. Baltimore: Warwick & York, 1914.

STERNBACH, RICHARD A. 1962. Assessing differential autonomic patterns in emotions. *Journal of Psychosomatic Research*, 6, 87–91.

STEVENSON, HAROLD W. 1970. Learning in children. In Paul H. Mussen (ed.), *Carmichael's Manual of Child Psychology*, 3d ed., Vol. I. New York: John Wiley & Sons. Chapt. 12, pp. 849–938.

STEVENSON, HAROLD W., AND RICHARD D. ODOM. 1965. The relation of anxiety to children's performance on learning and problem-solving tasks. *Child Development*, 36, 1003–1012.

STOLUROW, LAWRENCE M. 1961. *Teaching by Machine*. U.S. Department of Health, Education, and Welfare Cooperative Research No. OE-34010, Monograph No. 6.

STONE, CALVIN P., AND ROGER G. BARKER. 1939. The attitudes and interests of pre-menarcheal girls. *Journal of Genetic Psychology*, 54, 27–71.

STONE, CLIFF W. 1908. *Arithmetical Abilities and Some Factors Determining Them*. Contributions to Education No. 19. New York: Teachers College, Columbia University.

STRATTON, G. M. 1934. Jungle children. *Psychological Bulletin*, 31, 596–597.

STRUPP, HANS H. 1963. The outcome problem

in psychotherapy revisited. *Psychotherapy*, 1, 1–13.

STUBBS, E. M. 1934. The effect of the factors of duration, intensity, and pitch of sound stimuli on the responses of newborn infants. *University of Iowa Studies in Child Welfare*, 9 (4), 75–135.

STUMPHAUZER, JEROME S., AND BARBARA R. BISHOP. 1969. Saturday morning television cartoons: A simple apparatus for the reinforcement of behavior in children. *Developmental Psychology*, 1, 763–764.

SULLIVAN, HARRY STACK. 1953. *The Interpersonal Theory of Psychiatry*. New York: W. W. Norton.

SUTTON-SMITH, BRIAN. 1973. *Child Psychology*. New York: Appleton-Century-Crofts.

TAINE, HIPPOLYTE ADOLPHE. 1876. M. Taine on the acquisition of language by children. In *Mind*, 1877, 2, 252–259.

TANNER, JAMES M. 1970. Physical growth. In Paul H. Mussen (ed.), *Carmichael's Manual of Child Psychology*, 3d ed., Vol. I. New York: John Wiley & Sons. Chapt. 3, pp. 77–155.

TAYLOR, JANET A. 1953. A personality scale of manifest anxiety. *Journal of Abnormal and Social Psychology*, 48, 285–290.

TERMAN, LEWIS M. 1916. *The Measurement of Intelligence*. Boston: Houghton Mifflin.

TERMAN, LEWIS M. 1930. Lewis M. Terman. In Carl Murchison (ed.), *A History of Psychology in Autobiography*, Vol. II. Worcester, Mass.: Clark University Press; New York: Russell & Russell, 1961. Pp. 297–331.

TERMAN, LEWIS M., AND MAUD A. MERRILL. 1937. *Measuring Intelligence*. Boston: Houghton Mifflin.

TERMAN, LEWIS M., AND MAUD A. MERRILL. 1960. Stanford-Binet Intelligence Scale. Boston: Houghton Mifflin.

TERMAN, LEWIS M., AND MELITA H. ODEN. 1947. *The Gifted Child Grows Up*. Stanford, Calif.: Stanford University Press.

TERMAN, LEWIS M., AND MELITA H. ODEN. 1959. *The Gifted Group at Midlife: Thirty-five Years' Follow-Up of the Superior Child*. Stanford, Calif.: Stanford University Press.

THOMPSON, GEORGE G. 1959. Developmental psychology. *Annual Review of Psychology*, 10, 1–42.

THOMPSON, GEORGE G. 1962. *Child Psychology*, 2d ed. Boston: Houghton Mifflin.

THOMPSON, JAMES S., AND MARGARET W. THOMP-SON. 1966. *Genetics in Medicine*. Philadelphia: W. B. Saunders.

THORNDIKE, EDWARD L. 1898. Animal intelligence: An experimental study of the associative processes in animals. *Psychological Review Monograph Supplements*, No. 8.

THORNDIKE, EDWARD L. 1904. *An Introduction to the Theory of Mental and Social Measurements*. New York: Teachers College, Columbia University.

THORNDIKE, EDWARD L. 1910. Handwriting. *Teachers College Record*, 2, 83–175.

THORNDIKE, EDWARD L. 1936. Edward Lee Thorndike. In Carl Murchison (ed.), *A History of Psychology in Autobiography*, Vol. III. Worcester, Mass.: Clark University Press; New York: Russell & Russell, 1961. Pp. 263–270.

THORNDIKE, EDWARD L., ET AL. 1927. *The Measurement of Intelligence*. New York: Teachers College, Columbia University.

THORNDIKE, EDWARD L., AND ROBERT S. WOODWORTH. 1901. The influence of improvement in one mental function upon the efficiency of other functions. *Psychological Review*, 8, 247–261.

THORNDIKE, ROBERT L. 1968. Review of R. Rosenthal and L. Jacobson, *Pygmalion in the Classroom. American Educational Research Journal*, 5, 708–711.

THURSTONE, L. L. 1927. Psychophysical analysis. *American Journal of Psychology*, 38, 368–389.

THURSTONE, L. L. 1946. Theories of intelligence. *Scientific Monthly*, 62, 101–112.

THURSTONE, L. L. 1947. *Multiple-Factor Analysis*. Chicago: University of Chicago Press.

THURSTONE, L. L. 1951. Creative talent. In *Proceedings of the 1950 Conference on Testing Problems*. New York: Educational Test Service. Pp. 55–69.

TIBER, NORMAN, AND WALLACE A. KENNEDY. 1964. The effects of incentives on the intelligence test performance of different social groups. *Journal of Consulting Psychology*, 28, 187.

TIEDEMANN, DIETRICH. 1787. See Murchison and Langer (1927).

TIMS, MARGARET. 1961. *Jane Addams of Hull House: 1860–1935*. New York: Macmillan.

TRINCKER, DIETRICH, AND INGEBORG TRINCKER. 1955. Development of brightness vision in infants. In Yvonne Brackbill and George G. Thompson (eds.), *Behavior in Infancy and Early Childhood*. New York: The Free Press, 1967. Chapt. 19, pp. 179–188.

TWITMYER, EDWIN B. 1905. Knee-jerks without stimulation of the patellar tendon. *Psychological Bulletin*, 2, 43–44.

TYLER, LEONA E. 1965. *The Psychology of Human Differences,* 3d ed. New York: Appleton-Century-Crofts.

ULLMANN, LEONARD P., AND LEONARD KRASNER (eds.). 1965. *Case Studies in Behavior Modification.* New York: Holt, Rinehart & Winston.

VAN DE RIET, VERNON, AND MICHAEL B. RESNICK. 1973. *Learning To Learn: An Effective Model for Early Childhood Education.* HEW DRE Grant No. OCD–CB–336. Gainesville: University of Florida, Department of Psychology.

VAN DE RIET, VERNON, HANI VAN DE RIET, AND HERBERT SPRIGLE. 1968–1969. The effectiveness of a new sequential learning program with culturally disadvantaged preschool children. *Journal of School Psychology,* 7, 5–15.

WALK, RICHARD D. 1966. The development of depth perception in animals and human infants. *Monographs of the Society for Research in Child Development,* 31 (5), No. 107, pp. 82–108.

WALKER, RICHARD N. 1962. Body build and behavior in young children: Body build and nursery school teachers' ratings. *Monographs of the Society for Research in Child Development,* 27 (3), No. 84.

WALSH, ANN M. 1956. *Self-Concepts of Bright Boys with Learning Difficulties.* New York: Teachers College, Columbia University.

WARKANY, JOSEF. 1947. Etiology of congenital malformations. In S. Z. Levine (ed.), *Advances in Pediatrics.* New York: Interscience. Pp. 1–63.

WATSON, JOHN B. 1913. Psychology as the behaviorist views it. *Psychological Review,* 20, 158–177.

WATSON, JOHN B. 1916. The place of the conditioned reflex in psychology. *Psychological Review,* 23, 89–116.

WATSON, JOHN B. 1919. *Psychology: From the Standpoint of a Behaviorist.* Philadelphia: J. B. Lippincott.

WATSON, JOHN B. 1925. *Behaviorism.* New York: W. W. Norton.

WATSON, JOHN B. 1936. John Broadus Watson. In Carl Murchison (ed.), *A History of Psychology in Autobiography,* Vol. III. Worcester, Mass.: Clark University Press; New York: Russell & Russell, 1961. Pp. 271–281.

WATSON, JOHN B., AND ROSALIE RAYNER. 1920. Conditioned emotional reactions. *Journal of Experimental Psychology,* 3, 1–12.

WATTENBERG, WILLIAM W., AND CLARE CLIFFORD. 1964. Relation of self-concepts to beginning achievement in reading. *Child Development,* 35, 461–467.

WECHSLER, DAVID. 1944. *The Measurement of Adult Intelligence,* 3d ed. Baltimore: Williams & Wilkins.

WECHSLER, DAVID. 1955. *Manual for the Wechsler Adult Intelligence Scale.* New York: The Psychological Corporation.

WECHSLER, DAVID. 1958. *The Measurement and Appraisal of Adult Intelligence.* Baltimore: Williams & Wilkins.

WEISBERG, PAUL. 1963. Social and nonsocial conditioning of infant vocalizations. *Child Development,* 34, 377–388.

WEISS, L. A. 1934. Differential variations in the amount of activity of newborn infants under continuous light and sound stimulation. *University of Iowa Studies in Child Welfare,* 9 (4), 9–74.

WELLMAN, BETH L. 1932–1933. The effect of preschool attendance upon the IQ. *Journal of Experimental Education,* 1, 48–69.

WELLMAN, BETH L. 1945. IQ changes of preschool and nonpreschool groups during the preschool years: A summary of the literature. *Journal of Psychology,* 20, 347–368.

WESSLER, RICHARD L., AND MILTON E. STRAUSS. 1968. Experimenter expectancy: A failure to replicate. *Psychological Reports,* 22 (No. 3, Part 1), 687–688.

WHEELER, LESTER R. 1932. The intelligence of East Tennessee mountain children. *Journal of Educational Psychology,* 23, 351–370.

WHEELER, LESTER R. 1942. A comparative study of the intelligence of East Tennessee mountain children. *Journal of Educational Psychology,* 33, 321–334.

WICKENS, DELOS D., AND CAROL WICKENS. 1940. A study of conditioning in the neonate. *Journal of Experimental Psychology,* 26, 94–102.

WILSON, JAMES G. 1961. General principles in experimental teratology. In *Congenital Malformations: Papers and Discussions Presented at the First International Conference on Congenital Malformations.* Philadelphia: J. B. Lippincott. Pp. 187–194.

WINCHESTER, ALBERT M. 1951. *Genetics: A Survey of the Principles of Heredity.* Boston: Houghton Mifflin.

WINICK, MYRON. 1969. Malnutrition and brain development. *Journal of Pediatrics,* 74, 667–679.

WINICK, MYRON, AND A. NOBLE. 1966. Cellular response in rats during malnutrition at various ages. *Journal of Nutrition,* 89, 300.

WINICK, MYRON, AND PEDRO ROSSO. 1969*a*. The effect of severe early malnutrition on cellular growth of human brain. *Pediatric Research,* 3, 181–184.

WINICK, MYRON, AND PEDRO ROSSO. 1969*b*. Head circumference and cellular growth of the brain in normal and marasmic children. *Journal of Pediatrics,* 74, 774–778.

WOLPE, JOSEPH. 1948. An approach to the problem of neurosis based on the conditioned response. M.D. thesis, University of the Witwatersrand, Johannesburg, South Africa.

WOLPE, JOSEPH. 1958. *Psychotherapy by Reciprocal Inhibition.* Stanford, Calif.: Stanford University Press.

WOLPE, JOSEPH. 1961. The systematic desensitization treatment of neuroses. *Journal of Nervous and Mental Diseases,* 132, 189–203.

WOLPE, JOSEPH. 1964. The comparative clinical status of conditioning therapies and psychoanalysis. In Joseph Wolpe, Andrew Salter, and Leo J. Reyna (eds.), *The Conditioning Therapies: The Challenge in Psychotherapy.* New York: Holt, Rinehart & Winston. Pp. 5–16.

WOLPE, JOSEPH, AND ARNOLD A. LAZARUS. 1966. *Behavior Therapy Techniques: A Guide to the Treatment of Neuroses.* New York: Pergamon Press.

WOODROW, HERBERT. 1946. The ability to learn. *Psychological Review,* 53, 147–158.

WOODWORTH, ROBERT S. 1938. *Experimental Psychology.* New York: Henry Holt.

WORTIS, HELEN. 1963. Social class and premature birth. *Social Casework,* 45, 541–543.

WORTIS, HELEN, CARYL B. HEIMER, MARTIN BRAINE, MIRIAM REDLO, AND ROSE RUE. 1963. Growing up in Brooklyn: The early history of the premature child. *American Journal of Orthopsychiatry,* 33, 535–539.

YEH, S. D. J., AND B. WEISS. 1963. Behavioral thermoregulation during vitamin B_6 deficiency. *American Journal of Physiology,* 205, 857.

YLINEN, O., AND P. A. JARVINEN. 1953. Parotitis during pregnancy. *Acta Obstetricia et Gynecologica Scandinavica,* 32, 121–132.

ZBOROWSKI, MARK. 1955. The place of book-learning in traditional Jewish culture. In Margaret Mead and Martha Wolfenstein (eds.), *Childhood in Contemporary Cultures.* Chicago: University of Chicago Press. Pp. 118–141.

ZIGLER, EDWARD, AND EARL C. BUTTERFIELD. 1968. Motivational aspects of changes in IQ test performance of culturally deprived nursery school children. *Child Development,* 39, 1–14.

ZINGG, ROBERT M. 1940. Feral man and extreme cases of isolation. *American Journal of Psychology,* 53, 487–517.

ZINGG, ROBERT M. 1941. Reply to Professor Dennis's "The significance of feral man." *American Journal of Psychology,* 54, 432–435.

Name Index

531

Subject Index

Reinforcement (*cont.*)
  language skills, 376–380
  partial, 360–361; *r.* 380–381; 460–463
  positive, 420, 459
  schedule, 366–367; *r.* 381
    fixed-interval, 367
    fixed-ratio, 367
    variable-interval, 367
    variable-ratio, 367
  secondary, 324–325
Reinforcer, 359; *r.* 381
  conditioned, 360
  negative, 359
  positive, 359
  primary, 360
  secondary, 360
  unconditioned, 360
Relationship between poverty and intelligence, 227–241; *r.* 261–262, 266–267
  compensatory education group, 239–240; *r.* 261
  heritability group, 227–235; *r.* 261–262, 266–267
  language deficit group, 235–239; *r.* 262, 267
  psycholinguistic group, 240–241; *r.* 262
  summary, 241; *r.* 267
Relationship groupings, *r.* 200
  hierarchy of classes, 186
  multiplication of classes, 186
  multiplication of series, 186
  order of succession, 186
  substitution, 186
  symmetrical relations, 186
Relationship laws, *r.* 200
  associativity, 187
  closure or composition, 186–187
  identity, 187
  inversion, 187
  tautology, 187
Relaxation, 340–341, 414–415
Release therapy, 427
Reliability, *g.* 492
Reliability/achievement tests, 304
Remedial education, 4
Removal of positive reward, 426
Representativeness/intelligence tests, 248–250; *r.* 263
Repression, 398; *r.* 440
Reproduction, 43–51; *r.* 56–58
  endocrinology, 43–46; *r.* 56–57
    female, 44–45; *r.* 56
    male, 45–46; *r.* 57
    puberty, 43–44; *r.* 57
  fertilization, 46–47; *r.* 55
  intrauterine periods, 47–52; *r.* 58
    embryo, 48–52
    fetus, 52
    ovum, 47–48

Resistance to extinction, 361, 366; *r.* 381
Respondent, *r.* 349; 356; *r.* 381; *g.* 492
Respondent conditioning, 318
Response,
  conditioned, 320–323; *r.* 348, 349, 350
    emotional, 327–332; *r.* 351
    fetus, 335–336; *r.* 352
    newborn, 333–335; *r.* 351–352
    physical, 326–327; *r.* 351
  unconditioned, *r.* 348, 349
Responsibility, 452
Restricted communication, 241
Retrospective study, *g.* 492
Reward, 426
Rh-factor, 88, 151
Ribonucleic acid (RNA), 28–29
Right/wrong, 469–471
RNA (ribonucleic acid), 28–29, 42, 45; *r.* 55
Rocking/head banging, 173
Rorschach, 129–130
Roughhousing, 456
Routines, family, 450–451
Rubella, 62, 63, 151, 343

s factor, 218, 272, 507
Salamander, 97
SAT (*Stanford Achievement Test*), 303, 304
Scale for Handwriting of Children, 271
Schedules of reinforcement, 366–367; *r.* 380, 381
Schemas, 176, 177, 178, 189–192, 199; *r.* 201
  invention of new, 191–192
  primary circular, 189–190
  secondary circular, 190–191
  tertiary circular, 191
Schizophrenia, 9–10, 85, 156, 208, 481–482; *g.* 492
School phobia, 342, 417
Schwann's sheaths, 102–103; *r.* 135
SD (standard deviation), 302; *r.* 313
Secondary circular schemas, 190–191; *r.* 201
Secondary reinforcement, 324–325
Secondary reinforcer, 360; *r.* 381
Secondary sexual characteristics, 105, 106, 110; *r.* 137
The Secret Lives of Walter Mitty, 403
Self-acceptance, 427
Self-concept,
  attitude, 280–282
  effect of maturation, 110–117
  effect on achievement, 280–285; *r.* 312
  ethnicity, 283–285
  socioeconomic level, 282–283
Self-estimate/anxiety, 434

Self-fulfilling prophesy, 288–289
Selfhood, 144
Self-mutilation, 485–486
Self-regulatory fluctuation, 120; *r.* 138
Senility, 208
Sense deprivation, 192–194
  hearing, 192–193
  sight, 193
  smell/taste, 193
  summary, 194
  touch, 193
Sensory acuity of the infant, 98, 146–173; *r.* 197–198
  color discrimination, 147; *r.* 197
  hearing, 151–154; *r.* 198
  kinesthesia, 173; *r.* 198
  language readiness, 153; *r.* 198
  reading readiness, 150–151; *r.* 197
  shape discrimination, 147; *r.* 198
  sight, 146–151; *r.* 197–198
  smell, 155–156; *r.* 198
  taste, 154–155; *r.* 198
  touch, 125, 126, 156–173; *r.* 198
Sensory deprivation, 145, 151
Sensory functioning at birth, 144
Sensory-motor stage, 180, 182, 187–192; *r.* 200, 201–202
  coordination of secondary schemas, 190–191; *r.* 201
  invention of new schemas, 191–192; *r.* 201
  primary circular schemas, 189–190; *r.* 201
  reflex exercises, 189; *r.* 201
  secondary circular schemas, 190; *r.* 201
  tertiary circular schemas, 191; *r.* 201
Sensory processing of the child, 145, 174–192; *r.* 198–202
  implications, 192–195; *r.* 202
  Piaget, Jean, 174–175; *r.* 198–199
  Piaget's language, 175–180; *r.* 198–199
  Piaget's stages of cognitive development, 180–187; *r.* 199–201
  sensory-motor stage, 187–192; *r.* 201–202
  status at birth, *r.* 198
  summary, 195–197; *r.* 202
Sensory status at birth, 174, 192; *r.* 197
  audition, 151
  gustation, 154
  kinesthesia, *r.* 198
  olfaction, 155
  sensory processing, *r.* 198
  touch, 156
  vision, 146
Series multiplication, 186; *r.* 200
Servomechanism, 101–102; *r.* 135
Sex/anxiety, 433